Allan Seale's
Complete Guide to
Australian
Gardening

TREASURE PRESS

Freesia (Bergunden Strain)

Allan Seale's
Complete Guide to
Australian
Gardening

REED

First published 1985 by
Reed Books Pty Ltd
3/470 Sydney Road, Balgowlah NSW 2093

This edition published in
Australia and New Zealand by
TREASURE PRESS AUSTRALIA
a division of the Octopus Publishing Group
22 Salmon Street, Port Melbourne, Victoria 3207

ISBN 1 86345 033 5

Edited by Brenda Little
Designed by Margaret Howard
Illustrated by Helen McCosker
Photography by Ed Ramsay, Allan Seale

Typeset by The Typographers, Artarmon, N.S.W.
Printed in Singapore by Times Publishing Group

Contents

To the new gardener

We often hear that interest in gardening has suddenly soared. It is perhaps more correct to say that gardening activity and interest has been rekindled following the wave of post-war affluence. The motor car came within reach of most families after World War II, allowing easy access to surf, country, sports or social clubs and other activities.

Moreover, the arrival of rotary mowers made it possible to keep home surroundings reasonably presentable with minimum demand on time and effort. Most of the people that once went for Sunday strolls were now out driving further afield and not looking over fences to admire and take in gardening ideas.

Driving is no longer a novelty and rarely a pleasure. More people have home swimming pools and barbeques with accompanying outdoor living areas which they like to make as attractive as possible. This has centred more interest on the garden.

Most new home owners now want instant gardens involving large quantities of advanced plants and an increasing number of people without conventional gardens are satisfying their natural desires to grow things and enjoy attractive plant life around them by buying house plants and other plants for balconys or window boxes. Many of these plants have a limited life and the replacement rate is high creating a boom in the nursery and garden store business.

All of this may seem to link gardening with expensive buying sprees but that need not be so. Some of the loveliest gardens have cost their owners practically nothing. Apart from small initial outlay on a few seedling sized trees, they or sometimes friends have raised most of the shrubs from cuttings. The only recurring costs are for an occasional bag of plant food and perhaps a few packets of seeds or bulbs.

This is not to suggest that the nurseryman or landscaper is exploiting the garden enthusiast. It is just that when you choose to start from scratch as suggested you are using your own time and not paying for someone elses. In any case, the satisfaction gained from actually raising your own plants or growing a good tree from a tiny seedling is something which money cannot buy. Incidentally, the time to maturity when starting with small rather than advanced plants may not be as long as imagined. Quite often the small plants establish better and within a couple of years may bypass the advanced specimens. However, advanced plants certainly give the more satisfying immediate effect and therefore are difficult to resist, especially if starting a new garden or remodelling section of an old one.

Even though you may prefer buying plants as close to maturity as possible, at least experience the great satisfaction of raising at least some of your own seedlings or growing a few plants from cuttings. Easy and enjoyable ways to propagate your own plants is one of the many subjects fully explained in this book. It also tells how to care for and get the best results from seedlings, plus ways to make difficult soils productive without great effort. There is all the information needed to enjoy a supply of garden fresh vegetables throughout the year, even when space is limited and without frequent use of poisonous sprays. Growing of all flowers including annuals, perennials and bulbs is also well covered, together with the best planting times and ways to combine them for best effect.

Easy guides to pruning and general care of shrubs are given as well as planting recommendations for various climates, aspects and for different purposes. All types of house plants including ferns, palms, African violets, cyclamens and other favorites are catered for.

In compiling this book, the general aim, apart from offering a comprehensive guide to the successful growing of the widest plant range, is to give you ideas to make gardens more interesting, more enjoyable and easier to maintain. This applies particularly to old established gardens as well as the planning of new ones.

In both outdoor and indoor gardening it is not only a beautiful plant but the way it is presented and combined with others that creates the more interesting and pleasing effect. Above all else, the garden needs to be satisfying and easy to maintain. It should be a pleasure, not a chore.

Wishing you Good Gardening.

Allan Seale

MAKING A GARDEN

1. Designing a Garden

You can have a lovely garden without becoming a slave to it, even on a shoe-string budget. Planning a good garden is more complex than it appears but do attempt it, then if you decide to call in professional help you will be in a better position to assess the ideas put forward.

Good gardens, even large ones, need not cost the earth. There are many beautiful and substantial ones which involved no more expense than the cost of shrubs and trees bought gradually as areas were prepared for them, plus incidentals such as a packet or two of plant food and a few pounds of grass seed.

The luxury of annuals, bulbs and other perennials for colour, highlight and interest can be enjoyed when the budget allows. I know of one tightly budgeted but excellent garden with a productive vegetable plot; the cost saved by this home-grown produce is spent on the more ornamental part of the garden.

Garden construction involving large areas of stonework or rockeries can be expensive, but though rockeries can add interest they are not an essential part of good landscaping except, perhaps, as a means to cope with steeply sloping areas, and even then there are alternatives to expensive construction. In any case it is *your* garden and you are entitled to have the type of landscape that appeals to you.

A garden should be an individual creation which reflects personal tastes, not something that runs to a set pattern, so it would be audacious to lay down rules governing design. Any plan that is practical and not too costly is a good one, providing the result is functional, does not involve unnecessary maintenance and, above all, pleases *you*.

Many people have very little idea about how to start planning their garden. Even people with preconceived ideas often find it difficult to adapt them to their home site.

Starting points

Look at as many different gardens as you can, particularly those on sites similar to your own. Note, sketch or photograph those you find appealing, paying particular attention to shape of the garden and placement of trees or shrubs. Study magazine or garden-book illustrations. Although these examples and some of the grander gardens you see could be far beyond the dimensions of your site, there is often an overall shape, grouping of plants or general character that can be scaled down to suit you.

Site plan

Before starting definite planning, you will need a scaled map or plan of your home site, showing the house, boundaries and position of services such as sewer mains, gas, water and power pipes or wires and telephone lines, both overhead and underground.

A builder's block plan will simplify matters, as you can easily take a tracing from it. Otherwise you will need to measure the area using a 30-metre tape or a length of nylon non-stretch cord marked off in 10-metre sections, with one end marked in single metres. (Calcu-

lating is easier if you stitch coloured threads into the cord to show distances.)

Start by drawing in the boundaries, the position of the house and the distance of its points from boundaries, then add existing trees, water taps, power lines, meters and pipes. You will probably find it easier to plot this on graph paper using each large square to represent two square metres. Otherwise use a scale of one cm equals one metre. Double the scale for detailed planning of items like outdoor living areas or barbecues.

Now mark suitable areas for utilities such as clothes lines or hoists — these are still essential

This sloping site is effectively retained by a well-graded lawn, a few rocks and permanent plantings

and they can always be attractively screened from sight at a later stage. Clothes lines should be close to the laundry, and in direct sun. Have children's play areas within sight or earshot of the room adults use most of the day, and well away from driveways. The driveway itself, and essential pathways, can then be drawn on to the plan.

Until a well-considered plan has been finalised it is advisable to do all preliminary planning on tracing paper fastened to the master plan — this allows you to make modifications easily.

If you should like a swimming pool in the future, allow for it now, possibly adjoining the barbecue area. It can be put down to lawn in the meantime so that you don't have to change the overall plan and major plantings later.

Next, select your outdoor living, patio or barbecue area, which for preference should be handy to the kitchen. If possible have your family or living room running out to a partly covered paved area, or a deck with barbecue and outdoor dining facilities. If the paving meets the lawn without change of level the house will merge with garden happily and the paving will become an extension of your house.

Shrubs add both seasonal colour and background

Choose features that harmonise and add interest

Swimming pools can be designed to blend with natural settings

Paving can help to integrate house with garden

Garden pools add sparkle and interest

Planning

Planning is important — particularly for young home-buyers with a bare home site — if you wish to have a real garden rather than just a backyard. Landscaping can completely change the character of your home.

Use a simplified copy of your builder's plan, moving round cut-outs of the 'ultimate size' of the trees and shrubs you favour, making sure that they will not interfere with power lines or drains.

The artist's impression shows one possible treatment — outdoor areas in heavy use all year round are paved rather than grassed, yet a large area is devoted to lawn. The vegetable garden is in a sunny position; unsightly fences are screened by shrubbery and shaded areas are given over to hardy 'ground covers'.

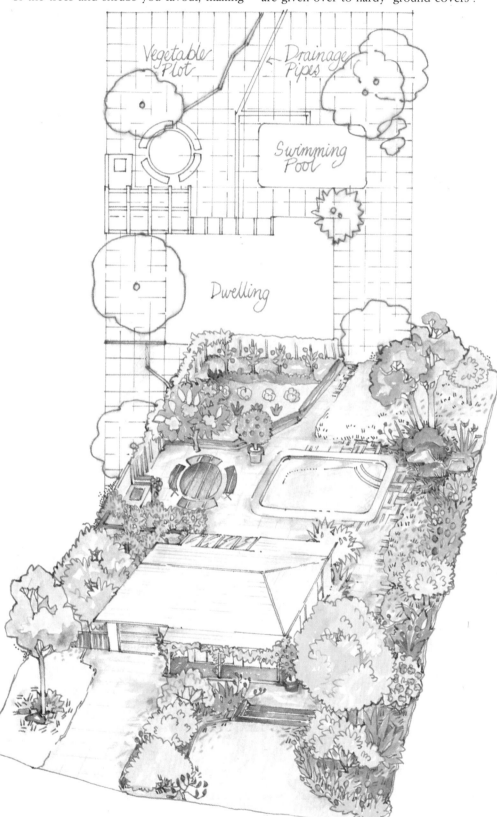

Sun and shade

The single most important thing to consider in planning a garden is the amount of sunshine it will receive in both summer and winter. Knowing where the sun will fall and which parts of the garden will be in shade throughout winter helps in selecting the appropriate plants and in obtaining the maximum benefit and comfort from your garden all year round.

The sun moves in a high arc during summer and a low one during winter. Therefore midwinter shade areas may extend at least three times as far as those in summer, varying according to latitude (the further south, the longer the shadow). You can make use of this to have the comfort of summer shade and winter sun. Plant high-branching trees close to a northern deck or barbecue area so that the low-angled winter sun streams in under them; in the summer the sun, being at a higher angle, will throw more shade more directly below the trees.

Similarly, you can plan a vine-covered pergola or an awning high and wide enough to allow plenty of sunlight beneath it during the winter months and yet provide welcome shade during summer. Keep this factor in mind when planning height and width of eaves, awnings or verandas. Also consider where shade will ultimately be thrown by trees, shrubbery or vines, because lawn grass often refuses to grow in shaded areas. To have to make the change from lawn to paving as the problem arises can be irritating and expensive.

Screening

Screening may be needed for privacy or to blot out unwanted or unattractive views. If you want to hide an ugly building but not the landscape beyond it, gauge the height of screening needed and plant shrubbery accordingly. Garbage cans kept near the back door can be screened by plants.

Winds

In an open or elevated area it is essential to consider the prevailing winds. People who live nearby will tell you of the direction of the wind; or some indigenous trees or shrubs will tell the story — they lean away from the wind.

Mark the area where wind protection is needed. If unfamiliar with the behaviour of the wind, the wind diagram indicates the way it jumps walls or solid barriers and gathers speed as it sweeps beyond them. A spaced planting of trees or shrubbery will filter or break its force and give appreciable protection over a greater distance than a solid barrier.

Right: Solid barriers such as a paling fence, a brick wall or trees with dense foliage create turbulence on both sides of the wind barrier. Slatted fences or trees and shrubs with light foliage will filter the wind and reduce its speed.

Below: A wisteria-covered pergola will allow plenty of sunlight beneath it during the winter months and yet provide welcome shade during summer.

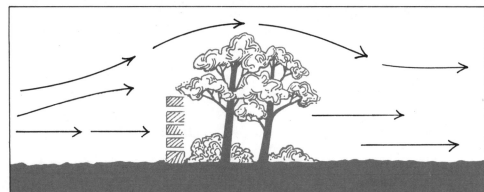

Silver beet looking at home amongst ornamentals

A 'star' garden design planted with succulents and bordered on the circle with buxus

A carefully planned garden spot of tree ferns, flax and polyanthus around a rock pool

Vegetable garden

Leave space for vegetable growing in a fairly sheltered, sunny area, clear of overhanging trees and near a tap.

A vegetable garden is often included with the general utility area and screened from the remainder of the garden. This is not essential as a well-tended vegetable garden is a thing to be admired. However, a screened vegetable garden is the ideal site for compost heaps, garden stakes and other 'backstage' materials.

Hobby garden

Mark areas on the plan which will be suitable for any special interests. For instance, a fernery or rock and fern garden could be given space in your outdoor living area. If your hobby is growing roses or dahlias, choose an open sunny area — if you enjoy growing fuchsias mark an area which will give them part-shade.

Major plantings

Now decide where trees and any significant groupings of shrubbery should go. Some people hesitate to plant trees because they feel they take up too much space or because they dislike fallen leaves. Leaves make valuable mulch or compost, but if constant leaf-fall worries you why not plant deciduous trees and have just one grand clean-up each autumn?

Trees are vital to the ecology. Gardens need them for natural character, summer shade and a habitat for birds.

Try to include at least one or two. If space is limited choose comparatively high-branching or umbrella-shaped types so that most of the space they take up is above head height.

Positioning trees

Work out where they would serve the most practical purpose, such as on the north or north-western side of your terrace or barbecue area to give relief from the hot midday and afternoon sun, or to shade a western window. It is possible to place trees so that you have summer shade and winter sun. Is your garden overlooked? A strategically placed tree will give privacy.

Trees growing slightly behind or at the front of a house frame it attractively. A tree masking the corner of a house makes the house seem bigger. A lightly foliaged tree placed about one-third of the distance from the house will make a shallow frontage look deeper. Make certain it would not obscure the entrance.

The vista from window or terrace will look more interesting and expansive if the branches of a tree mask harsh roof lines, power poles or other man-made additions that would otherwise spoil the outlook. Don't feel there must always be a purpose in your planning. You can plant just for the sheer pleasure a tree or trees give you.

Compromise

If you planted a tree in every position where it is needed in a small block you could soon have a jungle. Try to make your trees serve several purposes. One tree in the right position can not only shade the barbecue area but also screen an unwanted view from a living room window and provide a pleasant vista below its branches.

Decision can be often better done on the site than on paper. Hammer in a tall stake where the tree is needed, check its average spread or width in the 'Tree' and 'Shrub' list, then with a garden hose or rope mark out the area it would cover. Move the stake around until you can settle on the best position for all purposes. A grouping of several small trees might give a better effect than one large one.

When sketching your plan, cut out rough cardboard circles in scale with the average spread of the tree and move around to find the right position. For a grouping of trees, overlap the circles; the tree branches will intermingle when grown.

Precautions

Don't plant heavy-rooted trees like gums, jacarandas, ficus, elms, oaks or poplars near sewer pipes or drains. Gas or water pipes are less important in this respect, as the worst a heavy root can do is to lift or bend the pipe, but it is inadvisable to plant directly above them. If these pipes have to be replaced don't bother to take them up — just reroute the new ones. Beware underground power cables and telephone cables. Do not plant tall, spreading trees that may eventually foul or overhang power lines.

Permanent cover plants can also add seasonal colour — here kurume azaleas, rhododendrons and clipped golden euonymus

Weeping elm brings variety and form

Shrubs

Low, rounded or mounding shrubs usually look best in front of the house. Tall, slender ones break a smooth, flowing line but they are useful to mask hard corners and to make interesting contrast in group plantings.

Shrubbery in well-placed groups looks more interesting than evenly spaced fence-line plantings. Bare stretches of fencing between grouped shrubbery can be masked by brush-wood, climbing roses, creepers or espaliered plants.

This treatment helps to broaden the vistas of the garden and provides areas where you can grow annuals to give colour and variety; or easy-to-maintain and attractive ground cover, which can be easily taken up if you feel like planting something else. Bulbs, annuals and roses can be grown amongst many types of ground cover.

Points to watch

It is tempting to plant for immediate effect. Shrubs and trees planted too close together will soon look crowded and lose their characteristic shape and individuality. So, unless aiming for a dense drift of a particular shrub — note the average width shown in the 'Trees' and 'Shrubs' list and scale this on to the plan. Or, as suggested in 'tree-planning', use paper cut-outs made to scale, and shuffle these about into groups which fit the available space. Mark the height on each cut-out, so that you can estimate the amount of shadow the trees will cast and their effectiveness as a sun-screen.

Evergreen shrubs bordering the path to this grand house (above)

Overhanging wisteria and shrubs soften this entrance (right)

Kalanchoe, primula and wisteria bring colour to the evergreen shrubs in this garden (below)

Shaping the garden

Once utilities, outdoor living or play areas, paths and major plantings have been decided you can begin planning the shape of the garden. The grade or slope of the block must be considered. Steeply sloping blocks are dealt with separately, but on any site it is important to determine the direction surface water will run before finalising the plan of the garden. Do not allow water to run toward the house. If the slope is toward the house, plan for the water to be channelled aside before it reaches the building.

It is often possible to fashion a path which will act as a drain to take the water away from the house, or you can provide a slight depression in the lawn that will act the same way.

Decide if you need such diversion and, if you do, where the water will collect. Mark it on the plan. You can decide later how to plant the area.

Now decide the lines of demarcation between garden beds and lawns and the way paved areas will flow into lawn or garden. The general trend is toward a contrived series of curves, but some people are reverting to the evenly balanced straight beds so popular during the Victorian era.

To get the most interest into your garden try to have at least one or more points where the lawn disappears behind a clump of shrubbery, a retaining wall or the corner of a building. This is easier to achieve with curves which make shallow areas look deeper or narrow blocks broader by visually drawing out and stretching the shorter perimeter at the expense of the longer one. A vista can be stretched to the maximum by planning it diagonally across the block, and under the branches of a small, spreading tree.

Planning curves

I find that people planning their first garden tend to overdo the number of curves because it is hard to relate the scale of the plan to the site; what seems ideal on paper can look too fussy in fact.

So before finalising your design, test it on the site by laying a garden hose or length of flexible rope along the proposed line and move it around until it looks right. Don't be in a hurry to finalise the shape. First make sure there is sufficient width of garden for the shrubbery needed to screen fences, for general effect, and to give space for the planting of annuals, bulbs, perennials or ground cover. In small areas consider taking the lawn right up to the boundary fence or wall.

Mixed planting brings colour to this slope

Conifers and azaleas feature in this carefully planned border

Prostrate and erect conifers combine effectively to cover this slope

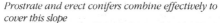

Paths

Paths, whether straight or winding, must be comfortable and safe underfoot. Whether earthen, gravel, or made from stepping stones laid in grass, a path is mainly functional.

Paths which lead to utility areas should be as direct as possible. A curved path is likely to prove an irritation when there is washing to be hung on a line or a barbecue to be lit and you could find your lawn worn bare by the necessity to find the quickest route from A to B.

In planning where paths should run, allow for flexibility in the initial stages; you have to live in a house or garden for a time before patterns of family behaviour and need are established. Don't be in a hurry to put down concrete paths. Remember that lawn and path should be on the same level if you are to have a good overall appearance and easy maintenance and don't put down paths or mower strips at the same time as laying down a new lawn. Wait until the lawn has settled, otherwise you are likely to face the irritation and expense, not to mention drainage problems, of having to bring in extra soil to make the level of lawn and path coincide.

Straight paths take care of the utilitarian aspect, curved ones should be used to make the garden more interesting and picturesque. A geometrical path from gate to front door is unimaginative; curve it slightly so that the house is out of view from the gate but the planting of a tree, a shrub, or the position of an outcrop of rock, leads the eye onward. If your garden has a good slope use curved paths made from stepping stones laid among attractive ground cover and gravel to lead to the lower levels of the garden. Shallow steps should have a wide tread. Use broad, flat stones and allow a lap of a few centimetres as the steps run downward.

These rough stepping stones attractively meander through rhododendrons and trailing perennials

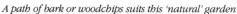

A path of bark or woodchips suits this 'natural' garden

An example of a 'crazy paving' path

Garden features

Once the 'bones' of a garden are decided you can turn your mind to the pleasant task of deciding the embellishments. What sort of boundaries would you like — fence or hedging? Is there room for a courtyard? What about a rockery, dry walls, garden seats? How would an area of paving fit into the plan? Or a Japanese or pebble garden? Where would be the best place for a small pool with waterlilies? One of the greatest pleasures in gardening is in learning what the options are and then adapting them to one's personal tastes.

Vines provide an attractive covering for pillars and fences (above)

A formal garden setting softened by informal plantings (right)

Gravel has been chosen as a low maintenance surround for this gazebo (below)

Railway sleepers make good steps (above)

Standard roses suit this formal setting (right)

Neutral paving and oiled timber are in character with this native garden (below)

Boundaries

Once your plan is drawn you will know both the shape of your land and the dimensions of the boundaries. There may be an existing fence or other barrier to mark the separation of your land from that of your neighbour, or, if you have a new house on a recently developed site, there may be nothing more than a row of pegs and a strand of wire. Now is the time to decide how to enclose your land and gain maximum pleasure from the effect created.

The once widely advocated American idea of no barriers between homes is now a thing of the past in Australia. Many gardens merge into roadside nature strips but there is usually a barrier of some sort between one property and another. It has been recognised that though neighbours may be close friends, the relationship lasts better if they do not have to live in one another's pockets. We all need privacy in which to express our individual taste. Plants make much friendlier and more attractive screens than man-made barriers. There can be neat, symmetrical hedges, shrubs allowed to grow and spread naturally or a mixed growth of plants which give a range of form, foliage colour and shape against the sky.

The formal hedge can create a charming effect in an otherwise informal garden if used as a foil for irregularly shaped or pendulous trees and other plants whose growth is spreading and informal. It is a practical choice too, for the width can be limited to less than one metre. Remember, however, that it will require regular trimming. Some people enjoy this chore; others hate it. Fortunately there are electrically powered hedge-trimmers that make the job quick and easy. A plant hedge is good as a replacement for a front fence or for use as a divider within the garden but, if used as a boundary marker, even when there is agreement between neighbours, there can be the question of trimming. If it is shared there could be the problem of performance. One neighbour might not do the job to the other's satisfaction.

Done regularly it is not difficult, as the line of previous growth is obvious and the clippers can be kept down to this level, but if trimming is left for some time an inexperienced clipper can achieve a topiarist version of the Loch Ness monster. It is then advisable to stretch a taut line to mark the top of the hedge and to work down from this. It is important to remember that while successful formal hedges may look perpendicular they actually slope in toward the top so that the base can receive the light and air vital to growth. Neglect this principle and you will have a hedge which thins out at the base or dies in patches.

The choice for formal or informal planting is wide.

Abelia chinensis Establishes quickly, reaching 2 metres in less than 2 years with a final height of about 3 metres. Leaves are a pleasant greenish bronze throughout the year. Clusters of mauve-flushed white flowers throughout the year, followed by tight clusters of green to bronze calyxes which remain attractive until spring. Left to grow naturally it will develop a fan-shaped formation of arching canes.

Photina glabra rubra makes a colourful hedge for cool and temperate districts. The new spring growth is a rich red. Keep it clipped and you will be rewarded by further flushes of glowing leaves. Height can vary from 1–3 metres according to climate. *Photinia robusta* has larger growth but less intense colour.

Coprosma (looking-glass plant) reaches 2–3 metres, has beautifully glossy leaves and is ideal as a hedge in coastal districts as it is unaffected by salty winds.

Evergreen hawthorns or pyracanthas. Ideal for a substantial, man-proof, thorny fence. The attractive *P. fortunii* has dense glossy foliage and clusters of shiny crimson berries in autumn and winter. *P. angustifolia* with bright orange berries spreads to 3 or more metres and will form quick cover when plants are set 2 metres apart.

Duranta with light green foliage and pale blue flowers grows to 3–4 metres with pendulous clusters of orange berries in the autumn.

Clipped hedges need maintenance but make an effective screen and background to this perennial border

Cotoneasters, thornless, with rampant growth, small white flowers and red berries make an easily controlled hedge as does *Euonymus japonicus variegata* which only grows to around 1 metre, is a pleasant gold-green and should be planted at 1-metre intervals.

Rosemary, sage-green, aromatic leaves, pale blue or lilac flowers is resistant to drought and can be trimmed to make a low hedge or be allowed to grow to 2 metres tall.

Dwarf box (buxus sempervirens), a glossy, small-foliaged plant, makes a useful, dense, low-growing formal hedge, as seen in many classical French and Italian gardens. It takes some time to become established and must be trimmed after the spring growth to achieve maximum effect.

Roses can make beautiful hedges. Tall, strong-growing types like 'Queen Elizabeth' or 'Buccaneer' planted about 1 metre apart will soon make a colourful and impenetrable fence at least 2 metres tall. 'Pearly-white Sea Foam', with the aid of a few stakes, will make a rambling, metre-high hedge while the old favourite floribunda, the red 'Lilli Marlene', is ideal for a low but not dense hedge. If you go in for a low post and rail division, try growing climbing roses along it.

Camellia sasanqua can stand full sun but take a little time to establish so, in the initial stages, the bushes, set about 2 metres apart, should be interspersed with plantings of marguerites or geraniums. The sasanqua new growth remains pliable for some months and the new canes can be interlaced with the old to form a delicate, living fence of glossy, dark-green leaves. The winter flowers give colour when the garden most needs it.

Different plants may be used alternatively for contrast in both colour and shape. 'Coast rosemary', the silver-grey westringia so resistant to salt winds, looks well combined with the purple-bronze berberis, with abelia and with yellow Drap d'Or or orange-and-red Chelsea Gem lantana, both of which bloom throughout summer and autumn.

Purple lantana (*L. montevidensis*), often used as a ground cover, can be raised with the aid of a few stakes or some wire netting to a height of more than a metre and one of the loveliest flowering fences I have ever seen was a random intermingling of this plant with pale blue plumbago.

A colourful fence is quickly created by growing ivy geraniums over supports about a metre high and combining them with white marguerites, dusty millers or Sea Foam roses.

Privet, whose white flowers have a drenching fragrance, was once widely grown as a boundary hedge, but it grows so quickly it needs frequent cutting and should not be planted if there is the possibility of neglect as the seeds will be carried into the bush by birds and will grow and present a menace to the environment.

The boundary fence can be wire, wood, brush, etc. but will always look better if draped with colour. Well-chosen creepers can add beauty quickly and easily.

This formal conifer planting provides wind protection and screening

If you have the space, large trees form a beautiful garden backdrop and screen

Courtyards

The courtyard developed in mediaeval times as a walled enclosure where herbs and vegetables could be grown, safe from wandering brigand bands. The art of espaliering then came into use so that as much fruit as possible could be grown in a small area. Apart from its practical use the courtyard can create atmosphere, and, if you have the space, is well worth considering.

I have seen tropical flowers and fruit growing happily in the trapped warmth and windless air of a courtyard in a temperature zone where the plants could not have survived if grown out in the open, and I know of a home on a windswept coastal headland which has a small courtyard dripping with ferns and foliage plants as lush as they would be in their native rainforest.

Construction can be quite simple.

You can use one side of the house and a protruding utility section, garden wall or dividing wall to make two sides of the courtyard. Bricks, concrete masonry, timber, timber-form fibrous cement sheeting, brush or melaleuca stick fencing could be used for the other two, or an existing paling fence could be used. In the latter case additional strength and privacy could be provided by nailing a narrower paling to the fence to cover all joints and lapped edges, and a pleasant appearance given by melding old and new palings with a coat of outdoor oil stain or water-based plastic paint.

You will have to consider the position of your courtyard in relation to the use of garden beyond.

A solid fence acts like a hurdle; wind will jump it and then come down on the other side at a distance of about twice the fence height. An open fence or screen of fairly open foliage breaks the intensity of the wind but does not curve its subsequent path downward.

Determine your windward side. The ideal would be a solid wall or fence there, with a taller row of growth just outside it.

A courtyard can easily become an extension of the house — perfect for outdoor living and for increasing the range of plants you can grow. Paving will help to integrate indoor and outdoor areas.

Bricks look well in any type of setting and can be laid in many different ways. One of the simplest patterns to lay is running bond, with the bricks laid either on the edge or flat. This is a 'directional' pattern which can be used to lead the way from one area to another. Stack bond, used with bricks of contrasting colours, is simple to lay and can look very pretty. Herringbone and basketweave patterns are more ambitious but are well worth the extra time and trouble.

Concrete paving blocks separated by a span-width of earth planted with ground cover, herbs or rockery or bedding plants gives a large area of easily maintained garden area which has little room for weeds.

A ground covering of loose river pebbles with stepping stones between them can look very attractive but, if the courtyard is likely

A courtyard planting of variegated flax and tree fern fronted by nandina nana and dwarf maple

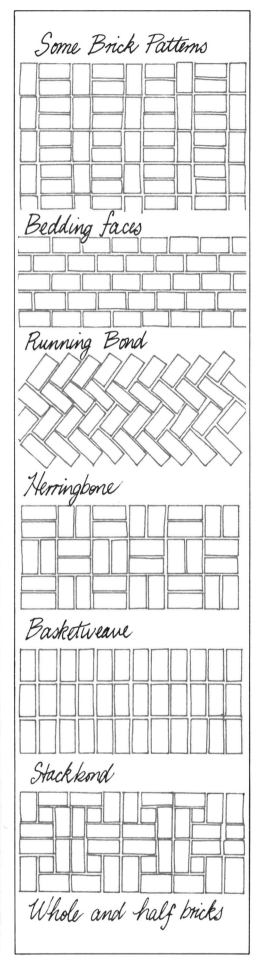

Some Brick Patterns

Bedding faces

Running Bond

Herringbone

Basketweave

Stack bond

Whole and half bricks

to be used for entertaining, a solid base is more practical. Blue metal or basalt, compacted, makes a firm, comfortable setting for Japanese-type gardens or ones which feature plants with spectacularly lush growth.

You can make paths by laying the paving blocks close together. You can also lead a path to a solidly paved area which features a sundial or a bird bath. This treatment is particularly suitable for creating an old-world or semi-formal effect.

The type of planting you choose has a strong bearing on the atmosphere you create. A few tall palms and bold-leafed plants suggest tropical island glamour, whereas upright conifers and an occasional urn spilling with geraniums or bedding plants give a Mediterranean touch. Tree ferns, moist mossy rocks and a few low-growing ferns can suggest a cool bushland dell in a shaded corner of the courtyard.

Whatever you choose, make sure they are plants that suit the aspect. Hibiscus are excellent on warm sunny walls, either espaliered or otherwise. So are acalyphas, which remain colourful almost throughout the year in all but cool districts.

Showy tropical to warm temperate climate creepers include allamandas, bougainvillaeas, lovely blue petrea, scarlet impomeas, clerodendrons and a variety of thunbergias.

Climbing, rambling or pillar roses against the walls fit beautifully into the old world-type courtyard. I have also seen panels of pillar roses like Titian used in contemporary settings.

For more shaded walls in temperate climates, try espaliering camellias or drape Chinese star jasmine. Sasanqua camellias espalier well and stand more direct sun and cold than the later flowering japonica types. For delightful wall decoration in cold districts it is hard to go past the many beautiful clematis, wisterias and espaliered flowering quinces, forsythia or ceanothus.

Bedding plants in containers bring welcome seasonal colour and variety. Also consider small trees such as Japanese maples and some of the smaller growing pines in containers. These can all be moved about to suit their increasing size or to provide a change of landscape.

Where space is limited, keep most plantings close to the wall. Creepers supported by a few wooden slats or light lattice-like frame on the wall are ideal. I know of a walled garden in Sydney's eastern suburbs where the white cement-rendered wall is covered with open, light-grade steel mesh. This gives the effect of 10 to 15 cm square tiles and is excellent support for the numerous creepers and espaliered camellias that give the garden a picturesque background and illusion of greater depth.

Nylon cord can also make effective and unobtrusive support for creepers or espaliers. It is strong, long-lasting, often available in a colour that will blend with the wall, and can be stretched in horizontal, perpendicular, diagonal or fan shape, depending on the extent of planting.

Clivias prefer shade and compete well with tree roots

To overcome heavy root invasion this entire courtyard planting is in pots

Paving

Paving can integrate house and garden, give a pleasant finish and permanence to outdoor living areas such as courtyards, patios, paths or driveways. In large gardens it is an excellent way to deal with difficult areas below trees where shade and dryness are too much for lawn grass. Whether paving with stone, brick or concrete blocks, initial preparation is much the same.

Grade the area to a slight slope so that water runs off in the most suitable direction. The slope can be as little as 1 in 100. Avoid path-slopes greater than 1 in 20 if their smooth surfaces are likely to become slippery.

Alternatively, use rough-textured concrete paving blocks or 'haunch up' bricks; by having them with one edge (usually the uphill one) fractionally higher than the other to create a slight ridging. The more obvious — and generally the most comfortable — way is to offset the grade with a few steps, but this (especially in courtyards used for entertaining) can create problems of personal safety and difficulty in moving trolleys or mowers.

After grading the earth, tread the area down well, give it a good soaking, let it stand for a week or so, then grade again. Before laying paving, the soil should be so firm that it shows no more than shallow surface-footprints.

When using bricks for areas that must take heavy loads (i.e. driveways) excavate sufficiently to be able to put down an 8–10cm layer of concrete, and cover by about 5 cm of sand as a cushion under the bricks. For other forms of paving — concrete, block or stone — just put down the 5 0cm layer of sand to allow accurate laying and cushion the load. With stone crazy-paving etc. it is essential to compensate for the varying thickness of the rocks.

Bricks

Many interesting patterns are possible. Some form of retainer or soldier-course helps to stop the bricks and their sand base from spreading. The course could be of cemented bricks up-ended, or hardwood timber lengths held in position by stout pegs. (If kept flush with the paving surface this timber can also be a useful guide to the general level.) Where stability is important the sand undercourse can be mixed with one part of dry cement to four of sand.

Crazy paving or random flagging

Depending on the size and type of area, start by positioning relatively large pieces of stone with their straightest side to form the edge of your work, then gradually fill in behind them. To cut stones you will need a bricklayer's hammer and boulster or a clutch chisel, with a comb for cutting and trimming which can also be used to chip off uneven or high spots on the stones. Use a sandbag three-quarters filled with dry sand to make an even base for cushioning the flags before attempting to cut them. Mark the cut and lightly tap along it before employing a sharper hit. Do not worry about trying to achieve a close, even fit as it looks better if small angular offcuts are used to fill gaps. Some unevenness in joints adds to the charm. A width of about 2 cm is needed for cementing between the stones.

Cement between crazy-paving by first damping the stones and sand below by hosing (but don't have their surface wet when cementing as it is then harder to remove spills). Mix three parts dry builder's sand with one of cement until uniform in colour then add enough water to make porridge-like but not so runny that the sand will sink to the bottom. If it is on the loose side, stir frequently. Trowel or pour this mixture just to reach the level of the stone, agitating it with a stick immediately afterwards in order to expel air and gain penetration to all crevices.

Top up where necessary, to fill joints evenly. For a smooth, more natural finish, wait until the cement is dry, and set, but not yet hard, then rub vigorously with a piece of dry hessian. (This is also the best way to remove spillage.)

Random flagging suits the informality of the planting it surrounds — spaces may be left for small plants between stones

Garden seats

What better way to give your garden a friendly, welcoming touch than to add an attractive seat beneath the trees?

Unless a tree is very wide and low-branching, a seat on the northern side of the trunk will be in shade during summer, when the sun is at its high angle, but reached by the lower-angled winter sun.

Since grass and other plants do not always grow well beneath a tree, a seat would make good use of what might otherwise be a difficult spot. And how delightful to sit in the sun and contemplate the garden vista, and how inviting a seat can look at the end of a garden path.

There are many types of garden seats to choose from. White painted timber or metal is a popular choice although stained timber in fairly basic designs is widely used in barbecue or similar outdoor living areas.

Stone benches with carved or fancy moulded supports have an air of elegance and are usually associated with formal gardens. In some of the more classical European gardens, one can occasionally see beautiful marble seats ornately carved with scrolls and cherubs. In the right setting these are superb. Marble is expensive, of course, but similar designs would be possible in well-finished concrete.

Rustic seats or benches, made from curved or twisted branches, have their charm, and fit particularly well into the more natural or bushland setting. You could make them yourself without being a particularly good carpenter.

There are no set construction rules, you just need two well-matched and sturdy uprights for the back-legs and back-rest, and fairly straight pieces for the front and back of the seats.

As an insurance against splitting or unstable joints, make the cross-sections butt beyond the uprights, use plenty of cross or diagonal braces, and pre-drill all screw or larger nail holes.

On steeply sloping sites, stone seats can be recessed into rock-retaining walls or random terracing. Finish the actual seat and back with fairly smooth random flagging, well cemented together and make sure that the seat slopes fractionally toward the front so that it does not become a water-holding trough.

Much the same idea can be used in brick retaining walls. The effect is usually better if bricks forming the front edge of the seat are butted forward a centimetre or two beyond the others.

A hexagonal or octagonal timber seat completely encircling a tree is picturesque and allows for a choice of aspect according to sun, wind or outlook.

Make sure the back does not fit closely against the tree. Room for expansion of the trunk is essential. It is better to have the seat free-standing and made in two or three sections so that it can be moved further out as the trunk grows.

Some form of solid paving is desirable below or in front of frequently used seats. It is surprising how rapidly grass disintegrates and earth is eroded to create depressions that can become puddles.

Solid paving is also desirable below fixed seats to eliminate the problems of grass or other growth in difficult-to-cut areas around and below the supports.

A garden seat can become a focal point as well as providing a place to enjoy the peace of the garden in comfort

2. House and Garden

The plants you choose to grow around your house and on its walls will go a long way toward defining its 'personality' and giving it an atmosphere to which people will react with pleasure. We can all remember 'that house with the wonderful orange creeper' or 'that house with those lovely window-boxes'.

The type of house you have and the colour of its walls will influence your choice of tree and shrub and shape of leaf and shade of blossom. Dramatic foliage and bold-coloured flowers will look marvellous against the white, clean lines of a 'Mediterranean' or 'contemporary' style of house; feathery leaves and pastel-coloured flowers would be lost against it. A house built from red or yellow brick will need the gentleness of colour and gracefulness of shape provided by a wisteria or campsis.

Architectural mistakes can be concealed behind a barricade of growing plants; line and balance restored by the repositioning of trees and shrubs. A house can be framed by the spreading foliage of just one tree; a Pencil Pine, upright as an exclamation mark, will balance a long, low roof-line, mark a boundary or lead the eye onward to a widening vista.

There are a few basic rules, the common sense of which is evident.

Do not plant tall trees, no matter how slender the type, in front of a window. Tall trees and shrubs should be planted where they can be seen to best advantage — against a blank wall or to mask a corner.

Don't site one dramatic plant too close to another.

Don't use too many narrow vertical shrubs in front of a building as these can have a disrupting effect, except perhaps when masking extremities or framing an entrance.

When planting window-boxes, go for a bold effect using a mass of one colour, rather than a mixture of colours, to contrast with another mass of a single colour, and lighten the planting by the addition of white or delicately coloured trailing flowers. Use colour in broad brush-strokes rather than in a fidgety, stippled manner.

Don't expect climbers to clothe your walls unless they are given adequate support. Complete plant food and compost mixed into the soil in which the climbers are planted will provide the necessary basic nourishment and a trellis made from latticed wood, plasticised wire or even from wire strung from nail to nail up the wall will give a tendrilled or twining plant the help needed to take off. Very few climbers are self-clinging; the ones that are, like the ivies, put out little suction pads which are so strong, that they will pull away not only the paint but part of the stucco.

Position is important. A north wall is the warmest in winter and the coolest in summer. A south wall takes the wind and is short on sun. A west wall can get very hot. An east wall gets morning sun but can be subject to frost in winter. By and large. a north wall offers the best all-round conditions in all climates to all climbers.

Plants for sunny situations
Agave attenuata (thornless)
Brassaia (Umbrella Tree)
Croton (warm climates only)
Doryanthes excelsa (Torch Lily)
D. palmeri
Dracaena draca (Dragon Tree)
Echium fastuosum
Fatsia japonica
Hedychium
Phormium (New Zealand Flax)
Strelitzia nicolai
S. parvifolia juncea
S. reginae
Yucca gloriosa

Plants for shady situations
Asplenium nidus
Aucuba japonica (Gold Dust Shrub)
Bromeliads (various types)
Clivia
Cordyline stricta
Doryanthes
Dracaena deremensis
Fatsia japonica
Mahonia
Monstera

Tall, vertical accent trees
Brachychiton acerifolium (Flame Tree)
Callitris rhomboidea (Port Jackson Pine)
Camellia japonica (most varieties)
Chamaecyparis lawsoniana aurea (golden)
C. L. erecta (bright green)
C. L. erecta glauca (grey)
Cupressus sempervirens stricta (Pencil Pine)
C. s. s. 'Swayne's Golden'
Elaeocarpus reticulatus (Blue Berry Ash)
Gingko biloba (Maidenhair Tree)
Hymenosporum flavum (Native
    Frangipani)
Lagunaria patersonii (Norfolk Island
    Hibiscus — may spread with age)
Liriodendron tulipifera (Tulip Tree)
Salix chiliensis (Pencil Willow)

Hanging plants
Campanula poscharskyana
Cymbalaria (Kennilworth Ivy)
Geranium (ivy types)
Gibasis (Hawaiian Bridal Veil)
Lobelia (trailing types)
Lotus berthelotii
Nasturtium

Carefully selecting trees, plants and flowers will add beauty and peace to your home

Friendly fences

Plants can often be used to replace conventional fences.

It is good landscaping to screen fences with shrubbery or creepers. But why bother to build fences to screen, when there are plenty of shrubs and other plants that will replace them efficiently?

Shrubs will appear more decorative and friendly because they look like an extension of the garden rather than a man-made barrier.

For their role as a hedge they can be chosen from the beginning to grow to the size wanted and left with a soft, natural appearance. You can compromise, if you wish, by trimming for denser growth.

Different plants may be alternated for contrast in both colour and shape. Silver-grey westringia or 'coast rosemary' (extremely resistant to salt winds) combines well with purple-bronze berberis. On a larger scale, conical variegated pittosporum, which grows upright, could be planted with comparatively squat bronze-green abelia.

Westringia goes well with abelia, too, and would also alternate happily with either yellow Drap d'Or or orange-and-red Chelsea Gem lantana. Both these lantanas are neat and compact, flowering right through summer and autumn, and they do not invade the entire garden. They are improved by fairly heavy pruning.

One of the loveliest flowering fences I can remember was a random intermingling of pale blue plumbago and purple lantana. They probably started off one on each side of the fence, then gradually combined.

Purple lantana (*L. montevidensis*, previously *L. sellowiana*) is also an inoffensive, non-invasive plant. It makes a mat of fine non-thorny stems and is often used as a dense ground cover. With the aid of a few stakes or a strip of wire netting, it can be raised to a metre or so.

If you want a substantial manproof fence, then plant the evergreen hawthorns or pyracanthas. Attractive *P. fortunii* has dark, glossy foliage and clusters of shiny bright crimson berries in autumn and early winter. *P. angustifolia* is heavily clustered with bright orange berries, but is more spreading — to 3 metres or so. For quick cover you could put in plants about 2 m apart.

Where little more than demarcation is needed, there are dense but low-growing plants such as dwarf box *(Buxus sempervirens)*. This glossy small-foliaged plant is used for the small formal hedges bordering many of the classical French and Italian gardens. It is fairly slow to establish and needs clipping after making its spring growth for a trim, formalised effect.

Then there is rosemary, which can be trimmed as a low hedge or allowed to grow unevenly from 1–2 m tall. It suits all but tropical districts.

Euonymus japonicus variegatus has naturally compact, rounded growth to one metre or more. It is a pleasant golden green. Plant a little less than 1 m apart.

Roses should not be overlooked for fences or hedges. Taller, strong-growing types like Queen Elizabeth or Buccaneer, planted about 1 m apart, will soon make a formidable but colourful fence at least 2 m tall.

Floribundas such as old favourite red Lilli Marlene are ideal for low, not-too-dense hedges. Pearly white Sea Foam makes a rambling, metre-high hedge with the aid of a few stakes.

Many of the climbing roses can be effectively grown along a low post-and-rail support.

Camellias also make a fine informal hedge, especially sasanqua varieties which stand full sun. Branches can be interlaced. Types like Hiruyu are suitable as the vigorous new growth remains pliable for some months. Set plants about 2 m apart. They take a few years to make good growth, so initially could be interspersed with marguerites or geraniums.

Ivy geraniums give wonderful effects trailed over supports about a metre high. They can be mixed with white marguerites, dusty millers, or even Sea Foam roses.

A planting of trees and shrubs can replace an ugly fence or cover an existing fence

Beautify your footpath

What better way to beautify your district and improve the environment than by starting with the street area outside your home?

This kind of improvement can cause a chain reaction. It often takes only one or two residents to upgrade their section of the nature strip before many more follow the example.

Also, the nature strip might be just the place for those trees or shrubs you want but lack space for in the garden, or even for annuals that need more open sunlight than the garden can offer. In other words, make the nature strip an extension of your garden, as so many people do already.

In fact, when we look back a few decades we realise that the footpath areas have improved tremendously, probably since power mowers came within reach of most households. Now the number of well-cared-for footpath lawns far exceed neglected areas. Many of the earlier ones were started just by mowing to keep down existing weeds and grass; then gradually they were improved.

Ask for advice at your Town Hall. Some councils give lists of trees they consider suitable for street planting in their localities and a few even supply trees.

The first consideration is to have something that does not obstruct road or footpath traffic by spreading until it is well above head height.

However, this should not exclude comparatively low-branching types such as liquid amber, dawn redwood or nyssa, if side branches are cut back sufficiently.

There are instances where height must also be considered, as unfortunately some councils still seem unaware of the need to have the electricity mains put underground. Not only are the poles and crossbars a blot on the landscape; trees must be small enough to keep below the wires.

Lopping the trees is far from the answer as this is an unnecessary expense and destroys their character — there is a notable exception at Richmond, NSW, where majestic plane trees are pruned so that the wires pass through a gap in their branches.

People living in tropical districts are fortunate in having beautiful and comparatively low-spreading trees like the glorious red poinciana. The lovely pink Cassia nodosa (or *C. javanica*) also is easily kept below wire level; similarly the pendulous golden *Cassia fistula,* the bauhinias and the Queensland umbrella tree.

For temperate areas there are the yellow-flowered river box (*Tristania laurifolia*), *Cállistemon salignus* and bauhinias; and others a little taller such as Cape chestnut, sapium, *Prunus vesuvius*, flindersia, the taller crepe myrtles, pepper trees and small gums such as willow gum (*Eucalyptus scoparia*) and New England peppermint (*E. nicholii*) which

do not lose character if top growth is eventually taken back.

In cold climates there are the hawthorns, laburnums, Japanese maples and flowering cherries. Deciduous trees allow a desirable balance of summer shade and winter sun plus a scene changing with the seasons, in many cases giving spring flowers or coloured autumn foliage.

If you want to grow bushy shrubs or densely foliaged trees such as conifers and variegated pittosporums, make sure they are placed so they will not block the view of anyone backing from a driveway on to the road, or of a nearby cross street.

We sometimes see delightful footpath displays of annuals. The success of these depends greatly on the control neighbours exercise over dogs and children, but I do know someone who is understanding and patient enough to interest neighbouring children in whatever he plants, and even gains their co-operation as guardians of the garden. Admittedly, he is retired and so is around the area for a good part of the day.

Flower beds running outside the fence usually fare the best as the fence gives some protection. Low-growing carpeting annuals such as alyssum and Virginian stock are probably the wisest choice for street planting.

Wall planting (Campanulas, alyssum, begonias, ivy, geraniums, etc.) makes a lovely curtain of colour

Violas are very colourful and long-flowering but they take a little longer to establish.

In several areas I have seen ivy used effectively as a low-edging or clipped border for footpath gardens, with spring annuals such as linaria or primula planted inside it.

One spectacular summer display I remember had long narrow beds of dwarf scarlet salvia edged with neatly-clipped variegated ivy.

Ivy is also an ideal cover on footpath areas too shaded for grass to grow well. It is not meant to take foot traffic but has the advantage of withstanding or at least quickly recovering from an occasional trampling.

Pig's face (*mesembryanthemum*) is ideal in all but very frosty areas for the sunny sloping banks of footpaths not likely to be walked on. Gazaneas also suit these situations. Both give a good show during spring and withstand long periods of dryness.

If you want something·easy but taller, plant cannas in reasonably moist sunny positions or agapanthus in tougher partly shaded areas. The latter, once established, compete well enough with the roots of most trees.

Above all, be philosophical about the footpath garden. If it works out and you enjoy it there is scope to go further. Expect an occasional disappointment but if it's too frustrating be prepared to abandon the flower idea and just mow the grass, which is still a worthwhile contribution to the district.

Above: Recessed rock garden beautifies footpath   *Below: Jacaranda-like Delonix regia (poinciana)*

Drape your fence with colour

One fence I frequently pass by is a striking mixture of lavender blue and bright golden orange. Here the choice is *Bignonia lindleyana* (now officially *clytostoma callistegioides*) which has masses of flowers like large jacaranda blooms, and orange *thunbergia Gibsonii*.

This type of combination can be practical because the *thunbergia* grows rapidly yet is gentle enough not to smother the slower developing *Bignonia*.

Other suggestions for possible combinations are the lovely coral pink antigonon and white mandervilla which are both summer flowering and grow in all but the coldest districts. Also, for more gentle growth, the sparkling little fire cracker plant, Manettia bicolor, with its multitude of bright red and yellow-tipped small tubular flowers, and Sollya, the Western Australian Blue Bell Vine.

The latter makes fairly dense fine caney growth that does twine to some extent but rarely covers an area more than about 2 m square.

Manettia flowers mainly during spring and summer. It also tends to keep to a little less than 2 m spacings. Both are happy in about half-sun.

Allamanda cathartica varieties are delightful in sheltered, warmer, temperate to tropical climates with their almost continuous masses of large golden yellow bells. They are wonderful mixers and in many north Queensland gardens intermingle with rich red bougainvillaeas, antigonon or 'purple wreath vine', *Petrea volubilis*. Petrea is occasionally found growing and flowering well in temperate regions but is more at home in warmer districts. Its large, lilac-like sprays of starry calyces hold their colour for many months after the small violet-like true flowers have fallen from their centres.

Congea is another outstanding tropical beauty, with rich rose to coral pink bracts that cover the wide-spreading vine densely during winter.

The bracts hold for many months, gradually fading to a dusty mauve-pink.

Cool-climate gardeners also enjoy wonderful bonuses, especially the lovely clematis that are really at home in cool to cooler temperate districts. Delightfully simple, four-petalled *Clematis montana* makes the most beautiful lacy veil over a fence, pergola or any other willing support. This starry-flowered beauty comes in crisp white (*alba*) and soft pink (*rubens*).

The large-flowered hybrid clematis seem to concentrate their effort into a lesser number of much larger and individually more spectacular flowers. These include six-petalled 'Barbara Jackman', with its cluster of glistening cream stamens contrasting against the deep purple rays that taper out toward the centre of each broad blue petal and 'Lasurstern' with still broader petals like rich, violet-blue velvet.

Our native Hardenbergias or 'False Sarsaparillas' make a charming mass of small violet-blue or lavender-blue pea flowers in spring and combine well with salmon-scarlet *Kennedia coccinea*, the Western Australian Coral pea.

Carolina jasmine, with its festoons of fragrant yellow bells, is another twiner that could be combined with Hardenbergia.

The only completely self-clinging creeper is the yellow-flowered Cat's Claw Creeper, *Bignonia tweediana*, or now officially *Doxantha unguis-cati*. It covers with brilliant canary yellow flowers, mainly in late spring.

Apart from the latter and bougainvillaea, all creepers or climbers mentioned are twining types, so on a solid fence or wall need some support to start them on their way.

Clematis montana with larger flowered C. 'Barbara Jackman'

Mauve wisteria drapes gracefully over a fence

Yellow Rosa banksia lutea pruned to drape fence

Climbers to grow against the north wall of a house

Antigonon (Coral Vine)
Bougainvillea
Petrea volubilis
Solandra nitida (Cup of Gold)
Solanum wenlandii (Potato Creeper)
Stephanotis

Climbers to grow against the east wall of a house

Clematis montana
Doxantha (Cat's Claw Creeper)
Hardenbergia comptoniana
Jasminum polyanthum
Lonicera
Mandevilla
Rose
Senecio
Solanum jasminoides
Wisteria

Climbers to grow against the west wall of a house

Aristolochia (Dutchman's Pipe)
Cobea scandens (Purple Bell Flower)
Doxantha (Cat's Claw Creeper)
Hardenbergia (Lilac Vine)
Ipomea
Pandorea pandorana (Wonga-wonga Vine)
Phaseolus caracalla (Snail Vine)
Pyrostegia (Orange Bignonia)
Solanum jasminoides
Trachelospermum jasminoides (Star
   Jasmine)

Climbers to grow against a south wall

Ficus pumila (Creeping Fig)
Hedera (Ivy)
Parthenocissus quinquefolia (Boston Ivy)
P. tricuspidata (Virginia Creeper)

Right: Doxantha (Cat's Claw Creeper)

Vitis vinifera (Ornamental grape)

Pink bougainvillaea intermingled with yellow allamanda

3. Overcoming Gardening Difficulties

Gardening on a sloping site

Where the site is exceptionally steep, the formal approach is to step it down in a series of regular terraces at right angles to the slope. A more popular treatment closer to our natural landscape is to use natural stone rockery-type retainers meandering in gentle zig-zag fashion down the contour.

In rocky areas it is often possible to make use of natural outcroppings of rock linking them with added rocks. The soil can be retained with good permanent ground cover plants.

Plants for a sloping site

A site that slopes at an angle of 30–45° will look good if plants grown in it contour the bank. Low-spreading shrubs, vines, ground cover, a few brilliant annuals and succulents, and the occasional taller shrub or small tree for sudden, dramatic accent, offer infinite variation. Trees or taller shrubs could be kept to the top of the site. Watering should be done by misting or using a fine sprinkler. If there seems to be any danger of soil-slip, a few strong shrubs at the bottom of the slope will hold the bank together.

Natural features

Natural features should be left undisturbed; these include trees, native shrubbery, even stumps, logs, etc. In fact, do not clear anything until ready to replace it with something else or give the area some other treatment — otherwise much of the existing topsoil may be lost. Clearing prematurely invites takeover by weeds.

In very rocky areas with shallow soil it is sometimes possible to bare flat, large boulders that can be used as a path or an open area. The soil removed can be used to build other sections to a good depth for cultivation.

Weathered bush rocks look very pleasant in rockeries or as retaining banks if they are not too obviously cemented, but this rock is expensive. Frankly, if the banks or rockeries are well planted it matters little whether they are constructed of choice stone or rubble from the site for it is not long before growth completely covers them.

Run-off water can be a problem if not controlled. In most cases it can be directed down pathways, but if the latter zig-zag down a slope you will need to use boulders to direct the flow or lower the path slightly where water would otherwise take the most direct course. Sometimes a natural watercourse can be preserved or you can make one and direct minor cross-drains into it.

The water course can be featured as a natural creek, even if it is dry most of the time. Instead of casing it with brick or concrete use a placement of rock or boulders, large river stones or a combination of both. This material must be substantial because running water develops a surprising propellent force.

Planting steep banks

Steep banks can be retained and integrated into the garden by planting them with a good permanent ground cover such as ivy, or with a mixture of low-spreading shrubbery.

If the banks are covered with unwanted grass or weed growth, kill it off and leave as a soil binder and protection cover while the wanted plants are establishing. This may not appeal to some people, because during the transition period it will not look attractive, but it is practical, especially when using the modern range of weedicides that leave the soil toxic for no more than a few days. (See 'Weed Control'.) After poisoning, leave for a few weeks, deal with new growth, then trample down the dead stubble as a mulch, removing only as much as needed when you make the planting holes.

Clay or shale banks will need soil-improvement before planting. Ivy is a good choice as it is self-clinging and, providing enough soil can be added to start the plants, it will soon spread and make roots.

As fallen leaves and similar material filter through the ground cover and decompose, a layer of more productive soil will build up over the surface of the clay.

With this gradual improvement in mind, either dig holes to hold enough soil to encourage the ivy or other cover plants, or drive in a few stakes to secure palings or timber troughs to hold soil for the cover plants. In Italy I have seen cover plants established on roadside cuttings in soil retained by a row of short stakes across the slope, with sticks or brush woven between them. Lack of permanence in the holding material is not important because once the cover plants establish their roots they bind the soil efficiently.

Colourful ground covers growing over rock-terraced slope

Timber walls

Timber, particularly treated pine and railway sleepers, makes effective retaining walls. Several methods are provided for interlocking some of the proprietary materials. The sleepers can either be stabilised behind heavy posts or bolted to a series of T-pieces keyed between alternate courses at the ends, or between joints. Precast, interlocking concrete beams are also available for large-scale embankments. This forms a substantial, open-type retaining wall with planting space between the beams.

Sleepers make an effective retaining wall

Railway sleepers make good steps and effectively retain slopes

Dry pack walls

Well-made, dry pack walls are effective embankment retainers and look very attractive, with trailing plants spilling from between the stones. The stones need to be at least 15 cm wide, but 20–25 cm is better. Their depth or length is not important although a few long ones (30–40 cm) will key the others in.

The wall will be more stable if the bank slopes back about 10° from the perpendicular. It is necessary to create a slope if none exists. Start by digging a foundation trench about one-third m wide and half as deep at the base of the bank, or correspondingly deeper and wider if the wall is over 1 m high. Lay a course of the heaviest stones in the base, if necessary packing sand or soil underneath to stabilise them.

Spread 3–4 cm of soil over the stones to give an even base for the next course; build up and firm soil behind them but don't attempt to achieve uniform depth. Lay the next course of stones, flattest side down, except where one will key easily into a gap used another way. Keep the outward face of each stone in line with the face of the wall by filling with soil and building up with some of the lesser or rougher stones behind or below it. Hold each stone in place while ramming soil between it and the bank.

Repeat this process until the desired height is reached, checking to see that the line of the wall is kept true. Use a plumb-line to check that the inward slope is maintained. Here and there use a wider stone or set one with the longest side into the bank to lock the wall to the backing.

Set stones so that the centre is approximately below the joint of the ones behind it, as you would in bricklaying. Where stones are not of similar length start a course by placing two or three large ones this way initially and then fill in between them with smaller ones.

Plants are set in new soil as the construction progresses, using enough water to settle them in, but not enough to make the soil sloppy. The top of the wall can be finished with flattish stones but this is not essential. Cement may be used if necessary.

Solid, random rubble stone walls can also be constructed this way but it is essential to have a wider footing with an agricultural drainage pipe behind it and rubble (or gravel backfill) above the pipe and between wall and bank. Weep holes at least 1 cm wide should be left between the stones every half- to one metre just above a drain at the base of the wall. This drain can be open or you can sink an agricultural drain and cover it with gravel.

Right: A grassed slope creates a feeling of space

Stone steps wind attractively through a setting of azaleas

Grass banks

Where a change of level divides a lawn, the easiest, most economical and most attractive treatment is to grass the dividing bank. This preserves the smooth flow of the lawn and creates a feeling of space. It is practical, providing the bank is graded to about 45°, and the top ridge and angle at the bottom is bevelled gradually to allow mowing. Soil cut from the ridge at the top of the bank can be raked down to smooth out the angle at the base.

Surface drainage could seriously erode the bank. The simplest and least obtrusive way to overcome the problem is to make a slight depression or ditch in the lawn 1–2 m back from the top of the bank.

Have a slight fall across, as well as down the slope, enough to take the water to one side or the other. Or make a diagonal ditch, starting two to three metres back from the bank at one side and about a metre from the top at the lowest end.

Steps

Making steps

These are essential when a grade would otherwise be uncomfortably steep or slippery. They can be an attractive feature of a sloped garden but you will need a ramped path if you want to use a wheelbarrow or lawnmower. Safety

Irrespective of whether you are building steps in concrete, brick, timber, cut or natural bush stone, there are a few important points that need to be observed.

Edges must be even, so if using natural bush stone, fill any gaps in the edges with cement, even though it might detract from appearance.

The steps must be of even height and have a width of tread that balances height. The wider the tread the lower the height of each step or 'riser', and the higher the step the narrower the tread, up to a certain point. The accompanying diagram gives the width of tread for height of riser.

Measure the height of the bank or rise where steps are needed. If you want low steps (which look best) and the height is 60 cm, with 10 cm risers, you will need 6 steps with treads 58 cm wide. This means the steps will either protrude or be cut into the bank approximately 3.5 cm. If you can't afford this space, try using steps with higher risers, say 15 cm, which will give an overall length of only 1.4 m because it involves 4 steps with depth of tread only 35 cm each instead of 6 at 58 cm.

Precautions

When using cut stones or flat bush rocks, do not lap them more than a couple of centimetres over the edge of the riser below. Unless the front edge of the riser is in good contact with the step above, the latter will tip when weight is placed on its front edge. This problem can be ameliorated by packing cement between the tread and riser, to bring the point of balance as close to the front of the tread as possible.

Riser Height	Tread Depth
10 cm	58 cm
11 cm	51 cm
12.5 cm	45 cm
13 cm	40 cm
15 cm	35 cm
16 cm	30 cm
17.5 cm	26 cm
18 cm	25 cm
20 cm	22 cm

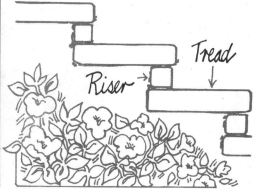

Gardening on rocky slopes

Success will depend on the use made of existing pockets of soil and the strategic positioning of plants grown in containers. Such soil as there is should be kept in prime condition by the surface build-up of organic material which will encourage.

It is better to bare your rock and to soften its outlines with containers spilling with plants than to attempt to garden in a few centimetres of soil with rock beneath it. Much of the art of gardening lies in the art of the possible: if your garden is made of rock, accept that you will never grow exhibition carrots or other root vegetables. Settle for plants in containers or succulents and similar plants that accept very shallow soil. Alternatively use some of the retaining methods mentioned earlier to retain a good depth of added soil above the shallow rock.

Large shrubs or small trees for moderately shallow soil

Acacia podalyriifolia (Qld Wattle)
Arbutus unedo (Strawberry Tree)
Calliandra
Callistemon viminalis (Weeping Bottlebrush)
Erythrina crista-gallii (Coral Tree)
Eucalyptus cinerea (Florist Gum)
Eucalyptus ficifolia (Flowering Gum)
Grevillea banksii (Scarlet Grevillea)
Hakea
Loropetalum (Chinese Witch Hazel)
Melaleuca nesophila (Tea Myrtle)
Nerium oleander (Oleander)
Parkinsonia
Pittosporum (All kinds)
Prunus (Flowering Peach or Brown-leaved Plum)
Photinia
Protea neriifolia (Oleander-leaved Protea)
Spartium junceum (Spanish Broom)

Low spreading plants

Arctotis
Ajuga (Carpet Bugle)
Alyssum
Bulbine caulescens
Cerastium (Snow-in-Summer)
Crassula (many kinds)
Dichondra repens (Lawn-Leaf)
Drosanthemum hispidum (Dew-Flower)
Duchesnea (Wild Strawberry)
Erigeron karvinskianus (Vittadinia)
Gazanias
Geranium incanum
Hedera (Ivy)
Heeria elegans
Hypericum calycinum (Gold Flower)
H. repens
Iberis sempervirens (Perennial Candytuft)
Japanese Spurge (Pachysandra)
Lippia Grass
Mesembryanthemum
Nepeta mussini (Catmint)
Nierembergia (Cup Flower)
Phlox subulata (Alpine Phlox)
Potentilla
Polygonum capitatum
Salvia leucantha (Purple Salvia)
Sedum
Stachys lanata (Lamb's Ears)
Vinca major (Periwinkle)

Upright plants

Agapanthus
Day Lilies
Dierama (Harebell)
Ferns
Gerbera
New Zealand Flax
Yucca

Shrubby vines

Bauhinia galpinii
Doxantha
Lonicera japonica
Phaedanthus
Plumbago
Pyrostegia
Trachelospermum

Medium-sized and small shrubs

Chamelaucium uncinatum (Geraldton Waxflower)
Cotoneaster (Prostrate varieties)
Clianthus puniceus
Echium fastuosum
Elaeagnus pungens
Erica
Escallonia macrantha
Grevillea rosmarinifolia
Lantana montevidensis (Mauve Lantana)
Leonotis leonurus (Lion's Ear)
Leptospermum (Tea-tree)
Leucospermum nutans (Nodding Pincushion)
Mahonia aquafolium (Holly Mahonia)
Melaleuca lateritia (Robin Redbreast Bush)

Gazania and alyssum

A colourful rock garden of campanula, alyssum saxatile, saxifraga and aubretia

Heeria with mesembryanthemum

Bringing birds back to the garden

A garden needs more than the visual beauty of plants; the melodious calls and busy flutter of birds really stir a garden into life.

Birds have more than aesthetic appeal. They are nature's controllers of the vast insect population, both of parasites and predators. Some birds are themselves predators of smaller predatory creatures such as frogs and lizards, while others are scavengers, cleaning away food scraps left by others.

Some birds, such as crows, are eaters of carrion and are perhaps unwelcome pests at times, but they make the environment more liveable and cut down the number of flies by removing dead animals.

Anyone can lure flocks of sparrows, Indian mynahs, pigeons and other scavenging birds by providing scraps of bread, grain or similar types of food. Encouraging the more beneficial insect eaters is a slightly different story, as it depends on providing a well-planted environment where they can enjoy seclusion as well as a natural balance of insect life.

Water or a bird bath, perhaps some form of feeding stations and, to some extent, honey-bearing flowers will also help. These flowers are usually regarded as the most important birdscaping element, but this is not necessarily so. They form a particular attraction only to the various spinebills and wattle birds, but even these birds are fairly diversified in their feeding habits and are also insect eaters.

I have watched wattle birds catch and devour large moths in flight after raiding the bread, honey, brown sugar and water mixture put out for rainbow lorikeets.

The wattle birds and other honey eaters are, of course, particularly partial to the flowers of banksias, grevilleas, bottle brushes and melaleucas, but they also seem happy to visit the flowers of a great variety of exotics, including abutilons (Chinese lanterns), hibiscus, single camellias, justicia, NZ flax, tecoma, bignonias, fuchsias and many others.

Our smaller insect eaters — wrens, brown fantails, silver eyes and pardalotes — carry out their aphid-hunting drives in citrus, camellias, roses and other exotics as keenly as they do in native shrubbery.

The wrens, silver eyes and fire tails build their nests as happily in a wistaria, asparagus or rambling rose thicket as they do in native shrubbery, and usually with better protection from currawong attack.

Some form of dense shelter is appreciated by the smaller birds. Most birds, large or small, revel in a bird bath, a wide container only 5–8 cm deep is more attractive to most birds than deep water. Either have the bath on a pedestal or with some overhead shelter but clear the area around it so that cats are less likely to stalk the bird while it is bathing.

Feeding stations will attract honey or nectar-feeding birds. There are inverted jar-type feeders that allow the honey and water mixture to ooze through a wick-like fabric. These birds are accustomed to picking up small amounts of similar solutions with the end of

Feeding stations lure birds to the garden

their long, penetrating, plunger-like tongues.

Small grain, such as Hungarian millet and canary seed, attracts finches, sparrows and redheads or fire tails, which have their appeal even though they're not particularly useful to the garden.

Any of these feeding stations should be located out of reach of cats. They can be suspended half a metre or so from a branch or on a thin bracket at least of similar length out from a high railing or a couple of metres up a wall.

A simple feeding platform can be made by suspending a length of board with nylon cord, swing fashion, from a tree or trellis. There is a theory that a swinging type of feeder is attractive to native birds but not to exotic invaders.

Allowing birds to become dependent on feeding station hand-outs is a mistake. Using it for a few weeks initially encourages birds to the area and they are then inclined to linger.

Confine feeding to prolonged wet periods, drought periods or other times when there may be little food about.

Plant grevilleas, melaleucas, etc, for the spine bills and wattle birds by all means. Most important, spray with care, only when insects get the better of the situation, and preferably only the parts of the garden where it is necessary.

Use low-residual insecticides like pyrethrum where possible, otherwise insects poisoned by potent chemicals can also poison the birds that eat them.

Melodious bird calls stir a garden into life

Rainbow lorikeets feeding

4. Special Gardens

Shade gardening

In gardening terms 'shade' does not mean total gloom but an area where direct sunlight does not fall. 'Semishade' is used to describe positions which have sun for only short periods of the day or where sunlight, though available day-long, is filtered through an overhang of leaves.

The shaded area of a garden can be a problem, but only if you allow it, for there are many ways to make it into an interesting feature area and a cool haven during summer.

The first thing is to give up all attempts to grow plants which obviously do not thrive there, and this includes grass. The soil in the shade beneath a tree is often poor and dry because the tree-roots are voracious feeders and take up all the available food and moisture. However, trees with deep roots such as the Eucalypts and Pines will not compete with shallow-rooted underplantings and if you plant beneath fibrous-rooted trees which have a spread of roots near to the surface they could actually benefit from the watering and attention you will give the new planting.

If you plant beneath a tree you must ensure there is adequate nourishment available. You can do this by spading out some of the tired soil and replacing it with good garden loam, to a depth which will give the new plants a good start, and then mulching around them with compost. Keep both the new soil and the compost away from the trunk of the tree, for if it becomes covered above its natural level the trunk could begin to rot.

If you decide not to attempt planting you could always pave the area and introduce colour with containers of plants which have been brought to the flowering stage in the sunlight and will continue to bloom in the shade. Or if you don't like too much paving leave panels of soil in which you can grow ground cover which will tolerate the situation, or you could introduce a small pool and make a cool mossy place where ferns would flourish.

Watering, always an important facet of the gardener's work, is more important than ever with regard to plants growing in the shade. Some plants handle lack of water better than others; the ones with big fleshy roots like the Agapanthus sustain it much better than ones with delicate fibrous roots which grow near the surface — azaleas are a good example. Small plants will need more frequent watering than deep-rooted shrubs, so try to make groupings of plants which require the same treatment, with the neediest ones being the most accessible.

The lists will help you to make your choice but nothing is better than personal experience. Few of us will not have learned that hydrangeas do better if they have a lot of water rather than what seems a normal amount, or that bromeliads need practically no watering at all.

Perennials for shaded positions
(Note: L indicates light shade only)
Acanthus, Acorus
Agapanthus (L)
Ajuga (L), *Bergenia*
Bromeliads
Chlorophytum
Crassula multicava (L)
Cyclamen neapolitan (L)
Clivia, Cymbalaria
Cyperus arternifolius (L)
Dietes (L)
Dracaena
Erigeron karvinskyanus
Helleborus orientalis (L)
Helxine, Hemerocalis (L)
Hosta (L)
Houstonia (L)
Impatiens, Iris ungicularis
Kohleria, Lamium
Libertia (L), *Ligularia*
Liriope muscari
Liriope japonica
Lotus peliorhyncus (L)
Lunaria (L), Maurandia (L)
Mazus (L), *Pachysandra*
Polyanthus (L)
Primula obconica (L)
Primula denticulata (L)
Saxifraga (various)
Schizocentron
Scilla, Tradescantia
Vinca major (L)
Vinca rosea (L)
Violet (all types) (L)
Zebrina pendula

Annuals for lightly shaded positions
Bellis
Browallia elator
Cineraria
Coleus
Lobelia
Nicotiana
Nigella (love-in-mist)
Primula malacoides
Schizanthus (Poor Man's Orchid)

Above: Clivia miniata

Left: Emphasis on white is a pleasant variation

Shrubs for shaded positions
(Those marked * prefer shade — others adapt to any but dense shade

Abelia
Abutilon
*Aralia**
*Ardisia**
*Aucuba**
Azaleas
Bauera
Begonia* (tree)
Berberis
Buxus
Camellia
Choisya
Clethra
Coprosma
Daphne
Elaeagnus
Eriostemon
Fatsia
Fatshedera
Ferns*
Fuchsias*
Goldfussia
Hydrangea
Hypericum
Ilex
Luculia
Nandina
Odontonema
Osmanthus
Palms
Phormium
Pittosporum tobira
*Plectranthus**
Posequeria
*Pseudopanx**
Punica
Raphiolepis
Rhododendron
Schefflera
Tree Ferns*
Viburnum suspensus
Viburnum tinus

Small plants for half-shade
Alyssum
Bellis
Bergenia
Coleus
Cineraria
Cymbidium (orchid)
Daffodil
Freesia
Hyacinth
Lachenalia
Lily of the Valley
Lobelia
Muscari (Grape Hyacinth)
Myositis (Forget-me-not)
Pansy
Polyanthus
Primula
Scilla

Succulents for shaded, poor soil
Crassula portulacea (Jade)
C. multicava (London Pride)
Sedum spectabile

Bulbs for shaded areas
Crinum (Veld Lily)
Haemanthus (Lily)
Moraea
Muscari (Grape Hyacinth)
Scilla (Bluebell)
Tritonia

Climbers for lightly shaded areas
Clematis hybrids
Clematis montana rubens
Clerodendrum splendens
Clerodendrum thompsoniae
        (Bleeding Heart Clerodendron)
Clytostoma callistegioides (Mauve Bignonia)
Doxantha unguis-cati (Cat's Claw Creeper)
Ficus pumila (Creeping Fig)
Hardenbergia comptoniana (Lilac Vine)
Hedera helix (English Ivy)
Hedera canariensis variegata
        (Variegated Canary Islands Ivy)
Hoya carnosa (Wax Plant)
Jasminium sambac (Arabian jasmine)
Lonicera sempervirens (Honeysuckle)
Maurandia barclaiana
Podranea
Rhoicissus capensis (Wild Grape)
Sollya heterophylla
Trachelospermum jasminoides (Star
  Jasmine)

Native plants for moderately moist, shady spots
Baeckea ramosissima
Banksia collina
Bauera rubioides
Bauera sessifolia
Boronia heterophylla
Boronia mollis
Boronia pinnata
Correa reflexa
Eriostemon myoporoides
Ferns of all types
Grevillea alpina
G. asplenifolia
Hibbertia sericea
H. volubilis
Platylobium formosum
Prostanthera lasianthos (Vic. Christmas
  Bush)
Pultenaea daphnoides
Westringia longifolia

Exotics for shade under trees
Azalea
Chlorophytum (Spider plant)
Clivia
Cineraria
Liriope muscari (Ribbon Grass)
Ophiopogon (Ribbon Grass)
Plectranthus
Polyanthus
Primula

Azaeleas, freesias and polyanthus grow successfully in dappled shade

Rock Gardens

A rockery can be the answer when a steep site looks bare and unattractive or a flat one looks uninteresting. You can grow a wide range of alpine plants, low-carpeting perennials and other dwarf plants in a rockery because the drainage is good and they provide a number of different aspects within a small area. They are not, however, essential ingredients of good landscaping and certainly not of easy-care gardening.

Don't think that cementing between the stones will keep out couch, nut grass or other running weeds; it won't, it will just impede drainage, make the weeds more difficult to get at and, more often that not, destroy the beauty of the time-sculptured bush or seashore stone which you have toiled to set in place.

Building a rockery

There are many different styles. Rocks, in their natural setting, are found with their heaviest and broadest side down, usually half-buried in the earth. They look at ease. If you balance them on their sides or stand them upright, they will not. You can cheat a bit by propping a broad, but comparatively shallow piece of rock on its side to make it look bigger and more dramatic, but you must support it well and make sure the back is well bedded into the earth.

Irrespective of the stone used, good planting will soon cover most of it. However, a few large pieces are preferable to a lot of small ones.

It will be easier to construct if you can make use of the natural sloping contour of the land — if the land is flat, you should build it up by digging out an area and banking up the soil you have removed to make a slope, which should not be less than 60–75 cm. A rockery on a very steep slope will be hard work to create and could present difficulties in maintenance, so think on a comfortable, rather than a grand-scale when planning your layout.

Keep the outline irregular, both at the lower front edge where the rockery joins the lawn or garden path and at the top where rocks should jut unevenly. The smooth contrived outline should be avoided.

If you start at the lower end of the rockery you should imbed the rocks in the earth to about half-depth at an angle of about 45° and tipped backwards so that you can fill in behind them with plenty of soil.

In some cases you may find it advantageous to fill the base of the space with clinkers, crocking or coke before topping up with soil. Dampen the soil and tramp down well. Place the next lot of rocks on the earth and bury the base of each of them in line with the top of the first course. Arrange them so that some are close to the first course and some further away, so that when the spaces are filled in the pockets of soil are irregularly shaped. Rocks should be placed with their most attractive side at the front and on view, and their less attractive one out of sight below the earth. You can construct as many growing pockets as you like, by the way you marry rocks or stones of one size with smaller or larger ones. There are no set rules or pattern of height, size and position; just arrange them and if they do not look 'right' rearrange them, making sure the larger rocks are safely 'bedded-in' and all are locked so as to give each other support.

A rockery looks at its best when you look upward and see it against a background of small trees or shrubs, even with one tall shrub against the sky. If the rockery is broad, have a path winding upward. If it is small, use the occasional small upright evergreen to break the line and catch the eye. It is far better *not* to use cement in the construction. If there is space to be sealed, do it with small pieces of rock clipped to size, if necessary.

Soil for the rockery

A great deal of the soil sold for garden filling, rockeries or top dressing is of poor quality. It may look good, but colour has little or no bearing on the quality of soil. The main complaint against the alluvial soils so widely available is that although they may appear gritty and free-flowing, they pack too densely, are airless, repress root development and so give very poor results. You can improve your own soil by adding river sand if the soil is clayey, or peatmoss if it is very sandy.

Some soil merchants sell a potting mixture, or seed bed soil, which is a mixture of river sand, peaty soil and sometimes loam. This is comparatively expensive but of better value than most close-textured, deeply quarried alluvial soils.

If you find yourself with the latter, mix in one-third mushroom compost, granulated tan bark or other organic material to improve aeration and general structure.

The soil in the pockets should be as good as you can make it to a depth of at least 30 cm.

In this steeply sloping rockery only some lower rocks are cemented.

Maintenance

Many attractive rockery plants such as armerias (thrifts), some of the dwarf campanulas, dianthus, candytufts, perennial asters, some of the achilleas, dwarf convolvulus, most succulents, verbenas, etc. will grow happily in most climates, but there are others in the alpine range which are only suitable for areas with cold winters and long mild springs, followed by fairly dry summers. These include some of the smaller herbaceous anemones such as *A. blanda, A. numerosa,* gentians, lewisia and to a lesser extent alpine phlox, arabis, alyssum saxatile, erysimum, etc. However, the latter group and others can be encouraged to grow in the warmer temperate regions with humid summers if given the right conditions.

One of the main problems with alpines in these more temperate areas, particularly the downy-foliaged types such as arabis, alyssum saxatile, burnt candytuft, some of the artemisias and others, is that they succumb to fungus rots during hot, wet summer periods. These rots usually start at the base of the plant, destroying the main stems, or in the case of arabis and other trailers, work gradually from the original root area outwards.

This can be overcome to some extent by giving them slightly elevated, well-drained positions, particularly if coarse sand or similarly gritty material is added to the soil to accelerate drainage. I find that the most important thing is to cover the soil around them with some sort of gravelly scree such as the finer grade of river pebbles or metal screenings.

This scree keeps the surface of the soil more open and allows water to get away quickly, keeps the plant drier by supporting it above the wet soil and prevents the soil from splashing up around the stems and lower foliage of the plant. This all helps to prevent fungus attack. Also, the plants look at home, growing over this gravelly scree as it is akin to their natural habitat.

Clumpy foliage plants such as alyssum saxatile, some of the dianthus and even English lavender can be affected by a mat of dead foliage collected below the plant. This can remain sodden for long periods and provide conditions inviting to botrytis and similar fungi during hot, humid summer periods. So clear away this dead material at the end of spring or in early summer, and trim some of the older excess base foliage to allow air circulation under the plant.

Watch your plants, particularly immediately after a few days of rain during summer when humidity is at its highest. If there is any sign of rotting or wilting, water the plant thoroughly with a complete fungicide, allowing it to penetrate well down the stem and into the soil around it. Then take cuttings from the still unaffected healthy outer growth. On trailing plants such as arabis, verbenas and alpine phlox, these outer rosettes of growth are inclined to self-layer and may already be making a little of their own root system.

Above, below: Livingstone Daisies

Below: Reddish Dissectum maple drapes attractively

Golden Euonymous and succulents add foliage colour

Dimorphotheca aurantica

Plants for the rockery

If you choose well you could have 50 different plants in a rockery 4 m long and about 1 m wide.

All the plants listed here suit cool districts and adapt fairly well to temperate areas unless otherwise mentioned, although excessive summer rain and humidity may be more difficult for them than dry heat.

Most of them like a light scree or surface mulch of pebbles to keep the soil more open and to stop wet soil from splashing up and clinging to stems and foliage.

The range of rock plants or evergreen perennials is vast but some of those more likely to be available are grouped here according to growth habit.

Trailing or carpeting

Arabis (Rock cress). Grey-green rosetted foliage covered with white flowers in spring. Spreads about 30 cm, needs sun.

Alpine phlox. Mat of grassy foliage; pink, ruby, mauve-blue or white flowers in spring. Best in cool districts where it spreads up to a metre. All but warmest temperate areas.

Aubretia (Rock cress). Similar to arabis, but less adaptable to temperate districts.

Androsace (Rock jasmine). Mat of silvery foliage, phlox-like flowers; white with red eye or pink with crimson eye. Cooler districts.

Anthemis (Camomile). Mat of fern-like foliage, with daisies. *A. nobilis,* small white; *A. tinctoria,* yellow.

Ajuga. Rosettes of dark glossy foliage, bluish flower spikes in spring. Grows anywhere. Variety Burgundy Lace has pink, bronze, cream foliage.

Achillea tomentosa. Mat of feathery grey rosettes, small golden flowers in spring.

Arenaria montana. Trails of fine foliage, scattered white flowers 2.5 cm across, in spring.

Campanulas. Some are clumpy, others carpet. All have delightful bells, usually blue, in late spring. Sun in cool districts, a little shade elsewhere.

Damperia diversifolia. A lovely native. Mat of bright green foliage studded for months with bright blue flowers. Give a cover of pine bark or pebbles in about half-sun.

Erigeron alpinus. Small mats of green with fine-petalled lilac-mauve flowers.

Erigeron (Babies' tears). Wiry trails, spread 1 m or more. Fine-petalled, five-cent-sized pink or white daisies.

Erysimum. Makes stubby mats packed with tiny bright-yellow flowers in spring. Best in cooler districts.

Frankenia pauciflora (Sea heath). Native with minute grey-green foliage, tiny pink flowers.

Lithospermum. Mat of dark foliage; bluest flowers all spring then spasmodically. Needs good drainage, at least half-sun.

Mesembryanthemum. Iridescent flowers, scarlet, orange, white, purple, etc. Tolerates long periods of dryness.

Scleranthus. Moss-like mounds of rich emerald green. Stands full sun.

Silene maritima. Mat of blue-grey foliage; dainty white flowers. Lightly broken sunlight in warmer temperate areas.

Thyme. Westmoreland and variegated lemon thyme, make upright clumps; others, such as caraway thyme and villosus, make low mats. All are aromatic. Well-drained soil with a pebble scree.

More upright and clumpy

Alyssum saxatile. Mounds of long, silvery foliage beneath a canopy of golden flowers, mostly in spring. Dislikes humid summers.

Armeria (Thrift). Mounds of fine foliage; globular heads of papery pink flowers, fine wiry stems.

Brachycome (Swan River daisy). Clumps of fine foliage; small mauve daisies mainly in summer.

Calocephalus. Dense filament of silvery stems make a 30 cm mound. Needs good drainage.

Daphne cneorum. Lovely 30 cm dome massed with pink flowers, late spring. For cooler districts.

Dianthus (or pinks). Numerous kinds make attractive silver-grey clumps with fragrant flowers like small carnations.

Hypericum reptans. Low mound of tiny foliage; buttercup-like yellow flowers.

Jasminum parkeri. Tiny shrub only 12 cm high. Yellow flowers, in summer.

Spiraea (Nyewood's variety). A miniature pink form about 15 cm high.

Kalanchoe

Mauve brachycome

Mesembryanthemum

Pebble gardens

If you are looking for easy maintenance go for pebble gardening but be prepared to put in some work in the initial stages. The pebble garden can be a boon in dry spots close to the house where the eaves keep off the rain or for the narrow strips in a garden which are too dry for many shrubs and most annuals. It can be very effective on a larger scale too. As with Japanese gardens, simplicity and style are the name of the game. In planning the garden consider the use of low-growing shrubs, rocks, water and stepping stones.

Choice of pebbles

Large-size pebbles look dramatic but can be misery underfoot and create difficulty if fallen leaves have to be raked from them. The alternatives are red gravel, crushed brick or crushed tile. You could try a combination of the two using the finer materials in the traffic areas and the larger ones to create effect.

Laying the garden

The first thing is to make sure the area is clear of weeds.

Oxalis, onion weed, nut grass, couch and kikuyu should be spot-sprayed with weedicides. Once they are cleared a 5 cm layer of fine gravel will keep other weeds down.

If you object to the use of weedicides put down black plastic sheeting and hope to smother them. You won't; they will still manage to push their way through any cuts in the plastic but at least you will have them under some sort of control. Anchor the plastic with lengths of 50 x 50 mm timber. This will also give you the height to which the pebbles should be laid.

You have a choice as to how to lay the plastic. If the site is on a slope use metre-wide sheets of plastic and, working from the top down across the slope, lay the sheets with the lower overlapping the upper by about 15 cm, so that water trickling down the slope will be able to seep to the soil beneath. If necessary the plastic can be raised very slightly using small pebbles or mounded sand to create the necessary gap. Set plants through a carefully cut slit in the plastic. On a flatter site use 2–3-metre-wide sheets and set plants through buttonhole slits in the sheeting and create a depression with the gravel or pebbles so that water will be guided down to their roots.

If you are laying a largish garden with stepping stones and featured rocks, flat bush stones, split flagstones, circular wooden blocks or manufactured concrete paving blocks, put them down first but with some sort of insulating material such as Sisalkraft tarred paper between them and the plastic. They all have sharp edges which could do unwelcome damage. Once they are safely in place you can spread the pebbles.

In an area where difficulties in growing are encountered plants can be set in containers and moved around as need be. Wide saucer-shaped containers are both decorative and useful and can be grouped with others of taller and more compact shape to make interesting features.

Low-spreading shrubs which suit pebble gardens are:

Coprosma Marble Queen — cream and green foliage

C. retusa variegata

Grevillea Royal Mantle

Chinese Star Jasmine, which twines upright; also makes a trailing mat of glossy foliage and fragrant cream flowers.

Juniper conferta

Sabina vulgaris.

Many species of ivy are also suitable, particularly for shaded areas.

Succulents suit pebble gardens

Prostrate conifers soften pebble gardens

Simplicity is the key to a good pebble garden

A Japanese garden

An area under trees where shade and the tree roots make ordinary gardening difficult could be the ideal place for the creation of a Japanese garden. Similarly, if you have a problem spot where water collects, you can turn disadvantage to advantage.

There are no *fixed* rules in the creation of a garden of this type but there has to be a 'feeling' for a type of design which is unlike the Western concept. The effect depends on balance and symmetry but not the conventional idea of equal numbers and equal spacing, the centring of a subject, or its equal spacing from the corners of a site. The basic elements of a Japanese garden are rock, plants and water; art lies in creating a relationship between them which is disciplined and restrained and which creates a feeling of peace. The triangle can be used to give a guide in grouping. An imaginary line from the centre of three subjects to be grouped should never create an equal-sided triangle; move them around until the shape looks more natural and the balance more subtle. Allow a single specimen, chosen for its beauty of form, to stand alone. In a Japanese garden space is vitally important. So is the choice of rocks. Do not mix sandstone with granite or ironstone; group the rocks in threes or fives and, if they have an obvious grain, place them so that the grain runs the same way. Rocks can be prostrate or upright; they must never look 'placed'. A garden with a change of level is more interesting than a flat one; soil can be scooped out to make room for a small pool and then piled behind it; once there is water in the garden there is the opportunity for imaginative treatments, involving stepping stones, bridges and the feature planting of small trees.

Personal taste no less than soil condition will determine how large a space will be given to a garden of this type; the underlying principles of peace achieved by balance and restraint can be carried out in projects both large and small.

River pebble mulch, stepping stones through water and stone lantern introduce Japanese theme.

A miniature Japanese garden

The sketch opposite shows how you can turn the drab bare area seen from a window looking on to a fence or wall into a miniature Japanese garden by using 'optical illusion'.

First 'frame' your vista with a small tree or vine; use soft, wispy grey plantings in the background (e.g. grey junipers, westringia, wormwood). Use the boldest and richest-coloured shrubbery in the foreground, reducing colour intensity further back. To create 'perspective' use shrubs, container plants and stepping stones, large ones in the foreground, smaller ones in the background. A small pool that tapers in width gives the illusion of distance. Dwarfed container-grown trees — particularly wispy maples — are excellent in any small garden scene. Try to achieve a 'natural' background — a series of bamboo screens are ideal.

Seaside gardens

A garden by the sea, open to strong salt-laden winds, can be both beautiful and productive if special care is taken in the initial planting.

One might imagine that a solid wall would be the best defence against the fierceness of the sea winds, but this is not so. Winds hurdle a solid obstruction and swoop downwards again a few metres beyond it; what is needed is a barrier of trees or shrubbery which, though easily penetrated, will slow down and break up the force of the wind and at the same time filter out much of the salt. Behind a front line defence of trees and shrubs with good salt-wind resistance, plants which are less hardy can be safely grown.

Many people who live overlooking the sea are reluctant to plant anything which will obstruct the view. Tall trees could be used to frame the view with low growers planted between them, or a series of low-growing plantings could be used as a wind-break which would preserve both the view and the garden. A picket-type or melaleuca-stick fence with a few centimetres between the uprights can make an immediate wind-break and speed the growth of the trees or shrubs planted on its lee side.

Tall trees with good salt tolerance

Lagunaria patersonii Norfolk Island Hibiscus. A rapid grower, happy in all but a cold climate, reaches 5 m in a few years and then slowly matures to twice the height. Pyramid-shaped with deep-green leathery leaves with a silvery-grey backing, small, leathery, starry-petalled flowers which change from creamy-white to pink. Its disadvantage lies in the sharp hair-like spines in the seed pods which irritate the skin if contact is made.

Araucaria heterphylla Norfolk Island Pine. A tapering conifer which grows to a height of 30 m with a base spread of about 10 m.

Choice can be made among the eucalypts, *E. botryoides* (Bangaloy), *E. gummifera* (Red Bloodwood), *E. leucoxylon* (Pink-flowered Ironbark), the broad-leafed paper-bark *Melaleuca quinquenervia*, Moreton Bay and Port Jackson figs, olives and Golden Lambert cypress.

Medium to small trees

Acacia longifolia (Sallow Wattle)
Banksia ericifolia
B. intregrifolia
B. serrata (Old Man Banksia)
Casuarina stricta (She-oak)
Leptospermum laevigatum (Coastal Tea-tree)
Pittosporum crassifolium
Tristania laurina (Water Box)

*Among the following salt-tolerant bushes and plants are many grey-foliaged varieties.
*Artemesia** (Wormwood)
Cassia bicapsularis
*Centaurea** (Dusty Miller)
Chamelaucium uncinatum (Geraldton Wax)
Eunonymus
Lavender*
Melaleuca hypericifolia
Metrosideros excelsa (New Zealand
    Christmas Bush)

Raphiolepsis (Indian Hawthorn)
Rosemary*
*Westringia** (Coastal Rosemary)

Plants with moderate salt tolerance

Bottlebrushes
Frangipani
Gardenia
Hibiscus
Leptospermum (Tea-tree)
Nerium (Oleander)
    For colour in the seaside garden:
Arcotis
Felicia
Gazania
Geranium
Mesembryanthemum
Pelargonium

Above: Mauve Lantana and strelitzia

Left: Blue Agapanthus with dwarf bamboo.

Below: French lavender hedge accepts seaside exposure. Violas are sheltered by N.Z. Christmas bush.

Water in the garden

A small garden pool adds charm to a garden, and, in the hot summers of the southern hemisphere, the sound of running water or the cooling effect of still water can be a real blessing.

In creating a pool you can be as imaginative and expansive as time and money will allow and, with fibreglass shells and electric pumps readily available, can have a water garden featuring fountains and/or waterfalls; but it is perfectly possible to create a pool a metre or two square (or round, or oblong) by using plastic sheeting as a water-retainer. The job is surprisingly inexpensive and quite within the range of the do-it-yourself handyman.

The type of plastic sheeting needed is the tough sort used by builders to make damp-courses for slab foundations.

Mark out the area for the pool and measure. Then buy a single piece of sheeting large enough to cover the maximum width of the intended shape, plus the height of the sides, allowing an extra 30 cm to tuck under turf or stones which will surround the pool. The pool can be any shape you wish but the sides should not rise more steeply than at a 45-degree angle. Steep sides tend to collapse under pressure or when wet.

The earth must be well firmed before you attempt to put the sheeting down. When you do lay it down be certain to smooth it out evenly. Anchor with stones light enough to give if you need to pull the sheeting into better shape and to make certain it is in all-over con-tact with the ground. Now begin to fill the pool. You will be able to tell from the level of the water if there is need to build up any low spots or to reduce ones which are too high.

When you have made certain the water-level is right you can begin to lay the 'coping stones' around the pool. You can achieve a pleasant effect by allowing the stones at the back of the pool to overhang the water — but be careful not to place them so that anyone stepping on the edge could overbalance and fall in.

Now is the time to show patience. Let everything settle for a week or two. Wait until after it has rained and the earth has dried out again if you can. If you have decided to have bold feature rocks around the pool now is the time to give them solid foundation.

When everything has settled to your satisfaction, siphon the water out of the plastic sheeting and mop up any residue. Make a stiff mixture — 5 parts sand to 2 of cement with water — then spade it all into the bottom of the pool, cover it with a sack, and then, using a piece of timber on which to stand, begin to work the cement layer up the sides of the pool, keeping the surface as smooth and even as possible and the layer at an even thickness of around 5–6 cm. Take the cement up and over the edges of the pool and under and around the coping stones so they are set firmly in place. Smooth the surface of the cement with dry hessian. When the job is completed wait about a day until the cement is dry enough for a final rub-down. Since it has been laid on the non-absorbent plastic it will not dry quickly.

After the final smoothing mist the pool with water once or twice a day for several days to 'cure' the cement. Then fill the pool. If it begins to pour with rain before you have finished rubbing down, fill the pool at once. Upward pressure from moist earth could crack the cement and you need the weight of water in it to resist the thrust. If you have to empty the pool at any time later don't leave it empty during wet weather.

If your land is wet enough to need the laying of agricultural drains, you could run the pipes to a sump in the lowest part of the garden and make it into a pool, complete with surrounding 'bog garden'.

If your land is steep you could build a concrete furrow down the slope, edge it prettily with rocks and plants and, from a concealed plastic hose attached to a nearby tap, allow a gentle, continual trickle of water to run down the furrow into a little pool below. The beauty of this is that the water can be regulated or completely turned off when not wanted.

Plants to surround a water garden.
Trees which continue to shed their leaves should not be chosen to overhang a pool; evergreen trees shed foliage gradually or in short, spasmodic bursts and can be more troublesome than deciduous trees which drop all their leaves in the one season.

Garden pools add charm and tranquillity to a garden

Nymphaea (Water Lilies) float peacefullly on pool

Cyperus papyrus (Papyrus Grass) and Canna lilies

Suggested plants for poolside areas

Trees
Artocarpus
Bananas
Brassaia (Queensland Umbrella Tree)
Cunonia (Butterknife Plant)
Palms
Strelitizia nicolai (Wild Banana)

Shrubs
Coprosma (Looking-glass Plant)
Hibiscus
Pentas
Prostrate Junipers

Accent plants
Cordyline
Dracaena
Fatsia japonica

Low-growing plants
Acorus variegata
Ajuga (Carpet Bugle)
Dichondra (Lawn-leaf)
Helxine (Baby's Tears)
Hypericum, creeping types
Lobelia *(L. erinus)*
Lysimachia (Creeping Jenny)
Myosotsis (Forget-me-not)
Zebrina

Medium-sized and tall bog-plants
Arum White (*Zantedeschia*)
Crinum
Elephant's Ear (*Alocasia*)
Ferns
Ginger-lily (*Hedychium*)
Japanese Anemone (*japonica*)
Iris (*I. kaemferi*)
I. *louisiana*
I. *monneri*
I. *ochreleuca*
Kniphofia multiflora (Bulrush Poker)
Lythrum
Primula denticula

Right: Iris kaempferi
Below: Iris ochreleuca

In addition to the plants which grow well in the moist rich soil of a boggy area there are many others which look at their best when grown in a waterside setting but do not like constant dampness around their roots. You can make very attractive plantings of these around a pool which has been constructed in a part of the garden where the soil is dryish — as long as you see they are watered regularly.

Plants not requiring damp soil but excellent in a waterside setting
Acanthus
Agapanthus
Azalea
Bamboos
Begonias
Dietes
Dwarf Cymbidiums
Eupatorium
Ferns, hardy species
Fountain Grass
Geranium
Harebell (*Dierama*)
Hemerocallis (Day-lily)
Juniper (prostrate forms)
Lantana montevidensis
Ligularia
Nandina domestica
New Zealand flax
Phygelius (Cape Fuchsia)
Red Hot Pokers (*Kniphofia*)
Shrimp Flower (*Beloperone*)
Spiraea, all kinds

In addition to the plants which grow around the pool there are those which will grow in the pool itself.

Plants to grow in the pool
Arrowhead (*Sagittaria*)
Lotus (*Nelumbium speciosum*)
Papyrus grass (*Cyperus papyrus*)
Pickerel-weed (*Pontaderia cordata*)
Water Lily (*Nymphaea*) Hybrids with red, pink, yellow or white flowers float on surface. The Blue Water Lily (*N. capensis*) stands well above water. Deep or shallow.
Water thyme (*Anachris canadensis*)

Water Lilies

Most types need at least half-sun to flower well and about 30 cm of water above the plants — large-flowered and longer-stemmed tropical types prefer a depth of about 50 cm. In artificial ponds (without an earthen base) water lilies need to be planted in pots at least 25 cm in diameter, or where depth is limited, in boxes filled with well-composted soil. In ponds of borderline shallowness I have had good results by leaving the crowns just protruding from a hessian sugar bag cut down in about a third of its size, loosely packed with compost and soil so that it can be 'splayed over' the pool base and anchored with a few flat rocks.

To keep the water cleaner, soak your planted-up pots, boxes or bags to expel air bubbles before immersing them in the pond as this minimises the amount of compost that will rise with the air bubbles. A layer of gritty sand or gravel over the soil also helps in this respect.

The hardier types have flowers of white, gold, pink or red; plants with blue or violet flowers usually need more heat. If you try to grow these in an area where the winter is cold you would be wise to lift them, pot-up and look after them during the cold weather and then return to the water in spring.

When plants have become overgrown and the flowers are being hidden by the leaves, take them out of the water and wash the soil from the roots. Then divide plant and roots into sections, keep just enough for replanting and either discard the rest or make a gift to friends and neighbours. This is best done in spring.

On the other hand, if there is need to increase your stock, snap off offsets growing on the roots, pot them up and keep the pots immersed in water in the shade. By the following spring the plants should be ready to be set out in the pool

You don't have to have a pool to be able to enjoy growing water lilies. A sunny balcony or a place in the garden which has sun for at least half the day and a container which will hold 15–20 litres of water will enable you to grow these exquisite plants.

Half-casks or shallow saucer-shaped containers will suit the white, cream and pink varieties, the deep blue tropical varieties need at least 45 centimetres of water beneath them.

Plant the rhizomes in seed-boxes filled with a 50–50 mixture of good garden soil and compost, cover the surface with a layer of sand, soak well and then lower carefully into the water. The layer of sand is used to prevent compost etc. floating free and clouding the water which should not be so cold as to shock the plants.

Planting should be done in spring but you can buy the rhizomes at any time of the year and keep them stored in damp sphagnum moss until planting time comes around. The important thing is not to let them dry out. A further important point to remember is not to be tempted to overplant. If you do you'll get leaves but few flowers.

Water Lilies (Nymphaea) in natural environment

Fish in a garden pool

Fish need light and clear water if they are to thrive.

If fish die or lie gasping for air on the surface of the water you will have allowed the oxygen in the pool to have become too scarce. Clear the pool of all fallen leaves which have encouraged the growth of algae and made the water murky and introduce a few plants such as those sold to oxygenate aquariums. As time goes on you will have to watch these do not take over too much space. But before doing this planting, jet a stream of water into the pool from a hose, making a splash and stirring up decaying rubbish which can then be dredged from the surface.

If scum is spoiling the appearance of the pool, gently lower a double-sheet thickness of newspaper on to the surface of the water and slowly draw it along to soak off the scum. Don't let the paper become too saturated before lifting it and throwing it into the compost heap.

Water Lilies (Nymphaea)

Fish need light and clear water

The small garden

Making the most of a small area

No garden is too small to be interesting, but the smaller it is the more important it is to plan carefully and select plants and materials which really suit your requirements and general aspect.

The materials you choose for paving or making walls and rockeries will have a greater impact than they would in a larger garden but this doesn't mean you should go for the exotic or expensive, quite the reverse — the spectacular can lose its appeal when you are confined with it. Harmony is the keynote.

The first essential is privacy and the screening out of any unsightly features. Bamboo makes a delightful screen but will take over if unrestrained. Grow it in low squat tubs so that both root and top growth are under control. A small tree, shrubs, climbing plants and tea-tree fencing can all be used to good effect. No matter whether you want to use your small garden for the intensive growth of flowers and vegetables or just as a place in which to relax, planning will be necessary.

General effect

A small garden can be made to seem larger and take on a pleasant air of 'mystery' if parts of it can disappear from view. A path can lead around the corner of the house, small peninsulas of shrubbery can hide a bed of flowers so that there are delights and surprises as one comes upon the unexpected. A small drift of bulbs or annuals, a grouping of ferns and weathered rock, a tiny ornamental pool, a stone lantern, or a garden urn filled with feature plants — the choice is wide.

One of the most charming but least contrived small gardens I have seen is no more than 8 m square. Instead of ornate paving, a broad circular walk made with well-compacted blue metal or basalt screenings is retained by a single circle of bricks. It is like a carousel, with a centre core of above eye-level plantings so that there is no point where more than part of it can be seen. This, apart from the variety of different plantings, increases interest tremendously because it stimulates speculation about what lies beyond the curve and every feature is a complete surprise.

The simple blue-grey base covering and broad curve create an atmosphere which is extended into the rest of the garden where there is a centre planting of bamboo in a large squat and attractively ornate bowl, a clump of papyrus and some large mossy rocks around a small pool.

Where the centre walk broadens to join another path which enters it obliquely the Japanese influence is accentuated by a small stone lantern and a bridge of split saplings over a damp, shaded area densely carpeted by helxine, whose tiny bright-green leaves set off the small drifts of polyanthus which add colour to the corner where tall tree-ferns create a filigree of sunlight and shade.

A small garden for outdoor living

A small garden lends itself to the 'extension of the house' concept so popular in our amenable climate.

The door of the house can open onto an area of even paving — stone slabs, brick, etc. Stepping stones and pebbles are excellent for picturesque effect where traffic is not heavy but in an area where a number of people are likely to be moving about a solid even surface is essential. Permanent seating can be fixed around walls softened by the leafy tracery of climbing plants or hanging baskets; an overhead vine or climber such as the non-edible Red Passion Fruit can be trained with very simple support, depending for detail on the layout and personal taste involved, to give shade. Daytime shadows are important; if the garden is to be used for entertaining at night, lighting will have a significant effect. Plants can be brought into focus or glamourised by soft lighting, hard corners and bare walls softened by shadows cast from a trailing vine or twiggy shrub. It isn't so much the space you have as the ingenuity you bring to the use of your space which matters.

Tree ferns create a natural setting

Alpine Phlox and yellow alyssum provide effective colour for cool climate gardens

A Tea-tree fence provides a soft background

Backyard into garden

Many small and narrow back areas of town-houses and city terraces have been changed from the utilitarian backyards to charming small gardens, and become an extension of the house in much the same way as early Egyptian, Persian or Moorish gardens. If sunny enough they can be hobby gardens brimming with flowers and vegetables.

Traditional Japanese landscaping suits a small area as it symbolises the natural landscape in miniature.

The shade that so often predominates in these small areas suits many of the appropriate plants such as clipped camellias, azaleas, aralias, moss and ferns.

Because most terrace-house garden areas are enclosed they already have privacy and a feeling of intimacy. Garbage tins or some architectural feature that would look out of character with the garden can be hidden by sheets of pressed metal moulded to look like a paling fence and they can be painted any colour. Tea-tree sticks make an attractive neutral screening.

No matter how attractive the walling or screening, it should be broken with planting to add interest and an illusion of depth. Good use of espaliers is one of the main contributors to this illusion.

Espaliers for the small enclosed garden are in many respects preferable to climbing plants. They are easier to keep within bounds and give the garden the mature character that normally comes only with trees.

You don't need special training or techniques to create pleasant espaliers. Basically, all you do is wait for some vigorous pliable canes or branches to develop then tie them down against the wall or fence in the way they look best. Occasionally clip off any growth coming toward the front.

Drama Girl camellias are suitable for quick espaliers as they grow faster than most other Camellia japonica varieties, the comparatively long caney new growth is easily trained and the huge rosy-red semi-double flowers are showy for at least 4 months in the season.

However, make sure the aspect is suitable. Camellia japonica varieties do best in temperate climates with dappled shade or direct sunlight for no more than an hour or two each day. *C. sasanqua* varieties tolerate more direct sunlight and also cold.

Citrus — particularly lemons — and hibiscus are also suitable for sunny walls. In cooler temperate to cold districts, berry shrubs such as cotoneaster, pyracantha, holly, laurel, gordonia or olive, or deciduous trees such as apple, pear or flowering quince do well.

Free-standing espaliers or cordons make pleasing space-saving hedges. Use stakes for a fence for the initial training and remove them later.

Introduce a free-growing small tree into the small garden. It gives character and beauty. You can achieve a most satisfying effect with one small upright or spreading tree, a seat, a few square metres of paving and a grouping of small shrubs or a low ground cover. An espalier or splay of ivy here and there will relieve fence or walling, place a colourful potted plant or two where highlight is needed and there you are!

The potted plant really comes into its own in the small garden. Room furnishing can depend, for effect, on a spot of colour here or a blaze of colour there; the potted plant can provide them both in the small garden and give scope for variety and change.

There are both small and large accents. Trees, no less than potted plants, have their place in the small garden.

Trees

More people would take part in helping to salvage our tree-depleted environment if they realised there are trees, both deciduous and evergreen, suitable for planting in a small area. Don't discount deciduous trees; they give summer shade and the sun can shine through their leafless branches in winter when it is most welcome.

Deciduous trees are not limited to cool districts. In northern tropical areas, low flat-topped poincianas give a brilliant display of orchid-like scarlet flowers in early summer. Rose-pink *Cassia javanica* and the hybrid Rainbow Cassia with pink to cream flowers are in spectacular bloom at the same time. *Cassia fistula* ('Golden Shower' or 'Pudding Pipe') make their brilliant cascade of golden flowers

Above: Lemon trees are particularly suitable for sunny walls

Below: Deciduous trees give summer shade and winter sun for outdoor living

in long pendulous sprays in summer in warm, temperate districts and in the tropics, after *Bauhinia variegata* (Butterfly Tree or bush) has displayed its rose-purple orchid-like flowers in spring. Prune after flowering to keep in check. *Sapium* (Chinese Tallow Tree) has beautiful autumn foliage and grows well in all but very cold districts and has a rounded top rarely more than 7 m high.

For temperate and cool districts the range of small- to medium-sized trees is extensive. The lovely spring-flowering crab apples (*floribunda* — has masses of red buds opening to pearly pink flowers and a wide, umbrella-like spread); various bronze-leafed flowering plums (*Prunus vesuvius festeri* — one of the best and largest, reaching to 8 or 9 m high and wide) and earlier flowering double-pink *P. blireana* (small with shady tree form — to 4 m high); the flowering cherries which suit all but warmer temperate districts; the exquisite Japanese maples; more open but taller and faster-growing 'Golden Rain' Koelreuteria, which inspired the Chinese willow pattern design and grows to 6 or 7 m. Take your pick!

Among the faster-growing evergreen shade trees for all but cold districts are *Pittosporum undulatum*, with dark foliage and honey-scented spring flowers and berries which can be messy underfoot; Fiddlewood, whose fan-shaped growth usually keeps to 6 or 7 m but can double it unless cut back periodically; Macadamia, renowned for its delicious nuts, and River box (*tristania laurina*) which, in average garden conditions, rarely exceeds 5 cm and withstands wet or dry situations, are all worth considering.

The broad-leafed paperbark (*Melaleuca quinquenervia,* 6–7 m) and slightly smaller prickly paperbark (*M. Styphelioides*) are also good. The native weeping bottlebrush (*Callistemon viminalis*) makes a graceful spread to about 6 m high and nearly as wide, and gives a wonderful display of silky brushes in spring — often to a lesser extent in autumn. Gordonia, grown in moderately cold to temperate climates, has white, crepe-like flowers from autumn to spring, and although treated as a large shrub, can be hurried into small-tree form by removing lower branches as it develops.

Flowering Weeping Cherry (Prunus subhirtella 'Pendula Rosea')

Flowering trees for a small garden
Small deciduous trees

Albizzia julibrissin Silk tree. Umbrella shape, H: 3–4 m, similar width; fine foliage topped with a canopy of silky pink and cream pompons in early summer; rapid grower but rarely long lived.

Bauhinia variegata Butterfly or orchid tree. Medium grower, H: 4 m, W: 4 m; spring-flowering, clusters of orchid-like mauve flowers with maroon centre markings followed by grey-green oval twin leaves that look like butterflies. *B. alba* is a slightly taller white-flowered type. All but coldest districts.

Cassia fistula Pudding pipe cassia or Golden showers. H: 6–8 m, W: 4–6 m; long compound leaves with bright green oval leaflets 7–8 cm long branches decked with long pendulous sprays of golden flowers in mid to late summer. Suits tropical to warmer temperate areas.

Cassia javanica Pink cassia. Umbrella-shaped tree, H: 4–6 m, W: 4–5 m; dense small foliage, clustered with pale to deep coral pink flowers in summer, suits semi-tropical to tropical areas. **Rainbow cassia** is a hybrid between this and *C. fistula*, with flowers ranging from yellow to coral pink.

Cercis siliquastrum Judas tree. Initially erect tree, H: 6–8 m, W: 4–5 m; small bauhinia-like foliage, branches clustered with small, deep rose-pink flowers in spring. Cool and temperate climates.

Koelreuteria bipinnata Golden rain or Chinese willow pattern tree. Slender-stemmed umbrella, H: 6m, W: 5 m; with large shapely leaves, sprays of small bright-yellow flowers in late spring, followed by mauve purple pods in autumn. Cool to temperate districts.

Lagerstroemia indica Crepe myrtle. H: 7–9 m, W: 4–5 m, but this and its hybrids are frequently pruned as large shrubs. All have clusters of red, pink, mauve or white flowers during mid-summer, foliage often colours in autumn. All climates. Larger leafed mauve to purple flowered. *L. speciosa* (Rose of India) needs semi-tropical to tropical conditions.

Laburnum Golden chain. H: 4–6 m, W: 4 m; resembling *C. fistula* but pea-shaped flowers in spring and gentler growth, seeds are poisonous. Best suited to cool climates.

Magnolia denudata Yulan tree. H: 7 m, W: 5 m; V-shaped growth with several stems — large white lemon-scented tulip-shaped flowers in late winter. *M. soulangeana* hybrids are usually a little smaller in growth and later flowering as varieties deepen in colour. Suit cool and temperate climates.

Malus Crab apple. Growth and flower varies with variety; *M. floribunda*, usually H: 5–6 m and as wide, like a low umbrella massed in mid-spring with red buds opening single pink to white followed by small yellow fruits. *M. purpureus*, H: 7–8 m, W: 4 m, with single wine-coloured flowers followed by dark fruits. *M. ioensis* is low-branching and shrubby with large double soft-pink flowers later in spring. All but tropical climates.

Prunus Flowering plums, cherries and peaches. Flowering plums more upright growth ranging from *P. cerasifera Blireiana* H: 4 m, W: 3–4m to *P. vesuvius Festeri* H: 9–10 m, W: 6–8 m. **Flowering peaches** need pruning, therefore growth is usually lower and more spreading. **Cherries** usually have a natural V shape, double varieties 4–6 m, some singles taller, depending on variety (check with nurseryman). All are suitable for cool to temperate climates with most cherries preferring the cooler conditions.

Small evergreen flowering trees

Acacia Wattles. Hundreds of species, including *A. baileyana* (Cootamundra wattle) with fine greyish foliage and golden winter–spring flower, H: 4–5 m, W: 4 m; quick-growing but often lasting only five to ten years; long slender-leafed *A. floribunda* with fingers of creamy yellow spring flowers, H: 6 m, W: 4–6 m; slightly more upright and larger leafed. *A. longifolia* (Sally or sallow wattle) and pendulous long grey-green leafed. *A. pendula* (Myall) with clusters of small ball-shaped lemon yellow winter/spring flowers, H: 9–10 m, W: 5–6 m. Except where mentioned, they are long-lived, adapt to all but tropical areas and the latter is drought resistant.

Callistemon viminalis Weeping bottle-brush. H: 6–8 m, W: 4–5 m; pendulous growth and scarlet brushes of flower in spring and spasmodically later; several hybrid forms are less spreading and with larger brushes. *C. saligna* (white bottlebrush) H: 7–8 m, W: 3–4 m is upright and features bright coppery pink new spring growth; it is also at home in swampy conditions.

Eucalyptus ficifolia Red-flowering gum. H: 7–9 m, W: 5–6 m; large umbrella shape, covered with pink to rich scarlet blooms during early summer. It is possible for seedlings to produce white or pale flowers but most seed is selected from stock with proven performance. Often short-lived in east coast summer rainfall areas especially in sand. All but coldest and tropical areas.

E. torquata Coral gum. H: 6–8 m, W: 4–6 m; ornate buds, showy coral-pink flowers in summer, especially suited to well-drained soils and winter rainfall.

Gordonia Poached egg tree. H: 6 m, W: 5 m; when not pruned as a shrub eventually makes umbrella-shaped glossy foliaged evergreen with attractive trunk, from late autumn to spring, displays 10 cm flowers with crepe-white petals surrounding an orange yellow centre. Cool and temperate climates.

Hymenosporum Native frangipani. H: 7–8 m, W: 5–6 m; just above head height; tapering pagoda shape, forming well-spaced tiers of dark glossy foliage, spangled during late spring with fragrant frangipani-type flowers that open limey-cream and age to mustard. Coastal native from central NSW and Queensland coast but growing happily in Hobart Botanic Gardens with protection from cold south-west winds.

Metrosideros excelsa New Zealand Christmas bush. H: 5–6 m, W: 5–6 m (aged trees sometimes much larger but stands cutting); dense umbrella shape, leathery foliage, massed with scarlet bottlebrush stamens in upfacing clusters from early to mid-summer; excellent resistance to salt winds; more suited to temperate to semi-tropical coastal districts.

Sophora tetraptera New Zealand Kowhai. H: 6–8 m, W: 5–6 m; pyramid shape, small pea-type leaves and massed in mid to late spring with pendulous golden yellow pea flowers; popular in Melbourne gardens. Cooler temperate districts.

Stenocarpus sinuatus Queensland fire wheel. H: 9–10 m, W: 5–6 m but larger in native forests; darkest green irregularly shaped leathery foliage; unique flower clusters, wheel-shaped in bud then opening to display spidery gold-tipped stamens; large drifts of flowers appear among the dark foliage — mostly in late summer but also in spring; may take seven to ten years to flower but worth waiting for; prefers fairly moist rich loamy or heavier soil but adaptable. More suited to humid coastal districts.

Virgilia Tree in a hurry. H: 8–9 m, W: 5–6 m, pyramid-shaped tree, small divided foliage, massed with clusters of mauve pink pea flowers in spring. May die out after 10 to 15 years but replacement is rapid; usually growing 2 m or more per year. All but coldest and monsoonal tropical climates.

Dissectum maples' colourful foliage brightens a garden

Callistemon viminalis

C — suits cool/cold areas
T — suits temperate areas
H — suits hot areas

Quick-growing large shrubs for screens

Leptospermum petersonii
Oleander
Photinia robusta
Pittosporum eugenoides
Pyracantha augustifolia
Rondeletia amoena

Quick-growing evergreen trees for screens

Citharexylum T–H
Cotoneaster pannosa C–T
Cupressus macrocarpa (varieties) C–T
Eucalyptus nicholii C–T
Hakea salicifolia C–T
Leptospermum laevigatum T
Leptospermum petersonii T
Melaleuca armillaris T–H
Nerium T–H
Pinus (various types for all districts)
Virgilia oroboides T

Evergreeen trees for small gardens

Acacia baileyana C–T
Acacia pycnantha C–T
Agonis flexuosa T
Arbutus uenedo C–T
Banksia integrifolia T
Bauhinia blakeana T–H
Callistemon salignus T–H
Callistemon viminalis T–H
Cassia multijuga T–H
Ceratopetalum gummiferum T
Citharexylum T–H
Conifers — see various species C–H
Cotoneaster pannosa C–T
Cotoneaster serotina C–T
Elaeocarpus T–H
Eucalyptus eremophila T
Eucalyptus nicholii C–T
Eucalyptus torquata C–T
Glochidion T–H
Hakea salicifolia C–T
Laurus nobilis C–T
Melaleuca armillaris C–H
Metrosideros T
Michelia champaca T–H
Olea C–H
Photinia serrulata C–T
Pittosporum rhombifolium T–H
Schefflera T–H
Sophora tetraptera C–T
Stenocarpus sinuatus T–H
Tamarix aphylla C–H
Tristania laurina T–H
Virgilia oroboides T

Deciduous trees for small gardens

Acer negundo C–T
Acer negundo variegata C–T
Acer palmatum 10–12
Albizzia julibrissin T–H
Alnus glutinosa C–T
Bauhinia variegata T–H
Betula (all types) C–T
Cercis C–H
Cornus florida C–T
Fraxinus excelsior aurea C–T
Koelreuteria C–T
Lagerstroemia indica rubra T–H
Liquidambar orientalis C–T
Malus (various types) C–T
Nyssa sylvatica C–T
Persmisson T–H
Pistacia chinensis T–H
Prunus (see selection) C–T
Sapium T–H
Stenolobium stans T

Rondeletia amoena

Cassia nodosa

Hakea laurina

Facelifting an old garden

There comes a time when even the mellow beauty of an old garden begins to fade; fortunately transformation will not cost the earth and the effort expended will be well worthwhile.

Consider your garden as a whole, starting with the approach.

Do you have a fence? Is it in a state of good repair? If you don't need it to keep in, or to keep out, children and animals, do you need it at all?

If you really want a barrier between your home and the outside world how about a living hedge rather than a man-made structure? The choice is wide. You could either have a formal, trimmed hedge or a mixed planting of shrubs allowed to take their own shape but kept neat by an occasional trim. Electrical hedge-cutters are very reasonably priced these days.

One of the most attractive hedges I have ever seen was cordon-shaped, like a double-espalier. The Camellia Sasanquas were planted about 1–1½ metres apart and their long, caney stems have been allowed to grow until they were long enough to be tied together and trained into an arch. The secondary growths were criss-crossed and twined into the main framework. The only work required to keep the decorative pattern was trimming of the new growth.

Don't clear away existing shrubbery until its potential is assessed. Stragglers might be rejuvenated by pruning, or large shrubs undercleaned to give small tree character.

A splash of colour in a shady spot 'lifts' the garden

Some prefer a natural setting for the garden

An open stretch of lawn highlights mixed planting of shrubs

Regrouping

If a shrub, tree or plant is not earning its way the gardener must face up to the fact that it either has to go entirely or be transplanted elsewhere. Fortunately it is easy enough to lift and replant most things and if there is not space in one's own garden there are surely friends or neighbours who would appreciate a gift.

Shrubs are best moved and replanted during winter when growth is more or less dormant, but don't expect much success in moving Australian natives, daphnes or luculias — they resent interference at any time of the year.

In many instances an area can be revitalised just by removing a shrub here and there to let light through or to give access to a view which will extend the garden vista. If there is no view you could put up a lattice in the empty space and train colourful flowers against it or introduce tubs containing feature plants, or tuck a seat in the space. There are many possibilities.

A splash of colour in a shady or difficult spot can give a real 'lift' to a garden. Dwarf begonias, which flower for a long time equally well in sun or shade, are invaluable. 'Gypsy', with a profusion of flowers above deep bronze foliage, comes in white, carmine, deep red, and white with a salmon-red margin. Just three or four plants, offset by a fern and a mossy rock with a surround of pinebark or pebbles, can do wonders for a dull corner.

Any 'dead' corner of a garden should be regarded as a challenge. Any introduction of light, space and colour can be for the better.

Overgrown gardens

Once the shape of individual trees and shrubs is obscured a garden loses character and becomes a shapeless tangle of greenery. Each planting should always be allowed to make its own statement. Deciduous trees and shrubs which have 'run past themselves' can be brought back into line by heavy pruning in late winter or early spring. Cut back deciduous caney shrubs as low as 1 m, then trim or pinch back new growth to encourage bushiness. This may mean a loss of spring flowers but it will strengthen the shrub and there will be many blossoms in subsequent seasons.

An overgrown conifer should be given a hard cut all over in early spring before new growth can begin. Leave the growing tip untouched and trim so that the columnar or cone shape of the tree is maintained.

If shrubs have become very overgrown it is possible to turn them into small trees; cotoneasters, feijoas, gordonias and murrayas lend themselves particularly well to such treatment. Look for shrubs which have an interesting trunk formation — this can either be a single trunk of unusual shape, or several trunks growing from the base of the tree. Trim away all dead, twiggy or untidy growth from the lower parts of the shrub and strip the main branches but leave growth at the ends. This should be trained into a flattened bun shape; the effect is traditionally Japanese and success depends on the positioning and balance of the bun-shaped growths.

Each planting of shrubs or trees should be allowed to make its own statement. Once the shape of shrubs, etc. is lost a garden becomes a shapeless tangle

WORKING
THE EARTH

5. The fertile soil

Know your soil

If you are a successful gardener there is always someone who will nonchalantly dismiss your achievement by saying that you must have good soil. It would be much nearer the mark to say that you must have good understanding of your soil. Soil is what you make it.

Some gardeners start with hungry and thirsty sand; others have earth which is as stubborn and unyielding as concrete, but even the meanest soil will become amiable with a little coaxing and understanding.

There are two extremes in soil type — pure sand and pure clay, and between them are various grades of loam. Sandy loams and light loams contain more sand and organic matter than clay, and clay loams and heavy loams contain more clay and organic matter than sand.

Test your soil

From several different parts of the garden dig up a tablespoonful of earth from a few centimetres below the surface and mix the samples together.

If the soil is not damp, moisten it, but only enough so that after kneading and squeezing it a few times, you can roll it into a ball.
1. Is it gritty rather than smooth, not sticky, and does it crumble as it dries? Then it is *sand*.
2. Is it gritty rather than smooth, not sticky, but does the ball hold together fairly well? Then it is probably *sandy loam*.
Make sure that it does not fit into the next category.
3. Is it only moderately gritty and slightly smooth and sticky? Does the ball of soil definitely stick together? Then it is probably *loam*. Check against category 4.
4. Is it only slightly gritty, fairly smooth, moderately sticky and does the ball of soil hold together so well that you can roll it into a pencil-like shape between the flattened palms and the shape will hold without crumbling? Then it is *clay loam*.
5. Is it hard to mould unless you add more water? Does it then become very sticky but will hold its shape well when rolled into pencil-shape or twisted into a ring? Then it is *clay*.

Your aim is to have a soil which holds water well but allows the excess to drain away freely. The soil particles should be grouped together in crumb-like colonies with space between them for the free movement of water and air which is so essential for healthy root growth. Both fine sand and clay soils pack too tightly to provide these conditions but both can easily be improved.

Improving your soil
Sand

Often described as 'the soil with the least backbreak but the most heartache' it needs little working, apart from weeding, but it dries out very quickly and always seems hungry and thirsty.

The first step in improving its water-holding capacity is to rake in a liberal layer of moistened peatmoss — a finger depth would be ideal. The peatmoss must be moistened either by soaking overnight or adding hot water just before use; if you apply it dry it will float out of the soil when you water. You could add some compost too. You could even use compost instead of the peatmoss, but this will disappear more rapidly from the soil.

Once this initial step has been taken, sandy soil can be kept in a healthy and productive state if you do what nature does and keep a layer of leaf mould or other organic matter as a mulch over its surface. Old grass clippings make a very good mulch. Don't bother about digging in, just keep the layer topped up as it thins out.

Sandy loam

Although this type of soil holds moisture a little better than a sandy soil, its fine particles still pack too densely to give the ideal conditions for plant growth, so treat as for sand by adding organic matter and keeping a surface mulch going throughout the year.

Loam

This is considered the ideal soil. It is easily worked and contains enough clay to hold moisture well and there is good air space between the crumbly soil particles. Avoid working it when it is wet so as to preserve the good texture.

Clay loam

It is even more important to avoid working this soil when it is wet or sticky. It should be just damp enough for a handful to hold together when moulded into a ball but dry enough to crumble easily. If it does not pass the test, delay work for a day and test again before proceeding.

Soil which contains clay should never be disturbed by digging, weeding, planting, walking on or any other form of agitation whilst at the wet and sticky stage. If this happens, the minute clay particles become dislodged from their crumb-like colonies and become suspended in solution with the excess moisture in the soil. This mixture of clay and moisture is better known as mud — the kind for making bricks! When it dries, it sets hard and the friable texture is lost.

The addition of lime will help to make loamy soils more crumbly because it hardens the soil water so that the clay particles do not go into solution so readily. Flocculation or precipitation takes place and the clay particles are formed into crumbs much in the way that soap particles are in limey water.

However, too much lime in the soil destroys the solubility of iron and to some extent phosphorus, sulphur and other elements essential to plant life. Its presence will upset acid-loving plants such as azaleas and magnolias.

Gypsum (calcium sulphate) is the only form of lime which will help soil structure without changing its activity.
Keep this soil well mulched.

Clay

Water does not readily penetrate clay soil so some system of drainage will be needed. See section 'Draining the soil'.

Since it is so tightly compacted, a clay soil is airless and plant roots cannot thrive in it, so it has to be lightened and crumbled. There are various ways of doing this.

If you have a large area of deep clay you can either spread good loam over the whole of it to spade depth, or you can build up beds of good loam with paths between them which will also act as drains to carry off surplus water. You might even consider covering the entire area with ashes, metal screening or other porous but permanent material, before laying down the beds or the paving for the paths. Or rough-dig the soil when it is just damp, breaking up the surface as much as possible and rake in a handful each of complete plant food and wheat per square metre. The fibrous roots of the wheat will separate the soil into crumbs. When the crop is about 25 cm high, chop and hoe into the soil.

Sawdust is a wonderful crumbler for heavy soils. You can compensate for the fact that it depletes soil nitrogen by sprinkling some complete food in with it. Before applying, break up the soil to at least finger depth. Give another application 6 weeks later and your soil will soon be ready for planting.

You can improve clay soil and bring it to the planting stage without delay by using the 'straw gardening' technique.

Put down a base mat of compressed layers of lucerne hay to a depth of 5–7 cm over the area you wish to plant. Spread a 10–12 cm layer of wheat or oaten straw and a scattered handful of complete fertiliser over it.

Mark the planting spaces and make a nest-like depression at each one. Place a generous handful of well-rotted compost in each and water well.

You can then plant tomato or other seedlings or the seeds of beans or zucchini. Daily watering will be needed during hot weather. If heat is intense you may even need to water more often. I find that potatoes are one of the easiest crops to raise by this method as they are able to survive any drying of the soil long enough to get their roots down and establish themselves.

'Straw gardening' builds up a wonderful surface mulch which earthworms will carry down to give an added depth of good soil.

Always keep a mulch of organic matter over a clay soil. It is needed to protect it against the unnecessary agitation of heavy rain or careless watering, to supply organic substances which prevent the fusing of the clay particles, to create the desirable crumb-like structure and to increase the teeming millions of useful bacteria which help to keep soil healthy.

Do not lay grass turves directly on to a clay soil. First put in drainage and then a 10 cm layer of sand or crumbly loam and remember that, contrary to general opinion, roses do not thrive in a clay soil. They are certainly more clay-tolerant than many plants but prefer a loamy soil with a clay sub-soil. Clay as a sub-soil conserves moisture and plant foods around their roots.

What organic matter does for soil

No matter what the nature of your soil is, the important thing is to mulch it.

Mulching

By keeping a mulch of organic material over the soil you automatically keep the soil in good condition, eliminating most weed growth, the need for digging and other forms of cultivation. A mulch encourages a lively earthworm population, so you can leave these busy little creatures to carry out any aeration that is needed. Their constant tunnelling from surface mulch to sub-soil does this very effectively.

The other important role of a surface mulch is to protect clayey soils from losing their good crumbly structure through the pounding of heavy rain or careless watering. In the same way a mulch prevents humus from washing out of sandy soil. It also conserves moisture and protects roots from excessive heat or cold.

What to use as a mulch

Fibrous compost, spent mushroom compost and spent hops are widely used as mulches. Straw — especially straw from stables — is excellent, though the latter tends to generate heat if applied thickly, so it is just as well to moisten and heap it for a few weeks before spreading it close to plants.

Seaweed makes a valuable soil-feeding mulch. This can be salty so it is as well to hose the seaweed in a place where salt-carrying water can run off safely before spreading it on the garden.

Lawn clippings are one of the most frequently used mulches. They are also a valuable material but, like stable straw, will generate heat if spread thickly when fresh and green. I prefer to moisten and heap them for a few weeks before spreading. It is usually easy to have a few conveniently placed hideaways behind shrubbery where the clippings can be heaped prior to spreading. Alternatively, once you have a good mulch established, it can be maintained by adding a light sprinkling of the green clippings to it each week or so.

Most leaves, including those of deciduous trees and gum leaves, will make valuable mulching material. Once gum leaves dry it is difficult for water to penetrate them evenly if they are spread more than about 5 cm deep. This initial water resistance can be largely avoided by moistening and heaping them for a few weeks as suggested for grass clippings. Another ideal mulching material is a mixture of gum leaves and grass which is taken up by the mower catcher from a leafy lawn. Again, it is best to moisten and heap this for a few weeks before spreading.

Wood chip made from feeding prunings through a hammer mill or shredder makes a good, long-lasting mulch. Sawdust and shavings contain little or no nutriment but give insulation and protection to the soil they cover, and help to lighten clayey soils. They don't take nitrogen from the soil unless dug in or applied more than about 10 cm deep; and in any case this can be overcome by watering them about once a month with one of the complete soluble plant foods or by sprinkling them with a little fertiliser.

Pine bark mulch also helps to keep the soil in good condition even though it has little or no nutritional value. It is more expensive than other mulches mentioned but is long lasting and more attractive for feature areas.

Compost as a mulch

Compost serves to improve the soil in the ways already mentioned but it cannot be considered the perfectly balanced plant food many people assume it to be.

Compost can only return to the soil those elements contained in the plant material used in the composting. Therefore, if this plant material was grown on deficient soils, the compost will be similarly deficient. This is why some gardeners add light sprinklings or waterings with complete plant food when making a compost heap. These additions also speed decomposition.

Exponents of organic gardening prefer to use completely natural additives such as blood and bone or animal manures, but the latter, with the exception of fowl manure, may be short of the phosphorus needed in most home garden soils.

How to make good compost

So much has been written about the making of compost that it often sounds a solemn and complicated ritual, but there are many ways to achieve good results. Any pile of spent plant life just moistened and heaped will naturally decompose to a valuable soil additive, though the moist centre will be ready to use perhaps months before the drier outer layer.

However, better compost comes more rapidly when available material can be collected, moistened and mixed together in a large enough quantity to encourage the generation of heat.

The heat generated as decomposition begins can be sufficient to kill most weed seeds and fungus or virus diseases that may be present in some of the plant material used. Therefore, if using a free-standing heap in the open (the type many compost enthusiasts still prefer) it needs to be at least 1.5 m in width and height, and preferably a little longer.

Both air and moisture are needed for a healthy beneficial type of decomposition.

Compost bins, pits and tumblers

To make a free-standing compost heap of strong construction is more difficult than it sounds.

One simple but easy way is to make an enclosure of wire netting a metre or more high, supported at corners and at the centre of the long sides with stout stakes. Just toss the layers of material in when they become available. With this and the free-standing heap, the exposed top and sides will still be whole and fibrous when the inside of the heap is soft brown compost.

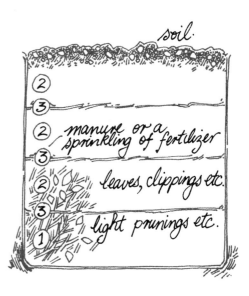

The principle is to lift the top layer and sides off, after 3 to 4 weeks, using this as the centre for another heap, then to pack the more decomposed material from inside the heap around it. In practice, most of us leave the heap until the inner material is ready to use, taking the top and side to start the next one.

I use three concrete bins with moulded lattice-like sides, earthen base and moveable boards or thin concrete slabs slotted down the front. One bin is filling, another is maturing and the other available for use when needed. When there are only few prunings about it may take a month or two to fill one, but every so often 30 cm or so of green matter with some organic complete plant food is added and generates a high enough temperature to heat the pile.

A few weeks after starting a new bin, I add about a span-depth layer from the top of the old one. This is then covered with a thin layer of soil and a little straw to slow drying and help the top material to mature. Another way, when you have a spare bin, is to fork the contents of the recently finished bin into it so that what was formerly the less-matured top is then at the bottom and the last used.

Compost in bins or heaps may take from 8 to 16 weeks to decompose fully to the soil-like stage for digging into the soil or adding to potting mixtures. The period depends on temperatures, moisture, the type of material used and whether manure, green grass or activators are added. Even though a good percentage of the compost is still fibrous, it is still very useful for surface mulching.

For rapid soil improvement I like to spread everything as it comes from the compost heap over the soil, then rake it over lightly several times. The coarse or still fibrous material flaked out is left aside to use for surface mulching after planting; the finer remaining material is dug in.

Compost tumblers can produce a good ready-to-use compost within a few weeks because of the easy daily turning and aeration. Before investing in one it should be realised that all material used needs to be shredded, otherwise whole weeds or even citrus skin halves will gather material and form tight balls during the turning action. It is also necessary to avoid excessive moisture from green material or the mix will not turn satisfactorily. Any large quantity of fresh grass clippings should be spread to dry for a few days or sufficient sawdust added to absorb condensation moisture.

Problems

With the definite exception of the above container I find that the greatest problem with other compost pits, heaps or bins is to keep them moist enough, particularly during summer. Once you have a heap of dry leafy material it is difficult to wet it evenly. So spread it out and saturate it before heaping. From then on just lightly water when the outside of the heap looks dry. Sogginess gives a sour ferment. Excessive water is also wasteful because it leaches valuable nutrients from the compost. For this reason, cover heaps or open bins against heavy rains.

What can be used in compost

All spent plant growth from the garden. Leaves can be stripped from the prunings and used. Heavy prunings should be shredded.

Avoid using bulbous weeds including oxalis, onion weed and nut grass, as enough of these will either escape or survive the heat to cause weed problems in the compost. Couch or kikuyu runners and Wandering Jew invariably survive unless they happen to be in the hottest centre of the heap, so it is as well to spread these in the hot sun for a few days before using them.

Grass clippings are valuable, especially when used as suggested earlier. Use all vegetable and fruit peelings in the compost but meat or processed food should be avoided. Egg shells are good, particularly if crushed. Newspaper or cardboard can be used, providing it is shredded and moistened. Mix it as much as possible with other ingredients so that it does not predominate in areas. Objections about lead in newsprint are unfounded, especially in these days of cheaper synthetics.

Gum leaves and most other leaves are excellent, providing they are moistened before being added and are confined to thin layers, or mixed in with grass clippings or other material. I hesitate to use large amounts of camphor laurel or she-oak (casuarina) leaves because they seem to contain substances that at least inhibit seed germination. However, these can still be useful as surface mulches in other parts of the garden.

Remember that it is hard to make really bad compost but some brews are better than others.

How to prepare the soil
Does your soil need draining?

Trees such as paper barks, bottlebrushes, pine-oaks, willows, poplars, swamp cypress and plants such as papyrus, flax, swamp heath, astilbe, day lilies, water irises, etc. are at home with their roots in soggy soil, but the majority of others — particularly citrus and camellias — develop root rot if the sub-soil remains wet for long periods.

This soggy sub-soil problem sometimes occurs above sandstone shelves that trap water, but more commonly where there is a heavy clay or shale and clay layer less than 45 cm below the surface.

Check the behaviour of sub-surface mois-ture by digging holes to spade depth at various points, 2–3 metres apart across the slope, preferably before or during periods of prolonged heavy rain. Water will collect in these holes but most of it should drain away within 24 hours (or certainly 48 hours) after rain stops. If not, some system of sub-soil drainage is needed.

Tile or cement agricultural pipes last the longest but flexible, perforated plastic pipes are now widely used. Installation of these is easier because they come in continuous lengths of up to 20 m or more.

Laying drainage pipes

Always plan the drainage system to make sure that there is a point of run-off for the water. The drains are laid across the slope 8 to 10 m apart with a slight slope to the lowest point. A fall of 5 cm in 20 m is sufficient. Trenches should be deep enough to lay the pipes on the solid clay sub-soil. For large-scale areas a herringbone system may be best, with the backbone or main drain carrying the water away. Where it is not possible to carry the water off your property, consider running it into a bog garden at the lowest point or into an underground sump filled with loosely-packed coarse rubble and surrounded by a few seepage-tolerant plants.

Pitfalls to avoid

I find that people tend to leave too much space between tile or cement pipes. This too often ends with soil blocking the pipes. Butt the pipes as close as possible — water will still enter. However, a 10 cm covering of gravel, clinker, ash, coarse river sand or similar material is desirable and speeds drainage.

Some people dig too deeply and start a grade too deep to maintain. You will find it is more practical to start the trench at the lowest point and work up to the highest. This stops it from filling with mud and water if weather is wet before completion.

However, to keep pipes from blocking under these circumstances, start laying from the highest point. Check pipes occasionally with a level on a length of rigid timber built up a little at one end to compensate for the grade. If any point is too low, build it up with firmly tamped soil over the entire width of the trench; otherwise water will be trapped where the pipe kinks downwards and it is at these points that silting and eventual blocking can occur.

Essential elements for fertile soil

It is essential that the soil contains all the elements found in the plant itself and that it retains them long enough for the plant to absorb them during its life. The chemical elements most needed by plants and most liable to rapid exhaustion are nitrogen, phosphoric acid (phosphorus) and potash (potassium).

There are other elements in the soil but they are used in such small quantities that they are lost from the soil only in exceptional circumstances.

Element	Effect
Nitrogen:	Makes leaf and stem
	Promotes quick growth (weight and bulk)
	Gives good colour and foliage
Phosphorus:	Promotes fruit and flowers
	Makes strong roots
	Ensures crop maturity
Potassium:	Promotes general health of plant and flowers
	Strengthens stems or stalks
	Increases size and flavour of fruits

Sub-soil

The condition of the sub-soil is a vital factor in the health of your plants; you can improve that too.

Deepening the sub-soil

Where topsoil is shallow the conventional, albeit drastic, treatment is trenching. Few people undertake this these days. The general approach now is to dig a trench a metre wide the full width of the area to about spade depth, and barrow the soil to the opposite end of the area. Then get into the trench and spade over the lower soil or, if very clayey, loosen it with a mattock or pick. If you can work in some compost so much the better. Do not bring clayey sub-soil to the surface.

Mark out another metre-side parallel area and shovel the soil from this into the first trench so that the sub-soil in this area can also be loosened and improved. Proceed this way across the area using the soil borrowed from the first trench to fill the last one.

Stony or rocky ground

Stones help to hold together light sandstone or ironstone soil can be accepted as part of the garden. They are only a nuisance where mechanical cultivators are used or if they are large enough to restrict roots of small plants such as annuals or vegetables. Shrubs and tree roots find their way between them.

Even where there is only shallow soil over large areas of rock it is surprising how tree roots spread over the rock shelves and find deeper crevices to penetrate. Where there has been only sufficient depth of soil to cover half the root-ball of young trees I have built up with rocks about a metre out from the trunk to retain the extra soil needed. All of these specimens are now fully grown without any signs of restricted root depth.

Quite often the depth of cultivation beds can be improved by building up with soil from the shallowest areas and leaving the latter paths. Lawns, particularly buffalo, couch and kikuyu grasses, will usually establish well where the average depth of soil over rock is only 12–15 cm. Some lawns are growing successfully with even shallower soil, but in this case frequent watering will be needed, especially during hot weather.

Acid or alkaline?

All successful gardeners know that some plants prefer an acid soil, others grow better in alkaline conditions. It is important therefore to establish the nature of your soil.

The rate of pH is the standard form of measuring the rate of acidity or alkalinity of a soil. The pH scale starts at 1 for extremely acid and goes to 14 for the very alkaline side. Neutral soil would have a reading of 7.

This acid/alkaline factor is important because only in the vicinity of the neutral mark are most elements appreciably soluble in the soil and unless they are easily dissolved

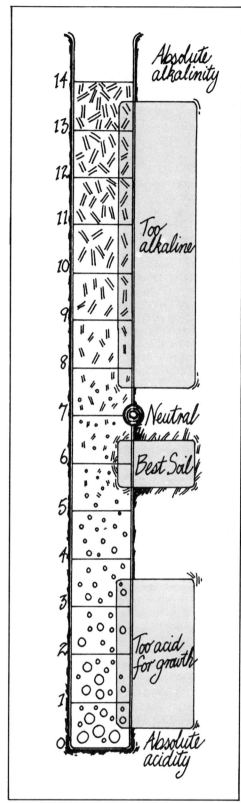

pH Scale and values
Soil is usually acid or alkaline and has according characteristics. Soil testing kits are available which indicate pH just by colour change on contact with a soil sample. This is then matched against the colour on the indicator chart provided.

in the soil water they cannot be taken up by the plant roots. Therefore in a very acid or alkaline soil it is possible to have deficiencies of elements that are actually present but unavailable to the plant. For example, essential elements such as potassium, phosphorus, boron and molybdenum begin to lose solubility as acidity increases (less than about pH 5.0). Similarly, as soils become alkaline or limey (about 7.0), manganese and particularly iron become insoluble and unavailable to the plant. Iron deficiency is quite common when soils have been heavily limed as lime reduces the acidity or inversely increases the alkalinity. The symptom is a yellowing of the foliage, particularly of the new growth, and it is referred to as 'lime-induced chlorosis' or iron deficiency.

Simple-to-use pH kits are available. They give a pH reading according to the colour changes the liquid registers when in contact with your soil sample.

This does not mean that you need to test your soil frequently, or for that matter take pH or acidity readings at all. Many plant lovers garden successfully without ever checking their soil pH. The main purpose of including this section is to make the gardener aware that over-acidity or over-alkalinity can affect the nutrition or general health of the plants, and to warn against the excessive use of lime and of acidifying agents when they are not needed. Only use the latter when you are growing acid-loving plants such as azaleas, rhododendrons, most ericas, magnolias and to some extent camellias, in soil that has previously been heavily limed or is known to be naturally limey or very alkaline. Over-limeyness or alkalinity may be encountered in soil around new buildings where mortar or cement has been dropped, or around new cement driveways and paths.

Soil in which azaleas and rhododendrons grow happily without any particular treatment can be regarded as moderately acid; just a little too acid for lettuce, cabbage, beet, onion, carrot, pea and bean crops. A light dressing of lime — say about three-quarters of a cup per square metre — applied once a year would be beneficial for these crops.

Hydrangeas usually indicate the acidity or alkalinity of a soil by producing pink flowers where untreated soil is limey and blue tones in acid conditions. There may be exceptions because colour is also dependent on the amount of aluminium in the soil, but these plants can be used as general indicators.

Acidity of the soil can be increased by applying 2 tablespoons of either sulphate of aluminium or sulphate of iron, or 4 tablespoons of powdered sulphur or flowers of sulphur per square metre. This will reduce the pH by 0.5 of a degree (say from 7 to 6.5) but this can vary in different soil types. Sulphate of ammonia, European peatmoss and hydrangea blueing tonics also have an acidifying effect on the soil.

6. Understanding plants and soil

Many people grow beautiful plants without knowing much about them. Some idea of their basic needs and the way they feed helps a gardener to understand them and enjoy them so much more.

First, consider the way they live.

For millions of years they have been doing what man has only achieved in fairly recent times in laboratory experiments: they absorb carbon dioxide through their leaves and, using light as energy, combine this gas with water to create sugar and starches.

Soluble nitrates, phosphates, sulphates and magnesium salt are dissolved in water taken up by the roots and then combined with sugar-type substances to form complex plant proteins and chlorophyll. It is interesting to find that this is similar in make-up to the haemoglobin of our red blood cells. Calcium is the main ingredient of plant cell walls as it is of our bone structure.

Plants, like people, can survive for a time on very little food, or on all sorts of rubbishy food and drink; but, like people, require sound nourishment to enable them to be at their best and need living conditions suitable to their own particular nature.

Light

All plants, except primitives such as fungi, need light to create and process the sugars essential for their make-up. Photosynthesis is the scientific name for the process.

The majority of trees, shrubs, garden flowers and vegetables need at least 6 hours sunlight each day to produce robust growth, but many of our popular house plants whose origin was below the dense tree canopy of tropical jungle can grow happily in very little light.

Palms, some ferns, philodendron and other such foliage plants will adapt to indirect or even full sunlight indoors, provided you give them time to adjust to the change of condition. Conversely, plants grown in bright light take time to adjust to the dimmer conditions indoors. Plants moved from indoors into direct sunlight are likely to burn badly.

There must always be a ratio between the amount of light, temperature, humidity and water for a plant to grow successfully indoors or out. Reduce one of these factors and the others need to be reduced accordingly.

A foliage plant will survive in a hot room if there is plenty of light, humidity and water and the same plant will probably stay reasonably healthy in comparatively poor light, providing temperatures are not high, watering is kept to a minimum and feeding is reduced as the growth rate slows down.

Humidity

Plants such as ferns and most of the foliage plants of jungle origin need relatively high humidity — around 40–50%. If they do not get it the foliage loses moisture too rapidly and the leaf tips and margins turn brown.

If the dry cold air of a closed room is heated by radiators or from the heat of the sun on the windows, humidity can fall dramatically and plants of this type kept indoors will suffer badly.

Plants from the dry areas of the world, such as succulents, accept very low humidity.

Water

A better understanding of plant needs is gained by appreciating that although roots need frequent contact with water they also need oxygen for their healthy development. Oxygen is also needed in the soil for the benefit of the seething population of bacteria that decompose organic matter and keep the soil healthy; unwanted gases must have the ability to escape or toxicity will build up in the soil to the detriment of everything growing there. The air and gas can only move freely if there is space between the soil particles — a saturated soil precludes this so care must always be taken when watering.

A happy medium is needed. A good general rule is to give the soil a thorough but gentle soaking and then don't water again until the surface begins to look dry. Ferns, sedge plants and young seedlings just developing their root system will appreciate more water. Seedlings, of course, should always be carefully watered until it is certain their roots have penetrated strongly and deeply enough for them to have become established.

Some cacti and house plants like a period of dryness between waterings, especially during winter.

The foods plants need

Nitrogen

Nitrogen is needed in relatively large quantities in all growth processes of a plant. It is a major component of the various plant proteins and also of chlorophyll — the green pigment of plants responsible for the energising of sunlight to perform that remarkable process of combining carbon dioxide from the air with water to form sugars, which are later converted to starches and other plant components. The process is called photosynthesis.

It is logical that when nitrogen is deficient, foliage will be pale or yellowish because of the absence of chlorophyll, and growth will be poor and stunted. Nitrogen promotes lush and vigorous vegetative growth. The main artificial sources of nitrogen are sulphate of ammonia, urea, calcium nitrate or calcium ammonium nitrate and, to a lesser extent, nitrate of soda (sodium nitrate), potassium nitrate and several forms of ammonium phosphate.

Phosphorus

Like nitrogen, phosphorus is concerned with the vital growth processes of plants and is a constituent of the living cell nuclei. It is also essential to the formation of strong root growth and the germination of seed. Phosphorus induces maturity and the formation and ripening of seeds, rather than lush vege-

tative growth. The addition of phosphorus to the soil can offset the over-vegetative effects of excessive nitrogen.

Phosphorus deficiency shows in poor, stunted growth but blueing rather than yellowing of foliage. Phosphorus-deficient roses usually have purplish tints on the undersides of the leaves which fall prematurely. Phosphorus-deficient cabbages and cauliflowers show dull purple tints, a condition more pronounced in certain varieties and with the effects of cold. Newly-sown couch grass lacking in phosphorus will be slow to germinate and when the grass does come through will be a deep slatey-purple rather than a bluish-green colour. The symptoms are more likely to occur when the area has been treated with one of the usual high- nitrogen-type lawn foods prior to sowing, rather than a phosphorus-rich lawn starter or complete plant food. These phosphorus deficiencies can be corrected by applying about one handful of superphosphate per square metre of garden area.

Superphosphate is the most widely used form of phosphorus. Fully soluble forms used in water-on plant foods include mono-ammonium phosphate, di-ammonium phosphate and occasionally potassium phosphate. Bone dust is a reliable but slow fertiliser. Fowl manure also contains reasonable quantities of this element.

Potassium

Potassium, usually referred to as potash, is not a component of plant tissue but is required in large quantities in all parts of the plant. It influences, or is sometimes regarded as a controller of, the amount of water a plant loses by transpiration. It acts as a catalyst in the formation and storage of starches, proteins, etc. Potassium-deficient plants are generally weak, particularly in the flower stems, and have brown and shrivelled leaf margins. The latter occurs mainly when the plant cannot take in sufficient water to deal with the high rate of transpiration from the leaves.

The main commercial source of potassium is potassium chloride — this is the most concentrated and relatively cheap form. Its main drawback is that if soil already has high chloride content, frequent use can create chloride toxicity, something occasionally seen in heavily fed roses and vegetables. Potassium sulphate will not cause the same trouble. Nitrate of potassium, another excellent source of potassium, has the advantage of also supplying immediately available nitrogen but is comparatively expensive.

Contrary to common belief wood ash does not necessarily contain a good percentage of potassium. It depends on the content of material burned. Green leaves and twigs produce far more potassium than mature wood. Compost, horse, cow and sheep manure, and particularly poultry manure, should not be exposed to rain as potassium leaches from them fairly readily.

Potassium becomes insoluble and therefore relatively unavailable to the plant under acid soil conditions. Symptoms of potassium deficiency occurring under these conditions can usually be corrected by the addition of lime. Appreciate too, that though the more available or soluble the potassium, the more rapidly it will leach from the soil during heavy rain or watering. For this reason relatively heavy applications of potassium are needed in tropical areas with high rainfall.

Calcium
Calcium forms a large part of the cell-wall structure in plants, much as it does in the bone structure of the animal kingdom.

Its deficiency results in collapse of the young tips or new shoots of plants. This is generally preceded by a distortion of the foliage with the tips of the young leaves hooked back and the leaf margin curled, or with irregular ragged formation of the leaves. Brown spotting and scorched areas are often present.

The first point of collapse in tomatoes is the base or blossom end of the fruit which becomes brown and sunken and prone to fungus attack. The more direct cause of the latter may be irregular or inadequate watering so that the necessary calcium has not been carried to all parts of the plant, especially the extremities.

Calcium deficiency occurs under very acid soil conditions, often where there is an excess of manganese or aluminium in the soil.

All forms of lime contain high percentages of calcium. Being a component of plant and particularly leaf cells, it is also present in most forms of compost.

Magnesium
In every molecule of that intriguing green leaf pigment chlorophyll there is one atom of magnesium. Cut off the magnesium supply from the plant and carotin or xanthophyl are formed, and the magnesium-deficient leaf takes on a yellowish colour, usually starting between the veins; brighter orange tints may also be present and the affected leaves usually fall prematurely. In some varieties of potatoes large dead areas appear between the leaf veins without much yellowing of the rest of the leaf. Magnesium is supplied inorganically either by magnesium sulphate (Epsom salts) or by dolomite, a comparatively slow-acting form of magnesium limestone. Most compost, particularly if made from green leaves and stems, contains an appreciable amount of magnesium.

Magnesium deficiency is more likely to occur in very acid soils or where large quantities of potash have been used, particularly sulphate of potassium.

Sulphur
Sulphur is a component of protein and certain oils in plants. Deficiency symptoms are similar to those of nitrogen deficiency, usually with leaves restricted in size and sometimes rolled at margins.

However, sulphur deficiencies are quite rare as there are large percentages of sulphur or sulphates in most fertiliser mixtures, in most organic material, and as impurities in the atmosphere, except in areas isolated from industry.

Trace elements
Although required in very small amounts, these are vital to growth. While they are not actual components of plant tissues they act like catalysts or oxidising agents assisting plants to absorb and utilise major and minor elements and in the formation of plant substances.

Iron
Although not a component of chlorophyll, iron assists in its formation. Therefore, when iron is deficient the symptoms are of yellowing rather similar to magnesium and nitrogen deficiencies. The main difference is that the latter two elements are relatively mobile within the plant and as nature tends to cater for the needs of young or new growth first, their deficiencies will be seen in the older foliage. Iron, on the other hand, is immobile in the plant so the yellowing will occur first in the new growth.

Iron occurs naturally in most soils but is rapidly rendered insoluble by the presence of lime. The remedy is to acidify the soil using sulphur, peatmoss, sulphate of aluminium or sulphate of iron which itself contains a large percentage of iron. Because of the tendency or iron to form insoluble substances in contact with other chemicals, the more positive remedy is the use of iron chelates applied either to the soil or as a foliage spray. Chelates do not readily combine with other substances and are relatively mobile within the plant.

Zinc
Zinc deficiency sometimes occurs in citrus causing a yellow mottling of the leaf. Apples and stone fruits deficient in zinc develop a condition known as 'little leaf' or 'rosette' and form clusters of very small foliage. It can be corrected by applying zinc sulphate to the soil.

Copper
Copper deficiency in citrus causes dieback of young shoots and sometimes a burning of the leaf margins, together with a type of rosette or formation of multiple buds. Excretion of gum may also be present.

Copper deficiency is treated by applying powdered copper sulphate (blue stone). Copper sprays such as copper oxychloride also help to arrest the deficiency.

Boron
Boron is mainly a regulator of nitrogen in the plant. Deficiency shows as cankers or sunken withered areas on beetroot, hollow cores in turnips together with a buff and pinking flush on the foliage, and death of the growing tip. It is also responsible for hollow stem in cauliflowers and excessive browning of the curd or complete failure to develop. It can also cause hardening of the skin of citrus and in lemons, particularly, hollow cavities with gumming between the flesh and rind of the fruit (also a brownish tint toward the centre of the fruit over the seed area).

Boron, like potassium, is readily leached from the soil, particularly under limey conditions, so it is possible to experience a temporary deficiency after long periods of rain, especially when the soil has become abnormally dry. It is therefore obvious that the condition may right itself. Otherwise it can be cured by adding sodium borate or borax, but care must be taken because although borax may be a nitrogen regulator and assist the intake of nitrogen by the plant, it becomes a potent herbicide, in greater concentration.

To treat an apparent boron deficiency in a medium-sized lemon tree do not use more than one tablespoon of borax, dissolved in a can of water and applied mainly under the outer foliage. Do not repeat this application within 12 months.

Molybdenum
Molybdenum is required at the incredibly low rate of a few ounces per acre but its deficiency can deform new growth on dahlias, pansies, forget-me-nots, cauliflowers, etc. In the latter it causes a related condition known as 'whip tail', where the leaves become distorted and twisted. In the young stages, leaves of both cauliflowers and cabbages have an upward cupped appearance with slight mottling. It is possible that the die-back of some shrubs, particularly camellias, could be associated with molybdenum deficiency.

Under normal conditions the deficiency is likely to show up only when soil conditions are very acid, preventing the solubility and availability of molybdenum to the plant. It may also occur after the use of fertilisers containing high concentrations of nitrogen and phosphorus. Corrective treatment is to spray with a solution of sodium molybdate (about one teaspoon per 4.5 litres of water), which is sufficient to supply the very small amounts needed. This treatment is used successfully in the commercial growing of rockmelons in areas where molybdenum is deficient.

Toxicity
Toxicities can occur through the excessive use of any of the trace elements especially of copper, zinc, boron and manganese. The latter toxicity may occur in very acid soils due to the greater solubility of this element in those circumstances. Symptoms are usually mottling or dark streaking particularly toward the margin of the leaf. Sometimes there may be a purplish banded effect in that area or a shrivelling of the leaf tip like that caused by potash deficiency, together with a yellowing. Beans show a yellowing between the veins with very fine brown spotting and in some cases a purplish overcast. Tomatoes usually show dead or brown patches here and there along the stems with lower leaves hanging and shrivelling. Some fungus diseases cause similar symptoms.

General diagnosis
It can be seen from some of the deficiencies listed here that accurate visual diagnosis of a deficiency is often difficult. This can be complicated further by the fact that more than one element may be deficient or there may be a deficiency of one and a toxicity of another. Also, there is the possibility that the various elements are present in the soil but are not

available to the plant because of insolubility caused by excessive acidity, alkalinity or excess of some other element.

The best advice is not to worry unduly about deficiencies. Be conscious of their possibility, due to heavy-handed use of soil acidifiers, lime, or individual rather than complete fertilisers. Do not apply any of these unnecessarily or at excessive rates. Remember that lack of apparent growth may be because the plant is resting because of the physical condition of the soil or too much or too little water. It could even be that the plant is suffering root damage from excessive fertilisers in the soil.

Feeding generally

Good gardens or good growth for that matter do not depend on frequent applications of fertilisers or even on the use of animal manures. In nature, all spent plant material falls to the ground, decomposes and is converted from organic to soluble inorganic salts. These salts are again taken up by the plant and so the cycle continues. Remember though that humans, the lower animals, birds and insects all feed off vegetation, so to keep the cycle complete, all waste products from these creatures and ultimately their dead bodies as well would need to be returned to the soil. This does not fit in with our lifestyle under close settlement. Therefore, we need to supplement the cycle.

Apart from utilising waste plant and household material for compost and supplying this to the soil, we can supplement fairly successfully with the use of animal manures, particularly poultry and sheep manure. However, the nutrient content of most farmyard manures depends both on the material that has been fed to the animals producing it and whether weathering and leaching action of rain have caused loss of ammonia and other minerals.

Concentrated artificial manures offer the most convenient way to supply plant nutrition in the home garden. Exponents of organic gardening frown on this method of feeding, and in some cases quite rightly so because they are often used excessively and there are many records of long-term bad results where one particular nutrient has been used excessively. However, there is no sound reason why artificial or inorganic fertilisers cannot produce crops equal in every way to those grown organically, provided they are used in complete balance, at sensible rates, and in conjunction with compost or similar organic material. This is logical when you appreciate that all organic material must be broken down by soil bacteria and converted to inorganic soluble salts before it can be taken up by the plant. These inorganic salts are in much the same form whether they are derived from organic material or supplied from packeted chemical fertilisers.

These days, when complete or mixed fertilisers are used rather than their individual components, any damage that occurs in the home garden is normally due to excessive feeding. Either the inexperienced gardener thinks that recommended rates of a handful or so per square metre cannot be enough and greatly exceeds the amount or believes that if a little is good then twice as much is twice as good. But this is certainly not the case.

To realise the damage caused by overfeeding you need to go back to classroom experiments on what probably then appeared to be the rather dreary subject of osmosis. The simple example of this is a container of water and salt solution both separated by a permeable type of membrane like egg shell or parchment and the result is that the salt solution draws in water, in an attempt to equalise itself.

This is just how root cells take in water and comparatively weak solutions of nutrient salts, transmitting them from cell to cell so that they disperse throughout the plant. However, once the solution of soluble salts in the soil becomes stronger or more concentrated than the fluid in the root cells, the action is reversed and the cell contents are drawn out. Unfortunately, the root cells are ruptured in the process and the plant's entire feeding system collapses. Even though the plant is surrounded by nutrients and moisture it dies of starvation and thirst.

The obvious message is to observe directions when using any concentrated fertiliser, to feed only when the soil is evenly moist, and to water well after feeding. It should be appreciated that a relatively safe solution of salts in moist soil will concentrate as the soil dries out. This is the danger — people get away with excessive feeding while the soil is moist, but the plants can suddenly collapse during a period of dryness, even weeks after feeding.

Plants in containers are frequently damaged by overfeeding because the soluble salts are unable to diffuse into the surrounding soil and concentrations become alarmingly high if the container's soil dries out.

This is also why, in sandy soil, it is advised that half the recommended rate of fertiliser be applied twice as frequently because sandy soil dries out very rapidly.

It is also why leaching of the soil is recommended prior to feeding house plants and other container-grown plants. Here the idea is to wash out any nutrient salts remaining in the soil before applying more.

Damage from excessive percentages of soil salts is not necessarily confined to the use of artificial fertilisers. As already explained, any organic material must go through a process of decomposition by soil organisms (to be converted from organic to inorganic soluble salts) before a plant can derive any nutrient from the material. Because the breakdown or decomposition of the organic material is relatively slow the release of nutrients is correspondingly slow, so likelihood of root damage is far less than with inorganic chemical fertilisers. Again, if damage does occur, it is normally when the soil suddenly dries out, particularly if this follows a long moist period that has favoured fairly rapid decomposition of the organic material.

When should I feed and how often?

Feed only when plants are showing some signs of active growth. Do not feed dormant plants because when the plant is unable to use the nutrients in the soil there is a danger of build-up of unused nutrient salts. Do not feed sick or ailing plants unless you are certain that the condition is due to a mineral deficiency. The main period of active growth is usually in the spring and this is the time to feed, but wait for signs of new growth first. Do not apply more than the rate recommended on the container and halve the rate if dealing with quick-drying sandy soil as already suggested. The rate should be reduced also when feeding plants in containers.

When applying plant foods, spread them mainly under the outer foliage because most of the feeder roots of a plant are concentrated here rather than close to the stem or trunk. Feed only when the soil is damp and water well after feeding.

Subsequent feeding depends on the growth rate of the plants. One feed in spring is usually enough for trees and ornamental shrubs. Summer fruits such as apples, peaches, pears, etc. respond to a second feeding when the fruit is half-formed. Citrus prefer an even supply of food to match their growth pattern so are fed initially in early spring and given a second feeding in early to mid-summer and then a little more again in autumn.

Rapidly growing vegetables and flowers benefit from a second application of the conventional dry mix or sprinkle-on type of complete fertiliser 6 to 8 weeks after the first one, or even a little earlier for quick-bearing crops such as beans.

The soluble type, complete-plant-foods or water-on fertilisers are far less concentrated than the dry mixes so are applied more frequently. As often as once a fortnight for plants in active growth; and for lettuce, spinach and silver beet as frequently as once a week is not excessive, providing the plants are well watered throughout the period.

Note that most of the water-on types of fertilisers contain extremely high percentages of nitrogen which promotes lush leaf growth and boosts size rather than encouraging productivity. It is excellent for leafy crops such as lettuce, cabbage, spinach, silver beet, etc. but makes tomatoes, beans, vine crops and flowers run to leaf rather than flowers or fruit. But if application is kept down until flower buds or fruit formation commences, it will usually improve size of flowers or fruit. How frequently these quick-growing crops need feeding will also be influenced by the amount of watering or rain received. Prolonged heavy rain or watering naturally leaches these nutrients from the soil and in these circumstances another light application of plant food may be needed sooner than it would otherwise.

What are complete fertilisers?

A complete fertiliser or complete plant food is one which contains a balance of the three major elements: nitrogen, phosphorus and potash. These are commonly referred to as 'major' elements only because they are required in much larger quantities than the 'minor' and 'trace' elements. A truly complete fertiliser or plant food will also contain the minor elements calcium, sulphur and magnesium, plus trace elements iron, manganese, boron, copper, zinc and molybdenum.

The analysis of a complete fertiliser or complete plant food will always be shown on the bag and is generally referred to in garden jargon as the 'NPK'. N stands for nitrogen, P for phosphorus and K for kalium which in this case is used to represent potassium because the two Ps would be confusing. When anyone refers to the NPK of a particular fertiliser it usually means the percentage of nitrogen, phosphorus and potassium that it contains. These are always expressed in that order. For example, if a fertiliser has an NPK of 5.6.4 it contains 5% nitrogen, 6% phosphorus and 4% potassium, which is fairly representative of a basic type of complete fertiliser.

Although we refer to major, minor and trace elements, the latter are just as vital to a plant's healthy functioning as the major elements. However, they are not always included in so-called complete fertiliser mixtures.

This omission is not necessarily detrimental to plant growth. There is usually sufficient elements present as impurities in the fertiliser, in most water supplies and in compost, provided the material making up the compost has not been grown in soil deficient in these minerals.

Under natural conditions, where mass growth is reasonably healthy, the soil will usually contain an adequate balance of all essential major, minor and trace elements. It is only when any of these elements are added in excess that the balance is thrown out. For example, deficiencies of boron and molybdenum may only occur after use of one of the higher powered or more concentrated complete fertilisers. Although both of these trace elements regulate the use of nitrogen within the plant, excessive application of nitrogen virtually recesses their presence to a stage where deficiency symptoms occur. Then there are other factors where one element will combine with another to form a compound which then becomes unavailable because this compound cannot be dissolved in soil water.

A common example of this is the excessive use of lime which readily forms insoluble compounds in contact with iron and so creates symptoms or iron deficiency, shown by a chlorotic yellowing of young foliage. The often recommended use of Epsom salts (magnesium sulphate) for greening of plants, particularly gardenias, may backfire if carried out excessively because it can form insoluble salts in contact with potassium. In this case the gardenia frequently fed with Epsom salts may start showing brown tips to the leaves — an early symptom of potassium deficiency. Deficiencies can also occur because something you have done to the soil makes certain elements extremely soluble and although this increases their availability to the plants, it also means that they are leached out more readily after heavy rain or watering. The use of lime, for example, can make both potassium and boron more soluble and so more subject to leaching from the soil.

The answer?

You don't need to be an analytical chemist to maintain a good balance of nutrients in the soil. These examples of possible adverse effects on the balance of soil nutrients are just to suggest that you let sleeping dogs lie. Don't dose your plants with copious quantities of one particular chemical just because you think it may be deficient or because someone suggests it is good for your plant.

You will find that you can have a happy, healthy garden by keeping the surface of your soil mulched with organic material just as nature does and if you feel a little extra feeding is necessary, as well it may be, use one of the accepted complete plant foods as directed on the package. Don't dose your plants with individual chemicals which are likely to do more harm than good.

How plants respond to different foods

If all is not going according to plan with your plants and you feel it's a feeding problem then answers to the following questions could give a clue to the problem — but remember that lack of light, too much or too little water or over-compacted soil might also be a factor.

1. Do plants look undersized, brown, with pale foliage, yet with plenty of small flowers and fruit?

This can be caused by lack of water or over-compacted soil, but more often is a sign of too little nitrogen. It is usually corrected by a mulch of good rich compost or by feeding with complete soluble plant foods, which, except for special vegetable food formulations, contain much more nitrogen than the dry-mix complete plant foods. Sulphate of ammonia, urea and nitrate of soda supply nitrogen alone.

2. Do plants look particularly robust, with foliage large and green but with few flowers and fruits?

This could be caused by lack of sunlight but more often is a typical sign of excessive nitrogen without enough phosphorus. These symptoms are particularly noticeable with tomatoes and dahlias. Rose foliage may eventually develop a bluish tint but couch grass seed is a more definite indicator; when phosphorus is deficient the seedlings are stunted and a definite slatey-purple colour (note that except in tropical areas it only germinates from mid-spring onwards when soil is warm). Correct by using a 'sprinkle-on' dry powder or granular-type complete fertiliser — or more positively with superphosphate, using up to 1 tablespoon per square metre. Bone dust also corrects it but its action is slower.

3. Do plants have weak pithy stems, poor quality flowers and leaves with brown tips and margins?

This can happen to some deciduous trees and shrubs and pot plants affected by wind or fertiliser burn or very dry atmoshpere, but is also a characteristic of potash deficiency. Cabbages and cauliflowers with this deficiency tend to roll their scorched leaf margins, usually upwards. All complete fertilisers contain a balance of potash. Sulphate of potash or miriate of potash are the main sources of supply and may be applied separately (2 teaspoons per square metre).

Note: It is impossible to make definite diagnoses from these symptoms alone. There are cases where toxicity from excess or deficiency of minor or trace elements can cause similar results; so can some diseases. It is intended only as an indication of behaviour when plant nutrients are badly out of balance.

Foliar feeding

Spraying the leaves with plant food does not replace the normal application of fertilisers but can be used to give an ailing plant or tree quick recovery through the quick absorption of nitrogen. Phosphorus and potassium, which take longer to absorb, are likely to be washed away by rain before the plant can absorb them. The process can be troublesome and sometimes expensive, but is worthwhile considering as a rescue operation.

7. Weed control

Weeds can make gardening seem frustrating and at times almost impossible in the way they overtake wanted plants. (A weed is really only a plant in a place where it is not wanted.)

Don't let weeds take the pleasure out of gardening

Most weeds can be controlled without heartache or backache and it can be surprisingly easy to get rid of the most formidable weed invasion, either by manual or chemical means. Once the worst has been overcome, most common weeds can be kept down by maintaining a surface mulch over the soil or by use of ground covers. An occasional scuffling of the surface soil will eliminate weeds soon after they germinate in vegetable or flower beds.

Where to start

Assess the type of weeds that predominate so that the most suitable method of control can be chosen. Annual weeds such as chickweeds, yellowtop, thistle, redshank, staggerweed, pigweed, capeweed, winter grass, summer grass, prairie grass, etc. are easily killed by cutting them just a centimetre or two below the surface with either a sharp hoe or well-sharpened spade held obliquely. Results are best if this is done on a warm, dry day. The same applies to the perennial weeds plantains, dandelions, catsear, paspalum, crow's foot and wire grass.

No need to burn the weeds even if they are seeding. Just heap them in some convenient place in the shade where they can rot down, and any seedlings that germinate from them can be treated in the same way. If you are not in a hurry to use the soil, chop off the weeds as suggested and as seedlings appear chop them into the soil before they reach the seeding stage. You will improve your soil by adding valuable organic material at the same time as getting rid of your weeds.

Chemical control

Chemical preparations such as Weedex, Polyquat, Gramoxone, Roundup and Zero will rapidly control most of the broad-leafed annual or perennial weeds and many of the grasses. All but the last two mentioned work only through green plant tissue and can be used close to brown-stemmed shrubs, roses or trees. They break down in contact with the soil within about 24 hours but are extremely toxic and must be used with care. Roundup and Zero are similar in action to the other preparations mentioned, but because they are a little slower to break down in the soil, some root absorption does occur and they may cause damage, particularly to roses. They are often used amongst trees and shrubs without ill effect but it is safest to avoid close contact with treasured plants.

Perennial grasses with underground storage stems such as couch, bladey grass, nut grass, Johnson's grass and kikuyu grass are difficult to control by manual or mechanical means. The last three mentioned can be controlled by

Roundup or Zero, at the strength normally recommended for general weed control and the others at about twice that strength. Nut grass particularly can have dormant underground corms, and several applications may be needed to give effective control.

It is safer to regard all herbicides as toxic and great care should be taken to avoid skin contact with the chemicals during mixing and application and with the weeds soon after treatment. Also avoid inhalation or contact with spray drift. It is wise to apply these chemicals with a fine-rose water can or special trickle bar which can be attached to a water can for the purpose, even though it may involve the use of more chemical.

Other lesser known chemicals still sometimes used for control of unwanted grasses are: Propon, Dalapon or Dowpon, which are applied as a spray to wet the maximum area of stems and foliage. It may take six weeks for a kill to become evident and thickly matted kikuyu grass will need a second application if regrowth occurs.

Another grass killer absorbed through the roots of the plant rather than the foliage is T.C.A. Results are better with this chemical if most of the foliage is cut down prior to application and the soil evenly moistened to allow complete penetration to the root area. To kill bamboo it needs to be applied at about twice the rate recommended for normal grass — one kilogram instead of the usual 500 grams to approximately 10 sq. m of area. T.C.A. leaves the soil toxic to most plants for about three months, although others have some resistance to it. For example, it has been effectively used as a selective herbicide amongst beetroot crops.

Long-lasting effect

There are a number of preparations sold under such names as 'path weeders' and 'total' herbicides which are useful for killing unwanted weeds along fence lines, footpaths, driveways, drains or other areas away from normal cultivation. They are safe to use as long as safety directions on the pack are observed. Although their effect may be listed as lasting 3 to 4 weeks, some of the ingredients such as Amitrole may persist longer, particularly in sandy soils and if washed to nearby areas will cause variegation or whitening of the foliage of shrubs, trees or other plants. This is usually only a temporary effect and the plant will outgrow the condition.

Couch and other persistent grasses in rockeries or amongst other plantings

Probably the safest way of eliminating these grasses in difficult situations without endangering nearby plants is to use Weedex, Polyquat or Gramoxone at twice the normal recommended strength. Before treatment, where possible, lift runners up that are intermingling with wanted plants and protect the latter with plastic or similar waterproof

material. Wear rubber gloves and even then do not handle plant material wet with the herbicide. Wash the gloves thoroughly before removing them.

Oxalis, onion weed and other bulbous pests

Eliminating oxalis by hand is not quite as impossible as it may sound. The initial disturbance inevitably distributes a number of loose bulblets or cormlets through the soil, but if these are removed when they make growth, before they have a chance to produce loose cormlets (with most types prior to spring or before they flower) the infestation can be gradually decreased and eventually eliminated. It requires patience but is worth trying. Onion weed is more difficult because the bulb is situated deeper than that of oxalis.

Chemical control — so far, unfortunately, there is no selective chemical that will kill these pests without damaging other plants. In soil away from the main root systems of wanted shrubs or trees, the most positive control is to have the soil fumigated with methyl bromide, a lethal gas to be used with the utmost care by experienced pest control operators only. The area to be treated is sealed down under plastic sheeting, the gas injected and left for 24 hours or longer, depending on temperature and other conditions. Even then there is danger that it may drift through the soil and escape to other areas. For effective destruction of the corms, at least 1 kg of the gas per 10 sq. m of area is needed and the soil must be well broken up and free from clods. The gas kills most weed seeds in the soil except clovers and mallow.

In cultivation, the best way to chemically eliminate these persistent weeds is to wet them thoroughly with Roundup or Zero, or in more closely planted areas with Weedex or Polyquat. When the weeds die, dig and water the soil to induce growth of dormant corms during the growing season. Treat new growth with the chemical when it is reasonably established, and if necessary, repeat the process several times.

Nut grass

Eradicating this pest is difficult because the thread-like roots may spread a span or two from the parent plant before producing a woody corm at their tip. When the soil is just damp and will crumble easily, lift it from about fork depth and gently crumble the clods so that the rootlets connecting the corms are not severed. The new season corms are usually not produced until mid to late summer so take action early in summer when the new growth is fully established.

Chemical control — Treat in the same manner as suggested for oxalis or onion weed, commencing in late spring when the grass is back into active growth. Armitrole may be used for nut grass control in areas away from wanted plantings, and where it is not intended to replant for several months. D.S.M.A., which is sold under various trade names for killing paspalum, is sufficiently toxic to nut grass to kill off the top growth and regular use should decrease the problem if not eventually eliminate it. This chemical is poisonous but can be tolerated by a number of ornamentals. However, try it out on a small scale to see that your wanted plants in question do have tolerance to the chemical.

Wandering Jew *Tradescantia*

Although often regarded as a serious pest, this weed is relatively easy to eradicate. When heavily matted it can be lifted with a rake and rolled up. Pieces of stem that remain can easily be removed when regrowth commences.

The main difficulty is destroying the weed when you have removed it. Spread over a rough lawn, most of it can be disintegrated with a rotary mower or most certainly with a mulching mower. Small quantities can be enclosed in a strong plastic bag firmly tied and placed in the sun, turning the bag to achieve a more even burn after a day or two. It can also be fed to fowls which will devour and recycle it.

Chemical control — Wandering Jew is rapidly destroyed if foliage is wetted with Weedex or Polyquat. When the weed is thickly matted some of the base stems may escape chemical injury. The treatment may have to be repeated a week later.

Some of the hormone-type, broad-leafed weed killers or tree and shrub killers will also eliminate Wandering Jew. Add two teaspoons of household detergent to every 4.5 litres of spray solution. Danger of damage from drift is minimised if, instead of spraying, this mixture is applied with a fine-rose water can or one fitted with a trickle bar, even though this may involve use of larger amounts of chemical.

Lawn weeds

This subject is covered under the 'Lawns' chapter.

Keeping weeds under control

As mentioned earlier, the easiest method of weed control once the initial infestation has been cleared is to scuffle the surface on a dry day. For small-scale weeding between plants an old sharp knife is ideal for the purpose as it can be used to sever the roots below the crown of the weed, without unduly disturbing wanted seedlings and nearby plants. To save bending, a sharpened crescent or L-shaped blade on a long handle is very useful; the enclosed or L-section can be used close to the stems of wanted plants without danger of up-rooting them or unduly disturbing their roots.

In vegetable gardens, or in flower gardens, particularly where sowings are made directly into the soil, prepare the beds several weeks in advance of sowing. Fertilise and even the surface, give a good soaking and allow the weeds to come through, then scuffle the soil as suggested and repeat the process after the weed growth has dried out. This will eliminate a lot of tedious hand weeding later.

Mulches

A continuous surface cover of still-fibrous

compost, leaf mould or dead leaves is sufficient to prevent most weeds from germinating. Grass clippings that have been heaped for a few weeks prior to spreading may also be used. Apart from controlling weeds, this mulch provides a buffer against heavy rain or watering, protects against extremes of temperature and gradually improves the soil by supplying humus as the organic material slowly breaks down. There is no need to dig — just add more mulching material as the previous layer thins out. Earthworms will take small particles of the organic material down below soil level and their tunnelling will keep the soil sufficiently aerated without digging.

Wood chip and pine bark are more permanent mulches. The latter is long-lasting and particularly useful where a slightly more glamorous appearance is preferred. However, a garden with plenty of shrubs and trees will eventually supply sufficient of its own mulch and the leafy cover of the soil will give a pleasantly natural effect.

Pebbles make an effective mulch with reasonable weed-repelling qualities. To deter persistent perennial weeds that might push through the mulch, first put down a layer of black plastic sheeting. Care must be taken to see that the plastic does not completely shed water from the area.

Therefore, when any slope is involved, the sheets should be laid across the slope starting at the top and working downwards, lapping each one by about a span. This prevents weeds from pushing through but allows water running down the slopes to filter beneath the sheets. On level ground several depressions and slits through the plastic should be made around the root area of shrubs or other plants. The slits in the sheeting may be covered with span-wide sheets of plastic to prevent weed penetration but allow entry of water.

Persistent weeds such as oxalis, onion weed

or nut grass can be effectively controlled with the chemicals suggested, organic or not, if they are applied through the mulch. This applies particularly to pebble mulches where soil may eventually work close to the surface and foster weed growth.

Establishing ground covers the practical way

Too many people plan ground covers to solve the weed control problem, then abandon the idea because it becomes impossible to hand-weed the cover plants whilst they are establishing. The best way to overcome this problem is to put down surface mulching material such as leaf mould, woodchip or pine bark and plant through it.

Eliminate existing weeds by the methods described, then lay the mulch at least 5 cm thick. If starting plants from runners, work in rows about 20 cm apart, raking back just sufficient of the mulch to allow planting of the runners, then before starting the next row, return the mulch closely around the newly set plants.

Set established potted plants 30–45 cm apart treating them as suggested for runners and lifting any trails of foliage before raking the mulch in to cover all soil around them. Give the area a thorough gentle soaking through the mulch.

By the time the mulch has decomposed and thinned out the cover plants will have thickened sufficiently to provide a weed-blanketing cover.

Eliminating unwanted trees

This section applies particularly to the eradication of privet which has become an invasive and quite serious pest in many areas.

Cut the tree down, leaving a stump 30–40 cm high. As soon as possible afterwards drill the stump with shallow downward cuts that completely encircle it in several layers. Bruise exposed areas of buttress roots with a heavy instrument and gradually trickle one part of 245T to five parts of kerosene into the cut and bruised areas. For a tree about 10 cm in diameter allow about one tablespoon of 245T (sold as tree or blackberry killer).

245T and similar preparations are volatile, so avoid damage to wanted shrubbery close by and improve effectiveness of the treatment by covering the stump with a plastic bag tied at the base or anchored with a shovel or two of soil. Leave the treated stump undisturbed for at least a month to give the chemical time to translocate to all areas of the root. Shallow cuts are far more effective than holes bored deeply into the stump, as the former takes the chemical into the downward conducting tissues where it has the most effect. Breakdown of the chemical in the soil usually occurs after about three weeks, so by the time the stump is dead it is usually safe to plant close by.

Chemical treatment is not necessary for young privets or similar trees under about 5 cm trunk or stem diameter which are usually fairly easy to grub out with a mattock or pulled out when the soil is well soaked after rain.

8. The gardener's calendar

January

Sow

Flowers

Yellow alyssum, columbine aquelegia, foxglove, polyanthus, primula obconica.

Iceland poppies should be sown thinly or planted out to 1 cm apart within a few weeks of germination.

Vegetables

All areas. Beans but *not* broad beans, beetroot, broccoli, Brussels sprout, cabbage, carrot, cauliflower, cress, kohlrabi, lettuce, parsley, parsnip, silverbeet. The herb dill, bush squash, cucumber, spring onion, sweet corn, zucchini — in all but very cold districts.

Tropical areas. All the abovementioned plus capsicum, egg-plant, okra, rhubarb and tomato.

Suggestions. Sow Long Scarlet or French breakfast radish with carrots. One improves the growth of the other and the radish will be ready to pull before the carrots are half grown. Do not plant dill within a metre of carrots — it retards their growth.

Celery and dwarf beans are good companions. Plant celery on the north side of the beans.

Plant

Seedlings of dwarf ageratum, marigold, phlox, petunia and zinnia. Petunias sown in spring will now be looking ragged. Rejuvenate by cutting back by one-third and giving a watering of complete plant food. Some may not withstand such drastic pruning.

Care and maintenance

Citrus

Any trees not fed during December should be given one-third of a cup complete plant food or citrus food per sq. m of soil. Water thoroughly after feeding.

If you cannot soak the soil thoroughly defer feeding until you can. Spray with white oil in the cool of the day for white wax scale.

Spray with white oil to which Malathion has been added, or with a Pyrethrum-type spray for citrus bug. Do not handle the buff, brown or black bugs — they eject an acrid fluid that stings and can cause temporary blindness.

Roses

Feed with complete rose food at the rate of one-third cup per sq. m. Alternatively, use half a cup blood and bone plus 1 teaspoon sulphate of potash. Water in well.

Mulch the soil around the bushes. Remove any dead or twiggy growth. Prune if necessary.

Pruning

In tropical to semi-tropical districts hibiscus pruned now will give a good flush of winter flowers.

Dahlias taken back to just above the second or third pair of leaves when about 50 cm high, then mulched and fed at fortnightly intervals when the flower buds are in evidence, will make compact plants with plentiful flowers.

Christmas bush — particularly New South Wales and Victorian types.

Special jobs

Irises

Divide and replant bearded irises. Take out the old centre clump and throw away. Replant healthy sections with the top of the rhizome above the soil.

Lawns

Do not trim too closely; the extra cover will help to prevent invasion by weeds. Soak thoroughly when needed and only rewater when the surface soil dries out so that the grass roots are encouraged to go deeper rather than to seek moisture on the surface.

Weeds

Summer grass, crow's foot and other summer weeds should be dealt with before they reach seeding stage. Use an old knife, a sharpened paint scraper or a chipping hoe to sever their roots just below ground-level. The plants can then be added to the compost heap.

Paspalum in lawns can be treated the same way or controlled by the use of D.S.M.A.-based sprays — but *not* in buffalo or Queensland blue couch lawns.

February

Sow

Flowers

Cineraria, pansy, primula and viola.

Vegetables

In all areas. Beetroot, cabbage, Chinese cabbage, cress, kohlrabi, leek, lettuce, parsley, parsnip, radish and silverbeet.

In all but cold areas. Broccoli, cauliflower, celery, onion, rhubarb and spinach.

In semi-tropical areas. Dwarf beans, tomato and zucchini. These can be sown throughout the year.

Suggestions. Sow lettuce and carrots

adjacently. Lettuce prefer more nitrogen than do carrots so water over *and* between the plants each week using a complete water-soluble food, but do not allow the feed to reach the carrots.

Onions, silverbeet and beetroot get on well together.

Plant

Flowers

Seedlings ageratum, petite marigold and phlox.

Vegetables

In warm temperate coastal areas. Dwarf bean seedlings.

In cool temperate areas. Brussels sprout seedlings.

Care and maintenance

Azaleas

Soak the ground around the plant thoroughly then feed with complete soluble plant food, a little weaker than the strength recommended.

If new growth is mottled, spray for lace bug.

Camellias

During dry periods soak the ground around the plant very thoroughly. Give an occasional watering with either fish emulsion or seaweed extract — both complete water-soluble plant food.

When the buds on the plant are the size of a pea, twist off all but 2 or 3 per stem.

Pruning

Fuchsias

In warm, frost-free areas prune now to give spring flowers. In other areas leave until late winter or early spring.

Hydrangeas

Though pruning is often left until July, doing it now will ensure attractive plants in spring.

Geraniums

Prune both Regal pelargoniums and Zonal geraniums to get the plants into good flowering shape by spring. Old plants become exhausted after a few years and can be replaced by cuttings from the sturdiest tip growth taken as prunings now.

Check for rust and spray with Zineb or Mancozeb if necessary.

Propagation

Take cuttings of evergreens, including gardenias, native plants and azaleas. Azalea cuttings taken now take longer to root than the soft-wooded ones taken in late spring or early summer but the success rate is better.

Layer evergreen magnolias, rhododendrons, daphnes and pieries.

Special jobs

Citrus

Check for collar rot. The condition shows as a lifting or cracking of the bark of the trunk about 75 cm from the ground, with soft, dead tissue apparent below it. Lemons are particularly at risk. Note: Do not worry if bark is scaly but the tissue is firm and green beneath it.

Bulbs

Buy bulbs for spring-flowering and store at moderate temperature in an airy place. Never transfer bulbs to a cold place or chill them in preparation for planting earlier than 3 weeks before the actual planting time.

Vegetables

Check zucchini, squash and pumpkin for mildew. Use the systemic fungicide Benlate or Karathane to control the fungus.

A level tablespoonful of sulphate of potash sprinkled around each clump of plants and watered in thoroughly also helps.

Lawns

If damage by 'dollar spot' or similar fungal conditions shows during a spell of warm, moist weather, spray or water with a solution of Mancozeb at the first sign of trouble.

If the lawn grass pales and dies suspect the presence of the black beetle and its larvae (a small grey-white grub).

AUTUMN
March

Sow

Flowers

Alyssum, calendula, English daisy, everlasting daisy, stock, sweet pea and wallflower.

Note: Sweet pea seeds dislike wet conditions. Do not sow in soggy soil or over-water while awaiting germination.

Dust with Captan or Bordeaux (copper oxychloride) before sowing if the soil is wet and only sow the seeds 1 cm deep, or pre-sprout the seed in damp vermiculite or sphagnum moss and then place it in the soil, roots downward and seed pod only fractionally below the surface.

Vegetables

In all but cool areas. Beetroot, broccoli, cabbage, Chinese cabbage, carrot, cauliflower (quick-maturing types), chicory, endive, kohlrabi, leek, lettuce, onion, parsley, parsnip, pea, radish, salsify, silverbeet, swede and turnip.
In semi-tropical and tropical areas. All the above plus bean, capsicum, cucumber, eggplant, rhubarb and tomato.

Peas sown in the tropics require attention as per sweet pea (see above).
In cool areas. Broad bean, cabbage, lettuce, onion, radish, spinach, swede and turnip.

The herb parsley can be sown in a container in a sheltered, sunny position.
Suggestions. Sow lettuce and onions near each other. Do *not* sow cabbage, cauliflower, broccoli or Brussels sprouts near the strawberry bed. Strawberries stunt the growth of all members of the cabbage family.

Lawns

Sow couch seed early in the month to repatch or resow a lawn so that it can become established before cold nights slow growth. If you prefer a mixed couch and bent grass lawn, sow the couch now and oversow with bent in mid-April.

Feed with a complete plant food or 'lawn starter', *not* a soluble lawn food. The latter is intended for established grass and will retard the germination of seed.

If there are cobweb-like patches or bruised-looking spots on the lawn in the early morning during a humid spell, spray or water immediately with Mancozeb to curb fungus infection. Aerating the lawn now as described in the 'Lawn' section will help to strengthen grass roots before winter.

If the soil where couch grass is growing is acid, or foods containing sulphate of ammonia and sulphate of iron have been used on it frequently, give a dressing of lime.

Plant

Flowers

Seedlings of Iceland poppy, pansy and viola for winter and spring display.

Vegetables

Seedlings of beetroot, broccoli, cabbage, cauliflower, lettuce and silverbeet.

Bulbs

Soft fleshy bulbs such as bluebells (*scilla*), grape hyacinth (*muscari*), soldier boys (*lachenalia*), dogtooth violet (*erythronium*) and fritillaria should be planted without delay. Daffodil, freesia, sparaxis and similar bulbs can be planted now or left until next month.

Plant tulip and hyacinth in cold districts, otherwise leave until late next month.

Plant anemone now for an early display but leave their 'teammates' — the ranunculus — until the middle of next month, particularly in humid, coastal districts.

Pruning

Camellia and chrysanthemum should be disbudded progressively as the buds form. Watch out for black aphis below chrysanthemum buds.

Disbud dahlia, leaving only 1 or 2 buds per stem. Tie plant to a stake at 45 cm intervals and scatter snail bait around the plants, particularly during damp spells.

Propagation

Mint Strike tip cuttings, several to a pot, and keep in a warm, protected spot.

Strawberries Divide and replant.
Violets
Divide and replant.

Special jobs

Basil

Pick for drying before the end of the month. Plants deteriorate when nights turn cool.

Fungus

Watch out for signs of browning on the lower, older foliage of shrubby and matting perennials such as lavender, arabis, dusty miller, etc. Fungus attack is more likely if the weather is wet or very humid.

Cut out and burn affected parts and spray the remainder of the plant with a complete fungicide such as Captan, Zineb, Mancozeb or Benlate.

If replacements are needed take tip cuttings from healthy growth.

Red spider

In dry weather, if bean foliage becomes buff-coloured and looks sandblasted, mist the plant frequently with water. If that is not enough, dust with sulphur or spray with wettable sulphur or Kelthane.

April

April is one of the busiest months of the gardening year. The soil is still warm but the air is clean and crisp and the sunlight bright but no longer fierce — nothing could suit gardener and plants better!

Sow

Flowers

Alyssum, calendula, candytuft, carnation, clarkia, cornflower, delphinium, dianthus, everlasting daisy, forget-me-not (*myosotis*), godetia, gypsophilia, honesty (*lunaria*), larkspur, linaria, Livingstone daisy, lobelia, lupin, mignonette, molucella (Irish green bell flower), nemesia, nemophila (baby-blue eyes), nigella (love-in-a-mist), Painted daisy, saponaria, statice, sweet pea, Virginia stock and wallflower.

Vegetables

In temperate areas. Cabbage, Chinese cabbage, cress, lettuce, parsley, onion, pea, radish, spinach and turnip.
In semi-tropical and tropical areas. All the above, plus: bean, carrot, chicory, endive, parsnip, potato, rhubarb, swede, tomato and turnip.
In cold areas. Broad bean, cress, lettuce, onion, radish, spinach and turnip.

Lawns

Sow bent grass, either as an entire lawn or for over-sowing couch to keep the lawn green during winter and early spring. If worried about invasion of winter grass in lawns, spray all but kikuyu lawns with Endothal when the weed first appears, then again one week later. This preparation also kills or retards clover.

Plant

Seedlings

Antirrhinum, Canterbury bells, columbine, hollyhock, schizanthus (Poor man's orchid) and scabious.

Bulbs

Anemone, daffodil, freesia, hyacinth, ixia, ranunculus, sparaxis, triteleia, tritonia and tulip.

Sprout the corms of anemone and ranunculus in a box of moist sand, vermiculite or peatmoss, or buy them in the bedding plant range. In all but cold districts tulips are a luxury, as they give a good show for the first spring only. Mark bulb plantings with pegs or small stakes so that they are not forgotten and damaged by cultivation.

Plant a bowl or two of hyacinths to flower indoors during winter as described in 'Bulbs', or grow some daffodils in a pot to bring indoors while flowering. You can use them in the garden, burying them to the rim of the pot to add interest and colour.

Fruit

Strawberries.

Vegetables

Broad bean, beetroot, cabbage, carrot, pea, silverbeet and turnip.

If you have a tough patch of soil that sets too hard for carrots, lettuce, etc. plant it with broad beans.

Good companions. Peas and turnips are a good combination for this month's planting, except in cold districts where frosts would damage the maturing pea pods. Keep the turnips about 50 cm on the northern side of the peas unless rows run north and south.

Care and maintenance

Divide clumps of Japanese irises if crowded. Divide last season's clumps of polyanthus.

Chrysanthemum

Stake and tie or stems will sag and kink as flower heads grow heavy.

Dahlia

Check for mildew. Control with Bordeaux or Karathane.

Remove blooms as they fade. Give soluble plant food every 2 weeks.

House plants

Discontinue feeding, except for cyclamen and plants in rooms kept evenly heated throughout the winter.

Iris

Feed with bone dust or a sprinkling of complete plant food. Mulch, but take care not to cover the rhizomes. Remove old foliage from centre of clumps.

Propagation

Take cuttings of carnations, coleus, geraniums and marguerites. Pinch out tips as cuttings take — continue doing this until September to have bushy plants which will flower through Christmas period.

Pruning

Prune cassia as flowers finish to keep bush looking attractive and to encourage another flowering in spring.

May

Sow

Flowers

Calendula, candytuft, forget-me-not, linaria, nasturtium, nemophila (baby-blue eyes) and Virginia stock.

Vegetables

In areas free from heavy frost. Broad bean, cress, lettuce and spinach. Do not plant silverbeet in cold areas.

In semi-tropical and tropical areas. All the above plus: bean, beetroot, cabbage, carrot, Chinese cabbage, endive, kohlrabi, parsnip, parsley, potato, radish, tomato and turnip.

Plant

In semi-tropical and tropical areas. Seedlings of the vegetables mentioned above can also be planted.

Trees and shrubs

Azalea, camellia, citrus, deciduous and rose (container grown).

Bulbs

Lily, Lily-of-the-Valley and tulip.

Flowers

Tropical areas. Amaranthus, balsam, celosia, cockscomb, cleome, coleus (part shade), cosmos, dahlia, globe amaranth, linaria, marigold, petunia, phlox, salvia and zinnia.
Semi-tropical areas. All flowers mentioned for March and April plus: begonia, petunia and, to a lesser extent, balsam, phlox and verbena.
Temperate areas. Sun: Alyssum, anemone, antirrhinum, larkspur, lobelia, nemesia, pansy, ranunculus, stock, viola and wallflower.
Shade: Cineraria, English daisy, primula and polyanthus.

Care and maintenance

Bulbs

Check to ensure that fibre is still moist but return it to cool dark situations without delay. If you can obtain some good-sized firm hyacinths, tulips or daffodils there is still time to start a bowl for winter flowers indoors. (Remember that planting one variety is preferable for general effect as different varieties flower at different times.)

Camellias

Can be moved this month except in cold frosty regions where they would experience less shock if moving was left until August. One point that must be stressed is that good recovery depends on cutting back to remove at least one-third of foliage. Even though they are now in bud or flowering it is better to sacrifice this year's display.

Chrysanthemums

Check for eelworm damage. Spray with Rogor.

Conifers

Are moved best in late autumn, so if there are any in the garden that need to be repositioned now is the time. Tall varieties need support against wind movement until they regain the anchorage of new roots. Where the conventional upright staking would damage remaining roots, drive in 1 or 2 long stakes, angled at 50–60° so that they cross close to the conifer trunk and tie them at this point.

Dahlias

If foliage has yellowed, cut stems back to just above ground-level — lift clumps, label, hose free of soil and store protected from frost and strong sunlight. It is also a good idea to mark names or colour on tubers with indelible pencil.

House plants

Should be given less water with the approach of cold nights, except in permanently heated rooms. Water only when the potting soil surface dries out, then water thoroughly. (Ferns are an exception as they need soil kept permanently damp but not soggy.)

Discontinue feeding orchids except those normally grown under heated conditions. Move cacti out of heated rooms, especially crab's claw (*Zygocactus*), as night temperatures in the vicinity of 10°C are needed to stimulate flowering. Cyclamen also need cool nights — if too warm the foliage yellows and flower buds shrivel.

Hydrangeas

If you want to change or deepen colour of flowers, start treating the soil around them this month.

Lawns

In temperate couch and buffalo areas it will pay to raise the mower a little so that it leaves the grass 1–2 cm high. If shaved low once growth ceases the lawn enters the winter brown stage at least a month earlier than necessary. This lack of cover also allows winter weeds to take over. If necessary spray again for winter grass — see 'April'.

Lilies

The true liliums should be planted as soon as possible before bulbs and roots become limp due to drying out. If existing clumps in the garden are becoming crowded there is still time to lift and replant all but November lilies and other early types flowering at a similar time. All need a well-drained rich soil.

Roses

Those grown in containers can be planted any time, but June–July are the main planting months for the widely sold ground-dug bushes so prepare the soil for them now, digging in a bucket or two of well-rotted compost where each one is to be planted or, better still, if planting a quantity, prepare the entire bed this way.

Pruning

Trim perennials.

WINTER

June

Sow

Flowers

Alyssum, candytuft, linaria and Virginia stock can still be sown in all but very frosty areas.

Vegetables

Tropical to semi-tropical areas. Beans, beetroot, cabbage, capsicum, carrot, chicory, choko, cress, herb, lettuce, spring onion, parsnip, salsify, silverbeet, sweet corn and tomato.

Fruit

Northern tropical areas. Cucumber, melon, pumpkin, squash and zucchini, Cape gooseberry.

Cooler semi-tropical areas. Sow the above in pots and transplant to the garden in late August, early September.

Temperate areas. Beetroot, broad bean, cabbage, Chinese cabbage, carrot, cress, kohlrabi, lettuce, onion, pea (not in areas with late frosts), salsify and silverbeet.

Plant

Flowers

Tropical to semi-tropical areas. All flowers mentioned for May.

Temperate areas. Seedlings of calendula, English daisy, dianthus, larkspur, Livingstone daisy, lobelia, nemesia, pansy, primula and viola.

Vegetables

Asparagus crowns, choko and potato (not if frosts persist — both).

Bulbs

Gladioli
Lilium (summer-flowering).

Fruit

Rhubarb crowns and deciduous fruit trees.

Roses

June, July — and in cold climates August — are the main rose-planting months, though stocks of many varieties will be sold out if purchase is left until the end of the planting season. If you obtain 'open-ground plants' (any but those actually growing in a container) and planting must be delayed more than a day or two, dig a wide hole in a cool shaded part of the garden, separate the plants but place them close together around the edge of the hole, fill in with enough soil to cover well above the roots, then fill the hole with water and keep it damp.

One of the main causes of failure is allowing roots to dry out before or during the planting process. So except where plants are to be held in moist soil as described above, do not unwrap until ready to plant, then stand the plants with their roots in a bucket of water while holes are being dug and prepared. Soil should be cool and damp, so do not dig holes in advance.

If a rose is being replaced, remove it with as much of the old roots as possible plus at least half a barrow-load of soil from the root area and exchange this with soil from another part of the garden where roses are not growing. Add up to one-third of the well-rotted compost to the replacement soil and mix in well. It would be an advantage to do this now, and give it time to settle down before planting.

Pruning. In warm and relatively frost-free districts start in June. Mid-to-late July is the favoured pruning time in most temperate districts, and in cold districts with late frosts, pruning is delayed until August or even early September when growth buds still look dormant. Inversely, if unusually warm conditions cause buds to swell and show signs of shooting, then prune without delay, even though there is some risk that heavy frosts could still follow and damage the soft new shoots.

Exceptions to winter pruning. Weeping standard roses (except Sea Foam) are wichuriana types including Dorothy Perkins, Lady Gray, Sander's White, Excelsa, etc. which are also still grown occasionally as ramblers. These flower only in spring on canes made the previous season so are pruned after flowering. This also applies to Banksia rose, Cherokee rose (*Sinica alba*) and to other old-fashioned roses that flower only in spring.

Other pruning

Pruning of apples, pears and stone-fruit can begin this month before new growth starts to show.

Late-flowering types can be left until August. Pruning should be light.

Cuttings. Hardwood cuttings — deciduous trees and shrubs.

Care and maintenance

Bulbs and annuals

Unless the soil is liberally mulched, lightly scuffle the surface to destroy chickweed, thistles, clover and other winter weeds. Choose a dry sunny day, otherwise chickweed, particularly, will survive and take root again on damp soil. Watch for bulbs that may be coming up now so that these are not damaged by cultivation — a good reason to identify planting areas with short stakes as suggested in April notes.

Don't worry if autumn-planted bulbs are not yet showing through. Some, such as freesias, sparaxis, jonquils and tritelieas, sprout foliage soon after planting but tulips and daffodils can take months. Types vary and those that make the earliest growth are not necessarily the earliest to flower. For example, King Alfred daffodil is one of the last to appear but the earliest to flower.

Dahlias

Lift and store tubers for replanting in spring.

House plants

Reduce watering of foliage plants as nights become colder, except where rooms are permanently heated. Water only when surface soil has dried out to the depth of about 1 cm, then thoroughly wet the potting mixture. Exceptions are ferns, palms, spathiphyllum agloanema, cyclamens, azaleas, camellias, tolmiea (pig-a-back), ardisia and aucuba (gold dust), which should be watered whenever surface soil looks dry.

Dry atmosphere can be a problem during winter months as the relative humidity of cold air is low and becomes much lower still when heated by radiators or sun on closed windows. This results in browning of leaf tips and in some cases the leaf margins.

Correct by moving plants away from heaters and group them so that moisture rising from their soil makes the area more humid. Place containers of water below them and near heaters or hot air vents, or stand the pots on trays of pebbles which are kept moist.

Do not feed while plants are dormant.

Spraying

Spray roses immediately after pruning with lime-sulphur solution to rid the plants of rose scale (which is defined by flakey, whitish crusting mainly on older canes) and to destroy spores of fungus diseases, particularly mildew and, to some extent, black spot.

Rake up and burn all old infected foliage and prunings as these carry spores that would re-infect new foliage next season. Hoe or turn in the top soil into the previous season's mulch. When covered with new mulch, disease-carrying foliage will rapidly decompose.

Do not use lime-sulphur spray if new growth is already commencing.

Fruit trees benefit from a spraying with lime-sulphur or 'dormant oil'. This treatment will minimise the carryover of brown rot spores (a disease particularly destructive to stone fruits), mites, woolly aphis and, to some extent, codling moth pupae which may be sheltering between cracks in the bark. Spray the trunk well.

July

Sow

Flowers

Very few flowers are sown during July except in tropical districts where those recommended for June can still be sown.

Vegetables

Sowing in all districts is as for June.

Good companions

Parsley is attractive enough to grow in any part of the garden. It appears to aid the growth of roses so why not plant a few clumps close under the rose bushes? Chives also seem to get along with parsley, look presentable in growth and tend to deter rose aphids in their immediate vicinity. If you feel that the roses would not be too overcrowded with yet another lodger, garlic helps to keep rose aphids at bay and reputedly, when grown with roses, will greatly increase their perfume.

Plant

Vegetables and fruit

Asparagus and rhubarb crowns in cool districts only. Mushrooms can be started in all districts *except* the coldest ones.

Other sowing for all districts is the same as for June.

Deciduous ornamentals and fruit, citrus and nut trees

Currant, gooseberry, loganberry, raspberry and strawberry.

If bare-rooted (growing in a container) observe the same precautions as suggested for rose planting as it is important that roots do not dry out. Do not plant deeper than soil line on stem especially in heavy soil, even though this may leave the graft above soil level. Although I do not favour staking young trees, it is desirable for tall 'open ground' trees for the first season until root-growth has a chance to develop, otherwise there may not be sufficient anchorage for the comparatively large top.

Pruning

Conifers

Growth of column or conical-type conifers can be thickened by giving them a light trim, removing a few centimetres of growth all over except for the apex or growing tip. Remove deposits of old foliage clustered in the crotches (junctions of branches with trunk) as it is here that borer and fungus activity starts. The strong jet of a hose can be helpful for this.

Roses

July is the main rose-pruning month for temperate districts. In coastal areas where frosts are not severe, mid-July is the favoured time and late July in cooler temperate areas. In cold districts pruning is best left until August as new growth stimulated by pruning can be damaged by heavy frost.

Stone fruits

Early-flowering stone fruits, particularly peaches, are approaching the flowering stage so should be pruned without delay. See also dormant spraying under June but do not use lime-sulphur if growth is already commencing.

Leaf curl can be minimised by spraying all parts of young twigs and branches with Bordeaux or copper oxychloride applied as buds begin to swell and first show colour. Spores of the leaf curl fungus carry over in the bud scales, infecting young foliage as it emerges.

Propagation

Hardwood cuttings of deciduous trees and shrubs can still be taken.

Care and maintenance

Flowers

Iceland poppies and, to a lesser extent, violas and pansies need to make a good mat of surface roots to develop vigour so carefully pull out weeds or confine and cultivate to very shallow surface scratching. Where possible mulch plants with partly decomposed but still fibrous compost as this retards weeds, preserves the soil in an open crumbly state and encourages surface root growth. Remove flower buds until plants are well established.

Feed polyanthus every 2–3 weeks with complete soluble plant food. Watch stock seedlings for aphis which causes distortion and flattening of foliage, particularly in the centre of the plant.

Frost damage

If evergreens such as hibiscus, gardenias and acalyphas are burnt by heavy frost, it is best to leave the damaged growth on the plant until frost danger is over. Although this may not look attractive, the damaged foliage gives some protection to the branches below it. Watering foliage of frosted plants before the sun reaches them helps to minimise frost burn (if taps and hose are not also iced up). However, plants that are kept a little on the dry side suffer less frost damage than others carrying maximum capacity of water.

House plants

As for June. Also check palm foliage for scale — see December. Remove any dead lower leaves from palms, philodendrons, ficus, etc. (Some lower leaf fall or browning is natural.) Remove old foliage from terrariums.

If plants wilt, the cause can be either dryness or overwatering. This might sound odd, but waterlogged soils prevent entry of essential oxygen; roots then fail to function and cannot take up enough water for the plant's needs, especially in the very dry atmosphere that develops when already dry cold air is heated. Root rot rapidly follows this wet condition. So if wilting occurs and the soil looks moist, let it dry out (if dry, water more liberally).

August

Sow

Flowers to sow or plant

This is a betwixt and between month, too late for poppies, violas and other spring flowers except in some of the coldest climates, and a little early for most of the summer flowers. However, if you have vacant space in the garden and are not in a heavy frost area, sow seed or plant seedlings (if available) of alyssum, candytuft, marigolds, petunia and phlox.

In tropical climates. Any of the flowers recommended for May can still be sown or planted out; but except for amaranthus and coleus these have a much shorter flowering period than when planted in autumn.

Vegetables

For tropical and semi-tropical areas. Sowings remain the same as those under June/July except that in warmer frost-free parts of the semi-tropical districts, cucumbers, pumpkins, zucchinis and similar may be sown direct into the soil rather than into pots. But remember that if these plants are exposed to cold changes they become retarded and are often bypassed by sowings made 4–6 weeks later.

Temperate climate sowings. The same as June/July, but tomatoes may be sown in containers now and moved under cover or to warm sheltered positions at night or during particularly cold changes.

Cool climate sowings. As recommended for June/July except for broad beans. Parsnips, swedes and turnips may be added to the list, and in most cool areas it is now safe to plant potatoes from sprouting tubers.

Good companions. August is a good month for planting peas in all areas, and for carrots, in all but the coldest districts. Both get on well together and seem to help each other so try teaming them up — giving carrots the sunnier side of the pea row. You will need to either stake the peas or leave about 50 cm between them. To make peas a worthwhile proposition for the space they need, sow a broad 8–10 cm wide row, with only 3–4 cm between seeds.

Plant

Bulbs

Agapanthus
Begonia — tuberous
Eucomis (Pineapple Lily)
Gladiolus
Hippeastrum
Hymenocallis
Iris (Bearded)
Lily-of-the-Valley (*Convallaria*)

Tube Rose
Valotta
Zantedechias (Calla Lily)

Divide and replant

If clumps of perennials have become over-large, lift and divide, discarding the old centre and replanting the vigorous outside growth. Plants which may require attention are achillea, agapanthus, aster, canna, *hemerocallis* (Day lily), *kniphofia* (poker), phlox, Shasta daisy and sunflower (*Helenium*).

Pruning

Camellias

If carrying a lot of wood on thin twiggy growth, will benefit from pruning before new shoots develop. As most types are approaching the end of their flowering, why not cut some large sections for indoor decoration from older well-established bushes? For a longer-lasting indoor display, delay flower drop by pinning through base of petals with two pieces of medium-to-thin florist's wire and then bending this down and twisting around stem.

Stems of spring-flowering blossom can be forced to flower early by cutting and bringing into indoor warmth 2–3 weeks before normal flowering time. Prunus, including peach and cherry, flowering quince, crab apple and forsythia can all be used this way but recut a little more off the stem every few days to assure that water intake continues.

Deciduous shrubs, etc.

Do *not* prune any of the spring-flowering shurbs, deciduous or otherwise, until *after* flowering as this would reduce their spring display. Pruning of deciduous fruit trees and grapevines is normally completed this month. Also remove old canes of loganberries and tie down new ones formed last season.

If not already done in autumn, prune autumn-flowering cassia (*C. bicapsularis*). Fuchsia, hydrangea and crepe myrtle by the middle of the month if you want to keep them as large shrubs rather than trees. Also prune back poinsettias when flowers finish, and ornamental winter-flowering peaches. (To prevent fruiting, cut just above base buds of the canes that have flowered — this gives more robust flower-packed stems.)

Roses

Pruning of perpetual-flowering types should be completed this month except perhaps in the coldest districts.

Other pruning

Abelia (if necessary)
Abutilon
Acalypha
Aloysia
Bauhinia galpinii
Bouvardia
Buddleia
Ceratostigma
Clerodendron
Cotinus
Erythrina (summer-flowering)
Heliotrope
Hibiscus (deciduous)

Hypericum
Lantana
Leonotis
Luculia (after flowering)
Melastoma (lightly)
Mussaenda
Plectanthus ecklonii
Plumbago
Pomegranate
Sambucus (Elderberry)
Stenolobium (Yellow Tecoma)
Tamarix (summer-flowering)
Tibouchina — lassiandra
Tweedia
Vitex

Care and maintenance

Azaleas

Check for petal blight which shows first as brownish or transparent flecks on flowers; premature shrivelling follows. Spray immediately symptoms appear, or if this has been a problem during past seasons, begin preventive sprayings each week from the time buds begin showing colour. Use Mancozeb or Benlate. Do not feed azaleas until flowering finishes.

Bulbs

As daffodils, jonquils and hyacinths finish flowering, pull off old flower heads to prevent seeding which saps bulb vigour. Watch tulips for aphis which cluster under or in cupped foliage.

Early planted lilium shoots can be badly damaged by slugs so protect with some well-placed baits.

Citrus

Should be checked early this month for woody swelling on stems caused by the tunnelling larvae of citrus gall wasp. If present, cut off and burn without delay as this year's brood of wasps begin emerging from these galls during the latter half of this month (even though they may be cut from the tree).

Citrus may be fed this month using no more than half a cup of citrus or complete plant food to each sq. m of area below the branches of the tree and just a little further out. Feed only when soil is damp, then water well after applying. Do not feed newly planted citrus for at least 6 weeks. August is a good month to plant citrus but in very frosty areas leave planting until late in the month or early September.

Ferns

Ferns (including maidenhair) showing a large percentage of browned or shrivelled growth may be cut back to soil-level then given a light dressing of rotted leafmould. Large, crowded clumps may be divided and are repotted now but first cut back all foliage. Keep soil damp but do not feed until new growth commences, then give no more than a complete soluble plant food, seaweed extract or fish emulsion at about one-third of normally recommended strength.

SPRING

September

This is a beautiful time of the year, so one of the most important things this month is making time to enjoy your own efforts, other people's gardens or the natural beauty of our bushland areas. Even if your contribution is no more than a few daisies in the corner of the garden, some greenery or a flowering plant on a window-ledge, you have helped to make spring a little more beautiful.

Sow

Flowers

Northern tropical areas. As for August.
Semi-tropical and warm temperate areas. As for August *plus* amaranthus, celosis, cockscomb, coleus and globe amaranth. They all need a warm situation if they are to germinate and make appreciable growth.

Temperate areas. Sow or plant out alyssum, antirrhinum, aster, balsam, begonia (all types), Californian poppy (*Escholtzia*), carnation, chrysanthemum, cleome (spider flower), cosmos, dahlia, gaillardia, gazania, gerbera, geum, gypsophila, kangaroo paw, kochia, marigold, nasturtium, ornamental basil, ornamental chilli, petunia, phlox, portulaca, rudbeckia, sapiglossis, salvia, statice, torenia, verbena, waratah and zinnia.

Cool areas. As temperate areas *plus* candytuft, cornflower, delphinium, godetia, linaria, lupins and mignonette.

Vegetables and fruit

All areas. Beetroot, cabbage, Cape gooseberry, capsicum, carrot, celery (not in tropical areas), chicory, Chinese cabbage, cress, herbs (all types), kohlrabi (not in tropical areas), lettuce, spring onion, parsnip, radish, rhubarb, salsify, silverbeet and tomato.
Tropical, semi-tropical and warm areas. As above *plus* beans, cucumber, egg-plant, marrow, melon, okra, pumpkin, rosella, squash, sweet corn and zucchini. Plants or cuttings of sweet potato can now be set.
Cool areas. As above *plus* peas, potato, swede and turnip.

Good companions

Tomatoes and basil have a definite affinity; they not only grow well together but the basil is reputed to improve the tomato flavour. It certainly does when they are cooked together. Basil is responsible for giving tomato sauce that tangy flavour. It adds wonderful aroma and zest to most meat and fish dishes including chicken and also vegetable or fruit salads. I find that it also repels white fly within a distance of about 1 m. Alternate it with the tomatoes or set a few plants close in front of them.

Another good September combination is sweet corn and cucumbers, keeping, of course, the latter toward the sunnier side. Corn does better when planted in several short rows, as pollination is surer than when in one long row.

Plant
Passion-fruit.

Pruning
Spring-flowering shrubs are pruned as soon as flowering finishes and before new growth starts and include acacia, bauhinia, boronia, bottlebrush, cistus, cytisus, chorizema, diosma, erica, eriostemum, eupatorium, grevillea, keeria, peach (flowering), pimelia, prostanthera, protea, raphiolepsis (Indian hawthorn), rondeletia, spirea, telopea (waratah), thryptomene, viburnum (except berry types) and westringia.

Note: Bottlebrush and Telopea: Prune when stamens start to fall as new growth begins very quickly.

Fuchsia: Tip-prune only for more compact growth.

Gardenia: Do not prune in very warm areas. Prune lightly elsewhere. Even if buds are forming they could fall if there were a sudden cold change.

Hibiscus: Evergreen (*H. rosa sinensis*). Prune early in the month but *not* in semi-tropical and tropical areas where January pruning is preferable.

Propagation
Gerbera
Temperate districts. Divide and replant if clumps are crowded with crowns (in warmer areas they are usually divided in late winter). Trim back roots to about finger length and leave only a few centimetres of foliage above the leaf stalk. When replanting have crown just slightly above soil-level, particularly in heavy soils. If leaves rather than crowns are overcrowding the clump, thin out all but 3 or 4 per crown.

Care and maintenance
Azaleas
Check for petal blight. Spray if necessary. See chapter 'Azaleas'.

Begonias (tuberous) and gloxinias
Check dormant corms for signs of shoots. If not yet showing, or if weather is beginning to warm up, place corms on trays of damp peat or sand, then pot in fresh potting soil when shoots appear.

Camellias
Feed.

Lawns
Feeding toward the middle of this month will help return green colour that disappears during winter from couch and bent in all but warm areas. It also improves appearance of other grasses.

Spring annuals
Once buds are plentiful and flowering commences, maintain vigour, lustre and flower size by feeding with water-soluble plant foods each fortnight.

Also, Iceland poppies that seem to be losing vigour can usually be rejuvenated by watering the plants with a weak solution of Condy's Crystals (potassium permanganate). Dissolve just enough to colour the water like weak tea.

Cinerarias
Check for scribble-like tracery in leaves, caused by leaf miner. Remove and burn leaves if only occasional ones are affected, otherwise spray with Malathion or Pyrethrum-type sprays at intervals of 4–5 days for a fortnight, or water foliage with Metasystox in a fine-rosed water can. (The latter liquid is very toxic so watering on should involve less risk of skin contact or inhalation than spraying.)

Fruit trees
Apples, pears and quinces need spraying against codling moth as flower petals fall. Note that this does not attack stone fruits which need not be treated for fruit fly until 5 or 6 weeks before harvest.

Garden flowers
Prolong flowering by removing old flower heads, particularly from Iceland poppies, sweet peas, pansies, violas, English daisies and calendulas.

Watch for aphis under foliage, causing crimping or distortion and below buds on flower stems of stocks, ranunculus, tulips, cinerarias and sometimes wallflowers. They also cause a flattened or stubby growth in stocks or cornflowers that have not yet made flower buds. They may also infest young foliage of maples.

Remember the ladybirds, beetles and their larvae, also birds such as wrens and silver eyes, normally keep this in check so explore other means of control before spraying with very toxic chemicals. Even soapy water or garlic spray is enough to control infestation by some types of aphids.

House plants
Warmth-loving foliage plants that are normally kept drier during winter should have a little more water when the weather warms up — give good soakings then allow the surface soil to dry out between times. Then feed, preferably with a soluble plant food when new growth commences.

Cacti should also have similar treatment to the above foliage plants when new spines (usually more colourful) begin to form at the tip or in the centre of the plant.

October

Sow or Plant
Flowers
Semi-tropical and temperate areas. Annuals such as nemesia, stock, primula, Iceland poppy, Livingstone daisy, Virginian stock, etc. will be finishing and ready to make good compost for future crops. Violas can usually be coaxed to linger longer by removing old flower heads and feeding occasionally with soluble plant food, so these can be left to give colour while petunias, phlox or petite marigolds are establishing close behind them.

The September list for all other areas still applies in October to all districts, plus amaranthus, celosia, cleome, cockscomb, coleus, and globe amaranth.

Seeds may be sown, or seedlings of flowers in this list planted out in all districts, except that in the northern areas (north of Rockhampton in the east and Carnarvon in the west) the flowering life of these annuals becomes shorter, with the possible exception of amaranthus, celosia, cockscomb and coleus.

Vegetables
In all areas. This month sow beans, beetroot, cabbage, carrot, Chinese cabbage, cress, cucumber, egg-plant, herbs, lettuce, marrow, melons, okra, spring onions, parsnip, pumpkin, radish, rhubarb, salsify, silverbeet, squash, sweet corn, tomato and zucchini.

In temperate and cool areas. As above *plus* celery, endive and leek. **In cool areas.** Only sow peas and kohlrabi. Plant seed potatoes. Sweet potato plants or cuttings and rosellas from seed are also suitable for warm and temperate areas.

Good companions
Capsicum and okra like being together and appear to help each other's growth. Okra is the taller, so keep the capsicums toward the sunnier side of the row or alternate them. (Pick Okra pods when young — no more than finger length — and try boiling them with tomatoes.) Keep cabbages a reasonable distance from tomatoes as they seem to upset each other.

Lawns
In temperate areas. October and November are the best months to sow kikuyu grass and establish runners of Queensland blue couch, buffalo or kikuyu. Bent is sown this month in cool districts but in warmer areas is best left until April. If considering a mixed couch and bent lawn, coverage and mixture will be more even if couch is sown now and bent added as an oversowing in April.

If sowing couch, use a standard complete

plant food or lawn starter, not a lawn food as the soluble types contain too much nitrogen and too little phosphorus for good germination and growth of new grass.

Feeding

Azaleas

May be fed lightly after flowering, with either a soluble plant food, a complete organic food, blood and bone or an azalea food. But play safe and use only about one tablespoon of these dry mixes per sq. m of area under and around the plants, applied when soil is moist then watered well afterwards. Remember that there are probably more azaleas killed by over-feeding than by starvation. A good mulch of leaf mould is more important for their well-being.

Camellias

Now in most cases in new growth, will appreciate another feeding if not fertilised with soluble food for two or three weeks or with dry mix camellia food or organic mixes for 6–8 weeks — actually it is better to apply any of these dry, or sprinkle on mixtures at about half the recommended rate twice as often. Watch for aphis on new growth of camellias or leaf-rolling caterpillars that web the tip leaves of new shoots together.

Lawns

Feeding with a good lawn food will enliven the lawn colour and thicken the grass, which apart from looking better will deter weed growth. Don't throw clippings away as they are excellent compost material, or if heaped for a week or so make a valuable weed-deterring and soil-improving mulch for the garden.

Passion-fruit

If growth is excessive, thin out some of the laterals; over-vigorous ones may be cut back or curbed by bending ends downward. Feed with one-quarter cup per sq. m of complete plant food. As vines have a productive life of only a few years, plant a replacement vine (not too close to the original one) every second or third year. Now is a good planting time.

Roses

In all but the coldest areas should be running up to flowers and will appreciate a little more feed if not fed since August. Use only about one-quarter cup of rose food per sq. m; apply particularly just under, and slightly out from, outer foliage of plants. Also during this active growing stage I like to add a heaped teaspoon per sq. m of sulphate of potash (potassium sulphate) *not* muriate of potash (potassium chloride). This helps vigour, strength of stem, improves foliage and flower quality and seems to improve mildew resistance.

Propagation

Chrysanthemum

Clumps should be separated and the strongest suckers planted out — or the tips from them used as cuttings. Break out top of young plants when about 12 cm high.

Dahlia

Clumps lifted in late autumn or winter may be divided and replanted, but do not divide tubers until shoots are showing. If they are still dormant move them to a warmer position and keep them moist.

Orchids

Remove old flower spikes, divide cymbidiums without delay (only if clumps are congested with old back bulbs). If plants are crowding the pot and back bulbs are comparatively few, repot into larger containers. If you have too many pots, try a few clumps in very lightly shaded parts of the garden, making slightly elevated pockets of rubble and leaf mould for them. Orchid enthusiasts with interests focused only on orchids frown on this, but cymbidiums look more attractive and often grow better this way.

Back cut epiphyte orchids such as dendrobiums as flowers finish. All orchids respond to soluble plant foods applied over the next few months, starting with the first signs of new growth. Most important, plants brought in under shelter or shade during the flowering period should be moved into at least half (or better still two-thirds) sun without delay. To avoid foliage burn when moving from full shade to full sun, condition gradually for about a week, perhaps under a tree where there is dappled shade, or under shade cloth.

Care and maintenance

Cyclamen

That have stopped flowering and which have foliage yellowing should be kept dry (allow surface soil to dry for 1–2 cm down until lightly watered again). Or remove and store corms in damp peat until sign of new growth appears in mid- to late December.

Fruit trees

Stone fruits will need spraying with Zineb or Mancozeb for brown rot, especially where there have been showery conditions. Use some of the same mixture on azaleas if petal blight is evident, and on geraniums to deter rust.

Fruit fly must also be considered in fly areas. Most fruits become susceptible to attack from about 6 weeks before ripening, so for November-ripening peaches it will be necessary to take precautions without delay. Spraying program is detailed under Fruit fly in pest section — but remember that some early peaches such as Watt's Early are sensitive to Rogor. Note that baits can be used effectively as an alternative to sprays. Also note codling moth treatment for apples and pears. Remove fruit setting on flowering peaches.

House plants

Should be watered more frequently and fed occasionally, as suggested under September. Repot if it seems necessary or if roots are showing through base of pot.

Lawns

Lawn fungus may occur in humid areas, particularly in bent grass. Watch for patches with web-like covering in early morning when the lawn is dewy. Grass under these patches develops a darker water- or oil-soaked appearance, then dies. Treat at the first signs of trouble by watering or spraying with Mancozeb or Benlate.

November

Sow or Plant

Flowers

In northern tropical districts the heat and the approach of the wet season make sowing or planting out very dubious endeavours.

All other districts. Ageratum, alyssum, amaranthus, aster, balsam, begonia (bedding types), Californian poppy (*Escholtzia*), celosia, chrysanthemum, cleome (spider flower), clianthus (Sturt's pea), cockscomb, coleus, dahlia, gazania, gerbera, geranium, gomphrena (Globe amaranth), gypsophila, kangaroo paw, marigold, nasturtium, Ornamental basil, Ornamental chilli, petunia, phlox, portulaca, rudbeckia, salpiglossis, salvia, saponaria, sunflower (*Helianthus*), Swan River daisy (*Brachycome*), verbena and zinnia.

Seedlings of phlox, petunias, dwarf ageratum or dwarf marigolds planted out early this month should commence flowering by Christmas time. Apart from available garden space, plant large pots or troughs with some of these; when they flower move them to vantage points or bring inside briefly for special occasions. Acalypha, gardenia, hibiscus which can be planted at any time in semi-tropical areas can now be planted in cooler areas for the soil is warming up and there is a long warm growing period ahead.

Vegetables

In all areas: Beans, cabbage, Cape gooseberry, celery, cress, cucumber, egg-plant, herb, leek (not in tropical districts), lettuce, marrow, melon, okra, parsley, parsnip, pumpkin, radish, rhubarb, rosella (not in cool areas), salsify, silverbeet, spring onion, squash, sweet corn, tomato and zucchini.

In tropical areas it is still possible to take sweet potato cuttings or set plants.

Lawns

Sow couch grass and keep the surface moist for at least 2 weeks after sowing.

Propagation

Azaleas

Many natives and other spring-flowering shrubs should be propagated by cuttings taken from the new top growths when they have lost their sappiness.

Dahlias

If inexperienced with dahlias, note that growth shoots come only from the collar of stem tissue attached to the neck of a tuber. If cut below this point the tubers make root but not top growth, so it is better to wait until shoots appear before dividing and planting. If there are numerous shoots from the one division, try removing some of these to strike as cuttings. These green plants also form tubers.

Dahlias should be staked when tubers are planted. Dahlias already in growth should be tied to the stake every 35–50 cm. See Dahlia section.

Pruning
Roses
Prune weeping standard and rambling wichuriana roses when flowering finishes. The weeping standard Seafoam (white flowers flushed with pink) is a perpetually flowering type and should be pruned in winter.

Shrubs
Tip prune new spring growth on spring-flowering shrubs to give compact bushy growth. This also applies to azaleas whether they were pruned after flowering or not. When a shoot has made several sets of leaves, or approaches finger length, pinch out the tip growth — do this progressively.

Tomatoes
Prune and feed. Tie tomatoes to their stakes as growth progresses and prune all but very small-fruited cluster types by breaking out the laterals (shoots that develop in the axil of leaf and stem). Keep well-watered and give a light sprinkling (about 1 teaspoon per running metre) of complete plant food below foliage every 4 weeks. Mulch the surface well.

Feeding
African Violets
African violets that have been dormant for a time should be flowering again now. If not, sprinkle about one-quarter teaspoon of super-phosphate around the edge of the pot, water well and move to a place where light is brighter but not into direct sunlight, through glass or otherwise. Alternatively, place the pot directly below a reading or table lamp that is on from early in the evening until late at night. This can induce flowering although reasonable light is

Lawns
Top dressing of lawns — particularly couch, buffalo and kikuyu — is usually done in November, but appreciate that this is not a yearly ritual and should only be carried out when the lawn surface is uneven, and only enough should be applied to fill minor hollows. Most top dressing soil, irrespective of colour, has little or no food value. Spreading a packet of lawn food will do much more to improve growth and colour than the average load of top dressing.

Care and maintenance
Chrysanthemums
Break off top 2–3 cm growth when plant is about 12 cm high. The 2 or 3 side shoots stimulated by this should also be pinched or broken out at the tips when latter approach finger length. Repeat process until late December to build up a many-stemmed, bushy plant. Stems should be tied to stakes as growth progresses.

Citrus trees
Should have frequent soakings but do not let

the soil remain continuously wet. Washington navel oranges, particularly, will drop fruit if soil is allowed to dry out.

Onions
Bend tops over to hasten maturity when bulbs are forming.

Silverbeet
Pale or dark brown spots may develop on the leaves after rainy or humid periods. This is a fungus leaf spot (septoria). Remove and burn worst affected leaves, spray remainder with Bordeaux or copper oxychloride which is removed safely by soaking leaves for a few minutes and rinsing prior to using. Although unsightly, diseased foliage is useable.

Stone fruits
Ripening from mid-December onwards will need protection from fruit fly in susceptible districts, starting from early this month (5–6 weeks before ripening). See Pests and diseases section for various treatments.

Brown rot prevention is desirable, especially immediately after showery conditions — spray with Zineb or Mancozeb.

SUMMER

December

Sow
Flowers
In all but tropical and semi-tropical areas. Ageratum, alyssum, balsam, Californian poppy, chrysanthemum, cleome, cyclamen, gazania, geranium (seed or cuttings), gerbera, gypsophila, nasturtium, Ornamental chilli, phlox, portulaca, polyanthus, primula, saponaria, sunflower, Swan River daisy, telopea, torenia, verbena and zinnia.

Vegetables and fruit
Sowings as for November *except* in cool districts where it is now too late for capsicums, Cape gooseberries, egg-plant and tomatoes, unless well-established seedings of capsicums and tomatoes can be planted in fairly sheltered northern aspects.

Plant
Flowers
Seedlings of celosia, cockscomb, coleus, dahlias, globe amaranth, kochia, petunia and salvia.

Propagation
December is a good time to take tip cuttings of most evergreens, including azaleas, boronias, camellias, daphne and tea-trees. If you find the latter too difficult, then try layering.

Feeding
Citrus
Benefit from a light feeding now. Spread about one-quarter cup of complete plant food or citrus food per sq. m of area below the foliage, then give soil a good soaking. Washington navel oranges, in particular, should not be allowed to completely dry out at this time of year.

Lawns
Feeding your lawns early in December will make them look their best at Christmas time. If weed invasion is heavy you can clean clover, cudweed and other soft types out by sprinkling it (about one handful per sq. m) with a soluble lawn food or sulphate of ammonia, preferably when it is dewy early in the morning. Train your lawn, shrubs, trees and flowers to withstand dryness longer by avoiding *frequent* light waterings.

Care and maintenance
Azaleas
Check for lace bug, which causes dull mottling or silvering of leaves. If foliage made since last spring shows symptoms then treatment is needed. Rather than spraying you can use a fine-rosed water can with Lebaycid or Rogor diluted to normal strength, applying just enough to wet foliage, as this does penetrate the leaf.

Ferns
Ferns need a good watering every day, even more frequently during heat-wave conditions. Apart from top watering, immerse fern baskets in water at least once a week. (If away for a day or two tie a water-filled plastic lunch bag with a fine pin-hole in the lowest corner above each pot.)

Fuchsias
Lighter foliage types, in particular, can suddenly die out during heat-wave conditions so be sure that roots are kept damp. If caterpillars attack foliage, spray either with Carbaryl or Thiodan, *not* Pyrethrum-type sprays in this case.

Dendrobium beetle
Which is about 1 cm long, orange-tan with black blotches, attacks new shoots of rock orchids, beech orchid and other dendrobiums, rasping away green tissues then laying eggs in pseudo-bulb which larvae may destroy. Catch them by hand (you have to be stealthy and quick) or spray with Pyrethrum-type sprays or Thiodan.

Red spider
Can take hold during hot, dry periods causing a dull sandblasted appearance on foliage of fuchsias, dahlias, beans particularly, and sometimes on indoor palms such as *neanthe* and *livistonia*. These tiny mites are clearly visible with a magnifying glass in bright light. Plants protected from weather are most susceptible, so frequent misting of foliage deters red spider. All but large container plants may be inverted so that foliage can be soaked in soapy water, or sprayed with wettable sulphur, or Kelthane, Malathion, Rogor or Lebaycid.

THE
FLOWER GARDEN

9. Bulbs for your garden

Bulbs add a freshness and charm to the garden, especially in spring. A small clump of golden daffodils strikes a cheerful note on the greyest August day; hyacinths bring fragrance and elegance with their finely-chiselled porcelain-like flower spikes and tulips give a special touch of magic.

The beautiful summer-flowering bulbs are more flamboyant. Nearly all bulbs increase and flower each year with little or no attention. Most are happiest in a mild-to-warm climate, whereas the spring-flowering tulips, hyacinths and, to some extent, daffodils are at their best in cool districts. There are bulbs for every climate but many of them are wonderfully adaptable.

Large drifts of daffodils or bluebells look lovely below deciduous trees, but in small gardens it is best to plant them among other flowering plants, then there is something to take over when the bulb display finishes.

Emphasise a clump of daffodils or tulips by a surround of low bedders like violas or alyssum. This keeps up the show long after the bulbs have finished. Bulbs look more natural when clumped together but if you prefer more formal bedding, space out the bulbs and underplant with a row of violas, bellis or other low-bedding plants between each row of bulbs.

Yellow or apricot violas below golden daffodils or orange tulips accentuate the colour theme or you could make a colour contrast. Although it looks untidy daffodil foliage must be left to yellow-off naturally, otherwise the next year's performance of the bulb will be adversely affected. One solution is to make clump-like plantings in bucket-sized plastic pots or similar containers and sink these to their rims in the garden prior to flowering and remove to a background area when the display has finished.

A few extra containers planted with bulbs will dress up any part of the garden that needs more interest and colour. They can also be used while flowering in areas too shaded to grow bulbs well, or brought indoors for special occasions. Anyone with a fairly sunny balcony or window ledge can enjoy quite a variety of well-grown bulbs in containers.

Bulbs and corms

Corms are loosely referred to as bulbs but differ from the true bulb in that they are made up of a solid mass of stem rather than leaf tissue. These bulbs are really buds containing within them flowers in miniature. Instead of multiplying by division like the true bulbs, each season corms produce one or more new bulbs on top of the old one. Corms include gladioli, freesias, ixias, babianas and watsonias.

The best known examples of true bulbs are daffodils, tulips, hyacinths, dutch irises and lilies. Because of the difference in make-up and habit, the performance of corms is influenced by growing conditions between planting and flowering time, while the true bulb's perform-

When planting bulbs such as daffodils and hyacinths: (1) mix 1 tablespoonful of fertiliser with soil in base and (2) cover with 2–3 cm unfertilised soil. Space bulbs around edges.

ance reflects the previous year's treatment. Therefore, the size of the corm has less bearing on its more immediate performance. With gladioli particularly, there is a general preference for deep rather than larger, flattish corms, although trials carried out in America were unable to establish any significant difference between their performance.

Freesias, anemones, ranunculi, etc. can give quite good performance during the first year from seed, or from tiny cormlets harvested from the previous season's late sowings, provided they are well grown. Seedlings would be several weeks later in flowering. The same applies to corms planted before they have had a reasonable period of dormancy since their harvest.

Gladioli and ranunculi especially need a 3-month resting period at least to produce flowers at 3 months or a little longer from planting, according to variety for gladioli, 3–4 months for ranunculi.

Wrong way (left) and correct way (right) to prepare planting holes for bulbs. If air space is left, bulb may die before rooting.

Preplanting care of bulbs

There seems to be a general impression that tulips, hyacinths and, to some extent, daffodils should be stored in a cool place between purchase and planting time. This is not so, as they remain dormant longer when storage temperatures are in the vicinity of about 20°C. Temperatures of 10°C or lower actually stimulate growth within the bulb and of the roots.

Chilling a few weeks before planting is often practised to force early growth and flowers, but with tulips, in particular, chilling or cool storage is dangerous if the bulbs are likely to be exposed later to appreciably higher air or soil temperatures. Temperatures above 20°C can kill the embryo flower within the bulb.

For this reason it is recommended that the chilling of tulips and hyacinths be left until late April or early May so that sufficiently cool soil temperatures are more likely to be available when they are removed from chilling, which usually takes about 3 weeks.

Planting
Preparing the soil

The impression that bulbs grow well in poor soil comes from the fact that true bulbs such as daffodils, hyacinths and tulips, when given correct moisture and temperature, will give much the same performance in either good soil or sterile sand — for the first season.

This is because the embryo flower is already formed within the bulb and the nutrient and energy it needs is stored inside the bulb during its previous growing season. It is possible to grow hyacinths or daffodils by setting the bulb in a hyacinth jar with its base just fractionally above the water, and keeping in a cool, dark spot for 6–8 weeks before bringing into the light. Naturally, bulbs grown this way rarely flower the following year.

Bulbs normally like good, well-drained soil. If the soil is not freely drained the bulbs will rot. To improve poor soil add well-rotted compost, manure or peatmoss but never use fresh manure.

Do not add lime to the soil unless it is very acid. Then use about half a cup of garden lime or dolomite per sq. m of garden. Tulips are an exception. They appreciate lime, so use up to twice this amount unless the soil is known to be limy or alkaline.

When planting a large area of bulbs, spread about 1 cup of bone dust or one third of a cup complete plant food per sq. m, plus lime if needed, and a layer of well-rotted compost.

Fork over thoroughly to mix in to the depth of 20–25 cm. Leave for a week or so for the soil to settle down. If in a hurry to plant lightly tread over the area to even it down, but *not* when soil is wet or sticky. Air pockets underneath may cause the bulb to die before its roots reach the moist soil.

Aspect

A few bulbs such as bluebells (*Scilla*) and agapanthus grow happily in light to moderate shade but others need at least half sun to flower properly the following season. Cool soil is important for success with spring-flowering bulbs such as tulips, hyacinths, daffodils, crocus, muscari and fritellarias and also most of the summer-flowering liliums.

A good surface mulch helps to keep garden soils cool. Bulbs do not mind tree roots and spring-flowering bulbs are ideal for planting under deciduous trees which provide plenty of sunshine during winter and spring.

Bulb size influences growth and flowering

Size and condition of the true bulbs have a very definite effect on their growth and flowering performance. True bulbs such as daffodils, jonquils, hyacinths and tulips; and in the summer-flowering range amaryllis, hippeastrums, liliums, vallotta, etc. are made up of layers of fleshy storage leaves and the flower is already determined in the bulb by the planting season. Development is dependent on nutrients and starches already stored within the bulb, so size obviously has some bearing. For example, when selecting bulbs of any of the larger trumpet-type daffodils, the diameter of the bulb at its widest point needs to be close to 2.5 cm. Length of the bulb has little bearing. Don't be confused by the large appearance of 'multi-nosed bulbs'. These are bulbs that have divided into several segments attached to the one button of base tissue and sometimes are enclosed within one papery outer fabric. These may not give a good result the following season unless at least one of the individual segments is to the size already suggested.

Some of the smaller-growing and smaller-flowering daffodils or narcissus produce smaller bulbs and types such as the bulbocodium (hoop petticoat daffodil) would normally not produce a bulb more than 10–12 cm in diameter. A good size for hyacinths would be 3–3.5 cm in diameter. Smaller hyacinth bulbs will probably still produce a flower but in most cases the size of the stem and the number of flowers is proportionately reduced. A good size for tulip bulbs is about 2.5 cm in diameter.

Planting guide

Bulbs are spoilt by being planted at the wrong time. The majority of bulbs bloom in the spring and must be planted in autumn so that they have about 6 months in which to develop.

One of the odd facts about bulbs is that they are planted at different depths. Tall-growing bulbs such as gladioli and lilies require the extra support of deep planting to hold them upright. The general rule is to plant large bulbs to twice the depth of the bulb and small bulbs slightly deeper than twice their depth.

Prepare the ground for planting by raking the surface and marking rows at the spacing required. Use a measure, such as a short stick cut to length, so that even spacing can be maintained. For a massed effect the rows can be set closer than conventionally specified spacing.

Make holes for the bulbs with a slender bulb-planting trowel or 'dibbler'. The handle

Bulb types

When selecting bulbs, you must be aware of the difference between the botanical definition and the everyday usage of the word *bulb*. To the botanist, only tulips, hyacinths, daffodils and a few others are considered *true* bulbs. But in common usage, crocus and gladiolus *corms*, dahlia *tubers* and iris *rhizomes* are referred to as *bulbs*. All of these store food that supports life until climatic conditions are right to renew growth.

True bulbs are the bases of stems enlarged and surrounded by fleshy, food-storing scales, which are actually rudimentary leaves. They usually have an oval or pear shape and a growing point at the central base. Bulbs live from year to year, adding layers of growth in *scales*. They have a *basal plate*, a disc-like plate on the bottom of the bulb, from which roots develop. Daffodils and tulips have a hard shell that helps protect the bulb and retains moisture. Lilies lack this covering and are easily damaged by rough handling.

Tubers are the swollen part of an underground stem. Like true bulbs and corms, they have leaf scales that can be almost invisible. The main body of a tuber is solid. Often, it is rounded or knobby, with the roots usually coming from the lower half. *Cyclamen, Anemones* and dog-tooth violets are typical tubers.

Tuberous roots are different from tubers in that the storage area is not part of the stem. Rather, the root holds the storage area, often separated from the stem. It is important that tuberous roots be connected to a stem with a bud. Without a bud they are unable to grow. *Dahlia* and *Ranunculus* are tuberous roots.

Rhizomes are underground stems that grow horizontally along the surface of the soil. Roots grow from the bottom of the rhizome. Leaves grow from the sides or top. Rhizomes grow horizontally, so it is possible for plantings to cover great distances. The bearded iris is a common rhizome.

Corms are composed of solid-stem tissue with a growing tip at the apex. Roots emerge from the sides. The corm becomes depleted by the end of the growing season. A new corm forms to replace the depleted one to continue growth the following year. *Gladiolus* is a typical corm.

of a trowel or a piece of thick dowelling is a good substitute. Mark planting depth on it. Avoid pointed dibblers — they leave an air space under the bulb.

Where clumps are no more than about 40 cm across, the bulbs can be planted closer than the recommended spacing, providing they are surrounded only by low plantings that will not shade them. The effect is better with closer planting.

I prefer to dig a hole to spade depth, a little wider than the clump will be, and tip in a good half-bucket of well-rotted compost and a generous half-cup of either bone dust or a complete organic food (or half this amount of one of the more concentrated complete fertilisers).

The compost will lose volume after further decomposition, so mix in equal parts of soil or enough to bring the level to within a few centimetres of the required planting depth.

To keep the bulbs out of direct contact with fertiliser add enough unfertilised soil as a base. If planting soft, fleshy liliums or gladioli it is an advantage to use clean sand, as it deters rots that may occur in wet soils, helps root growth, keeps the bulbs clean and makes them much easier to find when digging.

Set the bulbs toward the sides of the hole spaced at least twice their width apart. Before filling in the soil, define the perimeter of the clump with a few pegs or short stakes placed between the bulbs, or at least place a peg in the centre. This is more important than it sounds as some daffodils (tulips particularly) may take 2 or 3 months to show through and it is easy to forget their position and damage them by cultivation or even by planting over them.

General care of bulbs

Feeding

Bulbs need much the same type of plant foods as other flowers though the benefit from feeding will not be seen until the following year. Slow-release organic fertilisers are ideal for bulbs, standard complete plant foods also give good results. Fertilisers or plant foods should be kept out of direct contact with the bulbs.

Watering and mulching

Keep the soil around your bulbs moist but not soggy. Let the surface soil just dry out then give a gentle but thorough soaking. A light surface mulch of partly-rotted compost deters heavy soils from caking, slows rapid drying of sandy soil, keeps soil temperatures even, helps retard weed growth and so saves the need for cultivation.

Maintain watering after flowering until foliage yellows-off naturally. This foliage — with the aid of sunlight — supplies the energy which is stored for future use.

Importance of light

It is important to appreciate that the energy a bulb stores for the following years' flowering can only be built up by the action of light on its foliage.

With the exception of shade lovers, therefore, bulbs should be planted where they will get all the sun possible.

Daffodils, for example, grown in heavy shade are unlikely to flower a second year. If the leaves are removed before they are allowed to yellow naturally, food cannot be stored for next year's flowers to form. Tying the leaves together is not advisable because it excludes sun from the inner leaves — see 'Daffodils'.

Important: Remove spent flower heads before seed formation begins or they will drain vigour and retard next season's growth.

Lifting bulbs for replanting

It is not necessary to lift and store bulbs if the wet season does not occur when the bulbs are meant to be dormant. As a general rule, if bulbs need to be lifted for replanting, lift as soon as the foliage begins to die down or, in the case of tulips, as soon as the foliage begins yellowing. Do not reduce watering to induce premature yellowing.

Daffodils may be replanted immediately but it is better to store them after cleaning, in a dry area protected from extremes of temperature, until the normal replanting time the following autumn. Do not store at abnormally cold temperatures.

Liliums are an exception. These soft bulbs dry out readily so replant as soon as possible, or if storage is necessary cover them with slightly damp peatmoss or sand.

Naturalising bulbs

If the climate is right, spring or summer bulbs can be left in the ground in the same place for several seasons so as to develop naturally. Some bulbs are especially suited to naturalise because they are long-lived or because they multiply rapidly.

As the years pass, however, the flowers will become crowded and smaller, making it necessary to lift and divide the bulbs to increase the quality and quantity.

Naturalised Bluebells

Growing liliums

Liliums are beautiful, choice blooms for garden show or cut flowers for the house. Their flowering ranges from late spring to late summer according to the variety and the climate. In temperate districts the November Lily (*L. longiflorum*) displays masses of waxy, white fragrant trumpets by early November. Grows 1 m high; hybrids taller. These are followed later in the month by New Century or Asiatic Hybrids; low-growing (up to 60 cm) flower heads like starry cups or slightly reflexed, like tiger lilies, in shades of yellow and orange.

About a week before Christmas the Aurelian hybrids bloom — taller-growing, mostly trumpet types in yellow, gold, pink or white. The lovely 1–2 m tall *L. regale* (with large, gold-throated white trumpets, stained purple on the backs) also flowers at Christmas.

In early to mid-January the 1–2 m tall pink tiger lilies (*L. speciosum*) flower, also hybrids between the latter and the lovely large Golden-Rayed Lily of Japan (*L. auratum*). These crosses are usually classed as Parkmanii hybrids.

> **Note:** All flowering times can be nearly a month later in cool climates.

Climatic conditions

The later-flowering types are worth growing in temperate regions, but like most other liliums are at their best in cool highland districts, with good drainage and generous surface mulches applied during winter and if necessary renewed as hot weather approaches. Cool soil is essential.

Aurelian hybrids also prefer cool climates but do quite well in temperate districts with well-drained and mulched soil. Mid-Century or Asiatic Hybrids are more tolerant to warm soil so grow almost as well in warm–temperate as in cool districts.

Planting and care

In all cases (except with Madonna Lily *L. candidum*) the bulb should be covered by twice its own depth of soil, or a little shallower in heavy soils. It is worth digging 8–10 cm deeper so that some well-rotted compost and bone dust (or complete plant food) can be mixed in the soil. Cover with a few centimetres of unfertilised topsoil or clean sand in order to insulate bulb and fertiliser. Mulch the surface with compost, then add a sprinkling of complete plant food over it when new shoots show through. Protect agains snails at this stage.

Good drainage is essential. It is better to grow the plants in large, deep containers if soil drainage is poor.

Planting times vary according to flowering times. Early-flowering November lilies are planted in March. Asiatic Hybrids by mid-May and other late flowerers by the end of June. However, the shorter the time bulbs are out of the ground the better, as once they dry out and become limp it takes them a year or two to regain normal vigour.

Light requirements

In cool climates lilies flower better when in full sun. For temperate districts light shade is best for flower quality. All types do better when left undisturbed until clumps become crowded or when flower quality and quantity begin deteriorating.

Propagation

Propagate from seed, from bulb scales set as cuttings in damp sand, or from bulblets that form just below the soil level around the base of the stem.

Lilium (speciosum x Asiatic hybrid)

Lilium regale

Lilium Asiatic hybrid

Lilium Red Echo

Golden Clarion (Aurelian hybrid), Trendwell (spotted yellow) and Orange Destiny (Asiatic hybrids)

Growing problems and solutions

Bulbs which will not flower

One of the most frequent questions, particularly with daffodils, is why are my bulbs not flowering? The main point to remember is that all true bulbs, for example daffodils, jonquils, tulips, hyacinths (as distinct from the woody corms such as freesias, gladioli, babiana, etc.) have already produced the embryo flower within the bulb by planting time. Therefore, their performance will depend mainly on their treatment the previous season.

The most common reasons for non-flowering are:

1. Excessive dryness during the previous spring-flowering period and afterwards, while the foliage is still green.

2. Excessive shade the previous year, or foliage removed prematurely. It is only through the action of sunlight on the foliage that the plant can make sugars and starches which are stored within the bulb and are essential for the production of the next season's flowers. Therefore, if the foliage is prematurely removed, shaded or overshadowed by other plants, or is tied together for neat appearance, this essential food storage process is curtailed, or reduced.

3. Overcrowding of the clumps can be another factor. Daffodils may be left undisturbed in the soil for 3 to 4 years, depending on how closely they were planted initially, but depending on the rate of multiplication of the bulbs, they may become too congested to produce bulbs of flowering size.

4. Temperature can also have a bearing on the performance of tulips and, to a lesser extent, hyacinths and daffodils.

5. Varieties vary. Different strains of daffodils may vary in their performance. For example, many original strains of the old favourite King Alfred daffodil have a relatively poor flowering performance. A good effect in the garden is more assured by planting daffodils and other bulbs in clumps rather than single rows. Then if only 50% flowering is achieved, the clump planting still looks effective, whereas rows tend to look a bit 'tatty'. With clump planting it may be necessary to lift and replant every third year rather than every fourth.

Plant lilium bulbs at an angle to avoid water lodging in base — cushion bulb on clean sand if soil is clayey.

Bulb	Symptom	Cause	Remedy
Agapanthus	Failure to flower	New plants need at least a year to establish. Too heavily shaded or too much nitrogen	Patience. If foliage is generally lush, sprinkle one handful superphosphate around each clump in early spring
Allium	Black insects clustering below flower buds	Aphids	Pyrethrum-type spray or Malathion
Alstroemeria	Growth and stems stunted	Soil too compacted	Mulch liberally with an organic material, water liberally during early growth period
	Spotting and shrivelling of lower foliage	Fungus or bacterial spot	Spray liberally with copper spray
Amaryllis (Belladonna)	No flowers	Planted too deeply or clumps not sufficiently established	Either hose away soil or replant to expose neck of bulb. Best when clumps left undisturbed for several years
Anemone coronaria	Distorted, downward curled growth	Aphids	See Allium
	Poor, rusty or yellowish growth	Either insufficient drainage or excessive fertiliser	Improve drainage or flood soil to leach out excess fertiliser
Arum	See Calla	See Calla	See Calla
Babiana	Brown leaf tips	Overfeeding and watering but bulb infection is possible	See Freesia
Belladonna	See Amaryllis	See Amaryllis	See Amaryllis
Brunsvigia	See Amaryllis	See Amaryllis	See Amaryllis
Calla	Plants do not appear in spring	Tuber rot due to cold, wet conditions	Lift and store tubers in autumn where cold, wet winters are likely
Canna	Holes in foliage or leaves tattered	Snails	Use baits or spray with Methiocarb preparations
	Sections of stems collapse	Stem borer grub	Liberally spray or water Endosulphan to run down leaf into stem
Clivia	Flower stems or leaves eaten	Snails	See Canna
	Brown scalloped edges on leaves	Brown vegetable weevil	Spray with Endosulphan at first sign of attack
Colchicum (spring-flowering types)	Failure to flower	Winter too mild	Most types need sharp winterr and long, cool spring
Crocus	Failure to flower	Winter too mild	See Colchicum
Daffodil			
	Distorted foliage with reddish-ridged margin towards base	Bulb mite	Spray with Rogor, Lebaycid or Malathion
	Yellowing and twisting of foliage, without above symptoms	Basal rot	Destroy infected bulbs. Replant in soil with better drainage
	Failure to flower		See heading 'Bulbs which will not flower'
	Pale foliage with translucent streaks between veins	Mosaic virus (transmitted by aphids)	Remove and burn infected bulbs
Dahlia	See Perennials	See Perennials	See Perennials
Erythronium (Dog-tooth Violet)	Poor stunted growth	Bulbs may have dried out and softened before planting	Either replant immediately or store bulbs in damp peatmoss
	Foliage dwarfed and excessively twisted downwards	Green aphids	Pyrethrum-type spray or systemic such as Rogor
Freesia	Leaf tips shrivelled with brown stain	Can be due to excessive use of soluble fertilisers and overwatering	Flood soil to remove excess fertiliser, otherwise water only moderately
	Leaf tip damage with streaking continuing down between veins	Usually fusarium or similar fungus infection	At planting time remove husks to check bulbs, discarding any with sunken brown or black patches. Also improve drainage
Fritillaria	Poor stunted growth	Usually late planting	See Erythronium

Bulb	Symptom	Cause	Remedy
Gladiolus	Flower buds fused and not opening	Thrips	Spray alternately with Endosulphan and Rogor at 10-day intervals from the time plants reach four-leaf stage
	Whitish flecks particularly toward base of foliage	Thrips	As above
	Brown leaf tips	Thrip damage, excessive feeding, or bulb fungus attack	See Freesia
Ginger	Collapse of some leaves or stem	Stem borer	See Canna
Hippeastrum	Failure to flower	Poor growing conditions during previous season, or planting too deeply	Plant with neck of bulb exposed
	Distorted and ridged foliage	Bulb eelworm	See 'Daffodil'
	As above with red, ridged margins	Bulb mite	Rogor or Malathion spray
Hyacinth	Stored bulbs with downy white patches	Mealy bug or root aphids	Dip the bulbs in a solution of Rogor or Lebaycid made to normal spraying strength
	Light-yellowish mottling between leaf veins	Usually mosaic virus transmitted by aphids	Burn infected bulbs
Iris (Bearded)	Failure to flower	Deep planting or congested clumps	Plant with top of rhizome exposed, replant if clumps become sufficiently congested to exclude sun from centre
	Purplish-brown spots on leaves	Usually fungus leaf spot induced by wet conditions	Remove badly infected leaves and apply copper spray or Benlate
Iris (Dutch or other bulbous types)	Poor growth, yellow-streaked foliage	Virus	Remove and burn infected plants. Clean, virus-free stock should be produced from seed
	Brown leaf tips	See Freesia	
Jonquil	See Daffodil	See Daffodil	See Daffodil
Lachenalia (Soldier Boy)	Plants do not reappear at growing time	Bulb rot, due to wet, humid conditions during dormant period	Lift and store in dry, airy situation when foliage dies down. Replant in well-drained soil
	Stunted, deformed flower spikes	Aphids	At first sign spray with Pyrethrum or Malathion
Lilium	Poor growth, shrivelled foliage, scales of bulbs loose and rotted at base	Basal rot	Dip bulbs in spray-strength solution of Zineb or Mancozeb. Plant slightly on side in well-drained soil
	Brown blotches on foliage later turning whitish	Botrytis spot	Spray with Captan
	Pale, mosaic-like patches between leaf veins, poor growth	Virus (transmitted by aphids)	Destroy infected plants, grow virus-free stocks from seed
Lily-of-the-Valley	Failure to flower	Corms immature	'Pips' (shoots) need to be about 1 cm thick. A sharp winter and cool spring is also preferred
Muscari (Grape Hyacinth)	Failure to flower	Overcrowding or bulbs too soft	Lift and replant almost immediately within a few weeks of foliage yellowing. Also best with cold winter
Nerine (Spider Lily)	Failure to flower	Deep planting or clumps not well established	See Amaryllis
Nymphaea (Water Lily)	Small weevils or grubs eating foliage		If fish absent from pond, spray with Pyrethrum, otherwise lightly place twiggy branches to immerse leaves so that fish devour insects
Sprekelia (Jacobean Lily)	White streaking on flower petals	Thrips	Spray with Endosulphan or Pyrethrum
Tigridia (Jockey's Cap)	Light flecks on foliage	Either thrip or red spider damage	Spray with Malathion or Rogor
	Brown tips of foliage		See Freesia
Trillium (Wood Lily)	Poor growth, no flowers	Conditions warm or dry	Needs moist, cool soil
Tulip	Green or grey insects clustered below flower bud	Aphids	Pyrethrum or Malathion spray

Bulbs for special needs

Some bulbs for fragrance

Many bulbs produce some fragrance. These not only have pleasant scent but also a strong one.

Amaryllis belladonna
Crinum moorei
Eucharis amazonica
Freezia reflecta
Gladiolus tristis
Hyacinth
Lillium (trumpet and bowl-shaped)
Narcissus jonquilla
Narcissus tazetta
Tuberose (Polianthes)

Bulbs for rock gardens

Anemone
Babiana
Crocus
Cyclamen
Habranthus
Lapeirousia
Narcissus (Daffodil)
Sternbergia
Tritonia
Zephyranthes

Bulbs for hanging baskets

Only a couple of bulbs have a long bloom period and a trailing nature which make them suitable for hanging baskets.

Achimenes
Begonia

Bulbs for containers

Any bulb can be grown in a container for one year but, because of the extensive root system, few bulbs flower well year after year when grown in containers. Some bulbs, however, thrive under crowded conditions and can remain in the same pot for years.

Agapanthus
Clivea
Eucomis
Freesia
Hippeastrum
Ixia
Laperiousia
Muscari
Sparaxis
Tritonia

Shady areas

Anemone nemorosa
Begonia
Clivea
Cyclamen
Erythronium
Muscari
Scilla
Trillium

Moist areas

Canna
Hemerocallis
Iris (some species)
Zantedeschia

Unusual bulbs

Some bulbs not only look unusual but also have strange habits. Knowing what to expect helps you to handle them successfully and the results can be very rewarding.

Take for example a bulb of the autumn crocus (*Colchicum autumnale*). Sometimes it is quite large and irregular in shape, resembling a rather knobbly dark-brown tobacco pouch. Leave it sitting on your table or desk for a few days and, without contact with soil or water, it may suddenly throw a dozen or so chalice-shaped, papery flowers with long slender throats — like hungry fledglings craning their exceptionally long necks from the nest.

The tuberose, with spikes of heavily fragrant, waxy blooms, has its funny habits too. It is normally bought as a clump of small, thin bulbs surrounding a large centre bulb. This centre bulb usually flowers the first summer but then stubbornly refuses to flower again.

Therefore, the practice should be to lift the clump each winter, discard the centre crown that has flowered and replant the side shoots about 5 cm apart in rich, moist soil in a sunny position. Some of the larger side bulbs may flower the following autumn so any that are approaching 2 cm in diameter can be given a little wider spacing. The rest are dug in the winter when growth dies down and set out about a span apart to flower and produce offsets for the following season's planting.

Naked ladies, or belladonnas (*Amaryllis belladonna*), also have their funny little ways. They refuse to flower well unless left for a few years to clump up, with at least the necks of their bulbs above ground. Their foliage is carried from late summer through the winter and dies down in spring, so this is the time to move them if you really need to. Bulbs that have been moved will usually flower during normal time a few months after moving, but then are unlikely to flower again for several years.

Spider lilies, or Nerines, are a little like naked ladies in behaviour, but prefer their bulbs still further above the soil and are better with a good sunbaking and fairly dry summer conditions. Lycoris, the large golden-apricot spider lily, is from China rather than Africa where the climate is different, so is happy with wetter and milder summers.

Hymenocallis (Spider Lily)

Colchicum speciosum

Lilium henryii

Nerine bowderii

Growing bulbs in containers

Bulbs in containers outdoors

Bulbs can be enjoyed in so many different situations. With the possible exception of bluebells and hyacinths, which are artificially 'forced' in bulb fibre, bulbs need sunlight for at least half the day to grow well and continue producing flowers the following year. However, they can still be grown in containers outdoors and brought inside for periods of a few days while flowering.

Similarly, containers of flowering bulbs may be moved to bring colour and interest to difficult shaded or root-infested parts of the garden. Burying the container with rim at soil level or hiding it among ground cover will give the impression of a more natural and permanent appearance.

Add some colourful flowering annuals to pots, troughs or clumps of bulbs in the garden if you wish. This is in no way essential as in all cases the bulb foliage seems a perfect complement to the flower. However, the additions give variety and extra colour over a longer period. Make sure they are low growers that will not overcrowd or block sun from the bulb foliage.

White or mauve alyssum is a safe companion for any bulbs, especially for those such as freesias or sparaxis that resent much height close to them. Seeds or seedlings of alyssum can be set in the soil immediately after the bulbs and the latter will happily push their way through.

Violas make good partners for daffodils; English daisies (*Bellis*) and bluebells (*Scillas*) grouped in alternate clumps seem just right for each other.

Growing bulbs for indoors

There are two quite different approaches to growing bulbs for indoors. One method is 'forcing', where the bulbs are grown indoors in bulb fibre, to bloom earlier than their normal time. The other method is growing in soil with plant foods, drainage and sunlight.

Forcing flowers

Forcing is not the best term to describe this method of growing. What is done is to simulate the natural conditions that cause bulbs to bloom.

Bulbs grown this way cannot build up the necessary reserves needed to flower again the following year.

1. Select firm, good-sized bulbs. It is advisable to have one variety, as the bulbs will then flower at the same time, whereas mixtures are likely to give an uneven effect — especially with hyacinths, daffodils and tulips.

If bulbs are to be chilled they can be kept in the crisper of the refrigerator (10–12°C) for 3 weeks before planting.

2. Ensure that after chilling, the bulbs are not exposed to temperature increases of more than about 6°C as this can damage flowers, particularly tulips. So remove them from the

Cyclamen — commonly used as house plants

refrigerator only when ready to plant. It is better to delay planting, tulips and hyacinths particularly, until late April or early May so that after chilling it will be easier to find the cool environment needed.

3. Select any container with or without drainage but be sure there is at least 6 cm space below the bulbs when their necks are level with the container to allow for root development.

4. Use damp bulb fibre, not soil. If fibre is dry and difficult to moisten soak with hot water, leaving several hours to cool before squeezing out surplus moisture. If the container is not quite waterproof, or is liable to be stained by the fibre, line it with plastic and trim at soil level.

Firm enough of the moist bulb fibre in the base of the container to bring tips of bulbs to soil level or just below.

5. Space the bulbs at least 1 cm apart, then fill and firm fibre between them, particularly around the edge of the container. Water the

fibre and drain out the surplus by propping container on its side for 15 minutes.

6. To save worry about further watering, seal the container in a plastic bag, then wrap it in a thick brown paper bag and move to the coolest place possible. One way is to cover it with a few shovels of soil in a damp, shaded part of the garden (well marked with a few stakes).

7. Bulbs previously chilled should be left there for 6 weeks; those planted without chilling should stay for 8–9 weeks, but they should be checked after 5–6 weeks. Do not bring bulbs from cool darkness until large chunky shoots about 3 cm have formed and, more important, until root growth is well developed. The latter can usually be seen around the edge of the bowl or through a drainage hole; if in doubt check again after a week.

8. Move the container to a light but still fairly cool situation until the shoots have greened and leaves begin to unfold. It can then be

brought into normal room temperature, but away from heaters. Make sure the fibre stays moist.

Growing in soil for indoors

Bulbs grown in soil, provided that reasonable care is taken, will flower as well the next year in the same way as those cultivated in the garden.

Use any trough or pot that appeals to you providing the bulbs can be set in the soil with 3 times the depth of the bulb below it to allow for root growth.

For tulips, hyacinths and daffodils you need a container at least 25 cm deep: the average nursery bucket-sized pot. Freesias, sparaxis, babianas, bluebells, tritelias, lachenalias and summer-flowerers such as vallotas, eucomis and sprekelias which only need shallow planting will grow happily in troughs or bowls only 15 cm deep.

Soil

Any good proprietary potting soil will suit bulbs that are to be grown in containers out of doors. If you prefer to make up your own soil, 2 parts crumbly garden loam, 2 parts coarse sand and 1 part moistened peatmoss would make a good mixture. Mix in about 2 level teaspoons of complete plant food to each bucketful of this soil mixture.

Planting

1. Containers with side drainage slits do not need crocking, but those with a single drainage hole should be given a handful of charcoal or rubble in the base. Make sure this does not block the drainage hole; cover it with a large piece held clear of the base with a few small pebbles and built up with coarse pieces around it. I sometimes just cover the hole with a square of fibreglass insect gauze with a handful of small pebbles or charcoal on top.

2. For a pot 18–20 cm in diameter add about 2 teaspoons of bone dust or organic plant food with as much soil as you can afford in the base, allowing for another centimetre of so of unfertilised soil above this to keep the bulbs clear of direct contact with fertiliser. If you do not have the organic material suggested use half the amount of complete fertiliser.

3. Space bulbs about twice their width apart, perhaps a little wider for tiny bulbs such as triteleias and a little closer for daffodils. Grown this way they are best replanted at least every second year so they don't become too crowded. Fill in to within 1–2 cm of the container rim when the soil is pressed down gently. I like to use strawy compost or pine bark for the last 2–3 cm of covering as it looks better and helps to keep soil open.

Freesias and similar corms do not mind warm soil, but for daffodils, hyacinths, tulips, grape hyacinths and bluebells it is best to keep containers in a shaded place until growth appears, then (with the possible exception of bluebells) place them so that foliage gets sun but the container is shaded — even if only by other containers. Water whenever surface dries out, allowing just enough to give some run-off from drainage holes.

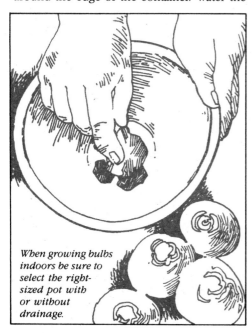

When growing bulbs indoors be sure to select the right-sized pot with or without drainage.

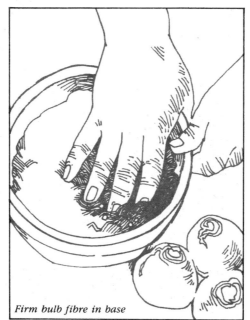

Firm bulb fibre in base

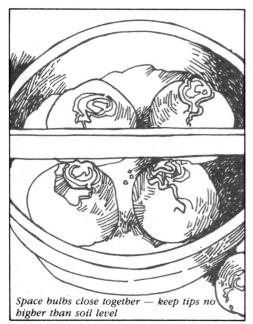

Space bulbs close together — keep tips no higher than soil level

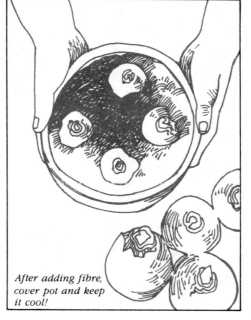

After adding fibre, cover pot and keep it cool!

A reference guide to bulbs

Spring-flowering bulbs

Allium (Flowering Onion) Some, like *A. roseum*, resemble a pink-flowered onion weed. Others, like *A. albopilosum*, have large, starry lavender or pale-violet heads up to 20 cm wide on stems nearly 1 m high. Most flower in late spring or early summer and may be replanted in at least half-sun, 7–9 cm deep during winter.

Alstromeria Plant in autumn for spring-flowering or spring for summer-flowering. Giver plenty of water during summer. Do not lift once established.

Anemone Poppy-flowered *A. coronaria* and its semi-double, finer-petalled variety *A. St. Brigid* are planted from corms from February to May for late winter and spring show. Red, blue and intermediate tone flowers on 20–14 cm stems; good for cutting or for bedding in sunny positions. Try interplanting them with yellow violas or pink English daisies (*Bellis*). Best treated as annuals. For other anemone species see section 'Perennials'.

Anomatheca see *Laperouisa*

Babiana stricta Resemble erect freesias but flower 2–3 weeks later. Flowers deep violet-blue, mauve and purple. Foliage broader and stiffer than freesias, prominently ribbed or veined and slightly downy. Treat as freesias.

Begonia tuberous see 'House plants'

Belladonna (*Amaryllis belladonna*) Called 'Naked Ladies' because the tall, smooth, fleshy flower stems appear before the foliage. Dinnerplate-size heads of fragrant, large pink trumpets, usually with paler centres; also *alba*, a creamy-white variety. Grow in full-sun or under deciduous trees, plant when dormant (November–December) with top half of bulb exposed. They flower best when undisturbed even though clumps are crowded.

Bluebell (*Scilla*) Dainty spikes with pendulous light-blue bells — they like moist, shaded spots or sun. For pleasant effect try mixing clumps with white primulas, polyanthus or English daisies. Autumn mulch of leafmould is recommended.

When clumps become crowded (every third or fourth year) lift and replant after foliage dies down, or store in damp peatmoss until February–April planting. Pink or white-flowering types are also available. The giant Spanish Bluebell has 38 cm tall spikes of large flowers.

Bulbinella Like miniature yellow 'pokers' but florets are starry rather than tubular; wiry erect stems to 60 cm and slender reedy foliage; flowering in late winter or early spring; divide in early winter if necessary.

Calla see *Zantedeschia*

Chionodoxa (Glory of the Snow) Beautiful blue flowers, strictly for cool areas.

Clivia miniata Excellent for shade; green-tipped, orange-red tubular flowers.

Crocus Late winter or spring types such as *C. biflorus* and *C. tomasinianus* have mauve to purple papery-petalled flowers which appear suddenly, often before foliage. *C. sativus*, with large lilac blooms and prominent orange stigmas, flowers in autumn. Most true crocus need a sharp winter and long, cool spring to perform well.

So-called Summer Crocus are *Zephryanthus* which are at home under warmer conditions.

Cyrtanthus (Ifafa Lily) 20–30 cm spikes of slender, pendulous, tubular flowers; coral red, golden buff or creamy rose. Spring flowers, then occasional later. Prefers half- to full-sun and good drainage.

Cyclamen persicum (Florists' cyclamen) see 'House plants'

Cyclamen neapolitianum see 'Perennials'

Daffodil Often appropriately called the 'heralds of spring', daffodils include the popular golden-flowered 'King Alfred' which finishes flowering before azalias, wisteria and most of the spring annuals reach the peak of their display. Old-timers such as the deeply-coloured 'Fortune' follow, then the gold and free-flowering 'Dr Roseby' and lastly, the pale creamy-yellow 'Emperor' which is more in line with the general spring show. However, stocks of good, golden late-flowerers are now becoming available.

Daffodil 'Hoop Petticoat' (*Bulbicodium*) Dainty little fine-foliaged spring-flowering daffodil growing only about 12 cm high, with a flared, papery, yellow trumpet and comparatively tiny petals.

Divide and replant daffodils every 3–4 years or every 2–3 years when closely planted in clumps. Bulbs should be lifted when foliage dies down and replanted from February–May. For cultivation details see under earlier headings dealing with soil and feeding, planting and general fare.

Dahlia see 'Perennials'

Erythronium (Dog-tooth Violet) More like large, long-stamened cream or mauve cyclamen than violets. Only worthwhile in cool climates, preferring a well-composted soil. The fleshy bulb should be replanted soon after lifting or stored in damp peatmoss if delay is necessary.

Freesia Modern hybrids have exceptional size, colour and stem length and are regaining the fragrance of the cream *Refracta alba* type. They need good drainage and at least half-sun.

Fritillaria imperialis Erect growth up to 1 m high with a whorl of pendulous, wide-mouthed orange-bronze to red bells below a large crest of rosetted strap-like foliage; slightly pungent odour. Needs cold winter, cool spring and well-composted soil. In wet districts plant bulbs on side so that water does not lodge in the hollow crown.

F. meleagris Has grass-like growth with chequered dark-brown and mauve (or green and white) nodding bells.

Grape Hyacinth (Muscari) Slender 12–15 cm spikes clustered heavily with tiny deep-blue bells in spring. Best in cool climates.

Hyacinth Their flower-packed spikes are fragrant and beautiful, appreciated either in the garden or indoors in bowls of bulb fibre.

Outdoors they are at their best in cool districts but are also worthwhile in temperate areas and re-flower for at least a few years in a cool, partly-shaded area of the garden; plant as suggested under 'clump planting'. They flower in early spring (late August, early September). In comparatively warm areas, particularly, it is as well to delay planting until late April–early May; lift bulb when foliage yellows and store it in ordinary (not cool) summer temperatures.

Ipbion see *Triteleias*

Iris (Dutch) Dutch Iris provide striking striking cut flowers with their three large arms and attractively marked fall petals and erect stems up to 1 m high. Colours mainly blue, yellow or bronze. Plant February–April in well-drained and preferably composted soil. Flower late September, early October. Where summers are wet it is best to lift bulbs when foliage yellows and store. For other types see 'Perennials'.

Ixia (Corn Lily) Slender, erect stems up to 10 cm long, with bunchy spikes of ruby-red, gold or buff oval buds that open to starry flowers. Bloom late September–October. Look best in clumps. Also earlier-flowering blue *I. capillaris*; more open-headed *I. paniculata* (Morphixia) in buff to salmon tones, lower-growing and usually flowering later in October, and lovely, soft-green *I. vidiflora* which unfortunately is often subject to a corm-attacking fungus. Treat as freesias.

Jonquil Many types. Those widely grown are varieties of *Narcissus tazetta*. 'Paper White', fragrant, all white flattish flowers in clusters on 40–50 cm stems; flowers May–June. 'Soleil D'or', orange cup with golden petals, flowers mainly late winter but occasional blooms in late autumn. Also numerous cream to yellow and white varieties. Best left to clump up for 5 years or so in sun to light shade. Cultivate as daffodils.

Lachenalia (Soldier Boy) All lachenalias prefer well-drained but not-too-dry and slightly limey soil. Ideal for borders, rockeries or container growing. Lift bulbs in wet summer areas. Store as suggested for bluebells or replant as soon as possible. *L. aurea*, yellow flowers, early spring; *L. pendula*, purplish red, flowers in September; *L. quadricolor*, tubular bells with reddish-purple and green both on tip of tube and overlapping petals, flowers in late winter, *L. tricolor*, erect 12–15 cm stems of long, pendant, yellow tubular flowers, shaded red at the base and tipped green, flowering in September or October in cooler climates.

Laperiousia (Anomatheca) Growth resembles freesia but with shorter-stemmed flattish heads of slender-petalled starry flowers in rosy-red to salmon with deeper maroon centre. Flower in mid-spring, but seedlings may bloom in late summer.

Leucojum (Snowflake) Clumps of dark, glossy green foliage, slightly arching stems with clusters of green-tipped white bells during winter. Best left undisturbed; sun or light shade.

L. autumnalis (Acis); dainty, small pink-tinted white bells on thread-like 10–15 cm stems that appear in late summer before the fine grassy foliage emerges; suit small rockery pockets or container-growing; preferably half-sun. Replant October to December if overcrowded.

Lilium see feature pg 85

Daffodil (Narcissus)

Clivia miniata

Sparaxis (Harlequin Flower)

Lachenalia aloides

Babiana

Sprekelia formosissima

Muscari see Grape Hyacinth

Narcissus see Daffodil and Jonquil

Ornithogalum chrysoides (Chincherinchee) Erect, 15–30 cm spikes on tightly-packed upfacing white bell-shaped flowers opening from the base, commencing mid-spring and lasting about 6 weeks. Different colours seen in cut flowers are achieved by standing the stems in dye.

O. arabicum: longer stemmed, large papery white florets with black eye.

O. undulatum (Star of Bethlehem): head of starry white flowers striped green on the outside of each petal.

Ornithogalums prefer a well-drained position with at least half sun. Lift and replant from December to February if overcrowded.

Ranunculus Ranunculi give warm colour to a spring garden. A soil rich in compost and plant food with half to full sun is preferred. Corms are planted claws downward with a covering of only about 4 cm of soil (up to 6 cm in light sandy areas). In humid coastal districts it is better to delay planting until late April. During wet conditions it is safest to first pre-sprout the corms in a tray of moist sand, then replant them like seedlings. Corm-grown plants are also available in the bedding plant range. Flower late September and October. Best treated as annuals. Can also be raised from seed started in early February.

Scilla see Bluebell

Scilla peruviana Broad, semi-erect foliage; heads about 10 cm wide with closely-packed, upfacing starry flowers, either buff with blue centres or entirely pale-blue; spring flowering; best in part shade. Divide in February if overcrowded.

Snowflake see *Leucojum*

Sparaxis (Harlequin Flower) Like brightly coloured red, orange, bronze or cream freesias with a centre zone of contrasting (usually black and yellow) harlequin markings; flower in late September or October. Treat as freesias.

Streptocarpus Rather like Sparaxis but red or rosy flowers are flatter and rounder petalled. Flower a little later than Sparaxis.

Triteleia uniflora (Iphion) Low clumps of slender, pale green foliage closely studded with starry pale-blue flowers from August to October; only about 12 cm tall. Increases rapidly; sun to half shade; the only objection is the onion-like smell when foliage is brushed or bruised.

Tulip Tulips bring colour, charm and character to the garden in mid-spring when the early daffodils have finished. They can be enjoyed in sun or shade in most climates for the first season, but then bulbs might as well be discarded in all but those climates with sharp winters and a long, cool spring.

Tulipa saxatilis Does well in warm and cool climates, but in very cold areas needs some shelter as the bright-green foliage emerges early. The flowers are mauve-pink with prominent yellow centres. It spreads from runners so is best confined by sinking a barrier around where the bulbs are planted — half an oil drum from which the bottom has been removed is an ideal barrier.

Watsonia Dense clumps of tall gladiolus-like

foliage and slender 1–2 m stems, with top-half studded with long, wide-mouthed tubular flowers in white, pink, salmon and terra-cotta shades. Excellent cut flowers, they sometimes naturalise, and in some areas of Western Australia, particularly, are becoming invasive. Spring-flowering. Can be, if necessary, replanted in January/ February.

Zantedeschia (*Z. aethiopica*) The white arum with large, handsome foliage and fleshy flower stems to 1 m or more tall. Grows well along creeks or damp areas, flowering mainly in spring and early summer, but can be brought to flower any time by keeping it dry to encourage dormancy, then resuming frequent watering.

Z. elliotiana The yellow Calla, or arum, with comparatively slender stems from 40–60 cm and finely-spotted foliage; flowering mainly late October–November but can be delayed until Christmas or later by storing bulbs in moderately cool, dry conditions, and planting about 10 weeks before blooms are required. However, if shoots are well advanced and tubers show signs of softening, they should be planted without delay.

Z. pentlandii A deep shade of orange-yellow with plain green foliage.

Z. rehmannii Small, pale-pink to light-purple blooms (paler in limey soils) on stems only 30–40 cm tall, flowering as *Z. elliottiana.*

All of the coloured callas are likely to rot in cold wet soils during the winter dormant period. Therefore, unless drainage is good, lift and store tubers after foliage yellows and replant from August onwards.

Summer, autumn and winter-flowering bulbs

Agapanthus (Lily of the Nile) Tough, bulbous, summer-flowering evergreens with strong and extensive root systems ideal for soil binding or competing with tree roots. Their long-stemmed, globular heads of blue or white trumpet-shaped florets are attractive during late November and December and useful for large Christmas flower arrangements. Sun to light shade; good drought resistance. Leave undisturbed but if necessary replant in winter.

Amaryllis see Belladonna

Brunsivigia Resembling Belladonna, but with more numerous, comparatively starry darker rose-red florets (bulbs have glossy scales whereas belladonnas are woolly). Treat as belladonnas.

Canna Handsome foliage and colourful heads of red, pink, yellow, orange, or red and gold flowers from mid-summer to autumn; suit wet or dry soils, need at least half sun; cut back when foliage yellows and if necessary divide and replant in late winter. In very cold districts lift and store clumps under protection from frosts.

Crinum moorei Very large bulbs to .5 cm high, with an umbrella of broad strap foliage and erect stems with clusters of slightly nodding large cup-like fragrant pink or white flowers in summer. Evergreen.

C. peduncularis, grows to 2 m high with dense elevated crown of broad rigid leaves over 1 m long and erect heads of spidery white

Bluebells (Endymion hispanicus)

Hippeastrum (Dutch amaryllis)

Ranunculus

'Golden Yellow' Freesia

Tulips

Bearded Iris

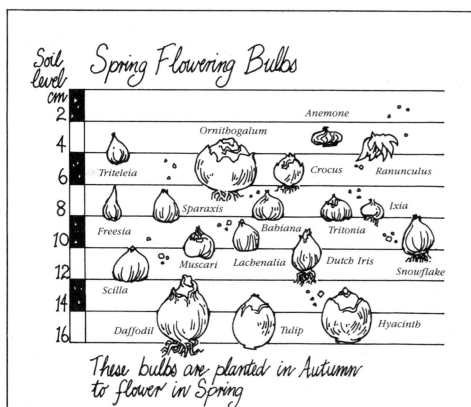

Spring Flowering Bulbs

These bulbs are planted in Autumn to flower in Spring

Depth of Planting

Summer Flowering Bulbs

These bulbs are planted in Winter or when foliage normally dies down

flowers from November to January. All but coldest areas; full sun to part shade.

Crocus see ***Zephyranthus***

Eucomis (Pineapple Lily) Long lax wavy foliage and 50 cm stems, the top 20 cm or so densely clustered in mid-summer with starry cream to mauve florets below a rosette of short foliage. The true petals and stamens fall to leave long-lasting, green flower-like calyces. Good drought resistance, but they appreciate plenty of water in spring and at least half sun. Plant bulbs with top half exposed.

Galtonia (***Hyacinth candicans***) Summer hyacinth. White, waxy fragrant flowers growing 1.2–1.5 m. Plant during dormant period in winter–spring.

Gladiolus Gladioli are corms rather than true bulbs and they respond to good feeding and plenty of water during the first season. Corms can be cool-stored to flower within about 3 months of planting providing they have first had a rest period of at least 3 months before harvesting. Main planting time is from August to November or in tropical areas February–June. Dig, clean and store the corms about six weeks after flowering. Actually these will be new corms formed above the originally planted and now shrivelled corm, which comes away easily a few weeks after lifting and drying.

Cormlets which usually occur plentifully between the new and old corm will reach flowering size the second year after planting.

Gladioli need good drainage and full sun. Thrips are their main enemy — spraying is often needed from the four-leaf stage onward.

Habranthus Open, soft, pink trumpets up to 9 cm wide on individual 10–15 cm stems in early summer. At least half sun; leave undisturbed for at least 4–5 years.

Hemerocalis (Day-Lily) see 'Perennials'

Hippeastrum Individually their blooms are probably the most spectacular of the summer-flowering bulbs; with heads of large open trumpets (velvety red, sometimes with white feathering or lovely lime or pink-tinted white) on stems to about 50 cm tall, and bold strap-like foliage. Prefer at least half sun, good enriched soil as suggested earlier for bulbs generally, and plenty of water during spring and summer. Plant with top third of bulb exposed (or a little deeper in northern areas). A comparatively dry winter period is acceptable. Best undisturbed unless crowded. Replant in winter if necessary. Main flowering November–December, but dormancy may be prematurely induced by drying, and flowers forced at any time.

Iris (Dutch) Provide striking cut flowers with their three large arms and attractively-marked fall petals, and erect stems up to 1 m high. Colours mainly blue, yellow or bronze. Plant February to April in well-drained and preferably composted soil. Flower late September, early October. Where summers are wet, it is best to lift bulbs when foliage yellows and store. For other types see 'Perennials'.

Lilium see Feature pg 85

Lycoris see Spider Lily

Montbretia

Polianthes see Tuberose

Spider Lily Both Lycoris and Nerine are grouped under this heading — differences between them are subtle. Both have large, nearly globular heads of spidery florets with six long narrow reflexed petals and prominent stamens. Nerines, particularly, are planted with the upper half of the bulb exposed; lycoris need their slightly more tapered bulb necks exposed. In both cases leave them undisturbed to produce crowded clumps in at least half sun.

Nerine bowderii A beautiful pink is amongst the most widely grown. There is also a white form: 'alba'.

N. fothergilli Major is spectacular orange scarlet with gold-dust sheen.

N. filifolia is low-growing, with fine rosy-red flowers.

L. sarniensis, the Guernsey Lily, is rich coral-red, but shy-flowering unless exposed to heat during summer.

All nerines flower during April or May.

One of the most outstanding and popular lycoris is *L. aurea*, with large heads of golden yellow flowers on 50–60 cm stems during March.

L. radiata has rosy red flowers with spidery stamens 8 cm long, during April.

Sprekelia (Jacobean Lily) Ornate, orchid-like large flowers in November. Petals resemble rich, crimson, satin-textured ribbon, with the top three gracefully arching, the lower ones protruding in close fan-like formation framing the bunch of long gold-tipped stamens. Stems only 12–18 cm long, so may be used in foreground plantings or containers. Leave undisturbed, but if necessary replant during late winter in a sunny position.

Sternbergia Often referred to as 'autumn crocus' because the bright yellow flowers of *S. lutea* appear from February to April. Will stand relatively dry spots under trees but need some direct sun. If necessary transplant during mid-summer, 8–10 cm deep.

Tigridia (Jockey's Cap) Slender 40–50 cm stems with flowers 8–10 cm across; broad saucer-shaped centres are gold, heavily-spotted red, surrounded by three flimsy silk-textured red, salmon or yellow petals. Prefer well-drained, sunny position. Replant in late winter if necessary.

Tritonias Like round, thin, silky-petalled freesias in bright scarlet (and sometimes silvery pink, salmon or orange). Flowers several weeks after freesias have finished; treat as freesias.

Tuberose (*Polianthes*) Stems 1–1.5 m tall, with double white heavily-fragrant flowers,

Flowering times for spring bulbs

	August	September	October
Anemones	○●●●●●	●●●●●●	●●●●●○
Triteleia	○●●●●●	●●○	
Ranunculi		○●●●	●●●●●○
Jonquils	●●●●●●	●○	
Freesias		○●●	●●●○
Crocuses	○●●●●	●○	
Sparaxis Tritonia		○●	●●●●●○
Ixia		○●●	●●●●●●
Lachenalia: Quadricolor	○●●●●●	●●●●○	
Tricolor	○●●●●	●●●●●○	
Scilla (Bluebells)		○●●	●●●●●●
Babiana		○●●	●●●●●●
Daffodils: King Alfred types	○●●●●	●●○	
Emperor	○●●	●●●●●●	○
Dutch Irises		○●●	●●●●○
Hyacinths: Forced or refrigerated	○●●●●●	●●●●●○	
Tulips: Forced or refrigerated	○●●●●	●●●●●●	○
Untreated	○	●●●●●●	●●●●●○

flushed pink on the buds, flowering mainly during summer. Clumps flower only once. Continued flowering is achieved by lifting clumps that have flowered in early winter and removing the torpedo-like offshoots from the sides. These are planted 4–6 cm apart in good rich soil, and replanted the following winter when they should reach flowering size. However, larger offshoots 2 cm or more in diameter may be planted direct into the garden as they are likely to produce flower spikes by autumn. Give them a warm sunny position, well-mulched or composted soil, and plenty of water during spring and summer.

Tulbaghia fragrans Broad, strap-like grey-green foliage, slender 30 cm spikes with loose heads of fragrant tubular, lavender flowers flaring to flat starry petals during autumn and winter; dormant during summer. Half to full sun and protection from very heavy frost is necessary.

Valotta (Scarborough Lily) Showy heads of brilliant, light red, upfacing trumpets on pencil-thin stems from clumps of neat deep-green, strap-like foliage. Good for containers, sunny rockeries or other foreground plantings where it can be left undisturbed for at least 4 years. Plant with the top of bulb just protruding (or even a little higher in heavy soils). If necessary transplant July–August. Flowers mainly in early summer with occasional heads later.

Zephyranthus (Summer Crocus)

Z. candida has 10–15 cm-high clumps of slender, bright-green foliage and numerous papery-petalled white flowers on single stems no higher than foliage, mostly in late summer, but can appear in spring if recent rains have followed a long, dry period. Replant in winter if overcrowded.

Z. grandiflora, sometimes known as 'Rain Lily' as the large trumpet-shaped pink flowers usually burst forth in northern tropical areas in January after the first rains. Grow to about 18 cm high. New hybrid zephyranthes are developing, including good deep-golden yellow ones. All grow in sun or part shade in all but the coldest districts.

10. Cultivation of perennials

What is a perennial?

Perennial is a very broad term covering every herb with a life of more than two years, other than the more definite woody shrubs. Even here the line of demarcation between perennial and shrub is rather indistinct.

There are many different and lovely perennials that will bring interest to the garden bed, the foreground of shrubberies and rockeries or will grow happily in containers for balcony or rooftop gardeners.

Many of these easily-grown perennials provide between-season colour for outdoor show, or cut flowers when few shrubs or annuals are blooming. For example, astilbe, campanulas and geraniums start their main display when most spring annuals are finishing; the long-flowering shasta daisies, perennial phlox, agapanthus and tall orange-red pokers all flower in plenty of time for Christmas displays. Early in the new year they are joined by perennial asters in a variety of forms and colours, long-lasting pineapple lilies, echinops and dahlias, the latter continuing at least until the beautiful chrysanthemums offset autumn foliage and bright berry shrubs.

Marguerites, kingfisher daisy and French lavender can be started or cut back after one flowering and give repeat flushes of bloom at almost any time of the year.

Red ranunculus add a splash of colour to this perennial border

Choosing perennials

There are both herbaceous and evergreen perennials to suit all climates. Some star performers of the classical British perennial border such as peonies, oriental poppies and bleeding heart only perform really well in districts with cold winters and long, cool springs.

However, there are interesting and beautiful perennials that can be grown without difficulty in temperate and sub-tropical districts. A few are at home in our far northern tropical zones.

Many pages would be needed to list and describe all the perennials that can be grown in this country. A large number of the better evergreen types is found among the rockery plant range in most nurseries. These include gems such as the deep blue carpet of *litho-spermum*, its adaptable Australian native counterpart, *Dampiera diversifolia*, chalky-white *arabis* and dainty *arenaria*. For brilliant gold there is *Alyssum saxatile*, *Achillea tomentosa* and *erysimum*.

Lovely alpine phlox, thrift, pinks and others come in shades of pink, mauve, blue, white and ruby-red. If they are pot-grown they can be planted any time.

One form of easy-care gardening with perennials is to lay fairly large, irregular paving stones over well-prepared, weed-free soil, covering two-thirds or more of the surface, then to plant your perennials in the gaps between the stones.

The effect is pleasantly informal, little or no space is left for weeds and there is room to wander between your plants without compacting the soil around them. The stones also protect the soil from heavy rain or watering.

A more ordered variation of the same idea is to lay a rectangle of square paving blocks in plain grid style — omit some to leave room for plants.

After the present spring show of blue delphinums, border pinks etc. fades there are clumps of Shasta Daisies, perennial phlox and blue salvia to give colour, through early to mid-summer, followed by perennial asters, lithrum and monarda to carry the display until golden glows, helianthus, etc., take over in autumn. The mauve erigeron now flowering can be cut back to give a later show, while there are still some gaps left for clumps of early spring daffodils or tulips.

Growing perennials

General care

Before planting, work well-rotted compost and a sprinkling of complete plant food into the soil.

Established herbaceous perennials will benefit from a surface mulch of fibrous compost, which will retard weeds and improve the soil.

Exceptions are downy-foliaged plants and the herbaceous peonies. Damp mulch close to the crowns of the peonies can induce a fungus disease which blackens buds and foliage. As these plants need liberal feeding, mulch is usually applied when flowers finish.

Snails and slugs can cause irreparable damage by attacking the young shoots as they emerge in spring, so scatter snail bait.

Keep a watch for aphids on young growth and rub them off. Spray with soapy water or a mild Pyrethrum-type insecticide which will also control caterpillars, etc.

Remove spent flowers to encourage more flowers and increase the vigour of the plant by preventing seeding.

Some perennials are subject to fungus rot during prolonged wet or humid periods during summer. The most susceptible are downy-foliaged plants such as *Alyssum saxatile, arabis, artemesia,* carnations, pinks and the herbaceous delphiniums, echinops, oriental poppies and a few others with woody crowns.

The problem can be minimised by removing old matted foliage and organic material from woody crowns, and substituting some coarse sand. A scree of pebbles keeps the surface more open and drier.

Thoroughly wet the crown and surrounding soil with Bordeaux or Captan. Benlate can be sprayed, particularly on carnations and pinks.

Fungus diseases are mostly encountered when plants are grown out of their environment, e.g. cool-climate or dry-area plants in warm, humid districts.

Dividing and propagating

Some of the tougher herbaceous perennials can be left undisturbed for many years — others, such as peonies, bleeding heart and, to some extent, helleborus are better left alone.

Most other herbaceous perennials, particularly those that produce suckers or stolons from the original crown, are best divided every year or every second year. Good examples of these are yarrow (*Achillea*), asters or michaelmas daisies, campanulas, helianthus, perennial phlox, obedient plant (*Physostegia*), and shasta daisies.

Leave until new growth commences in late winter or early spring when it is easier to select the strongest sucker or new crowns for replanting. Each crown is capable of producing a clump of stems, but for a rapid clumpy effect, three or even four crowns may be placed in a circle or triangle about 35 cm across. Cut back any well-formed leaves to prevent wilting. Long roots should be trimmed.

Dense, bulbous perennials such as day-lilies, pokers and agapanthus are divided by cutting between the divisions, trimming back roots and foliage to about finger length. This is better done in winter before new growth commences.

Perennials with woody crowns such as delphiniums, echinops, lythrum, gerberas and perennial lupins can be propagated by dividing the crown, leaving at least one shoot on each division.

There is a danger of the cut crown rotting, so dip the sections in a general fungicide mixed to normal spraying strength as a safeguard. Planting in a pocket of clean, coarse sand also helps.

If dividing a crown is difficult, cut a few shoots from the crown and root them as cuttings in a mixture containing plenty of coarse sand.

Replant woody perennials such as Russell lupins and echinops every second or third year, but there is no need to divide. Wash the old crown free of soil and remove the old roots and take a few shoots to rejuvenate stock.

Oriental poppies are also propagated by cutting the thick roots into sections about 7 cm long, then striking these in an upright position in coarse sand, leaving the tops exposed.

Lily-of-the-valley flowers best when allowed to establish for a few years but will eventually become congested with its own root mat. Grow several clumps or divide a bed into three or four sections; after three years divide one of the clumps. Continue this division every second year in late autumn or early winter — only roots carrying pips or crowns of at least pencil-thickness will flower.

Evergreen perennials are propagated from tip cuttings taken when the shoot has lost its soft sappiness. Trailing types such as alpine phlox, arabis and verbenas will layer, so sections carrying roots can be cut free and replanted.

Campanula, Aster, Shasta daisy

A guide to feeding and watering

Sufficient food for your plant needs can be provided in several ways.

Manure: Spread one shovelful per sq. m of cow or horse manure or about half the amount of poultry manure prior to sowing or planting. Be sure the manure is not too fresh.

Compost: Spread one shovelful per sq. m of fairly well-decomposed compost prior to planting or sowing. Some gardeners also like to add a small handful of a complete plant food per sq. m as well as compost. The compost does not always contain sufficient nutrients, especially phosphorus.

Complete plant food: Apply about one-third cup per sq. m.

Granular fertiliser: These impart nutrients gradually over a long period: 3, 6 or 9 months. This is a safe and reliable form of feeding; however, some preparations do not release enough phosphorus to promote good flowers. Instead, there is excess leafiness and no flower buds. This situation can be corrected by applying a light scattering (a small handful) of superphosphate per sq. m and watering in.

Water-soluble plant foods: Are ideal to boost and maintain flower quality if applied at the recommended strength about once every 2 weeks from the time the flower buds form.

Only feed when the soil is damp and water well afterwards.

Watering: Recently planted or divided perennials need to be kept damp until the new roots have a chance to spread. Then give a good soaking (1–2 cm below the surface of the soil) only when the soil has dried out. Use a gentle sprinkler which can be left on long enough to penetrate evenly to the sub-soil. Keep the soil protected with a surface mulch. This acts as a buffer to gently diffuse heavy rain or careless watering.

Avoid

1. Avoid frequent surface watering which
• brings feeding roots to the surface during dry periods leaving sub-soil dry.
• causes fertiliser or soil-salt concentrations in the damp areas.
2. Avoid heavy watering in clayey soils which
• causes surface crusting when dry preventing oxygen entering the soil.
3. Avoid heavy watering in sandy soils which
• washes out the organic particles leaving raw sand.

Growing violets for fragrance

Fragrant violets picked and bunched are a delight, but these same flowers, hiding their heads under the leaves as they sometimes do, are generally regarded as too modest to enhance the garden.

It is not always so. Some of the native violets are very perky, with flowers standing rigidly above the low carpet of small foliage.

Even the florist's violets (*Viola odorata*) are not always shy. Under some growing conditions their flowers are prominently displayed.

Excessive leaves that eclipse the flowers come in the second year of growth or when growing conditions are particularly lush. Violets flower more freely from new runners, so replant them each autumn.

Where they are established as a permanent ground cover, some of the taller foliage can be clipped back in autumn. An easy way to cope with a large area is to go over them with a rotary lawnmower set at a high cutting position.

Violets that get at least half-sun always flower better than those in shade. They make a decorative cover below roses, providing a natural leafy and attractive mulch during summer; their flowers and fragrance come in winter when the roses are dormant.

They make a pleasant leafy border or semi-permanent edging for beds of annual flowers or a leafy green mat below shrubs where their cover is dense enough to retard most weeds.

A good way to establish an easy-care cover of violets is to spread a surface mulch of leaf-mould or fibrous compost 2.5–5 cm thick and plant rows of violets about a span apart through the mulch. Rake back a band of mulch just wide enough to plant the row then rake it back again to cover the soil completely. Most mulches will remain intact until the violet leaf-cover thickens up.

Violets can also be grown on balconies or ledges as their comparatively shallow roots allow them to grow in low troughs, bowls, strawberry pots or even hanging baskets.

There are many varieties: the so-called red Admiral Avalon which is really a rosy-purple; pale buff-yellow lutea, white, and several doubles. However, the most popular are the deeper violet fragrant types such as Princess of Wales.

Wild violets are little charmers ideal for ground cover planting and most of them flower freely for a very long time.

One of the most widely grown Australian native species is *Viola hederifolia* which keeps producing prolific batches of dainty little pale-violet, white-edged flowers that stand well above the slightly lobed or scalloped foliage.

Some people regard this violet as invasive because it runs so readily but its mat of light bright-green can be very acceptable in areas where it is not competing with other low growth, or in part of the garden enclosed by a concrete path or mower strip.

This violet is ideal for hanging baskets as its enthusiastic runners trail gracefully and it flowers well in areas too shaded for other violets.

Dividing: Wild violets do not need regular dividing and if you want to propagate them just trim off foliage, lift roots or runners and set the knobby little crowns just below soil surface.

Florist's violets or varieties of *Viola odorata* are often left undisturbed for years but for the best performance divide, or more correctly replant, beds each year in early autumn. For this choose the more substantial of the new outer runners. If these are in short supply, lift the old corky-looking crowns, trim them off 2.5–5 cm below the lower leaves, trim off all foliage and plant them as cuttings.

Unless soil is very clayey they can be set into their permanent positions about a span apart and lightly shaded for a week or so with leafy twigs or they can be set out a few centimetres apart in shaded seed beds or boxes then planted out when new roots and foliage have formed.

They can adapt to most soils but will give better performance if you prepare the soil as you would for any seedlings, adding some well-rotted compost and a scattering of complete plant food. A scattering of lime also helps unless the soil is naturally limey or has been limed within the last year.

The charming carnation

Carnations were cherished for their delightful clove scent even before the Christian era.

The modern carnation was developed from the little fine-petalled *Dianthus caryophyllus*, its name coming from the Greek word *dios* — 'divine', and *anthos* — flower. Caryophyllus was the name for the clove tree which the carnation's perfume resembles.

Carnation-growing now seems to be regarded as a specialist's field. Don't be deterred. I have seen all types growing and flowering happily in a variety of containers, from block bottom plastic nursery bags to window boxes.

The present-day strains of bedding carnations are available from either seed or seedlings and are excellent for cutting or garden show. The blooms may not last as well as 'perpetual flowering' carnations but are prolific. They exhaust themselves in a season, so treat them as annuals. Plant in autumn for a mass of blooms from mid to late spring.

The more refined perpetual flowering carnations, such as Avonmore and Sim types, are regarded as perennials but even these do better if replaced every second year.

Many gardeners do not realise the advantage of pinching back or 'stopping' young carnation plants. This delays the flowering but makes a more attractive bushy plant. Break or cut the plant back to the top or second top joint when it has made 8–10 sets of leaves to force shoots to come from leaf junctions farther down the stem; treat these the same way when they have made about 8 sets of leaves. Keep doing this until you have a plant with many shoots, then let them run up to flower.

Some growers give an extra stopping to delay flowering. For example, although 'perpetual' types flower over a long period, plants

started in autumn are inclined to make a flush-flowering in late October or early November; an extra stopping in early spring and perhaps another later could bring the plants to a peak at Christmas.

This might suggest there are set times for stopping plants, but actually it is a progressive thing, done only when a shoot has reached about the eight-leaf stage. It is better for the plant if only one stem is stopped at a time. Keep plants compact by cutting flowers well down the stem.

The best cuttings come from the centre of a flower stem. A good soil for striking them is made by mixing 3 parts coarse sand with 1 part of moistened peatmoss.

Trim the top half of the leaves to reduce the risk of wilting and to let you see when the cutting has rooted and is making growth, for new centre leaves will be obvious above the trimmed ones.

Carnations grow in a variety of soils but prefer a sandy loam. Clayey soils can be lightened by mixing coarse sand lightly into the surface. Unless the soil is already limey dig in up to a cup of garden lime or dolomite per square metre.

A good drainage is essential, and if there is doubt about this use built-up beds.

Systemic fungicides such as Benlate or Bavistin make coping with fungus diseases comparatively easy.

For additional cultivation details see 'Reference Guide'.

Growing day-lilies

Day-lilies offer easy-care gardening with an abundance of showy flowers during late spring and summer in all districts. Most gardeners know the old double orange day-lily (*Hemerocallis fulva*), but it is surprising that more of the lovely modern hybrids are not yet widely used. Several hundred new varieties have been raised during the past 15–20 years.

Hemerocallis

These have new colours including ivory, lemon, soft mauve, purple, red and deep bronze, and larger flowers. The recently introduced tetraploids (their chromosomes are doubled by colchicine treatment) produce larger plants and flowers, have thicker flower stems and usually carry more flower buds. Miniature strains are also becoming available.

One criticism levelled at day-lilies is that the blooms last for one day only. The modern strains — especially under good growing conditions — can carry from 50–100 buds per stem, giving good continuity of flower. Regular watering during the flowering season will encourage extra flower stems.

Day-lilies are so adaptable that they will grow in practically any situation, standing long periods of dryness or over-wet soil in sun or shade but flowers are more profuse where the plants get at least half-sun and have occasional soakings in a reasonably well-drained soil.

A light feeding in spring and again as flowering begins will improve both the number and quantity of flowers. Use either a complete plant food or poultry manure scattered lightly around the clumps, then watered in well.

Day-lilies are planted or divided during winter when the clumps are dormant. Replant new stock before roots dry out, setting the crown at ground level. If dividing at other times, cut back the foliage to within a few centimetres of the crown. Dividing each year is not necessary. Flowers and appearance are best when clumps are undisturbed for at least two years.

Their long, tough roots make day-lilies excellent soil binders for steep banks or where something is needed to stop soil washing away. Their roots are more restrained and less avaricious than those of agapanthus.

Day-lilies are excellent in perennial borders and make attractive clumps between groups of shrubbery. Flower quality may not be at its best where other roots are competing for moisture and nutrients, but they do surprisingly well.

Some of the new tetraploid day-lilies include outstanding varieties such as Higashi: a beautiful porcelain-textured ivory white flushed with pink, blooms 15 cm across; Royal Diamonds: glowing terracotta red petals attractively interrupted by a rosy-red zone; Tallyman: unusual deep vermilion flower with a rich-gold throat; American Revolution: velvety, deep-wine red with tiny green heart blending into yellow before meeting the back red petals which fold gently back and Mountain Violet: rich-plum violet with distinct purple petal spot and small green throat. Some may cost as much as a dozen plants of other varieties.

Miniature day-lilies include gems such as Little Wine Cup: wine with small, green heart, blooms all seasons; Little Much: ruffled lemon with red eye marking above green heart edged yellow; Miniature King: butter-yellow blooms with a faint brushed halo of pink, gold heart; Lolabel: iridescent chrome-yellow.

Some gardeners like to raise their own new varieties from seed. Many day-lilies do not self-pollinate but will cross freely with other varieties or may be hand-pollinated. Seed pods ripen in autumn and seed may be sown immediately or kept until spring. Seedlings should flower in two years.

For additional cultivation details see 'Reference Guide'.

Hemerocallis hybrid (tetraploid type)

Geraniums for year-round colour

You can have colour from geraniums right through the year, if not from flowers then from the leaves.

They flower mainly through late spring and summer but the foliage of the fancy-leaf types is brightest in the cooler months.

Geraniums do well in a range of garden soils and any position that has some direct sunlight, good drainage, and isn't windswept. They can be grown to perfection in pots.

Most geranium enthusiasts have the greater part of their collection in pots, not because of garden space problems but so that plants can be moved about to best advantage for display. Gardeners in cold climates move them under cover during winter, then bring them out again when the more severe frosts are over. This is how the window boxes and chalet gardens in alpine areas of Europe suddenly burst into colour with geraniums in the warmer months. Another advantage of container growing is that it allows the plants to be enjoyed for indoor decoration but they should not be indoors for more than a day or two — geraniums need fresh air and sunshine.

The main secret of good growth is to prune each year and encourage bushy growth and flowerheads by pinching back the new shoots that follow pruning, and replacing old woody ones with cuttings taken from them while they still have some vigour left.

Pruning of geraniums grown for their flowers is best done progressively, as each branch finishes flowering, in one operation about late March or early April. Regal pelargoniums finish flowering earlier so should be pruned in February.

Fancy-leaf geraniums are pruned earlier still, generally in December or January. This means sacrificing some of the flowers but it allows the plant time to build up plenty of new growth before winter when foliage colour is at its best.

With zonal pelargoniums — geraniums, as we know them — the main stems or branches that have flowered are cut back to within about a finger length of the base or where they emerge from an older stem.

Any new shoots that have not flowered are pinched out at the tip (or cut back if this leaves them well above the general height of the pruned plant).

Regal pelargoniums do not take kindly to such heavy pruning. Since there is risk of losing the plant, leave a few leaves on one or two stems or strike some of the tip growths just in case the pruning backfires on you.

Ivy geraniums rarely require much pruning but if a plant is straggly the long stems can be cut back to a side shoot — once this is developed pinch out the tip to encourage denser growth. The ivy geraniums usually remain productive and attractive for a number of years but if one becomes straggly replace from tip cuttings.

Pinching back or tip pruning is additional to the main pruning.

Every time a new shoot gets to about finger length or makes four to five well-formed leaves, pinch out the tip growth and the pair of small immature leaves behind it to induce shoots to come from lower leaf junctions. Treat these the same way and keep up the tip pruning until flower buds begin to appear, or, in the case of coloured-leaf types, until a good-looking leafy plant is formed, hopefully by winter. Even then you can still cut back any growth that needs it as new shoots are also attractive.

Feeding: After pruning give some dry mix complete plant food mainly below outer foliage and water well. Repeat in 6–8 weeks but only after a thorough watering if the plant is in a container.

When flowers begin to show colour some people prefer to change to soluble plant foods which help to boost size and lustre of blooms.

Foliage colour of the fancy-leaf types is often brighter when the plants are kept a little underfed, so feeding can be suspended for the season when they reach a reasonable size.

For additional cultivation details see 'Reference Guide'.

Pelargonium zonal

Pelargonium regal

Pelargonium regal

Perennials for special purposes

Larger evergreen perennials

Centaurea cineraria (Dusty Miller)
Cheiranthus mutabilis (Perennial Wallflower)
Chrysanthemum fruticans (Marguerite)
Cineraria maritima (Silver Cineraria)
Felicia amelloides (Kingfisher Daisy)
Geraniums (various types)
Iris (tall bearded)
Lavandula dentata (French Lavender)
L. officinalis (English Lavender)
Dimorphotheca ecklonis (Black-eyed Susan)
D. barberae
See also page 117

Perennials suitable for cut flowers

Achillea (Milfoil, Yarrow)
Anemone
Aster
Astible
Chrysanthemum
Chrysanthemum maximum (Shasta Daisy)
Coreopsis
Dahlia
Delphinium
Gaillardia
Gypsophila
Helenium
Iris
Peony
Pyrethrum
Rudbeckia
Veronica longifolia subsessilis

Evergreen perennials for edging

Alyssum saxatile (Dwarf Goldentuft)
Arabis alpina (Alpine Rock-Cress)
Campanula
Cerastium (Snow-in-Summer)
Dianthus
Iberus sempervirens (Evergreen Candytuft)
Nepeta (Mussin Catmint)
Sedum
Viola cornuta (Tufted Pansy)

Perennials for background planting

Campanula (taller types)
Delphinium
Echinops ritro (Globe Thistle)
Hemerocallis (Day-Lily)
Salvia azurea
Thalictrum (Dusty Meadow-Rue)

Perennials for foliage effect

Achillea filipendulina (Yarrow)
Achillea tomentosa (Woolly Yarrow)
Artemisia (Wormwood — various)
Hosta (Plantain-Lily)
Lavendula officinalis (Lavender)
Nepeta (Mussin Catmint)
Santolina chamaecyparissus (Lavender Cotton)

Growing problems and solutions

Plant	Symptom	Cause	Solution
Acanthus	Foliage skeletonised or with large holes	Usually snails	Spray with Methiocarb, snail spray or apply snail baits
Achillea	Distorting of new growth	Aphids	Use Pyrethrum-type or Malathion spray
Ajuga	Ash-like patches over foliage	Powdery mildew	Spray with Benlate or general fungicide
Alyssum saxatile	Foliage suddenly drooping or wilting	Fungus stem rot	Remove and burn plant or affected section of clump, clean away mass of dead foliage below others. See heading 'Rock plants'
Amaryllis	See Bulbs	See Bulbs	See Bulbs
Anemone	Foliage crimped and twisted downwards	Aphids	See Achillea
	Stunted yellow or bronze foliage	May be poor drainage or due to heavy use of high-nitrogenous fertiliser	If appropriate improve drainage or minimise fertiliser concentration by flooding soil liberally
Arabis	Centre of plant darkening and softening	Fungus rot	See heading 'Rock plants'
Aster (perennial)	Ash-like film over foliage	Mildew	See Ajuga
Astilbe	Leaves with brown crisp margins	Usually due to dryness but occasionally potash deficiency	Keep soil continuously moist, otherwise see chapter 'Get to know your garden', heading 'Potassium'
Canterbury Bells Single, Double, or Cup-and-saucer types	Green or grey aphids on young growth or clustered under leaves which are usually curled downwards	Aphids	See Ageratum
	Leaves with dull sand-blasted appearance	Red spider mites	Dust with sulphur or spray with Folimat
	Powdery film over foliage	Mildew	See Ajuga
Carnation (Bedding types)	Flower buds hollow	Usually due to frost damage	
	Leaves with purple spotting or eruptions, or some shrivelling toward tips	It may be difficult to distinguish between several different leaf spots, rust or mildew damage	Benlate gives general control of all these diseases, except die-back which calls for new plants and soil
	White streaking of dark flowers, browning on pale ones	Thrips	Alternately spray with Rogor or Endosulphan (Thiodan) each week
Chieranthus (perennial wallflower)	Buff-coloured tracery in foliage	Leaf miner	Spray Lebaycid
Chrysanthemum (see also Shasta daisy)	Tiny black or brown insects clustered below flower buds	Black aphis	Use Pyrethrum-type spray or Malathion
	Segment of flower brown and sunken	Bud grub	Spray with Endosulphan at weekly intervals while problem persists
	Grey scribble-like tracery on foliage	Leaf miner	Spray Lebaycid
	Wedge-like blackening in lower foliage, followed by general shrivelling	Leaf eelworm (nematode)	Spray Folimat (with caution)
Crassula (multicava and others)	Numerous irregular small pits on foliage	Brown vegetable weevil	Spray Carbaryl each week while trouble persists
Dahlia	Lush foliage, few flowers	Feeding only with high-nitrogen soluble fertilisers or slow-release granules	Apply one handful super-phosphate around each plant and water in
	Dark-green, distorted top foliage	Can be earlier insect damage but also molybdenum or boron deficiency due to heavy feeding	See chapter 'Get to know your garden', heading 'Boron'
	Foliage with dull sand-blasted appearance	Red spider mites	See Canterbury Bells
	Edges of petals brown, tiny black insects in flowers	Thrips	See Carnation; also thrips under roses chart in 'Trees and Shrubs' chapter
	Foliage or blooms eaten	Apart from snails, probably loopers or heliotis caterpillars; also see earwigs	Spray with Pyrethrum-type sprays or Endosulphan
	Foliage or blooms eaten	Snails on foliage	Methiocarb spray

Plant	Symptom	Cause	Solution
Delphinium	Ash-like film on foliage	Mildew	Dust with sulphur or Benlate
	Sudden wilting	Crown rot	See Alyssum
Dianthus	See Carnation	See Carnation	See Carnation
Digitalis	See Foxglove	See Foxglove	See Foxglove
Erigeron	Grey powdery patches on foliage	Mildew	See Ajuga
Freesia	See Bulbs	See Bulbs	See Bulbs
Foxglove	Reddish-brown flecks on foliage	Rust	Spray with Zineb or Mancozeb
	Foliage with dull-brown paper appearance	Red spider mites	As for Canterbury Bells
Geranium (Pelargonium)	Yellowish spots on leaves, velvety brown circles on reverse side	Rust	Remove badly-infected foliage and spray with Zineb
	Brown rot at base of plant or cutting	Stem rot	Take tip cuttings from unaffected growth, discard and burn remainder
	Semi-transparent leaf blotches (mainly ivy type)	Bacterial leaf spot	Remove and burn badly-affected leaves and spray with copper spray
	Foliage or buds eaten	Looper or similar caterpillar	Pyrethrum-type spray or Carbaryl or Endosulphan
	Flower heads rotting during wet conditions	Botrytis rot	Spray with Captan or Mancozeb
Gerbera	Deformed flowers	Usually aphids damage in bud stage	Pyrethrum-type spray or Malathion
	Flowers with rotting centres	Usually bud grub	Spray with Endosulphan
	Flowers green	Greening virus, transmitted by aphids	Remove and burn affected plants
	White or cream, raised flecks mainly behind foliage	White rust	Spray with lime sulphur (late in day as young foliage may burn)
	Plant suddenly wilting	Crown rot	Save remainder by ensuring soil does not wash into crown and, if necessary, by lifting entire clump to raise crown slightly above soil
Helianthemum (Sun Rose)	Dull, lustreless, lightly mottled foliage	Red spider mites	As for Canterbury Bells
Lavender	Browning of lower foliage	Partly due to age but may be also downy mildew	Spray with Zineb; old plants best replaced with cuttings after about two years
Peony	Buds and foliage blackening	Botrytis (bud blast)	Avoid mulching or manuring plants until after flowering
	Failing to flower	Plants not yet well established or climate too warm	Best left undisturbed for many years; climate with long, cool spring is essential
Penstemon	Sandy mottling of foliage	Red spider mites	Dust with sulphur or spray Folimat. Misting foliage with water also helps
Polyanthus	Dull pale foliage	Red spider mites	As above
	Limp, stunted growth, small, downy white insects under leaf and sometimes on roots	Mealy bugs	Above treatment also controls
Shasta Daisy (Chrysanthemum maximum)	Tattered petals	Weevil or small brown beetle	Spray Endosulphan or Malathion
	Grey film over foliage	Mildew	Spray Benlate
Stokesia (Stoke's Aster)	Grey film over foliage	Mildew	Dust sulphur or use copper spray
Verbena	Grey film over foliage	Mildew	Dust with sulphur or spray Benlate
	Dull mottled foliage	Red spider mites	As for Canterbury Bells
Viola	See Pansy	See Pansy	See Pansy
Wallflower	Pale tracery in foliage	Leaf miner	Spray Rogor or Lebaycid

Perennials enduring shade

Aconitum wilsonii (Azure Monkshood)
Ajuga (Bugle Flower)
Bergenia
Convollaria majalis (Lily-of-the-Valley)
Dicentra eximia (Fringed Bleeding Heart)
Helleborus (Christmas Rose)
Hosta (Plantain-Lily)
Polygonatum biflorum (Small Solomons-Seal)
Thalictrum

Perennials enduring semi-shade

Anemone japonica (Japanese Anemone)
Aquilegia — hybrids (Columbine)
Asperula odorata (Woodruff)
Campanula (Harebell)
Digitalis (Foxglove)
Doronicum (Leopardbane)
Hemerocallis (Day-Lily)
Monarda
Primula (all types)
Pulmonaria
Silene caroliniana (Catchfly)

Perennials for well-drained soils

Achillea (Yarrow)
Anthemis tinctoria (Yellow Camomile)
Arctotis (Aurora Daisy)
Chrysanthemums
Dianthus deltoides (Maiden Pink)
D. plumarius (Grass Pink)
Echinops ritro (Globe Thistle)
Euphorbia (Milkwort)
Gazania
Geranium (all types)
Gypsophila (Baby's Breath)
Helianthus (Sunflower)
Limonium latifolium (Sea Lavender)
Lychnis chalcedonica (Maltese Cross)
Papaver orientalis
Phlox subulata (Moss Phlox)
Rudbeckia laciniata (Golden Glow)
Sedum Spectabile (Showy Stonecrop)

Perennials for wet situations

Acorus
Ajuga
Anigozanthos flavidus
Astilbe
Canna
Chlorophytum
Cyperus alternifolius
Dietes
Helleborus orientalis
Helxine
Hemerocallis
Hosta
Iris louisiana
I. kaempferi
I. spuria
I. pseudocorus
Lythrum
Ligularia

Mesembryanthum

Euphorbia wulfenii

Gazania and blue Kingfisher daisy

Heliopsis and Shasta daisies.

Chamomile (Anthemis nobilis)

Hybrid Gazania and Alyssum saxatile

A reference guide to perennials

Key to type of plant

How they grow — Code of types and characteristics

SE following the plant name means *shrubby evergreen*. Although regarded as permanent most of them become straggly after the first year's growth unless pruned back after flowering, and are better when renewed every second year from tip cuttings.

ER stands for *evergreen rockery-type* plant with semi-upright dome or cushion-like growth.

EC means spreading *evergreen carpeter* trailer or ground cover.

H is for *herbaceous*, meaning that the plant dies down in late autumn or winter, and remains as a dormant crown or rhizomes (storage stems) which produce growth or flower shoots again in spring.

A is for *alpine*. 'A' alone means that it is a recognised alpine plant needing cool conditions and good drainage, even though plenty of water may also be essential, especially during spring.

'A' following other letters suggests that for successful growth (in any but cool districts) it is as well to treat the plant as an alpine.

H is the average height of flower spikes; **W** is the average width of plant after one season's good growth.

P following main text is the type of propagation normally used.

Acanthus mollis (Oyster Plant) H. 2 m x 1–1.5 m. Clump (to .75 mm high) of large, handsome, dark, glossy leaves. Tall spikes of papery white, slate and buff florets appear in late spring or early summer. An exception to general herbaceous range as it dies down in midsummer, and foliage emerges again in autumn. Grow in sun or shade. P: seed; or divide during dormant period.

Achillea (Yarrow or Millfoil) Numerous species, all preferring sun, for cool and temperate climates.

A. filipendula H. 1–1.5 m x 30 cm. Lacy grey foliage clump, tall stems with flat heads of small golden florets in late spring. P: division in winter.

A. millefolium H. 30 cm x 60 cm. Dense clumps of finely divided olive-green foliage with ruby-rose flower heads paling to pinkish buff as they age; spreads vigorously. P: division during winter.

A. tomentosa H to EC. 12 cm x 15 cm. Silvery-grey, woolly rosettes with heads of bright golden flowers in spring. P: division of crown or cuttings during winter.

Aconitum wilsonii (Monkshood) H. 1 m x 20 cm. Slender stems of unusual, hooded, rich blue flowers in late summer. Prefers dappled shade or morning sun, cool to cooler temperate areas. P: divide in winter, best undisturbed for several years.

Acorus gramineus (Winter Flag) ER. 18 cm x 15 cm. Like a tiny, variegated flax; suits most light-to-heavy shaded areas. P: divide in winter.

Agapanthus ER. 1.5 m x 1 m. Tough, heavily rooted, soil-binding clumps with dark green strap-like leaves to .75 m topped by tall-stemmed globular heads of blue or white florets, mostly in early summer. Sun or part shade under trees; all but the coldest districts. P: divide in winter but best undisturbed.

Agathea see Felicia

Ajuga (Bugle Flower) EC. 18 cm (in flower) x 30 cm. Clumps of ground-hugging rosetted, smooth foliage. In cooler climates particularly it produces a delightful array of erect 15 cm spikes of blue flowers in spring.

A. *metallica* has deep bronze to green foliage.

A. *multicolor* is irregularly blotched with copper tones, and Burgundy Lace is mostly rosy-purple to bronze and cream. Grows in damp to moderately drained soils in full sun to shade. A good decorative gentle ground cover. P: division of clumps.

Alstromeria aurantiaca H. 50 cm–90 cm x 70 cm. Fleshy-rooted perennial with heads of brown-spotted orange trumpets during late spring and summer — variety Lutea is yellow. Ligtu hybrids come in mauve, pink and purple tones. Best in well-drained rich soil, undisturbed for at least 3 years, and mulched with compost in late winter. They prefer a dry autumn and cool winter.

A. *pulchella* (slender red trumpets with lime green tips) becomes invasive in warm temperate districts in light soils. P: seed or division of rhizomes in winter.

Altenanthera (Exhibition Border) ER. 15 cm x 15 cm. Bushy little many-stemmed clumps with slender red and bronze or cream and green foliage, often used for bordering or formal bedding designs in all but very frosty areas. (In the latter, cuttings may be struck in autumn and kept frost-protected for spring planting in the open.) Needs at least half sun. P: cuttings or seed.

Alyssum saxatile ER. 'A'. 30 cm x 45 cm. Long blue-grey leaves in dense rosettes, below slender-stemmed, wide-branching, cloud-like heads of tiny golden yellow florets, in spring and occasionally again in early summer. Best in cool climates as clumps are fungus prone during humid summers. Removing dead base foliage from below clumps helps deter fungus diseases. P: cuttings, or seed (for flowers in the first spring seed needs to be shown by mid-summer).

Androsace (Rock Jasmine) EC. 5 cm x 30 cm. Gentle trailer with small rosetted silvery foliage and lovely round heads of small phlox-like, pale pink flowers with crimson and yellow eyes. Best in cool to cooler temperate areas. P: cuttings or seed.

Anemone (Anemone japonica) H. 1–1.5 m x 70 cm. Suckers vigorously and has slender-branched stems with clusters of beautiful simple white poppy-like flowers with yellow centre stamens. There are also single and double mauve-to-pink varieties. Flowers mainly late summer and autumn. Cool to warmer temperate areas. P: division of crowns in winter, or seed.

Anemone japonica

Aurora daisy (Arctotis hybrida)

Floxgloves (Digitalis)

Perennial aster

Star daisy (Chrysanthemum parvifolium)

A. blanda H. 15 cm x 18 cm. Marguerite-like mauve, pink or purple flowers, for cool climates. P: seed.

A. coronaria — and St. Brigid types — best treated as annuals (see under Bulbs).

A. numerosa A. 12 cm x 15 cm. Delightful small daisy-like flowers in soft pink or blue; cool to cooler temperate areas with a winter mulch. P: division of roots during autumn or early winter.

Anthemis nobilis (Chamomile) EC. 12–15 cm x 30 cm. Fine, light green foliage, small white daisies. The herbal Roman chamomile is used for lawns.

A. cupaniana EC. 25–30 cm x 1 m. Grey-green foliage and a profusion of cleanly cut white daisies with more size and substance than above; flowers from early spring into summer.

A. tinctoria EC. 40–45 cm x 50 cm. Dark green fern-like foliage and bright golden daisies, mainly in late summer. P: seed or division of clumps in winter.

Anigozanthus (Kangaroo Paw) *A. flavidus* ER. 1.5–2 m x 1 m. Dramatic clumps of sword-like, bright green foliage and tall branching spikes of either lime green, buff-gold or bronze-red tinted, velvety, tubular flowers; the easiest variety to grow in humid areas or high rainfall districts, as it grows naturally in marshy areas.

A. manglessi the showy, rich, velvety red and green W.A. emblem, less than half *A. flavidus* dimensions, needs gravelly, quick draining soil, and prefers reasonably moist winter conditions but dry summers, otherwise subject to black leaf spots or 'ink disease'. Stands only moderate frost. P: division of clumps in winter or seed.

Aquilegia (Columbine) H. 50 cm x 40 cm. Also appropriately known as Grannies' Bonnets, slender-branched stems with slightly nodding flowers resembling wide-trumpeted daffodils; the long spurred cup usually creamy yellow with slender back petals in apricot, pink, lavender blue or maroon. The clumpy blue-green foliage is attractively divided. Flowers mainly mid-to-late spring in all but tropical climates; sun or part shade. P: seed sown by mid-summer to flower the first spring.

Arabis EC. 'A'. 15 cm x 60 cm. Dense mat of trailing rosetted grey-green foliage with chalk-white spikes of double or single flowers in spring; cool to temperate areas. P: use more vigorous rosettes with 3–4 cm of stem as cuttings; or layer.

Arctotis hybrida (Aurora Daisy) ER. 30–40 cm x 50–60 cm. Colourful, long-lived and drought-resisting large daisies in mauve, purple, mahogany and tawny shades with irregularly shaped grey-green foliage. Flowers mainly in spring; cool to semi-tropical areas with good drainage and at least half sun. P: seed sown in late summer; or cuttings.

Arenaria balerica EC. 2 cm x 18 cm. Emerald green moss-like carpeter with tiny white flowers.

A. caespitosa aurea similar to latter but in golden green tight hummocks, both prefer damp soil in part shade.

A. montana has more open growth, wandering, wiry stems lightly spangled with beautiful white 10-cent-size saucer-shaped flowers, mostly in spring. P: first two from division; *A. montana* from layers, tip cuttings or seed.

Armeria (Thrift) All varieties have tight tufts of thin fairly rigid grey-green foliage and globular heads of paper-like florets in pink, sometimes white and rosy red. Flower from mid-spring into summer.

A. maritima ER. 15–20 cm x 15–18 cm.

A. pseudo-armeria (A. latifolia) taller growing to 60 cm.

A. caespitosa varieties make small domes of tightly packed foliage only about 5 cm high with small pink to white flowers just above the leaves. Armerias prefer a slightly limy, well-drained soil, an open aspect and stand salty winds. In humid districts treat as A. P: divisions as cuttings or seed.

Artemesia absynthum (Wormwood) SE. 1.5 m x 1 m. Lacy silver-grey foliage with pungent aroma.

A. lactifolia ER. 1.5 m x 60 cm. Erect stems with silvery foliage.

A. nitida ER. 9 cm x 25 cm. Lacy silver leaves with silky texture, treat as A.

Aster novi-belgi (Perennial Aster, Michaelmas or Easter Daisy) H. 22–150 cm x 25–50 cm. Whether dwarf, medium or tall all types have erect spire-like sprays of fine-petalled daisies up to 20-cent-coin-size in white, mauve, lavender, pink, lavender-blue and purple. Flower late summer; cool and temperate areas; full sun. P: divide clumps in late winter or early spring, preferably annually.

A. alpinus mat of low foliage, single-stemmed lilac-blue flowers. Likes moist, heavy loam.

A. yunnanensis small lavender-blue daisies on 30–38 cm stems. Long flowering. Sun or part-shade.

Astilbe (Goat's Beard) H. 60 cm x 30 cm. Erect, plume-like spires of tiny florets in mauve, pink, white or rose-red in late spring; handsome, glossy, base foliage; prefers damp situation, half sun, in cool to temperate areas. P: division of crowns in winter.

Bergenia cordifolia (formerly *Saxifraga*) ER. 25 cm x 35 cm. Loose rosette or large smooth round leathery leaves with waxy stems of attractive pink flowers during late winter and early spring. Best in light shade. P: division of root stocks in winter.

Brachycome (Swan River Daisy) ER. 25 cm x 30 cm. Finely divided dark foliage, 10-cent-size finely rayed mauve to pink daisies on thread-like stems, mostly summer flowering, well-drained soil. P: seed or cuttings.

Caltha palustris (Marsh Marigold) H to ER. Clumps of heart-shaped dark glossy foliage, stems of flowers like giant golden buttercups to 5 cm across during spring and early summer, some double forms. Prefers sunny but wet situation, excellent marsh plants for cool to cooler temperate districts — may spread rapidly from its vigorous stolons. P: seed or division of clumps during winter.

Campanula (Hare Bells) H. Lovely sprays of bell flowers, mostly blue from mid-spring to early summer.

C. persicifolia 1 m x 30 cm;

C. poscharskyana 22 cm x 35–40 cm; lavender-blue flowers.

C. cochlearifolia and *C. isophylla* 10 cm x 30–35 cm; pale blue flowers.

Cool and temperate climates; dwarf types trail attractively, suit hanging baskets; some partly evergreen, best in part shade. P: division of clumps during winter or seed.

Canna H. Tall types to 2 m. Dwarf .5–1 m x 50 cm. Handsome bronze or green foliage, large heads of bright red, orange, yellow and orange or pink flowers during summer and autumn; suit wet or dry conditions in all climates, but remove and store roots during winter in cold districts. Prefer full sun. P: divide clumps in winter or seed.

Carnation ER. 40–60 cm x 30 cm. The tall, large-flowered Sim types are the popular florists' carnation but the more compact perpetual-flowering types are excellent cutting flowers, and if well grown are more attractive in the garden.

Carnations prefer an open, sunny position and good, well-drained, slightly limy soil, but do quite well in poor sand with some well-rotted compost added. In all soils also mix in either bone dust or a complete plant food (one-third cup per sq m) before planting.

Space the plants about 30 cm apart. For more compact growth and more flowers from perpetual-flowering types, break out the top joint of the plant when it is 10–12 cm high. Repeat this with each shoot following until a bushy, cushion-shaped plant is built up, then allow shoots to run up to flower. Apply light sprinklings of complete plant food (only about one level tablespoon per sq m) every six weeks. Water thoroughly but gently, then allow surface to dry out before watering again. Disbud to one bud per stem for larger flowers. Cut flower stems well down within 2–3 cm of the base to keep the plant compact and clumpy.

Sim types are treated similarly but plants are allowed to develop more height between 'stoppings' (or breaking out centres) and flower stems should be staked.

Propagation

Although perennials, carnations are at their best during their first year. Therefore it is always advisable to have new plants coming on from cuttings. The best or most vigorous cuttings are usually toward the centre of the flower stem. Break them off, trim back top leaves and base of stem and lowest leaves, then firm them into light soil, preferably a mixture of three parts coarse river sand and one of moistened peatmoss. Transplant when new growth shows above the original trimmed-back foliage.

Note: Knot root caused by eelworm (nematode) and collar rot can be a problem. The first can be controlled by treatment with chemicals such as Nemagon or impregnated Nemacur granules, which are mixed into the soil at planting time.

Collar rot is more difficult. Its spread can be checked by removing the infected plant and watering neighbouring plants with Benlate, wetting both stems and surrounding soil. Benlate can also be sprayed as a preventive during humid conditions.

Centaurea cineraria (Dusty Miller) SE. 1 m x 1 m. Bushy dome shape with long lacy silver-grey leaves, small mauve cornflower-like flowers. Grown mainly for foliage accent or contrast; likes well drained, open sunny position. P: tip cuttings, preferably in autumn or winter.

Cerastium (Snow-in-Summer) EC. 8 cm x 40–50 cm. Dense mat of small silver-grey foliage, topped with small saucer-shaped white flowers in spring. Good ground cover for banks or moderately dry sunny situations. P: layers or tip cuttings in late winter.

Chamomile see *Anthemis*

Cheiranthus mutabilis (Alpine Wallflower) SE. 50 cm x 70 cm. Bushy with short flower spikes varying from buff to mauve to purple. Also variegated form. Cool to semitropical; at least half-sun. P: cuttings from tips or side shoots.

Chlorophytum (Spider Plant) EC. 30 cm x 60 cm. Rosettes of slender strap-like cream and green variegated foliage with a decorative cascade of plantlets on old flower stems. Ideal drought-resistant trailer for baskets or ground cover below trees, best with half to full shade. P: replant plantlets or divide clumps.

Chrysanthemum (Japanese or florists' types) ER. 1.5–2 m depending on type and treatment. They need a well-drained, only moderately rich soil. Complete plant food or rotted manure should be added when planting out, but once growth is established the secret of good quality flowers lies in gradual feeding — just light dustings of complete plant food (or rose food) no more than 2 teaspoons per sq m, or ¼ strength soluble plant food each week.

Build up a compact plant by 'stopping' or removing tip of plant when it is about 12 cm high, then repeat this with each side shoot when it reaches finger length, until late December.

Stake each plant with three stakes around its outer limits, and tie stems over 30 cm. Disbud to one bud per stem for large, flowered types; for cluster types remove only centre bud. Exhibitors of chrysanthemums practise far more involved techniques — if interested, you can learn about them from chrysanthemum societies.

Check for black aphis, chiefly below buds; either rub them off or use a pyrethrum-type spray. Blackening of lower foliage is generally due to leaf eel worm (nematode). Control chemically by very toxic spray (Metasystox) or by stripping and burning the affected leaves and the few immediately above them. Remember that the pest or eggs could be transferred by the hands.

Chrysanthemum frutescens
see Marguerite

Chrysanthemum maximum
see Shasta Daisy

Clivia (Kaffir Lily) ER. 60 cm x 70 cm. One of the toughest and most decorative plants for shade areas. Establishes well under trees or in large pots. Clumps of dark green, firm strap-like foliage. *C. miniata* has showy heads of orange-red trumpets in spring. *C. hybrida* is brighter and a little larger in all respects. *C. nobilis* has clusters of pendulous tubular flowers. P: division of clumps in winter or seed.

Columbine see *Aquilegia*

Convallaria (Lily of the Valley) H. 20 cm x 15 cm. Needs cold winter and a fairly cool spring to flower well. Prefers well-composted or mulched soil and about half shade. Only roots with plump 'pips' or shoots flower the first year. P: division in winter, replanting with shoot 2 to 3 cm below surface.

Convolvulus mauritanicus EC. 15 cm x 50 cm. Dense trailer or ground cover, attractive with masses of lavender-blue flowers, mainly during spring and summer (non-invasive). P: layers or tip cuttings.

Coreopsis (Calliopsis) H to ER. 60 cm x 45 cm. Dense clumps of base foliage with flat 6–8 cm, bright golden flowers on slender branch stems in early summer; often naturalised in open areas. P: seed or division during winter.

Crassula multicava (London Pride) EC. 25 cm x 35 cm. Succulent with rounded, deep green leaves 3–4 cm across and fine sprays of tiny pink flowers in spring. Useful cover under trees in dry shaded parts. P: stem-pieces or plantlets on old flower stems.

Cyclamen (Cyclamen neapolitan) H. 8 cm x 12 cm. Charming little plant with small, heart-shaped marbled leaves and a profusion of erect little pink or sometimes white elfin-like blooms, mainly in autumn. Needs well-drained part-shaded cool to temperate areas. P: seed.

Cyclamen persicum see Flowering House Plants

Cymbalaria (Kenilworth Ivy) EC. 6 cm x 50–70 cm. Delightful carpeter or trailer with dense canopy of small-lobed foliage and tiny cream and mauve 'linaria' flowers; ideal for partly shaded rock walls or hanging baskets. P: seed or layers.

Cyprus Alternifolius (Umbrella Grass) ER to H. 1 m x 1 m. Elegant clumps of long stems crested with umbrella formation of slender strap leaves. Thrives in sedgy area, even in shallow pools or moderately moist, sunny or shaded situations or as container plant for well lit indoor area or outside. Dies down during cold conditions. P: division in winter.

Delphinium Treated as perennials (H) in cool areas and as annuals elsewhere. H. 1–2 m x 30–40 cm. Delphiniums give tall and stately spikes of flowers, mostly in beautiful shades of blue. They need at least two-thirds sun, good drainage and a well-manured or composted soil with bone dust or complete plant food added. Pacific Giants or similar hybrids reach 2 m or more under good conditions; Belladonna and other intermediate strains, 1 to 1.5 m; Butterfly grows to half a metre. In warm districts sow or plant out in autumn or winter. In temperate districts autumn planting is preferable. In cool districts spring sowing or planting is favoured unless seedlings have winter protection. Once established, crowns become dormant during winter, but are subjected to rotting during a wet humid autumn so in these warm areas are usually treated as annuals.

Dianthus (Pinks) Genus includes carnations and annual bedding type mentioned elsewhere. All ER to EC. Heights vary from 10–30 cm. Width from 12 cm to 30–40 cm. Species include *D. alpestris* with tightly packed, comparatively short-foliaged clumps and dainty fringed pink flowers; *D. deltoides* also clumpy, mostly with dark-eyed flowers; *D. subaculis*, very low matting with small, short-stemmed flowers. All prefer well-drained soil, and will spread over rocks from small but deep soil pockets or on gravelly scree. Adapt well to alkaline or limy soils. Most flower mainly from mid to late spring. P: remove some of the leafy 'crowns' as cuttings; these sometimes self-layer and may be separated for replanting.

Dietes see Iris

Digitalis (Foxglove) H. 1.5 m x 45 cm. Picturesque spikes of pendulous open bells in cream, mauve, pink or purple with darker centre colouring. Well drained soil; at least half sun; cool or temperate areas. P: seed sown by late summer to flower the first year.

Dimorphotheca ecklonis (Black-eyed Susan) SE. 75 cm x 1 m. Dark-foliaged, dome-shaped plant liberally spangled with dark blue centred white daisies during most of the year; *D. barberia* is rosy mauve. Sun or part shade, and under high branched trees where sun penetrates. P: seed or tip cuttings; *D. aurantica* (lower growing, with apricot and orange tonings) from seed.

Doronicum (Leopard's Bane) H. 40 cm x 40 cm. Bright green foliage and bright yellow, fine-petalled daisies in spring. Cool to temperate, at least half sun and fairly moist soil. P: divide in late winter or seed.

Echinops ritro (Globe Thistle) H. 1.5 m x 55 cm. Large green base leaves cut and serrated like Scotch thistle and in summer globular golf-ball-size metallic blue flower heads packed with bristle-like florets — retaining some colour when dried — well-drained soil in cool to semi-tropical districts. Seed and division of old crowns in late winter.

Edelweiss see *Lentopodium*

Erigeron alpinus EC. 20 cm x 30–40 cm. Very fine-petalled lavender-mauve daisies with raised yellow centre; cool to temperate areas; at least half sun; good drainage. P: cuttings, layers or division of clump in late winter.

E. karvinskyanus formerly *Vittadenia*, Baby's tears. EC. Wide-spreading mat of fine stems and foliage, with small white to pink daisies having almost hair-fine petals; can be invasive but attractive and effective cover for banks or even in light shade under trees.

Eryngium (Sea Holly) H. 70 cm x 40 cm. Similar to echinops with smaller flower cluster, and backed by deeply cut, spiky metallic-blue bracts. Other details as echinops.

Erysimum EC. 10 cm x 30 cm. Dense green mat in spring, covered with a lemon-yellow

Dahlias

Dahlia Give a long-lasting supply of summer and autumn flowers for garden show and cuttings and suit all districts. The cactus, hybrid cactus, decorative and other types come reasonably true from seed although none will exactly resemble the parent plant, and perfect 'show standard' types are very rare — named ones can only be secured by propagation from tubers or cuttings from tubers (green plants); compact-growing, bedding types are the ones most widely grown from seed or seedlings. Sow or plant out in spring, or in tropical districts during late summer or autumn. Need sunny, well-drained position with moderately rich soil.

Bedding types **Hi-Dolly, Unwin's Dwarf**, etc. grow only about 50 cm high and are usually raised from seed or bought as seedlings.

Named varieties of the following types are available in spring from tubers or green plants (plants raised from tuber cuttings):
Charm: medium-sized flowers in quilled or flat-petalled form, grow to about 1.2 m;
Pompon: golf ball-sized flowers 1–1.5 m;
Hybrid Cactus: types with semi-quilled petals to 1.5 m, and the large-flowered, broad-petalled decoratives grow to 2 m. Colours come in every shade but blue. Plant in spring (in tropical districts also in late autumn).

All types need at least two-thirds sun, well-drained soil, preferably with the addition of well-rotted compost, one-third cup of complete plant food and one-and-a-half cups of garden lime or dolomite per sq m (except where soil is already limy or alkaline).

Planting

Drive in stake then set tuber with shoot close to it, 5 to 6 cm deep, with the root end a little deeper. Water sparingly until foliage develops.

Cultivation

Break centre from plant to encourage branching when 4 to 5 sets of leaves have formed (25–30 cm high). Deep surface cultivated to about 5 cm deep until flower buds form (this helps to keep down height), then mulch soil liberally to increase root area and conserve moisture. Tie stems to stakes every 30 to 35 cm, making a firm tie around the stake and a loose one around the plant.

Watering

Give thorough but gentle soakings, allowing surface to dry out between waterings.

Feeding

Apart from initial feeding mentioned, give soluble plant food fortnightly after flowering commences but discontinue if plants become over-leafy.

Care

Disbud to one bud per stem. Remove old flower heads. Spray Bordeaux or Karathane if powdery mildew appears on foliage; use pyrethrum-type sprays for aphis or white fly, and snail baits around plants especially during wet conditions to keep these pests and slugs from flowers and foliage.

How to plant a dahlia tuber. Set stake when planting. Hole is filled gradually after shoots reach surface (above top of sprout).

As dahlia stem grows, it is tied in several places to the stake.

Disbudding dahlias when a large flower or long stem is desired. Remove three or more pairs of buds.

Dahlia, decorative type

In dividing a clump of dahlia tubers, cut old stalk as indicated by arrows.

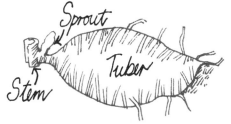

Dahlia tuber with section of old stem. Note sprout.

Dahlia, decorative type

Dahlia, hybrid cactus

Dahlia, decorative type

Dahlia, decorative type

canopy of flowers like tiny wallflowers. Cool to cooler temperate; good rockery or bank cover plant for sun or half shade. P: cuttings, layers or seed.

Euphorbia wulfenii SE. 70 cm x 90 cm. Dome shape, covered with clusters of bright green to golden buff flowers and bracts in spring. Needs good drainage, sun. P: early spring cuttings or seed.

Felicia ameloides formerly *Agathea* see Kingfisher Daisy

F. angustifolia. SE. 40 cm x 1 m. Low spreading, tiny-foliaged mat of stems massed with small lavender blue daisies in spring. Cut back heavily after flowering; spillover or foreground plant for sunny, well-drained aspects. P: cuttings.

Festuca glauca (Blue Fescue) ER. 25–30 cm x 25–30 cm. Dense tufts of fine blue-grey foliage; suit pebble gardens or rockeries in full sun. Needs good drainage. P: division in winter.

Filipendula purpurea H. 1 m x 30–40 cm. Fern-like foliage, large heads of rosy red florets in early summer. P: root division during winter.

Frankenia (Sea Heath) EC. 12 cm x 60 cm. Light mat of wiry stems with minute dull green foliage and tiny pink spring flowers, part shade. P: layers or cuttings.

Gaillardia H to ER. 45 cm x 35 cm. Clumps of serrated grey-green foliage, 8–10 cm flowers with dark-domed centre, surrounded by broad, overlapping satin-like maroon petals edged in gold. Well drained sunny position. P: seed or division in winter.

Gazania EC. 25 cm x 50–60 cm. Mat of slender, leathery foliage and single-stemmed bright orange, gold, cream or mahogany-toned daisies, many with contrasting eyes at the base of each petal; flower in spring, then spasmodically. Excellent on exposed sunny banks, rockeries and sea coast planting. P: layers, cuttings or seed.

Gentian H.A. 20 cm x 30 cm. Lovely rich blue alpine flowers for deep cool soil in cool climates. Need sun. P: seed or divide old clumps in winter.

Geranium ER. Geraniums give a brilliant flower display during summer, and the foliage of coloured-leaf types is at its best during winter. Other types are worth growing for their delightfully aromatic foliage. Growth habit varies from prostrate carpeters or trailers to upright 1 metre-high, or taller, bushes.

Cultivating: all geraniums prefer a well-drained soil, either in pots or in the garden, in half sun, and tolerate more wind and exposure than most other flowers. Performance and attractive plant habit depend greatly on the early training of the plant.

Most plants are grown from cuttings. For these, select sturdy tip growth, no more than finger length, striking them preferably in 3 parts by volume of coarse sand mixed with 1 part moistened peatmoss, or use light non-caking soil.

After a week or two move to full sun and at the first signs of growth pinch out the growing tip and give a light sprinkling (½ tea-

spoon) of complete plant food around the plant. When new shoots reach about finger length, again pinch out the tops and if necessary repeat until a compact bushy plant is built up.

Repot as needed and allow about a small level teaspoon of complete plant food scattered around the edge of a 15 cm pot, or a heaped teaspoon for a plant in the garden. When flowering commences water with half-strength complete soluble plant food each week, but discontinue and revert to standard dry-mix complete plant food if over-leafiness occurs.

Prune progressively when the flower buds on a stem finish, cutting it back to about finger length. By mid-autumn it may be as well to sacrifice a few flower buds in the pruning so that the plants are back in shape again by spring. When new growth comes after pruning, pinch back the tips as suggested for cuttings.

Regal pelargoniums become straggly if not pinched back thoroughly in early growth. Pruning back into older stems can often be too drastic, so if risking this, take cuttings first.

Ivy geraniums should not be pruned back heavily. If necessary cut back to a side shoot. Then encourage bushiness by pinching back tip growth.

The main geranium problem is rust which attacks a large percentage of *P. hortorum* varieties. These are the shrubby types grown for their showy, globular heads of bloom. Remove badly affected leaves (obvious by pale spots over leaf, rust-like circles underneath) and spray remainder of plant with Zineb or Mancozeb, directed mainly below foliage.

Trim back most of leaf blade, and trim roots to about finger length before replanting. Propagate by division or from fresh seed.

Gerbera (African Daisy) ER. 45 cm x 30 cm. Clumps of long-leafed crowns, erect-stemmed showy daisies, 9–12 cm across, in red, yellow, orange, pink or white, mostly single but full doubles also. Prefer deep, well-drained soil, warmth and plenty of sunlight and water during spring and summer. Where soils may be wet and cold in winter, plant with crown slightly above soil level and mound up to it with sandy soil. Excessive leafiness deters flowering — correct by breaking out all but 3 to 4 leaves from each crown in the clump; divide only when clumps become crowded with crowns, preferably during late winter in warm areas, elsewhere in early spring. P: seed or division during winter.

Geum H. 50–60 cm. Large base foliage, yellow or orange-scarlet, poppy-like flowers; dwarf forms also available. Sunny, well-drained position. P: seed or division during winter.

Gypsophila paniculata H. 20-70 cm. Finely branched sprays of dainty double or single pink or white flowers. Prefers deep, well drained and limy soil in cool to cooler-temperature districts. P: cuttings taken from selected roots when they shoot in spring.

Heeria see Schizocentron

Helenium H. 2 m x 40 cm. Heads of gold-orange or bronze short-petalled flowers with prominently raised dark centres, mainly in autumn. Much lower 60 cm-high strains are also available. P: division of clumps in winter.

Helianthemum (Sun Rose) EC. 22 cm x 60 cm. Bushy, dark foliage, spangled with small single or double flowers during spring and summer, in all colours but blue. Excellent for rockeries, sunny banks or pebble gardens with good drainage. P: tip cuttings or layers.

Helianthus salifolius (Perennial Sunflower) H. 1–2 m x 60 cm. Brilliant in autumn with numerous slender stems carrying a blaze of single golden flowers with contrasting black centres; average soil and at least two-thirds sun. P: division of clumps in winter.

Helichrysum bracteatum ER. 4 cm x 5 cm. Cushion of lance-shaped green to grey foliage with paper flowers to 5 cm across, usually deep golden yellow, sometimes white, with different stocks varying a little in flower size, colour and growth habit. Prefer at least half sun and good drainage. P: seed or cuttings.

Heliopsis scabra H. 75 cm x 60 cm. Somewhat similar to *helianthus* but single-stemmed, more substantial golden yellow flowers in autumn; also golden-orange forms. Sun and good drainage. P: division in winter.

Helleborus orientalis (Christmas Rose) Named because they flower at Christmas in the northern hemisphere. H. 12 cm x 40 cm. Deep green hand-shaped base foliage, stems of beautiful pendant 6–7 cm saucer-shaped, parchment-like, mauve-flushed flowers with rays of greenish bronze spots down the centres of the fine petals. There are also purple-tinted variations. Flowers turn green with age, lasting from mid-winter to spring.

H. corsicus is taller with larger and more erect clusters of 5–6 cm apple-green flowers, mainly in spring. Both prefer moist rich soil, sun in cool climates (elsewhere, part shade) and being left undisturbed. P: division in autumn or from seed sown when fresh (takes 2–3 years to flower).

Helxine (Mind-your-own-business) EC. 2 cm. Width varies surprisingly! Bright green, moss-like carpeter with rounded leaves no more than matchhead-size clustering on tightly matted, thread-like stems. In a moist, shaded spot it travels over rocks, brick, shaded lawns. P: any piece of the plant.

Hemerocallis (Day Lily) Adapts to very wet or dry situations in sun or part shade in any climate and is colourful in late spring/early summer with large heads of buds, several of which open every day into showy wide-mouthed coloured trumpets, lasting only one day — but there are usually enough buds to last for a month or more. P: divide clumps in winter but they may be left undisturbed for many years.

Heuchera sanquinea ER. 50 x 30 cm. Low attractive cushions of broad foliage long flowering, with slender 40–50 cm stems topped with 10 to 12 cm sprays of slightly nodding small coral red bells — dainty in the garden or as cut flowers. P: seed, then select best colours and increase by division or striking the woody side crowns as cuttings.

Hosta (Plantain Lily) H. 22–30 cm x 25–30 cm. Decorative clumps of ornate spoon-shaped foliage: *H. glauca* broad olive to blue-green leaves; *H. lancifolia* comparatively slender rich green; *H. undulata* is wavy-edged with its variegated form *variegata* boldly streaked with cream. All produce slender stems to 75 cm high with a loose spike of lavender or pale-violet bells in early summer. Prefer moist situation, better suited to light shade in cool or temperate districts. Snails love them so keep protected with baits during moist nights particularly. P: by division in winter, or seed.

Houstania ER. 5–6 cm x 12 cm. Small mound of fine foliage with tiny blue flowers on fine, erect pin-like stems mainly in spring. Needs moist, lightly shaded position. P: division.

Hypericum reptans ER to C. 8 cm x 30 cm. Small, blue-green foliage on slender branching stems, large soft yellow buttercup-like flowers in late spring and summer. Good rockery plant; sun or part shade. *H. calycinum* is taller (50 cm) with large yellow flowers and prefers light shade. P: tip cuttings or layers.

Iberis sempervirens (Perennial Candytuft) ER. 25 cm x 30 cm. Dense dark foliage shows up the rounded white flower clusters, mainly in spring; needs at least half sun. P: cuttings.

Incarvillea delavayi H. 30–60 cm x 30 cm. Clump of long, attractively divided foliage and spikes of large rose-pink flattened bells mainly in spring. Belonging to the begonia family, it needs a well-drained position and at least half sun. P: seed, established roots sometimes available in winter.

Inula H. 1 m x 1 m. Very fine rayed golden yellow daisies on individual stems, resembling *dorinicum* but a little finer and generally later flowering (summer rather than spring). P: seed or more usually by division in late winter–early spring — C & CT.

Iris There are iris species and hybrids suitable for either moist or dry situations.

Bearded Iris is the most widely grown, 50 to 70 cm x 70 cm almost evergreen clumps of handsome blue-green, lance-like foliage arranged like fans and large crepe-textured hooded flowers with silky gold-tipped beards down each satin-like tall petal, erect branched stems up to one metre in height, and in every colour including yellow and blue. They flower mainly in late spring.

They need plenty of sun, a well-drained crumbly soil with plenty of compost (and a little lime) and occasional dressings of plant food.

A clump only needs dividing when congested growth shades the centre. Replant any time after flowering. Cut back foliage in inverted V form, starting about 12 cm up the sides of the fans and lengthening toward the centre, trim roots and remove any soft sections of rhizome. Replant with the crown and

top of the rhizome ABOVE soil level. Feed when new growth commences and again in spring.

I. innominata — sometimes sold as Pacific Coast Hybrids. Dainty little irises only about 20 cm high, with erect slender evergreen foliage and silky-textured, rather open blooms in all shades of blue, apricot, yellow and copper with deeper veining running through the golden-blotched fall petals. Hybrid types flower throughout spring. They prefer a crumbly, reasonably moist but well-drained soil, without lime or animal manures. P: divide in autumn if necessary.

Iris kaempferi (Japanese Irises and Higo Irises) The best known water iris, with picturesque clumps of slender foliage about one metre high, and slender branched stems with large, flat beautiful flowers 12–18 cm across usually white to pale-lavender, with deep blue veining or deep blue with white veining mostly in late spring to early summer.

They also grow well in lime-free but well-composted garden soil kept moist from early spring to mid-summer.

For pool planting, I prefer to start them in plastic bucket-size pots of soil containing about 50% compost, kept moist in spring (if necessary by standing them in a saucer of water) then as growth establishes, immerse them to above the rim of the pot in a pond. They are removed and allowed to take their chances with rain from the time the foliage becomes untidy in late summer until early spring; suit cold to temperate climates. P: if necessary divide during winter.

I. louisiana tall, bright green, slightly drooping foliage and wiry, gently zigzagged stems to 1.5 m tall, carrying six or more triangular flowers with large, deeply veined falls. Colours range from deep violet to lighter blue, orange tan and reddish bronze, mainly during late spring. They grow in not-too-dry garden soil (no lime), in boggy areas or even in water, particularly in warm situations. P: if necessary divide in autumn.

I. pseudacorus (Water Flag). The yellow English water iris with dark veining through comparatively small ochre-coloured blooms; makes heavy clumps of erect foliage to almost 2 m high; suits large ponds or sedge areas. P: divided in autumn.

I. siberica. Graceful clumps of slender erect foliage 50 to 60 cm high, with straight slender flower stems held well above it during mid or late spring; blooms resemble small bearded irises, dark blue or lighter shades. P: divide in winter if necessary.

I. spuria. A species (or its hybrids) now becoming popular. Slender erect foliage to about 1 m, and erect solid stems carrying several large flowers with prominent broad-style arms, resembling Dutch irises. Mostly in shades of cream to lavender or bronze-yellow; foliage usually dies off during summer. Will grow in sedgy areas or average garden soil but prefer a lime-free, moist heavy loam. P: may be divided in autumn.

I. ungicularis (*I. stylosa*). Dainty, soft lavender-blue flowers in winter on stems only about 18 cm high. The slender, reedy

foliage tends to hide the flowers but this can be overcome by trimming back to about 10 cm high in April. Grows in sun or part shade with fair resistance to roots of nearby shrubbery. P: divide in autumn.

Dietes formerly *Morea* (One-day Iris) Dense clumps of reedy foliage growing to one metre high; wiry stems carry flat blooms about 6 cm across almost continuously. Adaptable, will grow in sedgy soil or dry, hard-baked areas, in full sun or part shade.

D. bicolor (Butterfly Iris) cream flowers with a contrasting brown 'eye'.

D. iriodioides white flowers with lavender-blue arms and a yellow blotch. P: for increase divide in winter, cutting foliage well back.

Jasminum parkerii SE. 16 cm x 18 cm. A real miniature shrub studded with light yellow jasmine flowers, mainly in summer. P: cuttings.

Kalanchoe blossfeldiana ER. 20 cm x 25 cm. Clumpy succulent with glossy foliage and bright scarlet 8 to 10 cm diameter heads of tiny flowers in late winter and spring. Needs at least half sun, good drainage and protection from heavy frost. P: division or cuttings from spring to autumn.

Kangaroo Paw see *Anigozanthus*

Kingfisher Daisy SE. 45 cm x 35 cm. Dainty, sky-blue daisies with yellow centres; in frequent flushes throughout year, treat as marguerites *Chrysanthemum fruticosa*. P: tip cuttings.

F. angustifolia SE. 40 cm x 1 m. Low spreading, tiny-foliaged mat of stems massed with small lavender-blue daisies in spring. Cut back heavily after flowering; spillover or foreground plant for sunny, well-drained aspects. P: cuttings.

Kleinia repens ER. 35–40 cm x 30 cm. Erect succulent with smooth stems and cylindrical leaves grown mainly for its blue-grey foliage; withstands dryness; at least half sun. P: cuttings.

Kniphofia (Tritoma or Red-Hot Poker) H. 1–1.5 m x 50 cm. Clumps of long, reedy foliage, flower spikes tightly packed with slender tubular florets; older types red in bud and yellow where the base florets are open, giving a 'hot poker' effect. Cream and yellow, also dwarf types available, some flowering in winter and spring. Widely grown *K. uvaria* flowers from late spring to mid-summer. All prefer spring and summer moisture but are drought-resistant and grow well with shrubbery; sun to part shade. P: divide clumps in late winter or when most foliage dies down.

Lavandula dentata (French Lavender) SE. 1 m x 1 m. Finely serrated grey foliage and torpedo-shaped flower heads tipped with lavender bracts; flowers almost continuously; full sun and good drainage. P: cuttings.

L. stoechas (Italian Lavender) SE. 60 cm x 70 cm. Flower spikes shorter than above with violet bracts. P: cuttings.

L. spica (English Lavender) ER. 60 cm x 35 cm. Clumpy, slender grey base-foliage, slim stems with spikes of small lavender florets in spring; at least half sun. P: cuttings.

Polyanthus

Bearded iris

Lavender officinalis

Peony

Platycodon and verbena

Lavender Shower see *Thalictrum*
Leontopodium (Edelweiss) H.A. 12 cm x 18 cm. Clumpy grey foliage, clusters of tiny florets surrounded by petal-like cream-white flannel-textured bracts. Early spring flowering if grown in an open and preferably elevated situation in a climate with a cold winter and cool spring. P: seed.
Liatris spicata (Gay Feather) H. 60 cm x 25 cm. Slender foliage, clustered florets like short bundles of rosy purple threads that open from the top down on an erect spike, spring flowering. P: seed and division of crown during winter.
Libertia grandiflora ER. 1 m x 40 cm. New Zealand native of iris family with handsome clumps of erect, slender strap leaves and slender-stemmed clusters of small white flowers in spring, leaving decorative seed capsules in autumn; needs at least half sun. P: seed or division of clumps in winter.
Ligularia ER. 25–30 cm x 40 cm. Good frost-tolerant foliage plant for damp shaded areas.

L. argenta boldly variegated, cream.

L. aurea maculata (Leopard Begonia) spotted gold leaves.

Both varieties have spikes of yellow, thin, floppy petalled daisies in late spring. P: division during winter.
Lilium see Spring and Summer Flowering Bulbs
Lily of the Valley see *Convallaria*
Limonium (Statice) many perennial varieties.

L. perezii E to H. 50–80 cm x 60–90 cm. Large-leaved, woody-stemmed shrubby plant with broad heads of papery violet-blue florets, mostly autumn and winter. *L. cosyrense* 22 cm x 25 cm has blue sprays; Purple Cloud has very fine florets giving a soft misty effect; well-drained position in sun; any but coldest or extreme tropical. P: seed.
Liriope muscari (Ribbon Grass) ER. 25 cm x 18 cm. Clumps of tough strap-like variegated foliage with spikes of small violet flowers resembling muscari (grape hyacinth), mostly in late summer. Best in shade; drought resistant, so are useful under trees. P: division in winter.

L. japonica or *Orphiopogon* (Dwarf Ribbon Grass) — still confusion about official name. EC. 12 cm x 22 cm. Dense mat of dark, slender foliage, excellent cover for complete shade under trees. P: division during winter.
Lithospermum EC. 8 cm x 40 cm. Branching, dark-foliaged trailer with five-cent-sized flowers of the richest blue, mostly in spring then spasmodically; needs half sun; cool to temperate. P: seeds, layers.
Lotus peliorhyncus EC. 10 cm x 50–70 cm. Tinsel-like mat of grey foliage with red pea-flowers in spring; good basket subject; needs good drainage; light shade to two-thirds sun. P: layers.
Lunaria (Honesty) H. 60 cm x 30 cm (biennial) Large base foliage, spike of single mauve stock-like spring flowers followed by disc-like seed pods. Pick and hang bunch upside down in dry place when pods yellow. When atmosphere is dry, pods easily separate

between fingers to expose the decorative, silver centre membrane. Cool to temperate; best in light shade. P: seed in autumn.

Lupin (Russell types) H. 1–1.5 m x 1 m. Lovely large densely packed spikes of florets in every shade including yellow and blue tones; mid-to-late spring; best in cool climates. Preferably deep, well-drained soil, otherwise it is advisable to replant clumps every second year. P: seed, or division of clumps in winter.

Lychnis calchedonica (Maltese Cross) H. 50–60 cm x 30 cm. Heads of brick-red florets shaped like a maltese cross usually in summer, likes cool and temperate climate. P: seed and crown division during winter.

L. Coronaria. Clumps of oval to lance-shaped grey foliage and slender 50 cm high stems of saucer-shaped ruby red flowers 2–3 cm across. P: from spring or autumn sown seed.

Lythrum Loosestrife H. 1.5 m x 50–90 cm. Slender spikes with clusters of small rosy purple florets; mainly summer; sedgy or well-drained soil. P: seed or crown division winter.

Marguerite *(Chrysanthemum frutescens)* SE. .5–1 m x 1 m dome-shaped bush, finely divided foliage and single-stemmed daisies 4–8 cm across in white, cream, yellow, mauve and pink with single or double 'cushion' centres.

Remove old flower stems well down into foliage; prune back after main flowering flushes without denuding stems of foliage. Old plants become straggly and are best renewed at least every second year. Full to half-sun in all climates. P: tip growth or side shoots as cuttings at any time.

Maurandia (Climbing Penstemon) H. 12 cm x 1–2 m. Bright green, small, ivy-like foliage, white-centred violet bells resembling penstemons in summer; prefers light shade; twines vigorously. P: seed.

Mazus (Fledglings) EC. 5 cm x 30 cm. Mat of light green foliage with small lavender flowers resembling open-beaked fledglings; summer; likes moist part-shade. P: division during winter.

Meconopsis betonicifolia, M. baileyi (Blue Poppy) H. 1 m x 40 cm. Clumps of erect large foliage, slender stems branching into clusters of soft, clear blue, crepey petalled flowers with yellow stamened centres. *M. grandis* is deep Prussian blue.

Both prefer moist, crumbly soil, morning sun only, or lightly dappled shade; cool or cooler temperate areas. Remove first flower-buds for perennial character. P: seed, which must be sown thinly to minimise damping off.

Mesembryanthemum (Ice Plants or Pig's Face) ER. 12 cm x .5 to 2 m. Under this heading are several closely allied genus including *Lampranthus, Oscularia, Delosperma, Drosanthemum* and others. All make good low cover of succulent foliage, and a brilliant display of shimmering silky-petalled daisy-like mauve, pink, purple, white, scarlet, orange or gold flowers, mostly mid to late spring. Suit all but tropical or coldest districts, drought resistant and

tolerant to salt winds. P: cuttings. For annual *M. criniflorum* see Livingstone Daisy.

Mirabilis jalapa (Four O'Clock or **Marvel of Peru**) H to ER. 1 m x 60 cm. Bushy plants with dark green foliage, carrying clusters of disc-shaped flowers to 3 m across with tubular 'necks' in pink, red, yellow-streaked red, etc. opening on cloudy days or late afternoon and closing in morning — some hybrid forms have perfume. Grown as annuals in cold frosty areas although they die down to a fleshy tuber. P: from spring-sown seed or from tubers dug in winter (may be stored away from frost in very cold areas).

Monardia (Bergamot) H. 45 cm x 40 cm. Rounded, almost spidery heads of scarlet rosy-pink, wide-mouthed tubular florets, mostly during summer; prefers moist crumbly soil in light shade or morning sun. P: division during winter.

Moraea see **Dietes** under Iris

Nepeta Faasenii (Cat Mint) H to E. 30 cm x 60 cm. Clump of numerous semi-upright stems with small wrinkled grey-green foliage, and massed with thin lavender flower spikes from mid-spring into summer. Spicy aroma attractive to cats; good border plant for well-drained, sunny aspects. Cut back in late autumn for best appearance. P: division in winter or cuttings.

Nierembergia caerulea, N. hippomanica (Blue Cup Flower) ER. 30 cm x 25 cm branching mound of fine foliage with 2.5 cm-sized, cupped violet-blue flowers almost covering the plant in summer; damp but well-drained soil; half sun or light shade.

N. rivularis 10 cm x 15 cm. Cleanly cut ivory white flowers. P: seed or cuttings in autumn.

Oenothera (Evening Primrose) H. *O. rosea* 30–50 cm x 60 cm. Large, upfacing pale rose flowers with deeper veining.

O. tetragonum 1 m x 50 cm. Large, soft, yellow blooms opening late afternoon; summer, at least half sun and any soil. P: seed or winter division of clumps.

Oriental Poppy see *Papaver*

Pachysandra EC. 25 cm x 50 cm. Closely set, fleshy bright green foliage, used as ground cover in reasonably moist, partly shaded areas. P: cuttings.

Paeony Numerous herbacious hybrids: H. 1 m x 1 m. Handsome hand-shaped foliage with erect stems carrying beautiful large crepey-textured poppy-like blooms up to small plate size. Rarely successful outside cool climates; prefers deep, rich, moist but well drained soil. Best when clumps are left undisturbed indefinitely; spring flowering. P: seed or division of crowns in winter.

Tree Paeony Plant similar to above but dies down to a stubby trunk rather than to below ground level. Prefers mild temperate districts with only a few hours of direct sun during morning. P: stem cuttings or seed.

Papaver orientale (Poppy oriental) H. 1 m x 1 m. Large clumps of grey-green, slightly hairy, divided foliage with striking saucer-shaped blooms up to 16 cm across, ruffled double or single with contrasting black centres and blotches at petal base, mostly in

bright orange red or scarlet but also in pink, white and mauve. Best in cool climates. Not to be confused with larger smooth-leafed and more erect *P. somnifera*, which is an annual, mostly lavender or mauve and a prohibited plant. P: seed or finger-length root cuttings taken in winter and struck in sand.

Penstemon (Pentstemon) H. 1 m x .5–1 m. Bushy with erect spikes of pendulous white-throated bells, in red, mauve or lavender to violet tonings. Early summer to autumn. Sometimes semi-evergreen but need cutting back in late autumn. Sunny, well-drained aspect in all climates. There are also several smaller completely herbaceous types. P: seed sown in autumn or cuttings.

Phlomis (Jerusalem Sage) E. 1–1.5 m x 1.5 m. Erect plant with large grey foliage and loose heads of yellow salvia-like flowers. Sun and good drainage; spring and summer. P: seed or winter division of clumps.

Phlox decussata (Perennial Phlox) H. .5–1 m x 1 m. Large, rounded heads of florets from early to late summer; white, mauve, rose and red tones. Half to full sun; warm as well as cold districts. P: division in late winter.

Phlox subulata (Alpine Phlox) ECH. 10 cm x 50–60 cm. Dense fine-foliaged carpeter massed with 5-cent-sized pink, mauve or rosy red flowers in spring then spasmodically until autumn. Best in cool climates but worthwhile for rockeries or other elevated positions with about half sun in temperate districts. P: layers or cuttings.

Physostegia (Obedience Plant) H. 75 cm to 1 m x 50 cm. Clump of erect stems topped with 10 cm spikes of closely set short mauve bells in summer. P: division in winter.

Platycodon (Balloon Flower) H. 40 cm x 40 cm. Balloon-shaped buds opening to upfacing starry-blue bells with deeper veining, also pale blue and white; needs at least half sun. P: seed or division in winter.

Polyanthus (hybrid strains) H. 22 cm x 15 cm. Modern hybrid strains have heads of large florets in every colour, including vibrant reds, blues and yellow during early spring; grow in full sun or part shade, preferably in rich moist soil. Feed with soluble plant foods when flower buds appear. New seedlings have greatest vigour (seed must be sown by mid-summer). P: for best results with second year plants, divide in late April, cutting the newly developed plantlets from around the woody crown and planting these up under seed bud conditions.

Polygonum amplexicaule H. 1 m x 1 m. Numerous woody stems with broad usually darker zoned foliage, carrying fine sprays of tightly clustered short tubular little flowers, in summer usually brick red. P: seed or division of crowns in winter.

P. affine H. 12–15 cm x .5–1 m. Spreading clumps of glossy base foliage, below erect flower-packed stems of tiny flowers — mainly in late summer. Some improved types like grape hyacinths in various shades of pink — best in cool to cooler temperate climates.

Primrose Similar to small single-stemmed polyanthus — treat as polyanthus.

Alstromeria, Ligtu hybrids

P. denticulata H. 40 cm x 20 cm. Slender stems with tightly packed globular heads of small florets in mauve, lilac or purple. Popular sedge plant for cool climates in shade or sun. P: seed. Usually grown as an annual.

P. obconica H. 22 cm x 12 cm. Large poly-anthus-like florets in tiers on a spike that produces new top buds for several months from early spring. Colours include white, mauve, lavender blue, pink and rosy purple; prefer moist light shade. Unfortunately some people are allergic to all parts of plant. P: seed or division in winter.

Pulmonaria (Lung Wort) Once used as a remedy for pulmonary complaints. 30 cm x 35 cm. Spotted foliage and sprays of large forget-me-not-type flowers changing from deep lavender to rosy purple. P: seed or winter division.

Pulsatilla (Anemone pulsatilla or **Pasque Flower**) HA. 20 cm x 25 cm. Clumps of finely divided foliage, large hairy-stemmed flower with six long violet petals cupped around a brush of centre stamens. Also cream *P. alba.* Best in sun with cool, well drained soil. P: winter division, or root cuttings in late winter.

Pyrethrum (Chrysanthemum coccineum hybrids) H. 60 cm x 35 cm. Shasta Daisy-like flowers with finely divided foliage. Colours include white, cream, mauve, pink and rosy wine-red, double or single with yellow centres. Spring flowering. Best in cool to cooler temperate districts. P: seed or division in late winter.

Romneya coulteri HP. 2 m x 2 m. Suckering woody perennial with attractive pale blue green foliage and beautiful crepey white poppy-like flowers 12 to 15 cm across with a centre cluster of golden yellow

Stokesia laevis (perennial aster)

Saxifraga caespitosa

Rudbeckia hybrids (Gloriosa daisy)

Phlomis fruiticosa (Jerusalem page)

Kniphofia (Red-hot pokers)

Rudbeckia lacinata (Golden Glow)

Santolina

stamens — may become invasive in light soils.

Rosemary see Shrubs and Herbs sections.

Rudbeckia lacinata (Golden Glow) H. 2 m x 60 cm. Tall, slender branched clumps with golden-yellow flowers like small show dahlias in late summer or autumn. P: winter division.

Rudbeckia hybrida (Gloriosa Daisy) Grown as an annual.

Salvia (Blue Salvia) *S. farnicia* is an elegant perennial with long, slender, pale violet-blue spikes not unlike English lavender. It is a delightful mixer, even with red salvia, giving a pleasant misting effect.

Santolina (Cotton Lavender) SE. 40 cm x 35 cm. Lacy, silver-grey foliage, yellow button-like flowers in summer. Cut back old plants in late winter or early spring. P: cuttings.

Satureia (Winter Savory) EC. 10 cm x 40 cm. Trailing mat of dense, light-green slender foliage, fluffy white flower sprays in late spring; good drainage and at least half sun. P: cuttings.

Saxifraga Four hundred or more species, mostly low-carpeting rock plants, for cool to cooler-temperate areas.

S. aizoon ECA. 12 cm x 10–15 cm. Rosettes of stiff slender foliage with granular, white-encrusted edges and slender sprays of small white-to-mauve flowers. Needs limy, gritty soil but fairly moist part-shade.

S. caespitosa EC. 10 cm x 25 cm. Mossy type with mat of pale green divided foliage, and massed with 5-cent-sized saucer-shaped white, pink or rosy-red flowers in spring. Needs moist semi-shade.

S. cordifolia Broad-leafed winter flowerer — see *Bergenia*.

S. sarmentosa (Mother of Millions). Rosettes of rounded hairy foliage, dark green with lighter veins; fine spikes of tiny flowers forming thread-like runners with plantlets; for moist shaded positions — easiest to grow in temperate areas. P: All propagated by seed or, more usually, by division of rosettes in late winter.

S. umbrosa ER. 25 cm x 15 cm. Loose leathery rosettes of foliage, wiry stem with branching filament of cloud-like tiny pink or white florets. P: All propagated by seed or, more usually, by division of rosettes in late winter.

Scabiousa H. 45 cm. Deep green mounded foliage, lavender-blue pincushion flowers. Late spring onwards.

S. parnasii. Dwarf, 7 cm. Silvery leaves.

Schizncentron formerly ***Heeria Rosea*** (Spanish Shawl or Creeping Lasiandra) EC. 5 cm x 1 m. Network of branching, fine red stems with small dark green foliage, covered with 10-cent-size, saucer-shaped bright rosy-purple flowers. Late spring. Dense mat over banks or moist rocks in light shade to half sun; ideal for hanging baskets. Needs protection from heavy frost. P: layers.

Scleranthus (Canberra Grass) EC. 5 cm x 30 cm. Moss-like carpeter making low, attractive emerald-green mounds; sun or shade, cool or temperate climate. P: division.

Sedum spectabile H. 40 cm x 25 cm. New spring growth like blue-green rosebuds, developing to erect stems with well-spaced scalloped blue-green foliage, heads of fluffy rosy-mauve flowers in summer. Also variegated foliage — both need sun. P: division in early spring.

Sedums Evergreen types — several hundred low-matting to clumpy, upright types with interesting foliage colours. Most are drought-resistant and ideal for rockeries, banks or container growing in full sun to half shade. P: stem or leaf cuttings.

Setrecia EC. 30 cm x 1 m. Spreading stems with waxy foliage that turns purple in sunlight; temperate to tropical. P: cuttings or division.

Shasta Daisy *(Chrysanthemum maximum)* H. The appealing, large-flowered single, lacy Chiffone and some of the larger doubles grow up to one metre high, and clump up 50–70 cm wide in the first season. Pincushions-centred Esther Reid rarely exceeds 50 cm x 40 cm. Main flowering is in early summer and if flower stems are cut back they continue until late autumn. At least half-sun in all districts. P: divide clumps and replant suckers in late winter or early spring.

Silene *acaulis* EC. 3 cm x 30–40 cm. Low mat of green foliage, spangled with stemless rosy-pink flowers in spring. P: layers.

S. maritima EC. 15 cm x 25 cm. Dense smooth pale blue-green foliage; white spring flowers. P: layers.

S. caroliniana ER. 22 cm x 24 cm. Bronze-green foliage with rose-pink spring flowers. P: cuttings or seed. There are also numerous taller pink or white-flowered silenes.

Solidago (Golden Rod)

Solomon's Seal see *Polygonatum*

Stachys lanata (Lamb's Ear) ER to H. 12–15 cm x 30 cm. Clumps of bold foliage like silver velvet; attractive contrast for bordering or foreground planting; flower spikes grow to 60 cm. P: division in winter.

Statice see *Limonium*

Stokesia (Stoke's Aster) H. 40 cm x 30 cm. Large, flat, double lavender-blue flowers, spasmodically from late spring to autumn. P: division in winter.

Swan River Daisy see *Brachycome*

Thalictrum diptocarpum (Lavender Shower) H. 1–1.5 m x 36 cm. Clumped dainty, fern-like foliage, tall branching stems carrying showers of pendulous lavender flowers with soft cream stamens. Best in moist, well-drained soil with about half sun. P: seed.

Thymus (Thyme) Numerous species and varieties suitable for well-drained paving areas or rockeries, with sun or lightly dappled shade; all evergreen and pleasingly aromatic.

T. herba barona 8 cm x 20–30 cm. Caraway thyme, lilac flowers.

T. lanuginosus 10 cm x 30 cm. Woolly thyme, lilac flowers.

T. nieciffii 5 cm x 30 cm. Dainty, fine silvery-green foliage, cerise flowers.

T. serpyllum vulgaris (Albus variegatus) 22 cm x 25 cm. Variegated lemon thyme.

T. serpyllum Westmoreland 25 cm x 5 cm. Dark green colour.

T. serpyllum Coccineus 8 cm x 30 cm. Masses of tiny crimson flowers. There are many more varieties. P: all from layers or cuttings — some come true from seed.

Thrift see *Armeria*

Torenia 0.25 cm x 15 cm. Similar to a little deep-blue snapdragon, with an open, pale centre and bronze-green foliage; suits rockeries or borders. P: sow or plant out in spring.

Tritoma see *Kniphofia*

Trollius eruopaeus H. 40–60 cm x 50 cm. Like tall sturdy-stemmed ranunculi with lemon yellow globe-shaped flowers, mainly in spring and ornately lobed dark glossy and leathery foliage, prefer wet soil with at least half sun. P: seed or if possible from divisions during winter which usually flower the first season.

Tuberose see Bulbs section

Tunica saxifraga Rosette ER.A. 15 cm x 25 cm. Finely branched sprays of small, double pink gypsophila-like flowers; sunny well-drained position. P: winter division or crown cuttings.

Verbena Various perennial types: ER to EC. 8–30 cm. Prostrate types spreading as far as one metre. Red, white, lavender and pink flowers in summer and autumn; all need sun and good drainage. P: cuttings or layers.

Veronica spicata H. 30 cm x 40 cm. Low mat of dark foliage; rich blue spikes of tiny flowers in spring and early summer; sun or part shade. P: division in winter. There are also several prostrate veronicas.

Vinca major variegata E. 15 cm x 1–2 m. Fine, flexible, trailing stems with glossy, oval, variegated foliage and 50-cent-size lavender flowers. P: layers.

Vinca rosea E. 40 cm x 30 cm. Bushy plant with dark glossy foliage spangled with 20-cent-size pink or white flowers mainly during summer, likes sun or light shade under trees. P: seed or cuttings.

Violet E. 20 cm x 50 cm. Princess of Wales with deep violet, fragrant flowers together with similar florists' types makes good, weed-resisting cover under light shrubbery where there is some sun and moisture. Best replanted every second year in well-composted, slightly limy soil. If foliage is tall and dense, clip lightly in early winter to improve quantity and display of flowers.

V. hederacea EC to H. 10 cm x 1 m or more. Native violet with slightly lobed, small bright-green foliage and erect white-to-mauve flushed flowers with a large deep lavender centre blotch; mainly during spring and summer; runs vigorously, especially in damp situations; sun or light shade.

Vittadenia see *Erigeron*

Wahlenbergia saxicola E. 10 cm x 12 cm. Fine base foliage, dainty erect sky-blue bells on thread-like stems; moist, light shade to half sun.

Wallflower see *Cheiranthus* and *Erysimum*

Planning your perennials by height

Preference is given in the following lists to the herbaceous perennials that need a little more planning, as planting is usually from crowns during their dormant season — winter in most cases. For easier planning they are grouped according to height.

> **C:** most suitable for cool climates
> **C–T:** cool to temperate climates
> **H:** adapt to warm semi-tropical areas

Plants less than 25 cm high

Anemone fulgens Brilliant red.

A. nemorosa, small pastel blue, pink or white; *A. blanda*, larger pastel daisy-like flowers. All bloom in late winter and spring; are dormant in summer and need cool, gritty soil. C.

Aster alpinus and dwarf forms of **Easter Daisy** C–T.

Convallaria (Lily-of-the-Valley) C.

Gentian Need cool, deep soil. C.

Geums Orange-red dwarf types. C–T and H.

Limonium (Statice) C–T and H.

Pulmonaria (Lungwort) With spotted leaves and flowers similar to Forget-me-nots. C–T.

Pulsatilla (Violet Pasque Flower). Treat as *Anemone fulgens*. C–T.

Veronica spicata With deep-blue flower spikes. C–T.

Plants growing to 60–65 cm

Aquilegia (Columbine) — All colours, spring-flowering. C–T and H.

Astilbe At home in moist, lightly-shaded positions. C–T.

Aster (Easter Daisy) C–T.

Campanula persicifolia (Harebell) C–T.

Dicentra spectabilis (Bleeding Heart) C.

D. formosa, lower-growing and smaller-flowered. C–T.

Doronicum (Leopard's Bane) C–T.

Eryngium (Sea Holly) C–T.

Frillaria imperialis Orange flowers. C.

Gaillardia Gold flowers edged with maroon. C–T and H.

Geum Flowers like small double-flowered orange and yellow poppies. C–T and H.

Gypsophila paniculata C.

Helenium C–T.

Helleborus orientalis Large, decorative, almost evergreen foliage and beautifully-marked flowers, in white or mauve during winter and spring. Likes damp, part shade.

H. corsicus has taller, densely-clustered spikes of green spring flowers. C–T.

Hemerocallis (Day-Lily) C–T.

Iris (Bearded) Spring-flowering. C–T.

Liatris (Gay Feather) Fluffy purple flower spikes in mid-summer. C–T and H.

Lilium (Asiatic Hybrid) Early-flowering, adaptable. C–T and H.

Monarda (Bergamot) With red or pink salvia-like florets radiating from knobby heads. C–T.

Phlox *(P. decussata)* Large, colourful flower heads during summer. C–T and H.

Platycodon (Balloon Flower) Violet or light-blue bell flowers. C–T.

Pyrethrum (*Chrysanthemum coccineum* hybrids) Like pink or red Shasta Daisies. C–T.

Stokesia (Stoke's Aster) Large, flat, lavender-blue flowers. C–T and H.

Plants growing taller than 75 cm

Anemone japonica (Wind Flower) C–T.

Astromeria C–T and H.

Aster (Easter Daisy) Taller types. C–T and H.

Canna Tall types. C–T and H.

Delphinium Better treated as annuals in warm climates. C–T and H.

Digitalis (Foxglove)Biennial rather than perennial but resows easily. C–T.

Echinops (Globe Thistle) C–T and H.

Helianthus (Sunflower) C–T and H.

Iris *I. kaempferi, I. louisiana*. Moist soil. C–T and H.

Kniphofia (Poker) C–T and H.

Lilium tigrinum, L. regale, L. speciosum and other taller hybrids.

Lupin C–T.

Lythrum (Loosestrife) Purple flower spikes, adaptable. C–T and H.

Meconopsis betonicifolia (Blue Poppy) C.

Papaver orientalis (Oriental Poppy) Huge double or single, red or pink, fluffy flower heads. C.

Peony Best left undisturbed. C.

Salvia farinacea (Blue Salvia) C–T and H.

Thalictrum (Lavender Shower) Soft, dainty, tall, slender, branching. C–T.

Shrubby perennials

There are a number of shrubby plants which can also be classed as perennials. Irrespective of official classification, they mix well with herbaceous perennials and evergreen rockery plants.

Blue Kingfisher Daisies *(Felicia amelloides)* are long-flowering. Smaller, lavender-flowered, spring-blooming *F. angustifolia* is most attractive if cut back heavily when its display finishes.

Marguerites make wonderful backgrounds and are a great standby for cut flowers. Trim back after each flowering flush and occasionally renew from cuttings. Shape by pinching out the tips several times when the growth reaches finger length.

Of the Lavenders, the French Lavender (*Lavandula dentata*) also fills in backgrounds attractively. It needs similar care and training but is usually only without flower for a short time in mid-summer. Italian Lavender (*L. stoechas*) grows only to about 50 cm, and English Lavender (*L. spicata*) has low, clumpy grey foliage with erect flower stems in late spring and summer.

Geraniums are valuable mixers — being cheerful, long-flowering and in great variety. The more popular flowering types (*hortorums*) start their main display in mid-spring but often produce some flowers almost throughout the year in warm areas. Ivy geraniums are similar and are wonderful as spillovers for banks, large rockeries or even for hanging baskets.

In winter, when flowers are less plentiful, there can be welcome colour from coloured leaf types which are at their best during cool conditions. I often use the golden-green type, Ann Tilling, with dark, chocolate-bronze Leonie Holborough. In spring their flowers also provide pleasing contrast — the former are bright red against the golden background, and latter a bright salmon over the dark foliage.

The secret of keeping geraniums attractive is to start new replacement plants from cuttings at least every second year, using solid finger-length tip-growths taken in summer. Pinch out the growing tips as soon as they have made a few new leaves.

Continue to pinch out each new shoot when it reaches about finger length until you have a good compact bush, even though this may delay flowering a little.

Geraniums or pelargoniums need plenty of sun and a well-drained soil, preferably with a little bone dust or complete plant food.

11. Growing annuals for display

It is widely held that annuals mean a lot of work for the gardener and, since their life-span is short, there is always need to consider what to do about the bare patch of ground left when their brief life is over. But annuals can be the most rewarding of all flowers — provided they are used skilfully.

First, and most important, never let the garden display be dependent on them. Annuals should have their place within a framework of permanent planting. So — if you are planning a new garden or remodelling an old one, leave space between trees, shrubs and strongly growing perennials for drifts of annual planting which will give seasonal colour.

If you like a formal layout use a bed of annuals to make the link between shrubs and the lawn. Or — if your garden depends on rockeries for effect — use one pocket out of three for seasonal planting so that variety and colour can be changed at will.

Annuals can be massed, in beds, borders or drifts, of one type and one colour only — the effect can be superb. Take your pick among phlox, petite marigolds, petunias, violas and primulas, or try a bank of multi-coloured nemesia. Alternatively, plant different types of colours and annuals together. There is no end to the different combinations which can be used to change the character of the garden from season to season.

For example — in temperate regions a lovely spring display would be a long, irregular border of violas, widening from a strip one plant wide to a drift, 10 or 12 plants deep, tapering away to eventually become hidden among a spread of gold and tawny-red nemesias intermingled with clumps of lacy white Primula deltacoides, backed, if the area is in full sun, by wallflower, ranunculi or Iceland poppies. For an even more spectacular effect try a clump of golden daffodils or a scattering of delicately-coloured freesias among the nemesia. Simpler, but just as lovely, is to have yellow and blue violas growing below the green and yellow of daffodils.

Next season, you may like to go predominantly yellow and white with white alyssum irregularly bordering yellow violas, then white primulas with clumps of yellow daffodils, backed with yellow wallflowers, yellow ranunculi or both. Or interplant pink English daisies with blue anemones, border them with white or mauve alyssum or blue violas and, for a backing, use stocks or poor man's orchid (Schizanthus), with a clump or two perhaps of white or carmine primula in front of them.

For shaded areas you could use medium-to-tall cinerarias bordered by dwarf types interspersed with clumps of primulas. You can have clumps of poor man's orchid or daffodils where there is at least half-sun. Shaded corners can make delightful nooks with a few ferns and primulas and perhaps a clump of bluebells or bright polyanthus.

For summer there are just as many — and even brighter — contrasts for sunny areas, such as a foreground clumped with petite yellow marigolds backed by a sea of phlox or petunias which gains tremendous sparkle from the yellow marigolds.

If you want contrast, use dwarf red salvia behind petite yellow marigolds and dwarf blue ageratum, with a background of scarlet and gold Prince of Wales feather (Celosia). These are just a few of many combinations — it's fun to make up your own.

Note: In more northern tropical areas the flowers suggested for summer planting in the cooler regions are planted in late autumn for winter and spring flowering.

Alyssum, violas, carnival and blue gem nemesia, bluebells and candytuft add striking colour to this garden bed

How to grow annuals

An annual plant will give a show of flowers lasting from between 2–6 months. Flowering times can be regulated by staggered planting.

Seed can be sown direct where the show of flowers is required, or can be sown in a seedbox and the seedlings brought along until strong enough to be planted out in the garden. See the list following giving plants which respond best to one or the other of these two treatments.

Soil

Annuals need crumbly and well-drained soil. Dig the soil to about 15 cm and spread a layer of well-rotted compost over the area and fork it lightly into the top. Unless manure is very well rotted it is best not used as it may burn the young seedlings. Peatmoss will help the soil retain moisture.

Seeds sown direct into the ground

Prepare the soil as described above, break down all the lumps on the top of the soil and level off the surface. It also pays to water the soil with a fine spray before sowing.

When the soil has settled down mark out rows for the seedlings. Use ribbon-like borders or squiggles for low-growing annuals such as dwarf phlox, alyssum, Virginian stock, etc. Taller annuals are best sown in roughly circular shapes 25–40 cm in diameter, not too closely crowded together. Use a garden stake or rake handle to scratch the furrows about 1 cm deep.

Sprinkle the seed thinly along the rows. For annuals such as alyssum and phlox drop a pinch of about a dozen seeds every 25 cm along the rows. Cover the seeds with a thin layer of crumbly soil or seed-raising mixture. Water lightly but thoroughly to begin with and keep the surface damp until germination takes place.

Transplanting seedlings

Before transplanting be sure the soil in the seedboxes is damp so that the earth will cling to the seedlings when removed. Lift each seedling retaining as much soil as possible. Place the seedling in a hole wide and deep enough to allow the roots to spread naturally. The seedlings should be planted at the same level they were in the seedbox. If the seedlings are planted too deep the stems may rot away.

Seedlings transplanted in hot weather should be shaded for a few days until they are established.

Watering

It is important to keep newly transplanted seedlings damp. Water lightly and thoroughly. Do not allow the soil to dry out until they are established. Once they are growing strongly allow the top 3 cm of the soil to dry out before watering again.

> **Remember:**
> • Do not water if the soil is damp less than 3 cm down.
> • Do not wet the surface only or the roots will remain near the surface.

Additional care hints

To improve flowers and prolong the flowering period small amounts of chemical fertiliser and liquid manure can be applied when the buds are forming.

To ensure the maximum flowering season remove dead and faded flowers. When they are not removed the plant diverts its energy to producing seed, resulting in a shortened flowering season.

Alyssum and English daisies border calendula (English marigolds) and ranunculus (perennial).

Raising your own annuals

All annuals are raised from seed. This also applies to biennials such as salvia, foxgloves, etc. and perennial Aurora daisies, columbines, polyanthus and other quick flowers often combined with annuals.

Seedbox mixture

To germinate, seeds need moisture, warmth and oxygen. The finer the soil particles the more closely they pack. This reduces the free entry of oxygen and water.

The ideal mixture is, therefore a coarse mixture of 2 parts coarse sand and 1 part moistened peatmoss. A number of good seed-raising mixtures are available with ingredients such as perlite and peatmoss or vermiculite which is light and flaky and holds large amounts of water within the particles, allowing plenty of space for oxygen to enter.

Sowing

Firm the dampened seed-raising mixture into shallow trays, boxes, seedling punnets or other suitable containers and even the surface. For fine seeds, lightly press rows about 1 cm apart over the surface. This enables you to sprinkle the seed more evenly along the rows and leave some spacing for easier handling and better growth.

To apportion fine seed evenly mix it with a small teaspoon of dry sand for each row. The seed and sand mixture can be distributed evenly if sprinkled against a ruler held with the lower edge just touching the row and the top angled out slightly.

Fine seeds need no further covering. Just gently press the surface with a flat dry surface to force the seed into contact with soil moisture.

Keep moist

Place the sown container in a plastic bag and keep in a shaded but light position to avoid drying out. Remove the bag and gradually condition to direct or lightly-broken sunlight as soon as the seedlings appear.

A good protection to break the force of hot sun (and equally important heavy rain or watering) can be made from fibreglass insect gauze. This can be pegged together as a sealed envelope around the seed container. It then has the added advantage of keeping out slugs, snails, caterpillars, etc.

Protect

Larger seeds such as pansies, columbines, etc. can be spaced individually. This may sound time-consuming but it saves at least the initial thinning out later.

Space

Thinning seedlings is important to avoid spindly growth and to deter damping off fungus which may occur in the moist, close regions between crowded seedlings. Many seedlings including poppies, primulas, ranunculi, will not progress until they are spaced out.

It is important to sow thinly and to space or 'prick' out as soon as the seedlings have made two true leaves, even though they may be still at the size when tweezers or toothpicks are needed to handle them.

Growing problems and solutions

Plant	Symptom	Cause	Solution
Ageratum	Foliage peaked and crimped upward	Green aphids	Use Pyrethrum-type or Malathion spray. If foliage is densely clustered, spray with Rogor or Lebaycid
Aster (China or annual)	Ash-like film all over foliage	Mildew	Spray with Benlate or general fungicide
Aster	Plant suddenly goes limp	Aster-wilt	No definite cure but drench surviving plants with Zineb or Captan
	Foliage with dull, sand-blasted appearance	Red spider mites	Dust with flowers of sulphur or spray with Malathion
Begonia (bedding types)	Leaves with brown-edged scalloping	Brown vegetable weevil	Spray liberally with Carbaryl
Bellis (English Daisy)	Raised orange pustules over foliage	Rust	Spray with Zineb or general fungicide
Brachycome (Swan River daisy)	Downward roll or curl of foliage	Aphids	Use Pyrethrum-type spray or Malathion
Calendula	Circular, bright orange cankers on leaves and stems	Rust	See Bellis
Canterbury Bells (singles)	Green or grey aphids on young growth or clustered under leaves which are usually curled downward	Aphids	See Ageratum
Carnation (bedding types)	Flower buds hollow	Usually due to frost damage	
Cineraria	Greyish-white tracery on foliage	Leaf miner	Spray with Pyrethrum-type spray 3 times at intervals of 3 days, or use Lebaycid
Cornflower	Centre of plant stunted and deformed	Aphids	See Ageratum
Hollyhock	Rusty spots on leaves	Rust	Spray with Zineb or Mancozeb
	Large holes in foliage	Usually snails but check for looper caterpillars also	For snails — spray with Methiocarb, snail spray or apply snail bait. For loopers — Pyrethrum-type spray or Carbaryl or Endosulphan
	Grey film on foliage and stems	Mildew	Dust with sulphur or spray Benlate
Larkspur	Foliage yellowing	May be effect of mildew or red spider mites	See Hollyhock
Lavender	Browning of lower foliage	Partly due to age but may also be downy mildew	Spray with Zineb; old plants best replaced with cuttings after about 2 years
Lobelia	Foliage and flowers suddenly disappearing	Tiny green stripping maggot	Either Pyrethrum-type sprays, Carbaryl or Endosulphan
Marigold	Dull cream mottling on foliage	Jassid (leaf hopper)	As above
	Foliage with sandblasted, dull appearance	Red spider mites	Dust with sulphur or spray Malathion
	Foliage eaten	These plants attract slugs and snails, but also check for caterpillars	Pyrethrum-type spray or Carbaryl or Endosulphan
Mesembryanthe-mum (Pig Face)	Raised, dull-yellow spots on foliage followed by shrivelling	Rust	Spray with Zineb or Mancozeb
	Lower foliage browning and shrivelling	Several types of fungi responsible	Use Zineb or all-purpose fungicide
Mignonette	Mottling or general dulling of foliage	Either jassid or red spider	Malathion or Rogor will control both
Nasturtium	Grey scribble-like tracery over foliage	Leaf miner	Spray with Rogor or Lebaycid
Nemesia	Seedlings rot at soil level	Damping-off fungus	Thin out crowded seedlings, avoid watering late in the day. In humid areas delay planting until late April
Painted Daisy	Buff blotching and streaking of foliage	Leaf miner	Spray with Lebaycid

Plant	Symptom	Cause	Solution
Pansy (Viola)	Crimped and mottled foliage	Aphids	Pyrethrum-type spray or Malathion
Petunia	Leaves eaten	Looper caterpillars or snails	Use baits or sprays for snails; for caterpillars use Pyrethrum or Carbaryl
Phlox decussata (Perennial Phlox)	Green flowers	Virus disease	Remove and destroy infected plants
Phlox drummondi (Bedding or Annual Phlox)	Sections of leaf white to transparent	Usually excessive feeding	Flood soil to remove excess food
Polyanthus	Dull pale foliage	Red spider mites	Spray foliage with Rogor or Lebaycid
	Limp, stunted growth, small downy-white insects under leaf and sometimes on roots	Mealy bugs	Spray foliage with Rogor or Lebaycid
Poor Man's Orchid	Foliage pale-yellow and clustered downwards	Red spider mites	Spray with Malathion or Rogor
Poppy (Iceland)	Flower stems zig-zagged or twisted	Either strong wind, or root damage by surface cultivation	Apply liberal surface mulch rather than till the surface
	Plants go yellow and limp	Virus wilt	Remove and burn affected plants
	Enlarged bud that does not open properly	Big-bud virus	As above
Poppy (all types)	Ash-like film over foliage	Mildew	Spray Benlate
Snapdragon (antirrhinum)	Numerous reddish-brown velvet-like spots over foliage and stems	Snapdragon rust	No cure but weekly spraying with Zineb helps to create resistance
	Small circular brown to transparent patches in leaves	Shot hole blight	Spray with Zineb or Mancozeb
	Dull, sandblasted appearance	Red spider mites	Dust with sulphur or spray with Malathion
Stock	Downward-cupped distorted centre foliage	Aphids	Spray with Rogor or Lebaycid
	Streaked flowers	Mosaic virus	No cure. Remove plants to prevent aphid transmission of virus
	Yellowish-brown leaves, black streak at base continuing down stem	Bacterial rot	No practical cure. Nurserymen can hot-water treat seed to prevent transmission
Sweet Pea	Plants suddenly wilt	Root or stem fungus	Sowings after early autumn humidity are usually less troubled, dusting seed with copper spray prior to planting deters early damping-off
	Brown, paper-like foliage	Broad bean virus transmitted by aphids, usually from its host, plantain weed	Removing plantain weed from vicinity before planting sweet peas
	Bud-drop	Usually due to cold nights and overcast days	Condition improves with sunshine and warmth
	Grey film over foliage	Mildew	Dust with sulphur or use Benlate spray
	Dull, mottled foliage	Red spider mites	Dust with sulphur or spray with Malathion
Verbena	Grey film over foliage	Mildew	As above
	Dull mottled foliage	Red spider mites	Use sulphur or spray with Rogor
Viola	See Pansy	See Pansy	See Pansy
Wallflower	Pale tracery over foliage	Leaf miner	Spray with Rogor or Lebaycid
Zinnia	Grey film over foliage	Mildew	As for Sweet Pea
	Flower centre damaged and tunnelled	Flower grub	Spray with Endosulphan (Thiodan)
	Plant goes limp and dark	Fungus wilt	Pull up and burn. Drench the rest of the plants with fungicide

Annuals to be sown direct
Winter and spring flowering
Sow during March (autumn).
Candytuft (*Iberis*)
Carnation
Centaurea cyanus (Cornflower)
  C. imperialis (Sweet Sultan)
Clarkia
Eschscholzia (Californian Poppy)
Gaillardia
Godetia
Gypsophila
Helichrysum
Larkspur
Linaria
Lupin
Mignonette
Nemesia
Sweet Pea
Virginian Stock (*Malcomia*)

Summer-flowering annuals
Sow during September (spring), except where otherwise stated. Most can be sown again in December for autumn flowering.
Candytuft (*Iberis*)
Centaurea (Cornflower and Sweet Sultan)
Cleome
Cosmos
Gypsophila
Helianthus
Helichrysum
Marigold
Nasturtium
Nemophila (Baby-blue-eyes)
  — also spring, full sun
Nicotiana (Tobacco Flower)
Nigella (Love-in-a-mist) — or autumn
Phlox
Poppy (Shirley)
Portulaca
Salpiglossis
Viscaria
Zinnia

Annuals to be sown and transplanted
Winter and spring flowering
Sow seed in March unless otherwise stated.
Antirrhinum (Snapdragon)
Arctotis acaulis
Belis perennis (Double Daisy)
Calendula
Cheiranthus (Wallflower)
Chrysanthemum (annual)
Dianthus (Pink and Sweet William)
Lobelia
Myosotis (Forget-me-not)
Nemesia
Poppy (Iceland)
Primula malacoides
Schizanthus (Poor Man's Orchid)
Stock
Viola

Summer flowering
Sow in spring when frosts are over.
Ageratum
Alyssum

Amaranthus
Aster
Balsam
Boronia
Brachycome
Calendula
Candytuft
Celosia
Cleome
Dahlia
Delphinium
Gaillardia
Helianthus (Sunflower)
Impatiens (Balsam)
Kochia (Summer Cypress or Burning Bush)
Lobelia
Marigold
Petunia
Phlox
Portulaca
Salpiglossis
Salvia splendens
Scabiosa
Verbena
Zinnia

Flowers for spring colour

Sunny aspects

Planted in autumn

30 cm or under: *Achillea tomentosa,*
Ageratum (frost-free areas only), *alyssum,*
anemone, *arabis, aubretia, bellis-perennis,*
dianthus, Forget-me-not, Livingstone daisy,
lobelia, Pixie lupin, *primula,* mignonette,
nemesia, pansy, *polyanthus,* dwarf stock,
Sweet William, *viola and* Virginian stock.

30–50 cm: *Alyssum saxatile, armeria,*
Aurora daisy, *calendula,* carnation, Everlasting
daisy (*acrolinium*), geranium, Honesty, Kingfisher daisy, linaria, Love-in-the-mist,
Ornamental kale, *mimulus,* Iceland poppy,
nemophila, ranunculus, schizanthus (Poor
Man's Orchid) and wallflower.

50–75 cm: *Aquilegia* (columbine), *clarkia,*
Big Gyp (*saponaria*), Canterbury Bell, *geum,*
godetia, gypsophila, Irish Green Bell flower
(*Molucella*) lupin, Painted daisy, Shasta daisy,
snapdragon, Bijou sweet pea and stock.

Over 75 cm: Cornflower, *clarkia,*
delphinium, *digitalis* (foxglove), hollyhock,
larkspur and sweet pea.

Lightly shaded areas

30 cm or under: Bergenia, *cineraria* (dwarf),
English daisy, Forget-me-not, *polyanthus,*
primula (all types) and Virginian stock.

30–60 cm: *Aquilegia and cineraria* (semi-
dwarf and tall).

Flowers for summer colour

Sunny aspects

Plant from spring to mid-summer or in monsoonal tropical districts during autumn.

30 cm or under: *Portulaca, ageratum,*
begonia (Thousand wonders), Petite marigold,
dwarf phlox, *torenia, dianthus, verbena,*
dimorphotheca, Californian poppy (*Esch-*
sholtzia) and dwarf salvia.

30–50 cm: Balsam, *brachycome* (Swan River
daisy), *celosia* (Fire Feather and Gold Feather),

gaillardia (perennial), *G. lorenziana,* petunia,
Mexican poppy, tall phlox (*drummondi*) and
zinnia (*linearis*).

50–75 cm: aster, Bonfire salvia, *viscaria,*
statice, gloriosa (daisy), *salpiglossis,* dwarf

Top: Ranunculi, a perennial but often grown as an annual

Bottom: English daisies, violas with a foreground of perennial alpine phlox

dahlia, zinnia (semi-dwarf) and *celosia* (Forest Fire).

Over 75 cm: blue salvia, marigold (tall African), zinnia dahlia (flowered types), *cosmos* (mandarin), *delphinium* (Pacific giants), *amaranthus,* dahlia (Charm Dec., etc.), *cleome* (Spiderflower) and *helichrysum* (Strawflower).

Shaded areas
Summer flowers for shade are less plentiful. *Impatiens* (30–50 cm) is a long-flowering standby. Bedding begonias (20–35 cm) flower where shade is not too dense. *Coleus* are brilliant and in all but cold districts.

Annuals for special purposes
Fragrance
Alyssum maritimum (Sweet Alyssum)
Antirrhinum majus (Snapdragon)
Centaurea moschata (Sweet Sultan)
Delphinium ajacis (Rocket Larkspur)
Dianthus chinensis (Chinese Pink)
Iberis umbellata (Purple Candytuft)
Lathyrus odoratus (Sweet Pea)
Bicornis (Evening-scented Stock)
Mathiola incana (Common Stock)
Reseda odorata (Mignonette)

Dried flower arrangements
Celosia cristata (Common Cockscomb)
Gomphrena globosa (Globe Amaranth)
Gypsophila elegans (Annual Baby's-Breath)
Helichrysum bracteatum (Strawflower)
Helipterum roseum (Everlasting Daisy)
Lunaria biennis (Honesty)
Limonium (Statice)

Yellow violas, white stocks and gold calendula provide pleasant contrast to ranunculi and bearded iris

Window boxes and planters

Ageratum houstonianum (Floss Flower)
Alyssum maritimum (Sweet Alyssum)
Centaurea cineraria (Dusty Miller)
Lobelia erinus (Edging Lobelia)
Petunia hybrida (Petunia)
Tagetes (Dwarf Marigold — various)
Verbena hybrida (Garden Verbena)

Annuals for special situations

Shady locations

Annuals are not lovers of shade, but a few succeed under partial shade.
Alyssum maritimum (Sweet Alyssum)
Antirrhinum majus (Snapdragon)
Begonia semperflorens (Wax Begonia)
Bellis
Centaurea imperialis
C. suaveolens (Sweet Sultan)
Cineraria
Clarkia
Coleus
Godetia amoena (Farewell-to-spring)
Impatiens
Myosotis palustris (Forget-me-not)
Schizanthus

Growing in poor soil

Alyssum maritimum (Sweet Alyssum)
Amaranthus caudatus (Love-lies-bleeding)
Calendula officinalis (Pot Marigold)
Celosia plumosa (Feather Cockscomb)
Centaurea moschata (Sweet Sultan)
Cleome spinosa (Spiderflower)
Eschscholzia californica (California Poppy)
Gaillardia lorenziana (Gaillardia)
Godetia grandiflora (Godetia)
Impatiens
Portulaca grandiflora (Rose Moss)
Tropaeolum majus (Nasturtium)

Edging annuals

Edging plants should be short and compact and flower for a long period.
Ageratum (Floss Flower — various)
Alyssum maritimum (Sweet Alyssum)
Celosia lilliput
Lobelia erinus (Crystal Palace)
Petunia hybrida (Petunia)
Tagetes (Dwarf Marigold)
Tropaeolum majus (Nasturtium)
Verbena hybrida (Garden Verbena)
Viola

Tall annuals for background

Amaranthus caudatus (Love-lies-bleeding)
Celosia argentea (Feather Cockscomb)
Cleome spinosa (Spiderflower)
Cosmos bipinnatus (Cosmos)
Delphinium ajacis (Larkspur)
Helianthus annuus (Sunflower)
Kochia scoparia (Summer Cypress)
Salvia farinacea (Mealycup Sage)
　S. splendens (Scarlet Sage)
Tagetes (African Marigold — various)
Zinnia (Zinnia — various)

A reference guide to annuals

Acrolinium see Everlasting Daisy

Ageratum (Floss Flower) Dwarf types are long-flowering and deep lavender blue, combining well with dwarf marigolds, dwarf phlox or bordering petunias, etc. Sown or planted mainly in spring but may also be grown through winter in warm districts.

Alyssum (Sweet Alice) Long-flowering carpeter in white, lavender or mauve-pink, for sun to part-shade, for borders, rockeries and between uncemented flagging. Sow seed direct or plant seedlings during spring in cold districts, or anytime elsewhere. Prefers slightly limy soil.

Alyssum saxatile see Perennials

Amaranthus A. *Tricolor* shows bright red and yellow tones from seedling stage; bronze-green *A. Salicifolia* types erupt in a mass of brilliant colour when plant approaches maturity. Prefers warm sunny position with plenty of water in early stages.

Antirrhinum see Snapdragon

Aquilegia see Columbine

Aster Popular cut flowers and wonderful garden show during summer when planted in mass. Check for aster grub that will web together centre leaves of the plant. Crego, the best of the soft, shaggy-petal types, makes a compact branching plant excellent for garden display. King Aster is a strong plant with exceptionally long stems and large blooms with quilled petals. The flowers have better weather resistance than other types, and last well when cut. They carry all the aster colours, as well as some interesting red and coral shades not found in other varieties. Flowers about two weeks later than Crego. Perfection, later flowering, sturdy with large blooms closely packed with short stubby petals.

Balsam Adaptable succulent-stemmed plants with crepey single or double-pink, red, white or mauve flowers. Modern top-flowering types display flowers well; on older strains they are partly hidden by foliage (which can be removed). Suit relatively poor soil — at least half-sun. Sow in spring or in semi-tropical areas in autumn. Sow direct, thin out or transplant to 25 cm apart.

Begonia (bedding) Many strains available, all carry a profusion of waxy pink, white or red flowers during the warmer months and in semi-tropical areas in winter–spring. Flowers are more prolific in half-to-full sun but they also grow in light shade. Thousand Wonders — compact dwarf type.

Bellis Perennis see English Daisy

Brachycome see Swan River Daisy

Calendula (English Marigold) Good for garden show and cutting but prone to attack by rust. Spray with Zineb for control and give full sun and good drainage.

Pacific Giant grows to 35 cm with good stems for cutting and has numerous medium-sized, two-tone flowers.

Campfire is larger but shorter-stemmed, deep orange. Large, easy seed to sow direct.

Lemon Delight, golden yellow flowers.

Honey Babe, dwarf, orange-gold flowers. Plant out by March for winter blooms, April–May for spring.

Californian Poppy Bright, quick cover for open, sunny positions where soil is not over rich; soft grey foliage below orange, poppy-like flowers. Best sown direct during spring or early summer.

Candytuft White hyacinth-flowered type growing to 30 cm and comparatively bushy. Umbrella type with pincushion-like flowerheads in pink and mauve. Sow in autumn. The latter can be sown in early spring for early summer flowering — needs good drainage and prefers limy soil.

Canterbury Bells Bushy plants with spikes of charming pink, blue or white bell-flowers for cool to temperate areas — singles treated as annuals, double or cup-and-saucer types as perennials. Full sun to half-shade, sow January to March.

Carnation Bedding types flower freely during mid to late spring from Feb–March sown seed or April transplants. Best treated as annuals. Need good drainage, full sun and preferably limy soil.

Celosia The old magenta type has been superseded by plants with brilliant scarlet or gold silky plumage in both dwarf (30 to 35 cm) to tall (70 to 75 cm) range. Needs warm conditions, so it is pointless sowing before October except in warm districts.

Forest Fire grows to 75 cm with rich scarlet flowers and bronze-green foliage.

Golden Delight has golden flowers.

Dwarf Golden Sunburst grows to about 38 cm. The type Fire Feather has red silky plumage, Gold Feather has gold plumage. Plants should be set about 22 cm apart.

Centaurea see Cornflower

Chrysanthemum Most Chrysanthemums, especially the popular florists chrysanthemums, are herbaceous perennials, and if specific or named varieties are needed it is necessary to propagate them from cutting or by suckers taken from the old clumps in spring.

However, there are now good strains available from seed or seedlings which are frequently treated as annuals, therefore they are included in this section.

There is also Chrysanthemum tricolor which is actually in the annual category. This is listed under its better known name Painted Daisy.

There are several different growing methods used to produce both a good show and cut flowers from the florists or perennial-type chrysanthemums. The more conventional one is to allow the young plants or seedlings a week or two to establish in a sunny, well-drained situation then when about 20 cm high to break out the top 5 cm. This encourages several branches to shoot from the sides and when about 12 cm long the tip growths are pinched from these to encourage further side branching. If time allows this pinching back or stopping process is continued until about mid-summer.

The result is that each of the side shoots favoured then produces a stem of flowers whereas otherwise the single plant would normally make one stem only.

Plants need staking and stems tying, preferably individually, every 25 cm or so.

Another method is to let the plants grow naturally then to cut them back to about 25 cm in mid-summer. Each flower stem may have all but one or two flower buds removed if one large flower is preferred to a cluster of smaller ones. However, the production of the very large exhibition-type blooms is different again as in this case only about 3 stems per plant are allowed to remain.

For good quality chrysanthemum blooms, feed gradually throughout growth, using only about a teaspoon per sq m of complete plant food every three to four weeks.

Chrysanthemums are normally planted in mid-spring. They make vegetative growth as days are lengthening then flower buds are stimulated by shortening days and therefore they flower naturally in autumn. The blooms or flowering potted plants seen in florists shops at other times of the year are obtained from growers with special control houses where lengthening or shortening days can be simulated by artificial lighting or darkening.

Chrysanthemum tricolor see Painted Daisy

Cineraria Showy heads of lovely rich-coloured daisies for lightly shaded parts of the garden with protection from heavy frost. Sow January to March, transplant April to May, or in cold districts during early spring.

Tall Branching, about 1 m high massed with medium-sized attractively coloured blooms.

Giants of California, semi-dwarf growing, 30–45 cm, with giant domed heads of exceptionally large florets. Strongly and attractively marked.

Tosca and Palette, true dwarfs growing only 20–25 cm; delightful for shaded rockeries or foreground drifts; combine well with white primulas.

Clarkia Upright pinkish-brown stems with crepey mauve to rosy-red flowers among grey-green foliage. Sow March to May, sun to half-shade; effect is best in clumps of 6 to 10 plants.

Cleome see Spider Flower

Cockscomb A form of *celosia* with broad, velvet-textured heads in red, purple, bronze, copper or gold. Like *celosia* it needs a warm aspect, both for germination and growth.

Coleus Colourful and beautifully marked foliage for partly shaded gardens or indoors, but needs good strong light for the best colour. Sow spring (or any time in semi-tropical to tropical districts). Pinch out tip growth to encourage branching.

Columbine (*Aquilegia*) Also appropriately known as Grannies' Bonnets, slender-branched stems with slightly nodding flowers resembling wide-trumpeted daffodils; the long spurred cup usually creamy yellow with slender back petals in apricot, pink, lavender blue or maroon. The clumpy blue-green foliage is attractively divided. Flowers mainly mid-to-late spring in all but tropical climates; sun or part shade. Sow seed by mid-summer to flower the first of spring.

Coreopsis (Calliopsis) 60 cm x 45 cm. Dense clumps of base foliage with flat 6–8 cm, bright golden flowers on slender branch stems in early summer; often naturalised in open areas. Sow seeds or divide during winter.

Cornflower (*Centaurea*) Deep rich blue or pink buttonhole-type flowers, popular for posies or short vases or as moderately attractive background plants. Need full sun and good drainage. Sow February to April, early spring in cool districts. Check for aphis and mildew.

Cosmos 1–2 m x 25–30 cm. These quick and easily grown favourites of grandma's day have returned to popularity. Old strains like Sensation with pastel pink, mauve, purple or white single blooms 8–10 cm across grow 2 m or more and are attractive as backgrounds to the summer garden or to quickly fill a bare corner.

There are now several semi-dwarf strains growing only from 1–1.5 m including semi-double orange **Mandarin, Flair, Sungold**, etc.

Cosmos grow well in any average soil with at least half sun and from early summer sowings often commence flowering about 6 weeks from sowing seed. May be sown direct into permanent positions, lightly covering the seed then firming down well and keeping moist until young plants are established. Sow from spring to mid-summer, or in autumn in warm northern districts.

Delphinium Give tall and stately spikes of flowers, mostly in beautiful shades of blue. They need at least two-thirds sun, good drainage and a well-manured or composted soil with bone dust or complete plant food added. Pacific Giants or similar hybrids reach 2 m or more under good conditions; Belladonna and other intermediate strains, 1–1.5 m; Butterfly grows to half a metre. In warm districts sow or plant out in autumn or winter. In temperate districts, autumn planting is preferable. In cool districts, spring sowing or planting is favoured unless seedlings have winter protection.

Once established, crowns become dormant during winter, but are subjected to rotting during a wet, humid autumn, so in warm areas delphiniums are usually treated as annuals. In cooler areas they are perennials.

Dianthus This name covers a large group of plants, including carnations, but in the seed and seedling trade one refers to various forms of Chinese or Indian pinks which make showy masses of flat, broad-petalled flowers, mostly red (or red with white markings). The annual bedding types usually give at least a second show if cut back after flowering; they have good drought resistance.

English Daisy (*Bellis perennis*) Dainty, quick-flowering and useful for spring bedding and borders, and for partly shaded areas of the garden. Handy as a 'fill-in' because seedlings can be planted to mid-winter or later in cool climates. Mostly light pink, but range from white to rosy purple — also larger-flowered but less prolific *Bellis monstrosa*.

Eschscholtzia see Californian Poppy

Everlasting Daisy (*Acrolinium*) Papery-flowered, slender-stemmed West Australian native that remains open and lasts indefinitely if bunched and hung head downward until dry — best sown direct in well-drained not over-rich soil, preferably in autumn, but early spring sowings are also made in cool to temperate areas.

Forget-me-not Useful as a 'fill-in', particularly for shaded areas. The burrs or hooked seed capsules can become enmeshed in clothing. Sow autumn or early spring.

Gaillardia Clumps of serrated grey-green foliage, 8–10 cm flowers with dark-domed centre, surrounded by broad, overlapping satin-like maroon petals contrastingly edged in gold. Grows 45 cm x 35 cm. Needs well-drained sunny position. Sow seed or divide in winter.

G. lorenzia About 38 cm high globular pompons in buff yellow and tawny shades. Sow direct in spring or transplant to 25 cm apart.

Globe Amaranth (*Gomphrena*) Globular, bright purple, papery flowers during summer and autumn. Leave sowing or planting until October except in semi-tropical to tropical areas.

Godetia The dwarf azalea-flowered types are the showiest; taller types are only colourful when grown under poor conditions. Both flower after most spring annuals have finished. Grows 25–50 cm x 20 cm.

Gypsophila The fine sprays of small white flowers add a softness to mixed plantings or cut flowers; sow any time. April sowing will give spring flowers.

Helianthus (annual) see Sunflower

Helichrysum see Straw Flower

Hollyhock The tall, stately, Old English picture-book flowers. When sown mid to late summer the annual types should flower in late spring, whereas perennial types rarely flower well until the second year. Best in rich, well-composted soil.

Honesty (*Lunaria*) 60 cm x 30 cm (biennial). Large base foliage, spike of single mauve stock-like spring flowers followed by disc-like seed pods. Pick and hang bunch upside down in dry place when pods yellow. When atmosphere is dry, pods easily separate between fingers to expose the decorative, silver centre membrane. Cool to temperate; best in light shade. Sow seed in autumn.

Impatiens Useful for summer colour in shaded parts of the garden; once established it seeds readily and often threatens to take over; sow or plant in spring; prefers a moist position.

Kale (ornamental) Attractive foliage, fringed, pink or cream and soft green. Sow Feb–March for display in winter, June–September. Prefers limy soil. Group 3 or 4 plants together to make a feature.

Kochia (Summer cypress) Neat little soft green, dense-foliaged bushes with a formal appearance; purplish-red in autumn. 1 m high. Plant 45 cm apart to make a hedge.

Larkspur Annual delphinium with tall slender spikes of blue, violet, pink or mauve flowers in late spring; prefers moderately rich soil and cool climate. Sow in April in a circle for pleasant clump effect. Seed needs cool nights to germinate well.

Calendula (English marigolds)

Pansies

Helichrysum (Strawflower)

Heartease, a perennial grown as annual

Rudbeckia hybrid (Gloriosa daisy)

Leptostyne Rounded bushy growth, bright yellow daisies on long stems. Remove old flowerheads for continuous display. Sow February for spring bloom.

Limonium see ***Statice***

Linaria Small spikes of florets like tiny snapdragons in mauve, purple, cream and tawny shades. Sow thinly in shallow furrows in mid-to-late autumn and don't bother to thin them out. About 30–40 cm tall.

Livingstone Daisy (*Mesembryanthemum*) Brilliant carpeter covered in fine-petalled, almost iridescent daisies with dark centres and contrasting zones of white and purpled-red or apricot, silvery-mauve and coppery-orange — but the catch is that they don't open until the day is warm and sunny. Best where the garden is slightly raised to give good drainage.

Lobelia Stocky, compact plants, densely foliaged in bronze-green and covered with deep royal-blue flowers from mid-spring into early summer. There are also dainty trailing types to suit hanging baskets or rockeries. Sow February–May.

Crystal Palace — compact plant.

String of Pearls — pink, mauve, white and blue flowers.

Love-in-the-Mist see *Nigella*

Lunaria see Honesty

Lupin Numerous types, from the low-mounding small pink or blue-spiked Pixie through to the hairy foliaged small-seeded or *Harwigii* type, with slender graceful spikes in various shades of blue; also tall bushy pearl types in pink or blue. All are easily grown, and may be sown direct into permanent positions.

Russell types, lovely large densely packed spikes of florets in every shade including yellow and blue tones; mid-to-late spring; best in cool climates. Preferably deep, well-drained soil, otherwise it is advisable to re-plant clumps every second year. Sow seed, or divide clumps in winter.

Marigold The yellow or orange-flowered African types are warmth-lovers, generally planted in spring or early summer to flower through the warmer months. The small darker-foliaged, smaller-flowered, russet and gold French types are more cold-resisting, so are planted in autumn for winter–spring flowers in all but very cold districts. There are many hybrids and dwarf-freckled or russet and gold types often used for summer display.

Crackerjack, African type, sturdy branching 1–1.25 m high. Large ruffled bright orange, gold-lemon and creamy-yellow flowers.

Jubilee, compact hybrid growing to 1 m high, with large ruffled orange, rich gold and sparkling lemon flowers.

First Lady, compact to 75 cm with medium-sized lemon-yellow blooms.

French types — once considered winter-flowering, now also grow well during the warm weather.

Petite Yellow, compact about 15 cm–25 cm high. Flowers for many months.

Petite Orange is an orange counterpart of Petite Yellow, with the same free-flowering habit.

Primula malacoides

Bellis perennis (English daisies)

Petunia 'Titan'

Aquilegia (Columbine)

Iceland poppies 'artist's glory'

African marigolds 'Jubilee'

Nemesia compacta

Freckle Face, maroon, blotched flowers, dwarf type. Marigolds are hardy, and may be sown direct where they are to flower, or transplanted to about 38 cm apart for taller types or 45 cm for petite. Protect seedlings against snails.

Maurandia (*Climbing Penstemon*) Bright green, small, ivy-like foliage, white-centred violet bells like pestemons in summer; prefers light shade; twines vigorously. Grows 12 cm x 2 cm. Sow seed.

Mignonette Insignificant greenish, buff or red-marked spikes. Grown mainly for its perfume. Sow direct in autumn (also in early spring in temperate-to-cool districts).

Myosotis see Forget-me-not

Nasturtium Good easy cover. They display flowers well if feeding is kept to a light sprinkling of complete plant food at sowing time. Rich soil encourages foliage. Sow direct in spring and early summer in cool areas; elsewhere at any time. Excellent for sunny rockeries, tubs or hanging baskets.

Nemesia Brilliantly coloured spring flowers. Need sunny, well-drained position. Early sowings may 'damp-off'. April sowings will flower in August.

Blue Gem — clumpy growth to 20 cm, small sky-blue flowers.

Carnival — taller with large mahogany, red, orange, gold and lemon flowers. The two varieties complement each other well if grown together.

Nemophila (Baby Blue Eyes) 25 cm across, 25–35 cm high, clumps of soft fern-like foliage with small saucer-shaped flowers in light sky-blue. Sow direct in autumn.

Nigella (Love-in-the-Mist) Beautiful mid-blue flowers, softly veiled in a mist of fine foliage. Sow direct in autumn or in early spring in cool districts. Likes full sun or part shade. Good cutting flower.

Ornamental Basil Metallic purple-black foliage; delightful aroma when brushed — try a clump or two with Petite Yellow marigolds. Sow spring or early summer.

Ornamental Chili 50 cm x 50 cm. Holds its erect multi-coloured fruits from summer right through to winter; useful for cutting. An attractive pot plant but definitely not edible.

Painted Daisy (Chrysanthemum tricolor) Similar to erect marguerites, with contrasting colour zones such as maroon and gold, mauve and lemon, etc. Good for cutting; transplant or sow direct in autumn, or early spring in cool districts.

Pansy Low-growing, beautiful flowers in deep, rich colours. Best in well-mulched, fairly moist soil with full sun. Remove blooms as they finish; sow or transplant in autumn.

Jumbo — strong grower with large, floppy petals.

Masquerade — similar to Jumbo but flowers later.

Roggli — dark blotched petals outlined in bright colour. Strong, erect blooms.

Ullswater Blue — rich blue flowers.

Petunia Ideal for a riot of summer colour, to bolster the spring show in semi-tropical or tropical districts, for pots, window or balcony boxes and rockeries. They revel in

heat, and although they appreciate reasonable moisture are excellent during dry periods. Most types flower better without overhead watering.

Phlox Give brilliance and sparkle in the garden, either massed on their own or combined with dwarf *ageratum* or petite marigolds. They can either be sown direct or transplanted from the seedbox. They need the sun for half the day and moderate feeding and watering but can do well even if neglected a little. Flowering will be prolonged if fed with complete soluble fertiliser and the plants are lightly mulched. Sow thinly in rows 25 cm apart and thin to 10–15 cm between plants. *P. drummondii* types such as Bright Eyes and Twinkle grow to about 40 cm. Flowers can have irregularly cut petals or a centre in a contrasting colour. Decorative and long-flowering.

Pin Cushion see *Scabiosa*

Polyanthus Not strictly annual but often grown as such. New hybrid strains have large brilliantly coloured florets in showy heads on heavy stems; ideal to feature in sun or partly shaded spots. Feed fortnightly with soluble plant food once they are established. Seed is expensive and must be sown before February (preferably November–December) to flower well the first spring. Also see under **Perennials**.

Poor Man's Orchid (*Schizanthus*) Pleasant, lacy foliage with 20-cent-size spikes of butterfly-like flowers in spring. They stand full sun but are also useful for part shade; allow to semi-trail in rockeries or baskets, or stake lightly for upright effect. Sow in March, plant out April–May.

Poppy (Iceland) If planted out by mid-April poppies are long-flowering from mid-winter to mid-spring; good for cutting or garden show. For best results give them full sun, protection from strong winds, and crumbly damp soil with surface mulching rather than cultivation. Remove flower stems until plants clump up with several crowns. Feed fortnightly with soluble plant food and if plants lose vigour, water foliage liberally with Condy's crystals (potassium permanganate) solution, diluted to weak-tea colour. Sow by mid-February and thin as early as possible.

Portulaca Succulent carpeter, border plant with double or single small poppy-like flowers in bright clean colours. Reputed to open only in strong sunlight but can be very colourful on bright overcast days and may even close in hot sun. Sow or plant in spring.

Primula malacoides (Annual types) A valuable lacy softener when mixed with other plantings, bordering Iceland poppies, or massed on its own. Grows in full sun but adapts to any area with reasonable moisture where shade is not too dense; also a good container plant. Gillham's White blends well with the bright orange-reds of *nemesias, calendulas* or wallflowers. *Carmine,* lavender, wine and white types mix well together or with *cinerarias,* stocks, English daisies and the softer-toned azaleas. *Primulas* prefer a well-composted soil with a dusting of lime; mix in a little superphosphate with seed-raising mixture or seedling soil, as

germination and growth are retarded if phosphorus is deficient and particularly where ammonia is plentiful (such as in heat-sterilised soil or if liberal quantities of animal manure have been used).

Rudbeckia hybrid (Gloriosa Daisy and others) Bold orange and bronze flowers, sometimes golden-yellow with black centres. Ideal for dry sunny banks where their warm colour can look spectacular. Flowers during late summer to autumn if sown in spring or early summer.

Salpiglossis An old-timer with 5 cm long buff or cream trumpet-shaped flowers prominently veined or overlaid with blue and bronze tonings. There are now also beautiful golden-yellow and lime tonings. Plant grows to .06–1 m tall. Sow direct, thin out to 15 cm apart.

Salvia Bright red flowers, *S. Splendens* types both dwarf and tall. Rainbow mixtures, purple, violet, rose and lavender.

Sapanoria (Big Gyp) Grows like white *gypsophila* but the rosy pink flowers grow up to 20-cent-size; sow direct any time, in at least half sun.

Scabiosa (*Scabious* or *Pincushion*) Pincushion-like flowers zoned with deep and pale lavender, lilac, to mauve-pink and purple. Once popular as cut flowers, older, taller types look ungainly — modern strains are relatively compact. Sow in autumn — or early spring in cool districts.

Schizanthus see Poor Man's Orchid

Snapdragon (*Antirrhinum*) Range from bright dwarf carpeters (25 to 30 cm) to stately plants with erect flower spikes up to 1.5 m tall — the latter look particularly effective in clumps and are probably safer used this way than having your display depend on them. Unfortunately all types are subject to snapdragon rust which will destroy the display prematurely unless you spray weekly with Zineb or Mancozeb; overseas rust-resistant Snapdragon strains are unfortunately not resistant to our Australian rust. Usually sown or planted out in autumn; spring sowings are worthwhile in all but tropical areas.

Spider Flower (*Cleome*) An interesting, quick-growing background plant. The pleasantly foliaged but rather prickly stems sometimes reach 2 m. Each is topped with a large globe of spidery pink lavender or white flowers with prominent stamens, which pale as they age but are enlivened late in the afternoon when a new circle of deeper ones opens. Drought-resistant, stands all but heavy frost. Sow in spring or early summer, and in warm northern areas during autumn.

Statice (Sea Lavender) Sprays of short-clipped florets like blue, yellow-pink or white crepe paper which hold colour when dried. Sow direct in autumn or winter (or in cool areas during spring) in a sunny position. *Statice* does not transplant well. Lightly cover the bulky seeds, which are the old florets. Thin out all but the strongest couple of plants at each spacing of about 30 cm. Cutting the stems encourages repeat flowering. *Statice* is usually treated as an annual.

Stock Lovely perfumed flower spikes for cut flowers or garden show. Column-type stocks produce only one large spike per plant, so need to be sown direct or transplanted 10–15 cm apart in circles about 40–45 cm in diameter. All branching stocks are effective when closely clumped; plants that finish flowering early can be pulled out without leaving an obvious gap.

Stocks need a well-drained, preferably limy soil, tilled occasionally to keep the surface weed-free. Before planting or sowing, work in some bone dust or complete plant food but avoid heavy feeding later, particularly with column stock as this stimulates undesirable secondary growth from flower centres. Watch for aphis, which causes distortion and flattening or downward cupping of centre foliage and for white butterfly or cabbage-moth-caterpillar; a cabbage dust or pyrethrum-type spray controls both.

Imperial and Perfection are semi-brush types which start flowering with one main central spike, then develop lateral spikes.

Austral is a branching type with heavy spikes of well-packed flowers.

Straw Flower (*Helichrysum*) West Australian natives with large crisp papery-petalled everlasting flowers, mostly in gold-bronze, pale purple or tawny tones. Best in moderate to poor soil with only about a level tablespoon of complete plant food per sq m added. Sown mainly in autumn or winter. Early spring sowings are successful in all but warm northern areas.

Sunflower Children love them and you can sow a clump where a bright background is needed, provided you will be viewing from the sunny side — otherwise the flowers will turn their backs on you! Sow in spring, or during autumn in semi-tropical areas.

Swan River Daisy (*Brachycome*) Dainty fine-petalled lavender, or mauve, daisies on low compact-to-semi-trailing lacy foliaged plants which flower mainly during summer and autumn. Sow seed in spring or early summer or in semi-tropical areas during autumn.

Sweet Pea The tall types make the most beautiful spring backdrop on a sunny fence or trellis, while dwarf types such as Bijou can be trailed over low dividing fences or left free-standing to twist into colourful mounds or spill over sunny banks. Both provide fresh, crisp, lightly fragrant flowers.

Sweet peas do not need the elaborate trenching and preparation once thought necessary. Just rake half a cup of garden lime per sq m with ¼ cup complete plant food into the surface soil then add half a bucket of well-rotted compost or cow manure to each running metre of row, and fork all this material into the soil getting at least half of it fairly well down. Don't turn the soil completely over — top soil is alive, so don't bury it; the seething population of micro-organisms it contains not only converts organic material into plant foods but also inhibits activity of the fungi that may attack your plants.

Give the soil a good soaking without puddling then leave it to settle down for a week or so. After a good surface scuffling to kill off weeds, it will be ready to sow. Germination problems are common with Sweet Peas but these usually occur early in the season, during wet conditions or when the seeds are watered too frequently after sowing, or when they are set deeper than 2 cm.

Sow shallowly and water carefully. You can prevent problems by adding ½ teaspoon of Captan, Zineb, copper oxychloride or Bordeaux to the seed-packet and shaking until all seeds are liberally dusted; or by pre-sprouting the seeds between moist paper towelling, or in a saucer of damp vermiculite. Make a furrow in the soil and place in seed, sprouted roots downwards and cover lightly with soil. When plants are 12 to 15 cm high pinch out the tops, place a few twigs to assist plants to reach the wire or trellis. For best results, when plants are at the budding stage they should be tied to the trellis and most tendrils trimmed off, as these ensnare and deform young flower stems. Prolong flowering by removing old flower heads.

Sweet William (*Dianthus barbatus*) The older types will not flower until the second year unless plants were set out by April. However, Sweet Wivelsfield and new hybrids such as Scarlet Emperor flower in early spring from autumn sowing or in late spring–early summer from early spring sowing or planting. Dwarf types like Magic Carpet and Wee Willie also flower quickly and are good for rockeries or foreground carpeting.

Torenia Look like a little deep-blue snapdragon, with an open, pale centre and bronze-green foliage; suits rockeries or borders. Sow or plant out in spring, 15–20 cm apart.

Viola Ideal for long-lasting colour. See Pansy for treatment required.

Apricot or Chantrylad — deep apricot flowers.

Blue Perfection — mid-blue flowers.

Crystal Giants — largest flowered type, strong-coloured flowers, blue, apricot, white, gold.

Lutens splendens — free-flowering yellow.

Toyland — small heartsease type, two-toned flowers, cream and purple, or lavender.

Virginian Stock Single mauve or pink starry flowers growing in low clumps about 22 cm high. Sun or part-shade. Sow direct from mid-autumn to early winter.

Viscaria 10-cent-size, disc-shaped flowers resembling Big Gyp (*saponaria*). Mauve, blue, pastel pink. Grows to 60 cm. Sow direct in at least half sun during spring (or in tropical areas, in autumn). Can grow clumped if clumps are given space around them.

Wallflower Renowned for fragrance and warm russet or gold tones; purple, mauve and cream shades are also available. Needs at least half sun, well-drained preferably limy soil. Sow or plant out in autumn or early winter. Grows best in a cool climate.

Zinnia Are among the brightest of the summer flowers and come in a dazzling mixture of all colours except blue. They grow quickly from seed or seedlings if you leave sowing or planting until at least mid-spring, when the soil is warm, but in warm northern areas they are started in autumn or winter. They grow best in a warm, sunny position with well-composted soil and plenty of water, given until flowering commences. Use a complete plant food when sowing or planting, but only apply soluble foods if it is obvious help is needed or after they have been flowering for a time.

Remove old flower heads. Pinch out the centre flower-bud to help the plant to branch out into compact form. Large flowered types growing to about 1 m and useful for backgrounds are: Dahlia Flowered, Brilliant Blue and Californian Giant. They can be allowed to grow only 10–15 cm apart in clumps — as long as there is space around the clumps otherwise keep them 30 cm apart.

Dwarf Coquette is a large-flowered compact, strongly branched type about 75 cm in many bright colours.

Hybrid zinnias are mostly semi-dwarf.

Z. Gaillardia — flowered, has two-toned flowers, large.

Z. linearis — orange flowers, small, massed.

Lilliput or Pompon types grow 60–70 cm, wide range of colours, round flowers.

12. Colour through the year

Transform your garden with spring blossom

It is the blossom trees that really turn a spring garden into a fairyland. Azaleas and the numerous annuals bring glorious masses of spring colour and wisteria and May-bushes contribute graceful cascades of beauty. But it is the flowering peaches, cherries, other prunuses and Crab apples that are scene stealers in spring.

These spring charmers are also most amiable and adaptable, growing well in all but tropical districts and flowering abundantly without special care. They are often of great practical value too, especially in small gardens. Here, because of their generous leafiness, they can double as small, summer shade trees.

Yet another advantage of these obliging trees is that they flower quickly — often the first spring after planting — except when heavily pruned back when a conventional vase-shaped fruit tree is preferred. Shaping is a case of personal preference, but most home gardeners generally prefer to let these trees grow quite naturally.

The flowering fruits or blossom trees are planted during the colder months when in their deciduous state. The most important point in the handling of these is to take care that the roots do not dry out at any stage. If planting must be delayed, cover roots with moist soil in a cool part of the garden.

The exception to winter planting is when nurseries have trees that have been established in containers. These may be replanted safely at any time providing the roots are not disturbed, but winter or early spring planting is still preferable because during cooler months it is easier to keep them moist until new farther-reaching roots become established.

Any soil, provided it is well drained, suits the spring blossom trees. That proviso merely means that it should be a soil that does not remain wet for a long period after heavy rain. If you have one of those heavy clay base-type soils it would pay to put in some form of drainage or to plant in an area built up at least 33 cm above the normal soil level.

The trees will establish much more quickly in heavy or clayey soils if a planting area at least a metre wide is prepared by digging in up to one-third of well-decomposed compost and, if you have it, some coarse sand. Alternatively there are also excellent crumbly pine-bark-based soil conditioners or planting soils which give a similar or even better result.

The most widely grown of the spring blossom trees are the various prunuses. As well as the numerous flowering plums (*P. cerasifera*), these officially include the flowering cherries (*P. serrulata* varieties) and the flowering peaches (*P. persica*).

Most of the more popular flowering plums follow their early spring flower display with a rich show of dark-purple bronze foliage which, in some varieties, remains dark throughout summer and autumn.

P. blireana is the earliest of the flowering plums, thickly clustering its twiggy growth with small, crepe-like, soft-pink double flowers.

Its foliage starts as bronze in spring then matures to a bronze-green. Growth is more restrained than most, reaching about 3 m, dense but more upright than spreading.

Moser's prunus (*P. moseri*) is a paler-pink form of *P. blireana*.

P. pissardii nigra is widely grown because of its darker, almost black-bronze foliage, from 5–7 m high with a top spread nearly as wide.

These flowering plums can be kept smaller by cutting to close above a lower branch. Heavy overall pruning stimulates too much erect growth. Annual pruning is not necessary.

The flowering peaches are perhaps the most spectacular with their profusion of long sprays packed with large florets in glowing pink, red and crisp white. There are both winter- and spring-flowering varieties. Pruning immediately after flowering is advisable.

The flowering cherries are superb. They range from early-flowering, simple, single blush-white *P. yedoensis* to a variety of white to deep-pink doubles with their numerous stems completely covered by large pendulous clusters of crepey pompon-like blooms.

The cherries are at their best in cool climates but also give a good display in all but very warm temperate areas.

Crab apples (*Malus*) also blossom in mid to late spring, some even later than the cherries.

Malus ioensis (Crab Apple) in flower

Above: Prunus Avium (Weeping Cherry)

Left: Prunus glanulosa (Dwarf flowering plum)

Below: Prunus persica versicolour (Variegated flowering peach)

Spring colour with petunias

Production of new hybrid petunias is big business, especially in the United States and Japan. This has naturally brought a bewildering range of varieties onto the world market, but only the outstanding ever find their way into the home garden range.

The Petticoat is a petunia with a difference. The blooms are large, deep, rich violet-purple that could look a little heavy if it were not for the contrasting ruffled white fringe that so effectively frames each flower.

The plant is also vigorous, long and free flowering and the blooms seem to have good weather resistance. This means that, unlike some varieties, the blooms are not readily collapsed by fungus during rainy periods.

In this case I speak from experience because I was able to try some plants, which I grew both in the garden and in hanging baskets.

Petunias are approaching peak flowering by August in semi-tropical to tropical districts, but in the former areas particularly, they can be started again for a colourful summer show.

Even in more northern monsoonal regions they can be grown in containers with some overhead protection.

Temperate and cool climate gardens may have all space for seasonal plantings packed with violas, nemesias, primulas and other spring flowers. Even so, it is not too early to start petunias in containers or in gardens where there is still space available.

Either start your petunia seedlings in permanent balcony pots or baskets, or set them out individually in smaller pots so that they can be tapped out later and transferred to the garden, where they keep colour continuity in gardens with mixtures of annual flowers.

For example, some of the lower foreground plantings like alyssum, violas and lobelias will, with reasonable conditions, keep flowering right through the spring and in some cases into summer. However, the nemesias and primulas behind them usually decide to bow out after the first few hot spring days. These can be conveniently replaced by your potted petunias.

Most northern hemisphere show gardens and parks replace their display of bedding plants and many other flowers almost overnight by growing great quantities of material in pots.

Naturally this type of gardening is labour-intensive and is not a general recommendation, but it does not take much effort and it can be fun to grow on a dozen or two potted seedlings. This is often enough for the more subtle type of colour highlight now preferred by many gardeners.

There are plenty of good proprietary potting soils available, or if your garden soil is not too heavy, keep 1 or 2 sq. m for the purpose, adding a good layer of compost occasionally, plus a scattering of complete plant food and lime. Till it over regularly to deter weeds. It can be replenished occasionally with a bucket or two of soil from the garden to compensate that added by the seasonal pots. One point: it is worth the little extra trouble to wash used pots, not only for plant hygiene but also because this makes it easier to tap out the soil ball.

Petunia seed is fine and hybrid strains are surprisingly expensive. Therefore, to allow easy spacing in seed boxes and give better results, most of the seeds offered by seed merchants are individually coated to look like tiny pellets of white clay. Initially this aid sometimes misfired because the coating failed to disintegrate and tended to smother the seed. The problem is now being overcome by using a softer coating, even though it may tend to crumble slightly.

Petunia seeds sown in spring flower later than spring-planted seedlings.

Before planting the seedlings out, mix a scattering of complete plant food through the soil to speed their maturity. Keep well watered, especially during early growth. One soaking with water-soluble plant food is beneficial to boost plant size if growth is slow, then apply again perhaps a week or two after flowering begins. Avoid frequent use of these water-on-type foods as most of them will produce sappy, leafy plants with few flowers.

Spring-flowering plants

Aubrieta deltoidea
Babiana stricta
Bellis perennis (English Daisy)
Campanula
Centaurea cyanus (Cornflower)
Cheiranthus cheiri (Wallflower)
Convallaria majalis (Lily-of-Valley)
Crocus flavus
Cyrtanthus mackenii
Delphinium
Digitalis purpurea (Foxglove)
Eranthis hyemalis
Erythronium dens-canis (Dog-Tooth Violet)
Eschscholzia californica (Californian Poppy)
Freesia refracta
Geum x borisii
Gladiolus byzantinus
    G. tristis
Haemanthus katherinae
Heuchera sanguinea (Coral Bells)
Hyacinthus orientalis
Impatiens balsamina
Incarvillea delavayi
Iris
Ixia viridiflora
Kentranthus ruber
Lachenalia aloides
Lampranthus aureus
Lathyrus odoratus (Sweet Pea)
Limonium sinuatum (Statice)
Linaria maroccana
Lobularia maritima (Alyssum)
Lupinus polyphyllus (Lupins)
Malcomia maritima (Stocks)
Matthiola bicornis (Stocks)
Muscari armeniacum (Grape Hyacinth)
Myosotis alpestris (Forget-Me-Not)
Narcissus (Daffodil)
Nemesia strumosa
Nemophila menziesii
Ornithogalum thyrsoides
Paeonia
Papaver orientale (Oriental Poppy)
Penstemon x gloxinioides
Polygonatum multiflorum (Solomon's Seal)
    P. capitatum
Primula x polyantha
    P. vulgaris
Pulmonaria angustifolia
Pulsatilla vulgaris
Ranunculus asiaticus
Scilla hispanicus (Bluebell)
Sparaxis tricolor
Tropaeolum majus
Tulipa (Tulip)
Watsonia pyramidata

Spring-flowering trees and shrubs

Acacia floribunda
    A. glaucescens
Aesculus x carnea (Horse Chestnut)
    A. hippocastanum
Akebia quinata
Alnus glutinosa
Angophora costata (Coast Red Gum)
Anigozanthos (Kangaroo Paw)
Azalea
Bauera rubioides
Bauhinia variegata
Berberis
Boronia megastigma
    B. serrulata
Brachysema lanceolatum
Brunfelsia bonodora
Buddleia alternifolia
Calliandra tweedii
Callistemon salignus (Bottle brush)
    C. viminalis (Bottle brush)
Cercis siliquastrum (Judas Tree)
Chamaelaucium uncinatum
    (Geraldton Wax)
Choisya ternata
Cordyline
Cornus florida 'rubra' (Dogwood)
Correa alba
Cotoneaster
Crataegus
Cytisus x praecox
    C. racemosus
Daphne genkwa
Deutzia gracilis
Diosma ericoides
Elaeocarpus reticulatus
Erythrina crista-galli
Eucalyptus melliodora
Forsythia suspensa
Grevillea (most species)
Hebe diosmifolia
Jacaranda mimosifolia
Jasminum fruticans
    J. polyanthum
Kalmia latifolia

Planting perennials for summer colour

Add new interest to your summer flower display by combining lovely, long-flowering perennials with petunias, annual phlox, marigolds and other bedding plants.

Winter is the planting time for most of the summer-flowering herbaceous perennials and the time when they are usually available in nurseries and garden stores. They would undoubtedly be more widely grown if it were not for the fact that at that time of year, most temperate climate gardens are already filled with spring flowers.

However, there is a way around this. Instead of letting the dormant crowns of your choice slowly deteriorate in their plastic sachet packs while trying to find a niche for them, plant them straight into pots of average potting soil kept in a fairly sunny outdoor position.

This way they establish far better than when half smothered by spring flowers which, in most cases, are spreading rapidly by the time early spring growth of the perennials begins. It also gives a far better chance of survival to shop-wearied, woody-crowned or soft-rooted perennials which may rot if suddenly transferred to average moist garden soil. This idea also makes overall weed control much easier, thus eliminating one of the main objections to clumps of perennials in the garden.

Most herbaceous perennials will grow on happily in a 12–15 cm diameter pot for a couple of months — at least until the spring annuals are due for the compost heap. Once established in the garden they are tough enough to compete reasonably with neighbouring plants, but where space is limited the

pot idea can still be continued when dividing them during future winters.

The comparatively wide and shallow azalea pots are quite suitable, easy to handle and need less soil than the deeper ones. I have also grown them in rectangular plastic 2 L ice-cream containers with drainage holes cut in each corner, but when replanting to the garden they are easier to tap out from the circular pots without disturbing their soil ball.

People without garden space can enjoy many of these perennials growing permanently in containers. The bucket-sized nursery pots will allow them to make a clump of reasonable size, even though it may restrict the spread of some. It can be an advantage to grow them almost to flowering stage in containers then place them where a highlight is needed among other plantings. This also saves them from overshadowing and crowding by taller subjects during early growth.

Some of the readily available and adaptable herbaceous perennials include the following:

Perennial Phlox have heads almost as large as hydrangeas in various shades of red, pink, mauve or white, making slender-stemmed showy clumps from 50–75 cm high. They reach their peak during December and January, provide excellent cut flowers, but if not cut back to more than about half their height will continue making colour until mid-autumn. They are best in a well-drained, slightly limey soil with at least half sun. Divide and replant at least every third year.

Shasta Daisy *(Chrysanthemum maximum)* are long flowering and adaptable, soon spreading into showy clumps nearly 1 m high and as wide. Their first flush of long-stemmed yellow-centred, white daisies comes in late spring and if these are cut back when needed or as flowers age, they continue spasmodically into autumn if conditions are not too dry. For

best results give them full sun and replant at least every second winter.

Perennial Aster, Easter Daisy *(Aster novi-belgii)* come in a great variety of colours and sizes. Some hybrids have tall flower-packed spires to 1 m or so high in ruby red, pink, mauve, lavender-blue and white. Others are miniatures growing only to about ankle height and ideal for rockeries. They flower mainly during mid-summer.

Balloon Flower *(Platycodon)* is a truly lovely relative of the campanulas with up-facing, long, starry petalled, cup-shaped flowers, mostly in deep violet with a few lighter blue and white strains. The common name comes from the large balloon-like flower buds. Flowering is mainly during late spring. These plants prefer a well-drained and well-composted soil in at least half-sun and also last well as cut flowers.

Astilbe which is sometimes known as Goat's Beard — hardly a fitting compliment for the soft, plume-like spices of minute florets in pink, mauve, white or rose-red. The base spread of glossy rose-like foliage is also attractive. Astilbe prefers a moist environment with some protection from hot afternoon sun. It is quite happy in sedgy pond-side areas or growing in containers standing in a water-filled saucer, a practice not recommended for most other plants. It flowers in late spring and early summer.

Perennial sunflowers *(Helianthus salicifolius)* — among the showiest plants in the autumn garden, each established clump with a display of 100 or more broad-petalled, black-centred, deep golden daisies on wiry-branched — almost leafless — stems, 1 or 2 m in height. There are several golden or yellow daisies related to the perennial sunflowers. These include the Golden Glow (Rudbeckia), the Gloriosa Daisy and Helenium.

Kolkwitzia amabilis (Beauty Bush)
Laburnum x watereri
Lambertia formosa (Mountain Devil)
Leptospermum laevigatum (Tea Tree)
Leschenaultia
Leucothoe fontanesiana
Magnolia x soulangiana
Malus (Crab Apple)
Melaleuca armillaris
Michelia figo (Port Wine Magnolia)
Parrotia persica
Pieris formosa forrestii
Pimelea ferruginea
Prostanthera ovalifolia (mini bush)
   P. rotundifolia

Prunus cerasifera (Flowering Plum)
   P. glandulosa (Dwarf Flowering Plum)
   P. persica (Flowering Peach)
   P. serrulata (Flowering Cherry)
   P. subhirtella (Flowering Cherry)
Raphiolepis indica (Indian Hawthorn)
Rhododendron
Ribes sanguineum
Robinia pseudoacacia
Rondeletia amoena
Sorbus aucuparia

Stachyurus praecox
Syringa vulgaris
Tamarix parviflora
Virgilia capensis
Viburnum
Weigela florida

Planting annuals for summer colour

There is still plenty of interest in the garden during October, even though the main spring display is now finishing in all but cool districts. Plenty of tasty vegetables and quick-blooming flowers can be planted now. Lawns can be easily and rapidly transformed to a flourishing, thick green carpet of grass, and fruit trees, shrubs, roses and house plants may appreciate a little attention.

A cheerful array of summer-flowering annuals can be planted to give a brilliant display by Christmas. Among these is a variety of bright petunias and plain or striped

phlox, such as one called Candy phlox. This has a different appearance and extra sparkle because mixed with its wonderful array of rounded petalled florets is a good percentage of dwarf Star phlox. These are the ones with ornately cut, pointed petals. Many have bright red or pink margins surrounding white star-like centres while others are red or carmine finely outlined in white.

These can be planted during October in all Australian climates. It flowers in 6-8 weeks from planting out, and flowering can be prolonged by pinching or clipping out old flower heads. Keep well watered and feed with a soluble plant food every 2-3 weeks from soon after flowering begins.

For a display of colour that is brilliant and different, try placing a few clumps of little yellow marigolds in a surround of Candy phlox. You might go a little further and splash in some dwarf blue ageratum, preferably close to the dwarf yellow marigolds. Queensland gardeners may not like the sound of ageratum because it has become a weed in some areas but there it is an older, taller, smaller-headed and far inferior type.

Above: Viola 'space crystals' and primula

Left: Antirrhinums (Snapdragons)

Below: Spartium (Spanish broom)

Above: Chrysanthemums, fancy quilled

Right: Browallia elata

Below: Virgilia capensis — a very fast growing tree

Summer-flowering plants

Acanthus mollis (Oyster Plant)
Achillea filipendulina
Actinotis helianthi (Flannel Flower)
Agapanthus orientalis
Ageratum houstonianum
Ajuga repens
Alstroemeria aurantiaca
Althaea rosea (Hollyhock)
Anthemis (Chamomile)
Astilbe
Callistephus chinensis
Canna indica
Celosia
Chrysanthemum frutescens (Marguerite)
    C. maximum (Shasta Daisy)
Clarkia elegans
Dahlia
Dianthus
Erigeron speciosus
Eucomis comosa (Pineapple Lily)
Gaillardia aristata
Galtonia candicans
Gazania x hybrida
Gerbera jamesonii
Gladiolus
Hedychium
Heeria elegans
Helenium autumnale
Helianthus annuus (Sunflower)
Helichrysum (Strawflower)
Heliopsis scabra
Hemerocallis fulva (Day-Lily)
Hymenocallis calathina
Impatiens
Lathyrus latifolius (Perennial Pea)
Lavatera trimestris
Liatris spicata
Lilium
Lobelia
Lunaria (Honesty)
Mimulus
Monarda didyma (Bergemot)
Oenothera biennis
Petunia
Phlox
Platycodon (Balloon Flower)
Polemonium coeruleum
Polianthes tuberosa (Tuberose)
Portulaca grandiflora
Romneya coulteri (Tree Poppy)
Rudbeckia hirta
Salpiglossis sinuata
Scabiosa (Pincushion)
Thalictrum (Lavender Shower)
Tigridia pavonia (Jockey's Cap)
Tritonia crocata
Vallota speciosa
Verbena x hybrida
Veronica spicata
Zinnia

Summer-flowering trees and shrubs

Abelia
Abutilon megapotamicum
Acmena smithii (Lilly-Pilly)
Albizzia julibrissin (Silk Tree)
Allamanda cathartica (C)
Aloysia triphylla (Lemon Verbena)
Astartea fascicularis
Backhousia citriodora
Bauhinia galpinii
Begonia coccinea
Beloperone guttata (Shrimp Plant)
Bignonia (C)
Bougainvillea
Brachychiton acerifolium (Flame Tree)
Brachysema lanceolatum
Buddleia davidii (Butterfly Bush)
Calliandra tweedii
Calluna vulgaris (Heather)
Calodendrum capense (Cape Chestnut)
Calonyction aculeatum (Ipomea)
Cassia fistula (Pudding Pipe Tree)
    C. javanica (Pink Cassia)
Castanospermum australe (Black Bean)
Catalpa bignonioides
Ceratopetalum apetalum (Coachwood)
Ceratopetalum gummiferum (NSW
    Christmas Bush)
Cestrum nocturnum (Deadly Nightshade)
Clematis
Cobaea scandens (C)
Cotinus coggygria
Delonix regia (Poinciana)
Dolichos lignosus (C)
Duranta repens
Eucalyptus calophylla
    E. ficifolia (Red Flowering Gum)
Fuchsia fulgens
Grevillea robusta (Silky Oak)
Heliotropium (Heliotrope)
Hibbertia scandens (C)
Hibiscus
Hydrangea macrophylla
    H. paniculata grandiflora
Hymenosporum flavum (Native Frangipani)
Hypericum calycinum
Jacaranda mimosifolia
Jasminum grandiflorum (C)
Koelreuteria paniculata (Golden Rain Tree)
Kunzea parvifolia
Lagerstroemia indica (Crepe Myrtle)
    L. speciosa
Lagunaria patersonii (Norfolk Is. Hibiscus)
Lavandula spica (English Lavender)
Leucospermum reflexum
Magnolia grandiflora
Melaleuca hypericifolia (Paperbark)
Melia azedarach (White Cedar)
Metrosideros excelsa (NZ Christmas Bush)
Nerium oleander (Oleander)
Passiflora (C)
Phaedranthus buccinatorius
Plumeria rubra acutifolia (Frangipani)
Prostanthera lasianthos (Vic. Christmas
    Bush)
Protea cynaroides
Sambucus nigra (Elderberry)
Sophora japonica
    S. tetraptera
Spartium junceum (Spanish Broom)
Spathodea campanulata
Spiraea bumalda (Anthony Waterer)
Styrax japonica

Tamarix pentandra
Telopea truncata (Tasmanian Waratah)
Tibouchina semidecandra (Lassiandra)
Trachelospermum jasminoides (C)
    (Star Jasmine)
Tristania laurina (Water Gum)
Yucca filamentosa

(C) following species denotes climber

Autumn-flowering plants

Amaryllis belladonna
Anemone japonica
Antirrhinum majus (Snapdragon)
Arctotis x hybrida
Aster novi-belgii (Easter Daisy)
Begonia semperflorens (Bedding Begonia)
Chrysanthemum frutescens (Marguerite)
    C. morifolium
Colchicum autumnale (Autumn Crocus)
Cosmos bipinnatus
Crocus sativus
    C. speciosus
Cyclamen neapolitanum
Dahlia
Delphinium
Felicia amelloides
Gerbera jamesonii
Helianthus salicifolius
Liriope spicata
Lycoris radiata
Nerine bowdenii
Pelargonium zonale
Physostegia virginiana
Rudbeckia (Golden Glow)
Schizostylis coccinea
Sedum spectabilis
Solidago canadensis (Golden Rod)
Sternbergia lutea
Stokesia laevis (Yellow Autumn Crocus)
Zephyranthes candida (White Autumn
    Crocus)

Autumn-flowering trees and shrubs

Arbutus unedo
Banksia ericifolia
    B. serrata
Bauhinia blakeana
Begonia coccinea (Tree Begonia)
Beloperone guttata (Shrimp Plant)
Brachysema lanceolatum
Caesalpinia pulcherrima
Calothamnus quadrifidus (Net Bush)
Camellia sasanqua
Ceratostigma willmottianum
Clerodendrum splendens
Cuphea ignea
Datura candida
Gardenia jasminoides
Grevillea banksii
Grevillea 'Robyn Gordon'
Hibiscus
Leptospermum squarrosum (Tea Tree)
Melaleuca quinquenervia
Plectranthus
Murraya paniculata
Prunus subhirtella autumnalis
Stenocarpus sinuatus (Qld Firewheel)
Strelitzia (Bird Flower)
Tibouchina

Winter colour from native plants

Some of the cool weather colour-makers are excellent propositions because they begin their display during winter and carry it through to spring. Others, such as *Grevillea banksii,* its progeny Robyn Gordon, and the bird flower (*Crotolaria laburnifolia*) seem to flower most of the year. Then there are a few cool-weather revellers, such as winter boronia (*B. ledifolia*) which reaches its peak during winter.

Winter flowerers include a great array of wattles (acacias) that range from small shrubs to small trees. Best known in the latter category are the Queensland Wattle (*A. podalyriifolia*) and the finer-leafed Cootamundra Wattle (*A. baileyana*).

Although these are not long-lived shrubs or trees, they re-establish rapidly, adapt to a wide variety of climates and are excellent for quick, temporary cover. Their fluffy golden flowers and their silver-grey foliage make a delightful foil for each other.

Grevillea banksii, which makes a 3 m-high dome of dark, attractively divided foliage, is excellent as a background plant. Erect spikes of red, waxy flowers stand proudly above the foliage during most of the year. Trimming them back as they fade keeps the succession of new flowers coming rapidly. The Queensland native grows in all but the coldest districts.

Grevillea Robyn Gordon, a hybrid between *Grevillea banksii* and the low-spreading *G.*
biternata, is at least as long-flowering as its parent with lighter, glossier foliage.

Many other grevilleas, including the widely grown *G. rosmarinifolia*, begin their flower display early in winter and continue until about mid-spring.

Crotolaria laburnifolia presents a handsome array of tall spikes clustered with large greenish-yellow pea flowers looking like birds attached to the stem by their beaks. Hence the common name — Queensland Bird Flower — although it is native to the north-west rather than the north-east of Australia. Its species name comes from the soft green leaves resembling those of northern hemisphere laburnum.

This amiable shrub grows 2–3 m high and produces about four flushes of flower a year, especially if old flower spikes are pruned back. Each flush lasts for many weeks, particularly through winter, in all but very cold areas.

Western Australia's Geraldton Wax (*Chamaelaucium*) is a delightful long-flowering shrub, clustered with sprays of pink, waxy, round-petalled tea-tree-like flowers that appear in early winter and carry through into spring. It is also a long-lasting cut flower.

It is sometimes regarded as temperamental and short lived, but this reputation comes mainly from its dislike of root disturbance, so stake it firmly so that the wind cannot loosen it in the soil.

However, this practice can be its downfall, because if the stake breaks the heavy shrub will topple and break most of its roots. It is better to start with a small plant in an area away from cultivation and let it sprawl or lean naturally.

Branches then develop close to the ground and it becomes self-bracing. Contrary to general opinion, it stands plenty of water provided drainage is good.

Growth is better in a slightly limey rather than acid soil and if the old flower stems are cut back before the new spring growth begins.

There are several lovely winter-flowering banksias. One of the most adaptable is small, dark-foliaged *B. ericifolia* which makes a dense mound to 3 m displaying numerous erect, orange-bronze brushes 25–30 cm long. This attractive shrub grows on the sea coast and in most mountain and inland temperate to semi-tropical areas.

The desert cassia, *C. eremophila*, is a sturdy shrub about 2 m high, which carries clusters of small, cupped, yellow flowers from mid-winter to spring. It is a drought-resistant stalwart for well-drained situations.

Many of the tea-trees give a good winter display. Some, such as *Leptospermum scoparium* and a few of its hybrids, have their main flowering period during autumn and winter.

Small-growing *Correa reflexa,* with its appealing pale green bell flowers, contrasting attractively with its dark oval foliage, blooms from late autumn to mid-winter.

It is followed on the sandy ridges of the east coast by the starry pink winter boronia (*B. ledifolia*), then before this loses colour in late winter or early spring, the golden-orange pea flowered *Dillwynia ericifolia* becomes a strong competitor for attention. *Eriostemons* also excel during late winter.

Winter-flowering plants

Bergenia cordifolia
Calendula officinalis
Coelogyne cristata
Cyclamen persicum
Eranthis hyemalis
Eucharis grandiflora
Euryops pectinatus
Galanthus nivalis (Snowdrop)
Gypsophila
Helleborus niger
Hyacinthus orientalis
Iberis sempervirens (Candytuft)
Kalanchoe blossfeldiana
Lathyrus odoratus (Sweet Pea)
Leucojum vernum (Snowflake)
Lobularia maritima
Manettia bicolor
Matthiola incana
Narcissus (Jonquil and Daffodil)
Papaver nudicaule (Iceland Poppy)
Primula
Rhipsalidopsis gaertneri (Crab's Claw Cactus)
Rosmarinus officinalis
Schizanthus (Poor Man's Orchid)
Schlumbergera truncata (Crab's Claw Cactus)
Senecio cruentus (Cineraria)
Strelitzia reginae
Viola cornuta
  V. odorata
  V. wittrockiana

Winter-flowering trees and shrubs

Acacia baileyana
Banksia ericifolia
  B. integrifolia
Boronia ledifolia
Buddleia salvifolia
Camellia japonica
  C. sasanqua
Cassia bicapsularis
Chaenomeles japonica (Flowering Quince)
Chamaelaucium uncinatum (Geraldton Wax)
Chimonanthus praecox (Allspice)
Coleonema pulchrum
Correa reflexa
Crotolaria laburnifolia
Cuphea micropetala
Daphne odora
Dillwynia encifolia
Epacris longiflora
Erica canaliculata
  E. willmorei
Eriostemon australasius
Eucalyptus citriodora
Euphorbia pulcherrima (Poinsettia)
Garrya elliptica
Gordonia axillaris
Hakea laurina (Pincushion Hakea)
Hebe speciosa
Jasminum mesnyi
Lavandula dentata (French Lavender)

Magnolia x soulangiana
Polygula myrtifolia
Protea mellifera
Prunus subhirtella 'autumnalis'
Reinwardtia indica (Yellow Linum)
Rhodoleia championii
Thryptomene calycina
Tibouchina (Lassiandra)
Viburnum tinus

13. How to make cut flowers last

Having grown the flowers one naturally wants to be able to enjoy them indoors for as long as possible. They will last longer if picked at the right time of day, the best stage of development for the species and are given immediate and considerate treatment — the most important thing is to get them into water with the least possible delay.

When to pick

Early morning or late afternoon — not in the heat of the day. Flowers picked in the evening last better than ones picked in the morning because they have built up food reserves during the day.

How to pick

Cut stems on the slant to give a greater area for absorption of water. Straight-cut stems could sit squarely on the base of a container and make the taking-in of water difficult. Trim off any ragged edges.

Take a small bucket of water around the garden with you when choosing flowers for cutting and put them straight into it.

Development of flower

Gladiolus, iris, poppy — in bud.
Rose — buds opening.
Carnation, daisy family, larkspur — flower three-quarters open.
Calendula, chrysanthemum, zinnia — flower fully open.

Flowers with woody stems will be able to absorb water in the vase much better if their stems are crushed and split 7–8 cm at the base; other flowers benefit if the stem is just scraped and gently slit.

Scraped stems

Anemone, aster, azalea, calendula, camellia, iris, larkspur, marigold, rose.

Crushed stems

Antirrhinum, chrysanthemum, geranium, stock, wallflower and most flowering shrubs.

Hollow-stemmed flowers or those from plants which ooze sap when the stem is cut will last longer if the end of the stem is seared either in a flame or by brief immersion in boiling water.

Heat treatment

Canterbury bells, dahlia, daisy, delphinium, foxglove, hydrangea, Iceland poppy, lupin, phlox, stock, wallflower, zinnia.

The hollow stems of delphinium, foxglove and lupin can be filled with water and sealed with a plug of cotton wool.

Flowers in the vase

Keep the leaves out of the water. They will rot very quickly and make the water smelly and polluted.

Keep vases away from sun, draught and heat from fires or radiators.

In hot temperatures spray the flowers with a fine mist of water to keep them fresh.

Aspirin, copper coins, coal, sugar and disinfectant are put into the water to help prolong the life of cut flowers — some people say they work, others are doubtful. There are proprietary preparations on the market which are worth trying but don't expect them to work if you cram flowers so close they can hardly breathe, or let the water become stagnant.

If you feel happier changing the water every day, by all means do so: strong-smelling flowers such as chrysanthemum and marigold transfer their characteristic odour to the water and it can become a bit too noticeable for enjoyment.

Above: Western Australian banksia

Right: Cut roses for vases when the buds are opening and scrape or cut stems under water to ensure they last as long as possible. A fine misting of water will keep them fresh

THE WORLD OF PLANTS AND GRASSES

14. The beauty of foliage

Add a touch of silver to your garden

Silver-grey foliage on its own gives a sense of depth and pleasant misty softness, yet it is such a spectacular foil for other colours. It makes golds glitter brightly, adds a radiant glow to reds and harmonises with pinks or blues.

These delightful results can be enjoyed on any scale from broad landscaping with shrubs or trees to the tiniest balcony garden. If thinking big, there are Queensland wattles with foliage looking as though cut from silver velvet, the finer silver-grey of Cootamundra wattle or silver-blue of Alligator juniper and Arizona cypress (*Cupressus arizonica*).

These all combine attractively with the pink blossom of flowering plums (*Prunus pissardi nigra* of *P. vesuvius*) then later make strong contrast against the purple bronze of their spring and summer foliage. The golden elm almost completes the spectrum and also looks brilliant when partly framed in silver.

Coming down in size, there are several silvery foliage plants acceptable for spotting among the other more definite colours. The most useful are the Dusty Millers, a name which includes several lacy-foliaged woody perennials.

One of the most popular of these is also known as Silver cineraria (*Senecio mauritima*). It has large deeply-cut leaves like silver-grey velvet lace, making a compact mound about 1 m wide and nearly as high. This ornate plant provides wonderful contrast for its own large branching sprays of tiny, bright golden daisies just above the foliage.

It is an amiable and adaptable plant that grows best in any fairly open sunny position. The species name (*mauritima*) means 'by the sea', suggesting that it is happy right on the coast — but it also does well in dry inland areas.

Centaurea gymnocarpa resembles the Silver cineraria with leaves cut a little finer, but is a little taller and has flowers like mauve cornflowers. Growth is more dome than cushion shaped.

Artemesias are also worthwhile members of the silver band. These vary in form from the large shrubby lace-foliaged Wormwood (*A. absinthum*), down through the wispy Ghost Bush (*A. lactiflora*) which forms clumps of erect silvery-white stems 1 m or more high, to several low forms only about ankle height. *A. nitida* is one of the most outstanding small rockery types. Lamb's Ears (*Stachys lanata*) can attractively carpet an area with soft downy silver foliage. It is used effectively as a border for semi-formal plantings such as dwarf red salvia, phlox and petunia.

In a less formal way, try clumping it between spring-flowering pinks, dwarf yellow wallflowers, geraniums or as a foil for any slightly taller, brightly-flowered plants. When in flower it makes spikes about 50 cm tall but these are not dense enough to oust its neighbours.

Cotton lavender (*Santolina*) is another silver softener but at the same time is quite eye-catching, especially in flower. It develops into a neat mound of rosetted leaves like tiny silver feathers, then in late spring is partly hidden below a mass of small golden flowers. This little gem is sometimes planted as formal edging around Elizabethan-styled gardens and can be clipped to keep it compact.

All of the true lavenders, particularly French (*Lavandula dentata*), can be used effectively in the silver-grey theme. Apart from its flowers and usually trim appearance, the foliage of this lavender is also pleasantly aromatic.

Raoulia is one of the most charming little silver carpeters. It makes a tight mound of tiny silver rosettes, each petal-like leaf smaller than a matchhead. Its flowers are just as tiny, resembling fuzzy drops of creamy-gold nestling among the silver. Raoulia is known in some areas as vegetable sheep because there are large mounds of it on the hillsides of its native Australia and New Zealand and from a distance it can resemble reclining sheep.

Some of these silver-foliaged plants are in the old-fashioned category and not always easy to buy. Most of the low carpeters mentioned are now creeping into the rockery plant range but in any case these, and all in the shrubby perennial class, are easy to propagate if you can locate them in your friends' older gardens.

The shrubby Dusty Millers all strike easily from tip cuttings about finger length or from similar-size side shoots from older stems. To avoid wilting, trim back all leaves to about one-third of their length immediately the pieces are cut from the plant, then keep them enclosed in a plastic bag until ready to plant.

A cutting soil made of 2 parts coarse sand and 1 part moistened peatmoss is ideal. Firm them in thoroughly and keep in a shaded sheltered position for 2–3 weeks.

Plants with grey or silvery foliage

Acacia cultriformis. Yellow flowers.
Acacia podalyriifolia. Yellow flowers.
Alyssum saxatile. Yellow flowers.
Centaurea cineraria (Dusty Miller). Mauve or purple flowers.
C. ragusina. Bright yellow flowers.
Chrysanthemum ptarmiciflorum
Dianthus. Pink flowers.
Feijoa (Pineapple Guava). Pink flowers.
Lavandula officinalis (True Lavender). Mauve flowers.
Leucadendron argenteum
Nepeta mussini (Catmint). Mauve flowers.
Romneya coulteri. White flowers.
Salvia leucantha. Blue flowers.
    S. argenta
Santolina chamaecyparissus. Yellow flowers.
Senecio cineraria. Yellow or cream flowers.
Stachys lanata (Lamb's Ear). Pink or mauve flowers.

Colourful plants for shady spots

Colourful foliage will give a lift to those areas too shaded for most summer flowers. Among the quickest growing shade-tolerant plants, with attractive foliage, are the New Guinea hybrid impatiens.

These plants also carry the typical impatiens or balsam blooms but each flower head is backed by a spectacular surround of unusually coloured large leaves.

Some varieties have dark, metallic purple-bronze foliage surrounding large, blood-red flowers. Other leaves display broad centres of glowing salmon-red to copper, contrastingly margined in dark green or bronze. Others are creamy ivory with dark margins and large pink to mauve opalescent flowers.

In climates with mild winters, these showy impatiens carry through happily until the following year but in cooler areas it is advisable to strike a few cuttings during late summer or early autumn, and keep them potted, in warm areas at least, until the following spring.

One surprising fact about these showy impatiens is that they reproduce from seed, usually with little variation from the parent plant.

Although the more common garden impatiens seed so freely, these New Guinea hybrids seem less inclined to set seed outside tropical areas. The only catch with trying to save your own seed is that the pods reach maturity quickly, then explode and fling their seeds far and wide. Impatiens does this by splitting and coiling the pod into spiral spring formation.

It is this unexpectedly sudden action that gives the plant its name, impatiens.

Impatiens propagate fairly readily from tip cuttings. Take these after new bursts of growth when they have lost most of their sappiness, and remove all but three or four top leaves. If the latter are large, then halve them.

A sandy soil, with a little peatmoss mixed in, gives good results. During hot, dry conditions especially, impatiens cuttings wilt quickly, so keep them in a plastic bag with a sprinkle of water until the minute you are ready to plant. Then, after watering thoroughly, enclose the container and cuttings in a plastic bag kept in a light but shaded position.

Coleus mix well with impatiens and are excellent for partly shaded areas of the garden or as container plants for brightly lit indoor situations. Although they grow well in shade, colours are much stronger where there is plenty of bright reflected light or an hour or two of early morning sun each day.

The same applies indoors. If foliage colour begins to fade, then move them closer to a window. Like the impatiens, many varieties of coleus carry through the winter in mild climates. However, they often become rather straggly toward the end of their growing season.

The old plants can be rejuvenated by cutting back in spring but it pays to start a few new ones from cuttings taken in late summer or early autumn. Select the younger shoots, removing any of the older stems entirely, and strike them as suggested for impatiens.

The important step to keep growth compact and bushy is to pinch out the growing tip once the cutting has made a few new leaves. Then, in turn, treat side shoots similarly as they reach about finger length or a little more.

If you have a large container, say one 16–20 cm in diameter, try setting two or three coleus in the one pot. The effect is much more dramatic.

Other ways to prolong the vigour and fresh appearance of coleus are to pinch out flower buds whenever they appear, and to feed occasionally with any of the water-soluble plant foods or seaweed extracts. Coleus and impatiens also like plenty of water, so give them a drink whenever the soil surface dries out.

Beautiful begonias

The huge begonia family contains a fascinating variety of plants. Some vie with the rose and camellia for beauty and perfection of flower, while others are grown for their appealing and often colourful foliage.

The begonia was introduced to England in the late 18th century and collections soon became a feature of all the large conservatories. It was found that the flowers of different species were easily crossed, and before long almost every head gardener had raised at least a few of his own hybrids.

The range therefore grew considerably and it was difficult to fully catalogue or keep up with the many new introductions. There are 200 distinct species and many hybrids.

The tuberous-rooted types (*B. tuberhybrida*) have glorious, large satin-textured flowers — either rose or camellia shape — in every colour but blue.

The basket begonias, with more numerous gracefully pendulous flowers, are also a form of this begonia (variety *Pendula*).

The tubers of *B. tuberhybrida* are planted in good fibrous, compost-rich soil during spring and the flowers come mainly throughout summer and autumn. Water is withheld as foliage begins yellowing after flowering and the tubers are then stored in sand or peatmoss for planting again the next spring.

Although they are often grown in glasshouses, this is mainly for protection rather than heat. They need an airy situation, preferring temperatures below 27°C. Propagation is mainly from seed or cuttings taken from the tubers.

A comparatively recently-introduced strain, *Begonia elatior* resembles the tuberous form but the flowers are smaller and more numerous. Since these do not form tubers, propagation is from stem cuttings of about finger length.

Fibrous-rooted or bedding begonias (*B. semperflorens*) have comparatively small and usually single waxy flowers from 10–20-cent size, but the blooms are carried in such profusion that they almost hide the attractive clumpy reddish-bronze, chocolate or green foliage.

Modern strains such as Gypsy and Thousand Wonders are ideal for mass planting in full sun or part shade as growth is usually only about 30 cm high. They are normally planted out in spring for summer flowering, but in warm frost-free areas can be grown outdoors throughout the year.

Propagation is from seed, which is very fine, and seed of the better strains is as expensive as gold. The clumps may be divided and replanted during early spring.

Tree begonias are grown partly for their handsome leathery 'angel wing' shape and often spotted foliage, but also for the showy pendulous clusters of waxy flowers that come in white and various shades of pink or red. These begonias are useful for lightly shaded parts of the garden or for containers on shaded patios or well-lit and reasonably airy indoor situations.

Most develop 1–2 m high and eventually sucker to form handsome clumps. Propagation is by planting pencil-length sections of the canes or tip cuttings of approximately that size, from early spring to autumn.

Many other semi-caney to shrubby-growing begonias carry attractive flowers. These include some of the large hairy-foliaged types such as hairy red-stemmed *B. scharffiana*, which has tall sprays of white flowers; *B. schmidtiana*, *B. ulmifolia* and their many hybrids.

Another handsome-foliaged group, generally known as rhizomatous types, spread by thick fleshy rhizomes or root stems. These include the well-known Cleopatra, with bright-green chocolate-streaked leaves; dark-green leathery-leafed Beefsteak Begonia (*B. erythrophylla*) and its curled or crested variety Cathedral Window (*B. erythrophylla helix*) which has red-edged translucent panels of lime green showing on the underside of the ruffled and upward cupped leaf.

All have wiry stems branching into fine sprays of small, waxy pink flowers and grow easily from a single leaf with the stem cut to 1–2 cm and gently pressed into light sandy soil, moistened peatmoss or a mixture of both.

Rex begonias are renowned for their beautifully marked and coloured foliage, some with a shot silk or opalescent gleam. Some of the well-known varieties include Merry Christmas — each leaf of which has a blood-red, satin-like centre surrounded by a broad zone of silver and pink, then bright-green and a surrounding purple edge; Her Majesty is dark, satiny ruby-red zoned with olive green and blotching of silver and pink, and Meteor which is a glowing rose-pink flecked with silver.

Iron Cross is not a true Rex type but usually loosely grouped in that class. The attractively-puckered, bright-green leaves have a broad, dark-brown centre pattern resembling an iron cross.

To maintain the full depth of their glorious colours, Rex begonias need a bright but well-ventilated sunroom-type condition or a sheltered outdoor spot in dappled sunlight. Excessive humidity may result in mildew.

Propagation by a single leaf as with rhizomatous begonias is effective. If you are striving for a number of plants from one leaf, it may be cut into wedge-shaped pieces — with the narrow base terminating in a cleanly cut section of one of the broader main veins. These pieces are set in a nearly upright position with the base 1–2 cm deep in moist sand.

Another method is to lay the leaf flat on a tray of sandy soil and sever the main vein in 5 or 6 places. Small plantlets are possible from each cut.

Other small caney begonias suitable for partly shaded parts of the garden include the Fuchsia begonias (*B. fuchsioides* and *B. cubensis*). Both have fleshy stems, small, glossy, waxy bronze-green leaves and dainty and pendulous pale pink flowers.

B. aconitifolia is yet another gem, making a clump of slender canes to about 75 cm high with deeply-cut pale olive and silver-spotted leaves resembling those of aconites.

Small clusters of silvery rose flowers intermingle with the foliage mainly during late summer and autumn. It propagates from tap or stem cuttings like the tree begonias.

Plants with large leaves

Acanthus (Oyster Plant). Shiny deep-green leaf.

Agave attenuata. Gigantic leaf rosettes, blue-green.

Aralia. Glossy leaves.

Arum lily. Green or speckled arrow-shaped leaves.

Bergenia (Saxifraga). Pink flowers, round leathery leaves.

Canna. Green or brown leaves.

Fatsia japonica. Glossy green leaves.

Hedychium gardnerianum (Yellow Ginger). Large green leaves.

Monstera. Large split leaves.

Senecio petasitis. Velvety green leaves.

Strelitzia. Bold leaves.

Plants with feathery leaves

Achillea (Yarrow). Green or grey. Flowers white, yellow or pink.

Asparagus fern. Green.

Astilbe. Plume-like flowers.

Centaurea cineraria (Dusty Miller). Silvery leaves, purple flowers.

Coleonema pulchrum (Diosma or Confetti bush). Small pink flowers.

Erica (heath).

Geranium incanum. Mauve flowers.

Tamarisk. Pink flowers.

Tree fern. Green.

Plants with grassy leaves

Bamboo

Liriope muscari.

Tristania conferta variegata (Variegated brushbox)

Above: Begonia rex

Below: A mixture of bronze, variegated and grey foliage.

Plants with variegated foliage

Abutilon (Chinese Lantern). Green and gold foliage.

Acalypha. All colours.

Acer negundo variegata.

Agave americana 'marginata'. Blue-green or yellow-striped leaves (thorny).

Aglaonema. Mottled with white, yellow and lighter green.

Alocasia macrorhiza 'variegata'. Dramatically blotched green and white.

Aphelandra squarrosa. Green and white.

Arundo. Green and white stripe.

Aucuba (Gold Dust Tree). Mottled green and gold.

Caladium bicolor. Silver, white, pink, red, bronze and green in combination (tropical).

Calathea. Cream and olive with underside patterns in mauve, pink and grey.

Codiaeum (Croton). All colours of yellow, green, red, pink and purple (tropical).

Coleus. Coloured variegations.

Coprosma (Looking Glass). Shiny green, cream and white.

Cordyline. Every imaginable combination of green, white, red and purple.

Dieffenbachia. Green and white.

Dracaena sanderiana. Green and white banded leaves.

D. godseffiana. Glossy green with white and yellow spots.

Euonymus japonicus. Gold marginal leaves.

Fittonia. Green with pink or white veins.

Geranium.

Hedera helix 'marginata'. Green and white foliage.

Hypoestes (Freckle Face). Green with pink spots.

Lamium. Marbled white leaves.

Manihot utilissima 'variegata'. Green and cream leaves with scarlet stems.

Maranta (Prayer Plant). Green with bronze markings.

Pilea cadierei (Aluminium Plant). Green and metallic silver.

Plectranthus hirtus 'variegatus'. Silver and green leaves.

Sansevieria (Mother-in-law's Tongue). Green, yellow and cream spiky leaves.

Saxifraga stolonifera (Strawberry Geranium). Green and white.

Tradescantia fluminensis 'variegata' (Wandering Jew). Green and white stripes.

Vinca major 'variegata' (Periwinkle). Green and cream.

Trees and shrubs with colourful autumn foliage

Acer palmatum (Japanese Maple). Red and yellow.

Berberis julianae. Scarlet.

Betula (Silver Birch). Gold.

Citharexylum. Apricot (spring).

Cornus florida.

C. baileyii. Purple-bronze.

C. sanguinea. Purple-bronze.

Fraxinus oxycarpa 'raywoodii' (Claret Ash). Deep, red-purple.

Fraxinus excelsior 'aurea' (Golden Ash). Golden yellow.

Koelreuteria paniculata (Golden Rain Tree). Yellow-orange.

Liquidambar styraciflua. Bronze, yellow and red.

Liriodendron tulipifera (Tulip Tree). Yellow.

Metasequoia glyptrostroboides. Coppery-bronze.

Nyssa sylvetica. Red, gold and yellow.

Pistacia chinensis (Chinese Pistachio). Purple, red and yellow.

Populus. Yellow and brown.

Quercus palustris (Pin Oak). Red and gold.

Sapium sebiferum (Chinese Tallow Tree). Gold, copper and purple.

Sorbus aucuparia (Rowan Tree). Yellow.

Spiraea prunifolia. Orange.

Tilia europea. Gold.

Ulmus glabra 'Lutescens' (Golden Elm). Deep Gold.

Viburnum opulus 'sterile' (Snowball, Guelder Rose). Orange-red.

Pistacia in autumn

Plants with bronze or reddish-purple leaves

Acalypha

Acer palmatum atropurpureum (Japanese Maple).

Ajuga reptans. Blue flowers.

Berberis thunbergii atropurpurea. Scarlet.

Cotinus purpurea. Purple-bronze flowers.

Fagus sylvatica atropunicea.

Iresine (Bloodleaf). Brilliant red and violet shades.

Prunus cerasifera 'Nigra'.

Strobilanthes anisophyllus (Goldfussia). Lavender flowers.

Zebrina pendula. Purplish flowers.

Crotons (Codiaeum) add colour to tropical gardens

Acalypha wilkesiana (Fijian fire plant)

Cineraria maritima

Left: A combination of coloured foliage keeps the garden interesting year round

15. Cacti and other succulents

If looking for plants that stand long periods of dryness, choose those with their own built-in water supply. Succulents have thick fleshy leaves and stems that store surprisingly large amounts of water. Not only that, they guard against wilting through loss of water during hot or windy weather by covering their leaves with a thick, waxy evaporation-proof skin.

Cacti are also succulents. The term succulent is loosely applied to almost anything with thick fleshy leaves and takes in a number of plant families, including some of the daisies, lilies and euphorbias.

In the case of cacti, the breathing pores are grouped together beneath a protective sheaf of hair and spines which in some cases also give sun protection.

The name cacti applies only to one particular plant family which has certain characteristics in common like flower form and fruit (which always forms below the flower petals). Some succulents, including a few of the euphorbias, aloes and agaves, have spines or spiky thorns but are not cacti.

All succulents are geared to survive drought or hot drying winds, with the possible exception of Crab's Claw or various strap cacti which grow naturally on trees in moderately moist, lightly-foliaged jungles.

The majority of succulents, and particularly the desert cacti, prefer to be kept fairly dry during winter but appreciate occasional soakings when new growth commences — in most cases during spring. New growth developing on any of the leafy succulents is quite obvious by formation of new leaves but the change is a little more subtle with leafless cacti. In this case it is the appearance of different coloured spines that lets you know that the centre of the plant is expanding or growing.

These new spines are usually a bright yellow, cream or pinkish colour, whereas the older ones are comparatively dull.

Cacti have beautiful flowers although the appearance of these may be scarce when they are grown indoors. Some need a fairly cool, winter period to flower. This applies particularly to the fairly rapidly-growing little Peanut cactus (*Chamaecereus sylvestri*) which needs winter temperatures around 13°C to flower well, therefore is unlikely to flower indoors. Another point worth noting about cacti is that during cool, wet conditions rotting is more likely to occur when splashed soil is crusted around the plant's base.

The best way to overcome this is to apply a screen or surface covering at least 1 cm thick of river gravel or other suitable aggregate. This not only stops soil from splashing but also keeps the soil surface more open, which in turn helps water to enter and get away more rapidly.

If base rot does occur, clean-cut damaged tissue then leave in a cool, dry place for a few weeks while the cut calluses. Then plant as a cutting in just-damp sandy soil.

Foliage of many waxy-leafed succulents can be colourful. Pleasant effects are possible by grouping types such as buff-gold *Sedum adolphi* with blue-grey Hen-and-chicken or *Echeverias*. Some of the latter also have pinkish-mauve tonings and their beautiful form resembles roses or lovely broad-petalled waterlilies, sculpted from pearly marble.

Graptopetalum paraguayens is also ornately sculptured, forming loose rosettes with thick, waxy, spoon-shaped petals in silver-grey to pale-blue-green flushed with amethyst. Cotyledons have similar formation and colouring, often with tall, waxy-pink stems of pinkish bells.

Kalanchoe marmorata has broad, pink to grey leaves attractively mottled with chocolate. *K. blossfeldiana* is dark grey-green with dense showy heads, and long-lasting clusters of small, deep-red flowers.

The tightly-packed, glossy jellybean-like foliage of *Sedum rubrotinictum* is flushed a rich, coppery-red during the cooler months, while that of *S. oxacanum* makes pleasant contrast in soft grey-green.

Cultivating cacti and succulents

Succulents are at home in well-drained rockery situations and are particularly useful for those frequently dry spots close to walls under the shelter of eaves. Here they can be effectively combined with rocks or a pebble garden.

Succulents are also excellent for balcony or terrace gardens, especially in those windy areas where container plants dry out rapidly. Because comparatively little soil is needed, they grow well in shallow bowls or troughs.

Desert soils are sandy or gritty and water drains away rapidly, but usually they are well supplied with organic matter from spent annual growth that matures rapidly in the showery season.

These low-rainfall desert areas are usually rather limey. Most garden loams can be made more suitable for cacti by raking in a 2.5 cm layer of coarse river sand or twice this amount if the loam is heavy.

Growing indoors

If growing succulents or cacti indoors, they need fairly strong light, in this case even an hour or two each day of direct sunlight through the glass. When there is not enough light for their needs, new growth becomes thin and unusually elongated.

Potting

A good potting mixture is about 2 parts medium garden loam, 2 parts coarse river sand and 1 part well-rotted compost. Unless the soil is limey, add about 2 teaspoons of garden lime or dolomite to each 10 L bucket of soil mixture.

Use at least 2.5 cm of broken crocks or coke in the base of the container to ensure good drainage and that this material doesn't block the holes.

See that the plant isn't covered deeper than its previous level. Set it with its base at soil level about 1 cm below rim of pot.

Firm it well, then scoop about 2 cm of soil from around the rim so water drains quickly away from the stem. Prevent the soil from levelling out by covering with about 1 cm of scree — blue-metal screenings, small pebbles, or crushed tile.

This surface covering also stops soil from splashing onto the stem of the plant and causing stem rot.

Most fleshy-leafed succulents also respond to the conditions suggested for cacti, although some also tolerate comparatively moist conditions in a well-drained garden soil. Roughly, it is the grey- or downy-leafed types that need best drainage and limey conditions.

Repotting

Small, rapidly-growing plants are best repotted each year; more mature plants every 2–3 years, preferably in early spring. Containers shouldn't be more than about 5 cm wider than the plant's spread, as the surplus soil is too slow to dry out.

A painless way to handle prickly plants is to fold a length of paper into a band, encircling them with this, and using the surplus ends like a cup handle. Pack soil around the plant with a pencil.

Watering

Water is needed most when new growth starts. In succulents, new shoots are an obvious indication of this. Cacti usually show brighter-coloured new spines.

Many succulents from Africa and the Mediterranean areas make new growth in winter. With cacti it is more frequently in spring, and at this time the plants will benefit from watering 2–3 times per week.

Wet the soil in the containers evenly. If the plant has been dry for some time, stand the container for about 10 minutes in a bucket of water. Let the soil dry out between waterings. True cacti, especially, need little more than a fortnightly watering during their dormant period, which is usually in winter.

Feeding

Avoid heavy feeding. Slow-acting bone-dust or cotton-seed-based fertilisers such as rose foods or seedling starters are ideal — a level teaspoon scattered around the edge of a 12.5 cm pot and scratched in lightly. In early spring.

Propagation

The usual method for branching succulents is by cutting. Use pieces of any length, cut cleanly with a sharp knife or razor blade, to avoid bruising. Leave fleshy stems for a few days until the cut section dries out.

Pot in a sandy, well-drained mixture with a minimum of water for the first few weeks.

Some succulents form plantlets at the base of severed leaves left to rest on a bed of sandy soil.

Cacti are usually propagated by removing 'pups' or new divisions that form round the plants. Large sections can be cut from tall types such as cereus. Don't bury them too deeply, but tie to a stake with the dried-out cut section covered by about 5 cm of sandy soil.

Raising cacti from seed can be fascinating. Scatter the seeds thinly, press into the surface of shallow trays of 3 parts sand and 1 of moistened peatmoss, or of seed-raising mixture. When about small pea-size, transplant about 2.5 cm apart in seed trays or boxes. Pot individually the second year.

Pests and diseases

Mealy bug is the worst enemy of cacti and some succulents: a small, downy, white aphid-like pest found in ridges of the plant at the base of the spines, sometimes in the roots. Small infestations are controlled by touching them with a camelhair brush dipped in methylated spirit. It is best to repot.

Control widespread attacks by spraying with Rogor or Malathion, adding about 1 teaspoon of household detergent to each litre of spray. Also water around each plant to wet the roots thoroughly.

Red spider or similar mites may also attack cacti or succulents, especially when under cover in a dry atmosphere. Symptom is a dull, lustreless or mottled appearance. Spray as for mealy bug.

Nopalxochia (German Empress cactus)

Echeveria

Rhipsalidopsis, one of the many Crab's Claw cacti

Left: Kleinia has interesting blue tones throughout the year

A reference guide to cacti

Desert-type cacti

Aporocactus. Grows on trees. Has long, slender stems that are ribbed and covered with fine spines.

A. flagelliformis (Rat-tail Cactus). Grown as a hanging plant; slender, carmine flowers borne freely along the stems.

Astrophytum (Star Cactus). This cactus is low-growing and globular in shape, but may become cylindrical with age. There are usually 5–8 ribs only; the areolae are set well apart along the ribs and the whole surface of the plant is often covered with small, white scales. The large yellow flowers are borne on areolae near the centre of the plant.

A. capricorne. Has 8 ribs and woolly areolae bearing a number of twisted spines.

A. myriostigma (Bishop's Cap). Usually 4 or 5 ribs but no spines.

Barrel Cactus see *Echinocactus grusonii*
Bishop's Cap see *Astrophytum myriostigma*
Cephalocereus. A large genus of columnar cacti normally reaching a considerable height; the ribbed stems are generally hairy.

C. senilis (Old-man Cactus). Is best known. Green-ribbed body wrapped in long, white hairs.

Cereus. Name used for a few species of columnar cacti, which bear large, funnel-shaped flowers which open at night.

C. aethiops and *C. azureus* have a blue, waxy coating on young stems; must be tall before their white flowers are produced.

Chamaecereus. *C. silvestrii.* Is small-growing with prostrate stems which are brittle and break off easily, but can be re-rooted. Has large, erect orange-scarlet flowers.

Cholla see *Opuntia*
Cleistocactus. One of the columnar cereuses. Spiny areolae close together make several slender stems from the base. The flowers are small and do not open wide.

C. straussi. Stems slender, erect and covered with white spines; flowers carmine.

Corypantha. These round or cylindrical plants are a few centimetres across and grow solitary or in clumps. Distinguished by the groove on the upper side of each tubercle, or protuberance, one or more of the spines is often hooked.

C. elephantidens. Spherical, with large tubercles and white wool on top.

C. vivifara. Smaller than *C. elephantidens*, with more cylindrical tubercles; it quickly makes clumps.

Dolichothele. *D. longimamma.* Yellow-green (glaucous) protuberances or tubercles, up to 5 cm long. Produces large, yellow flowers.

Echinocactus (Barrel Cactus). *E. grusonii* is the best known of this genus. The stem, at first spherical, becomes cylindrical with age, with many ribs and golden spines. Large specimens are sometimes seen — even small ones are very attractive.

Echinocereus. This cactus resembles the columnar cereuses. Although some species become cylindrical in time, they never form columns. The flowers are usually very large and showy.

E. delaetti. Ribbed, cylindrical stem entirely covered with white hairs.

E. rigidissimus (Rainbow Cactus). Short, stiff spines flattened against the stem, alternate zones being white and red.

Echinopsis. Spherical cacti with straight ribs, sometimes divided into tubercles; offsets are produced freely. The flowers are large with long tubes, white or pink.

E. eyriesii. Round with flowers up to 25 cm long, white with green throat.

E. multiplex. Globular plant with pink flowers.

Ferocactus. These large spherical cacti do not make offsets. The ribs are well developed and the spines are stout, sometimes flattened, and usually curved or hooked.

F. rectispinus. Has long spine, up to 120 cm.

F. wislizenii. Stout, with flat hooked spines.

Gymnocalycium. These cacti form low, spherical plants with wide ribs divided into tubercles characterised by a chin-like projection below the areola; the spines are variable and the white, pink or occasionally yellowish flowers are freely produced and usually large.

G. mihanovichii. The spherical body has alternate zones of light- and dark-green. Diameter about 5 cm. The variety of this species named *hibotan* is a tomato-red colour; it cannot be grown on its own roots but only when grafted on another cactus.

G. multiflorum. Large, bright-green plant, about 12 cm across with 8 or 9 stout, curved spines in each areola; pink flowers 5 cm across.

G. quehlianum. Bluish-green body and large flowers.

Indian Fig see *Opuntia ficus-indica*
Lemaireocereus. *L. marginatus.* Dark-green stems with 5 or 6 ribs along which woolly areolae are very close together.

L. pruinosus. The new growth at the top is glaucous-blue.

Lobivia. These cacti are medium-sized, round or cylindrical, usually very spiny and make offsets around the base. The flowers are usually yellow, sometimes orange or red.

L. aurea. Large, funnel-shaped yellow flowers.

L. famatimensis. Flowers may be yellow, orange, pink or blood-red.

L. pentlandii. Branches freely to form clumps. The flowers are orange-red.

Lophophora (Mescal, Peyote). Forms a low head, depressed in the centre, on a large taproot. Its few ribs are rounded, divided into low tubercles, and there are no spines in the areolae, only tufts of wool. Small pink or white flowers emerge from the woolly centre followed by little red fruits.

Mammillaria. Plants vary in size but are mostly round or cylindrical, sometimes solitary but more often making offsets or forming clumps. They are characterised by spiral rows of tubercles instead of straight ribs. There is an areola on the top of each tubercle and the spines vary in size and colour; in some there is wool in the axils as well as in the areolae. The flowers are small and produced in rings around the plant, not in the centre. In some the sap is watery but in others it is milky.

M. applanata. Hemispherical, with large, green tubercles and white flowers; milky sap.

M. bombycina. Hooked central spines, red flowers and watery sap.

M. bocasana. Branching type covered with handsome, hair-like white spines; yellowish flowers striped with red.

M. elongata. Small with golden spines.

M. magnimamma. Round, green stems; much white wool in the centre and on the areolae; flowers creamy-yellow; milky sap.

M. plumosa. A small plant, 30 cm across, covered with soft, feathery spines; forms clumps and should be watered with care. White flowers with a reddish mid-rib.

Mescal see *Lophophora*
Notocactus. This group includes round and cylindrical cacti with ribs in tubercles and large, yellow flowers.

N. apricus. Globular, with curved, reddish central spines.

N. leninghausii. Tall-growing plant with golden, bristle-like spines.

Old-man Cactus see *Cephalocereus senilis*
Opuntia (Prickly Pear, Cholla). The stems of this cactus are jointed. The joints may be flat, cylindrical or globose. The spines vary in number and type. The characteristic of this genus is that tufts of barbed bristles called 'glochids' are also produced in each areola. As these become easily detached, the plants should be handled with care. Because of their barbed tips, glochids are difficult to remove from the skin. Many of the flat-jointed plants make large bushes; growing of *Opuntias* was prohibited in most Australian states.

O. compressa. Native from Ontario to Alabama and Missouri, is a hardy, low-growing type with large, yellow flowers. Excellent for seaside plantings.

O. cylindrica. Cylindrical stems with lozenge-shaped protuberances bearing areolae but few spines. Flowers scarlet.

O. ficus-indica (Indian Fig). A large plant, cultivated for its edible fruit, its oval pads may be up to 30 cm long. Flowers yellow.

O. microdasys. Smaller than *O. ficus-indica* with no spines, but tufts of glochids that look like plush, and are white, yellow or reddish. Flowers yellow or tinged reddish.

O. polyantha. Flat, oval pads about 10 cm long, bearing yellow spines; produces yellow flowers regularly.

Oreocereus. A genus of columnar cacti, these plants have ribbed stems divided into tubercles. There are few spines but a large number of long hairs which wrap around the plant.

O. celsianus. White hairs and yellow spines.

O. trollii. Silky white hairs which almost cover the plant; golden-reddish spines.

Parodia. The straight or spiral ribs of these cacti are divided into tubercles and the areolae near the centre have much white wool; the large flowers are yellow or orange and are freely produced.

P. microsperma. A round plant, elongated when old.

P. nivosa. Has snow-white spines and bright-red flowers.

Rainbow Cactus see *Echinocereus rigidissimus*

Rat-tail Cactus see *Aporocactus flagelliformis*

Rebutia. This plant usually makes offsets from the base or sides of the plant; the flowers spring from old areolae, near the base in some species.

R. minuscula. Looks like a green golf ball; bears scarlet flowers with slender tubes.

R. senilis. Long, white spines surround the plant.

Rhipsalidopsis. An epiphytic type of cactus it has freely-branching, short, dark-green or reddish stems with narrow, flat joints.

R. rosea. Pink flowers (up to 30 cm across) produced freely at the tips in spring.

Star Cactus see *Astrophytum*

Trichocereus. These columnar cacti branch from the base; the spines are well developed and the white flowers, which are produced on old specimens only, open at night.

T. spachianus. A vigorous grower with curly white wool and yellow-brown spines. Branches at base when about 30 cm high.

Epiphyte cacti

Christmas Cactus see *Zygocactus truncatus*
Easter Cactus see *Schlumbergera gaertneri*
Epiphyllum. These are epiphytic, not desert cacti. The stems are flattened, often wavy or notched along the edge, with very small spines, if any, in the notches. The flowers are large and showy; many of the plants in cultivation are hybrids.

Schlumbergera Epiphyllopsis. This epiphytic cactus has short, flattened, jointed stems with elongated areolae on the top from which flowers and new joints develop.

S. gaertneri ephiphyllopsis (Easter Cactus). Bright-red flowers; numerous hybrids and varieties.

Zygocactus (Christmas Cactus). *Z. truncatus* are popular epiphytic cacti with interesting, flattened, jointed stems. From their ends (in mid-winter) emerge bright carmine, two-petalled blooms. Give less water in summer and put outside in the shade; bring in again before winter frosts and then, if necessary, repot in fresh soil.

A reference guide to succulents

Adromischus. Small South African plants with thick leaves and short woody stems, with small flowers in slender spikes.

A. cristatus. Thick, green hairy leaves on thin stalks, the wide top edge thinner and wavy; stems short, stout and covered with dry, brown aerial roots.

A. festivul. Larger leaves than *A. cristatus*, narrowed to the base, grey-green with darker markings.

A. maculatus. Flat, broad leaves marked with reddish-brown spots and edging.

Aeonium. Form shrubs with woody stems. Are not hardy in cold climates.

A. arboreum. Compact rosettes of green leaves on branched stems.

A. foliis purpureus, similar to *A. arboreum* but has dark-purple leaves.

A. domesticum. Shrublet with much-branched stem and small rosettes of roundish, hairy leaves toward the tips; small yellow flowers.

A. tabulaeforme. Almost stemless, with numerous leaves symmetrically arranged in flat rosettes. A pyramidal inflorescence rises from the centre, after which the rosette dies.

Agave. Leaves are thick, usually tapering, sometimes with spiny edges and are in rosettes on short stems. Are extremely large plants when fully grown.

A. americana (Century Plant). Spreading, greyish-green leaves. Several varieties have yellow, white or pinkish longitudinal stripes along leaves.

A. victoriae-reginae. A small type with very stiff, dark-green leaves edged and striped with narrow white lines.

Aichryson see *Aeonium*
Air Plant see *Kalanchoe pinnata*
Aloe. Natives of Africa, these plants vary in size, some having stems, others none. Some species, where the stem increases in height, become trees in their native habitats. The leaves are thick and tapering, sometimes with spiny edges, and in rosettes — flowers are usually orange or red. Aloes are spring and early summer growers and should be given adequate water during this period. Repotting or dividing can be carried out at this time.

A. arborescens. Develop a stem; have slender leaves with stout spines along edges.

A. aristata. The stem never lengthens but branches at ground level forming clumps. Numerous small, in-curved leaves, dark-green with white edges and spines on back and edge. Produces annual spike of typical red aloe flowers.

A. saponaria. Short-stemmed and forms offsets. Leaves fewer and much larger, pale-green with white oblong spots arranged in bands.

A. variegata. Leaves stand erect, arranged in three rows keeled on the outside; dark-green with white teeth along edge and transverse rows of white spots in irregular bands. Red flowers on loose spike about 30 cm high.

Astroloba Formerly called **Apicra,** is closely related to **Haworthia.** Leaves are arranged symmetrically up the stem.

A. pentagona. Five rows of leaves. Wide at the base, green, thick, firm and terminating in a sharp tip.

A. spiralis. Five rows of leaves, spiralled and blue-grey in colour.

Bryophyllum see *Kalanchoe*
Burro's Tail see *Sedum morganianum*
Candle Plant see *Senecio articulata*
Caralluma. Have stout, 4–6-angled leafless stems and small star-shaped flowers.

C. europaea. The commonest species with four-angled stems and clusters of small, pale-yellow flowers banded with purple.

Carrion Flower see *Stapelia*
Century Plant see *Agave americana*
Ceropegia. Mostly climbing or trailing plants with the exception of two: *C. dichotoma* and *C. fusca.*

C. dichotoma. Stout, erect stems; leafless for most of the year; curiously shaped yellow flowers.

C. fusca. Similar to *C. dichotoma,* but with chocolate-coloured flowers.

C. woodii. A trailing plant with thin stems rising from a corm and bearing small, heart-shaped leaves, dark-green with silvery markings and purple undersides.

Conophytum. A genus of stemless plants in the Mesembryanthemum family. Each pair of leves being so closely joined that a small, top-shaped body with a slit across the upper surface is formed — the surface may be flat, curved or lobed. The flowers emerge through the slit, after which the plant divides. Keep plants completely dry or almost so from June until December, by which time the outer pair of leaves should have dried up to a papery skin that splits when growth begins. This is a large genus of some 200-odd species.

C. calculus. Round, green head, without markings; yellow flowers.

C. frutescens. A lobed-top type and the earliest to bloom. Orange flowers may appear before watering.

C. globosum. Similar in colour to *C. calculus* but larger and kidney-shaped with mauve flowers.

Cotyledon. Woody plants from South Africa with slightly succulent leaves — they are usually attractively coloured.

C. orbiculata. Roundish, grey-green leaves with red edges.

C. undulata. Leaves have a wavy edge and covered with white meal. Produces orange or reddish bell-shaped, hanging flowers when larger.

Crassula. *C. arborescens.* A shrubby plant with fleshy, red-edged and spotted leaves.

C. cooperi. Forms mats of small rosettes of prettily marked leaves.

C. falcata. Tall with narrow greyish leaves, turned on edge; a wide head of bright-red flowers in summer terminates the stem, which later branches.

C. lycopodioides. Branching stems covered with overlapping, tiny, dark-green pointed leaves.

C. portulacea (Jade). Large with shining green leaves, red at the edges.

C. sarcocaulis. Small with tiny, blue-green leaves and bunches of pink flowers on ends of branches.

C. schmidtii. Low-branching stems with rosettes of leaves, the centres of which elongate into shoots bearing small, red flowers.

Crown of Thorns see *Euphorbia splendens*
Drosanthemum. This plant is one of the mesembryanthemums characterised by the glistening, nipple-like papillae on the leaves.

D. floribundum. Forms cushions of prostrate stems. Flowers freely, often in first year from seed.

Echeveria. The leaves are in rosettes, either stemless or on branching stems. They have a coating of wax or hairs on the surface which make them very decorative; flowers are red or orange in loose sprays produced in great profusion on most plants.

E. derenbergii. Glaucous-blue leaves in rosettes with red edges; bright-orange flowers.

E. gibbiflora. Larger than *E. derenbergii*, with rosettes carried on branching stems.

E. gibbiflora carunculata. Similar to main type but centre of leaf puckered with a large, irregular swelling.

E. gibbiflora metallica. Similar to main type but has dark, reddish-purple leaves.

E. glauca. Compact rosettes, rounded leaves with short tips, blue-grey with reddish margins.

E. harmsii. Small, erect shrub with hairy leaves in loose rosettes. Bright-red flowers about 3 cm long, 1–3 together on short stems.

E. leucotricha. Hairy leaves, mostly silvery, but brown on edges.

E. pulvinata. Low-branching stems with rosettes of green, hairy leaves, with crimson edges and large, orange flowers.

Euphorbia. Have columnar spiny stems and small, insignificant flowers. A milky juice or latex exudes if the skin is broken — in some cases this is poisonous.

E. caput-medusae (**Medusa's Head**). Cylindrical, spineless branches rise from a large spectacular central head, a new ring of branches being formed annually.

E. grandicornis. Singular stems and spines in pairs along angles.

E. heptagona. Ribbed columnar stems with solitary spines along angles.

E. meloformis (**Melon Spurge**). Has a low, round stem depressed in the centre, with about 8 wide ribs. Male and female flowers grow on different plants. The so-called spines are the remains of branching flower stalks which have become woody with age.

E. obesa. Round when young, becoming cylindrical; ribs more prominent at the top and

Aloe arborescens

its grey surface is covered with dull-purple, transverse lines.

E. pseudocactus. Segmented three-angled spiny stems with V-shaped dark-green patterning along stems.

E. splendens (Crown of Thorns). Has branching stems with irregularly scattered spines; bright-green oval leaves near tips of branches during growing period. Flowers small but surrounded by two conspicuous bright-red bracts.

E. submammillaris. Similar to *E. heptagona* but smaller and freely branching.

E. tirucalli (Milkbush). Erect stems, leafless and spineless.

E. virosa. Slow-growing erect plant with 4 or 5 ribbed stems; edges deeply waved and horny with 1.5 cm stout spines.

Faucaria. These low-growing mesembryanthemums have 2 or 3 pairs of thick leaves at right angles to each other; keeled at the back with a fringe of teeth along each edge.

F. tigrina. Large, stemless, bright-yellow flowers.

F. tuberculosa. Similar to *F. tigrina* but the leaves are not so long.

Fenestraria. Mesembryanthemums of this type are known as 'window' plants because of the translucent upper surface of the erect, cylindrical leaves which are held in rosettes.

F. aurantiaca. Large, yellow flowers.

F. rhopalophylla. Large, white flowers.

Gasteria. Can generally be recognised by the leaves which are arranged in two ranks instead of in a rosette, with no stem. The flowers are small, tubular with a swollen base, reddish with green tips and hang from long, arching flower stems.

G. lingua. Short, broad, dark-green leaves patterned in white.

G. verrucosa. Leaves about 15 cm long, pointed, greyish-green with white dots.

Glottiphyllum. These mesembryanthemums have soft-fleshed, green leaves closely packed in two ranks along short stems that are often prostrate. The large flowers appear from September to January.

G. depressum. Translucent green leaves and yellow flowers up to 6 cm across.

G. linguiforme. Wider leaves and larger yellow flowers.

Graptiopetalum. *G. amethystinum.* Has very thick, bluish-grey leaves, flushed with amethyst, on a stout, branching stem. Small, white flowers held in a loose cluster.

Haworthia. Related to the aloe but the plants are smaller, the leaves in rosettes and the small, white flowers held in long, loose inflorescences. Grow mostly from late winter to mid-summer and need less water in the resting period. Repot in September. Sensitive to strong sunshine and respond well to semi-shade conditions.

H. coarctata. Leaves reddish and in-curved.

H. cymbiformis. Stemless with rosettes of softer leaves. Prefers slight shade.

H. margaritifera. Has dark-green leaves with raised white dots on back and front.

H. tessellata. Small, low rosettes composed of a few very thick leaves with tips recurved; surface is covered with a network of fine lines.

Kalanchoe. The plants need more moist conditions than most succulents but grow quite well in a cool glasshouse or living-room.

K. blossfeldiana. Clusters of bright-red flowers. By selection a number of distinct varieties has been obtained.

K. daigremontiana. Produces plantlets along the notched edges of the large triangular leaves. Often seen as small specimens but if potted in richer soil will grow more freely and flower in a year or two.

K. pinnata (Air Plant, Life Plant). Leaves consisting of 3–5 oval leaflets which produce young plants along their scalloped margins if they are laid on moist soil, or kept in a light place without soil. Flowers are greenish or yellowish suffused with pink.

K. tomentosa. Leaves covered with silvery hairs, brown along the edges and in loose rosettes on branching stems.

Kleinia see *Senecio*

Lampranthus. Shrubby plants useful for planting outdoors in warm, dry climates, especially near the sea. The following can all be grown in pots but tend to become straggly — so should be started again from cuttings.

L. aureus. Yellow flowers.

L. blandus. Large, pale-pink flowers.

L. coccineus. Red flowers.

Life Plant see *Kalanchoe pinnata*

Lithops (Stoneface). Probably the most sought-after genus in the mesembryanthemum family. The top-shaped plant body consists of a single pair of united leaves, varying from a small slit to a definite fissure between the two lobes. In nature only the upper surface appears above the ground. The flowers (white or yellow) emerge through the slit across the top. The plants should be kept completely dry or nearly so during the resting period, from about June to December.

L. bella. Pale-grey with a sunken brown and yellow patterning on the surface; white flowers.

L. lesliei. Olive-green with red patches and yellow flowers.

L. olivacea. One of the 'windowed' plants, the centre of each lobe being translucent.

L. optica. Has a deep cleft between the two lobes which gape open and have translucent tips; colour normally grey but there is a purplish-red variety.

Medusa's Head see *Euphorbia caputmedusae*

Melon Spurge see *Euphorbia meloformis*

Mesembryanthemum. This name is applied to many plants that belong to the family *Mesembryanthemaceae,* especially to the shrubby types. They all come from South Africa and South West Africa.

Milkbush see *Euphorbia tirucalli*

Pachyphytum. The blue-green (glaucous) leaves are very thick, club-shaped and arranged in a loose rosette up a short, stout stem. The flowers are small.

P. compactum. Close rosettes; dark-red flowers with greenish tips.

P. oviferum. Larger leaves than *P. compactum,* more loosely arranged and with a dense, white coating; scarlet flowers.

Partridge-breasted Aloe see *Aloe variegata*

Pleiospilos. Usually consists of a single pair of thick leaves which look like chunks of stone; large, yellow flowers appear between the leaves in autumn at the end of the growing season, which starts during the summer. During the resting period keep the plants completely dry. Even when a new pair of leaves begins to grow in the centre, you should give no water until the old pair begins to dry up. They will then have passed on the nourishment stored in them to the growing pair.

P. bolusii. Brownish-green leaves with dark dots with the lower side rounded.

P. nelii. Similar to *P. bolusii,* but each leaf is the shape of half a sphere.

P. simulans. Leaves are very thick but spread out on the ground.

Sedum. Many of the species are hardy even in cold regions. Often regarded as rock-garden plants rather than tender succulents. Those that come from warmer countries can be grown out-of-doors in mild climates only. Colouring is at its best when grown in full sun.

S. dasyphyllum. A small plant with tiny, bluish succulent leaves which tinge red in the sun.

S. guatemalense. Fat, bronzy leaves about 1 cm long. Becomes green if not in sun.

S. morganianum (Burro's Tail). A hanging plant. Small, cylindrical, close-packed bluish leaves along long stems ending in small bunches of pale-pink flowers.

S. pachyphyllum. Erect, woody stems with slender, club-shaped leaves toward the ends, pale, yellow-green with red tips.

S. stahlii. Prostrate stems with fat, small, reddish leaves.

Senecio (Candle Plant). *S. articulata.* Keep dry or nearly so during summer so that the stems will remain short and glaucous — watering will make them long and green; leaves and flowers appear when watering is resumed in autumn.

S. haworthii. Erect with cylindrical pointed leaves entirely covered with a shining white felt. Keep dry in winter.

S. stapeliaeformis. Four-angled, dark, purplish-green stems with orange-red heads of flowers.

Stapelia (Carrion Flower). When their flowers open, many of these plants have an unpleasant smell that attracts flies for pollination. The stems are usually angular, leafless and rather soft. Give them very little water but do not keep them completely dry when resting.

S. variegata. Stems smooth and erect with spreading teeth; five-pointed, star-shaped flowers at base with wrinkled surface, yellow with purple markings. This variety has the typical, unpleasant odour.

Stoneface See *Lithops*

Mesembryanthemum

Kalanchoe tomentosa

Gymnocalycium mihanovichii 'rubra'

Kalanchoe blossfeldiana

16. Ground covers and trailers

Why not let ground covers take over the areas your favourite plants reject and where grass refuses to grow? The garden need not lose interest or variety because large areas are given over to ground cover. You can enjoy the most interesting collection of cover plants and still grow your favourite shrubs, bulbs and perennials with them.

One of the great attractions of ground cover is that it reduces the necessity to weed the garden.

Ground cover plants have the capacity to cover the ground with a low carpet of foliage. The carpet may be low and smooth or soft and thick. Ground covers, however, need not always be carpet-like. Some can form low mounds along the ground, others can be shrubby and create an undulating surface.

They are generally evergreen, spreading perennials or may be low-growing shrubs or succulents.

Trailing plants bring cascades of colour

Colourful cascading plants can bring beauty and interest to window or planter boxes, rockeries, embankments or bare walls. There is a wide range of decorative plants with naturally draping or contour-following growth style, many with permanently attractive foliage when they are not massed in flower. Apart from their individual appeal they are wonderful softeners to veil or mask severe lines of otherwise stark concrete edges.

Some of the tougher ones can even be grown in wall baskets to bring colour and to relieve the bareness of walls or fences.

All trailing plants are easily grown if in the right situation and climate. Therefore, to make selection easier, they are grouped here according to their needs. Annuals, perennials and more permanent shrubby subjects are also in their appropriate groups.

Spillovers or rockery plants are happiest in areas with cold winters and cool, spring conditions, but they also grow with some success in temperate districts, especially when trailing over rocks or masonry where stems are not encrusted with moist soil splashed up by rain or heavy watering. The latter seems to induce fungal rots during humid summer and early autumn conditions.

A pebbly scree or layer of gravel over the surrounding soil will give further protection in this respect. All need at least half-sun.

Yellow alyssum (*A. saxatile*) is one of the most spectacular, with masses of tiny golden florets on large, finely-branched heads giving a gold cloud effect above its rosettes of long silver-grey leaves. It can be raised from seed, which needs to be sown by February to flower the first year, or from late autumn cuttings, using side rosettes of growth with foliage cut back to at least half.

Arabis has contour-following stems studded with rosettes of short grey-green foliage, almost smothered in spring with thin-stemmed spikes of usually double chalky-white stock-like flowers. There is also a less robust single pink-flowered and a variegated foliage form.

Propagate arabis by using a healthy outer rosette of foliage with a few centimetres of stem attached, struck as a cutting, preferably in a mix of 2 parts coarse sand to 1 part of moistened peatmoss mix. Also, some stems self-layer.

Aubretia resembles a slightly smaller-foliaged, usually single-flowered, arabis in mauve to purple tonings.

Alpine phlox are the prime colour makers in cool climate gardens. Their dense carpet of small grass-like foliage spreads or drapes 1 m or so, and is completely covered throughout spring with starry pink, ruby, mauve-blue or white flowers.

Under good conditions they give spasmodic bursts of colour almost throughout the year. Propagate like arabis or by detaching self-layered stems.

Erysimum, from a distance, may resemble yellow alyssum but the much larger florets are in smaller heads and closely set above the dense foliage carpet. It is propagated like arabis.

Lithospermum pleases with a rich blue cascade of small flowers above trails of slender dark foliage. There is also a lighter blue variety, Grace Ward. This gem is harder to propagate than other plants mentioned. Stem layering is the most reliable home garden method.

The following plants grow equally well in cool or warm temperate areas.

Arenaria montana has thread-like trailing stems which carry small foliage and numerous upfacing round-petalled and saucer-shaped pure white flowers about 10-cent size. Stems layer easily or tip cuttings can be struck in autumn.

Snow-in-summer (*Cerastium tomentosum*) is a wonderful foil and pleasant contrast for neighbouring plants with its dense drape of small silver-grey foliage. All it needs is a well-drained spot in any climate and a light trim in late spring to remove the old stems that support its mass of small silvery-white spring flowers.

Campanulas, especially the numerous small evergreen types, are delightful spillovers for full sun or light shade. They are massed with mauve or lavender-blue bells for a long period between mid-spring and early summer and are very easily propagated by dividing clumps in winter.

The yellow Chamomile (*Anthemis tinctoria*) will spill and splay attractively when planted toward the edge of a wall. Mid-summer finds the plant covered with rich yellow daisies on stems about a span long and these often continue to appear during late summer and autumn. Foliage is finely divided and dense at the base of the plant. It's easily started from cuttings or by division during winter.

Verbenas are colourful and lovely, especially during late spring and summer. Many improved hybrid types are perennials and come in various shades of pink, mauve, red and white.

Spanish shawl, creeping lassiandra, Heeria elegans and schizocentron are some of the names that identify a tiny-leafed carpeter covered with bright carmine flowers in late spring or early summer. This little plant finds its way over bare rocks providing they are not too dry and is also excellent in a basket. It grows happily with about half sunlight and winter protection from heavy frosts.

Establishing ground cover
Remove weeds

First rid the ground of existing weeds.

Action should be taken during their active growth as some chemical treatments will not be effective during winter dormancy.

Persistent bulbous perennials such as oxalis and onion grass or perennial grasses such as kikuyu, couch and paspalum are very persistent and will probably need more than one treatment.

If the site you wish to prepare is heavily infested it could be worthwhile getting professional help and having the soil fumigated with methyl bromide. Since this gas is lethal and will kill any tree or shrub roots in the vicinity it should obviously be used with the greatest of care.

A less drastic treatment is to spray the stems and foliage of weeds with Roundup, Zero or Couch and Kikuyu Killer. These chemicals are absorbed by the plant and, since they are not selective, should not be used on an area where you wish grass to be retained. It will be 2–3 weeks before the weeds die.

Another method is to saturate the soil with a solution of TCA at recommended strength but, if you have to clear bamboo, use it at double strength. Apply when the soil is wet, not just on the surface but to a depth of several centimetres. Unfortunately, the soil will remain toxic for at least 3 months after using this treatment.

Stubborn blackberries can be dealt with during late summer or early autumn by spraying with a proprietary spray, especially for the killing of trees and blackberries.

General herbicides such as Zero, Weedex and Polyquot can be used to clear weeds. They work on green tissue, are toxic and should be handled with care, but they break down very quickly once they have made contact with the soil and it would be quite possible to start planting your new ground cover within a few days.

If you dislike the idea of using these chemicals then hand-weed the area to the best of your ability and be prepared to continue hand-weeding among the growing cover plants until such time as they have grown sufficiently to cover the ground and become strong enough to smother the weeds.

Mulch

The key to establishing ground cover easily and successfully is to use a surface mulch right after weeding. A layer of leafmould 3–4 cm deep makes an efficient mulch. Grass clippings can be used but only if they have been standing for a few weeks. If you use them when green they will heat up whilst decomposing, causing problems by 'felting' together and making a pad through which water will find it hard to penetrate.

Wood chips and pine bark also make efficient mulch that works well in conjunction with ground cover plants.

Some of the mulches are only temporary and will have decomposed by the time the ground cover plants have become strong enough to take over their role of blanketing weed growth, but the more expensive ones such as pine bark and pebbles, which are longer-lasting, can be used as features in themselves.

Planting and maintenance

Planting is simple. You only have to move the mulch cover aside, plant and then draw the mulch back around the plant when it is in place.

Ground covers — by and large — are low-growing perennials which smother weeds, carpet the soil and require little or no maintenance to remain attractive. Most of the ones widely used are content with any rain that may fall; some require a really dry position and others will benefit from being watered once a week or once fortnightly.

Ground covers for shade

Low-growing

Ajuga reptans (Carpet Bugle). Green or bronze leaves, blue flower spikes.
Bergenia cordifolia (Megasea or Saxifraga). Round, leathery leaves, pink flowers in mid-winter.
Chlorophytum (Hen-and-chickens). Green or variegated leaves in tufts.
Crassula multicava (London Pride). Round, grey leaves; pink flowers.
Convolvulus mauritanicus (Ground Morning Glory). Trailing green stems with small mauve flowers.
Duchesnea indica (Wild Strawberry). *Fragaria indica*, strawberry-like leaves and red fruit which is not edible.
Hedera (Ivy).
Helxine soleirolii (Baby's Tears or Mind-your-own-business). Tiny green leaves.
Hypericum. Yellow flowers.
Lamium maculatum (Dead Nettle). Variegated green and silver leaves.
Liriope spicata (Lily Turf). Tufts of strap-like leaves 15–20 cm long; mauve flowers.
Ophiopogon japonicus (Mondo Grass or Lily Turf). Tufts of narrow leaves 15–20 cm long; lilac flowers.
Plecanthus ciliatus. Dark-green purple-backed leaves, pale mauve flowers.
Polygonum capitatum. Pink flowers and pinkish leaves.

Saxifraga sarmentosa (Strawberry Saxifrage). Rounded, marbled leaves, white flowers.
Sedums (various).

Tradescantia fluminensis (Wandering Jew). Green leaves, white flowers.
Vinca major (Periwinkle). Blue flowers, also a variegated gold and green-leaved type.
Viola hederifolia (Wild Violet). Small, light-green leaves, flowers lavender to dark blue.
Zebrina pendula (Wandering Jew). Green and white foliage with purple beneath; purple flowers.

Dense, dry shade with root competition

Chlorophytum*
Clivia*
Ivy
London Pride
Mondo Grass

Dry, part shade with moderate root competition

Agapanthus
Bromeliad*
Chlorophytum*
Ivy
Lamium
London Pride
Liriope
Mondo Grass

Moderately dry — part shade

Campanula
Cissus*
Erigeron 'vittadenia'
Hardenbergia
Heeria*
Hibbertia
Ivy
Lamium
London Pride
Pachysandra
Polygonum
Plectranthus*
Trachelospermum
Vinca
Wild Strawberry
Wild Violet

Moist soil — part shade

Acorus
Ajuga
Arenania
Chlorophytum*
Fern
Heeria*
Hosta
Impatiens*
Ivy
Lamium
Lysimachia
Saxifraga
Wild Strawberry
Wild Violet

Ground covers for sun

Low-growing

Alyssum saxatile. Grey leaves, yellow flowers.
Arctotis. Greyish leaves; pink, cream and other coloured flowers.

Cerastium tomentosum (Snow-in-summer). Silver; tiny white flowers.
Chamomile (Anthemis tinctoria, German Chamomile). Tufts of deeply cut foliage, dark green above, grey beneath bright golden yellow daisies, 3–4 cm across on stems 30–50 cm high, mainly during early summer
Convolvulus maritima. Non-invasive perennial with small rounded foliage on trails to about 0.7 m long studded with lavender blue saucer-shaped flowers about 3 cm across, mainly during summer.
Dimorphotheca. Large, mauve-pink daisy flowers.
Drosanthemum. Tiny, shiny purple flowers, silvery leaves.
Erigeron. Tiny, white daisy flowers.
Gazania. Grey leaves, brilliant-yellow daisy flowers. Other types have variegated showy flowers.
Geranium (Ivy). Ivy-shaped leaves, flowers white, pink and red.
Iberis sempervirens (Evergreen Candytuft). Dark-green leaves, white flowers.
Lantana montevidensis. Small leaves, small purple flowers.
Lippia repens (Lippia Grass or Daisy Grass).
Nepeta mussini (Catmint). Grey leaves, pink-mauve flowers.
Sedum (Stone Crop). Tiny fleshy leaves which turn red in winter.
Stachys lanata (Lamb's Ear). Grey leaves and spikes of lilac flowers.
Thymus (Thyme). Small aromatic leaves, tiny whitish flowers.

Moderately dry — sun

Ajuga
Dimorphotheca
Erigeron 'vittadenia'
Gazania
Geranium
Grevillea
Hardenbergia
Juniper
Kennedia
Lantana montiv.
Lippia
Polygonum
Phlox subulata
Myoporum
Succulents
Trachelospermum
Thyme
Vinca
Wild Violet

Dry — very sunny

Arctotis (hybrid)
Cerastium
Chamomile
Dichondra
Dimorphotheca
Gazania
Lantana montiv.
Lippia
Mesembryanthemum
Succulents

Moist soil — sun

Dichondra
Lysimachia
Wild Strawberry
Wild Violet

Alpine phlox, white arabis and yellow alyssum add lively colour to this border

Shrubs for ground cover

Ground cover is not limited to carpeting runners. Low-branching shrubs planted close together can also be used to carpet the soil. Well-placed groups of the taller shrubs with drifts of low carpeters growing between them can look very attractive. When shrubs are being used as ground cover they should be set about one-third closer than the recommended spacing so that they will soon touch each other.

Low-matting prostrate shrubs

Grevillea biternata,. Light-green fern-like leaves. Rapid spreader. Grows well on rubble-type embankments in full sun.

G. laurina. Round leaves. Prefers to grow in leaf mould under the light shade of native trees.

G. obtusifolia. Deep-green glossy leaves, slow grower — likes full sun.

Juniperus procumbens

Dense, low-branching, medium-size shrubs

Grevillea alpina (varieties)
   G. lavendulaceae
     (particularly Canberra Gem)
   G. rosmarinfolia
   G. Robyn Gordon

Taller shrubs

Abelia
Azalea (Kurume or dense-growing
   indica types)
Choisya (Mexican Orange)
Coprosma (Mirror Plant — all types)
Cotoneaster horizontalis (Clusterberry)
Euonymus japonica
Hebe (Veronica)
Juniperus communis depressa aurea
   (varieties)
   J. conferta
   J. douglasii
   J. pfitzerania

Lantanas (dwarf)
Osmeria
Raphiolepsis (Indian Hawthorn)
Viburnum davidii
Westringia

Prostrate junipers make interesting cover

Arctotis hybrida

A reference guide to ground covers

Acorus Like a miniature clump of variegated cream and green flax only 15–20 cm high, clumps densely but slow to cover an appreciable area. Could be used for contrast of form and colour amongst *ajuga* or other low cover. Stands very wet or dry soil, almost full shade or sun but not for hot sunbaked situations. Propagate by dividing and replanting clumps, preferably in late winter-spring.

Agapanthus Tough clumps of strap-leafed evergreen bulbous plants with metre high or more stems carrying a globelike cluster of blue or white slender trumpetlike flowers in early summer. They flower best with at least half sunlight but grand as a cover below trees as they stand dryness and root competition well. They are also excellent soil binders. All but very cold districts. Propagate by dividing clumps in winter. Spaced 50–60 cm apart they should meet up in about a year.

Ajuga reptans Makes a spreading mat of rosetted usually dark bronze foliage with ankle-high spikes of blue flowers in spring. The latter are showiest in cool climates but *ajuga* is a good gentle cover in sun up to two-thirds shade. Especially suited to moist soil but withstands dryness. Clip off old flower spikes to encourage spreading. Propagate by removing rooted rosettes or runners any time, preferably avoiding mid-summer. Set plants 15 cm apart for quick cover.

Arctotis hybrida (Aurora Daisy) Quick growing silvery-grey foliaged plant with large bronze, yellow, purple or silvery-mauve daisies, mostly in spring. Long-lived and clumps up fairly thickly in well-drained positions with at least half sun. Drought resisting and tolerates root competition. All but extreme tropical districts. Propagate from autumn- or spring-sown seed or from cuttings — set plants 35–45 cm apart.

Arenaria balerica Creeping mat of bright green foliage only about 8 cm high, carrying small dainty white cup-shaped flowers on erect hairlike stems in spring. Not tough cover but attractive for foreground carpeting in cool to mild temperate areas. Propagate by division in autumn or winter.

A. montana More rambling than above with wiry stems and numerous larger flowers about 10 cent size. Long-lasting but not vigorous. Propagate from layers or cuttings in autumn or late spring.

Azalea Most attractive cover plant for not too densely shaded areas below trees. The Kurume types and most of the lower growing hybrid indicum types can be kept low and spreading by cutting back or pinching out centre of new growth from the early stages onward. Their growth tends to thin as shade deepens but weeds are rarely a problem amongst them, especially if a natural mulch of leafmould is allowed to remain around the plants.

Bromeliad Not generally accepted as ground covers but they add interest and are useful for dressing up shaded areas below trees. They grow in any or very little soil.

An example of successfully growing ground cover to add colour to the garden

Trailing species, geranium

Alpine phlox adds colour to border

A combination of alpine phlox and yellow alyssum saxatile

The main need is to keep water in the pitcher-like receptacle made by the leaf formation. These remarks apply to all the different *billbergias, neoregelias, aechmeas, nidularniums,* the hardier *vrieseas,* etc, which grow well outdoors in all but cold districts.

Campanula Low-growing evergreen types like *C. lactiflora, C. poscharskyana* cover quickly, are massed with starry pale blue flowers mainly during late spring, and grow well in part-shade. They make colourful broad borders or mats below all but very dense trees in both cool and temperate districts. Propagate by dividing clumps from autumn to late winter. Divisions set about 12 cm apart should make a continuous carpet in two to three months.

Cerastium tomentosum (Snow in Summer) Small silver-grey foliage, covered in spring with small erect cup-shaped flowers. Best in open, sunny, well-drained positions. In humid areas centres of clumps may die out, needing replanting about every second year. Propagate from cuttings or layers removed in late autumn or winter. Rapid grower.

Chamomile (*Anthemis nobilis*) Sometimes called Roman Chamomile. Low clumps or mats of finely cut light green foliage, branching sprays of small white daisies — sometimes planted as chamomile lawn but cannot be regarded as a weed-proof cover. Likes fairly heavy soil in cool to cooler temperate areas. It stands some foot traffic but stepping stones are suggested for main traffic ways.

Chamomile Yellow (*A. tinctoria*) A fine but dense grey-green foliaged plant with long-stemmed showy yellow daisies mainly in early summer. Makes good foreground cover in full to half sun. Propagate from cuttings or rooted divisions in spring — set plants about 20 cm apart.

Chlorophytum (Spider Plant) Large rosettes of green and cream straplike foliage with plantlets forming toward ends of long-branching flower stems. Excellent plant for dry shade under trees, drought-resistant because of its fleshy bulbous storage roots. Good contrast in front of dark-foliaged *clivias,* etc. Propagate by planting up plantlets.

Cissus (Kangaroo Vine) Both broad-leafed *C. antarctica (Rhoicissus)* and divided holly-leafed *C. rhombifolia* are dense, glossy-foliaged climbing plants that rapidly and attractively cover the soil in full shade or sun. They enjoy plenty of water during summer but withstand dryness well. Prevent them from climbing trees or shrubs they surround. Propagate from cuttings. One plant will cover about two metres square. Pinch back tips to encourage branching.

Clivia miniata An excellent cover plant for permanently shaded areas, it competes well with tree roots. Foliage is broad, stiff and dark green, flowers are heads of large orange-red trumpets in spring. *C. hybrida* is a little larger in all respects, clumps reaching about 80 cm in height. *C. nobilis* is an equally suitable plant but the later flowers being more cylindrical and slightly pendulous are less spectacular than the others mentioned. Avoid direct sunlight as this causes browning of foliage tips. Propagate by dividing clumps in winter or from seed which takes about a year to ripen and is slow to germinate.

Dichondra (known in New Zealand as **Mercury Bay Weed**) A good low-matting plant with closely set small kidney-shaped foliage like the native violet *(Viola hederaceae).* It grows well in sun or light shade with moist or fairly dry soil and stands moderate foot traffic. It can be invasive in rockeries, etc. Propagate from seed available from lawn seed suppliers.

Dimorphotheca ecklonis (Black Eyed Susan) Marguerite-like bushy daisy to 75 cm tall and at least as wide, with dark violet centre and violet flush to backs of petals. Included here because it grows well under trees providing they are high-branching enough to allow in about half sun, has reasonably bushy canes and can give a flower-packed appearance to a garden with little else to offer. Propagate from seed or cuttings.

Erigeron karvinskianus (*Vittadenia*) Fine-foliaged but densely matting and rapidly spreading plant covered with threadlike-stemmed fine-petalled pink-flushed to white tiny daisies, most profuse in spring but appearing throughout the year. Accepts light shade or full sun.

Ferns Shaded positions where the soil is reasonably moist can be transformed into charming bushland dells with a cover of ferns. Add to this atmosphere by including a few mossy rocks, a log or a shade-tolerant native shrub like dainty pink-flowered *bauera.* Also consider adding a small pond, both for appearance and to increase the moisture content of the area.

Most types of maiden-hair are suitable, especially the strong growers like Common Maiden-hair (*Adiantum aethiopicum*). Giant Maiden-hair (*A. formosum*) is also suitable but grows to 50 cm high and in light soils particularly can be a little invasive.

Some of the not too rampant fish-bone types (*Nephrolepis* or *Polypodium*) are also suitable. If transplanting (except from containers where roots are not disturbed) first cut back all foliage. It is hard to sacrifice immediate effect but it is the only safe procedure. If possible, transplant when new growth is not evident, preferably in late winter.

Gazania Low-matting leathery-foliaged daisy ideal for open sunny aspects. Resistant to salt winds and, once established, to drought — suits poor rocky situations where grass is hard to manage. Colours are mainly yellow and orange with some less usual larger and zoned burgundy and pink tones also offering — flower mainly in spring. Propagate from layers, side shoots with foliage trimmed back as cuttings, or seed. Set plants 50 cm apart.

Geranium Spreading geraniums make attractive and aromatic cover for well-drained situations with at least half sun. Amongst these are the ornately cut velvety-foliaged and deliciously aromatic types like the *Pelargonium quercifolium, P. graveolens,* P. Attar of Roses which smells like a rose garden in full bloom when the foliage is brushed or watered. There are other varieties with mint, apple, nutmeg and other spicy aromas. All are easily propagated from cuttings, taken preferably in late autumn then pinched back as growth progresses to keep them bushy. Allow plant-spread of at least one metre.

Low-matting geraniums like small purple saucer-shaped flowered *G. incanum* which usually need renewing after about two years. Ivy geraniums are excellent and free-flowering spillovers for sunny embankments.

Grevillea Native ground-hugging grevilleas include widely used fine light green-foliaged *G. biternata* which spreads about two metres and needs the taller flower stems trimmed back when finished; small dark-leafed *G. obtusifolia* which is relatively clumpy, rarely spreading more than one metre, and pleasantly meandering large oval-leafed *G. laurifolia* which grows naturally in light shade. The others need at least half sun, preferably more. Other slightly taller types like hybrid Robyn Gordon, and some of the *G. lavandulacea* forms are also attractively dense and make good cover plants.

Hardenbergia A good native cover or spillover plant for sun to half shade, covers in spring with sprays of lavender or violet-blue small pea flowers. If left to go its own way is a rampant quick-covering climber, therefore new growth needs turning back or trimming to keep it confined.

Helxine (Babies tears or Mind-Your-Own-Business) Dense bright green tiny-leafed ground-hugging carpeter for damp, shaded positions — even covers damp rocks or masonry. Propagate by transplanting small pieces.

Heeria elegans (*Schizocentron* or *Heterocentron* also known as **Spanish Shawl** or **Creeping Lassiandra**) Small-leafed ground-hugging carpeter bursting into a mass of 10 to 20-cent-size bright carmine flowers like small lassiandras in late spring. Best as a trailer over rocky banks, etc, in light shade. Stems self-layer, even on moist rocks. Use these to propagate, preferably in autumn or early spring before new growth commences. Resents heavy frost.

Hibbertia scandens One of many Australian native vines suitable for ground cover in sun to heavily dappled shade. Leathery, oval leaves, flowers like huge golden buttercups spasmodically throughout the year. Looks more at home if allowed to meander over an old log or some chunky rocks. Head back straying shoots into the area where needed or pinch back tips to encourage branching.

Hosta (Plantain Lily) Included here mainly because it is used as a ground cover in the northern hemisphere where it is successful because the ground is covered with snow or it is too cold for weed growth during its winter dormant period. It is a very beautiful plant with clumps of ornate spatulate-shaped variegated, blue-green or plain foliage to 20–30 cm high and dainty spikes of pendulous violet or pale mauve bells in early summer. Worth including for interest in lightly shaded moist spots amongst *Ajuga* or *Heeria*.

Impatiens sultanii (Busy Lizzy) There is a constant call for summer colour for shaded spots, and this plant is one of the very few that can oblige. A type of balsam, with thick brittle watery stems and heads of 20-cent-size flat, satin-textured flowers ranging through dark red, orange-red and various pinks or mauves to white. Some of the recent hybrid types have darker colours marked with white. All flower profusely during the warmer months, but are frost tender.

Regular types grow quickly to nearly one metre high, seed and self-sow readily, and if not controlled may smother dwarf azaleas and other small plants. More recent dwarfs should remain at about 25 cm but some eventually get taller in humid districts with mild winters.

There are also the New Guinea Hybrids with larger flowers and beautifully marked or coloured foliage which can be grown permanently in outdoor shade where winters are mild. Propagate from seed (if you are quick enough to catch it) or from tip cuttings kept in a humid atmosphere until rooted. Some gardeners root them in water.

Ivy (*Hedera*) There are many different shapes. Among the best for ground cover is Californian or Weber's Californian because it has very closely set overlapping foliage and a more branching habit than many others. Pittsburgh is similar with more angular foliage and is reputed to be more resistant to snow and frost.

Even these 'ground cover' types are capable of climbing and can strangle trees with their rampant adult growth. Checking over the ivy cover area about twice a year, particularly in spring, to head back or remove any climbing growths. An occasional trim in spring will also keep it from mounding high.

The types mentioned stand dense shade or full sun. For really tough situations the crested or parsley ivy (*Hedera helix* — Cristata) is the most vigorous and seems resistant to 'bacterial blight', a leaf spot which is showing up occasionally in some districts. Propagate ivy from sections of stem or tip cuttings taken when they have lost their spring sappiness. Root them under seed bed conditions before planting out into their permanent site.

Juniper Low-growing prostrate junipers make effective and attractive ground cover, especially in areas below eaves or where soil frequently dries out. All need at least half sun. Amongst the most suitable are *J. conferta* with twisted soft feathery grey-green growth, native of Japan and Rocky Mountains but adapts to heat, even in warm temperate areas. *J. sabina* with straight tapering featherlike branches radiating almost horizontally in all directions. There are several forms. Low clumpy *J. communis* Depressed Aurea

changes from gold to purple-bronze during the seasons, *J. horizontalis Douglasii* is blue-green. All need at least half sun, more for good foliage colour.

Average spread is about one metre, a little more for most *J. sabina* and *J. procumbens* types.

Junipers can be propagated by layering or from tip cuttings but unless you have a definite feel for this, buy plants.

Kennedia (Running Postman) Native vines that adapt to a variety of soils in sun or light shade, useful for ground cover if treated as Hardenbergia. *K. rubicunda* has large rounded foliage and large dark-red pea flowers. *K. coccinea* has small foliage and masses of smaller brighter red flowers, mostly in spring. There are about 10 other species.

Lantana montividensis (Purple Lantana) Too many people bypass this plant because of its name. This species is in no way invasive, rapidly forms a dense mat of stems and foliage that few weeds could penetrate and its continuous flowering keeps colour in the garden almost throughout the year. It is sometimes seen trained over fences or stumps but by nature is ground hugging, keeping to about 25 cm in height. It grows in full sun or half-shade and once established stands long periods of dryness and soon recovers from fairly severe frosting.

Lamium Low cover of silver and green variegated slightly hairy foliage, sometimes called Aluminium Plant but glossier, more erect *Pilea caderii* probably has more claim to the name. Also known as Dead Nettle because it is related to the nettle but without stings. As the weather warms in spring it sends out runners which root down and spread rapidly, earning it a reputation of invasiveness but it is easy to control either by cutting back or pulling out unwanted layers.

Lamium can be used as a temporary cover in shaded spots where *cinerarias, primulas* and other spring-flowering annuals are planted. Just pull out all runners and enough clumps to allow for your plantings of annuals in autumn, leaving an occasional clump or rooted layer every 60 to 70 cm.

The tufts of new silvery growths look attractive amongst the spring flowers, then as warmer conditions curtail the latter display, the lamium races into new growth to provide an attractive weed-free cover for summer.

Propagate from clumps or rooted layers with most of the growth trimmed off.

Lippia nodiflora (*Phyla nodiflora*) A tough little North Australian trailing plant with branching stems, small oblong foliage studded almost continuously with small cloverlike heads of tiny flowers, usually pink. One of the few covers that can be substituted for lawn grass as it stands some traffic. Weed infestation that may occur can be removed by setting the mower up a little. Needs at least half-sun and good drainage. Does well in dry inland areas. One disadvantage is that the flowers are very attractive to bees which may cause a problem with bare feet, thongs, etc. Propagate from layers or tip cuttings. If

purchasing do not confuse with *Lippia citriodora* which is a large woody shrub.

Liriope muscari (Ribbon Grass) Clumps of tough ribbon-like green and white foliage with spikes of small blue muscarilike flowers in summer. Attractive clumped for contrast amongst low-matting covers like *ajuga*, etc. Best in dappled to full shade, stands wet or dry soil. Propagate by dividing clumps in winter.

London Pride (*Crassula multicava* — *C. cordata* is a similar substitute) One of the best covers for dry shaded areas below trees. Waxy stems to about 25 cm with sets of opposite rounded to heart-shaped thick waxy olive green leaves 4–5 cm across. Finely branched spikes of tiny pink flowers appear in spring. Propagate by inserting stems into average soil — 15–20 cm apart.

Lysimachia nummularia (Moneywort or Creeping Jenny) Ground-hugging creeper or trailer suitable for damp situations in shade to half sun. Closely set pale green rounded 5 to 10-cent-size opposite leaves edge the soft stems. Can be invasive in damp areas of lawn, although easily killed by broad-leafed weed killer. Foliage may brown in full sun or severe frost. Propagate from layered stems. Covers rapidly during warmer weather while soil is damp.

Mesembryanthemum These include various forms of *Lampranthus*, which are the widely grown and showy Pig Face, smaller-flowered and shorter-leafed *Oscularis, Malephora* with glistening orange or yellow flowers, etc. All you have to do is acquire a piece of one that appeals, poke it into not too clayey soil, and it is bound to grow into a dense mat of succulent foliage with seasonal flower. All need at least half sun, and are ideal for exposed, often dry situations or where there are only small pockets of soil amongst rock. Suit all but the coldest and tropical districts.

Mondo Grass (*Ophiopogon japonicus*) Dense clumps of slender dark green tough but not stiff foliage — grasslike to about 15 cm high — ideal cover for completely shaded areas either wet or frequently very dry, or infested with dense tree roots. Not intended for traffic but is not damaged if occasionally trodden on. Propagate by division, preferably in late winter.

Myoporum parvifolium (Prostrate myoporum) Low-spreading plant with branching stems, closely set with leathery, dark green narrow leaves 2–3 cm long, studded with small starry white summer flowers. Ideal for sea coast but adaptable. Needs well-drained, sunny position. Propagate from cuttings, set plants one metre apart.

Pachysandra Glossy bright green cover plant to 25 cm high, seems better suited to cool districts — for shade or part sun. Propagate by cuttings.

Plectranthus ciliatus A plant that covers rapidly in warm, reasonably moist partly or fully shaded areas. The large slightly hairy deeply veined dark green leaves are purple backed, to 8 cm across and a little longer with squared stems growing to 15 cm in height, tends to smother smaller plants but ideal under large shrubs or for open shade. In late summer each stem carries a 12–15 cm broad spike of small mauve-flushed flowers.

P. oertendablii is similar to above with lighter veining. *P. australis* is smoother foliaged brighter green without purple backing. *P. saccatus* is a useful small low-branching shrubby species with small dense soft green lobed foliage and short spikes of lavender blue *salvia*-like flowers throughout summer.

Height rarely more than 75 cm, with a wider spread. One of the few summer-flowering shrubs that grow well in shade and accepts reasonable root competition. All *plectranthus* are easily grown from cuttings kept in a moist shaded position for a few weeks. They suit all but cold districts.

Polygonum capitatum (sometimes referred to as **Strawberry Grass**) Although not a grass, brown wiry stems are fairly closely set with dull green to bronze foliage, below numerous erect branching spikes of tightly packed flower heads like small pink strawberries. Sometimes regarded as a weed but can be used to make a pleasant cover in sun or preferably part shade. Needs little soil, therefore useful for a drape on rocky ledges.

Phlox subulata (Alpine Phlox) A very decorative and effective cover for cool climate gardens — dense mats of fine foliage, often completely covered with starry rose pink, mauve, pale blue or white flowers during spring and sometimes into summer. At least half-sun is needed for dense growth and prolific flowering. They also grow in temperate districts but not as well as in cool areas.

Propagate from rooted layers or from cuttings.

Saxifraga Several of the vast range are worth considering as ground cover for cool districts with moist lightly shaded situations. Among these are clumpy or mossy *S. cespitosa* with thin erect stems carrying small cupped pink or white flowers and *S. umbrosa* which carries dainty clouds of tiny pink flowers in spring. *S. cordifolia* with broad, leathery green foliage and sprays of waxy pink winter flowers is an effective clumpy cover in shade either in cool or temperate districts. This plant is now correctly named *Bergenia*.

Schizocentron see *Heeria*

Strawberry The wild strawberry is an efficient though in some ways over-enthusiastic ground cover which rapidly makes plantlets on the end of long runners capable of spanning mower strips, etc, but removing unwanted runners is not a serious problem. Foliage is softer and not as leathery as most fruiting types but makes a denser cover. Flowers are yellow, followed by red but unpalatable berries. It grows in sun or moderate shade in all districts.

Propagate from runners. The fruiting strawberries are suitable for ornamental borders but not as covers for difficult spots as they need ample sunlight and a reasonably rich soil.

Succulents There is a large range of succulents suitable for cover and colour in fairly dry positions with at least half-sun. Very little soil is needed, but good drainage is desirable. A variety of *sedums, crassulas, rosetted echeverias* and *graptopetalums*, pink or

marbled *kalanchoes, blue kleinea* which looks spectacular near buff-gold or bronze-red foliaged *sedums*, and many others are worthwhile. All grow easily from pieces at practically any time of year.

Also see London Pride and *Mesembryanthemums*.

Trachelospermum (Rhynchospermum or Chinese Star Jasmine) Handsome dark glossy foliage climber or twiner, easily kept in broad cushionlike mounds to about 2 m across. Fragrant cream flowers contrast pleasantly with the foliage in late spring. It grows happily in sun or shade but more rapidly in half-sun or broken sunlight. It grows well in all but the coldest districts.

Like many permanent easily controlled plants it is slow to make an appreciable dense spread but it is worth using a pinebark mulch, *lamium* or *ajuga* around it as a cover while it is establishing. Propagate from layers though it is usually more satisfying to purchase plants.

Vinca minor (Periwinkle) Glossy almost oval leaves on long slender stems topped with saucer-shaped mauve or purple flowers. Attractively variegated forms are widely available. Suits sun or shade, once established stands dryness well. *V. major* is similar but with larger flowers. Propagate from layers or cutting.

Wild Violet (Viola hederifolia) A delightful native carpeter making a dense mat of small kidney-shaped bright green foliage below numerous flushes of white to palest mauve flowers with contrasting violet centres. It covers rapidly and is invasive unless contained by a mower strip. Propagate by division.

Alpine phlox carpet below dwarf azaleas

Hibertia peduncularis

Maidenhair fern — good in damp and shade

Drifts of alpine phlox and other perennials provide long-lasting cover and colour

Heeria elegans (Spanish shawl)

White candytuft, alpine phlox and yellow alyssum

Mauve pink thrift (armeria) is adaptable to most conditions and is long flowering

17. The lawn

Planning a lawn

A swathe of lawn in healthy condition gives the garden it embraces an atmosphere of well-being and tranquillity, especially when it flows beneath the dappled shade cast by trees and shrubs. Gardening should always be a pleasure, not a penance and, though it takes time and energy to achieve a good lawn, there is no need to become a slave to the creation of that lovely stretch of green turf. The secret is to learn where grass will grow well and where it will not and to give up all idea of growing it where it will not be happy. Assess your shade areas. Consider the winter sun and the shadows it will cast from buildings, fences and dense shrubbery — grass needs sun for at least half the day if it is to make good growth. Don't worry about an isolated tree, particularly if the foliage is not dense, as the play of light and shadow over a lawn is very pleasant.

You will enjoy your lawn all the more if the maintenance is easy, so in your initial planning avoid strips of grass which are too narrow and corners which are too small to be comfortably dealt with by the mower. If your site slopes gently, let the grass cover the bank in a smooth unimpeded curve and add mower strips. These will save you from the continuous chase needed to keep grass from invading flowerbeds and will make edge trimming relatively easy but don't put them in until the lawn has settled down to an established level or you will have the chore of having to readjust them later. To be effective, lawn and mower strips should be on a level so that the mower can ride easily over the strips.

Creating interest

A garden becomes more intriguing when part of the lawn disappears from view. When limits are not defined there is not only an 'on-flowing' feeling but an agreeable one of speculation.

Create this effect by using gentle curves to bring a peninsula of growth out from the garden to partly hide the next bay of the lawn, or to carry the grass around behind a building or group of shrubbery. Use gentle curves instead of straight lines to lengthen the actual perimeter of the lawn and to give the impression of greater space. Generous curves look more restful than straight lines but avoid numerous small curves as these result in a 'fussy' effect.

Try out the plan in mind by placing a hose or soft rope to mark the intended curves and rearrange until the effect is pleasing.

Trees and shadows

Low-branching trees with dense foliage can make it difficult to grow grass directly below them, particularly when they have numerous surface roots. Nevertheless, trees give gardens a delightful character and their shadows on the lawn add interest and create patterns that change from hour to hour, and gradually vary from season to season.

Trees are seen at their best when the lawn goes (or appears to go) right up to their trunks. Actually it is more practical to keep the grass back a few centimetres from the trunk to eliminate those adventuresome and bent on tree-climbing runners that allude the mower and otherwise need hand-clipping. The effect will be the same as uninterrupted lawn flowing right up to the trees, but this way it is easier to maintain this pleasant appearance and, more importantly, avoids mower damage to the trees.

Planning paths

Grass soon becomes shabby and threadbare if exposed to much foot traffic. The family 'runs' will be fairly obvious even at the planning stage and you will be able to make provision by laying permanent paving; but habits and conditions do alter and you may find worn tracks across the lawn where the soil has become compacted and worn away by hurrying feet taking the shortest distance from A to B. You can take care of these incidental paths by supplying stepping stones which will not disrupt the smooth flow of the lawn and are often more attractive than a solid path. Providing they are set flush with the lawn, maintenance is easy. If the traffic is not enough to keep the grass from growing over them, just keep the edges trimmed. A quick run-around with a pair of strong scissors gives instant spruceness.

Site and soil preparation

It is essential to provide a good, even surface before putting in a lawn: this applies whether you lay turves, plant runners or sow seed. All too often turves are put down to cover tough clay but the results are never satisfactory — you need at least 12 m depth of good, crumbly, well-drained soil to grow grass well.

Grass is no different to any other plant and needs the same care and scope for good root growth: watering and feeding. In some respects it needs even more consideration than other plants because its foliage (a plant's food 'manufacturing' area) is frequently diminished by mowing, which naturally has a weakening effect.

If you have raw clay you are faced with a drainage problem as grass will not flourish in an over-wet soil. Depending on the extent of the problem you could put down agricultural drainage pipes over the clay then cover them with ashes before putting down the final layer of good soil, or just use a thick layer of ashes beneath the soil and don't bother with the pipes.

It is better to improve your own soil whether sandy or clayey, by the addition of compost or moistened peatmoss, than to rely on 'garden soil' bought at a nursery as they too often are alluvial-type soils which will compact. For grading or filling over poor clay use coarse river sand or bush sand to keep the soil open.

One of the best couch lawns that I know of

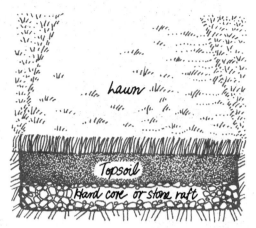

Where topsoil has been removed as on some building sites, spread a 15 cm layer of gravel over the clay base, firm, and cover with a similar depth of good topsoil. This can be an effective form of drainage.

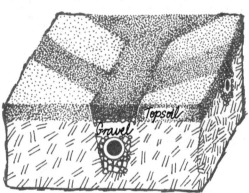

A herringbone arrangement of porous clay or plastic pipes sunk in gravel-lined trenches is the best but most expensive way to drain medium to large areas. The pipes, 8–10 cm diameter, are set 45–75 cm deep and fed either into a sump or outfall in a ditch or stream. To prevent soil falling in and blocking the flow ensure there are no gaps between pipes.

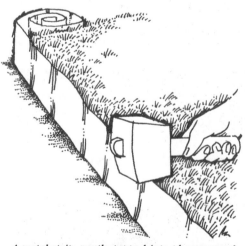

A metal strip, gently tapped into place around lawn edges, is an effective way to prevent damage. The top of the strip should be slightly below the lawn surface for ease of mowing.

is in a heavy, puggy clay area, where, after many unsuccessful attempts to grow grass, the owner put down a 10 cm layer of blue-metal screenings because he had noticed how eagerly couch grew into this material on roadside dumps. The success of this treatment was due to the tremendous aeration available to the roots in such a coarse, loosely-packed material, especially as the heavy clay below it still held plenty of moisture in easy reach of the roots.

Levelling

You may need a level spot for use as an outdoor living area. A rough level can be achieved by a line stretched across the site horizontally, broad and long, just above the soil so that the height can be corrected visually.

A more accurate way without special equipment is to drive in two sturdy pegs about 5 cm square and up to 1 m in height. On top of these fix a straight piece of timber about 2 m long. Level this with a spirit level by driving the higher stake a little deeper into the soil, then approximately above and in line with this fix a taut cord or line to stakes driven in either side of the area to be levelled. This line is adjusted to the same level as the straight timber guide by tapping the appropriate stake in deeper.

From this it can be roughly decided how much building up or cutting down will be needed at either end. When an approximate level is decided, drive in a stake directly below one end of the line with its top marking the level required.

Do this at the highest end first. Measure down this same distance at about 2 m intervals, along the line, and drive in more stakes with their tops marking this level. If the higher side has to be cut down then make a trench for the marker stakes so that the level can be clearly indicated.

The adjacent sides and opposite sides are then treated the same way. If necessary, the level can be checked this way between opposite corners. For the sake of the lawn it is advisable to remove topsoil off the site to be levelled so that it can be replaced over the excavated area later — otherwise all the acceptable soil will be at the built-up end.

If it is necessary to cut down to solid clay, consider laying drainage pipes with a slight slope and a few centimetres of clinker ash or similarly coarse non-organic material to help surplus water to drain off.

Also, unless space is limited, consider bevelling down the bank left on the high side so

that the sloping and levelled lawn areas can flow in together. In either case a slightly ditched surface drain would be an advantage at the top of the bank.

It is sometimes suggested that the mower strip should be higher than the lawn to allow for increasing height caused by top dressing, but top dressing should only be applied when needed to fill small pits or settlements in the lawn — certainly not as an overall covering.

The effectiveness of a mower strip also depends on having an even edge on the lawn side so that the various types of cutting wheels or mechanical edge trimmers can be used. However, this does not apply on the garden side and if necessary this edge can be deliberately varied, or to make it less obvious around rockeries, an occasional flattish foreground stone can be allowed to break into the strip providing it does not interfere with the mower.

A mower strip is essential where areas of gravel meet the lawn or where lawn grass gives over to ground cover below a shady tree, etc. An untidy no-man's-land invariably develops where grass runs into ground cover. Also, a rotary lawnmower can become a lethal weapon when trying to cut grass intermingled with gravel.

In some of these situations it is possible to use a path as a divider and mower strip. Ground cover can be incorporated with paving which is set below a seat beneath a tree and extended to the front on either side to form a divider between blocks of ground cover and lawn.

Making a mower strip

A number of prefabricated materials can be used for mower strip construction including bricks, paving blocks, straight-edged precast concrete strips or hardwood railway sleepers. For irregular curves, concrete formed on the site is often the easiest, providing, as suggested earlier, the lawn has settled down to its desired level.

When installing poured concrete strips the soil can be used as the mould, providing it is well compacted and just damp enough to hold its shape. However, for a more even edge, strips of flexible masonite-type fibre-board 8–10 cm wide can be used to keep at least the lawn edge true.

Start by spading along the line of the strip to clearly cut the edges vertically and to the required depth (at least 8 cm is desirable for strength and to deter sub-surface runners of

couch, etc.). Place the fibre-board edging strip with top edge flush with the lawn and held in place by some short pegs driven in a few centimetres below the top edge.

Pour a fairly strong cement or cement and blue-metal mixture, gently tamping it in to fill to the top of the fibre-board edging, then use the latter as a floating edge to even off and smooth the strip. The fibre-board mould may be removed after a few days. If you soak it before using it, it will crack away easily when it becomes dry.

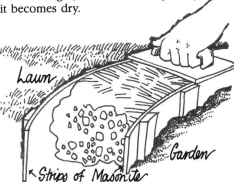

Preparing for a lawn on a steep, sloping site

When dealing with a slope too steep to comfortably walk on or mow, the usual approach is to divide it into a series of terraces.

Why not accentuate the pleasant effect of a long sweeping lawn by zig-zagging it partly across the contour?

This way a retaining terrace on fairly steep sloping rockery, built-in to about half-way across the slope — first from one side then further down from the other. Soil is then graded down from the higher point above each half terrace or retaining rockery so that the slope is shared both across and down the slope.

Appreciate that, except where there is a good depth of soil, the most satisfactory way to do this is first to remove the topsoil in both sections and replace it after the sub-soil has been graded down.

Where terracing or stepping down of the slope is desirable it is often possible to bevel the banks to a manageable angle and mow them. High mounds too steep to comfortably walk on can be mowed pulling a rotary-type mower up and down the slope with a rope.

On steeply banked lawns surface drainage can be controlled by making a gradual depression to act as a drain about 1 m back from the top of the bank. Where there is no cross-slope to carry off the water the drain can run at a slight diagonal, slanting about 2 m back from the top of the bank on one side and coming to within about 50 cm of it on the lower side. If this type of depression or drain is 1 m or more wide and only a few centimetres deep at its deepest point, it is hardly noticeable and does not cause mowing problems, but is capable of carrying off large amounts of water.

When your site is prepared and soil has been brought to the correct consistency, laid down and levelled, you can then consider how next to proceed.

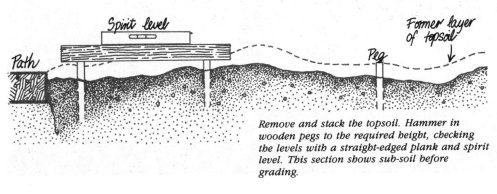

Remove and stack the topsoil. Hammer in wooden pegs to the required height, checking the levels with a straight-edged plank and spirit level. This section shows sub-soil before grading.

Planting a new lawn

Grading

After digging, breaking up and improving the soil, the next step is to grade the surface evenly. Grading does not mean levelling — that is only needed when the lawn is intended for bowls, croquet, practice putting or other lawn sports.

An efficient grader can be improvised by fastening ropes to the end of an old door, gate or solid window frame. A heavy plank with the pulling ropes fixed to screws close to the front edge is also effective. Any of these devices do a satisfactory job when pulled across the area, first in one direction then the other.

You can adjust their action by moving the points where the ropes are attached: if too far back the front edge digs in too much; if too far forward it skims over, rather than grading the surface. The idea is just to skim the soil from high spots and deposit it in depressions.

After grading there will still be some settlement, so to do a perfect job put a sprinkler on the lawn and give a thorough watering as suggested earlier.

Evenly treading over the area helps to settle it down, providing it is done when the soil is no more than just damp, certainly not when wet and sticky.

After treading and watering there are bound to be small areas that will settle here and there, so, just after the soil dries out rake the surface lightly and then give another grading. You should then achieve a perfect surface. Sounds like a lot of preparation but it is worth this little extra trouble because you have a lawn for a very long time. You could even water again and let it stand for 2 weeks before sowing. This will help to eliminate weed growth which may compete with the grass that you have sown. This is a definite consideration because weed growth usually comes through a lot quicker and tends to smother the grass.

When the inevitable weed growth does come through, wait until the soil surface dries out and forms a surface crust. Wait for a dry, sunny day and break up the crust with a rake or use a hoe and chip in a shallow way to get rid of weed growth.

In the event of prolonged wet conditions, rather than let the weeds get past the easy removal stage, kill by watering with a contact weedicide such as Polyquot or Weedex. These break down rapidly in contact with soil, allowing sowing a day or so after treatment. They are very toxic so label precautions must be followed.

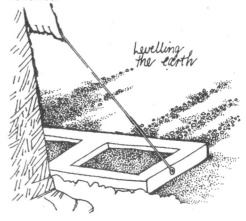

Levelling the earth

Fertilising before sowing or planting

Before sowing seed or laying turves it is also important to add fertiliser. To induce good root growth plenty of phosphorus is needed.

Bent grass, particularly suitable to cool climate, remains green during winter

Feeding can, however, be left until sowing or planting time but the advantage of applying it two weeks before (followed by a watering) tends to stimulate weed growth, particularly clovers, vetches, etc. The weeds can then be destroyed by lightly scuffling the surface on a dry, sunny day just prior to sowing or planting.

It is important to use a complete plant food or 'lawn starter', not a 'lawn food'. Lawn food is ideal for feeding established grass but not for seed germination or the root growth of turves or runners.

The type of formula to look for is one with an NPK (nitrogen, phosphorus and potash) percentage of approximately 5–7–6. Most of the lawn foods are in the vicinity of 17–0.5–7. The high-nitrogen and low-phosphorus percentages of the lawn food give a tremendous boost to established grass, but the deficiency in phosphorus retards germination and root growth of seed, causing failure, especially to couch.

Couch is very sensitive to the lack of phosphorus. The sign of phosphorus deficiency in couch as a result of using a common lawn food is deep, slatey, purple-coloured grass, rather than the usual bluish green. This deficiency can be corrected by spreading a handful of superphosphate per sq. m and watering well.

Lime

Lime is not always essential, depending on the type of grass sown. If you are sowing couch is is worth adding lime, especially if you know that your soil is acid.

Without obtaining soil tests or using testing kits, there are fairly obvious indicators of soil acidity in most areas. The presence of bracken normally suggests an acid soil. One of the best indicators is the hydrangea. Growing in normal untreated soil, in a natural limy soil, the flowers will be pink; in an acid soil they will be blue. There are a few exceptions because the blue colour particularly depends on the presence of aluminium in the soil and a few other factors, but it is a rough indicator. Therefore if the hydrangeas are blue your soil is at least a little acid and couch would appreciate the addition of some lime.

Use up to three-quarters of a cup of lime per sq. m. Spread it on initially — or you can add it with the plant food. One sometimes hears warnings about combining fertiliser and lime but if you use ordinary garden lime or dolomite you can combine it with a plant food, or even with animal manure without any worry.

Lightly dig or rake the lime and fertiliser into the soil.

Watering

After sowing, water the soil with a fine sprinkler. Thoroughly saturate the soil without leaving puddles. Keep the surface moist by watering lightly at least once daily during warm, dry days. It is advisable to *sow only as much as you can water comfortably* with a fixed sprinkler. This is to avoid the inevitable damage to the newly-sown grass and compaction of soil by walking over the area to change sprinkler positions. Therefore, try your sprinkler first, and position it where it will water the entire patch sown.

Choosing grass to sow or plant

The type of grass will depend largely on your climate. In most temperate areas where summers are hot and winters frosty, there is no ideal lawn grass because grasses such as couch and buffalo which tolerate hot summer conditions become dormant or brown off when chilly, winter weather arrives. Bent grasses are beautiful during the milder months but die off or brown badly if they become dry during the hot weather, and are rather fungus prone during warm and wet conditions.

However, in temperate areas with hot summers and cold winters there are ways to keep your garden looking at its best throughout the year. One is to sow a mixture of both cool and warm weather grasses as described under 'Grass mixtures'. Another is to plant or sow couch, then oversow it with bent during April, preferably before the weather gets really cold, so it will establish and remain green during winter and in early spring when most people like a good lawn to complement their display of azaleas, bulbs, spring annuals, etc.

All you have to do is to cut the couch fairly low and choose a still, wind-free day to scatter the bent seed as evenly as possible at about one-third of the rate recommended for normal sowing. Water just vigorously enough to wash the fine seed into the soil without excessive splashing or puddling, then hose frequently to keep the surface moist until the deeper green of the new bent grass is obvious.

Results will be better still if the lawn is given a light dressing (one handful per sq. m) of superphosphate or complete plant food (not soluble lawn food in this case) a day or two prior to oversowing. This will strengthen the roots of both the couch and newly-sown grass.

An alternative is to sprinkle just a light covering of spent mushroom compost after scattering the bent seed. This acts as a cover and moisture holder and as a soil improver. Do not use excessively to completely mask the grass. Any residue remaining will disintegrate after the first mowing.

To some extent 'tradition' determines the 'ideal' lawn. Various strains of white and strawberry clover are an accepted and important component of Rye and Kentucky Bluegrass lawn mixtures in Canberra, parts of Tasmania and Victoria; also in South and Western Australia but any type of clover is regarded as a lawn weed in most other areas.

Before definitely deciding, check the performance of the grass you choose in home gardens, parks, etc. in your neighbourhood. For a guide to selecting the best grass refer to 'A reference guide to grasses'.

Growing from seed

When to sow

Seed of couch, kikuyu and carpet grass may be sown at any time in tropical districts, but in temperate areas they are only satisfactory from October, when the soil is warming up, until late February — later sowings will germinate but usually not make runners before winter, except in comparatively warm areas. October or early November sowings are usually best because the grass has a longer period of warmth to establish and it is generally easier to keep the surface moist than in mid-summer.

Bent grass is best sown during April in temperate areas or in spring in cool districts. Bent is unsuitable for tropical areas.

Mixtures of cool and warm weather grasses such as couch and 'brown top' bent will give some result in spring or autumn, but for a good balance of couch and bent it is best to sow the couch in spring or early summer then oversow with bent in April — otherwise the quicker germination and upright growth of the bent seedlings tend to smother the couch, which by nature is more prostrate during early growth. The bent also often dies out during hot, dry, mid-summer conditions.

Sowing the new lawn

Before sowing, the soil should have settled down so that it shows no deep footmarks or footprints when walked over. The surface should be crumbly. Aim for a fairly settled soil with the top 2 or 3 cm raked into a crumbly state. That is the ideal seed bed.

The rate the seed is sown will depend on the grass. Rates for different grass seeds are given on the package, but for small-seeded grasses such as bent or couch, 2 gm per sq. m is ample, or 1 gm per sq. m for hulled or speedy couch, and for larger seeds such as rye, at least 4 gm per sq. m.

Even sowing is essential for good results. This can be achieved with the use of a well-adjusted seed sower but not with hand-broadcasting unless you confine sowing systematically to small areas and choose a still day. If sowing by hand divide the lawn into 2 m widths using a couple of ropes or garden hoses, then walk backwards within the strips, spreading a handful of seed over the 2 sq. m in front then step back another metre and spread another handful . . . and so on. Trying to broadcast seed over wider areas usually results in a zig-zagged fall and if there is any breeze a lot of seed will end up in the garden beds!

After sowing, covering the seed is easy providing you have a crumbly, reasonably dry surface. Just go lightly over it with a rake, backwards and forwards, ensuring the lawn seeds find their way down into the little furrows pulled behind the tines of the rake — and that is all the covering needed.

If you cannot do this, there are covers such as compost. Mushroom compost is ideal because it is relatively weed-free and fibrous. If birds or wind are likely to be a problem, fibrous material sprinkled over the surface will hold the soil and seed in place, will keep it covered and protected, retain moisture, and act as a buffer against heavy rain or watering.

Germination

The time taken for grass to germinate depends on the time of year it is sown and the type of grass. In a temperate climate couch may take 3–4 weeks if sown in September when the soil is still cool, but in November would probably germinate in 10–12 days. Hulled couch sown in warm soil germinates in 5 or 6 days. Bent grass in a similar time, in all cases, providing the soil is kept continuously damp.

After the grass seedlings have been well defined, allow the surface to dry out a little between waterings. Let the dryness extend down about 1 cm for a week then graduate to occasional soakings, rather than surface waterings.

When to cut your new grass

It is exciting when the first faint fuzz of green confirms that the seed you have sown is actually growing. Initially, you may need to crouch down almost at soil level and look across the lawn surface to see it, but in a day or so there is a wonderful transformation to a soft velvet-like green carpet of young grass.

Do not be in a hurry to cut your new lawn. As explained earlier, it is essential to have a good length of green foliage and sunlight on it to produce the sugars and starches that allow the grass plants to build up a sturdy frame and root system.

Let the grass get up to about finger length before cutting, then set the mower high enough to just take the tip off the grass. Maintain this height for a few weeks then gradually set the mower a little lower; there is no virtue in shaving the grass down almost to bare soil. The lawn will be much healthier, more attractive and relatively weed-free if the grass is cut no lower than 2–2.5 cm in height.

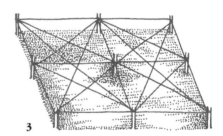

3

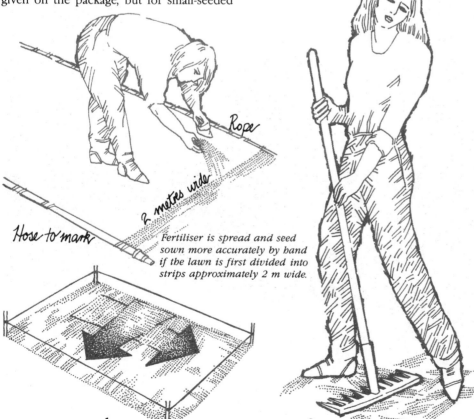

1

2

Fertiliser is spread and seed sown more accurately by hand if the lawn is first divided into strips approximately 2 m wide.

Sowing the seed

1. Measure out a sufficient quantity of seed for each strip and divide into two. Sow half the seed one way and the remainder across the line of direction as shown.

2. When the seed has been evenly spread, lightly rake the soil keeping the teeth at an angle to avoid burying the seeds too deeply, preferably no more than 3 mm. Gently tamp down the soil using the back of the rake with the handle upright.

3. One way to deter birds from eating seeds, even those coated with repellent, is to criss-cross thin black cotton 8 cm above the surface.

Growing from plants

Planting runners

The soil needs similar preparation to that outlined for sowing seed but with the surface raked a little deeper (6–8 cm) and just damp at planting time. Plant at the same times suggested for seed sowing of the various grasses.

The best way to plant evenly is to make furrows 25–30 cm apart and about 5 cm deep across the area. Place the runners end to end along these with a few centimetres between end and tip. Cover as you plant, holding the growing tip of the runner at about ground level with one hand, filling in soil with the other. This keeps at least the newer foliage exposed and allows more rapid establishment.

Oversow with bent or fescue seed immediately after planting runners to give quicker cover, prevent soil from washing and deter weed growth from the otherwise exposed soil. The running grasses will gradually overcome the bent or fescue as they establish.

Chopped sprigs are sometimes available. These are runners or turves that have been chopped into small pieces. Providing they are not allowed to dry out, each node or leaf junction is capable of providing roots and shoots. They should be broadcast at the rate of 1 handful or more per sq. m and covered with sandy soil at the times recommended for sowing seed of the particular grasses.

Laying turf

This involves more cash outlay but is desirable if quick cover is needed, especially for steeply sloping areas where storms may carry off seed and topsoil prior to germination or before growth is sufficiently established to bind the soil. It is also the wisest choice during hot weather where it is sometimes impossible to give gentle sprinklings frequently enough to prevent the surface drying during, or soon after, germination.

Carpet-like *rolls* of turf are available. These are machine-cut to an even thickness, so are very easy to lay evenly, by simply batting each strip closely against each other.

Sods or *squares* of turf, if hand-dug, may vary in thickness. To get an even surface it is best to have a wooden frame that is a little larger than the sod's size and just less than its average thickness (e.g. a wooden seed-box with the bottom removed). Each sod is placed face down on an even surface inside the frame and the base of the sod is graded level by a blade to remove any high spots.

The best way to lay turves evenly is to work forward, kneeling on a broad plank placed over turves laid so that each one is lifted into place but firmly pulled toward you without disturbing the level of the crumbly surface below it. Brush in a little sand to fill crevices between uneven sides where the soil may have broken away from the turves. Start in one corner, working diagonally across the site. Water well as soon as possible after the laying is completed.

Mowing turf

Turves should not be mown for at least 3 weeks after laying or until the grass has made about 3 cm growth, even though it may be tempting to tidy it up.

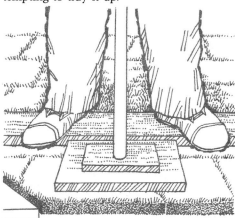

5. *Firm each row of turves after laying with a tamper made from pieces of wood, or use the back of a spade. Note that the level of the turf is about 1 cm above that of the path.*

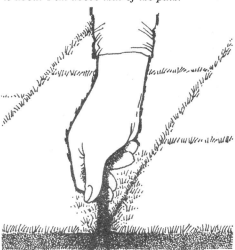

6. *Trickle fine sandy soil into any gaps between turves, filling all spaces to surface level. This helps to prevent drying out and to ensure quick establishment.*

7. *Brush the soil well in, using a birch besom or stiff broom, and loosen up flattened grass blades.*

1. *Mark out the lawn area, using a garden line and pegs for straight edges and a trickle of sand for those of irregular outline. Work from planks to avoid treading the ground.*

2. *Begin at a corner, using a full-sized turf and lay in straight lines lengthwise. Stagger each row, like brickwork, so that the joins do not align. Make sure each turf is pushed firmly against its neighbour.*

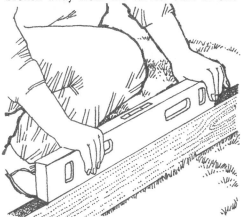

3. *Check critical levels with a straight edge, pegs and spirit level. Add or remove soil from beneath turves in depressions or on high spots.*

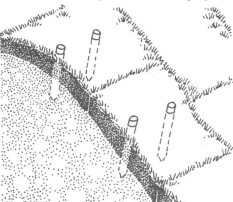

4. *On slopes, lay turves lengthwise and secure by driving 2 or more 1 cm diameter pegs, 15 cm long, into each turf. Knock the pegs below the level of mower blades as soon as the turves are established.*

Lawn care and maintenance

Fertilising

There's no point in feeding grass during its dormant period. Feed only when growth is likely. Spring is the obvious time to give the lawn its initial lift as soon as you see your grass beginning to grow. Feeding merely involves sprinkling the lawn food over the grass and watering it in. However, some lawn foods are so spectacular in their action that unless you spread them evenly, tney result in a zig-zag pattern of bright grass with dull, yellowish patches between them.

Roughly divide the lawn into 2 m wide strips. You can do this visually but it is better to mark each 2 m spacing with stones or stretch two hoses out to mark and fix the width, then move them along.

Walk backwards down the first strip sprinkling the fertiliser as you go. A 2 m width is chosen because this is about the maximum distance you can broadcast by hand and still get even coverage. Also, most lawn fertilisers are used at the rate of about 1 handful to 1 sq. m. Step back a pace, sprinkle 2 handfuls, step back another pace and another couple of handfuls . . . and so on. This way you get very even coverage. Then just move on and do the next strip.

Alternatively you could distribute half the fertiliser up and down the lawn and the other half across it. This works quite well but is more liable to leave gaps than using the 2 m wide strip method which is not as involved as it might sound.

Lawn foods, e.g. sulphate of ammonia, are very soluble and can burn the grass if you apply them when the lawn is wet or dewy. Wait until the grass is dry, complete your spreading and then water in thoroughly.

In most cases, lawn food is applied again in early autumn. Some people prefer to feed every 4–6 weeks. In this case use about half the amount previously suggested — say 1 handful to 2 sq. m. If the weather gets very dry during summer it is hard to keep moisture supply to the lawn, then it's just as well to stop feeding until the grass is again in a position to grow well.

Top dressing

Top dressing is usually needed to correct minor surface variations that may develop in new lawns. It should not be a ritual as most top dressing soils contain little or no nutrient

Aerate small areas of lawn by driving in a garden fork, moving it back and forth fractionally to widen boles. Do this when the soil is just damp.

Hollow tine forks are better for heavily-compacted lawns because they remove complete plugs of soil.

and progressively raise the lawn's height until it becomes a nuisance and an unnecessary expense. When top dressing is needed, apply only enough to fill small hollows. If there are hollows deeper than 3 cm, a better idea is to cut squares of sod cleanly with the spade, fill in the depression with soil, then replace the sods and firm down.

Inversely, if you have a hump in the lawn, lift the sods and take away the surplus earth, replace the sods and firm down.

As said before, bought soil can often be alluvial and so devoid of organic matter that it is like gel when wet and solid when dry. Use coarse river or bush sand if you must use top dressing — it may look coarse and the colour unattractive, but the grass roots will love it.

There are lawn levellers which do a good job in spreading top dressing evenly and rubbing the soil well into the grass. Failing these, use a 1 m length of straight timber, 8–10 cm wide and 1–2 cm thick, drilled in several places so that it can be wired to the head of a metal garden rake.

Top dress couch, buffalo or kikuyu about November, when new growth is active, and

bent in early spring or early autumn, but only if it needs it.

If the lawn is a little tired and thin, a feeding does more good than top dressing. The soluble type of lawn food usually gives more spectacular greening because of its high nitrogen content and it also retards the growth of clover. The dry-mix granule or sprinkle-on type of lawn food also promotes good growth but less spectacular greening.

Watering

Many people think that the more often they water, the better. This is not so — too frequent watering can have a very detrimental effect on the lawn.

It can encourage fungus diseases which cause bare patches, etc. but the worst factor is that it brings all the roots to the surface and the grass then becomes dependent on frequent watering. Come heat-wave conditions or sudden hot, dry spells, the roots are not deep enough to fossick for water. Your lawn will brown off badly. The best plan is to train your lawn to make deeper roots. Aerating will help but the frequency of watering is a very big factor. The best practice is to let the surface of an established lawn dry out and become reasonably dry for about 1 cm down, and then give it a really good soaking. Make sure that you allow enough water to get well down into the soil.

Soils vary — you may have to trowel down in one or two spots to see whether the water has really penetrated. In dry periods it will surprise you how little water had gone down, so make the soaking a thorough one.

Then let the surface dry out just a little further down before giving another soaking. Continue this way and you will find that the roots will move down into those deeper areas which are more constantly moist. Then you can safely go away and leave your garden for a week or two without the need to worry about lawn watering, except perhaps during extreme heat-wave conditions. On the other hand, frequent watering means that you have to keep to this practice to maintain the lawn in good condition.

The way you water makes a difference. Use a sprinkler that lets the water in gradually, without puddling the lawn surface. If puddles lie on the lawn you are watering too rapidly. A finer sprinkler takes longer — but it makes a difference to the soil. When soils are puddled the clay begins compacting and you lose aeration which the roots need to function properly. Correct watering does simplify the management of lawns.

Mowing

Avoid shaving the grass too low. Leaving the mower set to cut about 2 cm high will strengthen the grass, thicken it to minimise competition from weeds and encourage deeper root growth which in turn makes the lawn more drought-resistant. If you have been a 'low' shaver you will find that setting the mower higher will result in a greener, healthier lawn and after the second or third cut it will be at least as neat and trim as the lawn subjected to lower cutting.

Lawn problems

Bare patches under trees

Cause: These inevitably occur because of excessive competition for water, plant nutrients and, particularly, lack of light. Poor growth is often found on the shaded side of fences and buildings, etc.

Remedy: Use shade-tolerant lawn grass mixtures suitable for temperate and cool areas. These usually contain varieties of blue grass, bent and fescue.

Generally speaking it is better to replant your lawn, confining it to areas where grass grows well. Replace grass under trees and in other problem areas with shade-tolerant ground covers such as Californian Ivy, Mombo grass (*Ophiopogon*), or easy care, shade and wind-tolerant plants such as clivias, agapanthas, Spider plant (*Clorophytum*), London Pride (*Crassula multicava*), or if moisture can be maintained, azaleas and other shrubs tolerant to light shade.

Bare patches, compacted soil

Cause: This is more likely to occur in soils with a clay content which is frequently walked on when wet. The compacting prevents the soil aeration essential to root growth and also impedes the roots' physical progress.

Remedy: Improve aeration by prodding the soil with a hollow tined fork or an ordinary garden fork when the soil is just damp. Prod to finger depth every 10 cm. Move the fork backwards and forwards before withdrawing, to widen the hole. Aeration can be made more permanent by raking compost, vermiculite or other coarse or fibrous material over the lawn to penetrate the holes.

As suggested previously, a compacted track across the lawn probably indicates need for a path in this area. Where a solid path may disrupt the smooth flowing appearance of a lawn, stepping stones are a good compromise. They can look pleasant and add interest. Bare patches can be due to actual wearing of the grass as well as compacting.

Bare patches or patches of poor growth

Cause: May be due to areas of pure clay or shallow rock close to the surface.

Remedy: Dig out the clay to a depth of about 10 cm and replace with a good crumbly soil. If the rock is in a raised part of the lawn it may be bared and featured, or used as a base for groupings of appropriate plant containers. If this does not suit the landscape, try mounding the lawn gently to deepen the soil over the rocky area.

Grass dying

Cause: The uneven grass with wiggly yellowish lines is probably due to the activity of black- beetles and their larvae, or other similar grubs that eat the roots and underground stems of the grass.

Remedy: Flood the lawn thoroughly then water it liberally with Endosulphan, Carbaryl or Diazinon made about half as strong again as normally recommended spray strength and apply at least 4.5 L per 10 sq. m of lawn area. Then hose lightly to wash the chemical into

Above: Allowing lawns to disappear from sight gives an illusion of space

Below: Lawns allow for recreation and relaxation in the garden

the soil. Chemicals such as Fenamiphos are sold in granular form for treatment of black-beetles and lawn grubs and are scattered over the affected areas as directed on the container.

Dead patches in lawns

Cause: Usually a fungus growth which penetrates and destroys the grass seedlings, or spillage of petrol when filling the mower, or 'watering' by female dogs or puppies.

Remedy: Don't fill your mower on the lawn; train your dog! Water as soon as you notice the dying patch.

Lawn fungi

Cause: The fungi which cause brown patches in the lawn including 'dollars spot' where numerous patches are only about 5 cm in diameter, 'brown patch' which causes larger, irregular patches, and 'snow mould' where under moist conditions patches of white fungi are all treated the same way.

Remedy: At the first sign of damage, or better still, if small cobweb-like canopies of *fungus mycelium* are noticeable in the morning dew, spray the lawn either with Mancozeb or Benlate or any complete fungicide you have on hand. Treat the entire lawn or at least the area immediately surrounding the infected patches.

Dry, brown patch in summer

Cause: Sometimes when a fungus has attacked the grass it leaves the surface soil in the area water repellent and greasy, making it impossible for water to penetrate the soil.

Remedy: Soak the area with household detergent at normal washing-up rate — about 1 teaspoon to 4.5 L. Then hose with clear water. This should be done only once as frequent use of detergents will destroy the normal root functioning of most plants.

Moss or algae over the lawn area

Cause: Either drainage is not satisfactory or the lawn is watered too frequently.

Remedy: Water or spray the area with about 1 teaspoon of powdered copper sulphate (bluestone) dissolved in about 4.5 L of water. Or use a proprietary moss killer. Copper spray applied liberally at normal spray strength will also give some control of moss and algae.

Poor lawn colour

Remedy: If the lawn is not compacted (see Bare patches) or the area is not unduly shaded, a good, green colour can normally be obtained by feeding, when the lawn is in its normal active growth season. Couch grass, buffalo, carpet grass and other warmth-loving grasses may lose their healthy vigorous appearance or even appear to die out during cold conditions, and will give no response to feeding until their normal growth period returns when the soil is warmer. See Fertilising.

Unhealthy couch grass

Cause: Most of the couch grasses, particularly common couch, are happiest when the soil is slightly alkaline or limy. Frequent use of sulphate of ammonia or other soluble lawn fertilisers and particularly the use of 'weed and feed' preparations will gradually increase the acidity of the soil to a stage where the vigour of the grass declines.

Remedy: Apply a light dressing of garden lime or dolomite (say one half-cup per sq. m) once a year, or at least once every second year if these preparations are used frequently. Scatter the lime as evenly as possible, use the back of a rake or a broom to brush it into the grass and then water in well. Aerating the soil immediately prior to liming is beneficial. See Bare patches.

Lawn weed problems

Weeds grow mainly in bare patches or where grass is thin but rarely where there is a thick preventive cover. Leaving the grass to grow to 2 cm high not only strengthens it but gives sufficient cover to stifle most germinating weed species. It is particularly important to leave couch, buffalo and other summer-loving grasses a little longer during the last few cuts in late autumn. Otherwise, a point is reached where there is little or no recovery after the last low shaving and the soil surface is sufficiently exposed to invite an invasion of winter-growing weeds such as dandelion, clover, winter grass and others.

Set the mower a little higher to give an occasional feed to thicken the grass and minimise weed problems. Lawn foods high in nitrogen also retard the growth of clover whereas the basic fertilisers that contain relatively high amounts of phosphorus will encourage it.

Burning out the weeds

It is possible to use either the soluble complete lawn foods or sulphate of ammonia to burn out clover and most other flat-leafed weeds without appreciably damaging the grass. This is done by spreading these materials evenly when the lawn is still wet with dew. After the weeds shrivel and begin to brown (which may occur in half an hour or several hours, depending on moisture and temperature) the grass is then well watered to dilute the fertiliser and wash it into the soil.

It should be noted that grasses such as some of the bents may burn almost as rapidly as the weeds but this is not serious because, after a good soaking, regrowth of the grass occurs fairly rapidly and you should have a good, rich green lawn again within 7–10 days. This will certainly apply in spring when the grass is growing actively and soil moisture can be maintained.

Some gardeners apply this burning technique to couch in spring and other lawns when weed growth has taken over in winter, especially that of bindii or jo-jo, if it has been allowed to reach the prickly seeding stage, which makes selective spraying pointless.

Selective weed killers

Weed killers used for the control of broad-leafed weeds including clover, creeping oxalis, cudweed, dandelion, etc. kill some plants (and some grasses) and not others, partly because of the amount of chemical that is retained by the leaf blade of the plants involved. For example, because of their nature and angle at which they lie, grasses shed most of the chemical sprayed on them whereas relatively large amounts remain on a broad-leafed weed. Some plants are far more sensitive to these chemicals than others. For this reason do not add wetting agents to the sprays as you may with most insecticides, or mix them with other sprays unless the mixture is specifically recommended, otherwise they may lose their selectivity.

Care with lawn weed killers

It should be appreciated that, when using any of the selective broad-leafed weed killers, although a certain dilution may be recommended, it is always possible that dilutions even 100 times weaker (or in some cases the slightest trace of the chemical) can damage other plants. Tomatoes, lettuce, grape vines, zinnias, roses in young growth and a number of other ornamentals can be damaged by the slightest spray drift from the chemical, or even by minute traces remaining in the sprayer.

Always choose a perfectly still day, without any breeze, for spraying. In many areas complete freedom from breeze is possible very early in the morning. Avoid undue pressure so that the amount of fine mist from the spray is minimised, and keep the nozzle fairly well down toward the lawn so that there is less chance of spray droplets drifting to the surrounding garden.

Trickle-bar-type applicators attached to a watering can may overcome the problem of spray drift and for this reason are desirable even though they involve the use of far more chemical.

Because of the dangers from contamination keep a separate sprayer for the use of hormone weed killers. If you can't, the sprayer should be washed thoroughly in detergent — dismantling it if a syringe type, or leaving the container filled with a detergent solution overnight after its preliminary washing. In either case follow with several rinsings of litres of clean water pumped through the sprayer.

Some selective lawn weed killers such as those used for the control of bindii or jo-jo, winter grass and paspalum, apart from being toxic by mouth or inhalation can also be absorbed through the skin. Do not allow children or pets on the lawn for a few days after application or until the lawn has again been exposed to rain or watering. Walking barefoot on the lawn should be discouraged for the suggested safe period after application.

Many of the pesticides generally used for the control of black-beetle and other lawn insects are readily absorbed through the skin, so after applying, use the same precautions suggested in the above paragraph. Follow application of the chemical with a light watering to wash it from the grass into the soil.

Controlling some common lawn weeds

Paspalum

Paspalum can be controlled chemically in common couch (not Queensland blue couch) and bent lawns by the use of D.S.M.A. which is sold under several different trade names all implying paspalum killer.

Chemical control of paspalum may not always be necessary because, although this is a tough and persistent grass, its woody crown is comparatively shallow and is relatively easy to sever from the roots. With a sharpened mattock younger plants are easily removed by cutting just below the crown with a sharp knife or secateurs. Roots left in the ground will not regenerate, so there is no point in pockmarking the lawn with deep holes.

Crow's Foot (*Elusene*)
This tough grass is not easily killed by selective sprays but its crown is even shallower than that of paspalum so it can be easily removed in a similar manner.

Tufty wire grass, rat's tail or Parramatta grass (*Sporobolus*)
Another tough perennial weed with a very shallow crown. It can be easily removed with a sharp mattock.

'Horror' weeds
Persistent bulbous weeds such as onion weed, oxalis and nut grass are extremely difficult to remove from lawns as there is no selective chemical that will affect them without damaging the grass.

One tactic is to thicken the lawn by feeding regularly so that these pests cannot predominate. This rarely kills them. Another approach is to swab a herbicide, e.g. Zero, on to the weeds without touching the grass. One gardener I know twists two pipe cleaners together, twice, then wires them to each jaw of a pair of long-nosed pliers. The pipe cleaners are dipped into a container of herbicide, then used to grab the blades of onion weed or nut grass which are then gently pulled through them and given a good dose of herbicide on either side. A tedious job indeed. There is no other answer, except learning to live with these weeds and hoping that a more selective wonder herbicide will eventually come to the rescue.

Mullumbimby couch
A dark-green, fine, wiry-leafed, low-running grass that normally starts in damp patches then becomes rapidly invasive during wet periods.

This grass can be removed from among common couch or bent grasses by using the D.S.M.A. preparations mentioned under paspalum. These preparations are only effective while the weeds are actively growing in summer and under fairly high temperatures. Under extremely high temperatures some burning of the grass may occur. It is fortunate that black-beetles seem to seek out patches of Mullimbimby couch before they attack other grasses.

White root lobelia or poison pratia
This rapidly running weed with flattish, small bronze-green foliage can become a pest in couch because it tends to establish during winter when the grass is dormant. It has small, starry white flowers, a slightly milky sap and a prolific mass of fleshy, white roots that extend well down below the surface of the lawn. It has many deep perennial roots and is not seriously affected by the selective 24D-type weed killers when they are sprayed in the normal manner but, if these preparations are liberally watered on to already deeply moistened soil, the results are more effective. Apply at least 5 L at the spray-strength dilution to about 10 sq. m of lawn.

Hydrocotyl
One of several plants sometimes known as penny wort; a fairly common weed in sandy sea coast areas. Its tough disc-shaped bright-green leaves may extend to a depth of 50 cm or more, since it was obviously designed by nature to survive in sand dunes where the depth of sand over the runners may suddenly increase appreciably.

Treat this as white root lobelia.

Summer grass or American crab grass
Well known for its mass of slightly hairy green-grey blade-shaped foliage, rapidly spreading stems that root down as they progress, and the slender-armed antenna-like formation of slatey-purple seed heads. Summer grass is rarely a pest of well-established, evenly covered lawns as it only appears in thin or bare patches, particularly toward the edges of worn areas. Newly sown lawns are often threatened by a sudden invasion of summer grass, as its growth can smother recently-germinated couch, and in some cases appears before the latter.

Because summer grass only germinates as soil temperatures rise in late spring, its appearance in areas that have been carefully fallowed for weeks during late winter and early spring, often gives rise to the belief that the summer grass was in the lawn seed sown. Circumstantial evidence certainly seems to point to this but it is not so.

Summer grass invasion in new lawns can only be controlled by mowing to prevent it from smothering the grass seedlings, even though you may have to mow the new grass earlier than recommended. Summer grass in established couch or bent lawns can be killed by using paspalum sprays, but it should be remembered that it is an annual weed only, and nothing kills summer grass more effectively than winter chill.

Bindii or jo-jo (*Soliva*)
Makes its presence felt in late winter or early spring when its sharp, barb-like seeds are produced. Eradicate the pest as soon as the patches of pale and bright-green, fine carrot-like foliage begin to intermingle with your grass.

Preparations containing Bromoxynil will control this weed without damaging couch, kikuyu, or rye grass lawns. Most of these preparations include a percentage of M.C.P.A. which makes them effective also against creeping oxalis, clover, cudweed, dandelion and some other broad-leafed weeds. Bent, buffalo and fescue lawns which are sensitive to this chemical can be treated for bindii or jo-jo with 'weed and feed'-type preparations, soluble lawn foods, or sulphate of ammonia.

Winter grass (*Poa annua*)
This is troublesome in couch or buffalo lawns that have thinned out during the cooler months. It creates a patchy appearance because it is a much brighter green than these grasses, although if it was not for this 'weed' many of our temperate-to-cool area lawns would look considerably browner during winter.

Winter grass can be suppressed in couch, bent and buffalo lawns by the use of selective herbicides such as Endothal. Several applications are needed and care should be taken not to exceed the dilution recommended on the container.

In Endothal-sensitive grasses such as kikuyu and some types of fescue, the re-emergence of winter grass the following season can be reduced by frequently mowing with a catcher as soon as new seed heads appear but take care not to shave the lawn too closely as this provides scope for further invasions.

Creeping oxalis
This is not a bulbous weed like other types of oxalis. It spreads rapidly but is very low-growing, keeping within the height of closely-mown turf. Foliage is tiny like a very fine, small-leafed and pale-green clover, with minute, upright yellow flowers.

There are several hormone sprays sold as creeping oxalis killers and a few of the general broad-leafed killers also control this weed. Check label information before using.

Other weeds
Cudweed, capeweed, creeping mallow, daisy, dandelion, mouse-ear, chickweed, pigweed and plantain are all in the broad-leafed weed category and easily controlled as suggested under the heading 'Burning out weeds'.

Remember: easy ways to better lawns

1. Mowing
Avoid shaving the grass down low. Leaving the mower set to cut about 2 cm high will strengthen the grass, thicken it to minimise competition from weeds, and encourage deeper root growth which in turn makes the lawn more drought-resistant. If you have been a 'low' shaver you will find that setting the mower higher as suggested will result in a greener, healthier lawn and after the second or third cut it will be at least as neat and trim as the lawn subjected to lower cutting.

2. Watering
Water only when the lawn's soil surface dries out, then give a soak to penetrate down to the sub-soil. You can remove a small square of turf and trowel down to check the depth that the moisture has penetrated.

3. Feeding
Occasional feeding invigorates the grass, thickens it, minimises weed problems and, above all, keeps it an attractive green. Feed lightly every 6 weeks during the growing season of the grass. Do not feed during dry periods unless it is possible to maintain a reasonable level of soil moisture. Feed when the soil is moist, but the grass itself dry, then water liberally after the spreading of the lawn food is completed. This way you avoid any burn to the foliage.

Unless using a fertiliser spreader, hand-broadcast it, feeding strips only about 2 m wide at a time. You can mark out the strips with some garden stakes and a length of rope moving on as each section is completed.

A reference guide to grasses

Couch (Common Couch — *Cynodon dactylon*) is one of the best fine-leafed warm weather grasses. It runs and covers well, is reasonably hard wearing — is also resistant to most of the selective weed killers and has good drought tolerance.

On the debit side it runs fairly rapidly during warm weather and will invade flower beds and rockeries. It needs to be contained by a mower strip or by a sunken edge between lawn and garden so that runners can be controlled by regular edge trimming. Runaway couch can be killed by wetting with Weedex or Polyquot mixed at double strength. This will not affect the roots or brown woody stems of surrounding plants.

Couch does better if heavy soils are lightened as described under Soil, and if given full sun. It responds well to nitrogenous fertilisers such as the soluble lawn foods if they are applied during warm conditions when it is capable of growth. However, it prefers slightly limy soil. Therefore, if you use an acidifying fertiliser like sulphate of ammonia or 'weed and feed' preparations frequently add up to a cup of garden lime or dolomite per sq. m at least every second year in early autumn or spring and water well.

Couch lawns can be started from turves, runner sprigs (chopped up runners which are broadcast and covered with soil) or from seed. They should all be started after spring nights have lost their chill, and before summer has lost its warmth, as couch does not make runners once cool conditions arrive. Turves may be started in later winter–early spring and (if care is taken to prevent them from drying out) through late spring and summer also.

Sow seed at the rate of 2 kg per 100 sq. m. When the soil is warm it should germinate in 10 to 12 days.

Hulled Couch or **Speedy Couch** This is the same as the regular strain of Couch but the outer husk of the seed has been removed. There are nearly twice as many seeds per unit of weight, therefore 1 kg is sufficient for 100 sq. m and the seed germinates in half the time. This appreciably shortens the period where constant surface moisture must be maintained.

Queensland Blue Couch This makes a beautiful, very fine blue-green lawn with closely matting stolons or runners thinner than those of Common Couch. It is a little more frost sensitive and less resistant to wear than Common Couch, has less tolerance to drought, low-cutting and DSMA-type paspalum and Mullumbimby Couch killers.

Queensland Blue Couch is not grown from seed, but is started from turves or sprigs in spring or summer. Popular in semi-tropical or similar climates.

Bent Grass Is the finest grass for cool climates or for oversowing Couch or other warm weather grasses to keep the lawn green during winter. It is a brighter green than Couch. Brown Top Bent (*Agrostis tenuis* — sometimes known as New Zealand Bent and the most widely grown) is a fairly upright clumpy grass. It should be sown fairly thickly 1.5 to 2 kg per 100 sq. m during the mild weather of early spring or autumn. Seed takes 6–10 days to come through, depending on weather conditions.

Creeping Bent (*Agrostis stolonifera*) is distinct from Brown Top, being a true runner that covers rapidly and makes a beautiful lawn in all but the warmer climates. It is sometimes used successfully in lightly shaded aspects in temperate districts but is prone to fungus diseases during warm and very humid conditions. It is unsuitable for oversowing.

There are several hybrid forms, one of the most popular being Pencross Hybrid. Because of its running habit and fineness of the seed, 250 grams is sufficient for 80–100 sq. m.

Buffalo Broad-bladed vigorously running grass that makes a dense mat, even in shallow soils. It is more suited to warm temperate coastal districts, has tolerance to heat, dryness and light shade but browns off during frosty winters. When well established it tends to smother weeds, even paspalum, but is sensitive to most of the hormone-type and DSMA weed killers. Growth tends to become spongy after a year or two but can be corrected by whittling down with a rotary mower in mid-spring when the grass is showing signs of early growth.

Buffalo is not grown from seed, and can only be established from turves or more usually from runners planted in spring or summer. After planting the runners oversow with Brown Top Bent in spring, or in summer with Fescue, to give cover while the Buffalo is establishing.

Carpet Grass (or **Mat Grass**) Similar to Buffalo but coarser and brighter, almost glossy green, more cold sensitive and in frosty districts tends to disappear during winter. It has reasonable shade tolerance but resents close mowing and is sensitive to heavy feeding with sulphate of ammonia.

Carpet Grass is popular in warm coastal districts with mild winters. Broad-leafed Carpet Grass with a much wider leaf and flatter growth which needs very little mowing is widely used in the tropics, especially in

Stepping-stones minimise worn areas in lawns as in this Kentucky bluegrass lawn

monsoonal regions. It is started from runners in late spring–early summer, just prior to the wet season.

Carpet Grass (regular type used in warmer temperate and semi-tropical districts widely known as *Paspalum compressum* or more correctly *Axinopis affinis*) can be grown from seed, sown at the rate of 2 to 2.5 kg per 100 sq. m in late spring–early summer, or from runners planted at the same time.

Fescue There are several types of Fescue now popular in shade-tolerant mixtures. Chewings Fescue, with fine dark green upright growth, is widely used in grass seed mixtures as a nurse grass because it establishes quickly and gives rapid initial cover but dies out quickly when low-cutting is practised. It is also an excellent temporary cover for oversowing newly planted runners of Couch, Buffalo, Carpet Grass or Kikuyu, and mixes well with Kentucky Blue Grass. It prefers full sunlight but adapts to light shade.

Fescue can be sown at most times of the year but not in cold winter and hot summer periods. It is a comparatively large-seeded grass and is sown at the rate of 3–4 kg per 100 sq. m. Germination takes 7–10 days.

Kentucky Blue Grass This is a good quality hard-wearing lawn grass suitable for both cold and inland temperate districts. It has good tolerance to shade and dryness, therefore is excellent under trees, providing it is not subjected to close cutting. It is generally less suitable for humid coastal districts where it is subject to rust. Kentucky Blue Grass is started from seed sown in spring or autumn at the rate of 2 kg per 100 sq. m, usually emerging in 15–21 days depending on condi-

tions. Feeding should be confined to spring and autumn as it is relatively dormant in summer.

Kikuyu An extremely tough and vigorous grass for all but cold districts. It is the hardest wearing grass, has more tolerance to cold than Couch or Buffalo and better tolerance to shade under trees. One objection to Kikuyu is the toughness and density of growth under good summer conditions. If cutting is neglected for more than about a week it can be a problem with all but rotary mowers. It is very invasive but runners are relatively easy to control when the lawn is confined by reasonably deep mower strips or desiccant weed killers are used at the base of fences, edges of beds, etc.

In light soils particularly the runners are capable of matting below and lifting shallow paved paths but excessive vigour can be curbed by regular cuttings.

Kikuyu is usually started from runners in spring or early summer but seed is also available and should be sown at the rate of 125 g per 100 sq. m or at half the rate if Fescue is added for initial cover. Germination takes 10–15 days in warm soil. An oversowing of Fescue is recommended after planting runners to assure quick cover.

Perennial Rye Grass A dark, rich glossy-green grass that is hard wearing. It is often used in playing fields or nature strips, especially where low-cutting is not practised. It is also used on a large scale in some cool districts, sometimes mixed with White or Strawberry Clover since it is frequently in pasture making rich green cover. A cold-tolerant grass, it stands heat and dryness better than Bent or Fescue.

Its growth is tufty, giving a poor uneven effect unless sown thickly (4–5 kg per 100 sq. m). Rye Grass also resents low cutting. When cut low with a rotary mower particularly, the tougher leaf fibres are often left, resulting in a brown stringiness.

Perennial Rye Grass is best sown during spring or from mid to late autumn. Winter sowing is satisfactory in all but very cold districts, can be sown in summer providing the soil is kept moist until the young seedlings establish.

Grass mixtures Parts of western and southern Australia mixtures of Kentucky Blue Grass or Couch and Strawberry Clover are popular and give good results. In more northern and other warmer temperate districts mixtures of Couch, Brown Top Bent and Fescue are widely used. It is difficult to achieve even cover with these mixtures because in the last one, for example, the Couch germinates and grows best in warm conditions less suitable to Bent, and Bent and Fescue do better than Couch in early spring or autumn. Even if they germinate evenly young Couch has low ground-hugging foliage which tends to be smothered by the more erect Bent and Fescue.

For best results sow Couch in late spring or early summer and oversow with the Bent and Fescue in autumn. This is detailed at the introduction of this section.

Cheaper 'evergreen' mixtures containing Perennial Rye, Couch and Fescue are widely sold. These are suitable for nature strips, etc. but not for a quality lawn because of the tufty nature of the scattered Rye Grass — see 'Perennial Rye Grass'.

Kentucky bluegrass grows well under trees providing it is not cut too low

18. Ferns and palms

Ferns

Ferns are among the most popular indoor plants and usually give the most trouble. Overfeeding, lack of water and an over-dry atmosphere, combined with a lack of understanding as to which varieties can tolerate bright light and which cannot, contribute to the problems — but once a few simple factors are understood they can be trouble-free and luxuriously beautiful. Outdoors all species of fern need semi-shade and a constant supply of water.

Growing ferns

Aspect

Outdoor ferns need protection from strong wind; indoors they need to be protected against draught.

Although they are usually considered as delicate, shade-loving plants they can be grown in the sun if given adequate water and protection against wind. They will, of course, suffer burn during heat-wave conditions, particularly if the soil has become dry.

If you move a fern from a shaded indoor position into sunlight outdoors it will experience leaf burn; all transitions should be gradual.

A plant grown outdoors in the shade can be conditioned to sunlight by moving it first into bright indirect light, then into lightly dappled sunlight, then a few hours direct sun, etc. Similarly a plant from moderate indoor light can be conditioned to accept an area with some direct sunlight through glass. Provided it is remembered that the more light a plant receives the more water it will need.

Ferns indoors grow best in bright indirect light. This is defined as a position where a hand with fingers spread, held about 25 cm above a coloured card, will throw a distinct shadow.

Most ferns will accept moderately bright light (where the hand throws an indistinct shadow) although their growth rate will be less. A few, such as the holly fern (*cyrtomium*) and the fishbone or Boston ferns (*polypodium* and *Nephrolepis*), will grow in moderate to poor light though growth habit may be different, particularly that of the Boston or fishbone ferns. In bright light the fronds are relatively stubby but in moderate light they become much longer, more pendulous and weaker.

Soil requirements

For pots

Most of the proprietary potting mixes suit ferns, but they will be improved if a quarter by volume of crumbled, partly-rotted leafmould is added.

If you prefer to make your own mixture use approximately 3 parts good, crumbly garden loam, 2 parts coarse river sand and 2 parts rotted leafmould or moistened peatmoss (all by volume, not weight).

It is important to keep the mixture open and the addition of gravel and pine bark would not go amiss.

In the garden

Do not plant ferns in limy soil or soil that has been treated with compost containing lime.

Care and maintenance

Humidity level for indoor growing

Ferns prefer humidity in the 40% range — not over-moist, but an atmosphere just comfortable for everyday living. Low humidity results in brownish edges to the foliage and a dry, lustreless appearance.

A 5°C increase in temperature nearly doubles the amount of moisture the air can carry. This means that in a room with comfortable 40% humidity, a heater increasing the temperature from 15–20°C will lower the relative humidity to about 20%. Sun on closed windows has a similar effect.

One of the best ways to create and retain humidity is to place pots on trays with water in the base and sufficient thickness of pebbles or gravel to keep the pots just above the water. Trays or planter boxes with moist sphagnum moss or pine bark have a similar effect. Misting plant foliage with water on hot days also helps.

Freedom from draught is also desirable. Draughts rapidly diffuse or carry off the moisture you have coaxed to form around your plants. They also have a drying effect and can chill the plants or roots in wet soil.

Watering

Poor results with ferns are often due to the 'let the soil dry out between waterings' recommendation. Ferns, particularly the maidenhairs, will not tolerate dryness, especially under average indoor conditions. It is far safer to keep the soil surface damp at all times, which in most cases will involve watering daily. Avoid an over-soggy soil although some people do grow ferns successfully by keeping water permanently in the plant saucer. It may give good results in a bright warm situation, but is usually too much for ferns in average indoor conditions.

Types of water

The high chlorine content in tap water affects some types of maidenhair and bird's nest ferns. If you can smell or taste it in the water, use hot tap water that has been allowed to cool, or stand cold tap water in the sun for half-a-day or so before use.

Very cold water can shock some ferns, so reduce the chill but don't make the water noticeably warm.

Feeding

Ferns are not gross feeders. In nature they grow happily just with nutrients from decomposing leafmould or minute traces carried in soil seepage. A safe way to feed potted ferns is to top dress their soil with a handful or so of well-crumbled, partly-rotted leafmould applied in early spring before or when new growth is appearing.

Alternatively, feed with commercial complete soluble plant foods diluted to about one-third of the strength normally recommended, every 4–5 weeks during the warmer months of the year from the time the new growth begins. Before each repeat feeding, leach the soil thoroughly to remove any unused residues from previous feeding by soaking the container in a larger vessel of water for about 20 minutes. Drain slightly then gently pour another few litres of clean water through the soil to cause further run-off from drainage holes.

Soluble organic food such as seaweed extract and fish emulsion are also suitable and relatively safe for feeding ferns, but even with these it is wise to leach the soil after the second application.

Do not use the basic dry-mix fertilisers containing concentrated ingredients, e.g. sulphate of ammonia, superphosphate, urea or potassium chloride. Even though these may boost growth initially by improving size and colour of well-established fronds, they frequently burn the delicate embryo fronds just at or below soil level. The damage may not be noticed for several months until there is no new growth to replace the ageing fronds.

Ferns growing outdoors will appreciate a little rotted animal manure or rotted leafmould watered into the soil to keep it moist and crumbly. They will *not* like fowl manure which is too strong, and will burn the roots.

Repotting

This is usually done in late winter or early spring, but can be carried out any time if soil ball is not disturbed. If growth of plant is even but has reached the size of the pot, move to a container one or two sizes larger.

Large clumps with little growth coming from the centre, or uneven growth, may need dividing. This is done in late winter or early spring after cutting back all fronds to soil level. The clump may then be cut into segments, discarding areas of dead fibre. Most new shoots come from the outside of the clump, so each divided segment can be set toward the centre of a small container or several placed in a large one to give a pleasant even cover of growth. In fern baskets, set the segments only a few centimetres from the basket's rim.

Propagation

The outside growth of a clump of ferns will become strong while the centre is deteriorating. The young growth will split away fairly easily. Cut it away cleanly, trim the fronds and replant. Division can be made at any time of year but early spring will give least trouble in both warm and cool areas. Avoid extremes of temperatures, whether hot or cold, whilst subjecting the plants to pressure.

Do not overpot. Plant each cut segment in a 10 cm or even a 7 cm pot. They can be moved and grouped into a larger container once growth has been established. Do not be afraid to cut back top growth. The object of the exercise is to promote root growth; any excessive foliage left will only drain strength from the plant. Let your soil be damp at the time of repotting, soak as soon as is feasible, and then have the patience to leave the plant in a protected and shaded area until regrowth begins.

Some ferns do not divide or transplant easily — reproduction has to be made from spores. If you look on the back of a fern-leaf you will see them: patches of rusty, sooty, pinhead strips or blotches which are the life of the plant. The spores are like dust, almost invisible, and collecting them is not easy. I find it best to cover the leaf with a plastic bag and then to tap and shake it until the spores fall and are collected in the bag.

A mixture of peatmoss and sand or rotted leafmould and sand should first be drenched with boiling water to kill off any weed or algae seeds and, when it is cold, the spores can be dusted over the surface of the sterilised mixture.

Whatever the container used (large box or small pot), the atmosphere around it must be kept moist. You can use a plastic bag or frosted glass — just keep the container shaded and not too hot so that the spores can live and grow. It will probably be a month or even 6 weeks before the first new fronds can be recognised and the bag can be eased aside to give the tiny plants the air they need. When they have grown to about 2.5 cm high they can be lifted and planted 5–20 cm apart in the sterilised soil used for raising the spores, then gradually and carefully can be potted or transplanted. Loving care and total attention are required.

To raise staghorn and elkhorn spores shake them onto sheets of tea-tree bark that have been well soaked and when they have taken root and are large enough to handle easily, cut the bark into pieces and attach to whatever growing base you have; spongy wood is the best bet. This is still the best way to propagate staghorns although you will have to wait a long time to get good results. Elkhorns can be reproduced by simple division, but don't expect too much.

Growing ferns in a bush-house

Most ferns, apart from the more delicate Adanatiums and Maidenhairs, will grow happily in a bush-house. They will need potting-on year by year until they reach the largest size you can handle and you will have to be careful about watering at all times. It must always be enough but the soil must not be kept saturated nor allowed to become dry. *Asplenium, Ceratopteris, Dryopteris, Lycopodium, Nephrolepsis, Polystichum* and *Pteris* are all good subjects. The epiphytes (*Platicerium*), the popular stag horn or elk horn ferns, can be grown in a bush-house or in any spot where there is shade and they can be attached to the bark of a tree or any convenient piece of stonework, brickwork or timber, etc.

Tips to general care of ferns
- Give containers a half-turn occasionally if the growth tends toward light.
- Keep away from heaters or air-conditioning outlets, and out of draughts.
- Water every day.
- If foliage shows brownish outline, increase humidity and syringe with water occasionally during hot, dry periods.
- Remove dead fronds to keep plant looking more attractive.
- Be aware that all ferns naturally produce brownish spore clusters under foliage: on Maidenhair these are kidney-shaped, on fishbone circular spots, on Pteris marginal lines, etc.; so don't worry about this natural occurrence.
- Pinch off brown sections of foliage. If appearance is generally poor, cut back all fronds to soil level in late winter.
- Ants near ferns suggest presence of mealy bugs or scale. Glossy syrup-like appearance or black sootiness on foliage also indicates mealy bugs, scale or aphids.

Growing ferns in the garden

The magnificent tree ferns (*cyathea*), which give such atmosphere to a garden, need both shade and moisture. They can also be grown in large tubs and are well worth the attention they need.

Cyathea dealbata (Silver Tree Fern), *C. dicksonia australis* (Tasmanian Tree Fern) and *C. meduullaris* (Black Tree Fern) are the names to remember. With their strong trunks and huge, lacy spread of leaves they make a wonderful contribution to a landscaped garden.

Ferns can also be used as ground cover. *Andantium aethiopicum* and *A. formosum* (both maidenhairs) do well given filtered light and moisture, while Rasp fern (*Doodia media*) can cope with hot sun provided it has moisture at the roots.

Ferns for a poolside area are:

Gleichinia microphylla (Parasol Fern), *Pteris ensiformis* (Brake Fern) and *Sticherus flabellatus* (Shiny Fan Fern).

The bold and beautiful tree ferns

Tree ferns combine bold and beautiful form with lacy green softness and complement any type of landscape.

The softness may suggest that they are delicate, but this is far from so being. They may be seen covered in snow or standing like charred totems after a searing bushfire; then, amazingly, when rain comes, lush green fronds unfold from the slender trunks which seemed beyond hope of survival.

Of more direct interest to home gardeners is that they grow in any aspect, but are happiest in shaded areas where the choice of good landscaping subjects is limited. A group of three or so tree ferns will create a dramatic, pleasing natural effect, especially if the plants are unevenly spaced and of different heights.

Tree ferns indoors can be used either in the young stage among mixed plant groupings where a softening effect is needed, or on a grander scale and more dramatically when more mature. Although the spreading tops become weighty, they can be grown in relatively shallow containers providing they are wide enough to give good anchorage.

The main difficulty is supporting them until their tough root mat has spread sufficiently. Tall-trunked ferns could be first established in a sheltered outdoor area where a tripod of stakes or similar bracing can be used.

There are a number of different tree ferns, including the water-loving *Alsophila australis* from Tasmania; cibotiums from Hawaii, Malaysia and South America; tall, soft, green-fronded Cyatheas from the mountains of South America, and Dicksonias from Australia and New Zealand. They are classified mainly by the formation of their spore colonies or sori, which are close to the foliage edge below the fronds.

Technical differences are of little interest to most people, who appreciate tree ferns for their beauty alone. The main reason for mentioning them is that some species transplant more reliably than others.

By far the most adaptable, therefore the most widely used tree fern in Australia, is *Dicksonia antarctica*. This tree fern is distinguished by the trunk which is completely covered with a thick mat of dark, purplish-brown aerial rootlets.

The edges of the fronds are turned downwards partly to enclose the spore colonies.

Because of its mat of rootlets, this tree fern can be transplanted by cutting off the trunk at any height suitable, and planting the top. It is widely sold as a cylindrical totem without any apparent root system.

The same liberties cannot be taken with the Cyatheas or Coin-spot tree ferns. The latter are so called because, where old fronds have been shed, a bare woody coin-spot-shaped area is left between the short flake-like fibres covering the remainder of the trunk.

The surest way to re-establish cut tree fern trunks is to keep the base and the entire trunk moist by watering from the top or centre of the plant, initially at least once a day. If this cannot be achieved, fix a band of sphagnum moss or other water-holding material around the top of the plant so that moisture gradually trickles down to the remainder of the fibre.

When moving or replanting part of your own tree fern, cut back all mature fronds. This is hard to do as it temporarily destroys the fern's appearance, but if it is not done the fronds place an extra drain on the plant before it has time to establish soil roots and it will die off.

The stub of trunk left in the ground from the original plant will not make regrowth.

Ferns grown in hanging baskets

It is more difficult to give ferns growing in hanging baskets the moisture they need than ones growing in containers, so particular attention must be given to the way they are planted and the soil in which they are planted. It will be readily appreciated that a basket hanging in the air is exposed to more air movement than a container on the ground and, in hot or windy weather, the soil will dry out too quickly unless steps are taken to prevent it.

If you use a wire basket line it first with sphagnum moss and then with plastic sheeting, punched at intervals to provide drainage holes. To avoid souring of the soil by trapped water, put a handful of charcoal in the middle of the planting base. Soil must be open textured and the basket not over-filled — there has to be room for a run-off of moisture. If the soil becomes caked the texture is wrong — add more coarse organic material or lighten it with gravel and more charcoal. The soil must be kept both sweet and moist. Some plastic hanging baskets are fitted with a drip saucer; this can be used as a daily supply of fresh water but it must never be allowed to collect water which will become stagnant.

Phoenix robellini and Kentia palms

Growing problems and solutions

Problem	Cause	Solution
Shrivelling and browning of outer foliage	This is natural, because in most ferns the old foliage gradually dies off as the new growth develops	Trim off to improve appearance
Overall browning of foliage	Usually due to dryness	Unlike other house plants ferns need their soil to be kept at least just damp. Daily watering is generally required
Brownish edge to foliage	Generally due to dry atmosphere	Regularly misting foliage with water will help
Wedge-shaped brown or black areas in Maidenhair fern foliage followed by shrivelling	Leaf eelworm (nematode)	Pinch off and burn affected areas. For large-scale treatment spray with Metasystox (outdoors)
Brown hands on strap-like foliage such as pteris	As above	As above
Lack of young replacement growth when old foliage dies	Emerging embryo growth probably burnt by fertiliser perhaps a month or two previously	Ferns should be fed only very sparingly. Flood soil
Brown, velvet-like clusters or bands below foliage	These are the natural spore bodies of the fern	No treatment required
Downy whitish patches amongst foliage or on stems — may be followed by shrivelling with presence of sugary stickiness or black sooty mould	Mealy bug	Touch each insect with a swab moistened with methylated spirits or move outdoors and spray liberally with Folimat
Small brown dome-shaped incrustations on stem or leaf veins	Soft scale	Gently rub off with soapy cloth or spray as for mealy bug
Thin drawn foliage	Insufficient light	Move to area with bright indirect light
Tree ferns with creamy-white mottling on fronds	Leaf hoppers (jassid)	Spray either Pyrethrum-type preparation or Malathion
Tiny insects clustered on new growth	Aphids	Spray with soapy water or cover plant with soap lather, or spray with Pyrethrum-type spray holding pressure pack about 1 m from plant
Tiny grey to black sand fly-like insects hovering around plant	Mushroom fly, usually due to use of spent mushroom compost in potting mix	Use Pyrethrum-type spray as for aphids and, to destroy larvae which sometimes attack roots, flood soil with Malathion or Diazinon mixed at a little less than spray strength
Tiny white flies around ferns, usually causing some foliage mottling	White fly	Use Pyrethrum-type sprays as for aphids
Stag horns and elk horns Numerous small brown indentations on fronds	Tiny circular black stag horn beetle	Spray and water back of plant thoroughly, when moist, with Malathion
Fronds shrivelling, small holes in sterile fronds or back of plant	Tunnelling of stag horn beetle larvae	As above
Rusty velvet-like area below tips of fronds or in stag horns below junction of two arms	Natural spore bodies or in latter case, covering of spores	No treatment required
Area below the above, tunnelled with a churned appearance	Larvae of stag horn beetle	As stag horn beetle

Cyrtomium (Holly Fern)

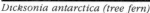

Dicksonia antarctica (tree fern)

Davalia pyxidata (Hare's Foot fern)

A cultivation guide to ferns

Adiantum (Maidenhair Fern)

A. aethiopicum (common maidenhair fern). Does well in hanging basket or damp open ground. Pale-green fronds grow to 60 cm.

A. formosum (giant maidenhair fern). Dark-green fronds grow to about 120 cm. Needs moist, shady position with rich soil.

Angiopteris evecta A large tropical fern. Fronds 180–300 cm long. Needs humid climate, shady position near creek ideal.

Asplenium *A. bulbiferum* (mother spleenwort). Has soft, finely-divided fronds from 30 cm to 250 cm long. Suitable for hanging baskets or on board.

A. falcatum (weeping spleenwort). Fronds 30–90 cm long. Hanging baskets or on board.

A. flabellifolium (necklace fern). Small fern suitable for hanging baskets or rockeries.

Blechnum Has fishbone-like fronds.

B. fluviatile (ray water-fern). Shady position in gravelly soil.

B. penna-marina (alpine water-fern).

Cyathea (Tree Fern). Grows well outdoors in damp soil and shady positions.

C. australis (rough tree fern). Can tolerate cold climates. Grows over 6 m.

C. cooperi (Cooper's tree fern). Prefers warm climate but transplants easier.

C. medullaris (black tree fern). Black trunk grows between 6 m and 15 m high. Has crown of 30 fronds.

Cyclosorus *C. nymphalis*. Pale-green fronds up to 150 cm long. Fronds clustered in crown. Requires damp soil, partial shade.

C. truncatus. Fronds up to 180 cm. Requires hot, humid climate.

Davalia pyxidata (Hare's Foot Fern). Grows in pots or hanging baskets. Has shiny, leathery fronds up to 75 cm long.

Dennstaedtia davallioides (Lace Fern). Fronds 150 cm high, dark green. Prefers rich soil, shady position.

Dicksonia Requires damp, shady position and protection from wind to prevent drying.

D. antarctica (soft tree fern). Grows 6 m.

D. fibrosa. Brown trunk with fronds about 240 cm long.

D. squarrosa. Grows to 6 m high with crown of leathery fronds up to 240 cm long.

Doodia (Rasp Fern). Harsh textured fronds. Prefers light shade, can grow in dry position.

Drynaria Grown outdoors mainly on board. Prefers hot, moist conditions.

D. guercifolia (oak leaf fern). Fronds resemble oak leaves.

D. rigidula. Most attractive of species. Leaves up to 2 m long.

Elk Horn Fern see *Platycerium bifurcatum*

Fishbone Fern see *Nephrolepis*

Giant Maidenhair Fern see *Adiantum formosum*

Hare's Foot Fern see *Davallia pyxidata*

Hypolepis distans Graceful drooping fronds suitable hanging basket.

Jungle Brake see *Pteris umbrosa*

Kangaroo Fern see *Microsorum diversifolium*

Lace Fern see *Dennstaedtia davallioides*

Microsorum diversifolium (Kangaroo Fern). Fronds are leathery, vary in shape.

Adiantum formosum

Adiantum aethiopicum (maidenhair fern)

Phoenix robellini (palm)

Licuala muelleri

Lycopdium (tassel fern)

Platycerium grande (staghorn)

Grows best attached to an old tree trunk.
Mother Shield Fern see *Polystichum proliferum*
Mother Spleenwort see *Asplenium bulbiferum*
Necklace Fern see *Asplenium flavellifolium*
Nephrolepis (Fishbone Fern). Will grow in poor or sandy soil, sun or shade.
  N. cordifolia (tuber fern).
  N. exaltata var. bostoniensis (Boston fern). Pale-green, feathery fronds. Grown in hanging baskets or pots.
Pellaea Leathery fronds on black or brown stems. Usually grown among rocks.
  P. falcata. Has fishbone-shaped fronds.
  P. paradoxa. Fronds usually heart-shaped.
Platycerium Grown on boards or trees, these attractive ferns have green, forked fronds which give an antler-like appearance.
  P. bifurcatum (elk horn fern).
  P. grande (stag horn fern)
  P. hillii
Polystichum *P. australiense* (austral shield fern). Dark-green fronds.
  P. proliferum (mother shield fern). Stands low temperatures, high altitudes. Grows well in coastal gardens.
Pteris *P. cretica* (cretan brake). Fronds 30 cm long. Variety *alba-lineata* has a white stripe down centre of each frond.
  P. macilenta. Quick-growing, prefers well-drained soil, part shade. Fronds 150 cm high.
  P. tremula (tender brake). Prefers moist, well-drained soil with partial shade. Fronds pale green.
  P. umbrosa (jungle brake). Prefers rich soil, dense shade. Dark-green, leathery, umbrella-like fronds.
  P. vittata (chinese brake). Prefers limy soil. Grows in shade. Fronds pale green.
Stag Horn Fern see *Platycerium grande*
Tree Fern see *Cyathea*
Todea barbara (Austral King Fern). A tree-like fern with short trunk. Between 2 and 14 crowns of erect, pale green fronds. Prefers shade, well-drained situations. Grows in large tubs or near creek.

Tuber Fern see *Nephrolepis cordifolia*
Weeping spleenwort see *Asplenium falcatum*
Willow spleenwort see *Asplenium flaccidum*

Palms

Palms have graceful form and bearing both indoors and in the garden, add beauty and elegance to the stateliest drawing room and are increasingly popular as a feature in contemporary settings.

Nearly all palms are adaptable to a variety of climates and aspects. Although they usually make the best growth in warm humid atmospheres, nearly all will stand temperatures down to 2°C for short periods.

However, judging by the number of questions and complaints about the behaviour of palms indoors, I feel they are one of the least understood house plants.

Growing problems and solutions

Palms, the most elegant, most popular and, under good conditions, the most permanent house plants seem to involve the most problems. This may be due to unsuitable conditions, lack of understanding or, in some cases, the condition of the palm initially.

Problem	Cause	Solution
Lower leaves yellowing and dying	Natural conditions as new growth develops	Trim off cleanly
Overall dead foliage	See 'Why palms die'	See 'Why palms die'
Large brown areas on foliage	Shade-grown plant moved suddenly to sunlight, or near room heaters	If extensive, trim off and wait for new replacement growth
Brown tips on foliage	Over-dry soil or, more usually, dry atmosphere	Trim off with scissors in natural leaf shape
Leaves with dull appearance, slightly crepe-like texture between veins	Either excessive dryness, root injury or roots not established	See 'Why palms die'
Irregular brown blotching on leaf margins	Usually due to overfeeding or continuously wet soil	Leach soil. Allow soil surface to dry between waterings
Foliage with dull sandblasted appearance	Red spider mites	Thoroughly sponge both sides of leaf with soapy water and mist with water occasionally. Alternatively, spray with Malathion
Yellow blotches on foliage	Either downy white or scab-like scales on opposite side	Gently rub foliage with soapy cloth
Numerous pale-tan to buff pinhead-like scabs on foliage and stems	Palm scale	Rub off with soapy cloth or toothbrush. For large-scale infection spray 2 tablespoons white oil plus 1 teaspoon Rogor or Lebaycid per 5 L of water in shaded, outdoor position
Downy white clusters below foliage	Downy scale	Remove with soapy water
Large areas of foliage eaten	Usually palm leaf rolling caterpillar	Monthly sponging of leaves helps dislodge this pest, or spray in outdoor shade with Endosulphan
New fronds with leaf tips apparently fused with whitish down giving a ladder-like formation	This is natural and more typical of Phoenix palms	No remedy needed
Fronds shrivelling and later dying after treatment with pressure-pack foliage foods	Application of spray excessive or pressure pack held too close to frond	Hold pack at least 50 cm away from plant and give only slight misting. Note that these foods should only be applied to healthy plants in environment suitable for good growth

Why palms die

It is unfortunate that palms leave some nurseries soon after repotting and before roots are established. Due to careless handling prior to potting the roots may have dried out completely and then general deterioration of the plant begins. It is possible that symptoms of the latter may not become obvious for several months and it is then too late to remedy the situation.

In all fairness it should be pointed out that these unestablished palms would not be handled by reputable nurseries. The more common occurrence is that the plants have been allowed to dry out too much, or in some cases the soil has been left saturated for too long and in either instance root damage will occur that may cause the plant to die during some period of stress, perhaps months later.

Over-feeding is another cause of permanent root damage. It is usually not appreciated that palms and many other house plants are in situations where the light is so reduced that they are still able to exist but not to make growth. Therefore, in these situations they need little or no feeding, and a sudden burst of plant food and particularly quick-acting foliage fertilisers can do more harm than good. The latter preparations can also have adverse effects when a plant has been existing on damaged or restricted roots which are not capable of taking up the comparatively large amounts of water suddenly needed to support extra growth.

Care and maintenance
Humidity
Palms prefer a humidity of at least 40% or more. Dry atmosphere results in browning tips but this can be minimised by keeping your palms away from heaters, air-conditioning outlets or closed windows with the sun on them. Ways to increase humidity are detailed in the 'House Plants' section.

Feeding
Palms respond to moderate feeding while they are growing actively. This is usually from spring to autumn, but varies according to indoor temperatures. When plants are grown in containers, the concentration of soluble plant foods or soil salts increases as the soil dries out.

It is wisest to avoid risk of root damage by using only about half the generally recommended amount of plant food and by leaching before feeding again. This applies whether feeding with soluble plant foods, slow-release granules, ordinary granulated or powder-type fertilisers or organic manures.

Remember also that the generally recommended rates are for plants under ideal growing conditions in active growth. Although types of palms and ferns recommended for moderate and low light survive happily in these situations, their growth rate will be much slower than those in high light. Under reduced growth conditions, reduce plant food rate still further — say to one-third or even a quarter strength.

It is sufficient to apply most soluble-type plant foods at the diluted rates every 6 weeks from spring to autumn. Powder or granular-type plant foods, including organic preparations, should not be applied more often than 10–12-week intervals in the warmer months.

Slow-release granules (6-month type) would normally be applied only once in spring, 3-month types in early spring and again in mid-summer. Occasional feeding through foliage with nutrient spray can be beneficial in the warmer months when growth is active.

Ferns need even less feeding than palms and are more easily damaged. The emerging embryo fronds are particularly delicate and very susceptible to damage at or just below ground level. Although feeding may appear to benefit a fern by improving size and colour of established fronds, it sometimes destroys the emerging ones. Few people appreciate the cause when the plant dies off suddenly, perhaps some months after the heavy-handed feeding.

When feeding remember:
- Feed only when growth is active.
- Feed sparingly, still more so if plants are in reduced light.
- Feed only when the soil is already evenly moist.
- Take care to avoid soil drying out after feeding.
- Leach soil before feeding again.
- Do not feed newly-acquired plants for at least 6 weeks.

Water

Too many palms grown indoors die or perform poorly because their roots have been allowed to dry out — mainly due to confusion with other house plants that need fairly dry soil during winter. However, overwatering has a similar effect because it causes root rot which prevents the plant from taking up essential moisture. In either case, there is browning of foliage tip then general browning and shrivelling.

A good rule is to water palms whenever the soil surface begins to look dry. However, palms in cool areas with only low to medium light need a little less water than those in high light and warmth. In this case, at least during the cooler months where rooms are unheated,

allow the dryness to extend just slightly below the soil surface.

Disregard advice to water at set periods, such as every second or third day, as this will vary according to temperature, light humidity, size of container and soil type. Rely only on the appearance of the soil. When you do water, apply enough to thoroughly wet the soil and cause a slight run-off into the drainage saucer (which should be emptied 10 minutes or so after watering).

General care
- Sponge foliage with a cloth dipped in slightly soapy water (not detergent) at least once a month. This not only removes dust but also deters red spider mites and helps to dislodge scale pests and caterpillars.
- Give palms one-quarter to half-turn every few weeks — otherwise growth tends toward the light source.
- Mist foliage during hot weather.
- Water whenever soil surface dries out.
- Remove dead or badly-yellowed lower leaves, but do not prune main stem or it will not produce new shoots.
- Keep palms more attractive by trimming off brown tips of foliage with scissors, slanted to stimulate shape of leaf point.
- Repot palms at least every 2 years.
- Use a sharp knife to clear roots matted in drainage holes — blocked drainage may result in root rot.

Check by inverting and tapping plant from container. Repotting is necessary if roots are matted over side of soil ball. Use a pot about two sizes larger, and a good potting mixture (or mix 2 parts by volume of crumbly, well-composted garden loam with 1 part of coarse sand and 1 of moistened peatmoss).

Add sufficient soil to bring soil ball just below rim of new pot and use a stick to pack new soil between soil ball and walls of pot. Stand in water until moisture appears on the surface but be careful not to agitate soil afterwards.

Putting palms out in the rain to 'freshen up' is a good idea, especially during the summer when there won't be an appreciable difference in temperature between indoors and outdoors. It is safer to pick a shaded situation because palms are damaged if forgotten and left in the sun. As suggested elsewhere, a species or palm may be seen growing happily in full sunlight because it has been conditioned to it, but the same type of palm grown indoors or even in a shaded outdoor position will burn badly when suddenly exposed to direct sunlight.

A reference guide to palms
Medium to small palms for the garden or for growing in containers
Burrawang *(Macrozamia communis)*. Attractive native; makes a broad funnel of dark-green fronds, eventually forming a scaly trunk to 1 m high. Best in a sheltered, outdoor position.

Neanthe bella. A delightful little indoor palm, similar to the parlour palm but with finer fronds; often grown in mixed bowls with

ferns, etc. Eventually forms a slender trunk, but less than 1 m high.

Parlour *(Chamaedorea elegans)*. Very dainty, with short decorative fronds on a slender stem. Grows 2–3 m.

Pygmy Date *(Phoenix robellini)*. Adapts well to moderate light. This dainty palm has a fountain-like rosette of finely-divided, glossy green feather-shaped, arching fronds, very soft in appearance but spiky at the base. After 5–7 years outdoors it develops a trunk and may eventually reach 3–4 m but is much slower in restricted light.

Raphis humilis. Very elegant for a low, wide container. Grows 1–3 m tall. For indoors or sheltered outdoor positions.

Palms with tall trunks
Palms with tall trunks are suitable for indoor decoration in their smaller stages, or for outdoor planting.

Bangalow *(Archontophoenis cunninghamiana)*. A graceful native palm with a dense top and arching branches and smooth trunk. Particularly suitable for not-too-exposed outdoor positions.

Cabbage Tree *(Livistona australis)*. Native palm with large fan-shaped fronds that need to be trimmed from the trunk as they age. More attractive in early stages; eventually reaches 15–20 m.

Cocos plumosa. Erect trunk with butts of old fronds clinging for many years, eventually becoming fairly smooth. The long arching fronds have irregularly twisted glossy leaflets, giving a soft plumy appearance. Grows 6–8 m.

Cocos weddelliana (Syragus). This has more regular fronds and a smooth trunk. Usually only 3–4 m.

Howea belmoreana. Similar to the kentia, with fronds at first upright and then gracefully arching but with close-set and narrower or more tapering leaflets, giving a softer appearance. Rarely exceeds 8 m.

Kentia *(Howea foseriana)*. A most popular house palm; in a container it remains 1–2 m high for many years, although outside it eventually reaches 15–20 m.

Large palms
Date *(Phoenix canariensis)*. Very long, stiff fronds in a dense rosetted head on a wide rough trunk, often with bunches of orange-hued dates. Grows 8–12 m high and at least as spreading.

European Fan *(Chamaerops humilis)*. Large, glossy dark-green pleated fan-shaped fronds on a fibrous trunk. Grows 5–6 m.

Wine *(Butia capitata)*. Same shape as the date palm but much lighter and more open in growth, with more arching, slender, grey fronds. Grows 4–6 m.

Palms that need bright light
Caryota
Cocos
Fan *(Chamaerops)*
Golden Cane or Madagascar *(Chrysalidocarpus)*
Lady Palm *(Rhapis excelsa)*
Livistona
Windmill *(Trachycarpus)*

19. Creepers and climbers

Creepers and climbing plants are functional as well as decorative. They give excellent value where space is limited and can be used in many different ways. They cover unsightly walls, rickety fences, tree stumps, the arbitrary fencing around garden pools; soften the lines of a house and cover pergolas and patios to give welcome shade. They offer the widest possible choice of colour and type of blossom; some are evergreen, others are deciduous. There is a climber or creeper for every situation. To choose the right one for a particular spot requires some understanding of the different ways plants are able to climb or cling.

Sucker discs

Hedera helix (English Ivy) and *Parthenocissus quinquefolia* (Virginia creeper) are examples of plants that climb with the assistance of sucker discs put out from the stem which attach themselves to a wall with great tenacity.

Petrea volubilis

Aerial roots

Hoya carnosa (Wax Plant) and *Monstera deliciosa* (Fruit salad Plant) put out aerial roots which, in the case of the Monstera, can be strong enough to force themselves through a wall.

Twiners

Their stems circle a support and grow upward; others put out hooks, prickles or tendrils, which enable them to get a purchase on a support and grow upward, and others, because they have a strong and whippy stem, need no support and grow upward in an arching and graceful fashion quite unaided.

Always give twining plants, or those that depend on their tendrils to enable them to climb, support in their early stages of growth. Twiners need sticks just thick enough for them to coil around but strong enough to stay upright under their weight. Tendrilled plants need a trellis.

A plant growing against wood can be given the help of a trellis of wire, wire mesh, plasticised wire or thin wood, held in place by rustless screws. If the plant is growing against a brick wall and you don't want to go to the trouble of plugging it to erect a trellis, drive a metal stake into the ground at the base of the wall, screw eyelets into the wood of the eaves or the fascia board and run wires between them. You can then train the plant along the wires. One of the most entrancing ways to make a display of a creeper is to build an arch or a series of arches over a path and train a wisteria to grow over the shapes so that the pendulous blossoms hang low and can be seen in their full beauty.

Planting and maintenance

Since the climbing plant will (hopefully) stay in place for a long time, it is worthwhile taking care during the initial planting. Consider the siting. Climbers often fail because they have been planted where they are under deluge from rain pouring from roof gutters.

Soak your new plant overnight but do not disturb the roots. Dig a hole of a sensible size to receive the plant, mix a little manure with some good soil and a light sprinkling of complete fertiliser and put it in the bottom of the hole and then cover it with soil. The feed should be kept out of reach of the young roots but be there for use as they grow. If the plant is not tall enough to reach the permanent support you have provided, hammer in some stakes to which it can be tied with soft material (strips of stocking will do) to train it upward in the right direction. Put in the plant, cover the roots with soil and firm down. A firm planting is essential. Water, then cover the soil around the plant with compost or a fine mulch of garden material to prevent the soil from drying out and caking.

Climbers can be rampant growers and, if not restrained, will lose much of their appeal. *Jasmine polyanthum*, with its starry flowers and drenching fragrance, is a joy but you would be wise to cut off all low-growing canes which would otherwise reach the soil, root and send up more growth. Other creepers which self-layer very quickly are *Akebia, Campsis, Doxanthus, Ficus, Hedera, Mulembeckia, Podreana* — you may still think of it as *Bignonia* — and Wisteria.

Above: Podranea rocasoliana (Pink bignonia)

Left: Wisteria sinensis

Creepers and climbers for special situations

Coastal areas

Aristolochia
Bignonia
Bougainvillea
Ipomoea tuberosa
Parthenocissus
Petrea volubilis
Podranea
Solandra
Solanum
Sollya heterophylla
Trachelospermum

Cold areas

Campsis radicans
Clematis
Clytostoma
Hedera
Lathyrus
Lonicera japonica
Parthenocissus
Podranea

Solanum jasminoides
Trachelospermum (Star Jasmine)
Wistaria

Dry inland areas

Bougainvillea
Doxanthus
Plumbago
Podranea
Pyrostegia
Senecio tamoides (Canary Creeper)
Solanum (Potato Creeper)
Tecomaria (Cape Honeysuckle)

Tropical Areas

Antigonon
Allamanda
Bougainvillea
Clerodendrum splendens
    C. thomsoniae (Bleeding Heart
    Clerodendron)
Ipomoea
Petrea volubilis
Pyrostegia
Quisqualis indica
Senecio tamoides (Canary Creeper)
Solandra nitida (Cup-of-Gold)
Thunbergia grandiflora

Ipomoea cardinalis

Clematis 'Nellie Moser'

Clematis montana

Above: Solanum jasminoides

Left: Bougainvillea

A cultivation guide to creepers and climbers

Key:
D — deciduous
SD — semi-deciduous
E — evergreen
C — self-clinging plant
S — plant requires support
T — twining plants or have tendrils. They make use of other plants or any available support.

Akebia quinata D, T. Attractively divided blue-green foliage, pendulous clusters of unusual lime to slatey-purple flowers in spring. Once established, is vigorous and freely self-layering. Deciduous in all but warm climates; good for cold to tropical districts.

Allamanda cathartica E, S-T. Tropical to semi-tropical creeper with glossy foliage and showy clusters of 5–7 cm wide, golden bells with broad, rounded petals. Prefers warmth, moisture and high humidity.

A. henderseni. Orange-yellow flowers with white spotted throats.

A. nerifolia **S.** Caney shrub, comparatively long foliage and tubular flowers with much smaller petals than *A. catharica*, more easily adaptable to frost-free temperate areas.

A. nobilis. Bright-yellow, lemon-scented flowers up to 12 cm diameter.

A. vilacea **S.** A reddish-violet form of above, usually with more shrubby growth.

Ampelopsis D (Virginia Creeper) see *Parthenocissus*

Antigonon (Coral Vine) **D, T.** Once established it makes a delightful summer or mid-autumn canopy of bright, coral-rose heart-shaped flowers above the crinkled mid-green foliage. Best in warm or warmer temperate districts. Plants can be started from seed in spring — they die down during the first winter in all but warm districts.

Aristolochia elegens (Dutchman's Pipe) **E, T.** Purple-banded, buff and white small vine, with heart-shaped leaves, flowers shaped like a Dutchman's pipe. Seed pods like fluted baskets. Best in part shade. Protect from frost.

Baubinia corymbosa E. (*B. scandens*). Dense, small, fern-like foliage eclipsed during mid-to-late summer by a mass of small, pale-rose flowers with reddish stems and stamens. Tropical to coastal temperate districts with plenty of water during summer.

Bignonia This is a case where reclassification of the genus has separated the earlier Bignonia species into several separate genera. These are:

Bignonia australis E. see *Pandorea pandorana*

B. jasminoides **C.** see *Pandorea jasminoides*

B. lindleyi see *Clytostoma*

B. rosea **SD.** see *Podranea*

B. tweediana **E.** see *Doxantha*

B. venusta **E.** see *Pyrostegia*

Billardiera scandens E, T. Twining Australian creeper with irregular, slightly hairy soft-green foliage and pendulous yellowish green

bell flowers neary 5 cm long. Gentle growth, rarely spreading more than 1–1.25 m. Grows in sun or part shade.

Blue Pea see *Lathyrus pubescens*
Boston Ivy see *Parthenocissus*

Bougainvillea E, S. Beautiful and vibrant summer colour provided there is ample support until well established. Tolerates poor soil but must have plenty of sun. Does even better when well fed. Prune back after flowering to keep growth under control.

B. Bridal Bouquet. Medium-growing, white blossom flushing to rose in the sun.

B. Carmencita. Vivid cherry-coloured or carmine, double flowers.

B. glabra **S.** (Varieties — shinier-leafed types), tolerates moderate cold in winter.

B. Laterita. A spring-flowering variety with brick-red bracts and loose growth which cascades attractively and makes a picturesque standard.

B. Louis Walthen. Unusual tangerine shade.

B. magnifica trailii. The strongest grower and hardy in all but cold mountain or southern climates. It carries masses of bright-purple bracts during spring and summer.

B. Mrs Butt. Rich, wine-red flowers and suitable for frosty areas.

B. rosea. Attractive dusty rose-pink, late winter and spring flowers. Needs frost protection. Was also known as *B. thomasii* in honour of the pioneer of the Indooroopilly Bougainvillaea Gardens in Brisbane.

B. Scarlett O'Hara. Like Mrs Butt, but with vivid red bracts.

B. Temple of Fire. Flowers brick to deep crimson-red. The only true dwarf shrubby type. Others are kept this way by pruning back vigorous growths and withholding feeding until flowering commences.

Campsis grandiflora (Chinese Trumpet Vine) **D or E, S, T.** Showy creeper with handsome, glossy divided foliage and clusters of large, wide-open, orange salmon trumpets displayed during summer. Deciduous in all but tropical climates. Brighter orange-red hybrid forms such as Madame Galen are self-clinging.

Carolina Jasmine see *Gelsemium*
Cat's Claw Creeper see *Doxanthus*

Cissus antarctica (Kangaroo Vine) **E, T.** Handsome, dark glossy-green irregularly-toothed longish leaves. New shoots covered in reddish-tan down. Clings with grape-like tendrils, climbing vigorously in warm, humid frost-free situations, half-sun or shade.

C. Rhomibifolia **T.** Is a similar South American creeper with leaves divided into three holly-like leaves.

Clematis. Showy flowers. Roots need shade with the rest of the plant in sun. Likes well-drained but deep, rich soil. Best in cool districts but grows well in temperate areas. A little lime is an advantage in acid soils.

C. aristata (Traveller's Vine). An evergreen species native to Australia and New Zealand, covered in spring with a mantle of creamy-white fragrant, star-like flowers. These are followed by unusual swirled, slender seed pods enclosed in silky grey down.

The plant prefers a cool, moist soil but is

extremely adaptable. Has fair tolerance to frost.

C. jackmanii **T.** Lavender-blue large blooms flowering on new growth in early spring and summer.

C. montana rubens. Four-petalled pinkish flowers about 5 cm across. Reddish spring growth. It bears on the previous season's shoots, so prune sparingly.

C. Nelly Moser **T.** Red and white large flowers, spring and early summer.

Clerodendrum splendens E, S. Large leathery foliage and clusters of brick-red flowers during summer and autumn. Suckers freely. For warm temperate and tropical areas.

C. tomsoniae (Bleeding Heart Vine) **T.** Caney vine with small blood-red flowers emerging from pendulous clusters of heart-shaped white calyces. Prefers light shade in warm, sheltered position. Cut back old canes in winter.

Clytostoma calliestegiodes (*Bignonia lindleyi*) **E, T.** Glossy-foliaged non-invasive and attractive evergreen with large lavender jacaranda-like bells in late spring and early summer. Ideal for temperate or tropical areas.

Cobea Scandens (Purple Bell Flower) **SD, T.** Fast-growing, soft-wooded creeper with large, decorative open-throated bells that open green and gradually deepen into violet. All but cold districts.

Dipladenia E, T. Yellow-throated pink flowers. Very decorative but a little sparse.

Doxantha unguis cati (Cat's Paw Creeper) (*Bignonia tweediana*) **E, C.** Cat's Paw Creeper', the new official name, is such an ugly name for a beautiful creeper; dense, small foliage intermingled with a mass of large canary-yellow bells in late spring and early summer. Grows in exposed positions in all but the coldest climates. Ideal for high fences around tennis courts, high walls or to cover dead tree trunks.

Fatshedera E. Hybrid between the shrub Fatsia and Hedera, the ivy, with large handsome fatsia-like leathery green foliage and long flexible but non-clinging canes. Grows in shade or sun, likes a warm position, but is frost tolerant. An attractive variegated form is also available.

Ficus pumila E, C. Strong vine with small, dense, neat foliage and coarse leathery adult growth. Should be kept clipped back. Excellent for binding embankments, old fences or consolidating loose rocky slopes.

F. pumila minima **E, C.** A miniature form of above with smaller foliage. Useful for decorating low walls, the base of stone pillars or pedestals, stumps or natural rock faces. Both types require temperate or tropical climate.

Gelsemium sempervirens (Carolina Jasmine) **E, T.** Small, dark-green pointed foliage, reddish-brown stems with clusters of yellow, bell-shaped fragrant flowers winter and spring. Stands light frosts.

German Ivy see *Senecio* (Lilac Vine)

Hardenbergia comptoniana E, T. Evergreen native. Small lavender-blue pea flowers carried in dense heads, spring. Rapid grower for all but coldest regions.

H. monophylla. Deep purple flowers, more evenly distributed.

H. violacea **E, T.** False sarsaparilla or purple coral pea. Sprays of purple flowers in spring.
Hedera (Ivy) **E.** Can stand sun or shade. Some more suitable as trailers or ground cover plants. The best to cover fences, walls, tree stumps are:

H. canariensis variegata **E.** Glossy foliage variegated cream-grey and dark green. Reddish stems. Dislikes severe cold.

H. helix **E.** Plain deep-green leaves.

H. helix (Cristata) **E.** Holly or parsley ivy. Large foliage ruffled and crimped at the edges.

H. helix (Goldheart) **E.** Small foliage, rich yellow with irregular dark-green margin. Good grower but more suitable for attractive tracery than quick dense cover. All ivies grow in cold to semi-tropical climates. All ivies are **C.**
Hibbertia volubilis **E, T.** Yellow flowers, found in sandy areas or in semi-rainforests.
Honeysuckle see *Lonicera*
Hoya carnosa (Wax Flower) **E, T–C.** Beautiful globular clusters of dainty pink porcelain-like flowers with red centres and waxy foliage. Prefers part shade in moderately warm aspects and should be allowed to dry out occasionally during winter. Flowers from old flower spurs so do not cut these.
Ipomea horsfallia **E, T.** Rich purple-bronze foliage and clusters of waxy magenta-red bells, with contrasting cream-tipped stamens. For tropical or warmer sheltered temperate areas only.
Ivy see *Hedera*
Jasminium azoricum (Azores or Summer Jasmine) **E, S.** Glossy evergreen foliage, sprays of starry white flowers, mainly in summer.

J. grandiflorum **E, S.** Smaller, less glossy foliage than *J. azoricum*. Fragrant pink-budded flowers during all but mid-winter months. Shrubby vine.

J. mesnyi (*J. primulinum*) (Yellow Jasmine) **E, S.** Large, yellow polyanthus-like flowers mainly during winter, and long arching canes that self-layer where they touch the ground.

J. nitidum **E, W.** Large, white star-shaped blooms about 38 mm across. A vine in tropical regions, elsewhere more of a caney bush.

J. polyanthum (Pink Jasmine) **T.** Because of the generous clusters of rosy-purple flushed buds that open white in spring only. Very fragrant and showy, but often spoiled by brown foliage in summer unless older canes that have flowered are cut out when the spring display finishes. Can self-layer to nuisance point, so keep stems clear of the ground.
Kennedia rubicunda (Coral Pea) **E, T.** Vigorous Australian native with 4 cm long, dull-red pea flowers in spring — withstands dry conditions well. All but very cold districts.

K. coccinea **T.** Smaller foliage but more prolific (salmon-red) flowers than *K. rubicunda*. Flowers well in moist positions with dappled sunlight.
Lapageria (Chilean Bell Flower) **E, T.** Flowers waxy rose bells, white spotted inside; some flowers creamy white. Likes the filtered light and humidity of a bush-house.
Lathyrus latifolius **E, T.** Fragrant white, pink or purple pea flowers; spring or summer.

L. pubescens. Downy foliage, tight heads of blue pea flowers.

Lonicera (Honeysuckle) **E, T.** Can be grown as shrubs or climbers. All are hardy.

L. brownii **SD.** Sometimes listed as *L. caprifolium* (pink honeysuckle). Reddish young canes, rounded foliage, clusters of long, pink trumpets opening creamy yellow at the tips. Flowers mostly in spring. If old flower heads are promptly cut back, a second flowering often follows. Can also be trained as a shrub. Very frost tolerant.

L. halleana **SD.** A fragrant strong-growing climber which needs to be kept off the ground to prevent it from layering down and straying. Clusters of large, creamy-white flowers turning yellow with age.

L. hildebrandiana **E.** Large tubular flowers; cream deepening to yellow.
Mandevilla suaveolens (Chilean Jasmine) **SD, T.** Attractive, dark heart-shaped foliage and clusters of large, fragrant, clear white trumpet-shaped flowers, summer–autumn. Best on protected wall in cold districts.
Manettia bicolor. Rapid twiner, dense, small dark satiny foliage, spangled with gold-tipped, bright red, 2–3 cm long tubular flowers during most of the year. For warm and tropical districts.
Mina lobata **D, T.** Quick-growing annual useful for short-term cover while permanent plants are establishing. Showy sprays of red and cream flowers during late summer or early autumn from seed sown in spring.
Muehlenbeckia complexa (Maidenhair Creeper or New Zealand Vine) **E, T.** Small, glossy-green round jade-like foliage growing alternately along wiry purplish-brown stems. Tiny fragrant flowers, will invade neighbouring plants unless checked. Likes half-sun or shade. Tolerates all but coldest climates but needs shelter from severe frosts. Graceful basket plant.
Pandorea jasminoides (Was Bignonia jasminoides). **E.** Dark glossy foliage, waxy-white trumpet-shaped flowers with rosy purple flowers in spring. Likes humid coastal conditions.

P. oxleyi **E.** Hardier species suitable to inland and all but very cold districts, resembles *P. pandorana* but with brown instead of purple marking.

P. pandorana (Wonga-Wonga, previously *Bignolia australis*) **E, T.** Bold dark-green foliage, large clusters of small, white tubular flowers with purple throat markings in spring. Prefers humid coastal conditions. Cv. 'Snowbells' is all creamy white.
Parthenocissum quinquefolia **D, S.** Known as *Amelopsis quinquefolia* or Boston Ivy. Large umbrella-like leaves divided into five pointed oval leaflets 7–12 cm long. Colours beautifully in autumn.

P. tricuspidata **D.** Previously *Ampelopsis veitchii* — also known as Virginian Creeper. Foliage resembles that of the grape but is richer green turning to vivid colours in autumn.

P. tricuspidata lowii. A smaller-foliaged type of above with more refined growth. Previously known as Small-leafed Virginian Creeper. All are **C.**
Passiflora caerulea (Blue Passion Flower) **E, T.** Finger-like leaflets usually arranged in

fives; petals creamy-white or mauve, rays or filaments tipped blue with a centre zone of white, then deep purple at the base. Non-edible fruits. For temperate and tropical areas.

P. coccinea **E, T.** Oval-leafed vine with brilliant scarlet flowers 12 cm across during summer and autumn, warmer temperate and tropical climates.
Pelargonium peltatum (Ivy Geranium) **E, S.** Pink, red, mauve or carmine flowers from spring through to autumn.
Perennial Pea see *Lathyrus latifolius*
Petrea volubilis (Purple Wreath) **SD, T–S.** Flowers like small double-violets backed by five longer starry lavender-blue sepals. (The latter hang like tinsel in long sprays for a month or two after the true flowers have fallen.) Tropical and frost-protected temperate areas.
Phaseolus caracalla (Snail Flower) **SD, T.** Fast-growing vine with bean-like foliage and fragrant, twisted, fluted snail-shaped flowers in cream, buff and lavender-flushed, blooming in summer and autumn. Temperate to tropical. Practically evergreen in warm districts. Dislikes frost.
Podranea rosea (or Ricasulona — *Bignonia rosea*) **E, T.** Caney growth, divided foliage. Sprays of large mauve-pink trumpets in late spring, early summer.
Pyrostegia ignea (Golden Shower previously *Bignonia venusta*). **E, T.** Bunches of bright-orange tubular flowers in winter. Best in warm districts, but stands fairly heavy frosts.
Quisqualis indica (Rangoon Creeper) **E, T.** Clusters of long, tubular flowers terminating in jasmine-like petals. Flowers vary from buff to pink or dark-red according to age.

Cut back in late winter and tip-prune — otherwise it becomes rampant in warm positions. Frost-free temperate and tropical, best with east coast humidity.
Rhynchospermum see *Trachelospermum*
Rose E, T. Fragrant creepers and climbers with long canes that can be trained against fences, walls and trellises.
Senecio (German Ivy) **E, T.** Dense but soft twiner with ivy-like foliage and flowers like small, cream marguerite daisies. Sun to shade in all but very frosty areas.
Solandra grandiflora (Balloon Flower) **E.** Spectacular creeper with balloon-like cream buds opening to giant cream, wide, trumpet-shaped fragrant flowers up to 30 cm long, mainly during spring.

S. nitida (Cup of Gold) **E.** Smaller foliage, flowers golden-yellow trumpets with purplish stripes. Both are rampant growers with arching upward, caney growth that needs training and regular pruning. Temperate and tropical plants needing protection from frost. They flower best in fairly poor soil.
Solanum jasminoides **SD, T.** Small foliage, dainty white, potato-like flowers, prolific growth.

S. wendlandii **T.** Blue to lavender flowers, potato-like, from mid-summer to autumn. Larger leaves.
Sollya fusiformis (Blue Bell Creeper) **T.** Western Australian wiry-stemmed, small but dense creeper with small, glossy foliage and dainty blue, pendulous bell-like flowers in

Clerodendron thompsoniae

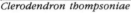
Allamanda cathartica

Pyrosregia

Quisqualis (Rangoon creeper)

Stephanotis floribunda

Parthenocissus tricuspidata

small clusters during spring and summer; good fence cover.

S. heterophylla **E, T.** Western Australian evergreen with clusters of starry blue summer flowers. Caney growth, may be trained as a creeper or can make a caney shrub. Temperate and tropical.

Stephanotis floribunda (Madagascar Jasmine) **E, T.** Long, leathery dark-green foliage, clusters of fragrant 5 cm long waxy-white bells, flaring to a five-petalled, jasmine-like mouth 3 cm wide. Flowers late in spring and summer. Warmer temperate and tropical areas.

Thunbergia alata (Black-eyed Susan) **E, T.** Dense, soft, light-green foliage, orange flowers about 4 cm across with four rounded lobes and a black centre.

T. coccinea. Red trumpet-shaped flowers.

T. gibsonii **T.** Similar to *T. alata* without the dark centre.

T. grandiflora. Light-blue flowers. Becomes over-vigorous in humid, tropical areas.

Trachelospermum jasminoides (Chinese Star Jasmine) **E, T.** Dense, dark-green glossy leaves, veiled with a lacy canopy of fragrant ivory propeller-shaped flowers in late spring to early summer. Does well in all except cold parts of the country. (There is a slower and stubbier variegated form.)

Virginia Creeper see *Parthenocissus*

Vitis (Alicante Bouchet or Ornamental Grape) **D.** Quick-growing, shapely grape foliage that colours beautifully in autumn. Can be cut back to within a few centimetres of the main stem to let the sun in during winter. All but semi-tropical or tropical districts.

Wisteria sinensis (Chinese Wisteria) **D, T.** Rampant if not cut back when long canes appear during summer; gives good summer shade and a glorious display of fragrant, pendulous lavender-blue flower sprays in spring.

W. floribunda (Japanese Wisteria). Has flower sprays at least twice as long as above and more leaflets (about 19 compared to a dozen).

W. multijuga (alba) **T.** White flowers in slender sprays up to 50 cm long, blooming about a fortnight later than Chinese Wisteria. All but tropical.

TREES AND SHRUBS IN THE GARDEN

20. Trees

The correct choice of trees for a garden is crucial. Many gardens are ruined by the growth of a lovely tree into a giant which overshadows other plants and steals the food they need. Some trees have roots which absorb so much water that nothing is left for their neighbours. Huge trees in a small garden can be a disaster.

There are a few golden rules.

• Plant evergreens on the boundary of the garden to ensure privacy. Do not plant them near the house where they would obscure light during the time of year light is welcomed.

• Plant deciduous trees near the house, not on the boundaries, for the obvious inverse reasons.

• If you want a shade tree in the garden don't go for a massive forest tree but choose smaller, spreading trees. These grow more quickly, do not rob the soil to the same extent and can be sited to provide shade for shrubs which flower well in shade and beneath which ground covers can provide both texture and colour. Shade trees are lovely near a swimming pool but not too close to be a nuisance when their leaves drop. (Evergreen trees drop their leaves — not in one autumnal deluge as do the deciduous — but spasmodically throughout the year.)

• Deciduous trees should be planted when they are dormant; late winter or early spring.

• Evergreens like moist soil and moist air after planting. This obviously is at various times in different parts of our continent.

• Provided the soil is well prepared in advance and watering is carried out intelligently, subsequently most trees grown in containers can be transplanted at any time.

• If you have an existing tree you would like to move to another position it can be done, within limits. Evergreens more than 185 cm need special care (see page 183). Deciduous trees more than 6 m high and with a trunk diameter of more than 15 cm are risky propositions.

Planting a tree

Location and soil

The position should be large enough to accommodate the tree when it's mature. It's a good idea to place a stake where you intend it to be and mark out the radius to see if you really have room.

Trees require lots of moisture but the soil must be well drained. Although it is desirable for the soil to be damp for planting, be sure to avoid wet conditions as sticky soil will set tightly around the roots and exclude oxygen essential for root development.

Planting

Make a wide hole so that well-rotted leaf mould or compost, moistened peatmoss or similar improvers can be mixed with the soil. This encourages the spread of roots into their new environment. When the planting soil is

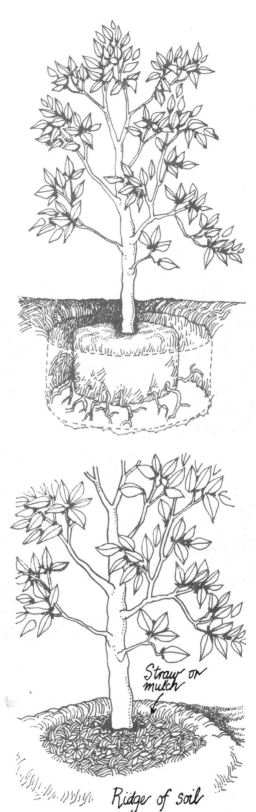

Straw or mulch

Ridge of soil

poorer than container soil, roots tend to remain in the original root ball.

Plant only when the soil is just damp, never when wet and sticky, otherwise it sets tightly and retards root growth.

Tread newly-dug soil down lightly before replanting. Do not plant deeper than previous soil level — or container soil level — and

mulch surface with leaf mould or other fibrous material to stop soil from caking and help to conserve moisture. Do not add fertilisers or manures at planting time.

Planting time

Deciduous trees bought growing in containers can be planted at any time but it is good practice to avoid the hottest months, especially if it is difficult to give them a good supply of water during their establishing period.

Deciduous trees such as prunus, crab apples, etc. may, in some areas, be available as open ground stock (plants dug and root-pruned during the dormant period). These can be replanted safely only during the winter months, taking care not to let roots dry out before or during planting.

Evergreen trees grown in nursery containers can be planted at any time although spring is the best time for warmth lovers or frost-tender types in other than warm districts, allowing them the longest period of warmth in which to establish.

Water

Gently soak the soil around the plant immediately after planting without disturbing or puddling the soil. This is easier if the suggested mulch has been applied.

Over the next few weeks, water again whenever the soil dries out for more than about a centimetre down, then about twice this depth for the next 8 to 10 weeks. From then, most trees should be able to fend for themselves, except during exceptionally dry or hot conditions.

Adding a newcomer

When planting a new tree or shrub among established growth, it is wise to water the entire area. The same applies when feeding the newcomer after it is established. This gives the plant a good chance to establish without undue competition, otherwise roots from nearby trees soon invade the favoured spot.

Step-by-step planting guide

Step 1. Dig a hole deep enough for the tree to be planted at the same depth as it was in the container. However, the hole should be at least twice as wide as the container to encourage new root growth.

Step 2. Make a mound of topsoil or improved soil at the bottom of the hole just high enough to bring the top of the plant's soil ball level with the surrounding soil so that it is not planted too deep.

Step 3. Without disturbing the rootball, position the tree in the hole. If the roots are spiralled around the base of the soil ball, carefully unravel, spread and cover them. If it is a bare-rooted tree carefully tease the roots outwards over the mound in the hole.

Step 4. Fill in the hole with improved soil. Firm down by pressing firmly around the young tree plant.

Step 5. Fashion a soil ridge slightly in from the edge of the hole. Fill with leafmould, grass or straw then gently flood in water.

Moving a tree

Trees can be rearranged like furniture — within reason. I have successfully moved mature trees more than 10 m high. Still larger ones have been transported long distances and replanted by landscapers with heavy equipment.

The key to moving trees successfully is careful handling at the right time of the year. Of equal importance is to cut back heavily immediately prior to the move. This is the hardest step for most people to take because of the desire to see the specimen looking its best in the new location.

Shrubs such as conifers and azaleas survive careful moving without prior pruning. Large camellias may appear 'not to have turned a hair' and continue to flower normally after the move but perform badly the following year, and if left unpruned will take several years to recover.

It is impossible to be certain about the chances of success because there are times when conditions are not favourable. It is unlikely that daphne and natives such as mature grevillea, banksia, Geraldton wax, mint bushes and gum trees will survive a move that involves cutting or disturbance of the root area.

The success rate is far greater if deciduous shrubs, roses and trees are moved when in their leafless or dormant state usually during winter.

It is also better to move most evergreens during their relatively dormant period during winter. Citrus, gardenias and in cold districts even camellias are better handled in late winter or very early spring. Always move them before new growth commences.

Young shrubs planted out only for a year or two, or camellias or conifers up to about 1 m high, can be moved by spading to cut all roots a span out from the trunk and attempting to lift the tree. If it does not respond to the lift make a spade-width trench outside the first cut to make it possible to cut in and sever anchoring roots.

Speed is essential, the root ball must not dry out. Dig the new hole in advance, at least twice as wide as the soil ball so that there is plenty of space to pack improved soil around the cut roots but no deeper. Progress is retarded and survival chances lessened if a plant is set deeper than its original level.

Have the soil just damp in the new position. It should not be wet or sticky. Slide hessian or similar material beneath the root ball and use this to lift the tree. Don't lift by the stem or trunk: soil will drop off taking young feeder roots with it.

Mound soil below the plant to bring it up to original soil level and position and carefully cut away jagged or broken roots.

When deciding how much to cut the roots, remember that most of the main feeders are below the outer branches.

Make a trench at least twice spade-width outside them to allow clean sawing of the roots. Cut below the root ball and rock the tree to loosen it. Water the root and surrounding soil as soon as possible. If the soil is too light or too heavy add compost.

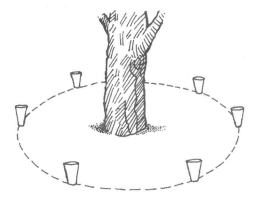

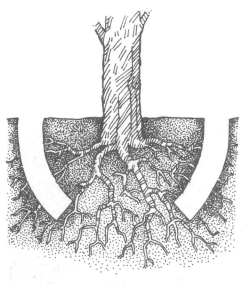

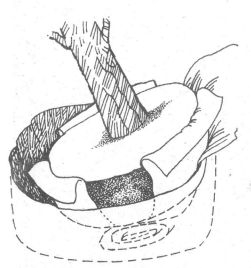

Conditioning large trees prior to moving

Stage 1. Mark out the estimated perimeter of the root ball using 6 stakes placed at equal distance apart. Using the stakes, mark out a circle divided into 6 segments.

Stage 2. Remove soil and cut roots in alternate sections. Cover cut root section with a piece of plastic, and while soil is being filled back into the trench, trickle compost to form a 'layer of encouragement' between cut roots and plastic.

Stage 3. Three months later deal with the other 3 segments in the same way.

Once the trench has been dug far enough under the soil base for all the tree roots to be severed, rock the tree, first backwards, inserting a strong sheet of doubled plastic beneath it, then rock forwards and manoeuvre the doubled piece of plastic out so that the tree is sitting on the opened sheet. It can then be lifted and carried to its new position.

In practice there is seldom the 3-month wait. The second trenching and lifting are done in one operation which then reduces shock by half.

Good tree management
Feeding

Feed young trees each spring by spreading half a wheelbarrow of well-rotted manure on top of the soil around the roots. Repeat in midsummer if possible. Compost may be used at anytime. However, be careful not to pile the manure or compost against the base of the tree or they may cause rot and death by raising the level of the soil around the tree.

The tree's feeding roots extend slightly beyond the rim of the outer branches and you should feed the whole area.

For mature trees water the ground the day before feeding. Using an iron bar drill holes about 5 cm in diameter to a depth of 46 cm over the root area approximately 90–100 cm apart. Use a balanced fertiliser (about 500 g for each 3 cm of the trunk but not more than 1.5 kg per tree) and divide it equally among the number of holes. Pour fertiliser into each hole, fill with water then fill with good soil or compost.

General care

Do not let vines grow over trees or cover any section of the trunk.

Do not build up soil around trees. This can cause their death. Added earth should be kept back from the trunk by a retainer of uncemented stone, brick, etc. Do not build up rockeries around trees.

Do not remove branches and leave a stub of old wood. This will die and leave a core of rotted wood extending into the heart of the tree, providing entry for fungus or borers.

Unless branches are removed correctly, they will split at the base and the splitting will extend into the main trunk with undesirable effects.

When branches have been broken off or cavities of decay appear, the rotten growth should be gouged out, fungicide applied and covered with a sealing compound. The cavity should then be filled to just below bark level with a mixture of 2:1 sand and cement dampened mixture, which is firmed down just inside the cambium level to allow the bark to grow over it.

Split branches can be splinted. If a branch splits away from the tree at junction level clean off the stump without biting too deeply into the bark of the tree.

Most trees are subject to inspect pests of one type or another. Keep careful watch and employ remedial tactics as advised in the section 'Pests and diseases'.

Trees for special situations

| C — cool climate |
| T — temperate |
| H — hot climate |

Evergreen trees resistant to salt winds

Acacia baileyana C–T
Acacia longifolia C–T
Angophora costata T
Araucaria hetrophylla T–H
Banksia integrifolia T
Callistemon viminalis T–H
Callitris rhomboidea T–H
Casuarina glauca T–H
Cupressus arizonica C–T
Cupressus (other types reasonably resistant)
Eucalyptus botryoides T
Ficus macrophylla T–H
   F. rubignosa T–H
Lagunaria T–H
Leptospermum laevigatum T
Melaleuca armillaris T–H
   M. quinquenervia T–H

Metrosideros T
Olea C–H
Pinus elliotti T–H
Quercus ilex C–H
Tamarix aphylla C–H

Trees for badly drained, over-wet areas

Evergreen

Callistemon (most types)
Casurina cunninghamii T–H
   C. glauca T–H
Melaleuca quinquenervia T–H
Tristania laurina T–H

Deciduous

Alnus glutinosa C–T
Poplar (all types, but most sucker badly)
Quercus palustris C–T
Salix (various types willow)
Taxodium distichum C–T

Trees for tropical areas

Acacia podalyriaefolia
Araucaria hetrophylla
   Norfolk Island Pine)
Bauhinia variegata (Orchid Tree)

Brachychiton (Flame Tree)
Calodendrum capense (Cape Chestnut)
Cassia fistula (Pudding Pipe Tree)
Castanospermum australe (Moreton Bay Chestnut)
Cupressus sempervirens stricta (Pencil Cypress)
Delonix regia (Poinciana)
Erythrina
Eucalyptus ficifolia
Grevillea banksii (Scarlet Grevillea)
Jacaranda acutifolia
Magnolia grandiflora (White Laurel Magnolia)
Plumeria (Frangipanni)
Spathodea campanulata

Trees for dry inland areas

Acacia (Wattle)
Brachychiton (Flame Tree, Kurrajong and Queensland Laceback)
Callitris
Casuarina
Cupressus macrocarpa
Erythrina (Coral Tree)
Eucalyptus

Erythrina (Coral Tree)
Eucalyptus
Fraxinus (Ash)
Grevillea robusta (Silky Oak)
Koelreuteria (Golden Rain Tree)
Phoenix canariensis
Pittosporum tenuifolium (P. nigricans)
Prunus cerasifera
   P. persica (Flowering Peach)
Santalum (Quandong)
Schinus molle (Pepper Tree)
Tamarix (Tamarisk)
Ulmus (Elm)

Trees for cold areas

Acacia (Wattle)
Acer (Maple)
Aeschylus (Horse Chestnut)
Arbutus unedo (Strawberry Tree)
Betula (Birch)
Catalpa
Cedrus deodara (Deodar)
Cercis siliquastrum (Judas Tree)
Crataegus (Hawthorn)
Cupressus macrocarpa (Monterey Cypress)
   C. sempervirens stricta (Pencil Cypress)
Eucalyptus (Gum)
Fagus (Beech)
Fraxinus (Ash)
Gingko biloba (Maidenhair Tree)
Hakea saligna (Willow Hakea)
Ilex aquifolium (Holly)
Koelreuteria
Liquidambar (Sweet Gum)
Liriodendron (Tulip Tree)
Malus (Crab Apple)
Pinus (Pine)
Platanus (Plane)
Podocarpus
Prunus (Flowering Peach, Plum, Cherry, Almond)
Quercus (Oak)
Salix (Willow)
Tamarix (Tamarisk)
Taxodium distichum (Swamp Cypress)
Ulmus glabra (Wych Elm)

Jacaranda acutifolia

Trees for colour

Trees for spring colour

Acacia baileyana (Cootamundra
   wattle) C–T
   A. decurens boormanii C–T
   A. longifolia C–T
   A. mollisima C–T
   A. pendulata (Weeping Myall) C–T
Malus (Crab Apple) C–T
Prunus cerasifera C–T
   P. persica C–T
   P. serrulata C–T

Trees for autumn colour

Acer (Maple species — except variegated
   A. negundo) C–T
Ash (species) C–T
Birch, silver C–T
Cornus florida C–T
Cratageus (species)
Ginkgo C–T
Koelreuteria C–T
Liquidambar (species)
Metasequoia C–T
Nyssa sylvatica C–T
Persimmon T–H
Pistacia chinensis T–H
Poplar (species)
Prunus serrulata (varieties) C–T
   P. campanulata T
Quercus coccinea C–T
   Q. palustris C–T
Sapium sebiferum T–H
Sorbus C
Tilia europea C–T
Ulmus (species) C–T

Gordonia

Above: Golden conifer

Left: Blue spruce and malus in spring blossom

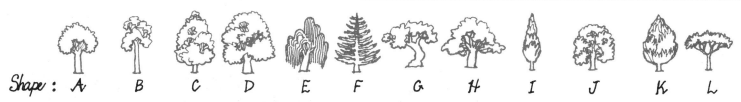

Shape: A B C D E F G H I J K L

Trees for small gardens

Evergreen

Acacia baileyana C–T
  A. pycantha C–T
  A. spectabilis C–T
Agonis flexuosa T
Arbutus unedo C–T
Banksia integrifolia T
Bauhinia blakeana T–H
Callistemon salignus T–H
  C. viminalis T–H
Cassia fistula H
  C. multijuga T–H
Ceratopetalum grummiferum T
Citharexylum T–H
Conifer (see various species) C–H
Cotoneaster pannosa C–T
  C. serotina C–T
Elaeocarpus T–H
Eucalyptus eremophila T
  E. haemastoma T
  E. nicholii C–T
  E. torquata C–T
Eugenia smithii T–H
Glochidion T–H
Hakea salicifolia C–T
Laurus nobilis C–H
Melaleuca armillaris C–H
Metrosideros T
Michelia champaca T–H
Olea C–H
Photinia serrulata C–T
Pittosporum rhombifolium T–H
Schefflera T–H
Sophora tetraptera C–T
Stenocarpus sinuatus T–H
Tamarix aphylla C–H
Tristania laurina T–H
Virgilia oroboides C–T

Deciduous

Acer negundo C–T
  A. negundo variegata C–T
  A. palmatum C–T
Albizia julibrissin T
Alnus glutinosa lacinata C–T
Bauhinia variegata T–H
Betula (all types) C–T
Cercis C–H
Cornus florida C–T
Corylus avellana C–T
Fraxinus excelsior Aurea C–T
Koelreuteria C–T
Lagerstroemia indica rubra T–H
Liquidambar orientalis C–T
Malus (various types) C–T
Nyssa sylvatica C–T
Parrotia persica
Pistacia chinensis C–T
Prunus (see selection) C–T
Salix matsudana C–T
Sapium T–H
Sophora japonica C–H
Stenolobium stans T

A reference guide to trees

E: Evergreen   **D:** Deciduous
H: Height: **W:** Width
C: For cool climates only
T: Temperate — where winter day temperatures are rarely below 10°C (50°F)
H: Hot, semi-tropical to tropical climates
Salt resistance — SH: high
                  SM: medium
                  SL: low
T–H: Suitable only to temperate and semi-tropical or tropical districts. **C–H** suits all districts.
Trees with **C** in the combination would resist heavy frost. Those rated **T–H**, unless otherwise stated, would survive moderate frost given protection the first winter.

Acacia (Wattle) *A. baileyana* (Cootamundra Wattle). Fern-like, silver-grey foliage, outer branches pendulous with mass of late-winter golden blooms. Dense, fairly spreading growth. H 5 m, W 3–4 m. SH. **Shape A.**

A. decurrens (Black Wattle). Erect, round-headed tree with finely cut, dark-green foliage, dark trunk, branches; masses of yellow flower, early spring. H 7–10 m, W 4 m. E, C–T. **Shape B.**

A. longifolia. Long, leathery, bright-green foliage, fingers of yellow, early spring. Good salt resistance. H 4 m, W 2–4 m . E, C–T. **Shape C.**

A. pycnantha (Golden Wattle). Bold, lance-shaped foliage, large fluffy, golden balls of flower in spring. H 3–5 m, W 2–3 m. E, C–T. **Shape C.**

A. spectabilis (Mudgee Wattle). Fern-like, blue-green foliage, profusion of small, bright, golden balls of winter-spring flower. Slender, erect growth. H 4 m, W 2 m. E, C–T. **Shape C.**

There are several hundred hardy wattles in the small-tree category, adaptable to a great variety of well-drained soils.

Acer (Japanese Maple). *A. palmatum* comes in many varieties, all with attractively-cut deeply-lobed foliage. The species is bright green. SL.

Variety *A. palmatum* 'Senkaki' has yellowish-green foliage, with red stems in winter.

All colour beautifully in autumn, prefer cool mountain climates but adapt to partly shaded positions in temperate climates except where summer heat is very dry. Average height in coastal districts 3–5 m and as wide, but they may double this height in mountain areas.

Smaller growing *A. palmatum* and other varieties are listed in the shrub section. **Shape A.**

A. platanoides (Norway Maple — like the plane tree). Erect, with fairly large five-lobed leaves. Prefers sharp winters but stands summer heat. Colours well in autumn. H 13–16 m, W 6–8 m. D, C–T. **Shape C.**

A. pseudo-platanus (False Plane Tree) sycamore. Large, coarsely lobed leaves usually downy on underside. Several varieties. H 12–14 m, W 6–9 m. D, C–T. **Shape C.**

A. negundo (Box Elder). Adaptable, quick growing; dense green foliage divided into 3–5 leaflets, turning yellow in autumn. Its two variegated varieties are popular — *agentia:* green/white variegated foliage; *aurea variegata:* green/gold. Neither colours in autumn. H 7–10 m, W 4–5 m. D, SM, C–T. **Shape C.**

Aesculus hippocastanum (Horse Chestnut). Large, divided fan-like foliage, candle-like spikes of white flowers, spring. H 15–20 m, W 6–9 m. D, C–T. **Shape D.**

Agonis (Western Australian Willow Myrtle). Spreading, with graceful pendulous outer branches; slender, weeping foliage. Wind, drought resistant. Not for frosty areas. H 5–6 m, W 5 m. E, T, SH. **Shape E.**

Albizzia julibrissin (Silk Tree). Quick-growing, small tree, wide umbrella shape, jacaranda-like foliage which folds at night. Silky, pompon-like pink and cream flowers above foliage, late spring. H 3–4 m, W 4–5 m. All but very cold districts. D. **Shape H.**

Alnus glutinosa (Alder). Birch-like, but with large, denser foliage. Adapts to wet soils, creek banks, etc.; coastal or cold inland districts. H 12–18 m, W 4–6 m. D, C–T. **Shape D.**

Angophora costata (Coastal Red Gum). Reddish-tan to mauve-pink bark, usually erect trunk, contorted outer branches. In sheltered area grows 20–30 m and is high branching, but may only be 7–10 m high and nearly as wide when exposed to wind. E, T. **Shape B.**

Araucaria heterophylla (excelsa) (Norfolk Island Pine). Tall, symmetrical conifer, with regularly placed, slender lateral branches diminishing in length up the tree. Cord-like, semi-erect branchlets clustered with small, rigid, dark-green leaves. Popular for sea coast. H 17–30 m, W 5–9 m. E. **Shape F.**

A. cunninghamii (Hoop Pine). Foliage softer, more tufted than Norfolk pine, often less symmetrical. H 13–17 m, W 5–7 m. E. **Shape F.**

Arbutus unedo (Irish Strawberry). Glossy-foliaged tree, sprays of small lily-of-the-valley-like flowers in autumn–winter, followed by large yellow then red berries. H 4–5 m, W 3–4 m. E. **Shape J.**

Ash see *Fraximus*

Banksia grandis. Western Australian species noted for long, slender, saw-toothed foliage. Erect, greenish-yellow cones spring. H 8–10 m, W 5–7 m. Prefers dry summer. E. **Shape G.**

B. integrifolia. Slender, toothed, leathery

foliage, dark-green above, grey beneath; greenish-yellow cones, winter to mid-summer. Resistant to salt wind. H 3–5 m, W 3 m. E. **Shape L.**

B. serrulata (Old Man Banksia). Gnarled, pinkish-brown bark, contorted branches; stiff, serrated foliage, and thick lime to mauve-grey cones. H 3–6 m, W 5 m. E. **Shape G.**

Baubinia. All have blue-green foliage divided in butterfly-like formation, with clusters of pelargonium-like flowers. SH. **Shape L.**

B. blakeana. Rosy-purple flowers, spring; occasionally till autumn. Frost tender. H 4 m, W 4–5 m. E. **Shape L.**

B. variegata. Spring flowers, slightly paler than above. Stands light to moderate frost. H 4–5 m, W 4 m. D. **Shape L.**

B. variegata candida. White-flowered form; slightly taller. **Shape L.**

Bay Tree see *Laurus*

Beech see *Fagus*

Betula verrucosa (Silver Birch). Gracefully pendulous outer branches. Small dark, glossy foliage turns gold in autumn, falls to display slender white trunk, branches. H 5–10 m, W 3–4 m. D. SL. **Shape D.**

Birch see *Betula*

Bottlebrush see *Callistemon*

Brachychiton acerifolium (Illawarra Flame). Erect tree with large, green, lobed foliage usually falling in spring to make way for brilliant, early summer cascade of small, waxy red bells. H 10 m, W 3–5 m. D, T–H. **Shape C.**

B. populneum (Kurrajong). Smaller, more angular foliage than above. Small white flowers. Adaptable, frost and drought resistant. H 10–14 m, W 5–7 m. E. **Shape D.**

B. hybrida. Hybrid between the two above species. Flowers more reliable than *B. acerifolia* but usually paler. **Shape D.**

B. discolor (Queensland Lacebark). Resembles kurrajong, with larger but sparser foliage, large rose-purple flowers, brown felted on outside. H 7–10 m, W 5 m. D, T–H. **Shape D.**

Brassaia see *Schefflera*

Caesalpinia ferrea (Leopard Tree). High-branching, round-headed tree; smooth, silvery-white trunk heavily spotted dark grey. Fern-like foliage bronze in spring, with small yellow flowers. H 17 m, W 6 m. D, T–H. **Shape B.**

Callistemon salignus. Slightly pendulous, slender foliage, pink new growth; creamy-white brushes, spring. Stands tough soil, poor drainage. H 5–7 m, W 3 m. All but coldest districts. E, SH. **Shape D.**

C. viminalis (Weeping Bottlebrush). Willow-like growth, red brushes late winter to early summer. H 6 m, W 5 m. E, SH. All but coldest districts. **Shape E.**

Calodendrum capense (Cape Chestnut). Handsome, rounded, dense-foliaged tree, spectacular with large heads of spidery pink flowers, late spring/early summer. May take 10 years or more to flower; grafted trees usually quicker. Protect from heavy frost first year. H 6–10 m, W 5–6 m. E. **Shape H.**

Callitris rhomboidea (Port Jackson Cypress). Dense column of fine, dark-green foliage best suited to light soil. H 8–13 m, W 2–3 m. E. All but coldest regions. **Shape I.**

Camellia see separate section

Cape Chestnut see *Calodendrum*

Cassia brewsteri. Graceful, spreading tree with pendulous, glossy divided foliage; long sprays yellow and orange-red flowers, spring. H 5–6 m, W 6 m. Frost free. E, T–H. **Shape E.**

C. fistula. Golden showers or pudding pipe tree. Large light-green leaves divided to rounded leaflets; long, pendulous sprays of large golden flowers, summer. H 3–4 m, W 4–5 m, frost free. D, T–H. **Shape E.**

C. multijuga. Quick-growing, erect, cone-shaped to rounded tree, massed yellow flower, autumn. Ht 6–9 m, W 4–5 m. E, T–H. **Shape C.**

Cedrus deodara (Himalayan Cedar). Graceful tree with slender, tapering trunk and lateral branches dropping at tips; wide spreading at base, gradually tapering to top. Foliage is blue-green, needle-like, almost completely covering branches. Needs regular moisture. E, C–T. **Shape F.**

C. atlantica (Atlas or Atlantic Cedar). More rigid growth and foliage than deodara; slightly ascending rather than pendulous tips. Best for cool climates. Stands dryness well. Variety *glauca* has blue-grey foliage. E, C–T. **Shape F.**

Ceratopetalum gummiferum (N.S.W. Christmas Bush) See Native Plants. **Shape C.**

Cercis siliquastrum (Judas Tree). Resembles small-foliaged bauhinia. Small, rosy-pink flowers, cluster branches, spring. H 6 m, W 3–4 m. D, C–T. **Shape C.**

Christmas Bush — N.S.W see *Ceratopetalum*

Christmas Bush — New Zealand see *Metrosideros*

Citharexylum (Fiddlewood). Quick-growing, spreading fan-shaped screen tree; bright, glossy foliage with some 'autumn' tints in spring. Tiny white, fragrant summer flowers. Cut to any size, does not stand heavy frost. H 6–9 m, W 5 m. E, T–H. **Shape H.**

Cornus florida (Dogwood). Pyramid-shaped, showy white flower bracts, spring. Variety *rosea* is pink. Autumn foliage. H 5–6 m, W 3 m. D, C–T, SL.

C. capitata — Benthamia (Himalayan Strawberry Tree). White spring flower bracts, red, fleshy, strawberry-like fruits, autumn. H 5–6 m, W 5 m. E.

Cotoneaster. Taller-growing types such as *C. pannosa* and *C. serotina* can have lower growth removed to create tree-like form. Outer growth is pendulous, with red berries autumn/winter. H 3–4 m, W 3–4 m. E. All but coldest and T. **Shape E.**

Cryptomeria japonica plumosa. Symmetrical, cone-shaped conifer. Softly curling foliage turns bronze, autumn/winter. H 10 m, W 3 m. E, C–T. **Shape F.**

Cupressis arizonica (Arizona Cypress). Dense, silver-grey foliage, quick growing. Salt and drought resistant once established. H 10–14 m, W 3–4 . C–T. **Shape I.**

C. macrocarpa (Monterey Cypress). Dark-green pyramid, short-lived on humid coast, better inland. H 14–17 m, W 5–6 m. E, C–T. **Shape I.**

C. macrocarpa brunniana (Golden Cypress). Erect, dense growth; bright green, golden tipped, spreading lateral in highlands. H 7–10 m, W 3–4 m. C–T. **Shape I or F.**

C. macrocarpa horizontalis aurea. Lateral, plume-like, golden-tipped under branches. Symmetrical pyramid. Stands sea coast or inland. H 10–14 m, W 5–6 m. E, C–T. **Shape F.**

C. macrocarpa erecta aurea. Quick-growing, more slender, open form of above *horizontalis aurea*. H 10 m, W 3–4 m. E. **Shape F.**

C. macrocarpa corybeare. Quick grower, pendulous, golden, thread-like outer branchlets. Remove growth reverting to erect form. H 5–7 m, W 3–4 m. E. **Shape E.**

C. sempervirens (Italian Cypress). Dark-green, upright column. H 7–10 m, W 2 m. E. **Shape I.**

C. sempervirens stricta (Pencil Pine). More slender form, for screen or windbreak where space is limited. H 2–3 m, W 1 m. E. **Shape I.**

C. sempervirens (Swane's Golden). Slender, golden form of above. H 5–6 m, W 1 m. E. **Shape I.**

Cypress see *Cupressus*

Cypress — Port Jackson see *Callitris*

Delonix regia (Poinciana). Beautiful wide-spreading jacaranda-like tropical tree massed with scarlet flowers, early summer. H 8 m, W 10–15 m. D. **Shape H.**

Dogwood see *Cornus*

Elaeocarpus reticulatus (Blueberry Ash). Native to east coast. Small, fringed white bells cluster branchlets in spring, followed by blue autumn berries. H 7–10 m, W 4 m. E, T–H. **Shape C.**

Erythrina variegata (Coral Tree). Spreading umbrella shaped, clusters of red pea flowers like small jets of flame at ends of twisted, thorny branches, winter. H 5–7 m, W 8–10 m. D, T–H. **Shape H.**

Eucalyptus (Gums, Box, Stringybark,). Over 600 species, mostly adaptable, quick growing. Popular garden types include available or suggested varieties for special purposes.

E. botryoides (Mahogany Gum). Stringy-barked, high branching, good resistance to salt winds, some frost resistance. H 15–20 m, W 6 m. E. **Shape D.**

E. cinerea (Argyle Apple). Rounded, opposite, silver-grey foliage. Decorative in younger growth, then rather sparse. H 10 m, W 5 m. E, C–T. SH. **Shape G.**

E. citrodora (Lemon-scented Gum). Quick growing, high branching, sparse foliage. Graceful, tall, slender, silvery-white trunk. Frost tender. E, T–H. **Shape B.**

E. cladocalyx (Sugar Gum). Dense, glossy foliage; smooth buff to grey trunk. Good windbreak, coast and inland. H 20–30 m, W 7 m. E. All but coldest districts. **Shape C.**

E. cladocalyx nana. Dwarf form of above. H 15–25 m, W 5–7 m. E, C–H. **Shape D.**

E. elata (Willow Peppermint). Tall, quick grower, fibrous trunk, pendulous foliage. Frost-free areas. H 15–25 m, W 5–7 m. E. **Shape C.**

E. eremophylla (Sand Mallee). Small tree for rugged inland conditions. Stands saline soil. H 6 m, W 3–5 m. E, T. **Shape D.**

E. ficifolia (Western Australian Red-flower-

Spathodea campanulata (African tulip tree)

Caesalpinia pulcherrima

ing Gum). Spectacular blossom, early summer. Seedlings vary from cream, pink to bright scarlet. May be short-lived but grows well when conditions suit. Usually best in deep, light soil. Resents heavy frosts. H 5 m, W 3 m. E, T. **Shape D.**

E. globulus (Tasmanian Blue Gum). Large, silver-grey juvenile foliage later slender, green, dense. H 20–25 m, W 10–14 m. E, C–T. **Shape D.**

E. maculata (Spotted Gum). Lime to pale-grey trunk, spotted slate grey. Native to shaly coastal areas. Frost protection, early stages. H 18–25 m, W 6 m. E, T–H. **Shape B.**

E. nicholii (Small-leafed Peppermint). Quick-growing small tree, slender, pendulous blue-grey foliage, low branching. Good screen. Suits poor, stony soil. H 6–8 m, W 5 m. E, C–T, SH. **Shape D.**

E. torquata (Coral or Coolgardie Gum). Pendulous, soft-green foliage, showy ridged pink buds open pink or red. Prefers well-drained or low summer rainfall areas, lower altitude. Moderate frost resistance. H 5–6 m, W 3 m. E, T. **Shape D.**

Fagus (Beech). Lovely foliage trees for cool districts.

F. sylvatica. Glossy, rounded foliage. H 20 m, W 10–14 m. D, C–T. **Shape D.**

F. sylvatica cuprea (Copper Beech). Coppery-red spring foliage, bronze-purple in summer. H 10–14 m, W 10 m. D, C to cooler T. **Shape D.**

Ficus macrophylla — *elastica* and *F. rubignosa.* Are all spreading trees with large, leathery, dark foliage, usually too spreading and heavily rooted for small gardens. H 10–14 m, W 15 m. E, T–H. **Shape H.**

F. hilli is higher branching with smaller, lighter foliage, but still with heavy root system. H 15 m, W 10 m. E, T–H. **Shape D.**

F. benjaminii, similar, is more pendulous, spreading. H 7–10 m, W 14–20 m, sometimes more. H. **Shape D.**

An attractive blue spruce among a back planting of conifers

Catalpa bignonioides

Ulmus procera 'Louis Van Houtte' (golden elm)

Fiddlewood see *Citharexylum*

Fraxinus (Ash). Hardy, deciduous tree.

F. excelsior aurea (Golden Ash). Has large divided foliage, buttery yellow in autumn. Winter stems yellow with black buds. H 5–7 m, W 5 m. D, C–T. **Shape D.**

F. raywoodii (Claret Ash). Quicker growing, taller than *excelsior aurea*, with finer foliage, claret colour in autumn. H 8–14 m, W 5 m. D, C–T. **Shape C.**

Gingko biloba (Maidenhair Tree). Large, soft leaves resembling giant maidenhair, turns gold autumn. H 10–15 m, W 5–7 m. D. Best in moist, cool climates or cooler T. **Shape C.**

Glochidion ferdinandi (Cheese Tree). Quick-growing, glossy-foliaged tree from rainforest areas, usually pyramid shaped. H 8 m, W 3–4 m. E, T–H. **Shape C.**

Grevillea robusta (Silky Oak). Erect, pyramid-shaped, stiff fern-like foliage, brushes of orange flowers, early summer. H 20 m, W 8 m. E, T–H, good frost resistance. **Shape C.**

Gum see *Eucalypt*

Hakea laurina (Pincushion Hakea). Broad, blue-green foliage, bronze tips, creamy pin-like stamens stud reddish globes of clustered florets, winter/spring. Well-drained soil, preferably with plenty of rubble near surface. E, T, SH. **Shape C.**

H. salicifolia — saligna. Dense, pyramid-shaped, quick-growing screen. Grey-green, bronze-tipped foliage. Adapts to poor. sandy soil or well-drained heavy loams. Can be cut to any size. E, all but coldest climate. **Shape C.**

Harpephyllum caffrum (Kaffir Plum). Boldly erect tree with dark, glossy foliage. Plum-like red fruits on female trees when male tree in vicinity. H 10–14 m, W 5–7 m. E, T–H. **Shape C.**

Holly see *Ilex*

Hymenosporum flavum (Native Frangipani). Slender, erect, glossy foliaged tree from north-east Australian coast. Fragrant late-spring flowers open cream, deepen to mustard.

Cassia fistula

Frangipani plumeria

Most Acer species have beautiful autumn foliage

The pencil-like stature of the poplar trees turning golden adds variety to this park

Hymenosporum flavum (native frangipani)

H 8 m, W 4–5 m at base, then tapering. With age, is high branching. E, T–H, SM. **Shape C.**

Jacaranda acutifolia (mimosaefolia). Fern-like foliage, glorious display of lavender blue, late spring/early summer. Golden winter foliage. Spreading umbrella shape when left uncut, otherwise develops taller growth. Deciduous in spring. H 10–14, W 14 m. T–H. **Shape H.**

Kaffir Plum see *Harpephyllum*

Koelreuteria paniculata (Willow Pattern Tree or Golden Rain). Quick-growing, high branching umbrella-like tree. Divided foliage, pendulous sprays of small, golden, early summer flowers. H 5–7 m, W 5 m. D, C–T, SM. **Shape A.**

Laburnum vossi. Soft green, small tree, pendulous sprays golden wisteria-like flowers, spring. Best in cool districts. H 3–4m, W 3–4 m. D. **Shape A.**

Lagerstoemia (Crape Myrtle). Unpruned, makes pyramid-shaped small tree with attractively-marked smooth trunk and limbs. Summer flowers, autumn foliage. H 5–6 m, W 3 m. Lower branching when pruned in winter. All but coldest districts. Also see Shrubs. SM. **Shape D.**

Lagunaria patersonii (Norfolk Island Hibiscus). Slender pyramid, leather oval foliage, small, waxy white to pink bell flowers, summer. Tolerates salt spray. H 10 m, W 4 m. E, all but coldest districts. **Shape C.**

Laurus nobilis (Bay Tree). Dense, rounded, small tree with dark, leathery foliage used for flavouring. Often formally trimmed. H 5 m, W 6 m. Sometimes taller in cool, moist positions. E, C–T, SM. **Shape D.**

Leopard Tree see *Caesalpinia*

Leptospermum laevigatum (Coastal Tea-tree). Tough, often gnarled seaside tree with coarse foliage and white spring flowers. Excellent for windbreaks in sandy areas. H 3–4 m, W 3 m. E, T. **Shape A.**

L. petersonii (Lemon Tea-tree). Glossy, bright-green foliage with lemon aroma. Good light screen. Ht 4–5 m, W 4 m. E. All but coldest districts. **Shape A.**

Leucodendron argentum (South African Silver Leaf). Long leaves covered in silky, silver hairs. Needs good drainage, resents prolonged summer rain. H 5 m, W 2–3 m. E. All but coldest to T. **Shape D.**

Liquidambar. Widely grown for autumn foliage. Tall, pyramid shape, large maple-like leaves. Variety *festeri* holds foliage longer, turns deep bronze, autumn. H 14–20 m, W 7–10 m. D, C–T. **Shape C** (Both).

L. formosanum monticola. Large 3-lobed leaves, bronze-tipped when young. H 8–10 m, W 5 m. D, C–T. **Shape C.**

L. orientalis. Smaller foliage, turning from gold to purple in autumn. H 5–7 m, W 3–5 m. D. **Shape C.**

Liriodendron tulipifera (Tulip Tree). Tall pyramid of large, bright-green fiddle-shaped foliage; gold in autumn. Unusual tulip-shaped lime-green and golden-orange flowers, spring. Grows about 60 cm a year. H 10–14 m, W 5–7 m, D, C–T. **Shape C.**

Macadamia see Fruits and Nuts

Magnolia grandiflora (Bull Bay). Tall, glossy-foliaged tree. Large, fragrant, white lily-like flowers, summer. H 10 m, W 5–6 m. E. All but Snowy Mountain districts. SM. **Shape D.**

Magnolia (deciduous) see Shrubs

Malus (Crab Apple). Grown mostly for spring blossoms which come after peaches and most other prunes, and for their colourful fruits. Varieties such as *M. aldenhamensis* and *M. floribunda* are usually umbrella shaped. H 4–5 m, W 4–5 m. C–T. **Shape A.**

M. ionensis is more compact, lower branching, to 4–5 m. *M. spectabilis* is more upright, 4–5 m. **Shape J.**

Maple see *Acer*

Melaleuca armillaris (Bracelet Honey Myrtle). Rounded, small tree with dark, fine foliage, cream brushes in spring. Stands wind and sea coast well. Adapts to most soils. Low branching, often to ground in exposed positions. Otherwise develops slender trunk. H 5–8 m, W 4–5 m. E, C–H. **Shape J.**

M. quinquenervia — leucadendron (Paper Bark). Round-headed tree with comparatively broad, pointed foliage, cream brushes, late summer. Stands salt wind, adapts to most conditions, including swampy soils. H 7–10 m, W 5–6 m. E, C–H. **Shape B.**

Melia azderach (White Cedar). Spreading shade tree with divided, glossy foliage, sprays small, pale-lavender spring flowers, followed by buff berries. H 7–10 m, W 7 m. Taller in warm coastal areas. D. All but coldest. **Shape H.**

Metasequoia glyptostroboides (Dawn Redwood). Pyramid-shaped conifer, bright fern-like foliage turns coppery-bronze, autumn. Rapid grower in moist, temperate areas. H 15–20 m, W 6–8 m. D, C–T. **Shape F.**

Metrosideros excelsa — tomentosa (New Zealand Christmas Bush). Dense, rounded, low-branching, dark leathery foliage covered with clusters of silky, red-stamened flowers at Christmas. Excellent salt-wind resistance. H 5–6 m, W 5–6 m. E, T coast. **Shape J.**

Michelia champaca. Pyramid-shaped, large light-green pendulous foliage, sweetly scented, spidery buff flowers, spring and occasionally summer. *M. longifolia* has white flowers. H 6–10 m, W 5–7 m. **Shape D.** (Both).

Native Frangipani see *Hymenosporum*

New Zealand Christmas Bush see *Metrosideros*

Norfolk Island Hibiscus see *Lagunaria*

Norfolk Island Pine see *Arucaria*

Nyssa. Lovely summer and autumn foliage tree, with erect trunk, lateral branches gradually shortening as they ascend. Oval leaves turn vivid red, gold, autumn. H 8–10 m, W 5–7 m. D. **Shape F.**

Oak see *Quercus*

Olive see *Olea*

Oleander see *Nerium*

Olea africana. Rounded tree, glossy, dark leaves, buff-bronze on underside. Small berries not edible.

O. europea, similar to *africana,* but with grey-backed foliage, provides the edible olives. Both are very adaptable, sea coast to mountains or inland. Can be pruned to any size and rejuvenated by hard winter pruning every 5–10 years. H 5–7 m, W 5–7 m. E. **Shape J.**

Paper Bark see *Melaleuca*

Parrotia persica. Resembles elm, but is silky bronze-green in spring, gold in autumn. Best in cool or cooler-temperate climates. H 6–10 m, W 3–5 m. D, SH. **Shape A.**

Peach see *Prunus*

Persimmon see *Fruit*

Pinus (Pine). *P. canariensis* is a quick-growing, gracefully pendulous pine with blue-green young foliage, deepening later. H 10 m, W 5 m. E. All but coldest districts. E. **Shape E.**

P. elliotti — caribaea (Caribbean Pine). Quick-growing, fine-foliaged pine for east coast or tropical districts with summer rainfall. H 24 m, W 7–10 m. E, T–H. **Shape K.**

P. patula (Mexican Weeping Pine). Quick grower with pendulous, blue-green foliage and reddish bark. H 10–14 m, W 6–10 m. E. **Shape E.**

P. radiata (Monterey Pine). Dense, dark-foliaged forestry pine, suitable for windbreaks. Grows quickly, adapts to variety of well-drained soils. H 25 m, W 8–14 m. E, C–T. **Shape K.**

Pistacia chinensis. Spreading shade tree, rich autumn foliage, resembles ash or rhus, but without rhus's toxic properties. H 6–8 m, W 7 m. D. All but coldest districts. **Shape H.**

Pittosporum crassifolium. Round, leathery, deep-green foliage, grey beneath. Fragrant, small purple-bronze spring flowers, excellent resistance to salt winds. Variegated form only reaches shrub proportions. H 5–6 m, W 3 m. E, cooler T to semi-H. **Shape C.**

P. eugenoides variegata. Column-shaped with grey-green cream foliage. H 5 m, W 3 m, larger in cool climates. All but coldest districts, and H. **Shape C.**

P. rhombifolium. Dark, glossy foliage, slender in early stages, later round headed with masses of brilliant orange berries, early autumn to spring. H 5–7 m, W 3–5 m. E, frost free T–H. SM. **Shape C.**

P. undulatum. Round-headed, dark-green dense foliage, quick growing in lighter soils of humid east coast. Fragrant, white spring flowers, then large dull orange berries. H 5 m, W 6 m. T–H, SM. **Shape H.**

Platanus hybrida (Plane Tree. Previously considered as *P. orientalis*). Large shade tree with lime and slate-blotched bark. Foliage like large maple leaves. H 14 m, W 6–10 m. D, C–T. **Shape D.**

Plum see *Prunus*

Podocarpus elatus (Illawarra Plum). Beautiful non-symmetrical conifer with broad head of dense, glossy, slender foliage. Young tips golden green. H 10–14 m, W 7 m. E, T–H. **Shape D.**

P. falcatus. Slightly larger than elatus, with blue-green new tips. Best in humid districts; cool to sub-tropical. **Shape D.**

Poinciana see *Delonix*

Populus nigra (Poplar). The slender Lombardy poplar, the silver or white poplar and spreading cottonwoods are picturesque especially in autumn, but sucker freely and have root problems for small gardens.

Prunus. Includes peaches, cherries, apricots, flowering plums. **Shape L.**

P. campanulata (Taiwan Cherry). Is earliest

flowering. Upright growth, covered in rosy-red, pendulous, bell-shaped flowers. August. Improved by heavy pruning after flowering. H 5–6 m, W 3–4 m. D. Best in temperate areas where frosts not severe. **Shape C.**

P. amanogawa (Column Cherry). Slender, column-like growth, soft pink, mid-spring flowers. H 5–7 m, W 2 m. D, C to cooler T. **Shape I.**

P. serrulata (Japanese Cherry). Many upright to spreading types with spectacular double white to deep pink flowers, mid-spring. H 3–5 m, W 3–5 m. D, C to cooler T. **Shape L.**

Beautiful weeping types such as *Cheal's weeping* are often grated to 2–3 m standards. (Always remove suckers from below graft.) Cheal's is improved by moderate pruning after flowering, but other *P. serrulata* types need little, if any, pruning.

P. subhirtella is a dainty, small single cherry, white-flushed pink, or pink. Popular weeping variety.

Of the flowering plums, *P. cerasifera* varieties are first to flower. Earliest is double pink *blireiana* and paler *moseri*. Both have pale-bronze spring foliage, bronze-green in summer. Ht 3–5m, W 3–4 m. D. **Shape A.**

P. cerasifera festeri has single pink flowers, larger purple foliage. H 5–6 m, W 5–6 m. E, C–T. SM. **Shape L.**

P. cerasifera pissardii has single, pale pink, early spring flowers, purple foliage. Variety *nigra* is still darker foliaged. SM. **Shape L.**

P. persica (Flowering Peach) 'Carson's' or 'Winter White'. Pink or red flowers in August, not suited to very frosty climates. Their later-flowering counterparts are usually listed as spring flowering.

Flowering peaches are generally low branching, but cutting the young tree higher than usual or rubbing off lower shoots creates a spreading tree. They are improved by cutting flowering laterals to within 2–3 cm of their base, right after flowering. Main leaders can be shortened back to a lower lateral. **Shape L.**

Queensland Nut see Macadamia under Fruits and Nuts

Queensland Firewheel see *Stenocarpus*

Quercus (Oak). *Q. coccinea* (Scarlet Oak). Comparatively slow-growing but noble tree with long, deeply-lobed foliage that colours brilliant red in autumn. H 14–20 m, W 7–10 m. D, C to cooler T. **Shape G.**

Q. ilex (Holly Oak). Young leaves are often holly-like. Dense, deep-green leathery foliage. Withstands hot, dry summers. H 20 m, W 7–10 m. E, C–T. **Shape D.**

Q. palustris (Pin Oak). Deeply cut foliage similar to *P. coccinea*, turning red in autumn but often remaining brown on tree. Quicker grower, stands soggy, badly-drained soil. **Shape C.**

Q. robur (English Oak). Less angular, bright-green foliage. Spreading shade tree, less glamorous than others in autumn. H 14–18 m, W 10–14 m. D, C–T. **Shape H.**

Rhodoleia championii. Small, light-foliaged tree from Hong Kong. Rounded, glossy foliage, yellowish new stems, pendant rosy-pink fringed bell flowers. H 5–7 m, W 3–5 m. E, T–H. **Shape D.**

Rhus see *Toxicodendron*
Rowan see *Sorbus*
Rubber Tree see *Ficus*

Salix (Willow). *S. babylonica* (Weeping Willow). A graceful tree for creek banks or near damp areas. Roots usually troublesome in small gardens. H 10 m, W 10 m. D, C–H. **Shape E.**

S. caprea (Pussy Willow). Upright caney growth, velvety spring catkins last well cut. H 7 m, W 5–7 m. D, C–H. **Shape L.**

S. matsudana tortulosa. Upright type grown for its 'corkscrewed' branches. Popular in decorative work. H 5 m, W 4 m. D, C–H. **Shape L.**

Sapium sebiferum (Chinese Tallow Tree). Rounded, with pendulous shield-shaped foliage; bright-green in summer; gold, copper, purple in autumn. H 5–7 m, W 5 m. D. **Shape D.**

Schefflera actinophylla (Umbrella Tree). *Brassaia.* Queensland tree. Slender canes carry umbrella-like head of large, divided, glossy foliage. Ideal for courtyards, swimming pool surrounds, etc. If too tall, lop back in spring to encourage lower shoots. Remove some canes if clump becomes too wide. H 3–5 m, W 3–4 m. E, frost free T–H.

Schinus molle (Peppercorn). Hardy, light shade tree with finely divided, willowy foliage; pendulous outer branches, clusters of small pink berries. Long-lived, stands hot, dry inland. H 6–8 m, W 5–8 m. All but Snowy Mountains. E. SM. **Shape E.**

Silky Oak see *Grevillea*

Sophora tetraptera (New Zealand Kowhai). Erect, fine-foliaged tree clustered with golden pea flowers, spring. H 5–6 m, W 3–5 m. D, C–T, SM. **Shape D.**

Sorbus aucuparia (Rowan Tree). Small tree with ash-like foliage, colouring beautifully in autumn. Bright red autumn berries. H 6–10 m, W 5–7 m. Best in cool climates. D. **Shape C.**

Spathodea campanulata (African Tulip Tree). Handsome, dark glossy foliage, heads of large, upright, crimson bells, summer. H 14–20 m, W 5–6 m. E, H. **Shape C.**

Steculia see *Brachychiton*

Stenocarpus sinuatus (Queensland Fire Wheel). Upright tree with dark-green glossy foliage, masses of spidery red flowers. Buds grouped like spokes of wheel. Slow growing. H 10 m, W 3–5 m. E, T–H, SM. **Shape C.**

Stenolobium stans (Yellow Tecoma). Small tree with divided, golden-green foliage, clusters of golden jacaranda-like flowers, late spring to winter. Winter prune, if necessary. H 4–5 m, W 3–4 m. D, T. **Shape D.**

Sycamore see *Acer*

Syncarpia glomulifera (Turpentine Tree). Erect, grey-brown, stringy-barked trunks, rigid oval foliage, dark green above, grey beneath; creamy blossoms, lantern-like woody nuts. Once established, wind, drought, borer resistant. H 10–15 m, W 5–10 m. E, T. **Shape B.**

Tamarix (Flowering Cypress). *T. aphylla* (Athel Tree). Pendulous grey-green, fine, rather sparse foliage. Clusters of tiny pink flowers, summer. Establishes in driest inland areas and near sea coast. H 8–10 m, W 5 m. E, C–H. **Shape A.**

T. juniperina (plumosa, gallica). Gracefully pendulous, fine foliage, feathery sprays, pink flowers, early summer. Can be winter pruned. H 4 m, W 3–4 m. D, C–T. **Shape A.**

T. parviflora, arching plume-like stems with sprays of deep pink flowers in spring, before the foliage. H 3–4 m, W 3–4 m. D.

T. pentandra purpurea, name still unofficial. Grey-green foliage with rather erect branched sprays of deep-pink flowers in late spring and summer. H 3–4 m, W 2–3 m. D.

Taxodium distichum (Swamp Cypress). Conifer with fern-like, soft green foliage turning rust colour in autumn. Grows to broad, spreading tree in swampy areas, more slender in drier soils. H 15–20 m, W 6–12 m. All but Snowy Mountains and tropical districts. **Shape C.**

Tea-tree see *Leptospermum*

Tilia europea (Lime or Linden Tree). Large shade tree, leaves turning gold in autumn. Small, fragrant, white summer flowers. Stands heavy pruning each winter, if necessary. H 15–25 m, W 10–14 m. D, C–T. **Shape D.**

Toxicodendron (*Rhus succedaneum).* Small spreading tree with brilliant autumn foliage, but contact can cause allergy symptoms with some people. Pisticia could substitute. H 4–5 m, W 4–5 m. All but coldest districts. D. **Shape A.**

Tristania conferta (Brush Box). Fine, spreading rainforest tree with bold foliage and smooth lime to coppery-tan limbs. In street, often pruned to mean, mushroom shape. Cut in winter, if necessary. Adaptable, but protect from frost for first year; inland. H 14–18 m, W 7–10 m. T–H. **Shape D.**

T. laurina (Water Gum or Kanooka). Umbrella-shaped small tree with oleander-like foliage. Clusters of small yellow flowers, summer. Stands wet soil, but adaptable. H 5–6 m, W 5 m. All but coldest areas. E. **Shape D.**

Ulmus (Elm). Some types, such as *U. procera* (English elm), make magnificent trees but sucker over a wide area, especially when roots are cut by cultivation. Too large and vigorous for average gardens.

U. glabra (Scotch Elm or Wych Elm). Less inclined to sucker. H 15–20 m, W 14–18 m. D, C–T. (Weeping forms are sometimes grafted on high standards.) **Shape E.**

Golden elms such as *U. procera vanhouttel* and *U. glabra lutescens* are less inclined to sucker and are smaller growing. Light, golden-green foliage, fan-shaped, low branching. H 10 m, W 8–10 m. D, C–T. **Shape L.**

U. parvifolia — chinensis (Chinese Weeping Elm). Beautiful spreading tree with smooth tan, mottled trunk, arching limbs, pendulous outer branches. Small glossy foliage, evergreen in some mild climates, otherwise D. H 10 m, W 10–14 m. C–T. **Shape E.**

Umbrella Tree see *Schefflera*

Virgilia oroboides *(capensis).* Rapid grower, tall pyramid-shape, spreading if lopped. Fine foliage, sprays of mauve-pink pea flowers, spring. Fairly long-lived in deep, well-drained soil, otherwise short-lived. H 7 m, W 3–4 m. E, T–H, SH–M. **Shape C.**

Wattle see *Acacia*
Willow see *Salix*
Willow Pattern Tree see *Koelreuteria*

21. Shrubs

Shrubs are the backbone of a garden and give a pleasantly natural character and feeling of permanence. They also provide a haven for bird life. Each shrub becomes an important and self-sufficient unit of the ecology as it recycles the atmosphere and the soil by taking up inorganic end products and returning spent foliage to maintain the soil's organic content.

Shrubs can be chosen to give year-round interest, colour, variety and can complement or contrast. They soften hard lines of man-made structures and effectively integrate house with garden. On the more practical side they can also be planted for privacy, as dividers, windbreaks or as weed-blanketing ground covers — yes, ground covers need not be low-carpeting plants.

You can enjoy an effective weed-preventing cover by planting drifts of any low-branching shrub whether it happens to be an ankle-high prostrate type or one which attains a metre or two in height. If you have a reasonable expanse of garden, a great deal of interest can be added by the variation in height and foliage texture between different drifts of shrubbery. How-ever, even in the smallest garden, a well-chosen variety of shrubs will also provide effective weed control.

In a garden of any size there are unending possibilities to create pleasantly balanced and complementary groupings. Try outlining a few possible combinations on paper.

You might start with a medium-sized dome-shaped shrub, then surround it with 2 or 3 casually placed smaller domes. Try the effect of a conical or spire-shaped conifer or similar taller shrub toward the background of the grouping. In another group try a fan-shaped abelia, dwarf prunus or flax. These all give complete contrast to the dome or gently mounded shapes.

To emphasise the pleasant form of each group, isolate it from neighbouring groups by a stretch of ground cover, cheerful bedding plants, low-growing perennials or bulbs which will give the garden seasonal colour highlight and added variety.

You can use a low and rapidly-spreading cover like silver and green variegated lamium which is easily removed if you wish to indulge in colourful hobby plants, or can be left as a maintenance-free cover from season to season.

This type of group planting is suggested as an alternative to the more conventional method of planting evenly-placed shrubbery along fences. Where sections of the fence are left exposed a shrub can be espaliered to cover the bare section. Alternatively, provide a lattice for an attractive creeper or a panel of brush fencing can be used as a background for a plant in a decorative container. These ideas add interest to a garden and can make it look more expansive by breaking the shrubbery line and increasing the length of vistas.

The majority of shrubs grow well in most soils providing they are well drained. For the few tolerant to over-wet soils see list under Shrubs for different purposes. However, shrubs are generally slower to establish in heavy clay soils which set hard after rain and in very sandy soils which dry out rapidly.

Shrubs give a natural character and a feeling of permanence to a garden. Leave some space for foreground planting

Planning shrubs for the garden

Choose the right position for your shrubs

Many shrubs can be moved satisfactorily but it is better to locate them correctly from the start. When selecting shrubs for your garden, apart from checking height and width, determine their preference for sun or shade. Some shrubs adapt quite well to either and the adaptable types should be allocated to the shaded areas where choice is more limited. It will be obvious from the lists that follow and give shrubs for different situations and purposes that the choice is much wider for sunny areas of the garden.

When planning shrubbery for a new garden, take into account areas where shade will gradually encroach as trees and larger shrubs gain size and plant the smaller shrubs on the sunny side, gradually stepping your planting up in height so that each shrub receives its share of sun. If, because of the location of the site, the position needs to be reversed, then the foreground shrubs should have tolerance to shade.

Appreciate also that the areas of shade will be much greater in late autumn, winter and early spring than in summer when the sun is at a much higher angle. During the latter period, shrubs shaded at other times of the year may be in full sun during the heat of summer. A great number of shrubs tolerate this situation but many, such as the Camellia japonica varieties, suffer foliage burn when exposed to full summer sun.

Do not overplant

This is a mistake frequently made when planting new gardens because it is so easy to be influenced by the immediate effect. Remember that though the result may look good initially, it could look hopelessly overcrowded within a year or two. Most catalogues and shrub labels indicate height but rarely width, which is an equally important factor when planning your garden. Average width of each shrub, as well as height is given in the alphabetical descriptive list of shrubs in this book.

It is worth the effort to mark each proposed shrub to scale on your landscape plan, or to position each one in its container on the site before final planting, making sure there is adequate space for its ultimate spread. However, when planting drifts of one particular shrub for a dense ground cover effect, the normal spacing is reduced by about one-third to a half.

Buying shrubs

Understandably most people are attracted to the larger advanced shrubs because these give a more satisfying initial effect. In many cases these are good value but they do not always retain their superior size and appearance. Under good conditions a smaller or cheaper plant may eventually surpass them because there is less shock from transplanting disturbance and also root growth has been less restricted by the container. This frequently applies to Australian native plants and others sensitive to root disturbance such as luculia, daphne, proteas, etc.

Try to avoid shrubs that look as though they have been in the container for a long time as these are likely to be in a root-bound condition with the roots closely entangled in a dense woody mass around the outside of the soil ball. With many of the nursery containers used these days, and particularly with well-advanced plants, it is difficult to check on this point, but indications are woody or old-looking top growth with old wiry-looking roots protruding from the drainage holes. In many cases a root-bound condition can be corrected at planting time, as indicated under 'Planting', but it is best to avoid buying root-bound plants.

Shrubs soften hard lines of structures and effectively integrate them with the garden

Planting shrubs

Planting times

Plants sold growing in containers can be planted at any time of the year, providing it is possible to keep the soil moist until they are established. For the latter reason, planting during the heat of summer is usually avoided, particularly in districts where hot, dry conditions may be experienced. When planting warmth-loving shrubs such as hibiscus, garenias and especially tropicals such as crotons, ixoras, acalyphas, etc. in all but semi-tropical to tropical districts, it is better to delay planting until early spring so that the shrub has the maximum period of warmth in which to establish itself.

Deciduous shrubs are still sometimes sold, particularly in cooler districts, in a bare-rooted state, that is, with roots wrapped or standing in moist sawdust, and not growing in a container. This category may include lilacs, the late winter- or spring-flowering fruit trees and roses. These can only be safely replanted during their winter dormant period. In some districts conifers and other evergreens are dug from nursery beds and sold with the root-ball wrapped in hessian. These can be replanted safely during winter or early spring which is the time that they are normally available.

There is a fairly general doubt about the wisdom of planting shrubs during their flowering time. This is quite safe, especially for azaleas, camellias and most of the spring-flowering evergreens because these plants do not make their new growth (which is the main drain on their root system) until flowering finishes. This is fortunate because, unless you know varieties well, it is preferable to buy azaleas, etc. when you can see the actual flower. The only time planting while in flower would not be advisable is in the case of deciduous shrubs, forsythia, flowering fruit trees, etc. sold in a bare-rooted state.

Soil

The majority of shrubs grow well in most soils providing they are well drained. For the few tolerant to over-wet soils see list under 'Shrubs for different purposes'. However, shrubs are generally slower to establish in heavy clay soils which set hard after rain and in very sandy soils which dry out rapidly. Ways to improve these conditions are suggested below.

Heavy clay soils: When planting out make a planting hole at least 50 cm wider than the soil ball of the shrub. Mix about one-quarter part of either rotted compost, crumbling leaf-mould, milled pine bark or similarly crumbly soil conditioner, plus the same volume of coarse sand with the soil you have removed. If sand is difficult to obtain increase any of the other ingredients to between one-third and one half part by volume.

After planting, carefully fork up the unimproved soil around the edge of the hole and partially integrate it with the improved soil. This will help new roots induced by the improved soil to accept their surroundings, and prevent root growth from stopping where the improved soil ends.

A spread of organic surface mulch around the plants will encourage earthworm activity and so improve the soil. The worms tunnel through the soil and improve aeration; they also take particles of mulch to lower levels and thereby extend the depth of root-inducing soil.

The main secret of improving tough soils or maintaining the desirable crumbly structure of clayey loam is to dig, plant or disturb only when the soil is just damp, never wet and sticky.

Another point to watch when planting in heavy clayey soil is to make sure that the planting hole, filled with comparatively crumbly and lighter soil, does not become a water-holding sump for the surrounding area. If there is a slight slope, dig to the same depth for a metre or so on the lower side.

Do not make the hole deeper than necessary. It is better to build up the soil surface surrounding the new shrubs rather than to dig into heavy clay to the soil container depth.

For large-scale plantings, apart from putting in a system of agricultural drainage pipes, it may be worth obtaining a load of river or bush sand to surface the garden and extend top soil depth. This practice works well when establishing Australian native plants, proteas, etc. in otherwise tough and slow-draining soils.

The soil level needed can also be achieved by cribbing topsoil from nearby areas where paths are to be laid. The extra height can be retained by stones, bricks or timber.

Very sandy soils: Most shrubs establish happily, even in almost pure sand, if a surface mulch is permanently maintained to conserve moisture, insulate against extremes of temperature, particularly summer heat and, at the same time, gradually build up the soil's organic content. Use any organic mulch such as leaf-mould, wood chip, dried grass or pine bark. Grass clippings that have been heaped for a few weeks are also suitable or may be sprinkled lightly in the green stage to augment the existing mulch.

As they develop the shrubs will gradually build up their own natural mulch of spent foliage. For people not yet on familiar terms with plants, it is as well to point out that evergreens (including conifers) shed their leaves as do deciduous shrubs. The difference is that the evergreens shed foliage gradually or in spasmodic bursts throughout the year while the deciduous shrubs have one grand leaf-fall during autumn.

Step-by-step planting

The way shrubs are planted has a definite bearing on their later progress. The main aim is to encourage new root growth to spread out into the surrounding soil and to develop strongly. Therefore, the physical condition of the soil is of the utmost importance. Although it needs to be in firm contact with the roots, it should also be crumbly so that minute spaces remain between the soil particles to allow the entry of small traces of oxygen essential for healthy root growth. This also allows free movement of water through the soil and gives the roots a chance to grow well.

One common fault is planting too deeply. This has a suffocating effect on the roots.

Another is the puddling of heavy soils or any loamy soil with a clay content. This breaks down the healthy crumbly structure of the soil and brings the ultra-fine clay particles into solution with the soil water. This forms mud, leaving the surrounding soil in an inert, airless state.

Step 1. Make sure that the soil in the container does not dry out prior to, or at, planting time. Give it a good soaking about half a day before planting.

Step 2. Have the soil in the garden only just damp at planting time, never wet and sticky, or very dry. This is particularly important in any soil with a clay content as disturbance when wet will cause it to set hard and airless.

Step 3. Make the hole only a few centimetres deeper than the soil in the container but at least twice its width. This will allow you to add plenty of improved soil to encourage the roots to spread out into their new environment. Otherwise, if the surrounding soil is inferior to that in the container, there is a possibility that the roots will refuse to leave their original soil and, in these circumstances, the plant can actually become root-bound after planting. See heading 'Improved soil'.

Step 4. Remove the shrub from its container without disturbing the soil ball. If the pot is large enough to handle this can be done by placing the fingers of one hand around the stem of the shrub to cover as much soil as possible, then inverting the container and giving the edge of the rim a few sharp taps on something solid. The soil ball should then slip out easily. If the container is too large to handle comfortably, but is of a type tapering slightly toward the base, lay it on the ground, place a piece of timber to cover part of the rim and give this a few sharp taps with a mallet. Roll the shrub slightly and repeat the tapping in several positions until the soil ball slips free. If necessary, it can be coaxed out with a garden fork levered on the edge of the container.

Shrubs in plastic nursery bags are easily cut free. Non-tapering metal cans, especially rectangular or flat-sided ones, need to be cut down one corner with tin snips and then along the base of at least two adjacent sides so that the shrub can be lifted free of the container, if necessary with a spade slid in below the soil ball.

Step 5. Carefully tease out and straighten any roots wound around the base of the soil ball, then place the latter on a small platform of improved soil which has been firmly mounded and high enough to bring the top of the container soil and garden soil to the one level.

Step 6. Cover the base roots that have been spread out with a few centimetres of improved soil, firm down gently then carefully tease out at least some of the roots wound around the soil ball, if necessary filling a little more soil below them to build up to the point where they emerge, cover, then repeat the process every few centimetres until the top of the soil ball is reached. If roots are tightly matted around the soil ball, most of the mat should be shaved off with a sharp knife. After such severe disturbance, the shrub should be either cut back (most leaves removed) or kept shaded for a few weeks.

Step 7. Rake a small water-holding ridge of soil around the shrub, just slightly out from the edge of the root ball. In this depression place a few centimetres of either compost that is still fibrous, leafmould, dead grass or other fibrous material, then give a good, gentle soaking. By placing this mulch of fibrous material over the soil before watering, the soil crusting or caking that might otherwise occur is eliminated. This keeps the soil open and therefore more conducive to the rapid formation of new roots. **Note:** Do not apply fertilisers or manures until about 6 weeks after planting and then only if new growth is evident.

Planting bare-rooted shrubs
The most important thing when planting bare-rooted shrubs is not to let the root dry out. Leave the shrub wrapped until ready to plant. If planting is to be delayed for more than a few days make a hole in a cool, moist, shaded part of the garden and cover the root area of the plant with moist soil. When ready to plant, unwrap and stand the root in a bucket of water, but do not leave soaking for more than an hour or so. Cleanly trim any jagged or broken roots.

Proceed as already indicated for 'Shrubs in containers', keeping the hole shallow but wide, and firmly mounding sufficient soil in the base of the hole to accommodate the spread of the roots and to bring the graft or bud union of the shrub to about ground level.

Fill in with slightly damp improved soil and at the same time gently firm the soil with the hands. Do not tread down as often suggested, for this is likely to damage roots. Make a water-holding ridge around the plant and fill with mulch and water as suggested for container-grown plants.

Planting hessian-wrapped or balled plants
Position the shrub with the hessian still intact, or if necessary, just loosened at the top so that it can be determined that planting is not deeper than the soil mark on the stem. If this mark is indefinite, the top of the soil ball should be covered with no more than a centimetre of soil. When the shrub is positioned, fold back the hessian from the top half of the soil ball, fill the hole and gently firm the soil, finishing off with a water-holding ridge of soil and surface mulch as suggested for container plants.

Staking
Staking is a convention frequently recommended for trees and shrubs but in most cases it is undesirable, especially for shrubs that resent root disturbance such as luculia, Geraldton wax and many other Australian natives. Too often well-meant staking is ultimately responsible for the loss of the plant because the upward training causes it to become top heavy, and once the stake rots it topples, breaking a large percentage of its roots at the same time.

In their natural state, especially in windy areas, these plants develop a natural lean away from the wind in their early stages and their lower branches then touch the ground and give them a self-bracing structure. Although a stake and support will increase the initial growth of tall shrubs or small trees they will be left with a comparatively weak root system which usually lacks wind resistance.

Where stakes are needed for protection it is better to put 2 or 3 a span or so out from the stem of the plant, and encircle them with a light tie. This will allow natural movement but still give some support.

A small picket made of 3 or 4 sticks placed on the windward side of a shrub will also give some protection and allow it to make more rapid growth.

Moving shrubs
Inevitably there are times when a shrub is found to be in an unsuitable spot, too large for its position or in the way of house extensions or garden replanning. Quite often it can be moved to a more suitable location.

Not all shrubs transplant readily. Some, like many Australian natives such as proteas, luculias, daphne and ones without an appreciable amount of fibrous root growth are difficult to transplant successfully. Others, including most deciduous shrubs such as camellias, azaleas, conifers and many other fibrous-rooted evergreens, normally survive a move well if the transplanting is handled with care and at a suitable time.

Time to move
Late autumn or winter is the safest transplanting time for most shrubs. Exceptions are warmth lovers such as gardenias, evergreen hibiscus, citrus and acalyphas which are best moved in late winter or early spring, just before new growth commences.

Conditioning shrubs for moving
One way to move most large evergreen shrubs successfully is to cut them back hard immediately prior to moving. Where it is desired to retain as much of the framework as possible, or in the case of shrubs that may be difficult to move, it helps to root prune them some months prior to the move. This practice is also advisable when it is known in advance that the move will have to be made at an unsuitable time of the year.

The best time to root prune without putting undue stress on the shrub is from late winter to early spring, or in mid to late summer when new growth has settled down to maturity.

Root pruning can be done by spading down around the shrub and cutting through most of the roots. This forces the formation of fibrous roots and minimises shock from moving because most of the new feeder roots formed are then within the root ball to be lifted.

For a medium to large shrub, start by marking a circle with a few short stakes 25–30 cm out from the main stem. Mark the circle into 6 roughly equal segments. Then, slanting the spade slightly under the shrub, tread it down to its full depth to cut all roots in alternate segments. The other segments are cut similarly a month or two later.

Keep the root ball (area within the circle) moist by trickling the hose into its centre at regular intervals. This helps to compensate for the reduced intake of water by the extensive root loss and to keep new roots within the root ball.

When ready to make the final move, again spade down around the shrub, this time a few centimetres outside the original circle and lift out a trench twice spade width on the outside of the cut. This trench is to allow room for cutting or spading in under the shrub to cut the remaining roots.

Final cutting of the few persisting roots is done by rocking the root ball from side to side to allow more access for the spade beneath it. Using the same rocking action, gradually pass a garden carry sheet or canvas below the shrub so it can be lifted with minimum damage to roots. Do this by rolling the first half of the sheet so that the roll can be worked under the soil ball then unrolling when the soil ball is rocked back over it.

Easier ways
Smaller shrubs with a spread of only about 50 cm can usually be moved safely by spading a circle 15–18 cm out from the base and slanting in slightly below the shrub. Spade around a second time, using a gentle lifting action. If the shrub fails to lift, dig a hole just outside the circle, wide enough to allow you to spade deep enough to cut retaining roots below the shrub. Make the move when soil is just damp.

Azaleas are relatively easy to transplant from late autumn to late winter as their roots are mainly in a fibrous mat 10–15 cm from the surface. This makes it comparatively easy to lift a wide but shallow soil ball, without need to cut the plant back.

Spade down and cut this root mat, if possible less than, or for a large spreading plant, not more than a span in from the outer foliage. Then spade in obliquely below the root mat until it is possible to lever the plant gently upward.

Replanting after the move
Make the new hole for the relocated shrub no deeper than the root ball but about a spade width wider. Pack good improved topsoil where there are gaps below the soil ball and also around it.

I find that an excellent medium for promoting new root growth is a mixture of equal parts well-rotted and crumbled leafmould and crushed sandstone. The latter is not available in some districts but suitable substitutes are coarse river sand, scorea, or similar crumbly rock. Alternatively use nursery potting soil or soil conditioners containing milled pine bark, peatmoss, etc.

Do not cover the soil ball with extra soil. Add a layer of well-rotted leafmould or fibrous compost and then gently but thoroughly flood the soil to settle the shrub in. After watering, do not disturb the soil, particularly if it is of a sticky nature.

Do not add manures or fertilisers when replanting shrubs. Forget these for at least 6 weeks then only use if new growth is developing. Apply at about half the normally recommended quantity which should be spread a little beyond the area of the original soil ball. For a month or two after moving a shrub, make sure that only the surface of the soil is allowed to dry out.

Staking

Temporary staking is advisable where wind is likely to cause movement of the roots. It is usually sufficient to place 2 or 3 stakes beyond the soil ball area and slant them toward branches where convenient ties can be made. Remove after a few months.

Care and maintenance

Watering

Newly planted shrubs need watering regularly until they have had time to make a normal root spread. As suggested under 'Planting' it is a good idea to ridge the soil a little out from the original soil ball to form a water-holding moat. This directs water down where it is needed to encourage the spread of roots. Otherwise, even with frequent surface waterings from hand-held hoses, it is possible for the area within the soil ball to dry out.

Water a wide area so that roots from neighbouring shrubs and trees are not attracted to the one favoured spot and cause root competition for the newcomer.

Once established, most shrubs can be trained to fend for themselves. Do this by watering initially only when the surface soil dries out, then let the depth of dryness increase between each watering. Except during very dry periods, the only time shrubs are likely to show signs of stress from lack of water is when new growth is being produced, usually in mid-spring. This applies particularly

to azaleas which have most of their roots close to the surface so, at this time, may show dryness stress before other shrubs.

The main point in good management of shrubs and the garden generally is to avoid the so-often-practised daily hosings. When water is needed, give a good soaking, and moisten the sub-soil evenly. Where possible, use a sprinkler that delivers the water gradually or gently enough to avoid puddling of the surface.

How long it should be left on to penetrate the soil will vary according to the extent of dryness, type of soil, the amount of growth, etc. It is as well to trowel down in several places to check penetration of moisture to sub-soil. There may be times when what seems like a thorough soaking has barely penetrated the surface mulch. The same applies to rain following dry periods.

Mulching

As already advocated, mulching helps to conserve moisture and assists its penetration into the soil, even though it may at times itself seem hard to wet. The cover of mulch also acts as a buffer against heavy rain, and therefore prevents surface puddling and preserves the desirable crumbly structure of the soil.

Feeding

Shrubs grown in a natural environment, where spent foliage or leafmould is allowed to remain on the soil, are reasonably self-supporting and should be able to survive without the addition

of manures, fertilisers or prepared composts. Ideally the prunings should be returned to the surrounding soil.

However, most people like to encourage a little more vigour or improve flower size and quality, particularly of camellias, gardenias, azaleas and other favourites. Remember that in this case the procedure should be much the same as applied to watering so do not feed only a favoured shrub, or you will encourage competition from the roots of neighbouring trees and shrubs, even from those up to 10 or 12 m away. It is a good practice to scatter plant food in other directions also. Even a few handfuls tossed over the fence may not be wasted.

When to feed

The main time to feed is when new growth is developing, particularly on a shrub that has been heavily pruned. Only feed when the soil is reasonably moist and give a good soaking afterwards.

Avoid feeding when shrubs are dormant as this can be harmful because nutrient salts not used by the plants can build up a concentration strong enough to cause root damage. This applies particularly when the soil dries out as then the concentrates increase. Azaleas, rhododendrons, ericas and many of our native plants are particularly sensitive to strong con-

Pieris forrestii, rhododendron and azalea shrubs combine to bring colour to this garden

centrations of soil salts. Their roots can be damaged by little more than half the rate tolerated by most other shrubs.

Azalea and rhododendron flower buds form several months before flowering time, often in late summer or early autumn. Feeding after this stage will induce a flush of new growth which reduces spring display by masking the flowers. Autumn or winter feeding may, in many types of rhododendron, abort the embryo flower buds, or cause a mutation to growth shoots rather than flowers.

How much and where

Apply plant foods mainly below the outer foliage of shrubs. Concentrations vary, but with standard sprinkle-on-type complete plant foods (also rose, camellia and azalea foods, which are suitable for most shrubs) a handful or quarter to a third of a cup per sq. m is sufficient. When using animal manure, about 1 L could be applied to the same area as these materials release their nutrients gradually over a longer period.

Do not feed newly planted shrubs for at least 6 weeks, then only if new growth is showing. Apply only about half the amount recommended for established shrubs, keeping it a little out beyond the foliage line.

Bark is a long-lasting mulch, conserving moisture and retarding weeds

Below: Shrubs make excellent cover for slopes

Pruning shrubs

Pruning is largely a matter of commonsense.

Late winter- and spring-flowering shrubs should be pruned as soon as flowering ends and before new spring growth begins.

Summer- and autumn-flowering shrubs should be pruned during the winter when flowering is over.

There are a few variations to remember: in all but tropical and semi-tropical districts leave pruning the evergreen hibiscus until early spring. In warm climates hibiscus are given a light pruning in January to encourage new growth and winter flowers.

The summer-flowering fuchsias can be pruned in winter, but in mild frost-free climates, a light all-over pruning will produce flowers in the following spring. Frangipani, which flowers in summer, should always be left unpruned. If it becomes invasive remove the offending branches in late winter. The beautiful New South Wales Christmas Bush, which flowers in spring, should not be pruned until January when it is seeding.

If a shrub needs special pruning it is described under the heading of that particular shrub. Otherwise the pruning procedures have been divided into **four** different methods — **a, b, c** and **d.** The pruning time and method are included in the description of each shrub genus: any variation for different species is also shown.

Method a: Bushy evergreens such as bottle-brushes, tea-trees, grevillias, etc. are pruned back after flowering, removing up to two-thirds of the flower stem or previous season's growth, leaving 2–4 sets of leaves at the base of the stem. Old wood or unwanted branches carrying only twiggy growth are cut out as close as possible to their junction with a main branch or trunk.

When new growth develops after pruning, tip-prune when about finger length, or 4–5 sets of leaves have been made to induce further branching and bushier, more compact growth.

Method b: For shrubs with caney growth such as abelia, spirae, forsythia, keeria, deutzia, etc. Old canes are cut out at ground level or more usually just above where a new one emerges from near their base. Newer canes are shortened back by about one-third to half their length.

Method c: Mainly for summer-flowering shrubs such as Crepe myrtle; the deciduous hibiscus; autumn-flowering Cassia bicapsularis, Vitex and poinsettias. The previous season's growths (the canes carrying the flowers) are cut back to within a short distance of the older branch. Leave only a stub of new growth, about finger length or a little longer. If numerous shoots develop on these stubs, rub off all but 3 or 4 evenly-spaced ones.

Method d: For diosma, buxus, golden privet, euonymus, dwarf honeysuckle (*Lonicera nitida*), lavender, etc. — bushy shrubs with shoots too numerous to prune individually. Just trim them to leave a few leaves at the base of the more recent shoots.

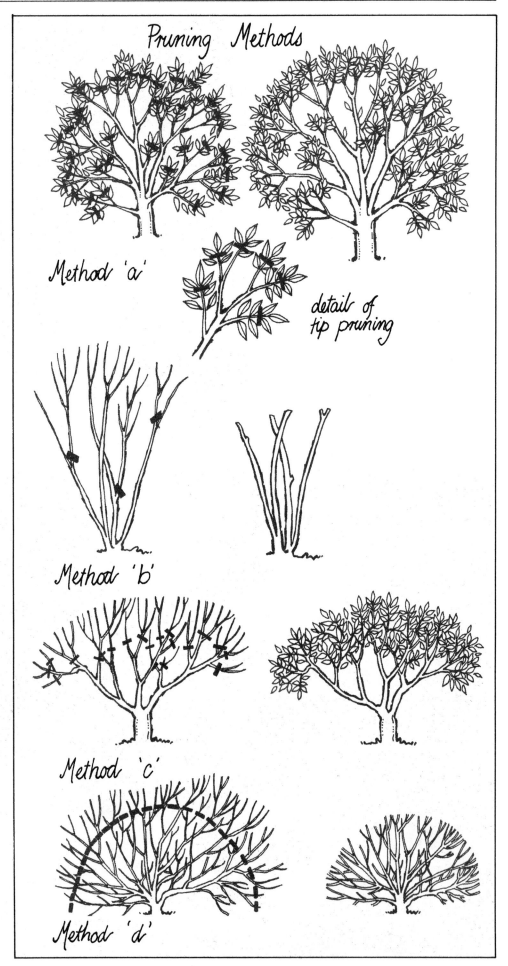

Pruning Methods

Method 'a'

detail of tip pruning

Method 'b'

Method 'c'

Method 'd'

Growing problems and solutions

The following are typical symptoms that occur in trees and shrubs. The remedies given are the least toxic of those considered to be worthwhile. Problems relating to native plants and fruit trees are dealt with separately.

Problem	Cause	Solution
Yellowing and falling of foliage		
One or two of the lowest leaves yellowing, browning or falling	Normal seasonal occurrence when new growth is forming	Remove old foliage. If excessive, see below
Excessive leaf fall	May be due either to excessive dryness or over-wet soils. See Citrus and Camellias	During dry periods soak soil thoroughly to below outer foliage, making sure moisture extends to sub-soil. Improve drainage in soils that remain moist for a long period
Overall pale yellow more pronounced on older foliage	May be due to deficiencies of nitrogen or magnesium	Water with complete soluble plant food
Pale yellowing mainly on new foliage	Probably iron deficiency	See heading 'Iron deficiency' in 'Understanding Plants and Soil' chapter. Also see heading 'Azaleas'
Scattered, variegated or white to yellow leaves	Could be due to nearby use of herbicide, particularly one containing amitrole	Flood soil to hasten leaching. Also see heading 'Camellias' in this chapter
Brown or black spots or patches		
Brown leaf tips Outdoors	In the garden is usually potassium deficiency	See heading 'Potassium' in 'Growing House Plants' chapter
Indoors	May be due to low humidity (dry atmosphere)	
Dry brown margins, particularly on deciduous trees	Probably due to wind burn but can also be potassium deficiency	See heading 'Potassium' in 'Understanding Plants and Soil' chapter
Irregular large brown blotches around margins of rhododendrons, oleanders, etc.	Usually due to concentrations of soil salts when dryness suddenly follows prolonged wet conditions	Flooding soil and mulching to aerate usually helps
Brown patches on margins of cordylines or dracaenas	May be due to use of perlite in potting mixture	Change to perlite-free potting mix
Brown spots on leaves	Usually due to fungus attack. Also see rose and vegetable sections	Use copper spray or Benlate
Brown patches that can be scraped off foliage	This is brown or red scale	White oil spray. See 'Pests and Diseases' chapter
Circular colonies of brown or reddish-brown spots below foliage (particularly on geraniums)	Rust (a fungus disease)	Spray with Zineb or Mancozeb
Large reddish-brown patches on grapevine foliage	Blister leaf mite	Spray with lime sulphur before buds burst or later with Malathion
Black sooty mould over foliage	The fungus responsible feeds only on sugary secretion, usually from scale pests but can also be due to aphids, mealy bug or white fly	Check for presence of any of these pests and see 'Pests and Diseases' chapter
Brownish blister-like formations on foliage of gum trees or Queensland wattle	Blister leaf saw-fly larvae	Spray with Rogor or Lebaycid
Greyish ash-like film or patches over foliage	Powdery mildew	Spray with Benlate or dust sulphur
Grey scribble-like tracery on the foliage	Tunnelling by leaf miner larvae	Spray with systemic spray such as Rogor or Lebaycid
Foliage eaten or misshapen		
Numerous small, scalloped sections around leaf margins	Probably due to unobtrusive, small brown vegetable weevil which feeds at night	Spray at night with Pyrethrum-type sprays — several applications needed
Curled and blistered foliage, particularly on peach trees	Curly leaf fungus	Spray with Bordeaux when flower buds show colour. See 'Pests and Diseases' chapter
Distorted rubbery foliage often with whitish bloom mainly on some azaleas and camellia sasanqua	Leaf gall	Pull off and burn affected leaves. Spray as for mildew
Round rubbery galls on gum leaves and some other trees	Usually formed and inhabited by the larvae of tiny wasps	Systemic sprays do not penetrate satisfactorily but usually not serious to the tree and will disappear in a season or two
Small irregular holes toward leaf centre	Usually due to earlier attack by leaf rolling caterpillar	See 'Pests and Diseases' chapter

Lack of flowers

Failure to produce flowers can be due to a number of conditions. If accompanied by excessive and lush vegetative growth it is usually due to excessive nitrogen and insufficient phosphorus. This condition is likely when plants are fed with soluble plant food that has a very high nitrogen ratio, or with sulphate of ammonia, nitrate of soda or urea. Similarly plants fed solely with compost derived mainly from grass clippings and other green, leafy material will also suffer from a lack of phosphorus. Correct this condition by applying about one handful of superphosphate per sq. m of area around the plants and watering this in well; or bone dust, which also contains a large amount of phosphorus, but this is not released until the material decomposes and therefore is much slower in taking effect.

Other factors

Some plants need 12 or, in some cases, 14 hours of darkness to stimulate flower production and therefore may not flower if given too much exposure to artificial light. Poinsettias are probably the most sensitive plants in this respect and may even refuse to flower if the light from a window reaches them at night. Chrysanthemums, Christmas or Crab's Claw cactus and kalanchoe all require similar long periods of darkness (short days) to induce flowering. Inversely, these plants may be induced to flower at any time of the year by putting them in a dark cupboard from 4 o'clock in the evening to 8 o'clock in the morning for approximately 6 weeks.

Some plants need cold nights to flower. In this category are various cacti, particularly the little peanut cactus, some bulbs and cymbidium.

Maturity

Most types of lilac, forsythia and to some extent some species of the rhododendron family need a fairly sharp winter to mature the wood sufficiently to produce flower buds. Many shrubs and trees need to gain a state of maturity before they produce flowers.

It is quite common for a shrub purchased in flower or fruit to fail to produce either again for a few years after planting out because, once the root growth is no longer restricted by the container, the plant runs to unproductive vegetative growth.

Light

Insufficient sunlight (particularly for camellias, azaleas and rhododendrons) is another factor responsible for lack of flowers. Excessive pruning can also cause it, particularly pruning at the wrong time of the year. The only time to prune shrubs such as weigela, guelder rose, flowering blossoms, etc. without losing flowers is immediately after their spring flowering. Shrubs that flower mainly on old wood such as Japanese cherries, crab apples, japonica, etc. need very little pruning and if pruned will invariably produce vegetative growth which produces very little flower for several years. In this case the tendency to produce heavy top growth can usually be checked by pruning again in summer.

Forsythia

Erica

Murraya paniculata

Problem	Cause	Solution
Leaf tissue removed, tiny veins still intact	28-spot ladybird or pumpkin beetle. Looper caterpillars in young stages may cause similar damage	Spray with Pyrethrum-type sprays or Carbaryl
Large irregular areas of leaf eaten, mainly between the major veins	Loopers or other types of caterpillars	Spray with Pyrethrum-type sprays or Carbaryl
Large, scalloped sections missing from foliage	Larger caterpillars or grasshoppers	Spray with Pyrethrum-type sprays or Carbaryl

Note that birds such as bulbuls, sparrows, pigeons, rabbits, possums and even rats can be responsible for disappearance of plant foliage

Bark, branch or trunk		
Cracks in bark	Occur naturally in many trees and shrubs with maturity. Where lower wood is visible or also cracked, may be due to rain or feeding following long period of dryness or neglect	Paint or spray cracked section with bituminous-type tree paint to discourage entry of fungus diseases or borers
Bark lifting or sunken brownish-grey sections on citrus trunks	Collar rot or scaley bark	See citrus section of 'Growing Fruit, Berries, Vines and Nuts' chapter
Liquidambar with corky ridges along branches	A natural character developing as branches mature	No treatment required
Dark-brown or black sunken sections on branches, particularly of maples	Either bacterial or fungal canker	If possible remove by cleanly sawing branch below damaged area then spraying with copper spray. In some cases only, cure is possible by cutting away affected bark, painting with copper spray then sealing with tree paint
Bark splitting and exuding gum below growing tip — particularly peaches, cherries, etc.	Peach tip moth	Spray with Rogor at first sign of damage
Holes in bark, sawdust-like castings, bark lifting with gumminess or fabric-like enclosure around branches		See heading 'Borers' in 'Pests and Diseases' chapter
Flower disorders		
Edges of petals chewed in scalloped fashion	Brown vegetable or similar weevil	Spray at night with Pyrethrum-type sprays — several applications needed
Petals chewed mainly from tips downwards	Earwigs	See heading 'Earwigs' in Glossary
Buds and large areas of petals eaten	Grasshoppers	Spray with Carbaryl or Endosulphan (Thiodan)
Numerous weevils in flowers — dahlias, roses, etc.		See heading 'Weevils' in Glossary
Flowers limp and shrivelling	Insufficient moisture, particularly during hot or windy conditions	Soak the root area well
Edges of petals shrivelled or transparent or fused in bud form as in gladioli	Thrips	Spray at 5-day intervals alternately with Malathion or Rogor or Endo-sulphan. Gladioli must be sprayed regularly from 4-leaf stage
Streaking of colours in flowers	White streaking, particularly on dark-coloured gerberas or carnations, may be due to a thrip attack. Otherwise colour streaking as in stocks, petunias, etc. is due to virus infection	There is no cure. Destroy to prevent further transmission by aphids. Do not sow seed from infected flowers
Poor size of flowers	Usually due to lack of water and insufficient feeding or generally too poor growing	Improve watering, feeding and cultivation
Bud drop	On gardenias can be due to sudden cold nights or presence of small weevil that punctures buds or girdles bud stems	For weevils spray with Carbaryl at intervals of 5 days until symptoms disappear. Camellias — see under heading 'Camellias' in this chapter. Can also be due to overfeeding or, with flowering house plants, to hot stuffy conditions

Nature of growth

It is worth noting that, in most cases, the more upright the growth the less productive it is and, inversely, the more lateral, the more productive. For example, some climbing roses produce vigorous, erect canes which will never flower while remaining in this position but become productive once tied down in a more lateral or arching position. The same applies to a number of climbing plants and to some extent to berry fruits such as loganberries.

Magnolia soulangeana nigra

Weeping Cherry combines with pink azalea to add colour to this garden

Colourful shrubs throughout the year

Winter flowering

Asterisk indicates those that need a frost-free area
Acacia baileyana
Azalea (some varieties)
Abutilon *
Banksia collina
  B. ericifolia
Buddleia salvifolia
Camellia japonica (varieties)
Chaenomeles
Chamelaucium
Crotalaria *
Daphne odora
Erica canaliculatus
  E. conica
Eriostemon
Garrya
Grevillea banksii
Hakea laurina
Leptospermum (some types)
Luculia *
Magnolia denudata
  M. stellata

Cytisus x praecox

Poinsettia*
Protea (some species)
Prunus mume
   P. campanulata*
Reinwardtia*
Ruellia
Tryptomene
Virburnum macrocephalum

Early to mid-spring flowering
Azalea
Brunfelsia
Chinese Witch-hazel
Cytisus x praecox
Diosma
Eriostemon
Eupatorium*
Geraldton Wax*
Lilac
Mint Bush
Peach (Spring-flowering)
Spiraea (White May)
Streptosolen*
Viburnum (varieties)
Weigela
Wisteria (may be trained as a standard)

Late spring
to early summer flowering
Abutilon*
Cuphea*
Deutzia
Erythrina
Fuchsia*
Hydrangea*
Oleander
Pentas*
Philadelphus
Rhododendron*
Rose
Rothmannia
Spanish Broom
Streptosolen*

Mid-summer
Abelia*
Bauhinia galpinii
Bignonia
Buddleia
Christmas Bush
Crepe Myrtle
Gardenia*
Hibiscus*
Hypericum
Jasminum azoricum*
Justicia*
Lantana
Marguerite
Murraya*
Pentas*
Vitex

Late summer and autumn flowering
Abutilon*
Buddleia
Camellia sasanqua*
Cassia bicapsularis
Gordonia
Hibiscus*
Justicia*
Lantana (varieties)
Pentas*
Tibouchina*

Shrubs and trees which produce attractive winter berries
Ardisia
Callicarpa dichomata (Chinese Beauty Berry, semi-deciduous shrub)
Cotoneaster
Craetagus (Hawthorn)
Holly
Pittosporum
Pyracantha
Sorbus aucuparia (Rownan Tree)
Syzgium (Lilly-Pilly)

Shrubs for garden features
Small, compact, rounded to clumpy evergreen shrubs suitable for foundation planting, large rockeries
General
Berberis darwinii
Calluna (all types cooler areas)
Cistus
Coleonema
Conifer (dwarf types)
Eriostemun myoporoides
Escallonia rubra pygmea
Felicia amelloides
Gardenia
Grevillea alpina
Lantana (dwarf types)
Nandina domestica nana
Pimelia ferruginea
Teucrium fruticans
Viburnum davidii
Ulex
Westringia

Prefers half-shade
Aucuba
Azalea (dwarf to semi-dwarf)
Daphne odora
Pieris

Adapts to half-shade
Buxus
Cuphea hyssopifolia
Eunonymus ovataus aureus
Goldfussia
Hebe
Lonicera nitida
Loripetalum chinense
Raphiolepis
Serissa

Shrubs for Japanese garden
Small
Acer palmatum dissectum
Aucuba
Ardisia
Conifer — see dwarf types in separate conifer section
Coprosma repens variegata
Cuphea hyssopifolia
Elaeagnus pungens aurea
Fatsia japonica
Hebe buxifolia
   H. hartiana
Indigofera decora
Kalmia latifolia
Lonicera nitida aurea
Loropetalum chinense
Mahonia (all types)
Nandina domestica

Pieris
Raphiolepis
Rosmarinus officinalis
Large
Abelia grandiflora
Camellia japonica
   C. sasanqua
Chaenomeles
Coprosma repens
Ilex
Kerria japonica
Magnolia stellata
Osmanthus
Pittosporum tobira
Pseudopanax
Rhododendron

Australian native shrubs
Acacia
Backhousia
Banksia
Bauera
Beaufortia
Callistemon
Calocephalus
Cassia artemisoides
Chamelaucium
Chorizema
Cordyline stricta
Crotalaria agatiflora
Eriostemon
Grevillea
Leptospermum
Melaleuca
Murraya
Myoporum
Prostanthera
Telopea
Tryptomene
Westringia

Prostrate or low-spreading evergreen shrubs
General
Abekia grandiflora tricolor
Cotoneaster pendula hillierii
Gardenia radicabs
Grevillea biternata
   G. Robyn Gordon
   G. obtusfolia
Juniper conferta
   J. horizontalis
   J. sabina
Lantana montividensis
Rosmarinus prostrata

Prefer half-shade
Bauera

Adapt to half-shade
Abutilon megapotamicum
Coprosma retusa variegata (trimmed)
Cuphea ignea
Eleaeagnus aurea (trimmed)

Dense, low-branching shrubs suitable for ground cover
General
Abelia grandiflora tricolor
Coleonema
Grevillea alpina
   G. obtusifolia
   G. biternata
   G. Robyn Gordon

Hebe (all types)
Juniper sabina (varieties)
  J. conferta
  J. douglasii
  J. horizontalis (varieties)
  J. procumbens
  J. davurica
  J. communis Depressa (varieties)
  J. Pfitzeriana (varieties)
Lantana Drap d'Or
  L. Chelsea Gem
Osbeckia kewensis
Pelargonium — particularly peltatum types
  (Ivy geranium) and rose scented
Westringia fruticosa

Prefer half-shade
Azalea indica
Bauera rubioides

Adapt to half-shade
Abutilon megapotamicum
Eriostemon myoporoides
Lantana montividensis
Raphiolepsis umbellata
Serissa
Virburnum davidii

**Large, quick-growing shrubs
to act as screens**
Abelia grandiflora
Coprosma repens
Cotoneaster pannosa
Feijoa sellowiana
Hakea salicifolia
Jasminum mesnyii
Leptospermum laviegatum
  L. petersonii
Oleander
Photinia robusta
Pittosportum eugenoides
Pyracantha augustifolia
Rondoletia amoena

Shrubs for special situations
Shrubs for shaded areas
Some shrubs really prefer shade and only do
well in it; others do well in shade but are
adaptable.

Adaptable
Abelia
Abutilon
Azalea
Berberis
Buxus
Camellia
Choisya
Clethra
Coprosma
Daphne
Elaeagnus
Eriostemon
Fatsia
Fatshedera
Goldfussia
Hydrangea
Hypericum
Ilex
Jacobinia
Luculia
Odontonema

Osmanthus Pieris
Phormium
Pittosporum crassifolium
  P. tobira
Raphiolepsis
Rhododendron
Schefflera
Viburnum tinus

Prefer shade
Aralia
Ardisia
Aucuba
Bauera
Begonia (tree)
Fuchsia
Nandina
Plectranthrus
Pseudopanx

Shrubs for cold areas
Abelia grandiflora
Azalea indica — *Rhododendron indicum*
Berberis (several)
Buddleia (Butterfly Bush)
Callistemon (Bottlebrush)
Camellia japonica
Ceanothus
Chaenomeles (Japanese Flowering Quince)
Coleonema (Confetti Bush or Diosma)
Cotoneaster (numerous)
Deutzia (Wedding Bells)
Elaeagnus pungens
Erica (Heath — numerous)
Erythrina
Euonymus europea (Spindle Tree)
Exochorda (Pearl Bush)
Forsythia (Golden Bells)
Gardenia jasminoides
Hibiscus syriacus (Syrian Hibiscus)
Hypericum (Gold Flower)
Lagerstroemia (Pride-of-India)
Lantana (hybrids)
Lavandula (Lavender)
Leonotis leonurus (Lion's Tail)
Lippia citriodora (Lemon Verbena)
Magnolia (numerous)
Mahonia aquifolium (Holly Mahonia)
Nerium oleander
Philadelphus (Mock-orange)
Pittosporum (several)
Punica (Pomegranate)
Pyracantha (Firethorn)
Rhododendron (numerous)
Ribes (flowering currant)
Rosmarinus (Rosemary)
Spiraea (May — several)
Viburnum (Snowball Bush)
Weigela

Shrubs for hot or semi-tropical areas
Abutilon (Chinese Lantern)
Acalypha (Copperleaf)
Beloperone (Shrimp Flower)
Bouvardia
Brunfelsia (Yesterday, Today and Tomorrow)
Datura candida (Moonflower)
Duranta repens (Forget-me-not Tree)
Erythrina
Euphorbia pulcherrima (Poinsettia)
  E. fulgens
  E. splendens (Christ-thorn)
Gardenia globosa

Hibiscus rosa-sinensis (Chinese Hibiscus)
Hydrangea macrophylla
Holmskioldia (Chinese Hat)
Iboza riparia (Misty Plume Bush)
Lagerstroemia (Pride-of-India)
Leptospermum (Tea-tree)
Leucospermum (Pincushion Flower)
Michelia (Port Wine Magnolia)
Mussaenda frondosa (White Flag Bush)
Nerium oleander (Oleander)
Plectranthus (Spur Flower)
Poinciana
Protea (several)
Reinwardtia indica (Yellow Flax)
Rhododendron indicum (Indian Azalea)
Strelitzia reginae
Streptosolen
Tecoma stans (Yellow Bush Tecoma)
Tibouchina

Shrubs tolerant to salt winds and sea coast conditions
Asterisk indicates those particularly able to withstand these conditions
Acacia
Acokanthera spectabilis
*Banksia ericifolia**
Brachysema lanceolatus
Buddleia salvifolia
Callistemon citrinus
Cassia artemisoides
  *C. bicapsularis**
*Cistus**
*Coprosma**
Cotoneaster
Cytissus
*Elaeagnus pungens**
Euonymus japonicus
Feijoa
Genista fragrans
Lantana
Lavandula
*Leonotis**
*Leptospermum laevigatum**
Melaleuca hypericifolia
Olearia
Pelargonium
Phormium
*Pittosporum crassifolium**
  *P. tobira**
Protea
*Raphiolepis**
*Rosmarinus**
Spartium
Tamarix pentandra
Tecoma capensis
Teucrium
*Ulex**
*Westringia**

Shrubs for badly-drained areas
Aucuba
Bauera
Callistemon citrinus
Cordyline australis
Cyperus alterifolia
  C. papyrus (Nile Grass)
Oleander
Phormium (Flax)
Russellia
Viburnum opulus

Growing some favourite shrubs

Azaleas and Rhododendrons

Strictly speaking, azaleas are rhododendron species and it is difficult to tell just where to draw the line. One prominent botanical authority suggested that 'azalea' should be reserved for the deciduous types, but the suggestion did not catch on. The public at large has learned to distinguish between the two by recognising the different habits of growth and physical characteristics.

Azaleas have scaley stems, seed heads and slightly hairy foliage. Even the larger types rarely grow more than 2–3 m tall.

Rhododendrons have smooth stems, tough leathery leaves and make very large bushes.

They both bring glorious colour to the spring garden.

Evergreen azaleas
Indicum types
Prefer temperate to semi-tropical coastal districts but grow well in cooler areas provided they have protection from wind and frost. They need sun for at least one-third of the day if they are to flower well. A partly-shaded area beneath trees suits them and, since they are shallow-rooted, grow well in the company of

For compact bushes and maximum blooms, azaleas may be pruned when flowers finish

Azaleas bring a splash of colour to this bank

Rhododendrons

Apricot tonings of mollis-type deciduous azalea

Rhodendron

Pink 'Rose Queen' and the red 'Princess Maude'

Rhododendron 'President Roosevelt'

deep-rooted trees such as the eucalypts whose leaves provide them with dappled shade.

Tall, spring flowering
Alba magna — white; *Exquisite* — pale-pink; *Magnifica* — rose-purple; *Splendens* — salmon.

They can be kept compact by pruning back as flowers finish and pinching back new growth when it reaches finger length.

There are hybrid types which have glossy leaves and flower in early winter continuing until spring. There are medium-sized types up to 1.5 m high, and dwarf types of less than 70 cm. Both varieties offer a range of double, semi-double and single flowers.

Gumpo azaleas
Only about .3 m high these small plants are covered with quite large pink, white or salmon-pink single flowers in spring. They are very useful in the rockery or at the front of the flower border.

Deciduous azaleas
Although they sometimes grow well in temperate climate they are more at home in areas with cold winters where there is leaf-fall in autumn. They are spring flowering and provide the rich gold, orange and apricot tones lacking in the evergreen azaleas. Most of them have a delicious, heavy fragrance.

'Mollis' types show large trusses of funnel-shaped flowers before the leaves come out. 'Ghent' types are usually taller and more branching with smaller flowers. 'Exbury', 'Ilam' and 'Knap Hill' are more recently developed hybrids which have larger flowers and heavier flowerheads. All require sun for about one-third of the day to flower well.

Azaleas indoors
A well-established azalea in flower makes a delightful indoor feature. In very cold climates, the sensitive *A. indicum* varieties can be enjoyed by bringing them indoors during winter and moving to outdoor shade when flowers finish in spring. Condition them gradually to a little direct or dappled sunlight — this should be the practice with all azaleas used indoors, as they need to be out in good light from the time new growth starts until flower buds are well formed.

Rhododendrons
These lovely plants vary in type from ones less than 25 cm high to trees up to 8 m. The most popular choice for garden growth centres on the medium-height compact shrubs which grow to 2–3 m in height and come into flower in mid-spring when the azaleas have finished.

There are many different varieties. Some of them are: Betty Wormald — pink-edged flowers; Countess of Athlone — lilac; Dr Arnold Endtz — rose-coloured flowers; Earl of Athlone — blood-red flowers; White Pearl — white-flushed to pink flowers.

Two dwarf types — 1–1.5 m high — which give flowers in mid-spring are: Elizabeth — brilliant scarlet flowers; Unique — apricot buds and creamy-yellow flowers.

Some rhododendrons flower well into summer. The lustre of their beautiful blooms will only be kept if they have the protection of light shade. Dappled sunlight or direct morning sun are ideal. Too much shade will mean no flowers. Rhododendrons flourish best in cool, moist, mountain climates. You have to take trouble to learn about the needs of the different types if you are to succeed with them in warmer districts. As a rule of thumb — keep to the early types if you live in even a temperate district.

Soil
Azaleas and rhododendrons prefer a light to sandy loam which is slightly acid — pH 5.5–6, but don't overdo acidity as they will not grow well in extremely acid soil down below about pH 4.3 They will also die in alkaline soils above pH 6.5, so keep lime away from them.

Exceptions are for very acid soils or where large quantities of acid German peatmoss is used in soil mixtures. Then a dusting of dolomite or garden lime is needed to bring the pH up to the 4.3–4.5 level, but be sure the soil is as acid as you think before venturing this far.

Azaleas and rhododendrons also resent heavy clay soils. However, they will grow well in clay areas if they are planted with the top third of the soil ball set above the soil level and a mixture of sand (or sandy soil and peatmoss) or rotted leafmould, is mounded up to (in the case of leafmould, slightly above) the soil ball.

Planting
Plant in a position where the roots will not be disturbed by cultivation; they have a wide but shallow mat of surface roots. Keep them away from plants that will be fertilised heavily. If the soil is clayey, plant as suggested in the previous paragraph.

In sandy areas, mix in up to one-third moistened peatmoss into the soil to prevent rapid drying out. Never plant deeper than the level of soil ball or the roots could suffocate. Always apply a mulch of leafmould below and around the plants — this keeps the soil cool, eliminates need for root-damaging cultivation, helps to retain moisture and gradually feeds as it rots down.

Aspect
The deciduous and Kurume azaleas do best in cool climates with at least half-sun. Other evergreen types and Kurumes in warmer areas are at their best in dappled sunlight, for example, under tall gums or with a few hours direct morning sunlight. A few of the medium-to-dwarf hybrids such as brick-red Phoebus and lower-growing maroon-red Dr Hugo Glasser will grow in full sun.

Other indicums such as Splendens and Magnifica are also seen heavily massed with flower in full sun, but the blooms seem to retain more lustre in part shade. The sunnier the position the more prolific and compact the plant. In full shade plants are usually leggy with few flowers.

Feeding
More azaleas have been killed by overfeeding than any other factor. If you use the various dry-mix proprietary azalea foods, give the plant no more than a light sprinkling — about 1 dessertspoonful per sq. m of area from trunk to outer foliage: a level teaspoonful is enough for a 25–30 cm-diameter pot; proportionately less for smaller pots. Sprinkle this plant food over the surface mulch, then water in.

Complete water-soluble plant foods are relatively safe but even these should be applied at half to two-thirds the normal recommended strength. A mulch of well-rotted cow manure is a safe food and soil improver but should not be applied as a complete layer more than about 1 cm thick.

In all cases, feed only when the soil is already evenly moist, and never before the new growth begins to appear after flowering. Then do not feed more frequently than at 6–8-week intervals from that stage until late February. There are excellent flower displays from long-established azaleas and rhododendrons which have only been fed naturally by fallen leaves that decomposed above their root area.

Watering
Since they are shallow-rooted, azaleas or rhododendrons should not be allowed to completely dry out, but it is surprising how many well-established plants depend entirely on rainfall and can survive drought periods well.

Do make sure they have plenty of water when new growth starts in spring and for a month or two afterwards. If the foliage shows signs of flagging, give a good soaking. Although roots are near the surface, water thoroughly enough to reach sub-soil, particularly during very dry conditions. Otherwise, with a moist surface and dry sub-soil, concentrations of soil salts could move to the root area — for these plants it could be dangerous. Potted plants should not be allowed to completely dry out.

Moving azaleas and rhododendrons
Both are comparatively easy to move because of their shallow root system. Cut a trench around large plants to the width of outer foliage, then spade under to cut lower roots at about three-quarter spade depth (or even shallower for plants under 1 m high) then gradually lift. If lifting below outer foliage is too difficult, cut it back.

Move plants any time from early winter to flowering time, although if heavy cutting is needed wait until August in all but warm, semi-tropical areas.

Replanting
Make a hole wider than the soil ball (so that you can easily fill in below the plant to avoid air pockets) but no deeper than the root ball. The latter should be covered only with partly-rotted leafmould after the move, not by soil. Ridge the soil out beyond the root ball to allow for thorough soakings.

Pruning
Azaleas can be made more compact by pinching out new spring growth when it reaches about finger length. Tall sappy growths that develop on types such as *Alba magna, splendens* and Exquisite, can be cut back just below the general line of the bush.

Old straggly plants can be rejuvenated by cutting back as flowers are finishing, or earlier, taking the main canes to within about 50 cm from soil level. Excess new shoots should be rubbed off, others pinched back to induce

Growing problems and solutions

Problem	Cause	Solution
Leaf disorders Intermittent yellowing, particularly the lower leaves of each stem	This is a natural seasonal happening, often in winter. May be more pronounced after soil has been wet for long periods	No treatment required
Pale yellowing mainly between veins of lower leaves	Probable magnesium deficiency	One teaspoon of Epsom Salts dissolved in a can of water. Watered over plant and the soil below when latter is moist. Do not make more than 2 applications yearly
Pale yellowing more pronounced on new or top growth	Possible iron deficiency but on Kurume azaleas is often due to excessive soil salts, particularly chlorides from frequent or excessive use of complete plant foods or azalea foods	Liberally flood soil with water and, to counter possibility of iron deficiency, water plant and soil with iron chelates as directed on container
Dull mottling of foliage progressing to overall bronzing or silvering	Lace bug	Spray with Pyrethrum-type sprays or Malathion directed mainly at underside of foliage, repeating in 5–6 days, or with Rogor or Lebaycid. See heading 'Lace bug' in Glossary
Browning and rolling of leaf tip	Leaf roller or leaf miner	Spray with Rogor or Lebaycid
Brown wedges in leaf	As above	As above
Foliage shrivelling from the tips and leaf margins	Usually due to lime or over-feeding, excessive cultivation, deep planting or a too-dry situation	Lift and replant if soil is actually covering original root ball. Otherwise mulch surface with leafmould or peatmoss and water liberally, especially during spring and summer. Azaleas prefer moderately acid soil
Grey powdery patches over foliage	Mildew	Use Bayleton or Benlate
Deformed thick rubbery leaves	Fungus gall	Remove and burn affected leaves then spray as for mildew
Twigs and branches dying back	Die-back disease	Cut out and burn infected parts, spray as for mildew. Sometimes more prevalent under excessively acid conditions.
Flower disorders Light brown or transparent flex on petals followed by premature shrivelling of flower which remains dead on bush	Petal blight	Spray at fortnightly intervals from the time buds show colour with Bayleton or other triadimefon preparations
Edges of petals tattered or lacy	Brown vegetable weevil	See heading 'Weevils' in Glossary
Large areas of petals or buds eaten	Grasshoppers or caterpillars	Spray with Carbaryl or Endosulphan

bushy growth. Heavy cutting may kill an old plant, especially if not previously pruned.

Rhododendrons may be rejuvenated in the same way as azaleas. Keep the bushes compact by cutting the flower stem down to just above the second or third leaf from its base, or above where there is a tier or whorl of small buds showing at the slight junction between new and older wood. Pruning by cutting off flowerheads to prevent seeding is usually enough. Heavily pruned rhododendrons may not flower the following year.

Non-flowering of rhododendrons can also be due to too much shade. In temperate areas if a wet autumn follows a dry summer the shrub will grow tall instead of producing flower buds. Feeding after the flower buds have formed (which can be as early as March in some cases) also has a similar effect. Erratic temperatures and light conditions can also cause some varieties to flower prematurely and poorly, with only one or two buds opening at a time.

Propagation
Azaleas
Propagation is best done in late spring when new growth is beginning to harden up.

Take pieces of this new growth, 5–7 cm in length. Cut just below a leaf junction. Make the cut clean and trim away all leaves on the lower half of the cutting.

Have pots ready containing a mixture of 2 parts coarse sand to 1 part moistened peatmoss. A 10–12 cm pot will do.

Insert the cuttings to half their length, 2–3 cm apart, around the edge of the pots. Firm in. Place a plastic bag over each pot, keeping it ballooned above it, either by the use of an elastic band or sticks or wire hoops set into the soil.

Keep the pots out of direct sunlight but in reasonable light for 5 weeks. Then begin easing the bag loose so that air can reach the cuttings. If they show signs of wilt they are not ready, so replace the bag until it can be moved without creating distress.

When cuttings are obviously established and have their own root growth they can be potted individually. Watch them as they grow and pinch out to make them grow bushy.

Grafting. The marcottage graft is made by cutting into the bark of the stem in two places 7–8 cm apart and then scraping away the bark between the cuts to expose the cambium (the inner tissue). This will girdle the stem. Make a deeper cut about 2 cm higher up the stem, circling it and then scrape down and remove the cambrium.

Wrap the entire section of the stem in damp sphagnum moss. Cover the moss with plastic to contain the moisture and secure in place. If you are afraid that the stem might break, splint it very gently.

Leave for 6–7 weeks then unwrap and inspect. If the plant has put out roots at the cut, sever carefully, pot up and plant out the new growth when the roots are really well developed but during the dormant period of the plant.

Rhododendrons
Don't try cuttings to propagate rhododendrons unless your thumb is very green indeed. Success is more likely from layering.

A low branch can easily be pulled down to the soil, and then, with the stem cut part-way through and held apart by anything small, and the cut pegged down into the soil for a little way and left in place for at least 3 months, you will eventually find a rooted section of stem which can be cut free from its parent to make a new plant. Plant in winter.

Air layering. A tall stem can be cut half-way through; held apart by a small object and the cut surrounded by damp sphagnum moss, held in place by elastic bands and covered with plastic to conserve moisture. The plant will put out roots at the cut. The stem can then be severed and the new plant set in place.

Pot plants
It is possible to enjoy both azaleas and rhododendrons growing in pots but there is a limit to the time such enjoyment is possible. The plant may do well for a year or two, even make some top growth, but once it becomes root bound the end is in sight.

Never buy a tall, woody plant in a small pot. Its condition makes it obvious it has been kept in the pot far too long.

If you are faced with such a problem don't transfer the plant from the pot to the soil and just hope for the best.

Tap the plant out of the pot, untwine roots which have gone in circles around the pot and trim them, teasing them free from each other. If necessary, cut away any woody section at the bottom of the pot. The roots should free to search out food in the new soil into which you will put them — they will then put out healthy new growth and your plant will begin to thrive.

Any plant which has been disturbed and replanted should be kept shaded for a few weeks while it is re-establishing itself. Trim back new growth put out in early spring to help it complete its rejuvenation.

Rhododendron 'Alice'

Rhododendron 'Earl of Athlone'

Rhododendron 'Mrs G.W. Leek'

Azalea 'Alba Magna'

Dappled sunlight suits azaleas and rhododendrons

Deciduous azaleas feature gold and orange tonings

Camellias

Camellias are among the most rewarding garden shrubs. Not only do their beautiful blooms come in winter when colour is most welcome, but their growth and shape remain attractive throughout the year, with very little pruning needed. Their compact form and glossy, dark-green evergreen foliage make them excellent landscape subjects. They would be worth a place in the garden even if they did not have such enchanting flowers. Not only this, they make wonderful pot or tub plants for the garden or balcony, etc. and in the coldest parts of the country can be taken indoors as house plants in autumn when the flower buds have formed, kept indoors to flower during the winter chill and then moved out into the garden as the earth warms up in spring.

Camillia reticulata

Camellia japonica

There are hundreds of varieties. They flourish in humid, temperate coastal regions. Given protection from hot winds and midday sun they will also grow quite well in dry, inland districts.

They do *not* like either tropical or very cold areas and flower well in winter. Light is needed for bud formation but full sun will scorch foliage. The red types — Moshio, Empress of Russia and Great Eastern — tolerate sun best.

All types of camellia need good drainage; the japonica types need it most. They will develop root rot if the soil around them remains wet for too long. If there is any danger of this, build up the soil to 50 cm or so above the normal level before planting.

Flower form varies through single, semi-double, informal double, formal double, ruffled peony, tight-cushioned, anemone-centred blossoms. There is little hope of keeping track of them all as varieties are being registered and named year after year. It seems that the camellia can never be other than beautiful.

A selection of japonica camellias

Alba Plena. Formal double. Large to medium blooms. Slow, dense growth. Good for tub. **Aspasia Macarthur.** Informal double, white-marked pink flowers. Slender, upright growth. **Australis.** Large informal double, bright-rose to cherry-red; golden stamens. Compact, upright growth. Mid-season.

Camillia japonica 'Lovelight'

Camillia sasanqua 'Hiryu'

Camillia japonica 'Drama Girl'

Betty Sheffield Supreme. Informal double. Petals edged with rosy-red fluted centre petals; showy stamens. Bushy growth, good for tub. Mid-season.

Blood of China. Informal double, dark salmon-red. Mid-season.

Bowen Bryant. Semi-double, bright pink saluenensis hybrid. Strong grower, sun-resistant. Mid-season.

Can Can. Pale-pink informal double. Silver tonings flushed rose; wavy petals. Tall, slender, strong grower. Mid-season.

Carter's Sunburst. Large, informal double, soft pink, flecked deeper pink; long flowering.

Chandleri. Bright crimson informal double 'waratah' type, occasionally flecked white. Large foliage, open growth. Early.

Clark Hubbs. Rich crimson informal double. Fringed petals; gold-tipped stamens. Long-lasting, compact growth. Good tub specimen. Mid to late season.

C.H. Hovey. Large, crimson formal double. Strong, irregular growth. Mid to late season.

C.M. Wilson. Large, powder-pink, double centred. Strong growth, slightly spreading habit, free flowering. Mid-season.

Dainty Maiden. Soft, flesh-pink semi-double with gold stamens among crepey centre petaloids. Long flowering, pendulous growth, dislikes full sun. Early.

Daitairin. Semi-double or double. Tight, pale-pink petaloids. Rounded, deep-pink petals in cupped formation. Long flowering, spreading. Early.

Debutante. Pale-pink informal double; central crest of petals. Long flowering, erect, slender. Early.

Dixie Knight. Large, red informal double. Strong, upright. Mid and late season.

Donation. Silvery-rose curved petals. Saluenensis hybrid with stiff, leathery, adult foliage and fairly loose growth. Stands full sun, excellent for tubs or espalier.

Doris Hirst. Large, double-centre, creamy-white with silky texture. Likes filtered sunlight. Early.

Dr Tinsley. Slightly cupped semi-double. White, pink-flushed at petal edges. Dense, compact growth. Slow to flower in early stages but worth waiting for. Mid-season.

Easter Morn. Large, beautifully formed soft-pink, formal. Dislikes sun.

Ecclefield. Large, white informal double, with high ruffled centre. Vigorous, upright, compact growth. Mid-season.

Eileen Samson. Rosy carmine, semi-double. Mid to late season.

Emperor of Russia. Bright, deep-red informal double; gold stamens. Strong grower in sun or shade. Dark foliage. Mid-season.

Emperor of Russia (variegated). As above but heavily marbled in white.

Fimbriata. Large, white formal double, fringed or feathered petals. Early flowering.

Grand Sultan. Large, deep-red formal double. Low growing. Mid to late season.

Great Eastern. Large, semi-double. Rosy to deep-red, reflexed petals spaced in trumpet formation. Strong, bushy, upright growth. Mid-season.

Guilio Nuccio. Large, coral-rose semi-double.

Deeply veined petals ruffled and waved high around golden stamens. Long flowering; good growth. Mid-season.

Hanafuki. Large, soft-pink semi-double with crepey, cupped petals around gold-tipped stamens. Upright, open growth. Mid-season.

Hawaii. Informal double, pale-pink, medium to large flowers last well. Medium growth. Mid-season.

High Jinks. Showy formal double pink, striped red, blotched with white. Free-flowering, vigorous upright growth. Mid-season.

Janet Waterhouse. Large, formal double; white. Low growth. Early.

Jean Lyne. Semi-double white, striped silvery pink. Vigorous, takes full sun. Mid-season.

Kamohonami. Single, white, attractively cupped; gold-tipped stamens. Dark, glossy, pendulous foliage. Erect, long-flowering. Early.

Kramer's Supreme. Large, crimson informal double blooms. Upright growth when young; stands full sun. Mid-season.

Lady Loch. Large, rounded informal double. Rose-pink ruffled petals, white at the edges. Vigorous, erect. Strong, dark foliage. Early to mid-season.

Laurie Bray. Large, semi-double. Waved, soft salmon-rose petals and yellow stamens. Colour strengthens with age. Vigorous growth, spreading, bushy. Dislikes sun. Good tub plant. Early to mid-season.

Lookaway. Deep rose-pink informal double, margined white. Tall, slender, medium-sized. Mid-season.

Magnoliaflora. Semi-double blush pink. Pointed, crimped petals in trumpet formation around creamy centre stamens. Bushy, shapely, ideal for tub. Mid-season.

Margaret Davis. Informal double. Soft ivory, deep rose at edges. Strong, upright, long-lasting. Early to mid-season.

Margarete Hertrich. Formal double, white. Bushy, upright growth. Excellent for cutting. Mid-season.

Margaret Waterhouse. Semi-double, soft-pink reflexed petals; creamy stamens. Free-flowering, likes sun. Upright saluenensis hybrid type.

Moshio (Australian Flame). Red, semi-double; golden stamens. Small to medium-sized star-like blooms almost cover dark, attractive foliage. Good for tub. Mid-season.

Mrs D.W. Davis. Large, soft-pink semi-double. Strong, upright growth.

Nancy Bird. Large, semi-double, white flushed pink at base with splashes of silvery rose. Free-flowering. Strong; likes sun. Mid-season.

Odoratissima. Loose, informal double. Small flat red flowers with incurved petals. Bushy growth. Sensitive to salt winds. Early and late season.

Polar Bear. Semi-double, creamy-white; yellow stamens. Medium growth. Early.

Prince Eugene Napolean. Mid-red formal double with slightly darker veining in reflexed petals. Bright, pendulous foliage. Mid-season.

Prince Frederick William. Formal double, rose-pink medium-sized blooms. Slow in early stages. Mid to late season.

Pukekura. Large, semi-double. White wavy petaloids; gold-tipped stamens. Branched, upright. Mid-season.

R.L. Wheeler. Rose-pink and white semi-double to double-centred. Upright, bushy growth. Excellent for tub. Mid-season.

Sawada's Dream. Formal double. Outer petals pink, paling to pure white at centre. Medium-bushy growth. Mid-season.

Shiro Chan. White species of C.M. Wilson. Bushy, spreading. Mid-season.

The Czar. Large, semi-double, deep red. Flowers well in young stage. Upright growth. Good for tub. Hardy. Mid-season.

Tiffany. Large, soft-pink informal double. Upright wavy petaloids; gold-tipped stamens. Vigorous, upright growth. Mid-season.

Tinsie. White centre, deep-red petals, sasanqua-like leaves. Open medium growth. Mid-season.

Tiptoe. Semi-double, soft pink, shading to cyclamen at tips of waved, spaced petals; amber-tipped stamens. Mid-season.

Tomorrow. Large, strawberry-red informal double. Free-flowering. Vigorous, upright growth, heavy foliage. Mid-season.

Tomorrow's Dawn. Deep to soft-pink with darker veining, and white bordering on petals and petaloids. Growth and flowering season as 'Tomorrow'.

Ubane (Toki no Hagasane). Semi-double soft pink to white. Slender, upright growth. Mid-season.

White Empress. White, semi-double. Fluted petaloids with gold-tipped stamens. Long-lasting. Vigorous, compact growth. Early.

White Nun. Large, semi-double. Pure white, rounded, outer petals fold back. Inner petals stay erect; lemon stamens. Free-flowering, long-lasting. Mid-season.

Wildwood. Large, light-pink, semi-double. Strong open growth. Mid-season.

Camellia sasanqua

These are smaller-leafed varieties, with more caney growth. They flower earlier than the japonicas and can withstand cold better. Sasanquas have the ability to adapt to full sun or shade; they will continue to flower in either. One of their greatest assets is a greater resistance to root rot than shown by other family members.

Susceptible varieties are often grafted onto sasanqua stock.

Hybrids

Hybridisation has long been practised in the camellia world. The late Professor Waterhouse (whose home in Gordon, near Sydney, has become a centre of pilgrimage for the camellia enthusiast) was responsible for many beautiful crosses. A lifetime study could be made of all the possibilities and new and interesting seedlings are being introduced all the time.

Camellias suitable for tropical and semi-tropical climates

C. granthamania — large, white flowers from Hong Kong; *C. hongkongensis* — large, crimson flowers from Hong Kong; *C. salicifolia* — white, slightly perfumed flowers, narrow leaves from Hong Kong; *C. sinensis* (Tea of Commerce).

Aspect

Dappled sunlight for *C. japonica*. Full sun to full shade for *C. sasanqua*.

Growing problems and solutions

Problem	Cause	Solution
Dull yellow spotting or mottling of leaf	Usually scale (check for tiny pear-shaped or brownish pinhead-sized scabs mainly on backs of foliage)	Spray 2 tablespoons of white oil per 4 L of water plus 1 teaspoon Rogor or Lebaycid
Glossy, creamy yellow mottling or marbling on some foliage only	Virus infection	Rarely of serious consequence. No positive cure. Do not propagate from tree
General yellowing and leaf fall	Can be due to excessive dryness, or to bad drainage and root rot	See heading 'Die-back of roses' in Rose section. Flood soil during dry conditions
Leaf fall and numerous dead twigs	Die-back, usually due to root rot in poorly-drained or slow-draining soils	Improve drainage, free drainage holes of containers. Camellias grafted or budded on sasanqua usually have greater resistance to root rot
Over-budding and plant heavily encrusted with flower buds	Due either to very dry early summer, root damage due to deep cultivation or, more commonly, when a large plant has been moved the previous season without pruning it back well	Remove all but one bud per stem and if appropriate prune back immediately after flowering
Pin-sized brown holes on edges of petals	Usually where spinebills or other honey-eating birds clutch edge of flower	Enjoy the birds enjoying the flowers
Leaves with dull creamy-brown sandblasted appearance	Red spider mites	Spray with Malathion or Rogor. Also mist foliage frequently with water. (Usually only likely when plant is under weather protection)
Very enlarged rubbery white or pale-green new growth on some sasanqua camellias	Leaf gall fungus	Remove and burn infected leaves or shoots and spray with copper spray or Benlate. (Usually disappears as conditions become warmer)

Soil

Camellias like acid soil but not acidity below pH 4.5. They will tolerate alkalinity up to pH 6.5. Good drainage is essential.

Camellias planted in containers need good, crumbly soil made from equal parts coarse sand, garden loam, rotted leafmould or cow manure. Moistened peatmoss can be used — 50:50 if the loam is sandy.

Planting

Camellias growing in containers may be planted at any time providing roots are not disturbed, although the cooler months (or when they are in flower) give them the best chance to readjust to change of environment. In cold districts spring planting is preferable.

When planting take care not to set them any deeper than container soil level. If the plant is in a root-bound condition, tease the roots out well and delay planting until winter. Trim back foliage and shade for a few weeks until new roots re-establish.

Keep soil moist but not soggy for a few weeks after planting. Once plants are established, give a good soaking once a week during dry conditions. Although camellias are surface feeders, let the surface soil dry out between waterings to encourage deeper root growth and greater drought resistance.

Plants in containers should not be allowed to dry out. Avoid any sogginess and check drainage holes. These can be blocked by roots or by earthworm activity. If the soil becomes soggy there is a danger of root rot.

Feeding

Feed camellias when new growth starts and give light feeding from then until winter.

Use camellia foods at the rate of about 1 tablespoon per sq. m of area (i.e. surface directly below the foliage) or half this rate for container-grown plants. Water well. Repeat every 8 weeks.

Soluble plant foods applied every 4–5 weeks are also beneficial. Always give a good soaking before feeding. Surface mulching is beneficial.

Disbudding

Flower quality is better when flower buds are thinned out to 1 or 2 per stem. Do this from about February onwards when the buds are pea-size and easily handled. To avoid tearing the stem, hold the stem and the base of the bud between finger and thumb of one hand and slightly twist the bud and lift it out with the other. Leave the buds that will look best in relation to foliage and stem position.

Moving

This can be done safely from late May to early August. For plants less than 2 m high cut a complete circle about 25 cm out from the stem, at about spade depth, then gradually lift the plant.

For larger trees, cut a cricle with a radius equal to 3 or 4 times the width (diameter) of the trunk, then dig a trench the width of a spade beyond this. This gives room to trim the roots below the bush. Gradually rock and lift the soil ball, and when it is free, gradually work canvas or hessian and 2 or 3 ropes below it so that the soil ball can be lifted intact. Do this when the soil is just damp — not at any other time.

Make a new hole twice as wide as needed so that plenty of good soil (but not fertiliser or manure) can be placed around the root area.

Make sure planting is no deeper than the previous one. Add a stake if wind movement is likely. Ridge the surplus soil a little beyond the root ball and fill the depression with partly-rotted leafmould or compost, then flood thoroughly.

Now comes the most essential part and usually the one that most people are reluctant to carry out. Cut the plant back heavily — this has to be done if the plant is to flower well in the future.

Rejuvenating

After a camellia has been flowering for 6–8 years it invariably makes a good deal of thin, woody growth and flower quality deteriorates.

Rejuvenate the tree in winter by removing all the side growths thinner than a lead pencil, cutting these as close to the main branches as possible. Then shorten back all branches to pencil thickness.

It is important to do this several weeks ahead of new growth starting. The tree will look pathetic but soon there will be an enthusiastic burst of new shoots. Rub off the surplus ones to achieve good, uncrowded even spacing of the remainder.

A compromise is to treat every second branch this way, then do the remainder the following winter.

Propagation

Camellias can be increased by cuttings, grafts, layering or by raising from seed.

Most nurseries increase their stock from cuttings. Layering, as described for rhododendrons, is simpler for the home gardener; grafting is something of an art, so why not try the simplest method? Camellias have big seeds which are easy to handle and if they don't come up true to their parent in either flower type or colour — they'll be lovely anyway!

When the flowers finish in spring, hard green woody fruits begin to form and make pods. They split open in late summer or early autumn and release the seeds. If you see a pod which looks as though it is about to split, pick it and keep it in gentle warmth until the pod breaks open, so that the seed is not lost to the garden soil.

The easiest way to sprout the seeds is to put them in a wide-mouthed glass jar three-quarters full of damp peatmoss or sphagnum moss on a shallow layer of sand placed over the moss. Gently cover the seeds with another thin layer of sand and damp moss. Put the lid on the jar and keep in a warm place for about 3 weeks.

Sort out the seeds which have developed a long tap root and put the others back in the jar until they too have sprouted successfully.

Trim the tap root to about 2.5 cm and plant in a small pot containing a mixture of 3 parts sandy loam to 1 of damp peatmoss. Plant with only the root beneath the soil and the seedcase sitting on top of it. Keep moist in a shady place. The trimmed root will be encouraged to put out small fibrous roots and, in a few more weeks, top growth should be under way.

The seedlings will naturally take a few years and great care before they reward you with any flowers, but the exercise is simple and more than usually rewarding.

Fuchsias

There are countless varieties of this graceful shrub which, although it prefers shade, can often be found doing surprisingly well in full sun. Flowering can last from late spring throughout the year, sometimes even into winter. The elegant, pendulous flowers — double, single, frilled and in many combinations of white, pink, red and purple — hold well and give a lengthy display.

Not the least of the charms of the fuchsia is the ease with which it can be trained into shape. Different species have different growth habits and you can have them growing in the garden as bushes, standards, espaliers, and hanging either over the edge of a container or rising above one in a pyramid. There are few plants more rewarding once their relatively simple needs are met.

Soil

In the garden. Light, medium not acid loam, enriched with compost and bone meal. If too sandy, add moistened peatmoss and more compost. If too heavy lighten with rotted leafmould or more compost.

In pots. Any good proprietary potting soil. If

Fuchsia hybrid

Fuchsia triphylla 'Garden Master'

you mix your own soil use a 4:1:1 proportion of loam, sand and peatmoss with 2 teaspoons of complete plant food per 10 L bucket.

In hanging baskets. Add more peatmoss to the mixture. Baskets dry out more easily than pots. Always line the basket with plastic (punctured in several places to allow drainage) and a layer of sphagnum moss. This not only holds the soil in place but helps it stay moist. Charcoal in the bottom of the basket will keep soil sweet.

Feeding

Avoid complete plant foods with a high nitrogen content. Phosphorus is needed to promote and sustain flowering. Consult pH table on plant food labels.

In the garden. 1 tablespoon complete plant food per sq. m.

In pots or baskets. Less than 1 teaspoon. Water in well. Repeat in about 6 weeks. While the plant is in flower give it a monthly dose of one of the water-soluble foods.

Watering

Fuchsias should not be allowed to dry out, neither should they be expected to thrive in a soggy soil. Watering should be generous but controlled during the long flowering period.

Fuchsia hybrid

Shaping and pruning

Bush. Cut off the centre shoot and top pair of leaves of a young plant. As shoots grow from the junction of the remaining leaves cut them back to 2 sets of leaves and, as side shoots grow from their leaf junctions, trim them back. The aim is to induce a compact dome shape.

Standard. Rub off all side shoots, leaving only the main stem to grow tall. Retain the top leaves. When stem is the height you desire, pinch out the centre shoot. As the side growth breaks, proceed as described for the bush type.

Espalier. Pinch out the top shoot when plant is about 30 cm tall. Fasten plant against a wall and train lower growths against it. When they are about 25 cm long, nip out their top growth. Allow plant to grow into a fan shape, keeping it neatly in shape against the wall.

Hanging basket and container-grown plants

Pinch out centre shoot. Allow the shoots which form in the leaf junctions to grow long enough to overhang the edge of the basket or container before stopping out again. Stop these again as often as needed to give the shape and bushiness to make a balanced picture.

Pyramid shape. The container is staked with the stakes tapering to a point. The plant (a strong upright is best for this type of treatment) is allowed to grow to 25 cm before the first stop. One of the two top shoots is removed and the other is trained to grow upright. Only 4 lower shoots should be left on the plant. They are trained outwards, evenly, and stopped after each shoot has made 3 pairs of leaves.

As the resultant shoots grow, they are stopped. It is then just a matter of repeating the stopping until the plant forms a tall, leafy pyramid. It sounds much more complicated than it is to carry out. Once growth begins it is easy to estimate where it should be encouraged to give the required shape.

Growing problems and solutions

Problem	Cause	Solution
Leaves eaten	Usually a greyish caterpillar	Spray with either Carbaryl or Endosulphan
Buds or flowers eaten	As above	As above
Leaves with dull sandblasted appearance	Red spider mite	Spray with a miticide. Mist foliage with water during hot, dry conditions also helps
Grey mottling or silvering of foliage	Thrips (small, dark, needle-shaped insects)	Spray with Endosulphan or Malathion
Leaves falling	Usual as colder weather approaches. Also due to hot, dry conditions	Mulch and improve moisture supply during summer
Sudden leaf fall	Can be due to use of Pyrethrum or Bioresmethrin sprays (some hybrid varieties are particularly sensitive to these)	For caterpillars, thrips, aphids, etc. use chemicals as suggested above
Sudden wilting and dying	Can be due to root or stem fungus but more commonly to heat-wave conditions	Keep plants well watered during these periods
Good growth but very little flower	Too little phosphorus in relation to nitrogen	Use complete plant food or if using slow-release granules, also supply about 1 level teaspoon of superphosphate per plant and repeat every 3 months during the growing season

Hibiscus

The original hibiscus (*Hibiscus rosa sinensis*) has undergone extensive hybridisation. A reasonably undemanding evergreen shrub, with spectacular flowers, it can be the glory of a garden.

There are hundreds of varieties. Flowers can be single, double, ruffled, two-toned. Plants vary in height from dwarf to 3–4 m in height.

There is an Australian native hibiscus that makes a tall, strong tree. It would take a book just to list the varieties. Older types are hardy and free flowering; the newer and more spectacularly-flowered hybrids from Hawaii and Florida take a little more care.

Deciduous varieties (*H. syriacus*) have smaller flowers than the evergreen species but are free-blooming over a long period from summer to late autumn and are quite hardy.

Soil

They tolerate all but acid and very heavy soils and, providing there is shelter from the blast of salt wind, do well in seaside areas.

Soil can easily be corrected by the addition of fibrous compost or peatmoss into the area where planting is to be made.

Feeding

Never feed during the early growth of the plant. Feed after pruning (see next paragraph) using a complete plant food, slightly below recommended strength, watered into the soil below the spread of the outer branches. As the plant grows feed in this way every 4–5 weeks. Always water well after feeding to prevent build-up of nutrients which could damage the roots of the plant.

When the shrub is in flower change to one of the liquid plant foods and feed at the recommended strength until early autumn.

During cold weather and winter the soil around the plant should never be more than damp. During hot weather keep a mulch around the base of the plant to protect the roots from overheating.

Pruning

Prune in early spring and shape the new growth. In warmer districts a second pruning in summer will encourage autumn and winter flowering.

Prune canes made the previous season by one-third, cutting to a bud growth facing inward. If you wish, leave some canes uncut to provide early flowers.

Pinch out new growth when it reaches 10–15 cm. Pinch out the shoots which form subsequently. This method of pruning will ensure bushy and compact growth and a profusion of flowers.

Propagation

Cuttings from the previous season's growth or tip cuttings taken during the growing season will provide new plants. Use a light, crumbly soil and keep the pot shaded or covered by a plastic bag until roots have become established. Success is often possible when cuttings are just thrust into the soil in a suitable spot in the shade.

Hibiscus flowers

Hibiscus flowers last just as well in water as out so can be used for table decoration or skewered on thin bamboo canes for use in large arrangements.

A number of the more recently introduced varieties, particularly, have flowers that last for 2 days. The one-day varieties can be used for night decoration by picking the flowers early in the morning as they begin to open, wrapping them in loose bud form in tissue paper and keeping them in the crisper dish of the refrigerator until late afternoon. They will open and last until after midnight.

Hibiscus 'Apple Blossom' is normally a tall grower

Growing problems and solutions

Problem	Cause	Solution
Numerous small holes giving leaves lacy appearance	Hibiscus beetle (small metallic black weevil)	Spray with Endosulphan (Thiodan)
Flowers infested with weevils	As above	As above
Tiny greyish insects clustered outside flower buds or on young growth	Aphids	Spray with Pyrethrum-type sprays or Endosulphan
Leaves yellowing and excessive leaf fall	Yellowing of older leaves is natural, particularly during late spring and late summer, or is due to dryness or lack of feeding or bad drainage. Can also be caused by use of Malathion, Rogor, Lebaycid or other organic phosphates, to which many hibiscus varieties are sensitive	Mulch surface, soak thoroughly during late spring and summer and apply 6–10 weekly dressings of complete plant food over this period. Improve drainage if necessary. Thiodan is a safer spray for most hibiscus pests
Excessive bud drop	Accentuated by fact that spent flowers fold back into bud formation before falling. Also flowers on most varieties only last one day. Hibiscus weevil, aphids or dryness and lack of feeding can be factors	See above treatments

Hibiscus

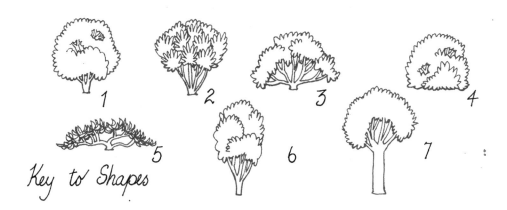

Key to Shapes

A reference guide to shrubs

E: Evergreen   **D:** Deciduous
H: Height: **W:** Width
C: For cool climates only
T: Temperate — where winter day temperatures are rarely below 10°C (50°F)
H: Hot, semi-tropical to tropical climates
Salt tolerance — **SH:** high
          SM: medium
          SL: low

Hydrangeas

Hydrangeas flower in early summer and need shade and plenty of water. Their large and beautiful flowers are white or tones of pink and blue which can range from red to lavender. The type of soil in which the plant is grown will largely determine the colour of the flower.

Soil

Alkaline soil (containing lime) for pink shades; acid soil (containing peatmoss, etc.) for blue shades.

You can deepen the blue of flowers by adding a little sulphate of ammonia to the soil around the plant. You can change pale-blue flowers into pink ones by adding lime to the soil. The best time to do this is after pruning (July) and when the plant is making growth in September and October.

An average dose is around 1 heaped tablespoon to a sq. m but be careful not to overdo it as too much lime could cause the leaves to yellow and drop. If this happens the plant will need a dose of iron to correct the deficiency caused by the lime.

Feeding

Give soluble plant food when the buds appear and from then on every 3 or 4 weeks. You could make the first of every month 'feeding' day.

The important thing is to keep the plant well watered but never flooded.

Pruning

The removal of the flowerheads after the flowering finishes can be followed by trimming in July or August. Cut out the old canes growing from the base of the plant but leave the stems which have carried the year's flowers. Shorten these back leaving a pair of buds. Cut out any weak and leggy growth.

For dwarf varieties cut out all stems which have produced flowers at ground level so that new growth from buds at the base of the plant can throw up new growth to carry the new season's flowers.

Propagation

Use the July or August prunings as cuttings. Take pieces of the previous season's flower stems, preferably with double buds at the top and insert to about half their length in sandy soil that carries about one-third peatmoss. One cutting per 10 cm pot will save trouble later. Cuttings shorter than 15 cm would not need quite such deep insertion.

Growing problems and solutions

Problem	Cause	Solution
Powdery grey patches on foliage	Mildew	Use copper spray
Purple-stained foliage	May be due to mildew but also to cold or soil condition	Treat as mildew if appropriate
White down on stems, sometimes also on ground below plant	Cottony cushion scale	Spray 2 tablespoons of white oil plus 1 teaspoon of Rogor or Lebaycid to 5 L water
Poor flower colour	Soil too neutral	Add lime for pink tones and iron sulphate or aluminium sulphate to acidify soil for blue tones. Commence treatment by late autumn
Lack of flower	Can be due to pruning	Prune back to plump double buds for flower or, in dwarf varieties particularly, allow all canes with terminal buds to remain
Lack of flower	Over-mild winters may be a factor with some varieties, especially in very shaded situations	A transition from 10°C (50°F) to 16°C (60°F) is needed by most varieties to initiate flower buds, but this factor seems less critical in sunny positions
Brown or burnt edges on flower petals	Sun scorch	Keep soil around plants well saturated during hot, dry conditions. If possible, shade during hottest part of day

Abelia Suit sun or part shade, in all but coldest regions. Prune in late winter, method **b**.

A. grandiflora, glossy bronze-green foliage and mauve flushed flowers in summer and autumn, makes good hedge. E 2–3 m x 2 m. Shape **1**. S–M.

A. chinensis tricolor, variegated gold, new growth flushed coppery pink. White flowers. E 1.5 m x 1 m.

A. schumannii, comparatively large, rosy, lilac flowers. E 1–2 m x 1 m.

Abutilon Maple-like foliage, flowers like small cupped hibiscus during summer and often into winter. Prune in late winter, method **b** or **c**.

A. Boule de Neige, white. E 1.5 m x .5 m. Shape **1**.

A. Eclipse, orange. E 2 m x 2 m. Shape **1**.

A. Jubilee, deep rose. E 2 m x 2 m. Shape **1**.

A. megapotamicum variegatum, prostrate pointed, gold splashed foliage, small pendant flowers, red with the cream petals protruding. Excellent spillover. E 0.6 m x 1–1.5 m. Shape **5**.

A. Savitzii, showy green and white foliage. E 1 m x 1.5 m. Shape **3**.

A. thompsonii, green foliage, mottled gold. E 1.5 m x 1–1.5 m. Shape **3**.

A. Yellow Gem, large clear yellow. E 2 m x 2 m. Shape **1**.

Acacias (The Wattles). Give a light pruning immediately after flowering.

A. acinacea (Gold Dust wattle). Slender 1.3 cm leaves; massed golden balls of flower, spring. Likes open, sunny, well-drained position. 1–2 m. Shape **2**.

A. buxifolia (Box-leaf wattle). Small, grey-green oval leaves. Arching sprays pale gold balls, spring. Adaptable. 2–3 m x 2–3 m. Shape **1**.

A. calamifolia (Wallowa). Long, thin, silvery-grey foliage. Fluffy heads yellow, spring. Drought resistant. 3–5 m x 2 m. Shape **2**.

A. cardiophylla (Wyalong wattle). Fern-like leaves, arching branches draped in small, bright yellow flowers, spring. Quick growing, adaptable. 2–3 m x 2 m. Shape **4**.

A. cultriformis (Knife-leaf or Dog-tooth wattle). Closely set, triangular blue-grey leaves. Arching branches, golden balls of flower, spring. Adaptable, drought resistant. 2–4 m x 3 m. Shape **2**.

A. drummondii Fern-like foliage, bright yellow fingers of spring flower. Needs good drainage. Can fail in East Coast wet summers. 1–1.5 m x 1 m. Shape **3**.

A. longifolia var. *Sophorea* (sallow or sally wattle). Broad, bright green leaves, creamy catkins, spring. Good sea coast shrub. 2–3 m x 2–3 m. Shape **1**.

A. podalyriifolia (Queensland wattle). Silvery blue-grey oval foliage. Massed large golden balls of winter flower. Foliage sometimes browned and disfigured by leaf miner, which cannot invade finer foliaged types such as *A. baileyana*. Most districts; sea coast. 3–5 m x 3 m. Shape **2**.

A. saligna (Golden Wreath wattle). Pendulous, sickle-shaped leaves to 15 cm long; spikes pale yellow flowers, winter. 2–4 m x 2 m. Shape **7**.

Acalypha (Fiji Fire Plant). Large, oval, pendulous leaves, bronze-margined pink, cream and green, or pink splashed with copper, black, green and similar combinations. Needs frost-free areas. Prune, method **c**, in late winter. D 2–3 m x 1–1.5 m. Shape **2. S–H.**

Acer see *Maple*.

Acokanthera spectabilis. Previously *Carissa* and *Toxicophlaea*. Large, oval, leathery, bronze-green foliage, heads of tiny white fragrant spring flowers, black fruits with poisonous milky sap. Damaged by heavy frosts. E 2–3 m x 1–2 m. Shape **4**.

A. spectabilis variegata. Showy cream, green and pink variegations. Prune lightly after flowering, method **a**. 1–2 m x 1–2 m.

Aloysia triphylla (Lemon Scented Verbena) (*Lippia citriodora*). Slender, tough, light-green and very aromatic foliage — insignificant spring flowers, better to sacrifice these by pruning in winter, method **c**, to make growth more attractive. All except coldest. E 2–3 m x 2 m. Shape **2**.

Andromeda. Rosemary-like, small waxy pink or white bells in spring. See *Pieris* which were previously listed as *Andromeda*. Prune lightly after flower, method **a**. Style **4**.

Aucuba japonica (Gold Dust). Adaptable shrub with glossy, large, oval, dark green, leathery foliage, heavily splashed with gold, Variety *crotonoides* has more profuse gold spotting. The former is male but all female types produce best berries. Aucubas are useful for shaded position, stand heavy frost and full sun, but scorch in dry heat unless protected. E 1–2 m x 1–1.5 m. No pruning needed. Shape **3. S–L.**

Baeckea ramosissima. Dainty pink teatree-like flowers, fine foliage; semi-prostrate. Flowers winter to mid-summer. About 30 cm. Shape **3**.

B. carnosa. Deep pink flowers fade to white. Suit light shade, hot dry districts. 1–1.5 m x 1 m.

Banksia coccinea (Scarlet banksia). Short, wide brushes; silvery-white buds open to scarlet. Broad, serrated foliage. From Albany district, WA. One of showiest banksias, but not widely adaptable. 2–3 m x 2 m. Shape **2**.

B. collina (hill banksia). Slender, dark-green foliage; plump honey-coloured brushes overlaid with styles like fine burnished wire. Prefers part shade. Spreading growth to 2 m. In moist gullies, to 3 m x 2 m. Shape **3**.

B. ericifolia, dome of closely set, fine, dark glossy foliage decked with 25 cm copper-orange brushes, autumn and winter. From East Coast exposed sandstone ridges, but adapts to inland. 3–4 m x 3–4 m. Shape **4**.

B. hookerana (acorn banksia). Heads taper to acorn shape. Silvery buds open to golden-orange with slender, serrated foliage 13 cm to 21 cm. Prefers dry summers, light soil. 2–3 m x 3 m. Shape **2**.

Bauera rubioides (Dog rose). Spreading semi-prostrate shrub, sparse foliage, dainty pink flowers like inch-wide umbrellas scattered over for most of year. Found along creek banks. Prefers moist position, some shade. 1–2 m x 2 m. Shape **5**.

B. sessiliflora, showy bauera. Flowers are close to stem, rather than pendulous, and profuse toward ends of branches; deep pink to magenta. Moist, sheltered position. 1–2 m x 2 m.

Bauhinia galpinii. Spreading shrub, brick-red flowers from late summer through autumn. Stands moderate frost only. D 2–3 m x 2–3 m. Prune after flowering, method **a**. Shape **5. S–H.**

Beaufortia purpurea. Adaptable, long flowering little shrub with small, closely set foliage; tiny crimson bottlebrushes. 1 m x 1 m. Shape **2**.

B. sparsa, showy shrub with larger, brighter brushes, mostly late summer. From warm, sheltered swamps, but adapts well. 1–2 m x 1 m.

Begonia. Tree Begonia. Long flowering caney shrubs with handsome foliage, useful for shaded positions with reasonable moisture. Flowers from late spring to autumn. Protect from frost and wind. Prune only if straggly, late winter, method **b**. 1–2 m x 1 m. Shape **3**.

Berberis. Compact shrubs for cool and temperate areas. If necessary prune to shape in winter, method **d**, then tip prune in spring. Shape **4**.

B. darwinii, small, glossy, deep green foliage, pendulous, lily-of-the-valley-like orange flowers in winter and spring, purple autumn berries. E 2 m x 1–2 m.

B. thunbergii atropurpurea, purple bronze foliage, brightening in autumn. D 1.5 m x 1.3 m. S–M.

B. thunbergii atropurpurea nana, dwarf version of above. D .5 m x .7 m.

B. thunbergii Kellers, light green foliage, splashed red and white, maturing to green and white. D 1–1.7 m x 1.3 m.

Bird Flower see *Strelitzia*.

Bird of Paradise see *Caesalpinia gilliesii*.

Boronia. Best in light, sandy soil (preferably with moistened peatmoss added to retain moisture) undisturbed by cultivation. Most varieties need light shade, especially in warmer temperate areas. Light pruning after flowering improves looks, can prolong life on short-lived types. Shape **3**.

B. denticulata, comparatively adaptable species from WA. Slender, toothed leaves; pink flowers, mid-winter to late spring. To 1 m x 1 m.

B. heterophylla (Red boronia). Cupped, rosy red flowers, spring. Deep green foliage. Needs moist soil. Short-lived, but quick growing. Raise from seed, or strike 5 cm tip cuttings about December. Compact, to 1.5 m x 1 m.

B. ledifolia (Sydney boronia). Low-branching pyramid of starry pink flowers, mid-winter to early spring. Once established, tolerates dry conditions. Seems best in poor bush sand with a light layer of leafmould. 0.5–1 m x 0.5–1 m.

B. megastigma (Brown boronia). Noted for perfume, fine foliage, and sprays of globular brown flowers with yellow inner side. Needs the same peaty soil as *B. heterophylla*, about half sun, or broken sunlight, and protection from wind. It may die out after two years and is replaced quickly from seed or cutting. Cuttings are said to make longer-lived plants. (There is also an all-yellow variety, *lutea*.) 1–1.5 m x 0.5–1 m.

B. pinnata, finely divided leaves, terminal heads of cupped rose-pink flowers, spicy aroma. Often found in same spots as *B. ledifolia*, but also extends into shaded, moist valleys where growth is more profuse. 1–2 m x 1–2 m. Taller in shade.

B. serrulata (Native rose). Diamond-shaped foliage on lateral stems, crowned in spring with rosy pink flowers. Hard to establish in cultivation. Grows naturally in warm, sheltered pockets along the East Coast sandstone ridges, usually with light protection, and a good mulch of leafmould. 0.5 m x 0.5 m.

Bottlebrush (*Callistemon*). They grow in over-wet soils, but have good tolerance to dryness. Keep compact by pruning just below brush as stamens begin to fall before new growth emerges from tip.

C. citrinus, crimson bottlebrush. Erect tree; lance-shaped leaves; silky, crimson brushes; mid-winter to mid-spring. 2–3 m x 2 m. Shape **2**.

C. viminalis, variety Hanna Ray, weeping bottlebrush with large scarlet pendulous brushes. 4–5 m x 3 m. Shape **1**.

C. viminalis variety, Captain Cook dwarf bottlebrush. Useful variety apparently derived from *C. viminalis*. To about 2 m x 1–1.5 m, with large semi-pendulous brushes, spring. Shape **1**.

Bouvardia. Soft wooden shrubs for positions protected from heavy frost. During summer and autumn they display dainty heads of waxy tubular flowers in white, pink salmon, red and crimson. Cut to one-third of height in late winter and mulch with compost. Semi-deciduous. 1 m x 0.7 m. Shape **3**.

B. humboldtii, glossy foliage and larger fragrant white flowers and is not pruned as heavily. E 1–2 m x 1 m.

Brachysema lanceolata (Swan River Pea). Dark foliage, and large smoky crimson pea flowers in winter and spring, all but the coldest districts. Prune after flowering, method **b**. E 1–1.7 m x 1–1.3 m. Shape **4**.

Broom see *Cytisus* and *Spartium*.

Browallia jamesonii see *Streptosolen*.

Brunfelsia bonodora (Syn *latifolia*) (Yesterday, Today and Tomorrow). Fragrant spring flowers open deep blue, fade to pale

Abutilon megapotamicum variegatum

Berberis darwinii

Cantua buxifolia

Bauhinia galpinii

Brassaia arboricola

Cotinus (smokebush)

lavender then white, light green foliage, evergreen in warm climates. All but coldest districts. 2–3 m x 1–2 m. Light prune after flowering, method **a.** Shape **4. S–M.**

Buddleia (Summer Lilac). Quick-growing shrub for all climates, needs hard winter pruning, method **b.** Shape **2.**

B. salvifolia, winter-flowering, upright heads of pale lilac flowers and rigid crinkly foliage, prune after flowering. E 2–3 m x 2–3 m.

B. veitchiana, long-stemmed sprays of lilac blue flowers in spring and summer. Also a form with variegated foliage. Both semi-deciduous. 3 m x 2–3 m.

Burchellia bubalina *(Syn capensis).* For warm climates, stemless orange red tubular bells, through spring into summer. Prune lightly after flowering, method **a.** E 1.7 m x 1.3 m. Shape **4.**

Buxus (Box). Tidy, small-foliaged evergreen, attractive all year round in all climates.

B. sempervirens, used for low box hedges in formal gardens or trimmed to low dome or other shape, untrimmed. E 1–2 m x 1–1.3 m. Prune when needed, method **d.** Shape **4.**

B. sempervirens aurea marginata, lower growing variegated form of above. E 1 m x 0.75 m. S–M.

Caesalpinia gilliesii (Bird of Paradise) *(poinciana gilliesii).* Fern-like foliage, heads of yellow flowers with prominent scarlet stamens in late spring, early summer. Often longer flowering in tropics. Stands fairly heavy frost. D 3 m x 3 m. Tip prune new growth if needed. Shape **2.**

Calliandra. Silky tassel-like flowers above fine dense foliage. May be pruned after flowering, method **a.** Shape **2.**

C. tweedieii, previously *Inga pulcherrima.* Crimson tassels in early spring and early autumn. E 3 m x 2 m.

C. portoricensis, white tassels in early summer. E 3 m x 1 m.

C. heterocephalus, large scarlet flower heads to 8 cm across set above the comparatively coarse foliage on long arching branches, mainly during spring and summer — more suitable to tropical or warmer temperate climates. E 2 m x 3 m.

Callistemon (Bottlebrush). Will grow in over-wet soils, and also tolerate dryness. Keep compact by pruning just below brush as stamens begin to fall before new growth emerges from tip.

C. citrinus (Crimson bottlebrush). Erect tree; lance-shaped leaves; silky, crimson brushes; mid-winter to mid-spring. 2–3 m x 2 m. Shape **2.**

C. viminalis, variety Hanna Ray, weeping bottlebrush with large scarlet pendulous brushes 4–5 m x 3 m. Shape **1.**

C. viminalis variety, Captain Cook dwarf bottlebrush. Useful variety apparently derived from *C. viminalis.* To about 2 m x 1–1.5 m, with large semi-pendulous brushes, spring. Shape **1.**

Calluna (Heather). Winter–spring flowering plant for cool soil and acid conditions, for cool to temperate areas. Shape **4.**

C. vulgaris, numerous varieties from

10 cm–1 m high. Trim lightly after flowering.

Calytrix alpestris (Snow myrtle). Stubby growth, heath-like foliage. Pink buds, starry white flowers. Prefers moist, peaty soil. 1 m x 1 m. Shape **3.**

C. fraseri (Summer fringe myrtle). Shrub with spreading branches, tiny foliage, starry lilac or purple flowers, summer. A WA species, found both in peaty swamps and fairly dry sand, prefers warm, sheltered positions. 0.5–1 m x 1 m.

C. scabra (Rough fringe myrtle). Pink or white flowers with long, hair-like awns to sepals. Prefers sand. 1–1.5 m x 1.5 m.

C. tetragona, fine-petalled white flowers, followed by flower-like red calyces. Minute foliage crowds woody stems. All States. Open, sandy areas. 1–1.5 m x 1.5 m.

Cantua buxifolia. Previously *C. dependans,* Sacred Flower of the Incas. Arching growth, pendulous clusters of tubular apricot-buff and rosy purple bells. Prune lightly after the winter–spring flowering, method **b.** All but coldest districts. 1 m x 1 m. Shape **1.**

Cassia arte misioides (Silver cassia). Compact growth, fine silvery foliage studded with buttercup-like flowers, spring. Sunny, well-drained position. 1–2 m x 1–2 m. Shape **4.**

C. eremophila, desert cassia. Needle-like but not prickly foliage, bright yellow flowers, mid-winter to late spring. Warm, dry situations. 2–3 m x 1.5 m.

C. bicapsularis, previously *C. candolleanda.* Massed with large yellow flowers in autumn. More compact if pruned after flowering, method **c.** Shape **4.**

Ceanothus arnoldii (Californian Lilac). Light blue flower heads in spring, cool to temperate areas. Prune after flowering, method **a** or **b.** E 2 m x 1.5–2 m. Shape **2.**

Ceratostigma. Deep blue small flowers in summer and autumn. Foliage colours in autumn. Prune back to about 25 cm in winter. Temperate and tropical. D 1 m x 1 m. Shape **4.**

Cestrum. Soft wooded shrubs for temperate and tropical areas — now officially including the *Habrothamnus.* Prune late winter, method **b.**

C. auranticum, suckering shrub with pendulous clusters of golden flowers in spring and summer. E 2–3 m x 2–3 m. Shape **1.**

C. elegans, previously *Habrothamnus elegans,* almost continuously with bunches of tubular red flowers and sometimes poisonous red berries. The larger and brighter flowered type frequently sold is correctly *C. newelli.* E 2–3 m x 2–3 m. Shape **1.**

C. nocturnum, 'Night Shade'. Clusters of greenish cream slender tubes, heavily fragrant at night. Flowers spasmodically on new wood from spring to autumn. E 1–2 m x 1–2 m. Shape **3.**

Chaenomeles (Flowering quince, cydonia or japonica.) Suckering shrubs, colourfully and decoratively clustered with waxy long-lasting blossoms during winter and early spring. Varieties include *moerloosi,* pink and white; *nivalis,* pure white; *rosea,* pink; *rubra grandiflora,* rich orange red. All

Brunsfelsia calycina

Calliandra tweedieii

Chaenomeles rubra grandiflora

Chaenomeles nivalis

Ceanothus arnoldii

Daphne cneorum

flower best on older wood, but prune lightly after flowering, method **b.** 1.7–2 m x 1.3–2 m. Shape **3.**

Cherry see *Prunus.*

Cherry Pie see *Heliotropium.*

Chinese Lantern see *Abutilon.*

Choisya ternata. Dark green glossy foliage, clusters of scented orange blossom-like flowers in spring and often again in summer. Stands heavy frosts. Prune lightly after flowering, method **a.** E 1 m x 1 m. Style **4. S–M.**

Chorizema cordatum (WA flame pea). Bushy semi-prostrate little shrub covered with slender spikes of orange-red pea flowers with a purple blotch in yellow-zoned centre; spring flowering. Cut back about one-third as flowers finish. Best in full sun. 1 m x 1 m. Shape **4.**

Christmas Bush. Each State has its own Christmas Bush. NSW, *Ceratopetalum gummiferum.* Grows in humid Eastern gullies, but needs fairly warm, sunny position to colour well by Christmas. The red calyces follow small, creamy spring flowers. Prune lightly in January before new growth appears, then feed with blood and bone or light dressing of fowl manure. Control leaf curl by spraying with two tablespoons white oil plus one teaspoon malathion–50 gallons of water. 5 m x 3 m. Shape **3.**

Prostanthera lasianthos, Victorian Christmas bush. Sprays small white purple-throated bells; lance-shaped foliage. In moist soil, sheltered position will grow in competition with other trees. 3–5 m x 3 m. Shape **3.**

Nuytsia floribunda, WA Christmas bush. Massed brushes of rich orange flowers. Hard to cultivate, as is parasitic on roots of host plants. Couch grass seed is planted with those of the nuytsia to provide a temporary host. Usually found in damp, sandy soils. 5–8 m x 2–3 m. Shape **2.**

Bursaria spinosa, Tasmanian Christmas bush. Spiky, small-foliaged shrub; large sprays of creamy, fragrant flowers. Sometimes known as blackthorn.

Cistus (Rock Rose). Small drought-resisting shrub. Sage-like foliage and poppy-like flowers in spring. All except humid tropical districts, good salt resistance. Varieties: *brilliancy,* deep rose with maroon blotch at base of each petal; *laurifolius,* broader foliage, crepey white flowers with yellow centre. Prune after flowering, method **a.** E 1 m x 1 m. Shape **4. S–H.**

Clerodendron ugandense (Blue Butterfly Bush). Sparse shrub, small summer and autumn flowers have both royal and light blue petals with prominent stamens. Cut well back in winter, method **c.** Temperate and warm climates. E 3 m x 2 m. Shape **2.**

Clethra arborea (Lily of the Valley Tree). Woody shrub, sprays of fragrant white flowers like lily of the valley, in late spring or early summer. Needs good deep soil, temperate areas. Prune after flowering, method **a.** E 3 m x 2 m. Shape **3. S–L**

Coleonema pulchrum. Previously *Diosma.* A dome of tiny pink starry flowers in spring. Fine, spicy foliage. All but coldest climates. Prune after flowering, method **d.** 1–1.5 m x 1–1.7 m. Shape **4.**

C. pulchrum nana E 0.5–0.7 x 1 m.

Coprosma repens. Adaptable shrub, rounded leathery glossy foliage, especially resistant to sea spray, city dust and fumes, full sun or total shade. All but coldest climates. Grows to 2–3 m and as wide, but prune to size or shape needed, method **d.** Shape **4.**

Cordyline australis. Rosette of slender rigid strap-like leaves for feature planting, rockeries, etc. Remains about 1.3 m high, similar width for several years then develops trunk, eventually to 3 m or more. No pruning — trim off old foliage.

C. stricta, dull green foliage, shorter and broader than above, quicker to gain height with slender caney growth to 4 m, eventually branching. May be cut to induce lower growth.

Cornus (Dogwood.) Hundreds of species, some grown for autumn foliage and others for beautiful spring flower bracts. No regular pruning needed — cutting occasional flower bracts, method **a,** induces new growth. Shape **2.**

C. florida, varieties have the large showy white or pink flower bracts in spring. These eventually develop small tree form, method **d.** 4–5 m x 3 m. Shape **2.**

C. baileyii and *C. sanguinea* are grown mainly for their beautiful autumn foliage and deciduous purple-bronze winter branches. Shape **3.** *C. baileyii* shows downy grey under the leaves. Both grow to 4 m high and about 2 m wide. Cool or cooler temperate areas. Shape **3.**

Corokia (Wire Netting Bush). Unusual twisted wiry stems and small foliage with grey reverse popular for bonsai—withstands salty winds. Prune only for shape. E 1–2 m x 1–1.5 m. Shape **2.**

Correa alba (White Correa). Tough little plant from exposed sea coast; rounded grey-green foliage, starry white flowers, winter. 0.5 m x 0.5 m. Shape **2.**

C. reflexa (Native Fuchsia). Shrub with pendulous, rather leathery bells to 5 cm long, mostly in winter. Numerous varieties with colours ranging pale green to red, or red with green tops. Leaves also vary. Prefers moist conditions similar to brown and red boronia, to which it is related. 1–1.5 m x 1–1.5 m.

Corylus (Filbert or Hazelnut). Small trees with pendulous catkins — for cool to cool temperate climates. Prune in winter, only when needed, for shape. Shape **3.**

C. avellana aurea, with gold foliage. D 3–5 m x 2–3 m.

C. avellana contorta (Crazy Filbert or Harry Lauder's Walking Stick Tree). Corkscrewed stems, to 2–3 m in moist, cool positions, but usually grown as container plant, 1 m high and as wide. Also favourite bonsai subject.

C. avellana purpurea, adaptable plant with purple-bronze foliage. D 3–5 m x 2–3 m.

Cotinus coggygria (Rhus cotinus or *Smoky Rhus).* Dense rounded foliage, small yellow flowers, then feathery pannicles of smoky-brown seed heads in late spring. Variety *purpurea* has deep purple-bronze foliage. Cool and temperate — winter prune,

method **c,** if necessary. D 2–3 m x 2–3 m. Shape **2.**

Cotoneaster. Numerous varieties from prostrate dwarf to small trees. Evergreen species suit cool and temperate areas. Deciduous types berry better in cooler districts. S–M.

C. franchetti, pendulous growth, orange-red berries, good hedge subject. E 3 m x 2–3 m. Shape **1.**

C. horizontalis, tiny glossy foliage, flat herringbone-like growth — red berries. Grows naturally to about 1 m, spreading or trailing to 2 m, but may be trained or espaliered upwards. Shape **5.**

C. horizontalis hodginsii, miniature form of above. D 0.3 m x 1–1.3 m. Shape **5.**

C. horizontalis variegata, silvery-margined form of above.

C. harroviana, leathery foliage, pink flowers, red berries that hold throughout winter. Unpruned grows to 5 m and as wide. Shape **1.**

C. microphylla, small glossy foliage, red berries. E 1–3 m x 1–2 m. Shape **3.**

C. pannosa, small oval silvery-backed foliage, red berries on pendulous outer growth. E 3–4 m x 3–5 m. Shape **1.**

C. parneyii, prominent foliage often colouring in autumn with large clusters of red berries. E 2–3 m x 2–3 m. Shape **1.**

C. pendula hillierii, attractive trailing type, round glossy foliage and red berries — good rockery subject. E 0.3 m x 1–1.3 m. Shape **5.**

C. serotina, quick-growing, pendulous, large clusters of lasting red berries. E 3 m x 3 m. Cotoneasters may be pruned in winter as berries finish. New late spring growth may be shortened back so that berries are not hidden. Shape **1.**

Crab Apple see *Malus.*

Crape Myrtle (*Lagerstroemia*). Showy late summer flowering, large shrubs or small trees, for all but coldest districts — often autumn foliage and smooth silvery-bronze trunks. Allowed to grow naturally they make attractive sparse-foliaged trees with terminal crepey-petalled flower clusters. For more flower and compact shrubby form, prune in winter, method **c.** All D. Pruned 2–3 m x 2–3 m. Shape **2.**

L. eavesii, large clusters of pale mauve flowers.

L. flos-reginae, bright pink, natural growth, tall.

L. heliotrope beauty, deep heliotrope.

L. indica alba, white.

L. indica rubra, tall vigorous grower in warm areas.

Crotolaria agatiflora (Bird Flower), previously *C. laburnifolia.* Blue-green foliage and long spikes of large greenish yellow pea flowers like small birds hanging by their beaks — flowers from late spring to early winter. Prune in late winter, method **b.** Stands all but severe frosts. E 2–3 m x 2 m. Shape **2.**

C. sempervirens, sparse shrub, large rounded foliage, spikes of large bright golden-yellow pea flowers in winter. Prune after flowering, method **a.** E 3 m x 2–3 m.

Crowea exalata (Small Crowea). Branching plant with slender leaves. Starry pink flowers are profuse in summer, but continue almost all year. Adaptable. 0.3 m x 0.5 m. Shape **3**.

C. salingna (eriostemon crowei), Red Wax Flower. Resembles large-flowered eriostemon, with lance-shaped, green-to-bronze leaves and large, waxy, saucer-shaped flowers, mostly in winter. Adapts to a variety of conditions, even flowering well just behind ocean beaches on East Coast. 0.75 m x 0.75 m.

Cuphea hyssopifolia. Compact tiny foliage, spangled with minute purple star-like flowers for many months. All but the coldest climates. E 0.5 m x 0.5 m. Shape **4**.

C. ignea (Cigarette Plant), previously *C. platycentra*. Low spreading shrub for temperate and warmer climates, continuous show of pendulous tubular orange-red flowers 3 cm long with ashen tip. Sun or part shade. E 0.5 m x 0.7 m. **S–M**.

C. micropetla, previously *C. jorullensis*. Caney growth, slender foliage, 7 cm, tubular creamy-yellow flowers partly sheathed in red calyx, during late summer and autumn. Temperate and semi-tropical. Prune late winter, method **d**. E 1 m x 1 m. Shape **4**.

Cupressus see Conifer Section.

Cydonia see *Chaenomeles*.

Cytisus. Resembling Spanish Broom but with softer growth— for cool and temperate climates. Prune after spring flowering, method **b**. Shape **1**.

C. albus, small white flowers. E 3 m x 2–3 m.

C. fragrans, bright yellow and fragrant. E 2 m x 1–2 m.

C. Lilac Time, soft lilac. E 2–3 m x 1.5–2 m.

C. Lord Lambourne, crimson and yellow. E 1–2 m x 1–2 m.

C. praecox, a dense dome of gracefully arching stems packed with small creamy yellow pea flowers in spring. 1–1.5 m similar width.

Dais continifolia (Pompon Tree). Small semi-deciduous tree covered for about two weeks in early summer with unusual pompons of pale mauve-pink flowers. Prune in winter for shape, if needed. Temperate and warm climates. 3–4 m x 2–3 m. Shape **2**.

Dampiera stricta. Deep blue flowers 1 cm across, brownish-green stems. Sparse foliage. Any light soil with part shade. Flowers spring–summer. 30 cm x 20 cm. Shape **3**.

D. diversifolia, charming blue-flowered ground cover for fairly moist part shade. Makes 60 cm mat of deep, rich blue, mostly spring, but long flowering. 5 cm x 50–60 cm. Shape **5**.

Daphne odora rubra (Red Daphne). Has reddish purple buds and back of petals. Charming shrub with dark glossy slender foliage and heads of cleanly-cut stars with a frosty pink flush. Very fragrant. Flowers during winter and early spring. Needs good drainage, light lime-free loamy soil (if heavy, add leafmould or peatmoss and coarse sand). Keep surface mulched to avoid caking and need for cultivation. Give an occasional good soaking during dry conditions, but avoid constant wet surface and over-feeding. More

daphnes are killed by kindness than collar rot, which is reputed to be their main enemy. Prune by cutting up to two-thirds of the flowers, method **a**, and 'heading back' runaway growths. Broken sunlight or morning sun suits them best. Mealy bugs or scale sometimes attack. Cool to temperate climate. E 0.5 m–1.3 m x 1–1.5 m. Shape **4**. **S–L**.

D. cneorum, slow-growing spreading plant with heads of fragrant rose-pink flowers in late spring. Cool to cool-temperate. E 0.5 m x 0.75–1 m. Shape **4**.

D. genkwa, like a small lilac, with heads of slightly fragrant flowers topping slender rigid deciduous stems. Needs light loamy acid soil. D 1 m x 1 m. Shape **3**.

Plain *D. odora* has white flowers, with comparatively caney growth. Also a variegated variety with yellow margined leaves. Shape **4**.

Datura cornigera (Angel's Trumpet) also **Brugmansia knightii**. Pendulous, creamy-white fragrant trumpets about 22 cm long. Several forms in cultivation especially *D. meteloides* with violet-flushed smaller trumpets. All mostly spring and summer flowering. Cool to tropic climates. Prune in winter, method **a**. E 2–3 m x 2–3 m. Shape **1**.

Deutzia (Wedding Bells). Caney shrubs flowering late in spring. Prune after flowering, method **b**, tip prune new shoots when 1–1.5 m high. Shape **1**. **S–M**.

D. candidissima, long sprays of double white flowers. D 2–3 m x 2 m.

D. rosea flore pleno, double white, flushed outside with pink. D 2–3 m x 2 m.

Dievilla see *Weigela*.

Dillwynia ericifolia (Heath Parrot Pea). Spreading small shrub, fine foliage, brilliant clusters orange flowers, spring, early summer. Best in light shade of tall gums. 1 m. Shape **4**.

D. juniperina, needle-like foliage, terminal clusters of yellow and brown flowers, late spring, early summer. Fairly open, sunny position. 1 m. Shape **5**.

Diosma see *Coleonema*.

Dogwood see *Cornus*.

Drejerella guttata (Shrimp Plant) or **Beloperone**. Small caney but dense shrubs with series of overlapping bronze-pink shell-like bracts suggesting a prawn or lobster tail. Small pale lilac flowers emerge on the hooded side. Temperate to tropical. Prune in winter, method **b**. E 1 m x 1 m. Shape **3**. *D. casheri*, has yellow bracts.

Dryandra formosa (Showy Dryandra). One of the loveliest of these unusual WA shrubs. Domed, silk-stamened yellow flowers 8 cm across are surrounded by a swirl of slender, glossy leaves, serrated to the midrib. The dryandras resemble South African proteas, to which they are related. Prefer dry summer climate and gritty soil. 3–4 m x 2 m. Shape **3**.

D. proteoides, has the typical protea bracts cupped behind the stamens; bronze yellow. Thin, erect shrub; finely serrated foliage. 2–3 m x 2 m.

Duranta repens. Thorny shrub, small

bright green foliage, pendulous small lavender blue flowers and orange berries, mainly in autumn and winter. Used mainly as tough hedge, temperate and tropical. E 3–4 m x 2–3 m, or pruned to any size, method **d**. Shape **1**.

Elaeagnus pungens aurea. Stiff glossy dark green and yellow variegated foliage. All climates. E 1–2 m x 1–2 m. Prune for shape in winter, tip prune later. Shape **5**. **S–H**.

Epacris impressa ('Common Heath'). Erect plant with small, closely set foliage and brush-like spike of closely packed, small white, pink or rose bells near top of each stem. Light, fairly moist soil; sun or dappled shade. Flowers winter and spring. Shape **3**.

E. longiflora ('Fuchsia Heath'). Sprays of pendulous, glass-like red bells tipped cream. Small, pointed foliage clings to arching bracts. Often found gracefully suspended where there is seepage. Flowers most of year. Best with part shade. 0.5–1 m x 1–1.5 m. Shape **5**.

E. microphylla ('Coral Heath'). Starry-faced, closely set white or pink-flushed bells, winter and spring. Often in sedgy areas. 1 m x 0.5 m. Shape **3**.

Erica. Heath-like plants for well-drained but moist acid soils where water easily penetrates below their close surface root mat during summer. Avoid cultivation or heavy feeding. Prune back lightly after winter–spring flowering, method **d**. Tip prune young plants. Best in cool or cooler temperature climates. Flower and plant size varies with variety. Shape **3**.

E. caniculata, earlier known as *E. melanthera* is massed with pale lilac flowers the size of a match-head. E 2–3 m x 2 m.

E. wilmoreana, has pink tubular flowers 4 cm long with comparatively slender growth, 1–2 m tall and to 1 m wide. Hundreds of species and hybrids with growth and flowers ranging between these species.

Eriostemon myoporoides ('Long-Leafed Waxflower'). Rounded shrub with slender foliage, starry pink-flushed flowers along stems, late winter to late spring. Variety of soils; open positions or below tall trees. Prune after flowering, tip prune new growth. 1–1.5 m x 1–1.5 m. Shape **4**.

E. lanceolatus (Pink Waxflower). Open, waxy pink flowers 30 cm across; long, slender blue-green foliage. Delightful but not easy to cultivate. Try warm, sheltered position among sandstone boulders. Flowers late winter, early spring. 1–1.5 m x 1 m. Shape **3**.

E. buxifolia, straggly but charming; white flowers, pink buds. Oval, dark green leaves. Prefers coastal areas. Spring flowering. 0.5–1 m x 0.5 m. Shape **3**.

E. verrucosa (Bendigo Wax or Fairy Wax). Short, stubby leaves, generous spikes of waxy flowers. Pink buds open white, spring. Prefers deep rich soil. 1–2 m x 1 m. Shape **5**.

Erythrina crista-galli (Boar's Tooth). Caney growth with long spikes of 7–8 cm long crimson pea flowers during summer. Cut well back to within few inches of woody trunk or heavy branches in winter. Temperate to tropic. D 3–4 m x 2–3 m. Shape **2**.

Cytissus scoparius hybrid

Coleonema pulchrum 'Nana'

Euphorbia pulcherrima (poinsettia)

Euphorbia wulfenii

Pachystachys lutea in tropical garden

Eupatorium megalophyllum

Escallonia. Glossy evergreens for cool to temperate areas. Prune after flowering, method **a**, rejuvenate occasionally by cutting well back during winter.

E. macrantha, clusters of small waxy rosy pink flowers during late spring and summer. E 3 m x 2–3 m. Shape **2**.

E. montevidenis, tall grower with white flowers sometimes flushed pink. E 4–5 m x 2–3 m. Shape **2**.

E. rubra pygmea, deep rosy-red flowers. E 1 m x 1 m. Shape **4**.

Eugenia leubmanni. Correctly *Syzygium leubmanni,* dense glossy foliaged shrub with small pendulous coral-red berries and pink new growth. Frost tender. E 2–4 m x 3–4 m. Trim new growth if necessary. Shape **4**.

Euonymus. Numerous species. Those useful for small gardens are compact evergreens, mostly with variegated foliage. They suit any climate including seaside, and may be clipped to any shape or size within the limits shown here. Shape **4**. **S–M.**

E. japonicus argentea, silver variegated foliage. E 3 m x 2 m.

E. latifolius albus, glossy deep green foliage, margined white. E 2 m x 1.3 m.

E. ovatus aureas, bright yellow new growth, centre of leaves later deep green, best colour in sun. Excellent tub specimens. E 1–2 m x 1–2 m.

Euphorbia. Hundreds of species from thorny ball-like succulents to trees. Those mentioned need protection from heavy frost.

F. fulgens, slender arching branches clustered with dainty brilliant scarlet rounded flower-like bracts. Needs warm position. Prune after flowering, method **b**. D 1.5–2 m x 1.5 m. Shape **3**.

E. pulcherrima (Poinsettia). Large brilliant scarlet bracts surrounding the green and yellow flower clusters in mid-winter. There are also pink and creamy-yellow variations. Prune after flowering, method **c**. D 3 m x 2–3 m. Shape **2**.

E. pulcherrima Henrietta Eck, a beautiful rich crimson, double with high-crested centre, sometimes single under poor growing conditions. Prune as above. Shape **2**.

E. splendens (Crown of Thorns). Semi-trailing plant for elevated planter boxes, etc. but when supported reaches 1–1.5 m. Clusters of bright orange-scarlet bracts along the thorny stems in winter. No pruning needed. D 0.5 m x 1–2 m. Shape **5**.

E. wulfenii, compact soft shrubby plant with heads of numerous small green and yellow bracts in winter and spring. Trim lightly after flowering. E 1 m x 1–1.5 m. Shape **4**.

Eupatorium megalophyllum. Dull green foliage, huge heads of fluffy mauve-blue flowers in early spring. Frost-free climates. Prune after flowering, method **c**. E 2 m x 2 m. Shape **4**.

Exochorda racemosa (Pearl Bush). Pearly white flowers like apple blossom with new lime-green foliage decoratively clustering the slender branches in spring. Prune lightly after flowering, method **a**. Cool and temperate areas. D 2–3 m x 2–3 m. Shape **2**.

Fatsia japonica. Dramatic plant, caney

growth crowned with handsome dark glossy green hand-shaped foliage. Stands sun, shade, indoor conditions and fairly heavy frost. E 1.5 m x 1–1.3 m not pruned.

Feijoa sellowiana (Pineapple Guava). Adaptable, compact and quick-growing, with rounded leathery foliage and in spring displaying pompons of crimson stamens backed by small still white petals. Guava-like fruits are stored after they fall until emitting a pineapple aroma. Any but coldest districts. Prune in winter if necessary, method **a** or **d**. E 4 m x 3 m. Shape **4. S–M.**

Fire Plant see *Acalypha.*

Forsythia viridissima. Shrubs massed with brilliant yellow, starry-petalled, open bell flowers in spring. Needs frosty winter to flower well. Prune after flowering, method **b**. D 6–8 m x 5 m. Shape **3.**

Frangipani *(Plumeria acutifolia).* For warmer temperate and tropical areas, large heads of fragrant, waxy white, yellow-centred summer blooms. Also several shades of pink. Prune in winter–early spring only when necessary to reduce size, removing entire branch or segment. Growth and flower come only from outer tips. Replacements may be started from segments, or small branches callused for a few weeks in dry shade after cutting in late August, then staked 8–10 cm deep in just moist light soil in warm position. D 3–4 m x 2–3 m. Shape **2.**

P. obtusifolia, leaves and petals more rounded, flowers white rather than cream. For semi-tropical to tropical areas. 5 m x 4 m.

Fremontia californicum. A rather sparse large shrub or small tree sometimes used as a wall espalier. Leaves with 3 rounded lobes, dark green above, underneath downy grey, saucer shaped golden yellow flowers to 7 cm across in spring. 2 to 5 m x 1.5–2 m. Shape **6** or as espalier shape **5.**

Fuchsia. Are graceful pot and basket plants, and useful for summer colour in not too densely shaded garden areas. Stronger growing, darker-foliaged kinds will also grow in full sunlight. Shape **1.**

They adapt to most well-drained soils, doing better if heavy clayey loams are lightened with compost or in sand with peatmoss added, preferring slight liminess (pH 6–7) to very acid conditions.

PRUNING: This is normally done in late winter, but early autumn pruning in frost-free areas will usually produce blooms in spring rather than early to mid-summer. Method **c** is preferred for bush types, method **b** for basket varieties, shortening canes about at the basket edge. In both cases tip prune later.

FEED: After pruning. Scatter bone dust or rose food, applying about 1 tablespoonful per sq. m, repeat in six weeks, then give occasional applications of complete soluble plant foods when flowering commences.

WATERING: Let soil surface dry out then give a good soaking. Losses can occur during heatwave conditions due to lack of water.

PESTS: Under dry conditions, or if plants are under cover, watch for dull mottling caused by red spider mites or patches of silver mottling from thrips. Also check for

Euonymus ovatus

Exochorda racemosa

Hydrangea

Genista fragrans

Ilex aquifolium 'Aureo marginata'

Ilex aquifolium (English holly)

leaf-eating caterpillars or loopers. Remedies are given for these pests in the 'Pests' section, but for fuchsias avoid using Pyrethrum or Bioesmethrin as these damage some varieties.

Gardenia. Small, glossy-foliaged plants with very fragrant waxy white flowers, mostly during summer. They prefer warm frost-free but lightly shaded situations. Main problems associated with gardenias are bud drop which often occurs with cold changes, but sometimes a small weevil that punctures the bud or girdles its stem is responsible.

Yellowing of base foliage is also common and natural in spring. If all foliage is pale then try soaking around the plant with 1 teaspoon of Epsom Salts (magnesium sulphate) dissolved in 8–10 litres of water, then follow up every 4–6 weeks during the warmer months with complete water-soluble plant food. Nematode (eel worm) also causes general debility.

Pruning in early spring makes plants more compact but delays flowering. Plants are best renewed after 5 or 6 years.

G. augusta, listed previously as *G. jasminoides* and *G. florida*. It is the largest of the prolific long-flowering double species continuing from late spring to autumn. E 1–1.5 m x 1–2 m. Shape **3. S–M.**

G. augusta (Professor Pucci), is a little larger in flower and foliage than above but with a slightly shorter flowering period. E 1–2 m x 1–2 m. Shape **3.**

G. globosa (Bell Gardenia) see *Rothmannia*.

G. radicans, almost a miniature form of *G. augusta* with flowers 5 cm across. Ideal for rockeries, low containers or underplanting. E 0.3–0.5 m x 0.7–1 m. Shape **5.**

Garrya eliptica. Dark green, dense-foliaged shrub with velvety lime to mauve-grey catkins during winter and spring. These are only worthwhile from male plants. Best in cool and temperate districts. If necessary prune in spring, method **a.** E 3 m x 3 m. Shape **2.**

Genista fragrans. Masses of small fragrant golden-yellow pea flowers in mid-spring. Prune back before these form pods, method **d.** Temperate and cool areas. E 2 m x 1–2 m. Shape **3.**

Geraldton Wax (Chamelaucium uncinatum). Beautiful shrub, with needle-shaped foliage, branching heads of dainty pink teatree-like flowers. Long-lasting cut flower, and lasts on plant July to October.

Grows in limestone areas. But adapts to acid-light loam or sand. In sand, seems to thrive on plenty of water providing drainage is good, but generally prefers dry conditions.

Losses often due to root disturbance, especially movement of top-heavy bush. Set young plants at an angle, or prune back, to encourage low branching to make the plant self-bracing. After flowering, remove all but a few inches of flower stems. To about 2–3 m x 2–3 m. Shape **2.**

Gold Dust Plant see *Aucuba*.

Goldfussia isopbylla. Slender purple foliage, pale mauve bells, mainly in spring and summer. Prune after flowering, method

b. Temperate and cool climates. E 1 m x 1–1.5 m. Shape **3.**

Gordonia axillaris. Glossy-foliaged shrub with large single white crepey-petalled flowers with prominent gold centre stamens. As flowers age, stamens and petals fall intact and right way up to form a beautiful and long-lasting floral carpet. Flowers from autumn to spring. Old woody plants may be rejuvenated by cutting back to main branches in late winter then tip pruning new growth. Alternatively, remove lower branches to give small-tree character, especially for Japanese-type garden. Best in temperate climates, but have good frost and cold tolerance. No pruning needed. E 3–4 m x 3–4 m. Shape **2.**

Grevillea. Adaptable, long-flowering shrubs. Great diversity of form.

G. alpina, mountain grevillea. Small, downward-turned 1 cm leaves. An upright-foliaged form has red and yellow flowers; a prostrate one, red flowers. 1 m x 1 m. Shape **4.**

G. dellachiana, a compact garden variety; red and cream flowers. A variety of *G. alpina*. 0.5–1 m x 1 m. Shape **4.**

G. apiciloba, leaves have prickly lobes; toothbrush-type yellowish green flowers have almost black styles. Hot, dry conditions. 1–2 m x 1–2 m. Shape **2.**

G. asplenifolia, upright shrub; slender, serrated leaves, brushes of red flowers, winter and spring. Grows well in part shade. 3 m x 3 m. Shape **3.**

G. banksii (red form), large, rounded shrub; fern-like foliage topped by spiky red brushes, most of year. There is a white flowered form. Most soils; all but coldest districts. 2–3 m x 2–3 m.

G. baueri, small, spreading plant; smooth oval foliage, salmon-red flowers, late winter-spring. 1 m x 1 m. Shape **5.**

G. biternata. Mat of finely divided foliage, heads of creamy-white flowers, winter-spring. Excellent for well-drained, sunny banks. 30 cm high, spread 2–3 m. 0.3 m x 2 m. Shape **5.**

G. hookerana, spreading shrub, wiry, finely divided foliage; brilliant red brushes, most of year. Best with dry summer, but fairly adaptable. 2–3 m x 2–3 m. Shape **2.**

G. juniperina, prickly spider flower. Small shrub; fine dark foliage, clusters red flowers, spring and summer. Also a prostrate form. Most soils. 1–1.5 m x 1.5 m. Shape **3.**

G. punicea, red spider flower. Sparse shrub from East Coast; clusters of spidery, blood-red flowers, late winter–spring. Sun to half shade. 2–3 m x 1–2 m. Shape **3.**

G. rosmarinifolia, handsome, spreading plant; dark, needle-shaped foliage, red-cream flowers, late winter to early summer. Variety of soils, climates. Light pruning after flowering keeps it more compact. A dwarf form, 1.5–2 m x 2–3 m. Shape **2.**

G. triloba, wiry, trident foliage, large heads, scented white flowers, mostly in spring. Adaptable. 2–3 m high, can spread to 3 m. Shape **2.**

There are also numerous hybrid Grevilleas.

Robyn Gordon is one of the longest flowering and most popular of these. It has large, bright red brushes and fern-like foliage. To 1.5 m high and as wide.

Hakea. A wide range from dwarf shrubs to medium-sized trees, which adapt well to hot, dry conditions.

H. laurina (Pincushion Hakea). Small tree with foliage like blunt eucalyptus leaves, bronze when young. Spectacular flowers, set close on branches, are red cushions with cream stamens, late autumn–early winter. Needs wind protection, or to be surrounded with a barrow or so of rubble to anchor roots. 5–6 m. Shape **7.**

H. multilineata (Lovely Hakea). Veined foliage and pinkish-red brushes overlaid by fine, creamy stamens, winter–spring. Grows well in Perth, some parts of Adelaide. Performance patchy around Melbourne, hopeless along East Coast. 3 m x 2 m. Shape **1.**

H. salicifolia (syn. saligna) (Willow-Leafed Hakea). Quick-growing screen or windbreak. 'Willow' refers to leaf shape; growth is fairly erect. Bronze new growth, white flowers, 6–7 m x 3–5 m. Shape **2**, but stands regular cutting.

H. victoriae (Royal Hakea). Spectacular, decorative foliage and formation. Rounded, veined and spiked stemless leaves form cups or hoods around the pink flower clusters. 3 m x 3 m. Shape **3.**

Hebe. Previously *Veronica*. Compact shrubs useful for foundation and foreground planting in cool to temperate climates. Small brushes of white, pink or lavender flowers mainly in spring. Trim after flowering, method **d**, and tip prune new growth. Size varies from low spreading types such as *H. hartiana*, small glossy rounded *H. imperialis* to taller, fine-foliaged *H. parviflora* which reaches about 2–3 m. Shape **4. S–M.**

Heliotropium (Cherry Pie). Small shrubs or woody perennials noted for their aromatic summer flowers. Prune in late winter, method **b** or **c**. Shape **5.**

H. aureum, lavender flowers and low-spreading golden foliage. Best in sun. E 0.7 m x 0.7–1 m.

H. Lord Roberts, violet flowers with deep green to bronze foliage. E 1 m x 1 m.

Hibertia peduncularis. Fine-foliaged mat; yellow flowers like small buttercups, mostly spring. Wonderful companion for *Dampiera diversifolia*; similar conditions. 5 cm x 25–30 cm. Shape **5.**

H. stellaris, thin, bronze-green stems with fine foliage and a showy canopy of dainty apricot-orange, saucer-shaped flowers, mostly spring. 25 cm x 30 cm. Shape **5.**

H. stricta, strong-growing, adaptable, yellow-flowered small shrub. Likes light shade of tall trees. 0.75–1 m x 0.5 m. Shape **3.**

H. volubilis, tough-flowered climber found behind sandy beaches or in semi-rainforests. Yellow lassiandra-like blooms.

Hibiscus. The evergreen hibiscus *H. rosa sinensis* · varieties revel in warm humid tropical to temperate coastal districts but adapt to any area where frosts are not severe. Deciduous types such as *H. syriacus* are suitable for cold districts. Both types flower freely throughout summer. Shape **2**.

The evergreen hibiscus (*rosa sinensis* and hybrid types) in temperate climates are best pruned in early spring so that new growth is in warm conditions. Use method **a**, but for very compact growth, shorten back to a 10–15 cm stub, tip pruning new growth twice when 10–12 cm long. Leave some of the lesser stems uncut for earlier flowering. In tropical areas they can be pruned in late winter, then cut back again in January to encourage a flush of bloom carrying into winter.

Deciduous *H. syriacus* and *H. mutabilis* are pruned in winter, method **a**.

Herbaceous types are cut to ground level in winter.

Feed with complete fertiliser at pruning time. For larger blooms, use soluble plant foods occasionally when buds start.

See 'Pests' for small black hibiscus weevils, green or grey aphids on buds or leaf-eating caterpillars and grasshoppers, but do not use Malathion, Rogor, Lebaycid or Meta-Systox on hibiscus.

Holly see *Ilex.*

Holmskioldia sanguinea. Caney growth, sprays of coppery-red, bougainvillaea-like flower bracts that hold from autumn to spring. Prune when most flowers finish in spring, method **c**. Semi-deciduous. 2–3 m x 2 m. Shape **2**.

Honeysuckle see *Lonicera.*

Hovea elliptica. Oval-foliaged shrub, clustered with small, blue peaflowers, spring. Warm, sheltered position; half sun. 1–2 m. Shape **3**.

H. longifolia, narrow foliage, slender stems; small lilac pea-flowers, late winter to spring. Often found in heavily treed gullies, but adapts well. Several forms. 0.5–1 m. Shape **3**.

H. trisperma, showy WA species. Rough, big leaves; bright violet-blue flower, winter-spring. Adapts to variety of climates, all but heavy clay soil. Easily raised from seed. 1–2 m. Shape **3**.

Hydrangea. Bring early summer colour to shaded positions. Most varieties can also be grown in full sun, but blooms may then scorch during hot dry weather. Pruning best done July–August, method **b**, but cut vigorous canes down to lowest or second lowest pair of plump, double buds. These produce late spring flowers, while more slender ones make growth that flowers much later, or next season. Unflowered canes (terminating in a bud) are left uncut unless they tower raggedly.

If unpruned for several years, most double buds are high up on new growth coming from old canes. Either cut back heavily, sacrificing main display for a season, or correct over two years by cutting half the canes close to ground, encouraging new base growth.

Dwarf hydrangea. A few, such as *Parsifal*, flower at tips of previous season's canes without producing side buds. Here the canes that have flowered are cut to ground level about February to stimulate new growth.

COLOUR: The only stable hydrangea is white. Acid soils usually produce blues, or they are induced by scattering about 2 tablespoons of sulphate of aluminium or sulphate of iron around medium-sized bush, preferably about May, then early August, and in October.

Pink is induced by lime, in very acid soils about three-quarter cup of lime per sq. m in May and September. Over-liming causes yellowish foliage, needing iron chelates for correction. Complete changes are difficult in large bushes, and can result in pale, indefinite colours, especially the first season.

Vigour is improved by feeding with complete fertiliser or fowl manure at pruning time, and flower size by soluble plant foods when buds form. See mildew and cottony cushion scale.

Hypericum. Twiggy shrubs with summer flowers like large buttercups. For cool, temperate and semi-tropical areas. Prune late winter, method **b**. S–M .

H. moserianum tricolor, low growth, variegated leaves margined red, small 5 cm yellow flowers. E 0.5–1 m x 0.5–1 m. Shape **5**.

H. patulum henyri, larger, deeper yellow flowers, rounded growth. Foliage colouring in autumn. Semi-deciduous. 1.3 m x 1.3 m. Shape **4**.

Iboza riparia (Moschosma). Light green, felt-like musky foliage, feathery sprays of tiny, just mauve flowers in winter. Prune after flowering, method **a** or **c**. Temperate and tropical, resents heavy frosts. D 2–3 m x 2–3 m. Shape **2**.

Ilex (Holly). Handsome foliage and autumn-winter berries on female plants, suit cool and cool-temperate districts. May be trimmed to shape. Fallen leaves retain their sharp spines, so can be a pest when hand weeding. Shape **2**.

I. aquifolium (English Holly), traditional dark foliage, long-lasting small red berries on female plants — subject to scale in some humid coastal areas. E 5 m x 3–4 m.

I. aquifolium, silver variegated, beautiful foliage with bold silvery-white variegations, slower growing than plain green. E 2–3 m x 1–2 m.

I. cornuta (Chinese Holly), spiny but less indented than above, berries less prolific. Best grower in temperate climates. E 3–5 m x 2–3 m.

Indian Hawthorn see *Raphiolepis.*

Indigofera decora (Dwarf Wisteria). Suckering plant, blooms like short pink and white bunches of wisteria. All but coldest climates. Cut back older canes after flowering. D 0.5–1 m x 1 m. Shape **3**.

Inga see *Calliandra.*

Irisene. Soft-stemmed plants with colourful foliage for humid, temperate and tropical areas in sun or light shade. Trim or tip prune in spring, method **c** or **d**.

I. lindenii, slender bronze foliage with pinkish veining when exposed to sun. E 1 m x 1 m.

I. formosum, tapering but wider foliage than *lindenii*, reddish bronze. E 1.5 m x 1.5 m.

I. herbstii, rounded, waxy, crinkled, beetroot-red foliage with semi-translucent rose veining. Variety *aurea-reticulatum* has green foliage with cream veining, occasionally splashed red. E 1–1.5 m x 1 m.

Jacobinia pauciflora. Dark-foliaged shrub, massed with showy little red and yellow flowers during autumn and spring. Prune lightly after flowering, method **d**. Temperate to tropical. Needs frost protection. E 1 m x 0.7 m. Shape **4**.

Jasminium mesnyii (Yellow Jasmine, previously *J. primulinum*). Long arching canes, studded with yellow semi-double, primrose-like flowers in winter and spring. Use as large shrub, espalier-type climber for quick cover, or spillover. Prune after flowering, method **b**. Canes touching ground self-layer. Any climate. E 3 m x 3–4 m. Shape **1**.

Justicia coccinea see *Odontonema.*

Kalmia latifolia (American Mountain Laurel). Lovely, soft pink blooms with exquisite form, buds like clusters of pale pink jelly moulds, opening with the ten gracefully arched stamens appearing to hold the flowers in their shapely form like the ribs of an umbrella. Deep green laurel-like foliage. Related to rhododendrons, growing in similar soils and climates but is difficult to establish and subject to die-back in warmer coastal soils. Best in lightly broken sunlight. Growth slow, rarely exceeding 1.5 m but occasionally 2–3 m and 1.5 m wide in cool, moist climates. Pruning — remove only old flower heads or tip prune new growth. E. Shape **2**.

Kangaroo paw *(Anigozanthos).* Interesting flowers on slender stems rising from clumps of bold, strap-like foliage. Often from arid parts of Western Australia but in cultivation most respond well to feeding in autumn as new growth begins.

Kangaroo paw is comparatively dormant during dry summers of native habitats. Summer rains or watering can extend flowering period, but with *A. manglesii* can cause heavy losses. Shape **3**.

A. bicolor. Showy red and green type similar to *A. manglesii*, but smaller; to about 0.5 m. Does well in damp, peaty soils, preferably with some shade. Flowers in about 18 months from seed.

A. flavidus (Albany kangaroo paw). Strongest grower. Rigid foliage 1 m high, flower stems to 3 m. May be yellow, dull green, or red. Long lived, long flowering, even in wet summers of Eastern States. Takes about four years to flower from seed, but can be increased by dividing clumps in autumn. Best in moist soil, at least half sun.

A. manglesii, red and green kangaroo paw. Showiest species. Vivid green flowers with bright red, woolly stems and calyx. Stems to about 1 m. Comparatively short lived, even in Western Australia, where it often dies out after 4 or 5 years. Control fungus disease causing blackening of foliage and die-back by spraying with Bordeaux or general-purpose fungicides.

A. pulcherrima, golden kangaroo paw. Showy with 1 m reddish branching stems, golden-yellow flowers. Reasonably moist,

Kerria japonica

Kolkwitzia amabilis

Luculia gratissima

Laburnum vossii

Montanao mexicana

Lagerstroemia eavesii (crape myrtle)

light soil. Flowers in about 2½ years from seed.

A. rufus, red kangaroo paw. Similar to *A. pulcherrima*; deep red to burgundy flowers with lime tips and throat.

A. viridis, green kangaroo paw. Low clumps, smooth green foliage, short stems. Flowers bright metallic green to soft gold.

Kerria japonica flore pleno. Lightly suckering with double orange pompon-like flowers to 5 cm across, carried along slender upright canes in spring. Best in part shade, prune after flowering, method **b.** Cool and temperate areas. D 2 m x 1.5–2 m. Shape **3.**

Kolkwitzia amabilis (Beauty bush). Resembles a refined Abelia with bunches of soft pink bells gracefully arching the slender canes. Best in cool climates. May be pruned after flowering method **b.** D 2 m x 1.5 m. S–L.

Kunzea baxterii. Like a brilliant red, silky-stamened bottlebrush. Long flowering, mid-winter–late spring. From dry-summer region of WA, but adapts well. 1–1.5 m x 1 m. Shape **3.**

K. parvifolia. East coast species; clusters of fluffy mauve flowers. Prefers light soils, but otherwise easy. 1–2 m x 1 m.

K. pulchella. Striking WA species. Flower clusters like red flowering-gum blossom, early spring to summer. Small silver-grey foliage. Should suit inland districts with hot, dry summers. 2–3 m x 1–2 m.

Lagerstroemia see Crepe Myrtle.

Lantana. Long-flowering and drought and heat-resisting shrubs for all but the coldest regions — easily managed and should not be confused with the noxious wild *L. camara*. Keep compact by heavy late winter pruning, method **b.** Shape **4. S–H.**

L. chelsea gem, orange and red flowers. E 1.3 m x 1.5 m.

L. drap d'or, free-flowering golden yellow. E 1.3 m x 1.3 m.

Lambertia formosa (Mountain Devil). So called because of long-eared, peak-nosed woody seed capsules which follow coral-pink protea-like flowers. Foliage dark green, slightly spiky. Keep compact by occasional pruning. Prefers light soil, at least half sun to flower well. 1.5 m in exposed position to 3 m and as wide with shelter. Shape **3.**

Lasiandra see *Tibouchina* and *Melastoma*.

Lemon Scented Verbena see *Aloysia*.

Leonotis leonurus (Lion's Tail). Heads of velvety orange-red, salvia-like flowers from early summer to late autumn. Prune back in winter, method **c.** Temperate to tropical, stands seaside conditions. E 6–8 m x 5 m. Shape **2.**

Leptospermum see Tea-trees.

Leschenaultia biloba (Blue leschenaultia or Mirror of heaven). An incredibly blue gem from WA, a sheer joy in early spring, when the tiny foliage has a blue mantle of flowers about 2.5 cm across. Rarely lives more than a couple of years in cultivation, but even one flowering is worth it.

Plants set out in early spring, flower the next spring or 18 months from autumn-sown seed. December cuttings offer some flower the following spring.

It is longer lived in light soils mulched with a scree of pebbles, crushed sandstone, brick or tile; and lightly broken sunlight. Light pruning after flowering also helps. In autumn, a dusting with cotton-seed meal or blood and bone, or watering with seaweed extract, seems to improve results. No other feeding or mulching. To 0.75 m with similar spread. Shape **5.**

L. formosa, red leschenaultia. Cushion of bright red flowers, often early winter to late spring. Yellow and pinkish-red colours. Usually 15–25 cm high, 50 cm wide. Shape **4.**

Leucodendron. South African shrubs with some resemblance to proteas. Prefer gritty, well-drained acid soils, fairly salt tolerant but rarely happy in warm humid coastal areas. Prune after flowering, method **a.** Shape **2.**

L. argenteum, silver leaf, long silky leaves like silvery velvet. Grows well in Victorian hills districts and parts of WA, but on more humid eastern coast often dies during summer wet periods. 5 m x 2–3 m. Shape **2.**

L. grandiflorum, reddish cones surrounded by pinkish leaves in late winter. E 1.5 m x 1–2 m.

L. salignum, yellow-tinged tip leaves surround bright yellow cones in the male trees and greenish ones in the female trees — late winter and spring — popular cut flowers in New Zealand. E 2 m x 2 m.

Leucospermum. Interesting and showy plants closely related to Leucodendrons and growing under similar conditions. Their stamens are more pronounced than the latter, with some resemblance to a fully mature waratah. Prune as flowers finish, method **a.**

L. bolussii has short, rigid, closely set foliage and showy terminal heads of pincushion-like flowers to 10 cm across. The numerous long orange stamens are yellow tipped. E 2 m x 2 m.

L. crinitum, each stem carries heads of brush-like yellow stamens with contrasting red at the base. E 1.3 m x 1.3 m.

Ligustrum (Privet). Once a popular hedge plant but now a pest, as seed is carried by birds and its vigorous growth congests many of our natural bushland areas. Shape **3** or **4.** The only two that should be allowed to survive, except as well-clipped hedges, are:

L. lucidum tricolor, the large-leafed type heavily variegated with cream. It is more controllable than the original species, but should not be allowed to seed and sections reverting to green need removing. E 3–4 m x 2–3 m.

L. ovalifolium aureo-variegatum, golden privet, a pleasant background for annuals or may be trimmed as a formal shrub. Colour is best in full sun. Trim to any size in spring, then later as needed, method **d.** 3 m x 3 m.

Lilac (*Syringa*). Sprays of fragrant spring flowers. Only suited to cold or cooler temperate districts except *S. chinensis.* Sprays of single, fragrant lilac-purple flowers. D 2–3 m x 2–3 m. Shape **2.**

S. vulgaris (English lilac). Upright caney growth usually suckering to a sizeable clump. Nurseries list a large number of double and single varieties ranging from white through mauve, pink, reddish purple to deep violet-blue. Prune lightly after flowering to encourage new side growths and more flower stems for the following year.

Remove one or two of the oldest woody canes after plants are well established and young replacement suckers are available.

Lilacs prefer a slightly limy soil.

Linum trigynum see **Reinwardtia.**

Loropetalum chinense (Chinese Witchhazel). Dark rounded foliage, graceful semilateral growth, clustered in spring with slender petalled creamy flowers. Cool and temperate climates, E 2–3 m x 2 m. Prune after flower, method **a.** Shape **2. S–M.**

Luculia gratissima. Shrub for temperate areas where frosts are not severe. Rounded heads of dewy textured pink flowers with sweet fragrance. Blooms from early to midwinter. After flowering, prune, method **a.** Old branches may be removed periodically but avoid general hard pruning.

Luculias give pleasure for many years if left alone. Treat similarly to Geraldton Wax — see **Chamelaucium.** Lightly mulch surface to keep down weeds and prevent heavier loams from caking. E 2–3 m x 2–3 m. Shape **2.**

L. tsetense is a white species with thicker stems, darker and usually denser foliage. E 2–3 m x 1–2 m.

Magnolia. Deciduous species. Like giant candelabras decked with large, waxy, tulip-shaped blooms from white to deep purple. For cool and temperate climates preferring the lighter acid soils, but adapt well to heavy soils if broken up around the plant by mixing in moistened peatmoss or rotted leaf mould before planting.

These magnolias are usually not pruned as they continue to flower on the same wood for a number of years. Cutting up to one-quarter of the blooms for indoors is enough to encourage some new growth.

Very old branches with numerous woody spurs eventually die out, so these may be removed to make room for replacement growth. Shape **3.**

M. denudata (Yulan Tree), previously *M. conspicua.* A tall-growing, fan-shaped tree magnificently arrayed with large fragrant white, bell-shaped blooms. It is one of the first to flower, in late winter–early spring. D 5–7 m x 3–5 m.

M. liliflora, also listed as *M. purpurea,* flowers are deep purple outside, more trumpet-shaped and thinner than *M. denudata.* Growth slender or slightly leggy. D 3 m x 2 m.

M. soulangeana, resulting from a cross between *M. denudata* and *M. liliflora,* very free-flowering, shaped like *M. denudata,* but flushed outside with rosy purple often deepening toward the base.

There are different variations of *M. soulangeana.* These include: *M. soulangeana alba,* fragrant white resembling *M. denudata* with just a faint pink flush at the base; *M. soulangeana Alexandrina,* early flowering white with deep purple-stained base; and *M. soulangeana Lennei* with stocky rounded goblet-shaped blooms evenly tinted light rosy-purple outside. In fact there are several variations of *Lennei,* including lovely large ivory *Lennei alba.*

M. soulangeana Rustica Rubra has the dark outer colouring of the *M. liliflora* parent. All deciduous. Height: *Lennei* more compact, rarely exceeds 3 m, others eventually to 5 m and about 4 m wide.

M. stellata (Star Magnolia). Lovely shrub with star-like, slender-petalled, pearly-white blooms 8–10 cm across, mostly in late winter. Variety **Leonard Messell** is a lovely soft pink. Cool and temperate. D 2–3 m x 2–3 m.

Portwine Magnolia (*M. fuscata*) see **Michelia figo.**

Mahonia lomariifolia. Decorative feature plant with erect canes each with a head of 30–40 cm long, ornate stiff leaves divided into serrated light green holly-like leaflets. Sprays of small yellow flowers in cooler climates followed by unusual dusty deep blue berries. For cool and temperate areas in sun or part shade. Also attractive plant for low containers. Slow growing, usually 10–12 cm each year to 2 m and suckering to several canes. Cool and temperate. E. Shape **3.**

M. aquifolium as above with only 7–9 rounder, darker blue-green leaflets, winter flowering and lower growth, rarely more than 2 m. E.

Maple (*Acer*). Beautifully shaped foliage, richly coloured in autumn. Most species best in cool or moist temperate districts. All are deciduous. Avoid pruning if possible.

There are many *A. palmatum* varieties. Taller growers are trees, shrubby varieties include:

A. palmatum dissectum, low growth, deeply cut leaves. Needs protection from full sun and hot winds. 0.5–1 m x 1 m, or often grafted on standards.

A. palmatum dissectum atropurpureum, dark bronze purple version of latter. Shape **5.**

A. palmatum dissectum 'tricolor', foliage splashed cream, bronze, pink and later green. Shape **5.**

A. japonicum, broad foliage, short pointed lobes, variety **Aureum** is gold in spring and autumn. 2–3 m x 1–2 m. Shape **2.**

A. japonicum filicifolium has beautifully and deeply cut large leaves. 2–3 m x 1–2 m. Shape **2.**

A. palmatum reticulatum, pale leaves, veins prominently marked in dark green. 2–3 m x 1–1.5 m. Shape **1.**

A. palmatum roseum marginatum has small foliage, variegated cream, faint rose margin, in early spring. 2–3 m x 1–2 m. Shape **1.**

Melaleucas are beautiful and usually adaptable trees and shrubs, mostly with flowers resembling bottlebrushes, to which they are related. The shrubby types include:

M. fulgens (Scarlet Honey Myrtle). Fine grey foliage; brilliant red brushes, spring. Light soil, at least half sun. 1–1.5 m x 1 m. Shape **3.**

M. incana, graceful, grey-foliaged plant; erect trunk, arching branches. Small yellow

Magnolia soulangeana

Magnolia stellata

Mussaenda philipica 'Luz'

Pentas lanceolatus

Psoralia

Pieris japonica

brushes, spring, early summer. 2–3 m x 2–3 m. Shape **1.**

M. pulchella (Claw Honey Myrtle). Feathery mauve flowers in claw-like formation. Main flowering late spring, early summer; a few showing almost continuously. 1–1.5 m x 1 m. Shape **3.**

M. radula (Graceful Honey Myrtle). Slender, blue-grey foliage, brushes of mauve flower along stems. A WA species, but adapts to most districts if soil not too clayey. 1.5–2 m x 1–1.5 m. Shape **2.**

M. steedmanii (Honey myrtle). With round tufts of brilliant red stamens spangled with golden pollen; short, pointed foliage. Adapts well, but shy flowerer in some localities. 1–1.5 x 1 m. Shape **3.**

Melastoma malabathricum (Pink Lassiandra). Shrub like *Tibouchina,* but with dense growth and mauve-pink flowers during summer and autumn. Native of India and Australia.

This is the shrub once listed as **Lassiandra rosea** that grows to 3 m high and as wide. The shrub originally known as **Melastoma** and also **Lassiandra microphylla** has smaller, dark-bronze hairy foliage, bright purple flowers 3–4 cm across and compact growth to 1.3 m. This is now officially **Osbeckia kewensis.** Shape **4.**

Michelia figo (Port Wine Magnolia) or previously **Magnolia fuscata.** Small, heavily fragrant waxy dull purple flowers during late spring and summer. All but cold districts. Prune only to rejuvenate after 12–15 years, 3–4 m x 3–4 m. Shape **4.**

Mint Bushes, the **Prostantheras.** Quick-growing shrubs with clusters of small, dainty bell flowers.

P. ovalifolia (Purple Mint Bush). Dense shrub covered with purple bells, spring. Often short lived due to digging in root area, heavy fertilising, or extreme summer dryness. Improved by light pruning after flowering. At least half sun. 2–3 m x 2 m. Shape **2.**

P. lasianthos see under Christmas Bush (Victorian). Shape **3.**

P. rotundifolia (Round-leafed Mint Bush). Similar to *P. ovalifolia,* but with denser, rounded foliage; bluish purple to lilac flowers, spring. Part shade, reasonably moist but well-drained soil. 2–3 m x 2 m. Shape **2.**

Moschosma see *Iboza.*

Murraya paniculata. Dark glossy foliage and clusters of very fragrant white orange-blossom-like flowers in spasmodic bursts during spring and summer. Tropical and temperate areas where frosts are not severe. If necessary prune for shape in late winter, method **d.** E 2–3 m x 2–3 m. Shape **4. S–M.**

Mussaenda frondosa. Light green foliage and prominent white leaf bracts pendant below the small orange flowers. Frost-free positions. Prune back in winter, method **b.** E 1–2 m x 2–3 m. Shape **5. S–M.**

M. erythrophylla, blood-red rather than white bracts. Needs warm frost-protected position. E 2 m x 2 m. Shape **2.**

Mussaenda. *M. philipica,* salmon red and *M. Queen Sirikit,* white flushed pink, both carry dense clusters of flower-like bracts in spring and summer, are suited mainly to tropical or semi-tropical districts. 1–2 m x 1.5 m.

Myoporum montanum (Boobialla or Water Bush). Waxy green leaves to 8 cm long, small white flowers and purple berries. Useful shrub or hedge plant for inland areas. Trim if needed. E 2–4 m x 2–3 m. Shape **2.**

Nandina domestica (Japanese Sacred Bamboo). Useful for shady corners, large containers, Japanese gardens and as gentle greenery for flower arrangements. Rigid caney growth with branching, finely divided dainty foliage. Bunches of cream flowers and sometimes red berries from female plants when successfully pollinated. All climates. E 1–2 m, clumps to 1.3 m. Variety **Nana** colours attractively in autumn and winter when in exposed position with fairly poor soil. Thin out old canes. E 0.6 m x 0.6 m. Shape **3** or **4.**

Nerium (Oleander). Hardy evergreens for all but cold mountain climates. Good summer display even under adverse conditions, providing they have a reasonable amount of sun. Prune after flowering, method **a,** or heavily to rejuvenate in winter. Shape **2.** Varieties:

  Delphine, single dark crimson;
  Dr Golfin, single deep cerise;
  Madonna grandiflora, double white;
  Monsieur Belaguier, single clear light pink;
  Mrs F. Roeding, semi-double salmon;
  Splendens variegata, attractive golden variegated foliage and single deep pink flowers.

  All grow to about 3 m when pruned as suggested and 2–3 m wide. Variety *splendens,* a single deep pink, often reaches 3.5 m and nearly as wide.

Net Bush *(Calothamnus).* Resembling bottlebrush, but with stamens in feather-like formation in one-sided bushes; needle-like foliage, rigid but not sharp. Adapt to most soils, but prefer sandy loam; withstand dryness and grow in sun or part shade. As growth is well established beyond the flowers, rejuvenate by cutting back about half the branches each year.

  C. quadrifidis (florets have four bundles of stamens). Long, grey-green foliage. Mainly spring flowering. 2 m x 2 m.

  C. villosus, short, closely set, needle-like foliage. Florets have woolly bundles of stamens. Rather spreading; to 2 m x 2–2.5 m.

Odontonema strictum. Previously *Justicia coccinea* or *Jacobinia carnea.* Caney plant with bold, dark-green foliage and terminal 10–20 cm spikes of rosy-red flowers from late spring to autumn. Prune in late winter then shorten back canes when each flush of flowers finish. Best in half shade. Coastal temperate and tropical areas. E 2–3 m x 1–1.5 m. Shape **3.**

Spirea thunbergii

Senecio petasitis

Schefftera arboricola

Spirea cantoniensis

Streptosolen jamesonii

Syringa (lilac)

Oleander see *Nerium*.

Olearia dentata (Toothed daisy bush). Spreading bush; toothed foliage, covered in small white daisies, mainly spring. Adaptable to sea coast or inland. 0.75 m. Shape **5**.

O. stricta, dark-green, narrow-leafed upright species. Massed with small lavender daisies, mainly summer. 0.75 m. Shape **3**.

Osmanthus. Shrubs grown for the fragrance of their small flowers, also attractive foliage. Prune lightly after flowering, method **a**. Shape **4**.

O. aquilifolium variegata (Japanese Holly). Variegated green and white toothed holly-like foliage and fragrant white flowers in early summer. E 2 m x 1–2 m.

O. delavayi, small buxus-like foliage, fragrant white summer flowers. Cool and temperate. E 1–1.4 m x 1.3 m.

O. fragrans, attractive holly-like foliage, white flowers with an apricot aroma in autumn and winter. Cool and temperate. E 2–3 m x 1–2 m.

Peach, Flowering see *Prunus*.
Pearl Bush see *Exochorda*.

Pentas lanceolata. Quick-growing summer and autumn flowering shrubs closely related to Bouvardias. They need a warm sunny position and occasional soakings during summer. Prune as flowers finish, method **a**. Shape **3** or **4**. Varieties include:

Blood red, 1.5 m x 1 m.

Candy stripe, red with broad pink margin to petals. 1 m x 1 m.

Carnea, mauve-pink, also light purple, deep red and white which appear to be without accepted variety names. E 1–1.3 m x 0.7–1 m.

Persoonia pinifolia (Geebung). Sparse but graceful Australian shrub with deep-green, soft needle-shaped foliage, terminal spikes of golden-orange flowers in late spring and early summer, followed by bunches of bronze-flushed green berries weighing down the pendulous outer growth in autumn. Trim back in late winter, method **a**. All but coldest climates. 3–4 m x 2–3 m. Shape **1**.

Philadelphus (Mock Orange). Caney shrub with sprays of 4 cm white, golden-stamened flowers in late spring. Prune as suggested for *Deutzia,* all but tropical areas. D 2–3 m x 2.3 m. Shape **1**.

Phormium tenax (New Zealand Flax). Dramatic clumps of erect strap-like foliage held by each crown in attractive fan formation. Green, bronze and variegated forms. Height varies from 2–2.7 m depending on position. They grow in wet or dry soil, any climate. Shape **3**.

Photinia. Attractive foliage shrubs grown mainly for spectacular red new growth. Trim, method **d** when spring growth loses colour.

P. glabra robusta, quick-growing hardy large shrub, small tree, or tall clipped hedge plant. Large foliage is red in young stages, when untrimmed plant reverts to deep green, at least until spring. All but tropics. E 5–7 m x 3–5 m. Shape **4**. S–L.

P. glabra rubens, smaller plant than above, young foliage remains rich red for several months, then gradually deepens.

Does not suit dry heat of Adelaide and inland areas.

Pieris. Small evergreens, often with colourful new growth and lily of the valley-like flower sprays in spring. For cool and cooler temperate areas, needing about half shade or lightly broken sunlight in the latter districts. Prefers similar soil conditions to azaleas. Prune, method **a**, after flowering or just trim off old flower heads.

P. forrestii, variety **chandleri**. Showy new spring growth changing from coppery salmon to cream and finally green. Also sprays of pearly-white spring flowers. Slow-growing to 2 m and similar width. Shape **1**.

P. japonica, has darker green foliage than above and an abundance of pearl-like flowers. E 1.2 m x 1 m. Shape **4**. S–L.

Pimelea ferrugenia. From WA, but adaptable to most temperate areas, including east coast. Small oval foliage closely set along generous sheaf of erect stems, massed with pink ricy pompons, late winter to mid-summer, when it is improved by a light pruning. Dome shape; to 1 m x 1 m. Shape **4**. S–H–M.

Platylobium formosum (Flat Pea). Flat, elliptic-to-heart-shaped foliage. Massed bright yellow and red pea flowers, winter–spring. At least some shade. 1–2 m x 0.5 m. Shape **3**.

Plectranthus ecklonii. Slender spikes of violet-blue flowers in summer. Grows well in the light shade of taller trees. Needs heavy pruning after flowering, method **c**, or in frosty areas in early spring. Temperate to tropical. Semi-deciduous. 1–2 m x 2 m. Shape **3**.

P. saccatus, small spreading soft-wooded under shrub with lavender-blue flowers and small, scalloped foliage. Useful for shaded areas under trees. Best with late winter pruning. Needs frost protection. E 0.7 m x 1–1.3 m. Prune late winter, method **b**. Shape **5**.

Plumbago capensis. Suckering shrub with heads of clear, light-blue phlox-like flowers from spring to late autumn. Attractive as a hedge or controlled rounded shrub. Prune back heavily in late winter. For more compact growth at cost of slightly delayed flowering, tip prune or trim new growth when about 15 cm long. E 1.3–3 m x 1.3–3 m. Shape **4**.

Podalyria calyptrata. Round silky-grey foliage in spring, clustered with mauve-pink pea flowers. Prune lightly after flowering, method **a**. 3 m x 2 m. Shape **2**.

P. sericea, growth more gentle than above with smaller, very silky-grey foliage and small lilac pea flowers about 1 cm across. Temperate. E 1–2 m x 0.7 m. Shape **3**.

Poinsettia see *Euphorbia pulcherrima*.

Polygala myrtifolia. Small purple pea flowers over a long period from winter into summer. Lightly prune, method **a**, after flowering. Temperate and semi-tropical. E 1–1.7 m x 1–1.7 m. Shape **4**.

Pomegranate see *Punica*.
Poinciana gilliesii see *Caesalpinia*.
Port Wine Magnolia see *Michelia figo*.
Privet see *Ligustrum*.

Prostanthera (Mint Bush). Quick-growing shrubs with clusters of small, dainty bell flowers.

P. ovalifolia (Purple Mint Bush). Dense shrub covered with purple bells, spring. Often short-lived due to digging in root area, heavy fertilising, or extreme summer dryness. Improved by light pruning after flowering. At least half sun. 2–3 m x 2 m. Shape **2**.

P. lasianthos see under Christmas Bush (Victorian). Shape **3**.

P. rotundifolia (Round-Leafed Mint Bush). Similar to *P. ovalifolia,* but with denser, rounded foliage; bluish-purple to lilac flowers, spring. Part shade, reasonably moist but well-drained soil. 2–3 m x 2 m. Shape **2**.

Protea. South African shrubs with fascinating flowers, related to Australian Waratah, but with outer bracts pronounced and extended in cone-shaped formation around it.

They prefer a gritty, well-drained soil. In otherwise difficult areas they have grown successfully when planted where a barrow load of lightly crushed sandstone or other lime-free rubble has been spread around the young plant. Better in milder mountain areas away from coastal summer humidity. Tip prune young plants, prune, method **a**, as flowers age. Shape **2**.

Among the most likely to be available are:

P. cynaroides — King Protea with huge, silvery-pink or sometimes rose-pink blooms 20–30 cm across.

P. nerifolia, which varies from silvery-white to pink or red with black feathering on the bract tips.

P. repens, also known as *P. mellifera* with reddish bracts and a long brush of red and cream stamens.

Prunus. This genus embraces most of the beautiful spring-flowering blossoms — not only the flowering plums which are commonly accepted as prunus but the flowering peaches, apricots, almonds and cherries. Even the evergreen Portuguese laurel once listed as *Laurocerasus* is now officially a prunus.

Nearly all prunus species are trees — exceptions are:

Dwarf Prunus, P. glandulosa previously *P. sinensis*. Massed with small pink or white (usually double pink or white) flowers in early spring. Left unpruned they make a rounded twiggy bush, but if cut to within about 10 cm of the ground immediately after flowering the plant makes numerous suckers forming erect canes carrying flowers almost along their full length. Within a few years the clump is 1–2 m wide.

The double white form is *P. glandulosa alba pleno,* and double soft rose *P. glandulosa rosea pleno*. Shape **3**.

Pseudopanax. Similar to the Finger Aralias, suitable as container plants for indoors or a reasonably moist position in the garden. In warmer temperate areas they prefer light shade. Suit Japanese settings and all but hot dry climates. Shape **3**.

P. carassifolium (New Zealand Lancewood). Pendulous, narrow bronze-green toothed foliage, wind resistant and stands heavy pruning if necessary, method **a.** Umbrella shaped. 2–3 m x 1–2 m.

Psoralea affinis. Often short-lived but quick-growing shrub covered with heads of pale blue pea flowers in spring. Prune after flowering, method **a.** Cool temperate to warm climates. E 2–3 m x 2–3 m. Shape **2.**

Pultenaea daphnoides. Upright shrub; small foliage studded with light-orange pea flowers, spring. There are numerous pultenaeas, but this one is adaptable, grows well in shade of taller trees. 2–3 m. Tip prune for more compact growth. Shape **1.**

Punica (Pomegranate). Extremely hardy withstanding very cold winters and hot dry summers. Prune lightly during winter or severely to rejuvenate, method **c.**

P. granatum nana is a miniature form with foliage, flowers and fruit proportionately reduced in size. Excellent for pot specimens or sunny rockeries. 0.3–6 m x 0.3–6 m.

Pyracantha (Fire Thorn). Hardy evergreen shrubs grown for their brilliant autumn berries. Suitable as hedges or individual specimens. Cool and temperate climates. Prune if desired after berries finish, method **a.** Shape **1.**

P. angustifolia, slender, leathery dull-green foliage, densely clustered thorny sprays of glossy orange berries. E 3 m x 3 m.

P. coccinea, dark green foliage, clusters of bright crimson-red berries. Sometimes listed as *P. crenulata* but it is considered that the true crenulata is a slightly inferior type of *P. coccinea.* E 2–3 m x 2–3 m. S–M.

P. rogersiana, dark green foliage, yellow berries turning orange-red. Variety *Flava* has yellow berries. E 2–3 m x 2–3 m.

P. yunnanensis, long, dark glossy foliage long-lasting orange-red berries turning deep crimson. E 3–4 m x 3–4 m.

Raphiolepis (Indian Hawthorn). Compact, leathery oval dark-green foliage, always attractive in any climate with excellent resistance to salt winds. Trimming off old flower heads in late spring, or method **a,** keeps them more compact. Shape **4.** S–H.

R. delacouri, erect heads of small pink flowers in spring. E 2 m x 2 m.

R. umbrellata ovata, dense growth, white flowers in spring. E 2 m x 2 m.

R. fergusoni, compact, dark foliage, heads of pink flowers. 0.5–1.5 m x 1 m.

Reinwardtia indica. Previously *Linum trygnum.* Winter-flowering shrub for warmer areas where frosts are not severe. Golden-yellow, petunia-like flowers cover the plant between June and August. Prune well back after flowering, method **b.** E 0.7–1 m x 0.5–1 m, but may sucker lightly.

Rhododendrons
see Azaleas and Rhododendrons.

Rhus cotinus see Cotinus.

Ribes (Flowering Currants). Small decorative spring-flowering shrubs for cool-mountain and southern districts. Lightly prune canes that have flowered. Shape **3.**

R. aureum, has pendulous yellow flowers with nutmeg-like fragrance and slender arching branches. D 1.3–2 m x 1.3–2 m.

R. sanguineum, light-green, three-lobed,

deeply veined leaves appear with the dainty pendulous bunches of rosy to coral-red flowers. D 1–2 m x 1–2 m.

Rondeletia amoena. Large oval dark-green foliage and rounded heads of small pink tubular and fragrant flowers in spring. Temperate to warm nearly frost-free areas. E 3–4 m x 2–3 m. Prune after flowering, method **a.** Shape **6.** S–H.

Rosemary *(Rosemarinus officinalis).* With slender rigid aromatic foliage often trimmed as hedge from 0.5–1.3 m or dense rather spreading shrub with small blue flowers from spring to autumn. Cool to temperate. Trim back in winter. E 1–1.7 m x 1–1.7 m. Shape **3.** S–H.

R. officinalis prostrata, is a delightful trailing form of above, in a suitable position gracefully spilling 1.3–2 m, ideal for dry walls or steep banks. Shape **5.**

Rothmannia globosa (Bell Gardenia) (was Gardenia *globosa*). Erect shrub with fragrant, waxy cream bells clustering the stems in mid to late spring. These are followed by seed capsules like small mandarins. All but cold districts. E 4 m x 2 m (very old shrubs develop spread). Trim after flowering, method **d.** Shape **6.**

Ruellia macrantha. Caney shrubs with large pointed oval bright green foliage and terminal heads of rosy-purple outward facing 5 cm trumpet flowers with white throats — mainly during winter and spring. Prune in spring when flowering finishes, method **b.** Temperate and warm areas. E 1–1.3 m x 1–1.3 m. Shape **3.**

Russelia equisetiformis (Firecracker). Arching canes with a horsetail formation of slender leafless green stems, pillarbox-red tubular flowers 3–4 cm long. May be tied to a stake making a tall slender shrub about 2 m or used as a spillover. Evergreen for temperate and warm climates. Untrained grows 1.3 m x 2 m. Prune back in winter if needed, method **b.** Shape **5.**

R. sarmentosa, an upright plant with well-defined rounded foliage and slightly larger flowers on erect spikes. Resents very heavy frost. E 1–2 m x 1.5–2 m.

Sambucus nigra aurea (Golden Elderberry). Large attractively divided foliage remaining golden during spring and early summer — sometimes black berries. Prune in winter, method **c.** Cool and temperate areas. D 3 m x 2–3 m. Shape **2.** S–M.

Senecio petasites. Large lightly-scalloped, velvet-like green leaves and russet late winter, buds opening in large heads of small, yellow daisy-like flowers. Shape **4.**

S. grandiflora is similar, with larger foliage. Prune as flowers finish, method **a** or **c.** Grows in sun or shade standing only light to moderate frost. Temperate to tropical. E 2–2.5 m x 2–2.5 m. Shape **4.**

Serissa feotida. Small glossy foliage and tiny white flowers in winter. Also variety *variegata* with thin creamy edge to foliage. Sun or part shade. Prune lightly after spring flowering, method **a.** Temperate and tropical. E 0.5–1 m x 1 m. Shape **4.**

Snowball Tree see *Viburnum opulus.*

Spartium junceum (Spanish Broom). Almost leafless upright green twigs, heads of fragrant yellow flowers mainly from mid-spring into early summer. Prune after flowering, method **a.** Salt wind and drought-resisting. Cool to temperate. E 2–3 m x 1–2 m. Shape **2.** S–H.

Spiraea (May). Hardy and adaptable shrubs for all but tropical areas. Prune well back after flowering, method **b.** S–H.

S. bumalda Anthony Waterer (Pink or Red May). Stems topped with large rounded heads of tiny carmine rose flowers during late spring with occasional heads throughout summer. D 1–1.3 m x 1–1.3 m. Shape **4.**

S. cantoniensis previously *S. reevesiana,* popularly known in Australia as White May. Graceful long pendulous sprays, clustered with round heads of tiny white flowers in spring. Most effective set on the edge of a lawn. Variety *flore pleno* is the dainty double White May. D 2 m x 2 m. Shape **1.** S–M.

S. prunifolia, wispy canes with loose clusters of small tightly double florets on slender individual stemlets. Softening amongst other shrubbery or in decorative work. D 2 m x 1–1.5 m with occasional suckers. Shape **3.**

S. thunbergii (S. gracilis) — slender foliage and thin arching sprays with tiny dainty tea-tree-like white flowers. Foliage colours in autumn. D 1–1.5 m x 1–1.5 m. Shape **4.**

Sprengelia incarnata (Pink Swamp heath). Spikes of star-like flowers that last well when cut, late spring–early summer. Prefers swampy conditions. 1–2 m x 1 m.

Strelitzia (Bird Flower or Bird's Tongue). *S. reginae,* clump of heavy stems branching into broad sword-like leaves about 35 cm long in all to 2 m high. The spectacular flowers are carried just above the foliage with a prominent bronze beak-like bud to 20 cm long. From this, orange and blue flowers continue to rise for many months. Plants are often in flower throughout summer and winter. No pruning — remove dead outer foliage. Shape **3.**

S. nicolai (S. augusta), heavy-trunked tree with some resemblance to its relative the banana palm but leaves are blue-green, more upright and rigid fan formation, growing 3–4 m and 3–4 m across. Flowers are white and blue. Dramatic appearance if occasionally cleaned of old foliage and flower.

S. parvifolia, more rigid and tapering than *S. reginae,* leaves only 15–20 cm long. Variety *juncea* is still taller but with small spoon-like leaves only 5–10 cm long at the stem tips. Makes a light and graceful feature plant. Flowers are similar to *S. reginae.* All strelitzias suit temperate to tropical climates.

Streptosolen jamesonii. Browallia *jamesonii.* Caney shrub with heads of small phlox-like, deep-orange flowers during spring and often extending into early summer. For all but very frosty areas. E 2 m x 1 m. Tip prune when young, prune after flowering, method **b.** Shape **1.**

Strobilanthes anisophyllus
see *Goldfussia.*

Sturt's Desert Pea *(Clianthus formosus).* Sometimes still known as *Clianthus*

Tibouchina (Lassiandra)

dampieri. One of the most spectacular Australian wildflowers. Spreading plant, with clusters of long, scarlet pea flowers each with a prominent black boss or dome in the centre.

A fast-growing plant from the dry summer areas, inclined to die out quickly in wet warm periods, and is best grown in a pot (15 cm or larger) in high rainfall areas so that it can be moved out of excessive rain. Needs gritty soil such as crushed sandstone and a little leaf-mould or compost with a dusting of lime.

Sow seeds direct, as it does not transplant readily. To germinate quickly, first soak seeds in hot water, or abraid by swirling in a bucket with a few rough stones added. Officially a perennial, but it does not carry well from season to season, and as it flowers quickly from seed, should be treated as an annual. 0.5 m x 0.5 m. Shape **5.**

Swan River Pea see *Brachysema*.

Tea-tree *(Leptospermums)*. Showy garden hybrids have resulted from crosses between New Zealand and Australian species. Some of these succumb to tiny scale pests, which result in incrustations of black sooty mould.

Tecomaria sambucifolia

Viburnum tomentosum

Weigela

Viburnum Macrocephalum

Berberis thunbergii atropurpurea

Buxus sempervirens carefully shaped

Chamaecyparis conifers — C. lawsoniana, C. pisiferanana, C. lawsoniana gimborniana

Chamaecyparis pisifera 'Filifera aurea'

Juniper pfitzeriana

Chamaecyparis pisifera 'squarrosa intermeda'

Topiary is the art of shaping plants into geometrical or animal forms. Yew and Buxus are the shrubs most often used for this technique

Control with white oil spray, 2 tablespoons per 4 litres of water. Shape **2**.

Among the most notable shrubby species are:

L. scoparium, mainly from NSW. Erect, with pendulous outer branches clustered with large, white or pink-flushed flowers, autumn/spring. Adaptable. 2–3 m x 2–3 m.

L. rotundifolium, squat, spreading shrub; dark green foliage contrasts with large, soft-pink flowers with glassy green centres. Grows well in parts of NSW, southern coast, but, surprisingly, I have seen it thriving inland at Forbes in an exposed position where the soil is no more than slightly acid. It seems to gradually deteriorate in acid sandstone soil. One of the loveliest tea-trees, well worth perseverance. 1–2 m x 2 m.

Tecomaria capensis. Caney plant, contained as dense shrub by cutting back in winter then trimming or tip pruning to desired form. Glossy green foliage, spikes of long tubular orange-red flowers from late spring to winter. Temperate and tropical. E 4–5 m and spreading unless controlled. Shape **2**.

Telopea see Waratah.

Teucrium fruticans. Slender greyish-white stems, small grey-green foliage and lavender flowers. Withstands dryness, salt wind and light shade. Cool to semi-tropical. E 1.3 m x 1.7 m. Prune out old canes if needed. Shape **3**. S–H.

Thevetia neriifolia (Yellow Oleander). Resembles an oleander with fragrant yellow flowers and finer, glossier foliage. Prune lightly after flowering. Frost-free temperate and tropical. E 2 m x 1.5–2 m. Shape **2**.

Thryptomene calycina (Heath Myrtle). Bushy, fine-foliaged Victorian wildflower. Massed with white, tiny-petalled teatree-like flowers, winter–spring. Reddish calyces follow. Well-drained soil, light shade in warm districts. 1.5 m x 1–1.5 m. Shape **3**.

T. saxicola (Payne's Hybrid). Spreading, slender, arching branches; sprays of tiny pink flowers, winter to late spring. Prune lightly after flowering. 1–1.5 m, about twice the spread. Shape **5**.

Tibouchina (Lassiandra). Robust and quick-growing in all but very frosty districts, with a show of large violet purple flowers in summer and autumn. Prune in winter, method **c**. Shape **2**.

T. granulosa, erect pyramid-shaped sprays massed with 5 cm rich lavender-blue flowers, are held well above the bush. E 3–4 m x 3 m.

T. macrantha was *T. semidecandra grandiflora* or **Lassiandra grandiflora**; very large violet-purple flowers and more compact growth, needs very little pruning. E 2 m x 2–3 m.

Also see **Melastoma** for Pink Lassiandra.

T. urvilleana previously *T. semidecandra Edwardsii* or **Lassiandra edwardsii**, very free-flowering with violet-purple flowers about 8–9 cm across.

Toxicophlaea see Acokanthera.

Tweedia caerulea or *Oxypetalum caeruleum.* Sparse shrub with heads of lovely clear light blue, five-petalled starry flow-

ers 20 cm across, during spring, summer and autumn. Arrow-shaped grey leaves. Prune winter, method **b**. All but cold districts. E 0.5–1 m x 1 m. Shape **3**.

Veronica see *Hebe.*

Waratah *(Telopea speciosissima).* Large, deep-red cone-shaped formation of florets, flamboyant surround of showy, lighter red bracts. Prefers humid east coast and mountain climate, and adapts from yellowish bush sand to heavier loams providing the surface of the loam is lightened by kneading in plenty of leafmould and a little sand. 2–3 m x 2 m. Shape **3**.

T. oreades (Gippsland Waratah), has red, rather loose, flattish flower heads above 8 cm. Similar requirements to *T. speciosissima.*

T. truncata (Tasmanian Waratah), has short, rather flat, bright-red flower heads a b o u t 10 cm across. Cool to cooler temperate.

Waratah plants are best at least started in light shade, so if in full sun protect with a cone of twigs, and let the plant grow through it.

Prune back before new growth starts from below the flower, which usually means before the flower is quite finished. Leave a few leaves at base of flower stem (previous season's growth). Rejuvenate old, leggy clumps by cutting within a foot or two of the ground. At pruning time feed with blood and bone, bone dust and cottonseed meal mixture, or animal manure.

Wattle see *Acacia.*

Weigela. Caney shrubs massed in spring with upright velvety-textured trumpet flowers 2–3 cm long. Cold and temperate areas. Prune immediately after flowering. Varieties include **Amiabilis**, light pink, **Amiabilis variegata** with cream foliage variegations, **Candida** pure white, **Eva Rathke** crimson and **Styriaca** rose-pink darkening with age. All but the last with reasonable pruning grow 2 m x 2–3 m, white *styriaca* is usually a little larger. All deciduous. Prune after flowering, method **b**. Shape **4**.

Westringia fruticosa. *Syn. rosmariniformis* (Coastal rosemary). Rosemary-like shrub with grey-green foliage, small, pale mauve flowers. A pleasant, adaptable background shrub, standing salt spray or dry inland conditions. Dense and compact, only about 0.5 m high or up to 2 m in sheltered conditions with liberal water. Trim for more compact form. Shape **4**.

W. glabra, smooth oval deep-green foliage and pale, lavender-blue late spring flowers. Adaptable but a little less salt tolerant than *W. fruticosa.* 1.5 m x 2 m. Shape **3**.

W longifolia, fine, mid-green foliage, massed with mauve-flushed white flowers in spring — like a soft mint bush. Suits light shade. 2–3 m x 2 m. Shape **2**.

Viburnum. Shrubs grown mainly for flowers and sometimes berries. Over 120 species and an increasing list as new hybrids are still evolving.

Deciduous types, prune after flowering unless grown for berries, method **b**. When

latter finish, trim old head back to just above the side shoots below.

V. betulifolium, birch-leafed, with white spring flower heads followed by masses of red berries from autumn well into winter. Best in cold to cooler temperate areas. 4–5 m x 3 m. Shape **1**.

V. burkwoodii, large fragrant heads of white-pink flushed spring flowers. Semi-deciduous. 2–2.5 m x 2 m. Shape **2**.

V. carlesii, dull green foliage, heads of sweetly scented white flowers in spring. 2 m x 1–1.5 m. Shape **2**.

V. macrocephalum (Chinese Snowball Tree). Large 12–15 cm flower heads change from green to white, mainly during later winter but occasionally from autumn onwards. Retains some of its large oval foliage during mild winters. 4–5 m x 3 m.

V. opulus (Guelder Rose). Small green bobbles in spring, gradually enlarging and paling to white hydrangea-like heads of flower. Shapely foliage like small grape leaves colouring in autumn. 2–3 m x 2–2.5 m. Shape **3**.

V. plicatum var. *tomentosum,* slightly hairy elm-like foliage with a circle of white florets surrounding the mass of pinhead-size fertile flowers, which develop to autumn berries and later turn black. 2–3 m x 2–3 m. Shape **1**.

V. plicatum var. *plicatum,* is now the rather confusing official title for *V. tomentosum sterile* which has a head of flowers similar to the Guelder Rose but quite different attractively pleated leaves. 2–3 m x 2–3 m. Shape **1**.

Viburnums, Evergreen. Prune after flowering if necessary, method **a**.

V. davidii, low-branching dense dark-green foliage, heads of tiny white flowers in spring. 1 m x 1 m. Shape **4**.

V. suspensum, large oval dark glossy green leaves, slender pendulous sprays of pearly-white flowers in late spring. 2–3 m x 2–3 m. Shape **4**.

V. tinus (Laurustinus). Dark-green, small laurel-like foliage, flat heads of pink buds in late winter–spring opening to tightly packed small white flowers. 2–3 m x 2 m. Shape **4**. S–M.

Vitex agnus castus (Chaste Tree). Divided foliage, spikes of small blue flowers early summer. Prune back to about half-size in winter, method **c**. Cool to semi-tropical. D 2–3 m x 2–3 m. Shape **3**.

V. trifoliata purpurea, grown for its purple-backed foliage which gives an unusual flutter of colour when stirred by a breeze.

V. trifoliata variegata, irregularly margined with cream, both are winter-pruned to about two-thirds size. D 2–3 m x 2–3 m.

Conifers

The variety of form and foliage colour of conifers gives scope for interesting groupings. One or two erect, slender types will balance and combine pleasantly with low-domed, rounded or prostrate forms.

They can be planted or grouped for an

immediate effect for they can always be moved easily in late autumn. When the soil is just damp, spade around the plant to cut the roots cleanly to about spade-depth. For most of the rounded or 'pyramid' types it is sufficient to make this encircling cut just below outer foliage. For slender, tall types (from .5–1 m high) cut about 20 cm out from the trunk, adding 10 cm in radius for every extra metre in height.

Topiary

The art of topiary goes back a long way. Many of the great gardens of the 16th century combined parterre (clipped hedging) with topiary but, as formality and contrivance lost ground to the informal and the natural, the art of topiary became unappreciated and skills lost. You need the long view and a special attitude of mind to attempt topiary today.

Yew and box hedging grow well in all but semi-tropical and tropical areas, but they take a long time to make a solid hedge. The small-leaved *lonicera nitida* grows much more quickly and soon becomes about a metre high. Abelia is coarser-leaved but grows even more rapidly. You can choose between a green or gold-leafed variety. When you have a solid hedge the design into which you will cut it is up to you. Just remember that a design which widens toward the top will throw a shadow and the lower foliage could be deprived of light and ruin the effect by shrivelling and browning.

Conifers can be trained, topiary-style, but they are tricky; ivy provides the ideal shortcut to success. Make the shape you desire, using stout wire, and then train the ivy over it. As the ivy grows the wire can be bent into a different shape if you so wish. From low-shaped hedges to tall, sculptured shrubs, design can be imposed on nature, but care is needed at all times. Watering and feeding must be controlled with intelligence. Rank growth with long spaces between leaves can ruin a desired effect.

A reference guide to conifers

As conifers are grown mainly for their shape or form, the following listings of dwarf and medium growers have been grouped according to shape. The height given (in metres) would, under average conditions, be reached in about seven years. Note: Taller growing conifers will be found alphabetically in the tree list.

Upright types

Chamaecyparis lawsoniana aurea densa. Gold, oval cone; H .5 m.

C. lawsoniana minima, deep green, broad base, tapering to pyramid; H 1 m.

C. lawsoniana aurea, slower-growing golden-green version of above. H .75 m.

C. lawsoniana erecta aurea, dense, upright golden-yellow; grows strongly. H 1.5 m.

C. lawsoniana fletcheri, soft green-grey upright foliage; suits partly shaded position,

loses slender form after 10–15 years. H 2–2.5 m.

C. obtusa crippsii, popular cone-shaped type with large fans of foliage generously tipped gold when in sun. H 3–4 m.

C. obtusa nana aurea, fan-shaped, gold-tipped. H 2 m.

C. obusta tetagona aurea, dark green in irregular bracts; tipped gold. H 2–3 m.

C. pisifera filifera, graceful, pendulous, cord-like foliage. H 1–2 m.

C. pisifera filifera aurea, slightly larger than above; long, fine, pendulous golden foliage, insignificant early, but develops into beautiful conifer. H 2–3 m.

C. Pisifera squarosa Cyno-virides, beautiful silver-blue feathery pyramid; sun or semi-shade; recently introduced. H 2–3 m.

C. plumosa aurea, broad-based tapering cone, dark green fern-like foliage tipped gold. H 2–3 m.

Cupressus sempervirens stricta (Swane's Golden) slender, golden pencil pine. H 4–5 m.

C. macrocarpa conybeare, gracefully pendulous golden, thread-like foliage in pyramid shape. Good quick-growing specimen. Remove any growth that reverts to upright form. E, H 5 m, W 3 m.

Cryptomeria bandai-sugi. Length of foliage varies, giving pagoda-like shape. H 1.3–2 m.

Juniper J. communis hibernica (Irish Juniper). Blue-grey foliage, slender upright form. Hardy adaptable type. E, H 3–4 m, W 1.6–3 m.

J. communis hibernica nana, smaller form of above, could be considered in dwarf collections as it gains height and width very slowly but in 10 years may reach 2–3 m under good growing conditions.

Picea glauca albertina conica. Miniature slow-growing spruce; conical. Dense grey-green foliage. H 1–1.3 m.

Thuya orientalis beverleyensis. Dense column of dark green-tipped gold. H 5 m.

Dome-shaped, fern-like foliage (developing cone or pyramid form with age)

Chamaecyparis obtusa nana. One of the finest dwarf, twisted fans of dark-green, moss-like foliage. Wider than height. Good for squat container. H 6 m.

C. obtusa nana aurea, slow growing, but taller than above. Larger, slightly pendulous fans, bronze to golden-green. H 1.7 m.

C. obtusa nana gracilis. Slow-growing, rounded. Rich, deep-green foliage. H 1.6 m.

C. obtusa nana kosterii, similar to the others. Apple-green foliage. H 6 m.

C. obtusa nana picta, similar to above. Dark green, silver-flecked foliage.

C. obtusa pygmea. Tiers of bronze-green fans. H 3 m.

C. obtusa nana spiralis. Similar to *nana.* Contorted branches. H 1 m.

Thuja occidentalis Rhinegold. Popular globe-shaped conifer. Soft, fine, golden young foliage. Bronze in autumn. H 1.3 m.

T. minima glauca. Blue-green dwarf globe, bronze-green in winter. H 6 m.

T. orientalis nana aurea. Dwarf golden variety, attractive in rockery or container, bronze in autumn. H 1.3 m.

Prostrate conifers

Juniper procumbens (Japanese mountain juniper). Dense mat blue-green foliage. H .3 m, W 1–1.6 m.

J. communis aurea. Spreading type, dense, fine foliage, grey-green in summer, grey-purple in winter. Golden-bronze new growth, hardy, needs exposed position for best colour. H .6 m, twice as wide.

J. communis var. depressa aurea. As above with larger foliage.

J. conferta, makes delightful, dense mat of silky golden-green tassles. H .5 m, W 1.5 m.

J. scopulorum repens. Prostrate, grey-green. Follows contours of site. H 1 m, W 1 m.

Sabina vulgaris. Sometimes listed under 'Juniper'. Feathery, deep green foliage, fanning horizontally. Quick-growing. H .6–1.3 m, W 1.5–2 m.

S. chinensis pfitzeriana. Spreads in V-like formation. H 1.5 m, twice as wide.

S. douglassii, slightly more upright than above. Slate-coloured in winter.

Podocarpus alpinus. Dark, glossy green foliage, semi-prostrate. H 1 m.

Dome-shaped, fine foliage

(*Chamaecyparis* means 'false cypress'. Many were once listed as *Retinospora; Pisifer* means 'fine foliage').

Chamaecyparis pisifera nana. Ruffled, dark-grey. Compact foliage, bronze-green in winter. Trunk usually divided. Hardy, attractive. H .6 m.

C. pisifera nana parslori. Brighter green than the above, growth a little quicker. H 1 m.

C. pisifera nana parslori aurea. A golden form, and variegated. Green-gold, cream foliage.

C. pisifera plumosa compressa. A compacted form. Tiny, dense foliage of moss-like appearance. H .5 m.

C. pisifera plumosa rodgersii. Dense, fine growth in tiny crests or undulations. Silvery grey-green toward base. Tipped creamy-gold. Holds colour all year. An attractive bonsai plant. H .6 m.

C. pisifera squarrosa intermedia. Silver-blue juvenile foliage. Later is longer and coarser and sometimes trimmed off. H 1 m.

Cryptomerias have long branchlets, densely spiralled with fine, scale-like foliage similar to Norfolk pine.

C. japonica nana. Dense, spreading globe of deep, bright green. Pale tassles of new growth. H 1.3 m.

C. japonica vilmoriana. Dwarf, dense globe. Winter foliage, bronze. New growth green. H .6 m.

Pruning conifers

Thicker and more even growth of conical grown conifers will be encouraged by lightly trimming all but the top growing tip in July. See *Pest Section* for problems.

22. Roses

Roses surpass the popularity of any other flower, yet are seldom used to best effect in the garden.

For centuries rose enthusiasts have insisted that these beauties should be grown in beds on their own and in a garden where space is limited. This means many drab periods between bursts of glory.

You can enjoy growing lovely roses without sacrificing the garden to them. They are not happy with the competition of taller growth close by them but there is no reason why bright splashes of low-bedding plants, bulbs and carpeting perennials cannot be grown below them.

Enthusiastic show-bench exhibitors do not favour this form of mixed cultivation because it makes it more difficult to carry out feeding and watering programs that will bring the maximum number of blooms to perfection at show time, but most home gardeners prefer a continuity of blooms for as long as possible, and to enjoy a variety of other plants with them. You can do this.

Rose breeders have given us a much wider choice than we once had; formerly people grew either the hybrid tea-type that gave a limited number of near-perfectly shaped blooms on individual stems, or the more compact floribunda varieties with numerous clusters of small, rather open blooms that make an excellent garden show.

Rose breeders have merged these once distinct strains, giving us compact, showy cluster-flowering types with perfectly shaped hybrid tea flowers. Some of the lovelier traditional and taller hybrid tea-type roses will undoubtedly remain for many years, but the new hybrid tea floribunda types are the answer for the gardener seeking both garden display and lovely blooms — and a variety of other plantings to happily intermingle with them.

For the balcony or window-box garden, one can obtain miniature roses, tiny blooms perfect in every detail, on plants small enough to grow in containers no larger than cyclamen pots (12–18 cm).

Above: Miniature rose, 'Over The Rainbow'

Below: Roses bring a burst of colour to the garden

Above: Miniature roses make an attractive container display

Right: Rosa banksia lutea (Banksia Rose), a thornless rose

A modern floribunda, 'Blessings'

Above: Hybrid tea, 'Esmeralda'

Left: A pillar rose, 'Titan'

Types of roses

Miniatures

Miniature roses include all types but in minute form. Ramblers, climbers and hybrid tea-types are all available in miniature form. They are suitable for low borders, ground covers or container growing.

Floribundas

These are the best landscape roses. They are hardy and disease resistant, more free-flowering than the hybrid teas but with smaller blooms. Floribundas have the same colour range as hybrid teas. They grow between 60 cm and 1.2 m high with a few reaching almost 2 m. Varieties such as China Doll — which grows no more than 60 cm high and is massed with clusters of small, flattish, double pink flowers — and crimson Marlena and bi-coloured Masquerade are suitable for low borders.

The 'fairy' variety with dense low-branching foliage and frequent clusters of small pink blooms is ideal for foreground planting. Larger-bloomed varieties such as the red Evelyn Fison, Lili Marlene, salmon-pink Bazaar, Apricot Nectar and the golden-orange Woburn Abbey are all taller (about 1 m) but still compact and showy.

Floribundas are good as border, barrier or combination plants. They are suitable for location along a driveway, pathway or in front of taller growing roses.

Hybrid teas

In 1867, a Frenchman, J.B. Guillot, crossed the then great rose of Europe, hybrid perpetual, with the delicate and graceful 'tea' rose of China. The new rose came to be known as 'hybrid tea'.

Hybrid teas are often considered the great roses of the world. Brightly coloured, elegant, with long stems and vigorous, they are usually grown for their perfection of bloom in beds for a dramatic display of colour. They are also grown for use as cut flowers. Their rich colours range from pure white through gradations of pink and red to crimson, copper, gold and yellow. They produce numerous flowers and many are fragrant.

Depending on the variety the hybrid teas grow between 75 cm and 2 m but the average is 1–1.5 m tall. There are also climbing forms of hybrid teas called climbing sports.

Hybrid teas are the roses most often used to make standard roses.

Grandiflora

Grandifloras are the newest of all rose classes. The differences between a hybrid tea and a grandiflora or a grandiflora and a floribunda are often small.

Grandifloras produce quantities of flowers similar to floribundas and the flowers have the size and delicate form of a hybrid tea.

Taller than either of the other roses, growing to 2.5–3 m tall, they make excellent background plants. Many are fragrant.

The grandiflora class was created especially for Queen Elizabeth II. It is essentially a large hybrid tea that produces hybrid tea-like pink flowers in sprays. The 'Queen Elizabeth' is considered one of the outstanding roses of all time.

Shrub roses

Most shrub roses are older varieties and don't have the brilliance of colour of the other types of roses. In general they are tough, low-maintenance plants with good versatility. They make good landscape plants, hedges and screens.

Shrub roses usually grow between 2 and 3 m and the shape varies. Some are upright while others are fountain shaped.

Standard roses

Standard roses are actually three different types of roses, all grafted into one. The three parts are the root stock, trunk stock (or standard) and the flowering top part.

Most commonly, hybrid teas and grandifloras are used for the tops but any type of rose may be grafted to the trunk stock. The trunk stock on which the flowering top is grafted usually stands about 1.75–2 m tall. A variation to the usual grafting of the more upright growing roses is the grafting of soft cane ramblers, (generally Wichuraina types) which will sometimes drape all the way to the ground. These varieties are called Weeping standards.

Pillar roses

Pillar roses are a less vigorous growing form of a larger-flowered climber. 'Pillar' is not a class of rose but is a terminology that has evolved in general usage to describe any rose trained to climb an upright post or pillar.

A good pillar rose grows to about 3 m high and flowers from top to bottom and tends to produce more flowers than other climbers. Titan is a lovely cherry-rose red pillar type; Golden Showers a glossy-foliaged yellow, and Cocktail, a long-flowering single red rose with a creamy-yellow centre.

Climbers

Climbing roses do not 'climb' naturally. They are the most vigorous forms of the various groups of roses notably hybrid tea and floribunda types. The long arching canes grow 3–10 m but must be tied or attached to a supporting structure — without any support they will sprawl on the ground in a tangled mound.

Large-flowered climbers. Have stiff canes which grow between 2.5–4.5 m long. Their flowers vary in size between 7 and 15 cm and usually grow in clusters of up to 25 flowers.

Climbing sports. Extra vigorous mutations of hybrid teas, floribundas or grandifloras are called climbing sports.

When a normal rose bush occasionally develops a vigorous cane without growth-stopping flower buds at its tip, buds taken and grafted retain all the characteristics of the original bush as well as its own peculiar characteristics of no growth-stopping buds at the tip of the cane. The new plant becomes a climbing rose — a climbing sport of the original plant.

Climbing sports are the least hardy of the popular climbers but their interest is in their beautiful flowers — the same flowers as the parent bush.

Ramblers

Ramblers are an older type of climber with twining growth and large clusters of small flowers. They have long, soft pendulous canes which grow 4.5–6 m long and need support. Most ramblers are of the wichuraiana type — the double pink Dorothy Perkins, the scarlet Excelsa and Sanders White. Flowers appear only once per season and are limited to red, pink, yellow and white.

Banksia roses

Similar to Wichuraians but with comparatively more woody growth. They produce clusters of dainty semi-double flowers in spring. Generally immune to the usual fungus diseases and are free from thorns.

Banksia lutea is a creamy yellow variety and *B. alba* is white and fragrant.

Growing roses

Position

Roses make their best growth in a sunny aspect — at least half a day's sun is essential, but performance will be better still with full sunshine. Reasonably open positions with good air circulation are preferred

Soil

It is often thought that roses prefer clay. They do have more tolerance to very clayey soils than many other plants but grow best in a crumbly loam with a clay sub-soil, which ensures an even supply of moisture and plant food within reach of the roots.

Good drainage is essential. If drainage is questionable (and if it is not possible to correct the position with drainage systems) then plant in beds raised 20–25 cm above the surrounding soil level.

Sand or very sandy soil can also produce good roses. Many beautiful displays of roses around Perth and other sandy areas of the Western Australian coast are proof of it. Many of these plants are budded onto root stocks suited to sand, e.g. *R. fortuneana*. However, on the less amenable east coast of Victorian and South Australia other stocks also give good results if the sand is permanently mulched with fibrous compost, straw, seaweed or similar organic materials. Adding peatmoss to the sand also helps, but does not compensate for the lack of surface mulch. Some varieties (usually the stronger growers) tolerate sandy soils better than others.

Soil preparation

Both heavy clayey soils and sand are improved by the addition of compost or similar organic materials. Horse manure is a good lightener for heavy soils and cow manure improves the structure of sand, but these materials should be added several weeks before planting — longer if manure is fresh or compost is only partly decomposed and still fibrous.

Roses also prefer a slightly limey soil, so if your soil is acid and has not been limed for a year or so, spread about three-quarter cup of either dolomite or garden lime per sq. m and dig it in well.

The ideal way to prepare the beds is to spread compost and lime a month or so prior to planting then dig the soil over and leave it in a loose, rough state. Work it over, breaking it up more finely, about a fortnight before planting.

However, if just planting a rose or two on the 'spur of the moment' and the soil is not the best, work in a little well-rotted compost, and if necessary some lime, then tread it down well to the right level before planting. Adding a good surface mulch after planting will make up for any lack of preliminary preparation.

Planning

Plant large busty roses a safe distance from pathways and patios. Make a point of finding the growth habit of roses from rose catalogues and growers' labels before planting. Place the tallest growers in the background, or in open positions on the southern side so that they do not shade smaller types, and step the height of the bushes down to the front or northern side of the bed.

If planting a border or bed for massed display it is more effective to use one variety. Mixed colours give a patchy appearance because of height differences and at different peak times for flowering.

Spacing

Single or even double rows, or groups of only 5 or 6 roses, can be set closer than those in large beds several rows deep, providing they are not closed-in by other tall plantings. For example, three bush roses could be set as close as 50 cm apart as plenty of light can penetrate around them, but in a bed with more than 2 rows of bushes it would be desirable to space them at least 75 cm apart to allow sunlight and reasonable access between the bushes. However, if bush roses are staggered you can get away with a minimum of about 60 cm between bushes in a mass planting; but another 10–15 cm would allow better maintenance of the plants.

Planting times

Container grown. Flowering roses in containers can be planted any time, providing the roots are not disturbed.

Open ground. The more widely sold 'open ground' or 'bare-rooted' roses which are dug in early winter, root top-pruned, and then sold with roots wrapped in moist sawdust or peatmoss can only be planted with safety during their dormant winter period from June to August.

In very cold districts August planting is more suitable but unless the roses are grown locally stocks are either sold out or making growth by this time. For this reason it is advisable to buy in winter and either 'heel' the plants (as described later under 'Getting ready to plant') or plant them out and pack straw loosely around them for frost protection.

Selecting and preparing roses for planting

Take care that the roots of your rose plants do not dry out. Keep them wrapped until ready to plant but if planting has to be delayed for more than a week, it is best to 'heel in' the plants by planting them in a wide, shallow hole or short trench large enough to comfortably accommodate their roots and covering the

latter with damp soil. If you have a large bundle of plants, open them up so that the soil can be filled-in completely between them, then water to expel air pockets.

Examine plants before buying. The bark should be plump and smooth but not necessarily green, as colour varies from bright green to dull bronze depending on variety. Look for any shrivelling — a dull, crepe-like marking, more pronounced at the top of the cane but often extending downwards. This is usually a sign that the roots have been allowed to dry. If you find yourself with plants showing shrivelling you might revive them by making a trench long enough to take the full length of the plant and after soaking the roots, patting them in and covering the canes as well as roots with soil. Leave them for 5 or 6 days. Recovery will depend on how far the plants deteriorated beforehand.

Soil at planting time should be damp, so if conditions are dry give a good soaking a day or two earlier.

Planting

Mark the holes but don't dig until ready to plant. Stand plants with their roots in a bucket of water while preparing the holes. Apart from keeping them moist, this also removes the 'puddling' of clay that many nurseries use to exclude air from the roots to help keep them dormant.

Make the holes just deep enough to bring the 'bud union' to about ground level and wide enough to allow a full spread of roots without bending, or even wider so that there is room to put some improved topsoil beyond the roots to encourage their spread — 30 cm is a good width.

If the soil is very clayey or of a heavy sticky nature, don't plant deeper than about 12 cm. If a rose has a long briar stock (i.e. more than 12 cm between root and bud union), keep the stock above soil level. Better to put up with someone telling you that it is planted incorrectly than to have the roots smothered.

Try the rose for depth, trim away any broken or jagged roots, then mound a few handfuls of topsoil in the hole to fit the spread of the roots.

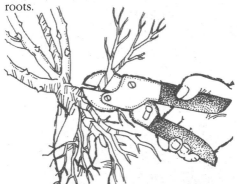

Half-fill the hole with improved topsoil (up to about quarter of compost rotted almost to soil consistency may be mixed in, but *no* fertiliser), then press down firmly to get the damp soil in contact with the roots. Do not add the 'conventional' bucket of water if the soil is damp — just fill in the remainder of soil and fashion some into a ridge slightly in from the edge of the planting hole.

Fill this surrounding saucer of soil with either fibrous compost, straw, leafmould, partly-rotted grass clippings or other fibrous material that will keep the soil open and prevent surface caking.

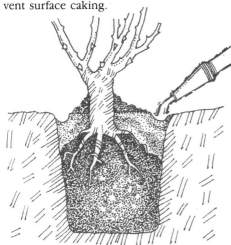

Now you can water. Allow about a bucketful per plant but don't 'slosh' it in too vigorously or this will defeat the care you have taken to prevent heavy soil from puddling and setting like cement; in sand it could force out all the organic particles scattered through it. So pour the water gently through the mulch. Another way to diffuse water evenly and gently is to spread a wet piece of hessian or old towelling around the soil at the base of the plant and pour through it.

Prune back the cane (or each cane) to just above an eye (or growth bud) pointing in the direction growth is wanted, starting the cut about .5 cm above the eye and slanting back to nearly behind it.

Standards, or Weeping Standards, are planted in the same way as Bush or Climbers, but as a stake is necessary, this must be positioned first, or root damage is almost inevitable. Use a solid 5 cm-square hardwood stake or, for a Weeping Standard, a length of galvanised water pipe for permanency. Stabilise against movement during wet or windy weather by setting the pipe in a 5 L can filled with concrete a few days before planting and then positioning below the root area.

The most important point about the stake (especially Weeping Standards which are top heavy) is to have the top of it extending a few centimetres into the branches beyond the bud union to prevent the chafing, and breaking, which would occur if the standard touched the top of the stake.

When tying, first make a separate firm tie around the stake, then another loose one around the standard. Use something lasting that will not cut, e.g. plastic or fabric-covered electricity wire, thick nylon cord, or galvanised or copper wire threaded through thick plastic tubing.

Weeping Standards develop a natural spread of more than 1 m. You can buy supports and hoop frames to hold them up.

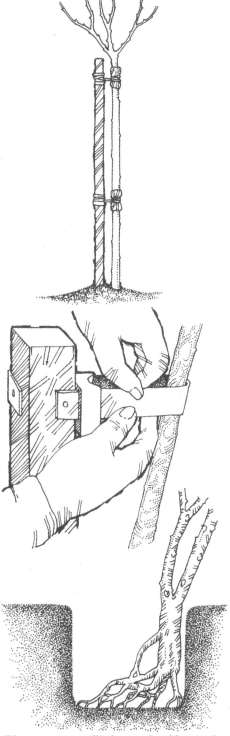

When setting out Climbers or Ramblers in the planting holes, place the stems to the back, nearest the wall or fence. The old soil mark should be level with the surface.

Old rose species, Rosa rugosa

Rosa rugosa hips

Low-growing hybrid tea, 'Lady Rose'

Standard roses, hybrid tea type

Old-fashioned shrub rose, 'Margaret Hilling'

Hybrid tea, 'Electron'

An old of climbing rose, R. Laviegata

A close view of R. Laviegata

Hybrid tea type

Climbing hybrid tea, 'Peace'

A close-up of the rambling rose, 'Dorothy Perkins'

Weeping standard, 'Dorothy Perkins'

Care and maintenance

Feeding

Newly planted roses should not be fed until new spring shoots are finger length. Feed sparingly, using no more than a tablespoon of complete plant food or rose food scattered out from the plant's base in a circle about 20 cm wide, then lightly raked into the soil or mulch and watered in. As an alternative to the rose food use about 2 cups of poultry manure spread around the plant.

Established roses may be given about twice the quantity recommended for new plants. In all cases this amount of manure or fertiliser may be applied every 6 weeks from the time new growth starts in spring through to mid-autumn, except during drought conditions where it is not possible to maintain a reasonable soil moisture. Never feed unless you can water thoroughly afterwards.

This feeding program differs from the recommendations of enthusiasts interested in exhibiting roses, because they time feeding and general treatment to bring the greatest number of blooms to their peak for show time, and encourage dormancy between these periods. Most home gardeners look for more continuity of blooms.

Watering

Rose bushes are usually healthier if the surface soil is allowed to dry out to the depth of 1–2 cm before being given a gentle but thorough soaking. The only exception is for about a week after feeding when it is safer to keep a little more moisture in the soil. Also, try to maintain a reasonable supply of moisture when bushes are in new growth. However, roses that have had time to establish a good root system have extremely good drought resistance and will recover remarkably after months of dryness.

It is only after a period of heavy feeding or where saline conditions are present that dryness can cause permanent damage.

Picking the blooms

With new roses, pick as lightly as possible to maintain maximum foliage as the plant depends on its leaves to produce the sugars and starches needed for vigorous growth.

To save unnecessary pruning later cut flowers as you would when pruning by making the cut above the third or fourth leaf from the base, favouring the one pointing in the direction the new growth is preferred, for the eye that will initiate this growth is in the junction of leaf and stem. Cut the same way as in pruning diagram.

The exception is with water shoots — those vigorous-looking, sappy stems carrying a candelabra-like formation of buds. Most growers prefer to leave at least the two lowest flower stems of the flower head until this new stem has matured properly.

Growing problems and solutions

Problem	Cause	Solution
Fuzzy brown or black spots with yellowish surround	Black spot fungus disease	See heading 'Black spot'
Greyish powder-like patches over leaves, young shoots and sometimes flower buds	Powdery mildew	Use Benlate or complete rose spray
Dull, sandblasted appearance of leaves	Red spider mites	Spray with Rogor, Lebaycid or Malathion
Dull, brownish-yellow markings between veins which may be yellowish, sometimes accompanied by shrivelling on leaf edges	Toxicity, usually of chloride	Avoid heavy or frequent use of rose fertilisers containing potassium chloride (muriate of potash), especially close to sea coast or in areas where water is heavily chlorinated. Water from chlorinated swimming pools will cause similar symptoms
Leaves small, yellowish-green sometimes with red spots and falling prematurely	Nitrogen deficiency	Soak root area with one of the complete, water-soluble plant foods
Leaves small and dark-green with purplish tints particularly on underside, growth weak and stunted	Phosphate deficiency	Apply handful of superphosphate per sq. m and water in well
Dead leaf margins and small, poor quality flowers	Potassium deficiency	Apply 1 level tablespoonful of potassium sulphate per sq. m and water in well or use a good rose food
Yellowing showing first toward centre of leaf between veins, and mainly on older foliage	Magnesium deficiency	Dissolve 1 teaspoon of Epsom Salts in a can of water and apply to area below foliage
Yellowing mainly around leaf edges and extending in between veins, mostly on older foliage	Manganese deficiency	Avoid over-limey soil, flood with water liberally or, if persistent, apply 1 tablespoon of manganese sulphate per can of water to area below foliage
More general yellowing, more pronounced on new growth	Iron deficiency	Apply iron chelates as directed on container and avoid over-liming
Yellowing first of the leaf veins and then generally along leaf midrib	Over-compacted or over-wet soils causing oxygen deficiency at roots	Dig soil to loosen when it is just damp and apply mulch or organic material to keep open. Avoid using water-containing detergents, or if drainage is bad, discontinue growing roses in that area
Leaves very dark-green and misshapen	Usually due to over-acid soil or heavy feeding with nitrogen which causes deficiencies of boron and molybdenum	If applicable, apply lime to correct acidity, otherwise apply a trace element mixture plus 1 heaped teaspoon each of superphosphate and potassium sulphate per sq. m of area and water in well. Then revert to use of complete fertilisers
Leaf fall	Apart from black spot and other factors already mentioned, this can be due to excessive use of Rogor or other organic phosphate sprays applied at higher than recommended concentrations	
Leaf burn	Can occur through over-generous fertilising or more frequently to too-strong concentrations of fungicides or rose sprays, or even to normal usage of sulphur and karathane preparations if application is followed by a hot sunny day	It is safer to apply fungicides late in the day or early evening. Use of a wetter agent minimises concentration of spray droplets in one area of foliage
Chewed foliage or petals	Usually attack by grasshoppers but caterpillars or, in some districts, earwigs can be responsible when foliage is young. Also check for slugs and snails	Spray with Endosulphan (Thiodan) or Carbaryl. If necessary use snail baits

Replacing old roses

When taking out an old plant, remove as much root as possible plus about a barrowful of soil from the root area. Exchange this with soil from a part of the garden where roses are not growing. The addition of well-rotted compost helps to offset the problems of 'rose-sick' soil.

Pruning

Roses, if left unpruned, continue to grow and flower but most of the growth goes to the top and the plant becomes very leggy. The bushes also become cluttered with dead or old unproductive growth.

The flower stem of the rose produces the

growth buds or shoots for the following season's stem. Notice that when a flower stem is left uncut, the new shoot comes from near the top of the flower. This is because of nature's form-rule that 'sap always flows more readily to the uppermost parts of the plant'. Nature probably worked this one out back in wilder days to help the rose fend for its share of light when it grew amongst many competitive plants!

A rose allowed to 'have its head' becomes leggy, the blooms tend to lose quality because the tops of the old stems, from where they start, are comparatively thin and less able to support them than sturdier sections nearer to the source of food and water supply. So this is where we take the initiative and either cut the flower stems or shorten the old ones at pruning time to force the new growth from the lower areas.

Nature apparently realised that if roses kept gaining height by the length of a full flower stem each season, only the birds could admire their beauty, so, after a year or two of seasonal skyward growth, this section of the plant loses vigour and new shoots (watershoots) develop, either from the plant's base or from well down on the main canes.

By pruning we speed development of more productive growth. Once a cane (main stem) or an upper section of it gets to the stage where it is producing only comparatively thin twiggy growth, cut it out, or back to where a newer cane emerges. Judgement between good and old twiggy growth is different with each bush because the poorest growth on a strong and vigorous grower is equivalent to the best on a weaker variety. If you have a below-standard cane, think carefully before removing it.

> **For details on rose pruning techniques refer to 'Pruning' chapter**

Cultivation problems and solutions

Scale

To treat this problem when roses are in growth, paint stems only with lime sulphur, mixed to the spraying solution recommended, or with 2 tablespoons of white oil per 4 L of water plus 1 teaspoon of Malathion.

Aphids

Are found clustered on young shoots or stems just below young flower buds. They weaken and sometimes deform the plant by sucking the sap. Ladybirds and their long, miniature dragon-like larvae eat at least 25 aphids a day; mantis, silver-eyes, wrens and other predators also feed on them so before spraying toxic substances on aphids try rubbing them off or spraying with soapy water. The Pyrethrum-type insecticides are the next choice as they only leave the plant toxic to predators for a few hours. They also effectively kill weevils and leaf-eating caterpillars.

Weevils and thrips

Are difficult to control in flowers as they are largely protected from sprays by the layers of petals. The best control is to carefully pull off ageing blooms and transfer to a plastic bag containing an insecticide or ammonia, or just tie tightly and leave in the sun.

Black spot

Black spot is a fungus infection; its spread and development are dependent on warm, moist nights or, more precisely, conditions where moisture or dewdrops remain on the foliage for at least 4 hours or longer at low temperatures. Therefore it is uncommon in areas where humidity is relatively low and summer nights are not dewy.

Spores of the fungus are carried over on old infected foliage that remains from the previous season. (For this reason it is a good idea to hoe in leafy mulch and foliage during the dormant winter period just after pruning, otherwise the spores are released from these dead leaves, float in the air like dust and some eventually lodge on the new season's rose foliage.)

To develop sufficiently to gain entry to the leaf, they must remain in a water droplet for about 4 hours when temperatures are in the 25–30°C range or up to 12 hours in the 10–15°C range. Do not water the foliage late in the day so that it will remain wet at night. Foliage watering at other times is not detrimental. It can wash off black spot spores but will also remove the residue of sprays. Dewy nights are the main problem.

Control of black spot disease is achieved by spraying at least once a week with a rose spray or fungicide that will remain in a film on the leaf and go into solution with any water droplets that should kill or at least prevent the black spot fungus from developing. During showery periods or where there is overhead watering this protective spray film readily washes from the leaves as has been mentioned. The answer is to use a good sytemic fungicide that will remain on the leaf for some time and prevent the disease from entering or at least from taking hold.

Weekly sprayings with Triforon have given good results against black spot and other sprays of this nature are being developed. One that also controls powdery mildew has some advantages as it eliminates the need for applying a second fungicide.

Burn rose prunings, and at pruning time spray with a clean-up fungicide such as lime-sulphur spray to help eliminate transmission of black spot. If you prefer not to dig in surface mulch apply another layer of mulch over the old one, some weeks before new rose growth is due to start. This will speed decomposition of the old and presumably affected foliage, and spores carried by the latter will be rendered harmless in nature's melting pot of soil organisms.

Failure to grow

This can be due to a number of factors. The more common ones are planting too deeply in heavy clay soils (roots should not be deeper than about 10 cm) and poor drainage. Too much water around the roots usually kills a plant.

Root damage can be caused by chafer or similar grubs (usually whitish-grey with small orange heads which curl into a crescent when disturbed). If their presence is suspected flood the soil with an insecticide such as Carbaryl or with Endosulphan.

Overfeeding will also cause root damage, especially if soils containing high rates of fertiliser or soluble soil salts are allowed to dry out. Remember that smaller but more frequent than recommended applications of fertilisers or rose foods are usually the safest, particularly in quick-drying, sandy soils. Apply fertiliser only when the soil is moist and water well afterwards. Do not feed newly planted roses until new growth is well developed, and then only sparingly, otherwise future growth could be seriously retarded.

Rose sickness occurs when a new rose is planted where an old one has been removed. The rose-sickness is due to deficiency of trace elements needed by the roses, eelworm (nematode) infestation causing knotting and distortion of the roots and possibly a build-up of toxic substances exuded by the roots of the previous roses.

To avoid danger of 'rose sickness' remove as much of the old root as possible and at least half a barrow load of soil from the root area and replace with soil from a part of the garden where roses are not growing. The removed soil will not be detrimental for plants other than roses. When planting the new roses the addition of plenty of well-rotted compost mixed in with the soil and a surface mulch of compost will help to avoid future problems.

Dieback

Dieback can be due to a number of factors, including black spot and bad pruning practices, such as leaving an old cane stub instead of cutting it to as close as possible above the newer cane or removing the old growth during summer instead of the winter. The remaining dead tissue may then extend down to envelop the newer growth. Cutting new canes too high above a leaf junction or eye may also be a factor.

Downy mildew, which was only recognised as a serious rose disease during recent years, seems to be a major cause of dieback. This starts with leaf shrivelling and a purplish streaking of the stems which is often followed by splitting or canker.

Treatment of downy mildew is to cut back to an eye or healthy cane junction well below the obviously affected area, burn prunings and spray thoroughly with Mancozeb, making sure that this also covers all cut surfaces. Repeat the spraying a fortnight later and if symptoms occur again.

This same treatment should be carried out if dieback appears to be due to other causes. Regular but not excessive feeding and watering is also recommended. Some rose varieties are prone to dieback and/or downy mildew than others.

23. Australian native plants

A native garden can be one of the easiest to keep in order, not because Australian native plants are the easiest to grow, or are trouble-free, but because the garden is relatively maintenance-free. Leaves and twigs are an acceptable part of the ground cover. They look natural, and once you build up a good cover of mulch and living plants there is little or no weed invasion.

Digging is unnecessary, and once you have the soil under control is undesirable. Root disturbance is not appreciated by any plants and most of our Australian plants resent it more strongly than others.

If starting with a completely cleared site decide first on the most suitable utility areas, children's play areas and so on, and then select trees or major plantings where they are best suited for both shade and aesthetic reasons.

If you feel a lawn is needed, then have one, even though some people may say that lawns don't go with native gardens. They certainly do with bush gardens, but can be a problem in shaded areas overhung by trees simply because they just don't grow well in these aspects.

Devise some way of preventing couch or kikuyu from finding its way into surrounding bush setting. The conventional cement mower strip may look a little too contrived here but you could overcome this by keeping the edges even and true on the lawn side to make maintenance easy, and running it into irregularly-placed and varying-sized flat bush stones on the other.

Pea gravel or similarly exposed aggregate, bedded into the cement of the mower strip, can also give a more natural effect, especially if, here and there, it runs into a drift of slightly coarse river pebbles or river gravel which can be used as a mulch around most native plants. Alternatively, you could design a split stone path between lawn and native garden.

The lush green of lawns and exotic plants need not be in conflict with an Australian native or bushland garden. Flora from our exposed hilltops or heathland country and the predominantly sunny slopes may be dull olive to grey-green in tones, but most of the natural growth in our more protected valleys and in coastal rainforest areas is just as lush and rich green as most exotics and blends beautifully with azaleas or rhododendrons, cymbidium orchids, rich green maples and camellias.

Grevilleas are among the most adaptable native shrubs. Being long flowering, their great attraction to nectar and insect-eating birds lasts for many months, in a few cases almost continuously.

Probably the longest flowering grevillea is G. banksii which, in reasonably open situations, makes a large rounded shrub to about 3 m high with dark-green fern-like foliage and erect spikes of usually red flowers almost throughout the year.

Next comes one of its smaller-growing progeny, G. Robyn Gordon, which has spreading growth, usually only about 1 m high and rarely without glistening red brushes of flower.

Some of the tall-growing, handsome-foliaged toothbrush-flowered grevilleas such as G. Ivanhoe, which makes fairly erect growth 3–4 m high, and the more spreading pink-flowered but otherwise similar G. asplenifolia, are also long flowering in open or lightly shaded aspects.

Some of the medium-sized grevilleas with beautiful growth are the various G. lavandulacea varieties and hybrids, such as Canberra Gem, with dense clumps of upright stems,

Acacia sublata (Awl Wattle), made more compact by top pruning. It suits cool to warmer temperate districts and flowers during summer and autumn.

Casuarina, Banksia serrata and Grevillea 'Ivanhoe'

Cassia artemisioides (Silver Cassia)

Callistemon 'Gawler' hybrid

Acacia retinoides, like many of the adaptable wattles, rapidly provides soft screening as well as bright golden flowers. It grows 4–8 m high and nearly as wide.

Eriostemon myoporoides, grevillea lavandulacea and dillwynia combine to bring colour to the garden

densely clad in dark glossy green slender foliage with red flowers.

Other grevilleas, such as *G. biternata, obtusifolia, laurifolia* and some forms of *G. juniperina,* have prostrate form which is ideal for ground cover planting.

The bottlebrushes (*Callistemons*) are also extremely adaptable subjects that grow in heavy or light soils, have good drought resistance but in most cases also accept badly-drained or even sedgy soil.

They include the 5 m tall, cream-flowered *C. salignus,* noted for its silky pink new growth, the erect shrubby 3–4 m *C. citrinus* with bright-red brushes, the gracefully weeping 4 m high *C. viminalis,* the larger brushed form Hannah Ray, and the relatively dwarf form Captain Cook, which rarely grows more than 2 m. As with the grevilleas, there are many other worthwhile hybrids and variants.

The banksias are beautiful and include a few varieties such as the rich scarlet Albany banksia (*B. coccinea*) which is a challenge to grow in most areas outside its native habitat, and others such as long, golden orange-covered *B. ericifolia* which is widely adaptable. The latter makes a dense 3 m high dome of fine dark-green foliage, and is happy on the coast or inland, providing the position is well drained.

The Waratah (*Telopea*), which most plant lovers want to grow, is unpredictable, growing well in a variety of different aspects and, at the same time, refusing to budge in others that may seem identical and that may be regarded as its natural habitats. Although a great deal of research has been undertaken on this plant, there is, so far, no reliable success formula, except that it resents fertilisers that are high in phosphorus and in some cases bushfires seem to contribute to its well-being. In any case, it is worth trying and it could be rewarding.

Other natives such as the lovely blue *leschenaultia,* brown boronia and red and green kangaroo paw (not adaptable flavida varieties) are short-lived in many districts but are quick to flower, so are worth planting even if they give only one season of pleasure.

Apart from the bottlebrushes, some of the *melaleucas,* swamp heath (*Springelia*), *Banksia robur,* the Albany kangaroo paw (*Anigosanthus flavidus* varieties) and a few other exceptions, most native plants need well-drained soil. If drainage is doubtful, put in a system of agricultural drainage pipes or plant in beds built up at least 30 cm above the surrounding soil.

Heavy clay soils will also grow a wider range of native plants more successfully if first dug over deeply, then covered with from 5–15 cm of coarse river sand. In all cases a surface mulch of compost will benefit. Keep up the organic content of the soil, save the need for root-disturbing weeding and create a more natural appearance by maintaining a cover of leafmould or woodchip over the soil.

Don't be too impatient. Small plants often surpass those planted as advanced specimens. Do not overcrowd or overshadow. Check height and spread and allow for it when planting.

Paths

To create a pleasantly relaxed, natural bushland atmosphere paths need to be of natural material, to meander a little across the contour of the site or around trees or groups of shrubbery. Avoid regular edges and create interest and surprise by occasionally narrowing the path between some tall, dense, bushy shrubs or groups of shrubbery, then widen it where you have a more open area with an interesting collection of smaller plants.

Flat bush stones look picturesque but it is wisest to keep these for stepping stones or secondary paths between low plantings or native ground covers. Plain earth with a normal cover of leaves makes the most natural looking path. If you have heavy soil that becomes sticky when wet, or busy access paths that tend to become eroded by foot traffic, use a topping of blue metal screenings or wood chip. Both are comfortable underfoot. However, on sloping sites contour paths often become watercourses, so some well-placed flat stones, or stepping stones, will help to prevent running water from gouging out the soil.

Another way around this problem is to use shallow steps of timber here and there, to retain soil and lessen the grade. Hardwood pieces (10 cm x 5 cm), just a little longer than the path width and held by stout pegs at either end, will serve this purpose — or you may prefer the more natural look of lengths of saplings or small logs used the same way. If you need steep steps, select stone that looks as if it belongs to the site. If this is too difficult you could use lengths of railway sleepers or solid logs as risers, with earth firmed in behind them. These wooden sections can be held in place by cutting or bolting them into a sleeper framing either side of the steps or, in a less regular style, by angle iron pegs near either end, providing these are driven in lower than the top of the riser.

Ground cover

There are many low, spreading plants that can be used as ground covers below taller plants. They look natural and decorative and help to deter weed growth and protect the soil. To establish them successfully you will have to give the natural bushland cover of leaves, bark, twigs, stone or a mixture of these materials.

Unless you have an unspoilt bushland area, relatively free from weeds, spread a mulch 2–4 cm thick of leafmould, woodchip or pine bark either before planting or immediately after. This prevents competitive weed growth and saves the tedious and root-disturbing chore of weeding while the cover plants are establishing.

It also helps water to penetrate the soil evenly, improving drainage and aeration by keeping it more open, and stops soil from splashing and the coating of the young plant stems and foliage which can foster fungal and bacterial diseases.

When planting just rake the mulch clear of the spot then replace it immediately afterwards, preferably before watering, as then surface puddling and caking will be avoided.

Buying plants

Most people planning a new garden are impatient to enjoy the end result, so advanced plants are tempting. These may be good value but after the first season or two they can be surpassed, both in size and quality, by smaller and cheaper specimens which were planted at the same time. A young plant experiences less shock from transplanting disturbance and the roots have not grown sufficiently to suffer restriction within the container.

Another point in favour of starting with smaller plants is that larger plants often have had to be staked and this causes them to lose a lot of their natural character as well as their wind resistance.

However, whether buying small or advanced plants, avoid those that look as though they have been in their containers for a long time as these are likely to be root bound, with roots tightly matted in a fibrous mass which takes the shape of the container. Except for plants in small tapered containers it is difficult to tap a plant out to check its roots so avoid woody and old-looking trunk and stems with wiry roots protruding from the drainage slits of the pots.

Preparing the site
Clearing weeds and pest shrubs

If you are lucky enough to have completely unspoilt surroundings, disturb them as little as possible.

Unfortunately these days you rarely find unspoilt bushland close to roads or habitation; there is usually some degree of invasion by lantana, privet, blackberry, kikuyu, couch or other weeds of cultivation.

The best way that bushland areas can be restored to their natural state is by systematically clearing small areas, hand-pulling where possible and covering the disturbed area immediately afterwards to prevent other undesirable plants taking hold in the cleared soil by leaving the uprooted plants or weeds covering the area they were removed from, with the roots above the soil so that they dry and die more quickly.

Chop large weeds or shrubby plants into smaller sections to keep things looking reasonably tidy and, if privets or other noxious weeds are seed-infested, remove them and cover the area with other acceptable organic material. I find it doesn't take long to cut prunings into short pieces and spread them as mulch around the shrub they came from; you can keep a reserve heap of this material to supply cover where needed.

Persistent grasses of cultivation such as kikuyu, couch and others cannot be removed by hand.

Poison the unwanted grasses and weeds such as kikuyu, couch and other runaway grasses by using chemicals such as Zero.

Mist most of the weed foliage without causing run-off into the soil, as this can affect some trees and native shrubs. Poison the weeds 3 or 4 weeks before planting. For weed infestations amongst numerous native shrubs you intend keeping, use Polyquot or Weedex.

These may be applied with a fine-rosed watering can or one fitted with a special trickle bar. Apply the chemicals right up to brown-stemmed shrubs as they destroy only green plant tissue and decompose within days when in contact with soil. However, they are very toxic to animals and humans, so it is imperative to observe label instructions carefully. For this reason, watering can application is advised rather than spraying.

Pest shrub or tree

Lantana, a common invader of many areas, has formidable, prickly stems but is shallow-rooted and easily killed by grubbing out the main roots then pulling out emergent seedlings. Chop the stems and foliage into manageable lengths and leave them covering the soil to prevent it from eroding and to deter other unwanted growth.

Privets, camphor laurels and other noxious trees

If too large to grub out cut down to a stump 25–30 cm high, then without delay frill the stump with several layers of *shallow* downward-sloping cuts and saturate by trickling in 1 tablespoon of Tree and Blackberry Killer (now 245T without harmful 'agent orange') mixed with 5 tablespoonfuls of kerosene. This is enough for a stump 10–12 cm in diameter.

Bruise exposed roots leading from the stump with the back of an axe and trickle in the mixture. To prevent volatile fumes from the chemical affecting nearby wanted plants and to increase effectiveness of treatment, tie a large plastic bag over the stump, and secure the edges of the plastic with a little soil.

Blackberries can also be treated with Tree and Blackberry Killer but in this case the chemical should be diluted with water as suggested on the container label and sprayed to wet both foliage and canes as thoroughly as possible. Do not cut down vines prior to treatment as effectiveness depends on covering the largest foliage area possible. Leave canes standing after treatment until completely dead. Early to mid-autumn treatment is usually the most effective. Spray drift from this chemical can damage wanted plants in the area, so choose a still day for spraying.

Soil

Where possible leave all branches and twigs covering cleared area. This will not only prevent weed growth but will return nutrients to the soil that the unwanted growth took from it. A mulcher will convert foliage and smaller branches into a fine mulch which presents no fire danger. Heavier branches and trunks can be strategically placed to retain soil and mulch in a natural looking manner.

There are a number of Australian native plants tolerant of, or adaptable to, heavy clay soils or soggy conditions, but most prefer quick-draining and fairly light soil. If the soil is heavy or clayey and remains wet for long periods after rain you could just concentrate on plants listed as suitable for this situation, but you can enjoy a far greater variety of plants by building up at least part of the area with lighter soil.

Be careful because a lot of so-called 'garden soil' sold is brown or dark-grey alluvial loam that looks good, but sets so densely that roots are starved for oxygen and a plant can make little or no progress. Far better to choose bush sand or coarse river sand. The latter is an excellent topping, even for some of the lighter loams, because it keeps the soil open, allowing good penetration of air and water. It is an excellent growing medium when mixed with a little compost, rotted leafmould or peatmoss.

A gravel mulch also helps water penetration, keeps the soil open and prevents silting material from splashing over plant stems and lower foliage. A coarse river sand topping helps in the cultivation of dry summer plants such as leschenaultia, Sturt's desert pea and red and green kangaroo paw, but unless there is some cover from leafmould or other plantings it may get a little hot for brown and red boronia, bauera, epacris, ferns and other lovers of cool, damp soil.

There are several ways to build up the soil simply and in an attractive but natural way. The new soil can be tipped in nearly flat-topped mounds with gently graded sides ascending to a broad crown a metre or so above the original soil level. Where space does not allow this the soil may be retained almost vertically or in one or more steps using logs, railway sleepers, rocks or neutrally coloured concrete blocks or bricks as retainers. Weep-holes must be left to assure escape of excess water.

A built-up bed caters for a range of natives because those needing keen drainage can be located near the top and others preferring more moisture on the lower and damper levels.

Lime

Lime is not generally considered desirable for native plants but slightly limy soils are preferred by eremophilas, desert cassia, desert pea and most other plants from the low-rainfall inland areas of Australia. Some others from Western Australia, Geraldton Wax for instance, grow naturally in limy or slightly alkaline to neutral soils but can adapt well to fairly acid soil conditions.

Therefore, garden lime (ground limestone or calcium carbonate) or dolomite (calcium magnesium limestone) could be added sparingly (say half a cup per sq. m) when growing the plants mentioned in some of the acid soils from comparatively high rainfall areas.

This also applies for the more general range of plants in strongly acid Hawkesbury sandstone and similar soils, especially when these areas have not had bushfires for some years.

Soil-testing (pH) kits can be obtained from comprehensive garden stores to give fairly accurate indications of acidity or alkalinity (limyness). As a rough indicator, flowers of hydrangeas are usually blue in acid soils, pink in alkaline. Presence of bracken usually indicates moderately acid soil conditions.

Planting

Aspect

Although many native plants are adaptable, give those from other areas the conditions they prefer and separate them according to their likes, keeping those which prefer moist conditions at a lower level. Ones that prefer dry summer conditions can be built up in more elevated positions so that they can be watered separately from the others. Some of the dry summer plants can only be grown in wet areas in containers given protection from prolonged summer rain.

Note the aspect where the plants grow best in their native habitat or, if from a distant area, how they grow best in other native plant collections. Those that grow in shaded gullies can be planted on the southern side of a dense, foliaged shrub tall enough to shade them during the hottest part of the day. Others such as the Sydney boronia, tetratheca, dampiera and fan flower can be planted on the southern or eastern side of the more wispy foliaged plants, e.g. Grevillea serissa and lambertia.

In quick-drying, sandy soils it is an advantage to start the plants in spring or autumn so that they are well established before the heat of summer.

Although many native plants are found growing in full sun, they are invariably protected by taller plants in their early stage and establish quicker if some initial protection is given. I have found that this applies particularly to waratahs, boronias and some of the smaller grevilleas. So when starting small plants in exposed conditions or plants that have been under shade cloth in nurseries, try poking in a few twiggy sticks on the northern side or in a pyramid over them. Let them gradually grow out from this protection.

When planting make sure that the top of the soil ball or level of soil in the nursery container is set no deeper than normal soil level.

Avoid later settlement of soil by treading over areas that have been dug prior to planting, then digging the hole for the plant no deeper than the actual soil in the container but about twice as wide so that soil can be properly packed around it.

The exception is when a planting area in pure sand is improved with peatmoss mixed in below the root area, but in this case it should be firmed well before planting.

When digging, treading or planting any soil with a clay content (one that cakes or sets hard), have the soil at the just damp state only. If it is obviously moist or sticky delay planting until later.

Also with the above type soil it is good practice to mulch some leafmould, dry grass or other organic material around the plant immediately after planting and before watering as this then stops the surface from caking afterwards, and so improves aeration of the soil and induces stronger root growth.

Surface mulching or even a surface scree of pebbles also stops soil from splashing and coating around the stems and lower foliage of plants. This splashing is undesirable because it increases the risk of rotting or damping off during wet or humid periods, particularly with greyish foliaged plants, dampieras, leschenaultia, Sturt's Desert Pea, etc.

Root-bound plants (those with roots tightly matted around the soil ball) rarely progress well. Sometimes roots fail to emerge from this tight ball and the plant dies during the first dry period. Filling around the plant with a good root-inducing mixture (say 3 parts coarse river sand to 1 part well-rotted leafmould or compost) will help roots to spread. However, it is worth spreading the roots manually when planting. Unwind ones coiled around the base of the container or gently pull the base of the root wall outwards, spreading them as much as possible. Then build and firm soil up to make a platform for a few likely looking roots a little further up; spreading, covering, firming and repeating the process.

Some people may say it is dangerous to disturb the roots of native plants. This is so but I maintain that it is better to risk losing the plant than have it remain permanently crippled. The alternative is to obtain another plant with roots in a better condition: with any but large containers it is easy to check in the nursery by upending the pot with one hand over the soil and tapping it out on the edge on a solid rail, bench or similar surface.

If you do have to disturb roots, compensate by pruning the plant back by about one-third and shade it for a week or two under some foliage supported by stakes.

Banksia serrata

Growing native plants in pots

Many native plants can be enjoyed in pots, on balconies or other areas where there is no soil, also where soil is not suitable or drainage is poor. Container growing also makes it possible to enjoy dry summer subjects such as leschenaultia or Sturt's Desert Pea in wet summer areas, as the containers can be brought under shelter during long wet periods.

A good standard soil mixture for pots is 2 parts coarse sand, 1 part good crumbly garden loam and 1 part well-rotted compost or rotted cow manure. Some growers omit the loam, using an extra part of sand.

Results are usually better if the container can have some protection from full sunlight, especially in summer, as this makes the soil surprisingly warm and can damage or retard root development. Sometimes it is possible to place the actual container but not the plant in it where it is shaded by another plant, low railing, a few rocks or by a grouping of other containers. A trailing plant over the northern side of the container can also have the desired effect.

Tree ferns grow in shade and damp

Grevillea 'Royal Mantle'

Nuytsia floribunda (Western Australian Christmas Bush) with red Banksia coccinea

Caring for native plants

Staking

Staking is a convention frequently recommended for trees and shrubs but is often undesirable, especially for shrubs which resent root disturbance, such as Geraldton Wax and many other Australian natives. Too often staking is responsible for the loss of the plant because the upward training causes it to become top heavy, and once the stake rots, it topples, breaking a large percentage of its roots at the same time.

In their natural state, especially in windy areas, plants develop a natural lean away from the wind in their early stages, and their lower branches then touch the ground and give them a self-bracing structure. Although a stake and support will increase the initial growth of tall shrubs or small trees they will be left with a comparatively weak root system that usually lacks wind resistance.

Where stakes are needed for protection it is better to put 2 or 3 a span or so out from the stem of the plant and encircle them with a light tie. This will allow natural movement but still give some support.

A small picket made of 3 or 4 sticks placed on the windward side of a shrub will also give some protection and allow it to make more rapid growth.

Hypocalymma cordifolium

Grevillea 'Robyn Gordon'

Prostanthera nivea

Ptilotus obovatus

Watering

For the first few months, while new plants are establishing, it is good practice to let the soil get quite dry for 1–2 cm below the surface, then give a good soaking. This encourages roots to penetrate the soil and make the plants more self-reliant.

Treatment from then on depends on your selection of plants. This is where plants native to the district can then look after themselves, because they are the ones conditioned through the ages to stand the long wet or dry periods typical of the district.

It is for this reason that in the Perth area, with normally dry summers, the local government is urging people to grow local native plants in their gardens to conserve water. Some of the east-coast natives would not survive in the Perth or Adelaide areas without artificial watering.

On the other hand, once established in their own district they can be left to depend on rain except when growing in pots and perhaps in raised beds with light soil where drainage is particularly keen.

However, most plant lovers like variety and are always seeking something different so have plants from many areas in their collections. Also in the majority of cases natives are intermingled with exotics.

The only safe recommendation is to give a good soaking whenever dryness penetrates more than a few centimetres below the surface. To some extent you can compensate for moist or dry preferences by putting such types as leschenaultia, desert pea or red and green kangaroo paws in more elevated, quicker-drying pockets of soil — while baueras, epacris, brown boronias, Albany kangaroo paw, etc. are in lower areas where it is easier to maintain a damper soil.

Finally, when you do need to water, if possible use a sprinkler that covers a wide area. This minimises root competition from trees or strong growers that otherwise send their roots into favoured areas where plants are watered individually.

Mulching

As already advocated, a mulch helps to conserve moisture and assists its penetration into the soil, even though it may at times itself seem hard to wet. The cover of mulch also acts as a buffer against heavy rain, and therefore prevents surface puddling and preserves the desirable crumbly structure of the soil.

Fertilising

Most native plants exist happily in low-fertility soil, gaining sufficient food for their needs from decomposing leafmould with occasional droppings from insects, birds and other animals. Few will tolerate strong fertilisers, particularly those that contain superphosphate.

If feeding is needed, organic fertilisers such as blood and bone are safest because they release inorganic nutrients slowly as they break down. A light dressing of cow manure that has partly decomposed is also effective. Some growers also use water-soluble nutrients such as Zest, Thrive or Aquasol, but with some fertiliser-sensitive natives even these are safer

applied at half-strength and then only when the soil is moist, preferably just before new growth starts.

Avoid feeding when shrubs are dormant as this can be harmful because nutrient salts not used by the plants can build up a concentration strong enough to cause root damage. This applies particularly when the soil dries out as the concentrates increase then.

Propagation

Most shrubby natives can be propagated from cuttings. Tips of new growth with 3–8 cm of stem may be taken when they have hardened sufficiently to lose their sappiness, or use side shoots to this size broken off with a small heel of the old wood attached.

Remove the lower half to two-thirds of foliage using, for example, a nail to dibble a hole, firm them in about one-third their depth and 2–3 cm apart close to the edge of a 12 cm pot almost filled with a mixture of 3 parts coarse river sand and 1 of moistened peatmoss, all well firmed down and watered.

Cover with a plastic bag and keep in good light but out of direct sunlight until roots appear which may take from 4–10 weeks, then remove cover and gradually condition to sunlight.

Most natives also germinate readily from seed providing it is fresh and sown at the right time. Late autumn or early winter is sometimes preferred in warm humid climates for waratah and other seedlings inclined to damp off earlier in autumn. In cool climates spring is the best time.

Use either proprietary seed-raising mixture or mix equal parts of coarse river sand, good crumbly garden loam and well-rotted compost blended well together. Preferably sterilise this by spreading in a metal dish and baking in an oven set at 75°C (200°F) for about 20 minutes, or until heated through to the centre.

When cold, fill into pots or seedling punnets, firm evenly, sprinkle seed thinly over surface and cover with either vermiculite, coarse gritty sand or fine gravel, press down gently and stand to about two-thirds the height of the soil in water until the surface is moist.

Keep moist by soaking as suggested, or syringing gently when needed, but when seedlings appear, allow the surface to almost dry out before watering again.

Seeds of leguminous plants (those with bean-like pods such as wattle, cassia and pea flower) need abraiding between sandpaper or to have boiling water poured over them then left to soak for 3 or 4 hours before planting.

Seedlings need thinning out or carefully replanting into individual pots when they are close enough to be touching, but leave this until the true — or in the case of wattles and eucalyptus, juvenile — leaves have formed.

Note that some seeds come through in a week or two. A few very slow ones such as Christmas Bells (*blandifordia*) may take from 6–12 months.

Pruning

Avoid heavy pruning of natives especially when the shape of the plant is acceptable. Growth can be made bushier and in many

cases the vigour of the plant improved by a light pruning after flowering to prevent seeding. As a general rule leave at least 2 and preferably 4, or sometimes more, leaves to the base of the flower stem which, in most cases, is the wood made during the last growing season.

It is desirable to prune before new growth starts. In the case of some natives such as bottlebrush and waratah it is necessary to start before flower colour completely fades as new growth is very quick to shoot from the end or base of the flower respectively before it finishes.

The main part of pruning for more compact form is to follow the initial cutting by tip-pruning or pinching out the tip of new growth, usually when it is about finger length, providing the new base leaves already look mature. This encourages further branching.

Native creepers have a special charm

Most of Australia's native climbing plants are in the well-behaved or easily controlled category and some of them provide good dense cover that remains attractive throughout the year.

Among the most appealing climbers in the native plant range is Pandorea 'Snowbells'. During late September and October Snowbells is almost covered with dense sprays of creamy-white bells that contrast beautifully against a background of handsomely-divided dark glossy-green foliage. Occasional flower clusters appear until January.

Snowbells is a free-flowering and vigorous form of the Wonga-wonga vine (*Pandorea pandorana*) which, in earlier days, was listed either as bignonia or more usually as *Tecoma australis*. The more common form has pretty purplish markings inside the narrow flower bell.

This and other Pandoreas are worth growing for their handsome foliage alone. Also, the old flowers fall before browning which keeps the vine permanently attractive. Their native habitats range from Queensland to Tasmania, and from fairly open situations to dense rainforest country where vines make early growth in almost complete shade, then make their way to the tree tops to flower.

Pandorea jasminoides has comparatively large and beautiful palest pink, bignonia-like flowers that flatten to about 4 cm across at the top to display a maroon centre.

These come in scattered clusters rather than in a mass like the Wonga-wonga vine or Snowbells.

Happy Wanderer, a good free-flowering selection of *Hardenbergia violacea*, was introduced as 'Climber of the Year, 1981'.

This is another adaptable native that grows happily in well-drained soil, whether in full sun or half shade.

This species is native to all states except Western Australia, occurring on the coast in the highlands and inland districts. It is widely adaptable and stands tough, dry conditions. A tea-tree or similarly bushy shrub covered by the vine in spring is a delightful sight. In the garden it is best on a wire fence, pillar or as a stump cover but be aware of its wandering habits because it is not above taking over a nearby shrub.

The Kennedias are an amiable group of native climbers, closely related to Hardenbergias. They are widely used as scrambling ground covers for banks, but also make attractive fence covers or light screens.

One of the showiest is the coral creeper (*K. coccinea*) from the comparatively moist but well-drained soils in the jarrah forests of southwestern Australia. In spring it is tightly clustered with small, light scarlet/orange pea flowers about 1 cm long, and is a glorious sight when draped over logs or low bushes in sheltered, fern-covered areas of the forest.

K. rubicunda, one of several species referred to as 'running postman', is the most vigorous east Australian variety with large, but comparatively sparse, dull leathery green leaves and pea flowers about 5 cm long. This is a tough vine that adapts to a variety of soils and aspects.

Traveller's Joy is one of the common names for *Clematis aristata*. The name implies that water is close by to where it grows, but although in spring it often covers trees along watercourses with a delightful lacy canopy of creamy-white starry flowers, it is also found in all Australian states on paddock fences and other supports, well away from water. The flowers are followed by spidery, quaintly twisted seed awls, covered with silvery hair.

Plants for special purposes

For lightly shaded areas with average moisture
Banksia collina
Bauera rubioides
Boronia pinnata
Boronia mollis
Boronia megastigma
Cordyline stricta
Dampiera stricta
  D. diversifolia
Dillwynia ericifolia
Eriostemon myoporoides
Grevillea asplenifolia
Hibbertia stricta
  H. volubilis
Hovea longifolia
Lambertia formosa
Prostanthera lasianthos
Persoonia pinifolia
Platylobium formosum
Pultenaea daphnioides
  P. flexilis

Plants with good resistance to salt winds
Acacia baileyana
  A. longifolia (variety *Sophorea*)
  A. podalyriifolia (most acacia species have reasonable resistance)

Banksia ericifolia
Cassia artemisioides
Correa alba
  C. reflexa
Crowea saligna
Geraldton Wax (*Chamelaucium*)
Hibbertia volubilis
Leptospermum laevigatum
Melaleuca hypericifolia
Myoporum
Oleria dentata — *O. tomentosa*
Westringia fruticosa

Trees for seaside planting
Araucaria cunninghamii
  A. excelsa
Banksia integrifolia
Callitris rhomboidea
Casuarina equistifolia
  C. stricta
Cupaniopsis anacardioides
Hibiscus tiliaceus
Lagunaria patersonii
Leptospermum petersonii

Shrubs for wet soils
Albany Kangaroo Paw (*Anigozanthus flavidus* varieties)
Banksia robur
Beaufortia sparsa
Bottlebrush (*Callistemon* — especially *C. citrinus* varieties)
Cordyline stricta
Epacaris impressa
  E. longiflora
  E. microphylla
Sprengelia

Shrubs for heavy clay soils
Albany Kangaroo Paw
Bauera rubioides
Callistemon — varieties
Grevillea asplenifolia
  G. *banksii*
  G. *juniperina*
  G. *rosmarinifolia*
  G. Robyn Gordon
  G. Royal Mantle
Leptospermum petersonii

Plants to attract native birds
Acacia
Agonis
Albizia
Angophora
Baeckea
Banksia
Billarderia
Boronia
Busaria
Callistemon
Callitris
Calytrix
Cassia
Cassinia
Casuarina
Ceropetalum
Chamelaucium
Chorizema
Coprosma
Correa
Dillwynia
Dryandra

Elaeocarpus
Eremophila
Eriostemum
Eucalypt
Eugenia
Gompholobium
Goodenia
Grevillea
Hakea
Hibbertia
Hymenosporum
Kunzea
Lambertia
Leptospermum
Melaleuca
Olearia
Pittosporum
Prostanthera
Sollya

Flowers for the vase
Acacia
Actinotus
Anigozanthus
Baeckea
Banksia
Blandfordia
Boronia
Callistemon
Calytrix
Ceratopetalum
Chamelaucium
Crowea
Darwinia
Epacris
Eriostemon
Grevillea
Hakea
Helichrysum
Lambertia
Melaleuca
Prostanthera
Telopea
Thryptomene

Palms
Archontophoenix
Calamus
Caryota
Howeia
Livistonia
Orania
Ptychosperma

Ferns
Adiantum
Asplenium
Athyrium
Azola
Blechnum
Cyathea
Dicksonia
Lycopodium
Lygodium
Marsilea
Nephrolepsis
Ophioglossum
Platycerium
Pyrossia
Todea
Vittaria

Chorizema cordatum (W.A. Flame Pea)

Anigozanthos flavidus hybrid (Kangaroo Paw)

Pandorea pandorana

Hardenbergia comptoniana (Native Wisteria)

Hibbertia scandens

Wattles bring a splash of winter colour

Australia's wattles begin to splash their brilliant gold across our otherwise sombre, grey-green hillsides during winter, and that is why 1 August was chosen as 'Wattle Day', to honour our national flower. This is a time when other colour is at its lowest ebb, so their cheerful sparkle is even more appreciated.

There is great diversity in the wattles. More than 600 of the 800-odd recorded species are native to Australia. These range from low-spreading rockery-type shrubs to massive trees 10–20 m high. Some are broad foliaged, others soft and fern-like.

A remarkable thing about them is that all start their seedling stage with finely divided foliage then gradually, but completely, change into their adult leaf form which, in some cases, is as broad as a gum leaf.

Botanically, all of our wattles are acacias except, ironically, the one responsible for this purely Australian title. This is the creek wattle, Callicoma, which at first glance resembles acacia. It grew in the first settlement along the Tank Stream, as it still does along many creeks of eastern Australia. Its long, flexible 3–4 m stems were ideal for weaving the wattle or fabric for the wattle and daub huts of the first settlers. Therefore, this and all the acacias which appeared similar in flower were all known as 'wattles'.

Apart from flower brilliance, the foliage of many wattles is very beautiful. Among the loveliest are the Queensland wattle (*A. podalyriifolia*), which has foliage like silver-grey velvet, and the finely divided blue-grey Cootamundra wattle (*A. baileyana*). The latter, particularly, makes a pleasant, soft background for other trees and shrubs, and also gives an illusion of distance to a landscape.

The Cootamundra wattle is worth considering, especially in larger landscapes, for combining with, alternating with, or as a background for the numerous exotic prunuses, particularly for the dark-foliaged flowering plums.

Acacia baileyana

Acacia saligna (Golden Wreath Wattle)

Acacia podalyriifolia (Queensland Wattle)

Acacia decurrens

It is a wonderful foil for the soft-pink, early-spring prunus blossoms and for the dark-purple bronze foliage that follows.

Similar combinations could be made with dark-foliaged maples, most autumn foliage, the pink of Cape chestnuts, the scarlet of the Western Australian flowering gums (*Eucalyptus ficifolia*) or of the flame trees.

Admittedly, the Cootamundra wattle and many others are short-lived, sometimes with a lifespan of only about 7 years, but they are quick to grow and flower so there is not long to wait for a replacement.

This quick-growing but short-lived character can also be used to advantage. These trees are excellent planted between or just beyond other plantings to that they give quick screening and a sense of establishment while permanent, slower-growing trees are developing and establishing themselves.

One of the quickest growing and very adaptable medium-sized species is the Sallow wattle (*A. longifolia*), which has broad, pale-green foliage and fingers of yellow flowers in spring. It can grow about 3 m in a year, eventually making a round-headed or pyramid-shaped tree about 5–6 m high. It is relatively long-lived and widely used in California as a street tree. Another variety, *A. longifolia sophorae*, is also widely used for sand binding and reclamation work on the seafront, so naturally has good salt-wind resistance.

Another taller and even quicker grower is the Cedar wattle (*A. elata*). It grows rapidly to about 20 m, has large, fern-like mid-green foliage and fragrant cream flowers in early summer. At its best in coastal districts, it needs some protection from heavy frost in early growth, but has established well in Canberra's Botanic Gardens.

Other tall, attractive wattles include the black wattle (*A. decurrens*), growing to 15 m with a slender, dark trunk and rounded head of feathery, deep-green foliage covered in golden flowers during early spring. Unfortunately it is subject to borer attack in some districts. *A. mollissima* is similar, with white flowers in late spring.

Weeping Myall (*A. pendula*) has slender green foliage and graceful willow-like growth which carries clusters of yellow flowers during early spring and grows 7–10 m tall. These trees are excellent for inland climates.

Blackwood (*A. melanoxylon*) is a valuable timber tree which, in moist gullies, grows to 30 m but less in exposed positions. It has slender foliage to 15 cm long and pale-yellow flowers, mostly in spring.

There are many smaller wattles for small gardens. Apart from those mentioned initially there is the Wyalong wattle (*A. cardiophylla*), with feathery pale-green leaves and small yellow flowers. It grows about 3 m high.

Snowy River wattle (*A. boormanii*) grows 2–3 m and has a mass of golden spring flowers.

Dogtooth wattle (*A. cultriformis*) grows 2–3 m, with blue-grey triangular foliage and deep-golden spring flowers.

Small, scrubby prickly wattle (*A. brownii*) grows about 1 m and is spangled with large, golden balls among the short prickly foliage.

Growing problems and solutions

Before embarking on chemical treatment remember that native birds and insect predators depend on plant-attacking insects for their existence. Some foliage loss or damage should be accepted as being part of the natural environment. Webbing caterpillars, sawflies, etc. can be squashed on sight and the large, hairy eucalyptus-strippers that shelter beneath loose bark can be trapped by tying a collar of hessian around the tree with the top half of the hessian hanging over to provide an attractive daytime shelter for the pests.

Badly eaten or stripped foliage, webbed leaves
Cause: Caterpillars or beetles.
For Scarab beetles, Christmas beetles and their stubby larvae
Control: Spray with Carbaryl or Endosulphan.
For larvae of moths or butterflies (*Lepidoptera*)
Control: Spray with Dipel, a bio-insecticide that attacks the intestines of caterpillars and is harmless to birds and other natural predators. The caterpillar must ingest the insecticide for it to be effective, so spray thoroughly using a wetting agent to make certain all leaf surfaces are covered.
For webbing caterpillars
Dull green caterpillars that web together leaves of the Flame tree or Kurrajong; Sawflies — long purplish-black caterpillars, usually massed and seething; smooth, slender brown caterpillars that are common to *Leptospermum* (tea-tree), *Callistemon* (bottlebrush) and *Melaleuca* (paperbark).
Control: Remove webbed leaves and squash caterpillars or spray with Carbaryl or Endosulphan, using a wetting agent to ensure penetration of the tent-like web.

Burnt-foliage appearance of gum trees
Eucalyptus. Large blisters on the leaves.
Cause: Tunnelling of a tiny caterpillar known as blister leaf sawfly. The adult is a small, buff, winged moth-like fly.
Control: Spray with semi-systemic insecticides such as Rogor, Lebaycid or Metasystox if it is possible to spray the tree safely. Even though unchecked, the infestation usually lasts only a season or two then disappears for some years.

Scorched-looking gumtree foliage
Cause: Lerps or lace lerps. Small, white lacy incrustations, resembling the skeleton of a fish or a fan, are shelter for the tiny larvae of psyllids (scale-like creatures) that cause leaf browning by sucking the sap.
Control: Spray small trees with a systemic chemical as suggested for the control of blister leaf sawfly. Like the latter pest, the infestation rarely persists for more than a couple of

seasons. Large trees can be treated by injection. You can have it done professionally — if you do it yourself drill a series of holes 1 cm in diameter and 12–15 cm apart, 1 m up from the base of the trunk at a downward angle of about 40°, and at a similar angle to the face of the trunk, not directly in toward the centre of the tree. This way they penetrate the greatest area of conducting tissue which is a few centimetres from the bark.

For a tree trunk about 25 cm in diameter mix 3 teaspoons of Rogor or Lebaycid with 2 tablespoons of water and 2–3 drops of household detergent then using an eye dropper, oil can or capillary tube, fill the holes with the mixture.

When the mixture has been absorbed, plug the holes with pieces of dowelling the same diameter as the drill used for boring the tree, tapping in to just below the bar so that the latter can grow over it and seal the wound. This type of injection usually gives the tree immunity for about 2 months from the time of treatment but this varies according to the growth rate of the tree.

Brown blistered foliage of wattles
Queensland wattle (*Acacia podalyriifolia*)
Cause: The unsightly brown blistering, particularly prevalent in mild to warm districts, is caused by a leaf miner which tunnels the leaf.
Control: As recommended for the blister sawfly. If infestation gets out of hand you could replace the tree with a Cootamundra wattle (*A. baileyana*) which, although a little larger and more spreading in growth, has similar silver and gold colouring.

Dull, sandblasted appearance of foliage
Cause: Red spider mite or thrips. These attack during hot, dry conditions or when the shrub is protected from the weather by higher foliage or an overhead canopy. Thrips (dark insects about the size and shape of a needle-point) create a more silvery effect.
Control: Spray with Malathion, Rogor or Lebaycid and in the case of thrips, also with Endosulphan and Carbaryl. Frequent misting of the foliage with water will also deter these pests.

Downy white substance
Particularly on the branches of some species of wattle trees
Cause: Cottony cushion scale, an Australian native scale which occasionally also attacks exotics. Closer inspection may show the presence of numerous, small light-brown or buff egg sacs.
Control: Spray with Rogor or Lebaycid mixed with about 1 tablespoon of white oil per 4 L of diluted spray mixture plus a few drops of detergent to assist wetting of the water-repellent webbing.

Rubbery or wart-like leaf gall

Cause: The gall often contains the larvae of a tiny wasp, or sometimes it may be parasitised by a secondary invader.

Control: Systemic sprays rarely penetrate the gall. Heavy infestations are unsightly but rarely cause permanent damage to the tree and like many other native tree pests may disappear entirely within a year or two. Parrots, particularly the Rosellas, seem to enjoy feeding on the galls.

Twig, branch and trunk damage

Cause: Cup moth caterpillar, a fleshy, rectangular, usually pale-green with swordtooth-like protrusions at side and rear. Four clusters of cactus-like spines protrude at either end and inflict a painful sting if the caterpillar is disturbed. The adult is a small brownish moth with rounded wings and body. The case enclosing the pupae is egg-shaped, shiny brown or grey, smooth, hard and woody and looks like a part of the twig to which it is attached. It removes the top section of wood cleanly leaving a woody cup.

Control: Squash. Heavy infestations on not-too-tall trees can be controlled by spraying with Carbaryl or Endosulphan while the caterpillars are feeding.

Scale on gum trees

Cause: Small, globular, usually pale-brown scale insects about match-head size and closely clustered on the twigs and branches.

Control: Spray with a mixture of 2 tablespoons of white oil and 1 teaspoon of Rogor or Malathion per 4–5 L of water.

Damping off or collar rot

Cause: Fungus attack of stem and upper root system — probably the most common cause of plant wilt and death. It affects plants from cooler regions (especially those from the dry summer areas of Western Australia) which are growing in areas with high summer rainfall. Downy stemmed or foliage types such as Sturt's Desert Pea, some of the perennial straw flowers and ghost or skeleton bush (*calocephalus*) are particularly susceptible.

Control: There is little positive control for this type of fungus disease when plants are grown out of their own environment. The detrimental effect of prolonged summer wet and humidity is greatly accentuated if soil is allowed to splash up and crust around the stems of these plants. Plant them in a stony scree or pebble mulch suitable for alpine plants. This eliminates soil splashing, improves drainage, keeps the surface of the soil open and aerated and also eliminates the film of surface moisture that encourages progress of 'damping off' fungi such as Pythium.

Holes in the bark and branches

Cause: Borers. One of the commonest borers is the longicorn. The adult is a formidable-looking slender beetle, up to about 4 cm long with a still longer wiry antenna, often arched back over its body. Colour varies from brown, grey to light mottled combinations.

The female longicorn usually lays its eggs in cracks or crevices of the bark. The larva, a large whitish grub, tunnels through the soft conducting tissues of the wood just below the bark and a severe infestation can completely ringbark the tree.

Longicorn attack different trees in different ways. For example, they can burrow straight through a branch or limb of a pittosporum causing it to snap and fall off.

A tree is seriously damaged and weakened by longicorn activity but death usually follows from fungus attack.

Symptoms are not always obvious. Smooth-barked gums or Angophoras show a patch of scaly bark or cracks, usually with some gum exuding but often the only signs are the holes left by the beetle as it tunnelled out after emerging from the pupa stage.

Control: Injection of insecticide into the holes is of little avail because the hole is merely an indication that the cycle is finished and the adult has left. If entrance to the hole is blocked with sawdust-like fibre it shows the adult has not yet emerged and it is worth injecting Malathion, Endosulphan, Thiodan or similar insecticides, then plugging the hole with putty.

Always check for tunnelling or damage below the bark. Lift all loose bark and use a strong jet of water to clean the wound of pulverised wood and other material left by the borers. Mix copper spray with sufficient water to make a paint-like consistency and apply to wound.

When dry, plug all holes with putty. It is very important to stop entry of water which could induce fungus attack. Seal the entire area with tree paint to encourage new bark to grow over the wound.

The tree should then be fed with a complete plant food containing trace elements to speed recovery and help to ward off further attack. Tests have shown that trees secrete gums and other resinous substances that engulf the borer larvae in a very early stage of development. Apply the plant food when the soil has been thoroughly soaked, using about 1 handful per sq. m, mainly to the area below the outer branches.

Trees in home gardens are often weakened because their natural cover or the leafmould around them is removed. In nature the decomposition of this material plus bird and animal droppings supply nutrients for healthy growth.

Deep section of trunk gouged out

Cause: Borers. This type of damage is more likely when the trunk of the tree has been covered by ivy or other creeper which provides a harbour for the pests and masks the damage they have caused.

Control: Treat with insecticide as for sapwood borers. Remove most of the collar of bark growing in toward the cavity. Slice this back to the normal line of the bark on the trunk.

Drive a number of nails about halfway into the wood on either side of the cavity then using a fairly strong mixture of 2 parts sand and 1 part cement kept just dry enough to remain intact, pack the hole to just below the bark. The nails will hold the cement in place and the bark will gradually grow over the cement. When dry, paint cement and the freshly cut edges of the bark with tree paint.

A collection of sawdust-like material at the junction of a branch and the main trunk of smooth-barked trees

Cause: Deeper penetrating borers. The grub responsible may penetrate 20–30 cm or more, usually in a downward direction.

Control: Treat by clearing the hole and probing with a piece of copper wire. If this does not appear to have killed the grub, inject an insecticide, for example, Malathion, or use methylated spirits. It is then important to plug the hole with putty. Citrus as well as native trees can be affected.

Ring-barking

The initial symptom is a fabric from 1–5 cm long covering part of the stem. In some cases the fabric is fine and much the same colour as the stem or it may be coarse like a mixture of web and sawdust. In this case the larva or grub may be greenish-grey to pinkish and up to 3 or 4 cm long. It feeds on the bark and sapwood below the fabric quite often completely ring-barking the branch.

Cause: Ring-barking borer. This pest attacks a number of shrubs and trees, both native and exotic.

Control: Remove the fabric and find the hole which is rarely more than about 5 cm deep as it is only used as an extra protection should the fabric covering be removed by predators.

Probe the hole with copper wire or inject methylated spirits or an insecticide. Putty the hole after the grub emerges or the insecticide has dried away.

If ring-barking is very deep it may be necessary to prune off the affected branch. However, the coating of the wound with tree paint often induces regrowth of bark and sapwood.

Pine branches dying

Cause: Pine weevil borer which girdles the bark.

Control: Early each spring clear away old foliage matted in junctions between branch and trunk using a strong jet of water. As a preventive spray or at the first sign of damage apply Endosulphan (Thiodan) in sufficient volume to wet all parts of the trunk and lower branches. Do this during mid-spring then again toward late spring: the time the adult is most active. Chlordane, which is more toxic but longer-lasting, may be used in mid-spring.

Any dead branches should be sawn off level with the trunk and the exposed wood painted with tree paint.

Alyogyne heugeli (Lilac hibiscus)

Banksia ericifolia

Banksia integrifolia

Brachycome (Swan River Daisy)

Cassia odorata

Calothamnus quadrifidus

Acacia cultriformis (Dog Tooth Wattle)

Callistemon viminalis

Dryandra formosa

Boronia serrulata (Native rose)

Boronia pinnata

Callistemon viminalis cultivar

Calytrix tetagona

Christmas Bells with Angophora cordifolia

Agonis flexuosa

Dampiera

A reference guide to native plants

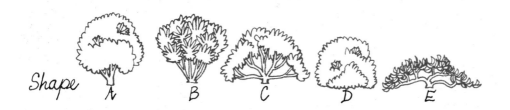

Shape A B C D E

Acacia (the Wattles) Give wattles a light pruning immediately after flowering.

A. acinacea (Gold Dust Wattle) Slender 1–3 cm leaves; massed golden balls of flower, spring. Likes open, sunny, well-drained position. 1–2 m. Shape **B**.

A. brachybotrya (Grey Mulga) Short, stubby, silvery foliage. Flowers in small clusters among foliage, winter to late spring. Very drought resistant.

A. browni Bushy shrub with large golden flowers, short, needle-like foliage. Needs regular moisture. Coastal NSW.

A. buxifolia (Box-leaf Wattle) Small, grey-green oval leaves. Arching sprays pale gold balls, spring. Adaptable. 2–3 m x 2–3 m. Shape **A**.

A. calamifolia (Wallowa) Long, thin, silvery-grey foliage. Fluffy heads yellow, spring. Drought resistant. 3–5 m x 2 m. Shape **B**.

A. cardiophylla (Wyalong Wattle) Fernlike leaves, arching branches draped in small, bright yellow flowers, spring. Quick growing, adaptable. 2–3 m x 2 m. Shape **D**.

A. cultriformis (Knife-leaf or Dog-tooth Wattle) Closely set, triangular blue-grey leaves. Arching branches, golden balls of flower, spring. Adaptable, drought resistant. 2–4 m x 3 m. Shape **B**.

A. Drummondii Fernlike foliage, bright yellow fingers of spring flower. Needs good drainage. Can fail in East Coast wet summers. 1–1.5 m x 1 m. Shape **C**.

A. farnesiana (referring to Farnese Gardens in Rome) Thorny Wattle, occurs naturally in most temperate parts of the world. Foliage fine, flowers large, deep gold with a heavy perfume, which is extracted commercially. Its 1 cm thorns and bushy growth make a formidable hedge.

A. floribunda (Sallow or Sally Wattle) Dark green, slender leaves, catkins of creamy flower, spring. Likes plenty of water. 3–5 m x 3 m. Shape **A**.

A. howitti (Sticky Wattle) Short, dark green foliage, new growth sticky to touch. Pale yellow flower-heads, late spring. Shapely small tree. East Gippsland.

A. longifolia var. Sophorea (Sallow or Sally Wattle) Broad, bright green leaves, catkins of creamy flower, spring. Good sea coast shrub. 2–3 m x 2–3 m. Shape **A**.

A. myrtlifolia (Myrtle-leafed Myrtle Wattle) Prominent oval leaves about 5 cm long, upright in regular formation on upright growth. Showy yellow flowers, spring. Attractive, adaptable. Most parts of Australia.

A. nervosa (Rib Wattle) Foliage resembles

A. myrtlifolia; large, golden-yellow, sweetly perfumed flowers in winter. Best in warm areas.

A. oxycedrus Stiff, lancelike leaves 5–10 cm long, sharp-pointed. Long fingers of creamy-yellow flower along stems, late winter, early spring. Grows naturally in poor sandstone. East coast.

A. podalyriifolia (Queensland Wattle) Silvery blue-grey oval foliage. Massed large golden balls of winter flower. Foliage sometimes browned and disfigured by leaf miner, which cannot invade finer-foliaged types such as *A. baileyana*. Most districts; sea coast. 3–5 m x 3 m. Shape **B**.

A. pulchella Compact, spreading, fine-foliaged shrub with large, showy, golden flowers. Prickly spines at base of foliage. From WA.

A. rubida (Red-stem Wattle) Similar to golden wattle of east coast — broad foliage 5–7.5 cm long, clusters of smaller flowers. Leaves and stems reddish in winter.

A. saligna (Golden Wreath Wattle) Pendulous, sickle-shaped leaves to 15 cm long; spikes pale yellow flowers, winter. 2–4 m. Shape **C**.

A. vestita (Weeping Boree Wattle) Gracefully pendant growth, downy leaves about 1 cm long, pointed. Long sprays of bloom, mid-spring to mid-summer. NSW.

A. vomeriformis Low-growing, attractive in rock gardens, small, prickly foliage, flowers along the branches all spring. Vic., NSW, Tas, SA. 60 cm.

Acrolinium see Everlasting Daisy

Actinotus belianthii see Flannel Flower

Anigozanthos see Kangaroo Paw

Baeckea Heath-like shrubs with small flowers with tiny rounded petals.

B. camphorosmae (Camphor Myrtle) Has camphor smell in crushed foliage, pink flowers in clusters at end of branches. This species from WA, the others from eastern Australia.

B. carnosa Deep pink flowers fade to white. Suit light shade, hot dry districts. 1–1.5 m x 1m.

B. crenatifolia White flowers in summer, round foliage.

B. linifolia Narrow foliage, small white flowers, spring.

B. ramosissima Dainty pink tea-tree-like flowers, fine foliage; semi-prostrate. Flowers winter to midsummer. About 30 cm. Shape **C**.

Banksia coccinea (Scarlet Banksia) Short, wide brushes; silvery-white buds open to scarlet. Broad, serrated foliage. From Albany district, WA. One of showiest banksias, but

not widely adaptable. 2–3 m x 2 m. Shape **B**.

B. collina (Hill banksia) Slender, dark green foliage; plump honey-coloured brushes overlaid with styles like fine burnished wire. Prefers part shade. Spreading growth to 2 m. In moist gullies, to 3 m x 2 m. Shape **C**.

B. ericifolia Dome of closely set, fine, dark glossy foliage decked with 25 cm copper-orange brushes, autumn and winter. From East Coast exposed sandstone ridges, but adapts to inland. 3–4 m x 3–4 m. Shape **D**.

B. robur Caney growth, serrated foliage, bronze in young stages, cones blue-green in bud, opening to lime. Grows in swampy areas. 1.5–2 m x 1.5 m. Shape **C**.

B. hookeriana (Acorn banksia) Heads taper to acorn shape. Silvery buds open to golden-orange with slender, serrated foliage 13–21 cm long. Prefers dry summers, light soil. 2–3 m x 3 m. Shape **B**.

Bauera rubioides (Dog Rose) Spreading semi-prostrate shrub, sparse foliage, dainty pink flowers like inch-wide umbrellas scattered over for most of year. Found along creek banks. Prefers moist position, some shade. 1–2 m x 2 m. Shape **E**.

B. sessiliflora Flowers are close to stem, rather than pendulous, and profuse toward ends of branches; deep pink to magenta. Moist, sheltered position. 1–2 m x 2 m.

Beaufortia purpurea Adaptable, long-flowering little shrub with small, closely set foliage; tiny crimson bottlebrushes. 1 m x 1 m. Shape **B**.

B. sparsa Showy shrub with larger, brighter brushes, mostly late summer. From warm, sheltered swamps, but adapts well. 1–2 m x 1 m.

Blandfordia (NSW Christmas Bells) Colourful perennials native to peaty bogs where they enjoy semi-shade, but they can adapt to moist, loamy garden soil and are sometimes found on dry sandstone ridges. Seed can be raised in a vermiculite-based seed-raising mixture or one made from equal parts sand and peatmoss or leafmould and will take from 6–12 months to make appreciable growth. Transfer to pots and grow on until large enough to plant out.

B. flammea prineps Yellow-flowered type, long bells.

B. grandiflora Red bell-shaped flowers tipped with yellow, 20 or more flowers to the spike, with long thin leaves.

B. nobilis Smaller flowered type. Reasonably adaptable.

Boronia Are exclusive to Australia and have a characteristic spicy scent. Best in light, sandy soil (preferably with moistened peatmoss added to retain moisture), leave undisturbed by cultivation. Most varieties need light shade, especially in warmer temperate areas. Light pruning after flowering improves looks, can prolong life on short-lived types. Shape **C**.

B. denticulata Comparatively adaptable species from WA. Slender, toothed leaves; pink flowers, midwinter to late spring. To 1 m x 1 m.

B. heterophylla Red boronia. Cupped, rosy red flowers, spring. Deep foliage. Needs moist soil. Short-lived, but quick growing.

Raise from seed, or strike 5 cm tip cuttings about December. Compact, to 1.5 m x 1 m.

B. ledifolia Sydney boronia. Low-branching pyramid of starry pink flowers, midwinter to early spring. Once established, tolerates dry conditions. Seems best in poor bush sand with a light layer of leafmould. 0.5–1 m x 0.5–1 m.

B. mollis From shaded gullies of the east coast, caney growth massed with rose-pink starry flowers in mid-spring. 2–2.5 m x 2 m. Shape **A**.

B. megastigma Brown boronia. Noted for perfume, fine foliage, and sprays of globular brown flowers with yellow inner side. Needs the same peaty soil as *B. heterophylla*, about half sun, or broken sunlight, and protection from wind. It may die out after two years, and is replaced quickly from seed or cutting. Cuttings are said to make longer-lived plants. (There is also an all-yellow variety, *lutea*.) 1–1.5 m x 0.5–1 m.

B. pinnata Finely divided leaves, terminal heads of cupped rose-pink flowers, spicy aroma. Often found in same spots as *B. ledifolia*, but also extends into shaded, moist valleys where growth is more profuse. 1–2 m x 1–2 m. Taller in shade.

B. serrulata Native rose. Diamond-shaped foliage on lateral stems, crowned in spring with rosy pink flowers. Hard to establish in cultivation. Grows naturally in warm, sheltered pockets along the east coast sandstone ridges, usually with light protection, and a good mulch of leafmould. 0.5 m x 0.5 m.

Brachysema lanceolatum (Swan River Pea) Dark foliage, and large smoky crimson pea flowers in winter and spring, all but the coldest districts. Prune after flowering. 1–1.7 m x 1–1.3 m. Shape **D**.

Callistemon (Bottlebrush) Spring-flowering ornamental shrubs and trees will grow in wet soils, and have good tolerance to dryness. Keep compact by pruning just below brush as stamens begin to fall before new growth emerges from tip.

C. brachyandrus Slender, small red brushes with golden anthers. 3 m x 2 m. Shape **B**.

C. citrinus (Crimson bottlebrush) Erect tree; lance-shaped leaves; silky, crimson brushes; mid-winter to mid-spring. 2–3 m x 2 m. Shape **B**.

C. rigidus Sharp pointed leaves.

C. rugulosus Scarlet bottlebrush, with narrow leaves.

C. teretifolius Bearded bottlebrush, stamens bearded at base, prefers dry conditions.

C. viminalis variety (Hanna Ray) Weeping bottlebrush with large scarlet pendulous brushes 4–5 m x 3 m. Shape **A**.

C. viminalis variety (Captain Cook dwarf bottlebrush) Useful variety apparently derived from *C. viminalis*. To about 2 m x 1.5 m with large, semi-pendulous brushes, spring. Shape **A**.

C. violaceus A reddish-purple variety of citrinus.

Calothamnus (Net Bush) Resembling bottlebrush, but with stamens in featherlike formation in one-sided bushes; needle-like foliage, rigid but not sharp. Adapt to most soils, but prefer sandy loam; withstand dryness, and grow in sun or part shade. Rejuvenate by cutting back about half the branches each year.

C. quadrifidis (florets have four bundles of stamens) Long, grey-green foliage. Mainly spring flowering. 2 m x 2 m.

C. villosus Short, closely set, needlelike foliage. Florets have woolly bundles of stamens. Rather spreading; to 2 m x 2.5 m.

Calytrix alpestris (Snow Myrtle) Stubby growth, heath-like foliage. Pink buds, starry white flowers. Prefers moist, peaty soil. 1 m x 1 m. Shape **C**.

C. fraseri Summer fringe myrtle. Shrub with spreading branches, tiny foliage, starry lilac or purple flowers, summer. A WA species, found both in peaty swamps and fairly dry sand, it seems to prefer warm, sheltered positions. 0.5–1 m x 1 m.

C. scabra Rough fringe myrtle. Pink or white flowers with long, hairlike awns to sepals. Prefers sand. 1–1.5 m x 1.5 m.

C. tetragona Fine-petalled white flowers, followed by flower-like red calyces. Minute foliage crowds woody stems. All States. Open, sandy areas. 1–1.5 m x 1.5 m.

Cassia artemisioides (Silver Cassia) Compact growth, fine silvery foliage studded with buttercup-like flowers, spring. Sunny, well-drained position. 1–2 m x 2 m. Shape **D**.

C. eremophila (Desert Cassia) Needlelike but not prickly foliage, bright yellow flowers, midwinter to late spring. Warm, dry situations. 2–3 m x 1.5 m. Shape **D**.

Chamelaucium uncinatum
  see Geraldton Wax

Christmas Bush NSW (**Ceratopetalum gummiferum**) Grows in humid gullies, but needs fairly warm, sunny position to colour well by Christmas. The red calyces follow small, creamy spring flowers. Prune lightly in January before new growth appears, then feed with blood and bone or light dressing of fowl manure. Control leaf curl by spraying with two tablespoons white oil plus one teaspoon Malathion–50 gallons of water. 5 m x 3 m. Shape **C**.

Victoria (**Prostanthera lasianthos**) Sprays small white purple-throated bells; lance-shaped foliage. In moist soil, sheltered position, will grow in competition with other trees. 3–5 m x 3 m. Shape **C**.

West Australia (**Nuystsia floribunda**) Massed brushes of rich orange flowers. Hard to cultivate, as is parasitic on roots of host plants. Couch grass seed is planted with those of the *nutysia* to provide a temporary host. Usually found in damp, sandy soils. 5–8 m x 3 m. Shape **B**.

Tasmania (**Bursaria spinosa**) Spiky, small-foliaged shrub; large sprays of creamy, fragrant flowers. Sometimes known as Blackthorn.

Chorizema cordatum (WA Flame Pea) Bushy semi-prostrate little shrub covered with slender spikes of orange-red pea flowers with a purple blotch in yellow-zoned centre; spring flowering. Cut back about one-third as flowers finish. Best in full sun. 1 m x 1 m. Shape **D**.

C. ilicifolium (holly-like leaves) and *C. dicksonii* (narrow, pointed leaves), neither as showy as *C. cordatum*.

Clianthus see Sturt's Desert Pea

Cordyline australis Rosette of slender rigid straplike leaves for feature planting, rockeries, etc. Remains about 1.3 m high, similar width for several years then develops trunk, eventually to 3 m or more. No pruning — trim off old foliage.

C. stricta Dull green foliage, shorter and broader than above, quicker to gain height with slender caney growth to 4 m, eventually branching. May be cut to induce lower growth.

Correa alba (White Correa) Tough little plant from exposed sea coast; rounded grey-green foliage, starry white flowers, winter. 0.5 m x 0.5 m. Shape **B**.

C. reflexa (Native Fuchsia) Shrub with pendulous, rather leathery bells to 5 cm long, mostly in winter. Numerous varieties with colours ranging pale green to red, or red with green tops. Leaves also vary. Prefers moist conditions similar to brown and red boronia, to which it is related. 1–1.5 m x 1.5 m.

Clematis aristata (Traveller's Joy) Climber, creamy, starry flowers followed by hairy seeds.

Crinum peduncularis Lilylike plant with handsome rosette of rigid, broad leaves 1 m–1.5 m long. Spikes of large, spidery, white purple-stamened flowers, early summer. 2 m. Stands swampy conditions or sea coast. Prefers warm, sunny, sheltered pockets.

Crotolaria laburnifolia (Bird Flower) Softwood shrub with blue green foliage and long spikes of large greenish yellow pea flowers like small birds hanging by their beaks — flowers from late spring to early winter. Prune in late winter. Stands all but severe frosts. 2–3 m x 2 m. Shape **B**.

Crowea augustifolia Small shrub from S.W. Australian forests, with starry white to blush pink flowers clustering the upper stems. .75 m x 1.75 m.

Crowea exalata (Small Crowea) Branching plant with slender leaves. Starry pink flowers are profuse in summer, but continue almost all year. Adaptable. 3 m. Shape **C**.

C. dentata Beautiful WA shrub, to about 60 cm. Small, pointed, slightly toothed foliage, starry white flowers close above reddish stems.

C. saligna (eriostemon crowei) (Red Wax Flower) Resembles large-flowered eriostemon, with lance-shaped, green-to-bronze leaves and large, waxy, saucer-shaped flowers, mostly in winter. Adapts to a variety of conditions, even flowering well just behind ocean beaches on east coast. 0.75 m x 0.75 m.

Dampiera stricta Deep blue flowers 1 cm across, brownish-green stems. Sparse foliage. Any light soil with part shade. Flowers spring–summer. 30 cm x 20 cm. Shape **C**.

C. diversifolia Charming blue-flowered ground cover for fairly moist part shade. Makes 60 cm mat of deep, rich blue, mostly spring, but long flowering. 5 cm x 50–60 cm. Shape **E**.

Darwinia leiostyla

Epacris microphylla

Eriostemon australasius

Chamelaucium uncinatum

Grevillea triloba

Grevillea rosmarinifolia

Dillwynia ericifolia (Heath Parrot Pea) Spreading small shrub, fine foliage, brilliant clusters orange flowers, spring–early summer. Best in light shade of tall gums. 1m. Shape **D**.

D. floribunda Has stiffer growth, flowers in spikes among foliage. All States.

D. juniperina Needlelike foliage, terminal clusters of yellow and brown flowers, late spring–early summer. Fairly open, sunny position. 1 m. Shape **E**.

Dryandra formosa One of the loveliest of these unusual WA shrubs. Domed, silky-stamened yellow flowers 8 cm across are surrounded by a swirl of slender, glossy leaves, serrated to the midrib. The dryandras resemble South African proteas, to which they are related. Prefer dry summer climate and gritty soil. 3–4 m. Shape **C**.

D. proteoides Has the typical protea bracts cupped behind the stamens; bronze-yellow. Thin, erect shrub; finely serrated foliage.

Epacris impressa (Common Heath) Erect plant with small, closely set foliage and brush-like spike of closely packed, small white, pink or rose bells near top of each stem. Light, fairly moist soil; sun or dappled shade. Flowers winter and spring. Shape **C**.

E. longiflora (Fuchsia Heath) Sprays of pendulous, glass-like red bells tipped cream. Small, pointed foliage clings to arching stems. Often found gracefully suspended where there is seepage. Flowers most of year. Best with part shade. 0.5–1 m x 1–1.5 m. Shape **E**.

E. microphylla (Coral Heath) Starry-faced, closely set white or pink-flushed bells, winter and spring. Often in sedgy areas. 1 m x 0.5 m. Shape **C**.

Eriostemon Resembles Boronia. The main difference is that it has five petals, ten stamens while Boronia has four and eight. Petals are heavy, waxy, and have less scent.

E. australasius (lanceolatus) (Pink Wax Flower) Lancelike foliage, large petalled, slightly cupped, waxy-pink flowers, lat ly to September. Prefers acid sandstone ιι, light shade.

E. banksii (Banks' Wax Flower) Large-leafed species from Cape York.

E. buxifolia Straggly but charming; white flowers, pink buds. Oval, dark green leaves. Prefers coastal areas. Spring flowering. 0.5–1 m x 0.5 m. Shape **C**.

E. crowei. See *Crowea saligna.*

E. difformis, sub species 'Smithianus'. Small foliaged shrub with starry white flowers in autumn — best in well drained light shade. 1 m x 1 m. Shape **D.**

E. glasshousiensis (Glasshouse Wax Flower) Attractive, free flowering. Large, soft, spatula-shaped foliage when in mild coastal districts, but smaller, stiffer leaves when in more extreme inland areas.

E. lanceolatus (Pink Wax Flower) Open, waxy-pink flowers 30 cm across; long, slender blue-green foliage. Delightful but not easy to cultivate. Try warm, sheltered position among sandstone boulders. Flowers late winter–early spring. 1–1.5 m x 1 m. Shape **C**.

E. queenslandicus (Wallum Wax Flower)

Neat shrub resembling a dwarfed *E. myoporoides*.

E. myoporoides (Long-leafed Wax Flower) Rounded shrub with slender foliage, starry pink-flushed flowers along stems, late winter to late spring. Variety of soils; open positions or below tall trees. Prune after flowering, tip prune new growth. 1–1.5 m x 1–1.5 m. Shape **D**.

E. spicatus Attractive, narrow-leafed WA variety. Upright spikes, mauve-pink flowers.

E. verrucosa (Bendigo Wax or Fairy Wax) Short stubby leaves, generous spikes of waxy flowers. Pink buds open white, spring. Prefers deep rich soil. 1–2 m x 1 m. Shape **E**.

E. verrucosa (variety Mrs J. Semmens) Beautiful double, with pendulous growth.

Eugenia leuhmanni Correctly *Syzygium leuhmanni* Dense glossy foliaged shrub with small pendulous coral-red berries and pink new growth. Frost tender. 2–4 m x 3–4 m. Trim new growth if necessary. Shape **D**.

Everlasting Daisy (*Helipterum*) (*Acrolinium*) *H. roseum* With crisp, papery flower heads 7 cm across, pink or white. Annuals, flowering in spring from autumn-sown seed. Fairly sunny position. Sand or clayey soils. 0.5–1 m x 1 m. Shape **C**.

Helichrysum bracteatum Golden everlasting, or strawflowers. Larger heads than *helipterum*, in gold tones. Sow spring, for summer flowers. 1 m. Shape **C**.

Flannel Flower (*Actinotus helianthii*) Daisy-like flower, looks as if cut from creamy flannel, tipped green. Foliage is silver-grey, lacy. Best in fairly warm, deep sandy soil. Flowers mostly spring–summer. Shape **C**.

Fan Flower (*Scaevola aemula*) Prostrate, spreading plant; sparse foliage, fan-shaped mauve-blue flowers to 3 cm across. Spring–summer. Shape **E**.

S. crassifolia Thick, rounded foliage, flowers as *S. aemula*. Grows on exposed sea coast, or dry inland.

Geraldton Wax (*Chamelaucium uncinatum*) Beautiful shrub, with needle-shaped foliage, branching heads of dainty pink tea-tree-like flowers. Long-lasting cut flower, and lasts on plant July to October.

Grows in limestone areas, but adapts to acid light loam or sand. In sand, seems to thrive on plenty of water providing drainage is good, but generally prefers dry conditions.

Losses often due to root disturbance, especially movement of top-heavy bush. Set young plants at an angle, or prune back, to encourage low branching to make the plant self-bracing. After flowering, remove all but a few inches of flower stems. To about 2–3 m across. Shape **B**.

Gompholobium (Golden Pea) Upright stems with large, yellow pea flowers with dark brown to black buds, late winter–early spring. Leaves in sets of threes.

G. latifolium Lance-shaped leaves, large, yellow pea flowers. Prune after flowering to encourage compact growth.

G. grandiflorum Smaller type with fine foliage. Grows well in coastal sandstone areas, NSW, Qld.

G. minus grows only 15–20 cm high, with

Leptospermum squarrosum

Grevillea rosmarinifolia

Hakea laurina

Leschenaultia formosa

Persoonia pinifolius

Dryandra formosa

fine foliage, creamy-yellow flowers. There are at least 20 other species growing throughout Australia.

Grevilleas Adaptable, long-flowering shrubs. Great diversity of form.

G. alpina (Mountain Grevillea) Small, downward-turned 1 cm leaves. An upright-foliaged form has red and yellow flowers; a prostrate one, red flowers. Shape **D**.

G. apiciloba Leaves have prickly lobes; toothbrush-type yellowish green flowers, have almost black styles. Hot, dry conditions. 1–2 m. Shape **B**.

G. asplenifolia Upright shrub; slender, serrated leaves, brushes of red flowers, winter and spring. Grows well in part shade. 3 m x 3 m. Shape **C**.

G. banksii (red form) Large, rounded shrub; fernlike foliage topped by spiky red brushes, most of year. There is a white-flowered form. Most soils; all but coldest districts. 2–3 m x 2–3 m.

G. baueri Small, spreading plant; smooth oval foliage, salmon-red flowers, late winter–spring. 1 m x 1 m. Shape **E**.

G. biternata Mat of finely divided foliage, heads of creamy-white flowers, winter–spring. Excellent for well-drained, sunny banks. 30 cm x 2–3 m. Shape **E**.

G. dallachiana A compact garden variety; red and cream flowers. A variety of *G. alpina*. 0.5–1 m. Shape **D**.

G. hookeriana Spreading shrub, wiry, finely divided foliage; brilliant red brushes, most of year. Best with dry summer, but fairly adaptable. 2–3 m x 2–3 m. Shape **B**.

G. juniperina (Prickly Spider Flower) Small shrub; fine dark foliage, clusters red flowers, spring and summer. Also a prostrate form. Most soils. 1–1.5 m x 1.5 m. Shape **C**.

G. punicea (Red Spider Flower) Sparse shrub from east coast; clusters of spidery, blood-red flowers, late winter–spring. Sun to half shade. 2–3m x 1–2 m. Shape **C**.

G. rosmarinifolia Handsome, spreading plant; dark, needle-shaped foliage, red-cream flowers, late winter to early summer. Variety of soils, climates, 1.5–2 m tall, as wide. Light pruning after flowering keeps it more compact. A dwarf form, 1.5–2 m x 2–3 m. Shape **B**.

G. triloba Wiry, trident foliage, large heads scented white flowers, mostly in spring. Adaptable. 2–3 m high, can spread to 3 m. Shape **B**.

There are also numerous hybrid Grevilleas that suit native gardens. **Robyn Gordon** is one of the largest flowering and most popular of these. It has large bright red brushes and fernlike foliage. To 1.5 m high and as wide.

Sandra Gordon is a small tree decked with tapering brushes of golden yellow flowers mainly during spring and early summer.

Grevillea **Royal Mantle** makes an excellent dense contour following ground cover with closely set attractively toothed foliage and still prostrate brushes of purplish red flowers in spring.

Hakea There is a wide range from dwarf shrubs to medium-sized trees. They adapt well to hot, dry conditions.

H. laurina (Pincushion Hakea) Small tree with blunt eucalyptus-like leaves, bronze when young. Spectacular flowers, set close on branches, are red cushions with cream stamens, late autumn–early winter. Needs wind protection, or to be surrounded with a barrow or so of rubble to anchor roots. 5–6 m. Shape **A**.

H. multilineata Veined foliage and pinkish-red brushes overlaid by fine creamy stamens, winter–spring. Grows well in Perth, some parts of Adelaide. Performance patchy around Melbourne, hopeless along east coast. 3 m x 2 m. Shape **B**.

H. salicifolia (syn *saligna*) (Willow-leafed Hakea) Quick-growing screen or windbreak. 'Willow' refers to leaf shape; growth is fairly erect. Bronze new growth, white flowers, 6–7 m x 3–5 m but stands regular cutting. Shape **A**.

H. victoriae (Royal Hakea) Spectacular, rounded, veined and spiked stemless leaves form cups or hoods around the pink flower clusters. 3 m x 3 m. Shape **C**.

Hardenbergia comptoniana (Native Wisteria) Sprays of small, lilac-blue pea flowers, spring. Vigorous in most soils, best in fairly sunny position. Shape **E**.

H. violacea (syn *H. monophylla*) False Sarsaparilla or Purple Coral Pea. Sprays of purple flowers in spring. Excellent creeper where it can romp freely, or be trained on fence or trellis. Light shade to sun; most soils. Shape **E**.

Hibbertia peduncularis Fine-foliaged mat; yellow flowers like small buttercups, mostly spring. Wonderful companion for *Dampiera diversifolia*; similar conditions. 5 cm x 25–30 cm. Shape **D**.

H. stellaris Thin, bronze-green stems with fine foliage and a showy canopy of dainty apricot-orange, saucer-shaped flowers; mostly spring. 25 cm x 30 cm. Shape **D**.

H. stricta Strong-growing, adaptable, yellow-flowered small shrub. Likes light shade of tall trees. 0.75–1 m x 0.5 m. Shape **C**.

H. volubilis Tough-flowered climber found behind sandy beaches or in semi-rain forests. Yellow lassandra-like blooms.

Hovea elliptica Oval-foliaged shrub, clustered with small blue pea flowers, spring. Warm, sheltered position; half sun. 1–2 m. Shape **C**.

H. longifolia Narrow foliage, slender stems; small lilac pea flowers, late winter to spring. Often found in heavily treed gullies, but adapts well. Several forms. 0.5–1 m. Shape **C**.

H. trisperma Showy WA species. Rough, big leaves; bright violet-blue flower, winter–spring. Adapts to variety of climates, all but heavy clay soil. Easily raised from seed. 1–2 m. Shape **C**.

Kangaroo Paw (*Anigozanthos*) Interesting flowers on slender stems rising from clumps of bold, straplike foliage. Often from arid parts of WA, but in cultivation responds to feeding in autumn as new growth begins.

Kangaroo Paws are comparatively dormant during dry summers of native habitats. Summer rains or watering can extend flower-

ing period, but can also cause heavy losses. Shape **C**.

A. bicolor. Showy red and green type similar to *A. manglesii*, but smaller; to about 0.5 m. Does well in damp, peaty soils, preferably with some shade. Flowers in about 18 months from seed.

A. flavidus (Albany Kangaroo Paw) Strongest grower. Rigid foliage 1 m high, flower stems to 3 m. May be yellow, dull green, or red. Long-lived, long-flowering, even in wet summers of Eastern States. Takes about four years to flower from seed, but can be increased by dividing clumps, in autumn. Best in moist soil, at least half sun.

A. manglesii (Red and Green Kangaroo Paw) Showiest species. Vivid green flowers with bright red, woolly stems and calyx. Stems to about 1 m. Comparatively short-lived, even in WA, where it often dies out after four or five years. Control fungus disease causing blackening of foliage and die back by spraying with bordeaux or general-purpose fungicides.

A. pulcherrima (Golden Kangaroo Paw) Showy, with 1 m reddish branching stems, golden-yellow flowers. Reasonably moist, light soil. Flowers in about 2½ years from seed.

A. rufus (Red Kangaroo Paw) Similar to *A. pulcherrima*; deep red to burgundy flowers with lime tips and throat.

A. viridis (Green Kangaroo Paw) Low clumps, smooth green foliage, short stems. Flowers bright metallic green to soft gold.

Kennedia Good climbers for use as screen, ground cover.

K. coccinea Scarlet-orange pea flowers in spring.

K. rubicunda (Running Postman) Tough, adaptable.

Kunzea baxterii Flowers like a brilliant red, silky stamened bottlebrush. Long-flowering, midwinter–late spring. From dry summer region of WA, but adapts well. 1–1.5 m x 1 m. Shape **C**.

K. parvifolia East coast species; clusters of fluffy mauve flowers. Prefers light soil, but otherwise easy. 1–2 m x 1 m.

K. pulchella Striking WA species. Flower clusters like red flowering-gum blossom, early spring to summer. Small silver-grey foliage. Should suit inland districts with hot, dry summers. 2–3 m x 1–2 m.

Lambertia formosa (Mountaindevil) So called because of long-eared, peak-nosed woody seed capsules which follow coral-pink protea-like flowers. Foliage dark green, slightly spiky. Keep compact by occasional pruning. Prefers light soil, at least half sun to flower well. 1.5 m in exposed position, to 3 m and as wide with shelter. Shape **C**.

Leschenaultia biloba (Blue leschenaultia or Mirror of Heaven) An incredibly blue gem from WA, a joy in early spring, when the tiny foliage has a blue mantle of flowers about 2.5 cm across. Rarely lives more than a couple of years in cultivation, but even one flowering is worth it.

Plants set out in early spring flower the next spring; or 18 months from autumn-sown seed. December cuttings flower the following spring.

Likes light soils mulched with a scree of pebbles, crushed sandstone, brick or tile and lightly broken sunlight. After flowering dust with cotton-seed meal or blood and bone, or watering with seaweed extract, in autumn. No other feeding or mulching. Prune lightly when flowering finishes. To 0.75 m with similar spread. Shape **E**.

L. formosa (Red leschenaultia) Cushion of bright red flowers, often early winter to late spring. Yellow and pinkish-red colours. Usually 15–25 cm high, 50 cm wide. Shape **D**.

Melaleucas Beautiful, adaptable trees and shrubs, related to *Callistemon* (Bottlebrush). The shrubby types include:

M. fulgens (Scarlet honey myrtle) Fine grey foliage; brilliant red brushes, spring. Light soil, at least half sun. 1–1.5 m x 1 m. Shape **C**.

M. hypericifolia Large shrub with stiff but pendulous branches clad in hypericum-like foliage and red bottlebrushes along stems. 3–4 m x 2–3 m. Shape **D**.

M. incana Graceful, grey-foliaged plant; erect trunk, arching branches. Small yellow brushes, spring, early summer; a few show-tolerant of poor drainage. 2–3 m x 2–3 m. Shape **A**.

M. pulchella (Claw Honey Myrtle) Feathery mauve flowers in claw-like formation. Main flowering late spring, early summer; a few showing almost continuously. 1–1.5 m x 1 m. Shape **C**.

M. radula Slender, blue-grey foliage, brushes of mauve flower along stems. A WA species, but adapts to most districts if soil not too clayey. 1.5–2 m x 1–1.5 m. Shape **B**.

M. steedmanii Round tufts of brilliant red stamens spangled with golden pollen; short, pointed foliage. Adapts well, but shy flowerer in some localities. 1.5 m x 1 m. Shape **C**.

Melastoma malabathricum (Pink Lassiandra) Shrub like *Tibouchina*, but with dense growth and mauve pink flowers during summer and autumn. Native of India and Australia.

This is the shrub once listed as *Lasiandra rosea* which grows to 3 m high and as wide. The shrub originally known as *Melastoma* and also *Lasiandra microphylla* has smaller dark bronze hairy foliage, bright purple flowers 3–4 cm across and compact growth to 1.3 m. This is now officially *Osbeckia kewensis*. (Originally from China.) Shape **D**.

Mintbush see *Prostanthera*

Murraya paniculata Dark glossy foliage and clusters of very fragrant white orange blossom-like flowers in spasmodic bursts during spring and summer. Tropical and temperate areas where frosts are not severe. If necessary prune for shape in late winter. 2–3 m x 2–3 m. Shape **D**.

Myoporum montanum (Boobialla or Water Bush) Waxy green leaves to 8 cm long, small white flowers and purple berries. Useful shrub or hedge plant for inland areas. Trim if needed. 2–4 m x 2–3m. Shape **B**.

M. debile Prostrate form with blue-green foliage, tiny starry white flowers and pealike

fruits in green or red. 0.3 m x 1 m. Shape **E**.

Net Bush see *Calothamnus*

Oleria phlogopappa One of the most popular daisy bushes, with small grey-green foliage 3–5 cm long and during spring almost covered in 10 to 20 cent sized lavender blue to mauve daisies. There are also white and pinkish forms — like most olearias, needs pruning well back and lightly fertilizing after flowering to keep growth attractive. For temperate and cool climates. 1.5 m x 1 m.

Olearia Dentata (Toothed Daisy Bush) Spreading bush; toothed-foliage, covered in small white daisies, mainly spring. Adaptable to sea coast or inland. 0.75 m. Shape **E**.

O. stricta Dark green, narrow-leafed upright species. Massed with small lavender daisies, mainly summer. 0.75 m. Shape **C**.

Pandorea pandorana

(Wonga Wonga Vine) Climber, glossy foliage, clusters creamy-white bells. Free flowering. Adaptable.

P. jasminoides Large pale pink flowers.

Pimelea Long flowering, adaptable to most soils and climates.

P. ferrugenia is showiest. From WA, but adaptable to most temperate areas, including east coast. Small oval foliage closely set along generous sheaf of erect stems, massed with pink ricy pompons, late winter to mid-summer, when sit is improved by a light pruning. Dome shape; to 1 m. Shape **D**.

P. hispida (The Rice Flower) White or pink-flushed flower heads like clustered grains of rice. 30–60 cm.

Persoonia pinifolia (Geebung) Sparse but graceful Australian shrub with deep green soft needle-shaped foliage, terminal spikes of golden-orange flowers in late spring and early summer, followed by bunches of bronze-flushed green berries weighting down the pendulous outer growth in autumn. Trim back in late winter. All but coldest climates. 3–4 m x 2–3 m. Shape **A**.

Philotheca Closely resembles eriostemon, but with the 10 stamens fused together at base.

P. australis Rarely exceeds 30 cm. Densely packed, fine foliage lying close to the stems, attractive, mauve-pink eriostemon-like flowers, late spring. Found in sandy soils of east coast.

Pimelea ferrugenia From WA, but adaptable to most temperate areas, including east coast. Small oval foliage closely set along generous sheaf of erect stems, massed with pink ricy pompons, late winter to mid-summer, when it is improved by a light pruning. Dome shape to 1 m x 1 m. Shape **D**.

Platylobium formosum (Flat Pea) Flat, elliptic-to-heart-shaped foliage. Massed bright yellow and red pea flowers, winter–spring. At least some shade. 1–2 m x 0.5 m. Shape **C**.

Prostanthera (Mintbush) Quick-growing shrubs with clusters of small, dainty flowers.

P. lasianthos see under Christmas Bush (Victorian). Shape **C**.

P. ovalifolia (Purple Mintbush) Dense shrub covered with purple bells, spring. Often short lived due to digging in root area, heavy fertilising, or extreme summer dryness. Improved by light pruning after

flowering. At least half sun. 2–3 m x 2 m. Shape **B**.

P. rotundifolia Round-leafed mintbush. Similar to *P. ovalifolia*, but with denser, rounded foliage; bluish-purple to lilac flowers, spring. Part shade, reasonably moist but well-drained soil. 2–3 m. Shape **B**.

Pultenaea daphnoides Upright shrub; small foliage studded with light orange pea flowers, spring. There are numerous *pultenaeas*, but this one is adaptable, grows well in shade of taller trees. 2–3 m. Tip prune for more compact growth. Shape **A**.

P. flexilis Tall and broad arching branches with narrow oblong leaves and showy masses of orange-yellow and red pea flowers, in mid-spring — grows in deep shaded gullies or in full sun where it is more compact. 2–4 m x 2 m.

Rhododendron lochae Australia's only rhododendron, native to mountainous areas in northern Queensland. Although of tropical origin it can be grown in all but gardens of cold districts where temperatures drop below zero.

A small open plant that flowers in light shade, or bush house conditions, an acid soil enriched with plenty of leafmould and preferably a little sandstone rubble or other coarse material added to keep it open. It can also be grown permanently in a container 25 to 30 cm in diameter. Unlike northern hemisphere rhododendrons the clusters of waxy red bell flowers come mainly in late summer. Unfortunately plant breeders have not yet succeeded in crossing this tropical form with larger flowered exotic species. Open growth to 1.5 m x 1 m. Shape **C**.

Sprengelia incarnata (Pink Swamp Heath) Spikes of star-like flowers that last well when cut, late spring–early summer. Prefers swampy conditions. 1–2 m x 1 m.

Sturt's Desert Pea (*Clianthus formosus*) Sometimes still known as *Clianthus dampieri*. One of the most spectacular Australian wildflowers. Spreading plant, with clusters of long, scarlet pea flowers each with a prominent black boss or dome in the centre.

A fast-growing plant from the dry summer areas, inclined to die out quickly in wet warm periods, and is best grown in a pot (15 cm or larger) in high rainfall areas so that it can be moved out of excessive rain. Needs gritty soil such as crushed sandstone, and a little leafmould or compost with a dusting of lime.

Sow seeds direct, as it does not transplant readily. To germinate quickly, first soak seeds in hot water, or abraid by swirling in a bucket with a few rough stones added. Officially a perennial, but it does not carry well from season to season, and as it flowers quickly from seed, should be treated as an annual. 0.5 m x 0.5 m. Shape **E**.

Swainsonia Over 60 species in Australia, one in New Zealand. Leaves are finely divided into small opposite leaflets, some fernlike. Flowers in long racemes from the leaf axils. Petals rounded, outward curved or pouched, upturned or hooked.

Most are low-spreading shrubs, with small pink or red flowers. Some species such as *S.*

Melaleuca fulgens

Pultenaea flexilis

Pimelea sylvestris

Telopea speciosissima (Waratah)

galegifolia (goatsrue) or *S. greyana* are poisonous to stock. The animals become addicted to the plants, which affect their nervous system.

Swan River Pea see *Brachysema*

Tea-tree (*Leptospermum*) Showy garden hybrids have resulted from crosses between New Zealand and Australian species. Some of these succumb to tiny scale pests, which result in incrustations of black sooty mould. Control with white oil spray, 2 tablespoons per 4 litres of water. Shape **B**.

Among the most notable Australian species are:

L. laevigalum and *L. petersonii*

L. scoparium Mainly from NSW. Erect, with pendulous outer branches clustered with large white·or pink-flushed flowers, autumn–spring. Adaptable, 2–3 m x 2–3 m.

L. rotundifolium Squat, spreading shrub; dark green foliage contrasts with large, soft-pink flowers with glassy green centres. Grows well in parts of NSW southern coast, but, surprisingly, I have seen it thriving inland at Forbes in an exposed position where the soil is no more than slightly acid. It seems to gradually deteriorate in acid sandstone soil. One of the loveliest tea-trees, well worth perseverance. 1–2 m x 2 m.

Telopea see Waratah

Tetratheca Attractive little plant with rosy pink, four-petalled bell-shaped flowers on short, slender stems.

Thryptomene calycina (Heath Myrtle) Bushy, fine-foliaged Victorian wildflower. Massed with white, tiny-petalled tea-tree-like flowers, winter–spring. Reddish calyces follow. Well-drained soil, light shade in warm districts. 1.5 m x 1–1.5 m. Shape **C**.

T. saxicola (Payne's Hybrid) Spreading, slender, arching branches; sprays of tiny pink flowers, winter to late spring. Prune lightly after flowering. 1–1.5 m, about twice the spread. Shape **E**.

Waratah (*Telopea speciosissima*) Large, deep-red cone-shaped formation of florets, flamboyant surround of showy, light red bracts. Prefers humid east coast and mountain climate, and adapts from yellowish bush sand to heavier loams providing the surface of the loam is lightened by kneading in plenty of leafmould and a little sand. 2–3 m x 2 m. Shape **C**.

T. oreades (Gippsland Waratah) Has red, rather loose, flattish flower heads about 8 cm across. Similar requirements to *T. speciossima*.

T. truncata (Tasmanian Waratah) Has short, rather flat bright red flower heads about 10 cm across. Cool to cooler temperate.

Waratah plants are best at least started in light shade, so if in full sun protect with a cone of twigs, and let the plant grow through it.

Prune back before new growth starts from below the flower, which usually means before the flower is quite finished. Leave a few leaves at base of flower stem (previous season's growth). Rejuvenate old, leggy clumps by cutting within a foot or two of the ground. At pruning time feed with blood and bone, bone dust and cottonseed meal mixture, or animal manure.

Westringia fruticosa (syn *rosmariniformis*) (Coastal Rosemary) Rosemary-like shrub with grey-green foliage, small, pale mauve flowers. A pleasant background, and most adaptable, standing salt spray or dry inland conditions, where it is dense and compact, about 0.5–2 m high in sheltered conditions with liberal water. Trim for more compact form. Shape **D**.

W. glabra Has smooth oval deep green foliage and worthwhile pale lavender-blue late spring flowers, resembling some of the Mintbushes. It seems adaptable but a little less salt tolerant than *W. fruticosa*. 1.5 x 2 m. Shape **C**.

W. linearis Fine, mid-green foliage, massed with mauve-flushed white flowers in spring — like a soft mintbush. Suits light shade. 2–3 m x 2 m. Shape **B**.

W. longifolia Fine, mid-green foliage, massed with mauve-flushed white flowers in spring — like a soft mintbush. Suits light shade. 2–3 m x 2 m. Shape **B**.

CONTAINER GARDENING

24. Gardening in pots

Even though you may not have a plot of ground you can still enjoy gardening. Many shrubs, flowers and vegetables grow quite happily in containers on a sunny terrace or balcony. Even if you *do* have a garden, container-growing can prove advantageous. Those awkward spots, where tree roots rob the soil of moisture and nutriment or where drainage is a problem, can be enlivened by the presence of plants growing in good soil in a container that can be moved whenever necessary.

Container growing gives flexibility — you can move the pots around so that flowers are always seen to best advantage, can bring them into the house to enjoy them when you come home from work in the evening and use them — either indoors or out — for decoration on special occasions. You can bring flowers to the bud stage in the sun and then transfer them to a spot that needs enlivening for their flowering period. For handicapped people and for those who find bending uncomfortable and exhausting, container growing means that gardening can be done at bench level and in comfort.

Containers

A container that narrows toward the top or has an inverted rim will cause trouble when the time comes to remove a plant from it. Unless there is very good reason otherwise, always choose a container that tapers toward the base; not only will the 'knocking-out' of a plant be easy but the sides of the pot will be less exposed to the hot rays of the sun than will those of pots with straight or outward curving sides.

Protection of the plant roots is very important; if the soil becomes overheated a plant will die. Even the shaded side of a container exposed to full sun could be too hot. Protection can be given by placing tubs, pots, etc. so that one gives shade to another — you could also position the containers on the southern side of a low wall so that while the flowers and foliage are seen above it, the roots are protected against the sun.

Another way of giving cover is to plant small perennials or rockery plants which thrive in the sun around your big plant and to allow them to spill over the sides of the container. Cerastium, vinca major and vittadenia are only a few of the attractive little plants which will give both colour and cover but will not take too much nutrient from the soil.

What size container do I need?

A container should be a little wider than the root spread of the plant it contains, unused soil soon becomes stagnant.

Slow-growing plants such as conifers and camellias planted in an over-large container should be given the company of some low-growing annuals which will quickly take up the space and be decorative as well as useful. Use common sense to avoid overcrowding.

A half-cask or concrete tub 50 cm x 50 cm will house a 2–2.5 m camellia quite happily for several years, providing the plant is kept compact and in proportion by judicious pruning when the flowers have faded.

Drainage

Good drainage is essential in all container growing.

Shards of terracotta pot, the traditional 'crocking' material, take up soil space so as an alternative you could cover the drainage holes with a square of fibreglass insect gauze. This will allow excess water to drain away and will prevent worms from entering the pot; invaluable as these creatures are in the garden they are positively detrimental in a pot for they alter the tilth of the soil and can block the drainage holes with their castings.

To give a free flow of air and water both in and around a container, stand it on bricks placed flat side down. In the case of a wooden tub this also gives protection against premature rotting.

Cement containers

Thoroughly hose out new containers to remove any vestige of lime; then while still damp, wet the inside even more thoroughly with a solution of aluminium sulphate: 2 tablespoons dissolved in 600 mL water. Allow to stand for 2–3 days days then hose out again.

If this seems too much trouble you could line the containers with plastic sheeting, but be certain not to cover the drainage hole.

Potting

Soil

Any good proprietary potting soil will do. The addition of 1 heaped teaspoonful garden lime or dolomite to a 10–12 L bucket of soil will benefit most flowers and vegetables. Notable exceptions to this are parsley, tomatoes and potatoes.

If you wish to mix your own soil a good general mixture is as follows:

3 parts by volume garden loam as crumbly and well composted as possible
1 part moistened peatmoss
1 part coarse river sand
Add 1 heaped teaspoonful complete plant food to each bucket of soil mixture

If your loam is heavy or sticky add an extra part of sand; if it is sandy add an extra part of peatmoss.

Potting-on

Most plants need potting-on as they grow and this is quite simple when the pots are small enough to handle easily.

Spread your fingers on either side of the plant stem over the top of the pot and then turn the pot upside down and tap the edge against something solid. This will loosen the soil and enable the plant and soil to be removed easily. It will be even easier if the pot has been lined with plastic sheeting. If you should find the roots still stick, or the pot is

too fragile for you to dare tap the rim, run a sharp-bladed knife between the soil and the side of the pot. Few plants, apart from some sensitive natives or plants as difficult to rear as proteas and the daphne, will mind. When potting-on observe the usual good garden practice of using a new pot (while bigger than the old one) that is only large enough to contain the expected new growth of roots. An extra 5 cm in width will do nicely.

Large plants

Large plants and even small trees can do well in containers and, because their roots are confined, will stay within reasonable proportions. They only need an occasional repotting and root pruning to keep them attractive and healthy for many years.

Repotting and root pruning

If a large tub specimen is beginning to lose its healthy vigour in spite of your usual good care, the time has come for action of a more positive nature.

First dampen the soil well, then, using a piece of board to protect the rim, roll the container over onto its side and tap the rim gently, rotating the container slowly and carefully.

If the root-ball does not loosen sufficiently you will have to cut it away from the sides with a spade or knife. Lift the plant out, cut away the tangle of outer roots and loosen the soil clinging to the rest. Make certain that any cut is clean and all dead roots are removed.

If the container has been crocked, take out the crocks and wash them, then replace. If fibreglass gauze has been used, take it out and hose it down and then replace. Cover this with some fibrous compost or rotted turves and firm into place with 2–3 cm soil.

Now lift the plant and carefully position onto the soil. Dribble in the new potting soil slowly and carefully, making certain there are no air pockets and that the roots are in good contact with the new soil. Firm the soil as you go. The plant must not be allowed to wobble. When the pot is filled prune back about one-third of the top growth to balance the reduction you have made in the root system and place the plant in the shade and out of the wind to give it the best chance to recuperate. The best time to carry out these procedures is about 3 or 4 weeks before new growth is expected to start.

Once a plant has reached the stage where it has outgrown a 50–60 cm diameter container, the time has come to be drastic. You could not pot it on — the size of the container needed, when filled with plant and soil, would be almost impossible to move. The answer is to reduce the size of the plant.

This is done by removing the plant from the pot and cutting away one-third of the root growth and up to half of the top growth. Twiggy growth should be removed and branches taken back to where they are pencil thick. Repot carefully as per instructions previously given, keep the plant in the shade and water very carefully. When growth resumes, pinch out the top bud and trim any new shoots so that shape is created. With good care you will soon have a healthy plant of the right proportions.

Climbers for container growing

Climbers too can be grown in pots.

Gentle twiners such as Carolina jasmine, Chinese Star jasmine and *clematis* can be trained to grow in columns, circles or umbrella shapes or can be trained against a wall or support in the conventional way, while growing in a pot. *Gelsemium* (Carolina jasmine), *Trachdospermum, plumbago*, and the beautiful Dipladenia, all require minimum training and pruning to give of their best.

A light sprinkling of complete fertiliser every 3 or 4 weeks after growth commences is all the plants need until the flower buds form. It is extremely necessary to water the fertiliser well. Once in flower, a fortnightly dose of water-soluble fertiliser will keep the plant growing well.

Climbers suitable for growing in containers
Abutilon (Can be trained)
Allamanda
Dipladenia Bougainvillea
Gelsemium sempervirens
Hedera helix
Hoya carnosa
Plumbago
Pyrostegia ignea
Sollya
Stephanotis
Thunbergia
Trachelospermum jasminoides

Grapes
Grapes, both for fruiting and for decoration, can be grown in wooden wine casks or any container more than 35 cm in diameter provided the soil is never allowed to dry out during spring and summer.

Flowers in containers

Low-growing flowers and bulbs look their best when grown in troughs or squat containers with low sides. You can buy inexpensive fibre cement containers shaped like a saucer and ranging in size from about 40–60 cm in diameter, which give a wide display area in relation to their size. If you don't like the cold look of the cement you can either paint them to suit the surroundings or give them a more attractive appearance by painting them with a neutral brown paving paint, both inside and out, and then throwing sand over them while the paint is still wet so that they take on a pleasant sandstone look.

Tall flowers usually have longer roots and since their height may require them to be staked for best effect, a container about 25 cm deep will be necessary. It is always important to choose a container of a height proportionate to that of the plant. There is often no need to plant directly into a container as the plastic pots in which plants come from the nursery can be used inside an ornamental one and then replaced when the show of flowers is over. This is one of the best and easiest ways of using growing flowers. Ingenuity will provide many occasions when a humble plastic pot can be hidden among surrounding greenery.

Fruit trees in pots

If you want a decorative plant for a large container, why not try a lemon, cumquat, mandarin, tangelo, grapefruit or an orange tree?

These useful and decorative citrus not only grow and look well as container specimens, but containers are the safest way to grow them if the garden soil is sticky and clayey, or if drainage is doubtful.

Theoretically, any type of fruit tree can be grown in any sized container. Ideal containers for easy-care growing are half casks or tubs 50–60 cm across and nearly as deep.

Soil
Most proprietary potting soils are suitable for summer fruits, citrus and other evergreens including guavas. A good mixture is 1 part moistened peatmoss, 1 part coarse river sand and 2 parts good crumbly well-composted garden loam.

If grown in small containers, in principle the trees should be heavily pruned then removed from their containers and root-pruned every 4–5 years. However, I have seen reasonably healthy trees that have been growing undisturbed in 30 cm pots for 10 years or so. Roots restricted by the container size automatically keep the plant more dwarfed, but more frequent watering and gradual feeding are needed in this root-bound state.

Drainage needs to be checked occasionally because the tree's own roots sometimes block the drainage hole, trapping water in the container and causing root rot. Worms can also be responsible for causing poor drainage. If present in container soil, they can be eliminated by watering with Carbaryl or Malathion mixed at ordinary spray strength.

It helps to keep the container 1–2 cm above the ground by standing its rim on 3 or 4 tiles or paving blocks.

Citrus are not the only fruits which can be grown in a container; peach, fig, guava, avocado and mango are all suitable subjects.

All citrus need at least half a day's sun to fruit well, and full sun is normally recommended. In hot weather shade the pots so that the soil does not become too hot. Always protect citrus against strong wind which can cause leaf deformity and die-back.

Watering
Water whenever the surface of the soil dries out and until there is a run-off from drainage holes.

Feeding
Citrus perform best when an application of complete plant food or citrus food is given in early spring, again in mid-summer then about April. Use 3 teaspoons for a 60 cm tub.

Before feeding, leach out any residues of salts from the soil by flooding a bucket of water slowly through it.

Shrubs suitable for container growing
Abelia
Acalypha wilkesiana
Acer palmatum
Ardisia crenata
Aucuba japonica
Azalea
Bauera rubioides
Begonia coccinea
Buxus microphylla
Callistemon citrinus 'Endeavour'
  C. 'Captain Cook'
  C. 'Little John'
Camellia japonica
  C. reticulata
  C. sasanqua
Chamaecyparis obtusa — *Nana Aurea*
  C. obtusa — *Tetragona aurea*
Citrus
Codiaeum (with cold protection)
Coprosma repens (Marble Queen)
Cotoneaster conspicuus — *Decorus*
Cryptomeria japonica
Cunonia capensis
Daphne odora — *Rubra*
Drejerella guttata
Erica
Euonymus japonicus
Euphorbia milii
  E. pulcherrima
Fatsia japonica
Fuchsia
Gardenia
Grevillea (Robyn Gordon)
  G. (Royal Mantle)
Hebe diosmifolia
Hibiscus
Hydrangea
Hypericum
Jacobinia carnea
Juniperus conferta
Kalmia latifolia
Laurus nobilis
Lonicera nitida
Loropetalum chinense

Trees suitable for container growing
Albizia julibrissin
Arbutus unedo
Banksia integrifolia
  B. ericifolia
Caesalpinia ferrea
Callistemon salignus
Cedrus atlantica — *Glauca*
  C. deodara
Cupressus macrocarpa — *Brunniana Aurea*
  C. sempervirens
Eucalyptus caesia
Fagus sylvatica
Ficus benjamina
  F. elastica — *Decora*
Ginkgo biloba
Leptospermum petersonii
Melaleuca quinquenervia
Olea
Pittosporum eugenioides
Podocarpus elatus
Schefflera actinophylla
Tristania conferta
  T. laurina

Azaleas grow well in containers. This wooden half-barrel makes a good pot

Loropetalum (Chinese Fringe Flower) kept dwarfed in a container

Cumquat nagami are both edible and attractive

A dwarf pine growing successfully in clay pot

A corner of the garden can be brightened by adding containers of flowers which can later be moved

Nemesias make a colourful container display

This Kentia palm, growing happily in its red pots, decorates an entrance.

Azaleas grown in containers enables a gardener to have colour and greenery in areas in which plants cannot be grown

Magnolia
Nerium oleander
Pieris japonica
Pinus
Pseudopanax
Punica
Raphiolepis
Rhododendron
Rosa
Rosmarinus officinalis
Russelia
Sabina
Taxus baccata
Thuja occidentalis
Viburnum tinus
Westringia fruticosa

Hanging baskets

Hanging baskets look delightful when planted with cascading petunias, trailing lobelia, dwarf ageratum or petite marigolds. Never hang baskets above eye-level or you will lose much of their effect.

Plants grown in wire baskets dry out rapidly so you must take steps to preserve moisture by lining the baskets with a layer of paperbark and then one of black or dark-green plastic with holes cut into it to allow excess water to drain away. Sphagnum moss makes a good liner, used either with the paperpark or on its own. A layer 3–4 cm thick will hold the soil safely and retain quite large quantities of water. It is a good idea to put a saucerful of charcoal in the basket too. The charcoal will take up excess water and gradually release it to the soil, which it will also keep sweet.

Plants for hanging baskets

Achimenes longiflora
Adiantum hispidulum
Asparagus sprengeri
Asplenium bulbiferum
Azalea
Begonia semperflorens
  B. tuberhybrida pendula
Campanula
Chlorophytum
Cissus rhombifolia
Clerodendrum thomsonae
Coelogyne cristata
Columnea microphylla
Convolvulus mauritanicus
  C. tricolor
Crassula multicava
Cymbalaria muralis
Ficus pumila
Fittonia argyroneura
Fuchsia procumbens
Gardenia jasminoides radicans
Gazania x hybrida
Gelsemium sempervirens
Hedera
Impatiens
Ipomoea
Lantana montevidensis
Lobelia
Nemesia
Passiflora
Pelargonium peltatum
Petunia

Philodendron scandens
Platycerium bifurcatum
Polypodium aureum
Rhoicissus rhomboidea
Rosmarinus lavandulaceus
Saxifraga stolonifera
Schlumbergera truncata
Sedum
Selaginella
Senecio
Sollya fusiformis
Stephanotis floribunda
Streptosolen jamesonii
Thunbergia alata
  T. gregorii
Tradescantia fluminensis
Tropaeolum majus
Vanda tricolor
Zebrina pendula

Sink gardens

The original 'sink gardens' were made in discarded stone sinks from English cottages. The sinks were about 50 cm–1 m long by 50–60 cm wide and were only about 12–20cm deep.

It will be hard to come by a genuine stone sink today but the shape is easily created by using a tomato case as a mould and using cement, reinforced with strips of wire netting to give strength, as the material. The sink should be sloped, at the base, toward a drainage hole.

Before introducing soil make certain the drainage hole is kept clear by the use of insect gauze or strategically placed crocks.

Spread charcoal or crushed coke over the base of the sink to at least 1 cm deep. Cover this with a layer of fibrous compost or leaf-mould. Then add soil made from a mixture of equal quantities of garden loam, moistened peatmoss, coarse sand and charcoal or perlite, or finely crushed coke.

Small, colourful flowering plants or the shallow-rooted herbs make excellent subjects for a 'sink garden'. If you wish to be more ambitious you can create a landscape in miniature.

The miniature garden

There is considerable art in the creation of these little worlds. Everything must be kept to scale. A small, young plant of a type which will eventually grow large may look right in the short term but will soon ruin the whole effect, so choice must be restricted to the naturally dwarf-growing types. The bonsai method is very useful for keeping small conifers in shape.

In creating a landscape a small tree no more than 20 cm high can represent a towering cedar; small rockery plants and flowering shrubs, moss and the tiny-leaved carpeters give the green of grass and meadow, and small capfuls of water hidden among a pile of carefully chosen stones the glint of highland pools. Contrived they may be, but gardeners down the years have taken pride and pleasure in creating them.

Terrariums

Terrariums are not only decorative and fascinating in themselves, but they also allow you to grow plants that can be difficult under ordinary indoor conditions.

This is possible because the terrarium becomes another world, a micro-climate automatically free from draughts, with the atmosphere steeped in humidity that is protected from diffusion by the surrounding air. Reduced evaporation results in slightly higher temperatures; water vapour condenses when the glass is cool and returns to the soil; oxygen and carbon dioxide are recycled by the plants. Therefore the container can be completely sealed and left for months or, if growth is not too abundant, even for years without attention.

Many different types of containers can be converted into an attractive terrarium. The easiest to plant and maintain are glass bottles or bowls with an opening large enough for your hand to pass through but it can be an interesting challenge to plant narrow-necked carboys or even clear-glass wine flagons.

Tools to manipulate the plantings can be easily made. Bind an old fork, a cane or dowel and then do the same with a teaspoon. It is possible to plant very narrow-necked bottles using a couple of straightened out wire coat-hangers with one end loosely looped as a handle, and the other bent into a horseshoe shape. These wires are ideal for lowering plants, and for making depressions, and raking and firming the soil.

Soil is gradually poured in through a paper funnel so that it does not splatter the sides of the bottle. Trim off dead leaves with a razor blade glued into a split end of a dowel. Use the hooked wire already described as a holder and lifter. If necessary, the glass can be cleaned by attaching a small wad of cloth to the same wire.

Soil

Most potting soils can be used for terrariums but for sealed containers it is preferable to avoid mixtures largely composed of compost that may decompose rapidly. Two parts coarse sand mixed with 1 part peatmoss over a handful of crushed charcoal in the base of the container is ideal.

The general appearance of many terrariums is spoiled by using too much soil — this probably comes about by inserting enough to cover the soil ball of plants. This is not necessary: in this perpetually moist atmosphere, plants can survive with a much reduced root area.

I reduce the root ball depth to nearly half by using my fingers to press up the soil ball's base and move the roots outwards, also removing a little of the topsoil.

Arranging the terrarium

Select your plants, aiming for a variety of contrasting shapes and foliage colours; remove their pots, then arrange them experimentally in a similar-sized mound of soil outside the terrarium.

The effect is better with something tall and wispy toward the centre and low, bold shapes in the foreground. Bush moss or Club moss (Selaginella) or low trailing plants can be used as fillers to hide the soil between comparatively tall or slender plants.

When the arrangement is satisfying, transfer it to the terrarium. Avoid overcrowding or your little glass world will soon become a dense jungle! Plants with spreading roots or heavy foliage can be wrapped in a cylinder of paper, which is loosened and removed by the all-purpose wire hooks when the plant is in place.

Water by spraying down the sides of the glass as this will avoid splashing of soil. Try not to over-water, but if this does happen, tilt the container to one side and use a sponge or wad of towelling on a wire to mop up the water that collects.

A terrarium sealed with cork does not need watering, but open types should be watered whenever the soil looks dry.

How to plant a bottle garden

6. A spool on a stick can be used to tamp and firm soil.

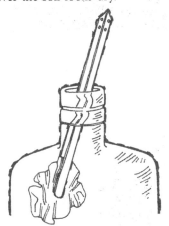

1. Dampen paper towel with window-cleaning spray and clean and polish bottle. Let dry before planting.

3. Roll larger, leafy plants in paper cylinder to slip them through the neck without damage.

4. Use wooden tongs to lower small plants through the necks and to manoeuvre all plants into position.

7. Use a bulb syringe to wash sides of glass, water roots into place and settle soil. Use it dry to blow dust and soil particles off glass or leaves. Shaping and pruning can be done with a razor blade taped to a stick. Pick up prunings with tongs.

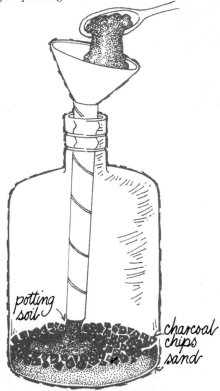

2. Add 25 mm layers of sand and charcoal chips — then a deep layer of potting soil using a funnel and paper tube extension to help keep dust down and off sides of bottle.

5. A spoon taped to a stick is great for digging planting holes, positioning plants, covering roots, and shaping the terrain.

Plants for bottle gardens and terrariums

Asparagus plumosus
Asplenium bulbiferum
  A. flabellifolium
Blechnum penna-marina
Calathea makoyana
  Codiaeum variegatum pictum
Collinia elegans
  Ficus pumila
Fittonia argyroneura
Hedera helix
Maranta leuconeura
Microsorium scandens
Peperomia caperata
  P. magnoliaefolia
Pilea cadierei
Pyrrosia confluens
Saintpaulia ionantha
Sansevieria trifasciata
Scindapsus aureus
Syagrus weddelliana
Tradescantia fluminensis
Zebrina pendula

With careful planning a great variety of vegetables can be grown in small containers (left: beans, middle right: carrots)

Tom Thumb tomatoes

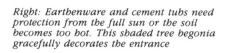

Growing trays offer versatility and give a better display for flowers

Right: Earthenware and cement tubs need protection from the full sun or the soil becomes too hot. This shaded tree begonia gracefully decorates the entrance

Above: Window-boxes provide an opportunity for colourful plantings at window-level
Below: Petunias and Celosia decorate the entrance to this house

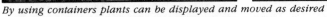

By using containers plants can be displayed and moved as desired

Window-box garden

The window-box is one of the best-known containers for people who are determined to have a garden, no matter how small the space.

Window-boxes give the windows above them a friendlier look, and offer the apartment dweller, with a sunny window-ledge, a way to grow a huge variety of herbs, small vegetables or flowers.

Make sure that the window-box is well supported and not a safety hazard, that it has drainage and that the drainage or run-off water will not create a nuisance.

Use any of the soils recommended for container gardening. Where rapid drying occurs, choose herbs such as thyme, marjoram and others listed in the herb section for drier soils. If growing vegetables (e.g. lettuce) that need a moist soil, add about one-third peatmoss to the soil to improve its water-holding properties.

Geraniums and petunias are excellent flowers for sunny window-boxes as both can stand periods of dryness.

If you happen to have direct sunlight through the glass, it is possible to grow quite reasonable mint, parsley, probably chives and basil indoors. Should the window be open most of the time, then the range can be extended to other herbs and most plants that could be grown in an outside window-box.

Without direct sunlight chives, mint and parsley will grow but will probably be thin and drawn. Cress is a good crop for shaded areas, does better in indirect light than full sun, and needs little soil. A seed-box or plastic tray only 2–3 cm deep will grow both garden and water cress, providing the latter can be kept fairly moist.

Sow garden cress thickly, using about 1 teaspoon of seed for a box 30 cm square. Harvest with scissors as you need it from the time it is 10–12 cm high, which in warm weather is only 4–5 weeks from sowing; sow a tray every few weeks.

Vegetables in containers

You can still have vegetables even if you are without a garden plot in which to grow them. An ordinary plastic bucket with holes punched in it for drainage, some good potting soil, a packet of seeds and a little care and attention and you will be able to grow carrots that are long, straight and juicy.

I once demonstrated this on a television program, sowing a circle of carrot seed within 1–2 cm of the rim of one of these pots. Within 11 weeks the planted-up container was returned to the studio and the soil bowl carefully tapped out to show a yield of 27 good-sized, long young carrots. The same pots are also ideal for a single tomato plant which, if a tall type, can be supported on a stake wired to the individual pots or the latter placed alongside a wall with trellising for their support.

However, there are now good self-support-ing dwarf types that need no staking and so are ideal for pot growing.

Three to four plants of climbing beans can be allowed to one of these bucket-size plastic pots and supported against a wall with trellising as suggested for the taller tomatoes. One rooftop gardener has an excellent semi-mobile-type garden and trellis suitable for climbing beans. Sixteen to 20 L (kerosene tin-type) brown painted metal containers are enclosed in a redwood frame open except for the base board and another covering the tops of the cans. The uprights at the back extend 2 m or more to support a light, lattice-like framework for supporting the beans. The same idea could be used for climbing peas, tall-growing tomatoes, or for training the more viney types of cucumbers.

Soil for containers

Most proprietary potting mixtures are suitable for growing vegetables in containers. These soils can be made more to the liking of lettuce and beans, in fact all vegetables except rhubarb, parsley, tomatoes and potatoes, if a little lime is added. Use about 1 heaped teaspoon of either garden lime or dolomite mixed through every 10–12 L bucketful of soil mixture.

If making up your own container soil, a good mixture would be about 3 parts by volume of good crumbly garden loam, 1 part of moistened peatmoss and 1 part of coarse river sand. Unless the loam is well-composted top soil, it would be as well to add 1 part of either mushroom compost or well-rotted stable manure. If clayey or sticky, add 1 extra part of sand, or if very sandy — an extra part of peatmoss.

The volume of the mixture can be increased and the weight reduced by adding up to one-quarter of perlite.

Granular foam polystyrene (used for stuffing pillows, etc.) is often used by nurseries as a soil lightener. Up to one-third by volume may be added to a soil mixture for this purpose. It is water-repellent so will reduce the water-holding capacity of the mixture so compensate by adding an extra part of moist peatmoss or vermiculite.

These are only a few variations that can be used for potting soils. Many nurseries now use a composted mixture of sawdust and chicken manure as a soil substitute. While this gives good results it dries more rapidly than conventional mixes so more frequent watering is needed using this.

Good drainage is essential

Any container used for growing vegetables must have drainage holes that allow excess water to drain away freely. In wide shallow containers, in particular, it is essential to have drainage holes well spaced around the perimeter of the base; rectangular ones should have at least a drainage hole at each corner. Otherwise, if the container is on an uneven surface, water will be trapped and become stagnant. However, there is no need to waste soil space by filling the base with crocking material as previously recommended.

Drainage material in containers must allow excess water to escape without taking the soil with it. One of the easiest and most space-saving methods is to cover the drainage hole with pieces of fibreglass insect gauze about 5 cm square. If the soil is fibrous and crumbly it is unlikely that extra covering will be needed, but as a precaution and to speed water escape, cover each gauze square with about 1 cm of either crushed charcoal, gravel, rice hulls or other open material that does not decompose rapidly. In containers more than about 25 cm wide put 1 cm thick layer of this type of material over the entire base.

Filling the containers

The soil mix should come within 2–3 cm of the container's top when the material has settled down. Initially loosely fill to the brim, then gently but firmly press the just damp soil down, especially around the sides and in the corners of rectangular containers. It will probably be necessary to add 1–2 cm of soil. If the margin between soil surface and the top edge of the container is greater than suggested, it may cause the seedlings to become leggy. On the other hand, if the soil is closer to the rim, watering becomes difficult.

Your container crop

The Small Fry tomato is becoming popular as a balcony plant. It bears a long crop of plum-size fruits on fairly bushy plants which can be allowed to spill from elevated containers or may be trained upright on stakes.

This tomato crops well under cool conditions, either early in the season or late, and often it will carry through well into winter in frost-protected positions.

Apollo is another prolific tomato suitable for growing in containers. The fruits are medium to small, in generous clusters. The plant grows to about 2 m.

Tomatoes prefer a soil with plenty of compost but which has not been heavily limed within recent months. Feed either with tomato food, complete plant food or specially prepared soluble vegetable food. Some of the other soluble foods contain high proportions of nitrogen and because of this they produce lush bushes but little fruit.

Plant pills or Osmocote are also suitable when the plants are in containers.

Fruit fly baits give control of this pest without any need for recourse to poisonous sprays. Use tomato dust for other insect and fungus pests on the plant. For taller tomatoes it is often easier to have the pots against some type of trellising or support rather than trying to stake the individual pots. It is also worth running a wire through each pot to tie it to the support so that it is not moved accidentally after the plant has been tied.

I have also used several bucket-sized pots or oil drums ganged together in a banana case with stakes or trellising nailed to the back.

Golden Nugget pumpkin is the newsiest development in vegetables for many years and looks like making pumpkins a more popular home garden crop. It makes a bush only about 60 cm wide and the same height. This means you could grow individual pumpkin plants in bucket-size nursery pots or plastic bags.

The fruits, small and rounded, about the diameter of a saucer, have a good pumpkin flavour. The skin is golden orange and in fact a bush carrying the pumpkins is decorative.

Golden Nugget starts fruiting 10–12 weeks from the time of transplanting and the mature pumpkins can be stored for 2 or 3 months.

Pumpkins grow in almost any garden soil or potting mixture but are happier when plenty of compost is present or with a light scattering of complete plant food, a few plant pills or a teaspoon or so of Osmocote per plant. Both of the lastmentioned materials feed gradually and supply nutrient for at least the duration of the crop.

Patio Pik cucumber also grows in the type of container suggested for Golden Nugget pumpkins, or in reasonably wide troughs or window-boxes. The slightly trailing plants look quite decorative.

The green straight-sided fruits may be used at any time from gherkin size to full maturity but, like all cucumbers, have a nicer flavour before the seeds have filled out. You may care to pickle them as gherkins in the young stages.

Soil and feeding needs are about the same as for pumpkins but keep the plants well watered on hot days.

Zucchinis, bush marrows and squashes make plants 75 cm–1 m across, but you can accommodate three plants in, say, a plastic garbage can, with each plant set 10–12 cm from the edge. A great depth of soil is not essential so if you can find containers of a similar width with only 25–30 cm depth, use them by all means. I have seen good results from two plants of zucchinis in one of those foam-plastic fruit cases but here the plants would need watering twice daily during hot, dry conditions. These shallow fruit containers will take at least 6 plants of lettuce or dwarf French beans.

Lettuce, onions, radishes, beetroot and most herbs have fairly shallow roots and grow happily in boxes or plant troughs only 15–18 cm deep. Silver beet and cabbages can also be grown in shallow containers but I find that they maintain vigour and crop longer with a container depth of at least 18 cm.

There is a small cabbage variety called Superette which is proving popular because of its modest size and the fact that it is a quick-maturing type. It is able to produce solid hearts in about 10 weeks from transplanting.

Cabbages prefer a limey soil and should be given regular watering and feeding to encourage firm, leafy hearts.

The care of plants grown in containers
Watering
The smaller the container or amount of soil in relation to plant size, the more often water will be needed. If the container itself is exposed to direct sunlight there will be greater water loss by evaporation, except perhaps where containers are made of well-insulated substances such as foam polystyrene (spongy plastic). It may be possible to position the container so that those with low-growing plants protect others with taller plants from sunlight by shading the containers.

In any case, irrespective of circumstances, the safest procedure is to water whenever the soil surface looks dry, allowing enough water to cause some run-off from the drainage holes.

Feeding
Because of the limited amount of soil in the containers, care is needed in feeding them. When using dry-mix complete plant foods give your pot plants only about quarter the amount recommended for an outdoor garden, and twice as often — say 1 heaped teaspoonful per sq. m of area every 6 weeks instead of 1 tablespoonful every 3 months. This would mean as little as half a teaspoon of complete plant food to a 25 cm pot, or just less than a quarter teaspoon for a 15 cm pot; use even less of high-powered concentrates e.g. nitrophoska, and twice as much for organic materials such as blood and bone or cotton seed meal-based fertilisers.

Water-soluble-type fertilisers should be used at half the recommended strength, but on leaf vegetables such as lettuce, cabbage and silver beet may be used weekly instead of fortnightly.

Important
With all plant foods or fertilisers apply only when the soil is moist, water again after applying any of the dry or sprinkle-on types, then, before feeding again, give a good soaking allowing enough water to encourage liberal run-off through the drainage holes. This will help to leach out excess unused fertilisers or soil salts which might otherwise build up to a concentration that could damage roots.

Be careful that no more than the surface of the soil dries out for a week or so after feeding because when the soil dries out, its solution of soluble salts becomes more concentrated and can cause root damage.

In other words, enjoy your container plants — but don't kill them with kindness!

Potted plants make an entrance
A trimmed box, bay tree or other potted shrub can so effectively say 'welcome' when it is placed beside an entrance. The shaping of shrubs, whether in columns, spheres or domes, gives them greater impact and seems to make them more a part of the architecture.

If you prefer, however, indulge in more natural, free-form growth. It would be difficult to find anything more arresting and appealing than a naturally formed azalea or rhododendron in flower, or the elegance of a well-grown camellia.

Many low-spreading plants are adaptable to shaded or sunny entrances. These include the variegated coprosmas which mound and spill delightfully and the dense Indian hawthorns (*Raphiolepis*) which grow in sun or shade.

The graceful mounding or spilling Chinese star jasmine, with fragrant cream flowers in early summer, drapes decoratively from tall urns or low bowls. There is a more clumpy, slower-growing variegated form.

All the shrubs mentioned can be made more compact but still retain pleasant undulating or other irregular form by just occasionally trimming or pinching back new growth.

For a softening effect, the Japanese sacred bamboo (*Nandina domestica*) is ideal and looks particularly attractive when given room to sucker and clump up in a wide bowl. The canes reach 1 m or so in height with a broad head of ornately divided, fern-like leaves.

Fatsia or *Aralia japonica* has a similar growth habit but is much bolder and more dramatic with large, dark, hand-shaped leaves. It grows in full shade or sun.

The Mahonias, with long, frond-type leaves divided into holly-like leaflets, could be described as about halfway between nandina and fatsia. In cool climates they carry sprays of dusty blue berries.

Ardisia is another caney gem with small heads of dark, glossy green foliage above glistening red berries. For best effect, set several well-developed plants in one low container. It is more attractive when protected from full sunlight.

Another bold and attractive foliage plant for shaded areas is the gold dust shrub (*Aucuba japonica*). It is semi-caney in growth, but can be kept dense and compact by pinching out tip growth during its early stages. It takes quite cold conditions. The colourful crotons, related to Aucuba, are ideal for tropical to semi-tropical situations.

Tree begonias look effective where there is scope for a fairly tall entrance plant. Hybrid forms range from 1–2 m tall, some with large silvery foliage. They are best in bright, indirect light.

Small-foliaged evergreens such as box and yew are traditional for formal shaping because they are easy to work and very long lived. Their drawback is slow growth.

More rapidly growing substitutes include dwarf honeysuckle (*Lonicera nitida*), small-leafed privet (grow it only where it can be controlled and prevented from seeding), *Cotoneaster horizontalis* and *Hebe buxifolia* (Veronica). All need at least one-third sun.

For a fairly quick formal shape for permanently shaded or sunny entrances, grow Californian, Pittsburgh or other fairly small-leafed ivy over a wire shape. For an inverted cone or column, use 3 or 4 lengths of fencing wire poked into the soil and fastened where necessary with thinner wire. For a dome or sphere on a standard, the wires can be twisted as one at the base then bowed out at the top.

Remove the ivy's side-branching pieces until they reach the point where spread is needed. Pinching back tips will encourage more branching growth. Feed it occasionally from spring to autumn for more rapid growth.

In positions with at least half-sun, bay trees or cumquats make decorative standards. Cumquats can often be bought as standards, but it is easy to train them just by removing lower branches close to the main stem.

25. Growing house plants

Environment is the key to success with house plants. There is often the impression that all house plants are from steaming jungles and therefore revel in warmth and humidity. This may apply to many of the foliage plants but there are exceptions. For example the Pig-a-back *Tolmiea* is from the cool coast of eastern Canada; some begonias are stimulated to flower by cool rather than high temperatures; many cacti need cool conditions to flower and others need periods of short days. African violets like humidity and warm nights but cyclamen do not.

It is important to carefully understand the needs of your plants and select a position and provide conditions in the house or room that will best suit them. A wide range of plants, especially foliage plants, will adapt to a variety of different conditions or environments.

The majority of foliage plants we grow indoors, for example philodendrons, dieffenbachias, aphelandras, scindapsus, umbrella trees, etc. are from jungle areas where humidity is high, temperatures fairly warm and constant, and have an adaptability to fairly low light. Some, such as the scindapsus (pothos), many of the philodendrons, monstera, ficus and some palms, start their life where light is restricted beneath the great leafy canopy of the jungle, then gradually make their way out into sunlight. This could explain why some grow happily in moderate light indoors while in warm humid areas the same plant may be flourishing outdoors in full sunlight.

Although plants may be adaptable, the transition from one extreme to another must be gradual.

Light is essential for active growth, the greater the amount of light — providing conditions are warm — the greater the growth rate, and therefore the greater the amount of water needed.

Hence the general rule that should be regarded as a key to the successful growing of house plants: *Keep light, temperature and water in the same ratio.* Increase one, increase the other; reduce one, reduce the other.

A plant, therefore, accustomed in nature to high light and warmth may adapt to a moderately lit room at a lower than accustomed temperature if water is reduced proportionately.

Create a garden room for your house plants by enclosing a veranda

Acclimatising and potting your new plants

Most plants are usually temporarily upset by complete changes of environment. It is often not appreciated the extreme changes to which a new plant may be subjected. From ideal nursery conditions in hot or draughty transport, to be jostled in retail stores and subjected to dull and cool conditions by day and hot and stuffy at night, then too often there is a traumatic period in hot closed cars, sometimes even in direct sunlight, before its new home is reached.

The best way to acclimatise the newcomer is to leach its soil, give it the type of light recommended for the specific plant, also doing what you can to improve the humidity, then to leave it alone except for watering whenever the surface soil dries out. Do not feed for about 3 months unless there are bursts of new growth in the meantime, and then feed only sparingly.

Leaching

Saturate the soil, immersing the container in water for about 10 minutes. Remove the plant and when run-off from drainage holes is subsiding, slowly pour another few litres of water over the soil and allow to drain away.

Use water at room temperature or remove the chill from tap water.

Repotting

Most house plants can be left for at least a year in their original containers, and in many cases for a number of years without need for repotting. As with most aspects of house plant growing there can be few definite rules because growth rate will vary considerably with aspect and other conditions.

Be guided by the appearance of the plant. If it is a clumpy type, such as *Spathiphyllum*, fern, pilea, etc. that completely fills the pot, ficus or philodendron that appears packed with roots, or with numerous roots coming from the base of the pot, it probably needs repotting.

If foliage pales and becomes smaller irrespective of other care then repotting may be required. As a final check carefully tap the plant from its container to see the condition of roots. If roots are tightly matted around the soil ball, repot.

Choose a container about 5 cm larger in diameter than the previous one if it was up to about 20 cm, or about 10 cm larger if replacing a still wider one.

Drainage

Containers with side slits for drainage around the base do not need crocking or other added drainage material. Types with a large centre hole can have the usual pile of soil-reducing base crocks replaced with a square of fibreglass insect gauze over the base, with a small handful of lightly crushed charcoal, gravel or similarly coarse material over this.

Add sufficient potting soil to bring the soil level of the plant to within 2 or 3 cm of the pot rim. Then with the potting soil only slightly damp so that it runs freely, pour it in several stages between soil ball and walls of new pot, packing it in at the same time with a piece of dowelling or similar aid. Also give the container a slight tamping to settle the plant in. This is done by lifting it fractionally and dropping it several times on a firm surface — if the pot is a breakable type first insulate with cardboard or similar material.

When the soil level is readjusted (without completely covering the old soil ball), give a good soaking by standing the container in water to about two-thirds height of the soil ball.

Do not feed after repotting for at least six weeks. This encourages roots to venture out into the new soil.

Some people prefer to first tease some of the roots out if the plant is in a root-bound condition or even to shave off the outer woody mass in alternate strips. This does help the plant to recover better ultimately, but it needs a good humid surrounding such as one of those 'holiday care' plastic plant tents for at least a few weeks while roots are recovering.

Potting soil

Garden stores and nurseries have good ready-mixed potting soil available that will suit most house plants. Exceptions are anthuriums which prefer a coarser, more open mixture. This can be achieved by adding 1 part crushed charcoal or weathered pine bark, rice hulls or similar material to 3 parts by volume of potting mixture, or by using an orchid compost.

The latter is intended mainly for cymbidium and Slipper orchids. For dendrobiums, cattleya, etc. add at least half of coarsely chopped tree-fern fibre or similar material to keep the mixture more open.

If you prefer to make your own potting soil a good mixture is the John Innes Potting Compost which consists of:

7 parts good crumbly and previously composted garden loam
3 parts moistened peatmoss
2 parts coarse river sand

To every 5 L of mixture add about 1 level teaspoon of garden lime or dolomite and either about 1 tablespoon of dry powdered fowl manure or 2 teaspoons of bone dust. Note that the plant food additions are not exactly the same as specified for the English mix but the closest substitute from ingredients generally available in other areas.

There are many potting mixtures with quite different components which all give good results. The main aim is for a mixture that remains crumbly, allows air and water to enter readily and excess to drain away freely, but holds reasonable amounts of moisture. It also needs to give the roots good anchorage.

For an indoor garden effect group house plants ensuring a colourful display

Caring for house plants

Plants and light

Light is essential to life. It provides the energy needed to build sugars and other carbohydrates which are the plants' major components. Some house plants can survive with low light intensity, others with medium light, but most prefer high light.

Very bright light (500–1000 f.c.) Direct sunlight through glass. Suits herbs, some succulents and plants usually grown outdoors but is not often recommended for the general house plant range in our climates.

Bright light (200–500 f.c.) Bright light near a sunny window but not direct sunlight (through glass or open window). Bright light could be described as a position in a room where there would be no noticeable difference when the light was switched on during a normal day. The light should be bright enough to cast a definite shadow when your finger is held about 10 cm above the plant foliage.

Moderate light (75–150 f.c.) Strong enough to cast a light shadow when a pencil or finger is held about 10 cm above a sheet of white paper, or a room where the artificial lighting is switched on by day does not make appreciable difference, good light to read by. Usually a position within about 2 m of a sunless window or up to twice the distance from a window with direct light.

Low light (25–75 f.c.) Four to 5 m from a bright window; just enough light to read by comfortably, but where artificial lighting switched on by day would give a brightening effect.

Duration of the light is important. Most foliage plants will survive happily with as little as 6 hours per day of their specified light requirement. The longer the period of required light intensity the more abundant the growth. Flowering plants usually need at least 10 hours, some as much as 14 hours.

Poinsettias and chrysanthemums can be stimulated to make flower buds by artificially shortening days or lengthening nights, so commercial growers induce them to flower at any time of year by darkening the growing houses at a predetermined time each afternoon to simulate long nights.

Artificial light can compensate for lack of natural light. Both fluorescent tubes and incandescent light globes give off all the rays that make up the spectrum of sunlight.

In fluorescent light, blue rays predominate, which is good for growth of foliage plants but will rarely produce flowers. With incandescent light red rays predominate and cause spindly stems on foliage plants but help to induce flowering. The ideal is a combination of fluorescent and incandescent lights or special plant light tubes which are now widely used by nurserymen.

The latter are expensive but desirable because, like fluorescent tubes, they are cool, and for maximum results may be set to within centimetres of the plants without burning them; whereas incandescent bulbs need to be at least 20 cm from plants to avoid burning. Floodlights have the same properties as incandescent lights and though excellent for highlighting groups or specimen plants, are hot, so need to be about 1 m from the plant.

You will need to add an incandescent lamp for flowering plants and group the latter about 50 cm from it.

Remember when using lamps that placing them above plants may not be enough for branching or very leafy types, as foliage may obscure light from lower growth. Side lighting may be necessary, or perhaps a mirror to double the light.

THE INTENSITY OF LIGHT IS EXPRESSED IN FOOT CANDLES OR CANDLE POWER — f.c.

One 150-watt incandescent globe gives high light (150–500 f.c.) at 50 cm medium light (75–150 f.c.) at 75 cm low light (25–75 f.c.) at 1 m
One 40-watt fluorescent tube gives very high light (500–1000 f.c.) at 15 cm high light (150–500 f.c.) at 25 cm medium light (75–150 f.c.) at 25 cm low light (25–75 f.c.) at 1 m
Two 40-watt fluorescent tubes give high light at 75 cm medium light at 1.3 m low light at 1.75 m

---

Light can stop flowering

Growth of flowering plants responds to light similarly to foliage plants, but in some cases flowering or more correctly the formation of flower buds is stimulated by lengthening night or long night periods. This applies particularly to poinsettias which will not flower during their normal winter period if exposed to lights at night, as this has the effect of shortening the night. Zygocactus and kalanchoes also need short nights for about 6 weeks to produce flower buds. Chrysanthemums are similarly light sensitive. With this knowledge nurserymen are able to artificially manipulate night or day length and produce these plants in flower at any time of the year.

ACCURATELY DETERMINING LIGHT INTENSITY (Foot Candles — f.c.)

Using a camera with a built-in light meter — set the ASA film speed at 200, and the shutter speed to 1/125 of a second. Place a piece of plain white paper on the plant or supported facing the light where it will be. Focus on the paper, centre the light meter needle (taking care not to block the light with the camera) then read off the f stop (which is usually on the section you have been turning to centre the needle). Calculate the f.c. (foot candle) as follows: f2.8=32 f.c., f4=64 f.c., f5.6=125 f.c., f8.0=250 f.c., f11=500 f.c., f16=1000 f.c.
Foot Candles or Candlepower (f.c.) is purely for the enthusiast

---

Plants that adapt to either bright, moderate or low light

Asterisks indicate plants suitable for very low light situations

Aglonema (Chinese Evergreen)*
*Aspidistra**
Brassaia (Dwarf Umbrella Tree)
Bromeliad (need bright light to flower)
Chlorophytum (Spider Plant)
Cissus antarctica (Kangaroo Vine)
Dracaena deremensis (varieties)*
Fatshedera
Fern (Holly and Boston)*
Ficus elastica (Rubber Tree)
Hedera helix (Ivy — varieties)
Maranta (providing light is not very low)
Monstera
Palm (particularly *Neanthe Bella**
Philodendron (leathery-leafed types such as *P. oxycardium*)
Poinsettia (for flower, needs bright light for growth)
*Sanseviera**
Spathiphyllum
Syngonium

Plants for moderate light only

Anthurium scherzerianum
Aphelandra
Asparagus Fern (all types)
Begonia Rex
Calathea
Dieffenbachia
Dizygotheca
Dracaena terminalis
Fatsia japonica
Fern (all types)
Fittonia (Nerve Plant)
Hedera helix (Glacier — variegated Ivy)
Hedera canariensis (Large-leaf variegated Ivy)
Palm (Kentia, Phoenix)
Rhapis
Pepperomia
Pilia (Aluminium Plant and others)
Rhoeo
Schefflera
Scindapsus
Tolmiea
Tradescantia

Watering

How often should house plants be watered?

This is something that can never be answered in terms of time or quantity. The amount of water needed will vary with size of container or amount of container soil in relation to size of the plant, relative humidity which affects evaporation from the soil and amount of water lost from the foliage, temperature and light. Actively-growing plants require comparatively large amounts of water, whereas dormant ones, particularly when temperatures are low and light is restricted, need very little.

Water is essential to all plant life and small amounts of oxygen are essential for the healthy functioning of plant roots. Oxygen normally penetrates through the tiny pores between the soil particles, but when the soil remains wet for long periods, these soil cavities are filled with water and roots cannot function properly, and are unable to transmit water to the rest of the plant — even though they may be saturated themselves. If the over-wet state continues the roots suffocate and eventually succumb to fungus rot.

Therefore, the answer to this most frequent of all house plant questions is: allow the surface of the potting mixture to become just dry then give a good soaking — enough to cause slight run-off from the drainage holes. In unheated rooms during cold conditions, especially if light is restricted, the surface dryness of soil in which leathery foliage plants are growing may be allowed to extend about 1 cm down in the soil and further still for desert cacti and snake plants. It is safest to keep the soil surface just slightly damp for most ferns and palms.

What type of water?

To most people water is water but variation in the chemical content of your supply can affect plants. Temperature is also more important than is often appreciated. It has been proved that very cold water can shock the roots of many plants, particularly those of jungle origin. It has a retarding effect on growth, and on some occasions the plant can show resentment by developing leaf spots.

It is easy to avoid risk of shock by taking the chill off the water — it should not feel warm to the hand but not cold either. Keep the can you use for watering filled so that the water is at room temperature when needed again.

Mineral content of water varies considerably. In many inland areas it is fairly hard. This is not greatly detrimental to plant growth but continuous use can reduce soil acidity to a state where foliage colour becomes pale, due to an iron deficiency. Also, white precipitate will develop over the soil and on unglazed pots.

In most cases the 'hardness' can be overcome by boiling the water so develop the habit of tipping the residue from your electric jug or kettle into a container for plant watering. Do not use water treated with water softeners.

Chlorine is used in varying degrees to purify water supplies. It is not detrimental in minute traces, but if it can be smelt in water it will have a retarding effect on most plant growth and can cause yellowing or blotching of the foliage in dracaenas and cordylines. It is easy to minimise the chlorine content of water by either standing it in a container in the sun or by boiling it, and the idea already suggested of saving water from the electric jug or kettle will solve this problem also.

Some water supplies have the addition of fluoride to minimise tooth decay. Plants can display their resentment of fluoride by a browning of the leaf tips and margin. Amongst the most sensitive are cordylines, dracaenas, yuccas, spider plant (*chlorophytum*), some ferns and palms.

Control: Use a fluoride filtering system or water the plants with a little lime water made by mixing about 2 teaspoons of hydrated lime with 4.5 L of water every 3 months or so. Allow about half a cup to a 15 cm pot but do not use on lime-sensitive plants such as azaleas, ericas and pieris.

How to water

Most people water from the top, others from the bottom. In the latter case the containers are placed in a dish of water that comes one-third to one-half up the side, and left until moisture begins to creep about the surface soil. They should be allowed to drain for a few minutes before returning to their plant saucers.

This method has advantages where plants such as African violets or gloxinias have foliage covering most of the soil, also where it is desirable not to 'water-spot' foliage. A minor drawback of watering from the bottom is that it tends to bring soil salts to the surface, which leaves a whitish precipitate over the soil and pot rim. If this salting becomes pronounced it can be counteracted by leaching (gently pouring several litres of water over the soil to achieve good run-off from drainage holes).

Watering from the top is not detrimental if done gently so that the soil surface is not compacted by puddling, and if water is poured evenly over the surface. When applied only in one spot it may travel downward without diffusing to evenly wet the potting mixture.

Except for the few plants already mentioned which need only a minimum of moisture during cold conditions, when you do water, water thoroughly until water begins running out of drainage holes. Make sure that this excess is not allowed to lie in plant saucers. It is desirable to go around the plants about half an hour after watering to tip out any water in the plant saucer.

Danger of over-watering

Everyone knows that water is essential for plants to survive but it is not always realised that small amounts of oxygen are also essential for root functioning. This oxygen from the air normally penetrates through the minute spaces between the soil particles.

However, when the soil is saturated these spaces are completely filled with water and oxygen is excluded. If the soil remains in this wet, airless state for long periods the roots are unable to take up water for the plant, even though they may be swimming in it.

The symptoms a plant then shows — limpness, wilting and dying of foliage — are much the same as those caused by excessive dryness. Even if moderate watering is resumed, it may take some time for destroyed roots to be replaced and normal vigour to return. Note that blocked drainage holes or run-off water allowed to remain in the plant saucers may cause deterioration of roots in lower half of the container, even though the topsoil may only appear fairly damp.

Temperature

Comfortable home temperatures whether natural or artificially induced will suit most house plants but plants of jungle origin resent sudden changes of temperature.

These changes occur in winter, more frequently than people realise, in both temperate and cool districts. Living rooms are heated 20–25°C during the evening then heating is switched off for the night and room temperature may drop to 10°C or lower in cold districts. Rooms with large areas of glass cool rapidly and the area near a window can become very cold in a short time.

Most plant growth stops when temperature drops to 4–5°C. Growth of some plants, e.g. Elatior begonia and cineraria, is stimulated by moderately low temperatures (10–12°C). Growth of most foliage plants increases as temperatures climb, at least to about the 30°C mark, providing light intensity also increases. With low light and high temperatures, growth becomes weak and drawn. *Dieffenbachias* (Dumb canes) near glass will collapse when the night temperature drops to 5°C, whereas others in a similar position in an unheated room can survive. Inversely, cyclamen enjoy chilly nights and stop growing and flowering once nights are warm.

It is certainly not suggested that any house plants should be placed near heaters. Apart from the undesirable changes in temperature, humidity can be extremely low in these situations as detailed under 'Humidity'.

Avoid draughts, not only because they chill foliage and soil but because they lower humidity dramatically by removing the moisture vapour that collects naturally around a plant. It follows that it is also advisable to keep plants away from the direct air current from air-conditioning ducts.

There is no reason why house plants should not do well in air-conditioned rooms. Most systems do not seem to dry the air as much as many conventional room heaters. I have seen sensitive plants such as African violets and maidenhair ferns growing happily within 1 m of an outlet — but they did have protection against the direct air current.

Humidity

Most house plants prefer a relative humidity of between 40–50%. This is not, as is often imagined, damp atmosphere that encourages moulds, damages furniture, etc. but is a healthy climate for comfortable living. It is when relative humidity gets down below about 25% that breathing passages and skin feel uncomfortably dry. Then most plants, with the exception of desert cacti, snake plant and a few others, show their discomfort by losing foliage lustre and beginning to brown at the tips of the leaves or leaf margins. The relative humidity figure is the percentage of moisture the air is capable of holding. Warm air holds far more moisture vapour than cool air so when warm air with a high moisture content is suddenly chilled, most of the moisture it is carrying is precipitated as rain, or condenses in contact with a cold surface such as cold glass.

An increase of 11°C doubles the amount of moisture the air is capable of holding, but in a closed room, if there is no moisture available for the air to pick up when the temperature is increased, the relative humidity of the room can drop by about half. Fortunately there are simple ways to regulate humidity and avoid this undesirably dry atmosphere.

Simple humidifiers

The simplest way to offset low humidity is to provide a good area of moist surface. With any rise of temperature the rate of evaporation from the moisture will increase and maintain sufficient humidity around the plants.

One simple method is to place the plant containers on trays of pebbles with sufficient water in the base to keep the pebbles moist without wetting the container soil. Alternatively, moistened pine bark may be used, or sphagnum moss which is capable of holding large quantities of water without becoming soggy. You can also group plants together so that evaporation from the soil and moisture lost from foliage create a moist micro-climate around them. Protection from draughts is essential, otherwise the evaporated moisture will be carried away from the plants.

Feeding

The art of feeding your plants properly is to give them only as much food as they need, and only during periods when they need it, which is when they are making active growth. Because of reduced light and temperature, many house plants can do little more than exist and are incapable of making any appreciable growth. So plant nutrients can only be utilised very slowly. Frequent application of plant foods will cause a build-up in the soil which will eventually damage the plant roots so feed only when you notice the plant is making new growth, using either slowly-soluble granules, plant pills or the completely water-soluble plant foods, including fish emulsion and sea-weed extracts.

Use soluble plant foods at about one-third to a half of the normally recommended strength every 3 or 4 weeks while growth is active.

As a safety precaution, leach the soil before feeding again so that any unused residues are washed out and root damage is avoided.

Foliage plants should be given enough food to keep them healthy but not so much that they become great monsters.

Some flowering plants, e.g. cyclamen, need very little feeding after flowering commences. Others, e.g. African violets, need plant foods with a higher rate of phosphorus than the majority of the complete soluble types available. These points are covered under the headings of the particular plants.

For safety leach the soil before feeding. This removes unused and dangerous residues of plant foods and other soil salts.

Do not feed sick plants

This does far more harm than good — rather like stuffing food into a sick child. Check the plant for pest and disease, leach the soil thoroughly, give moderate light and humidity then leave it except for occasional watering when the soil dries. Feed very sparingly when signs of new growth are evident.

Do not feed new plants

It is usually impossible to tell whether the plant you have bought has been on the plant pill, fed with slow-release plant foods mixed with the soil or has been on a fortnightly ration of some rapidly devoured soluble food.

Even though you may detect the beady traces of resin-coated slow-release granules in the soil, it is difficult to determine whether these have been recently added or have served their span. A safe rule is to leach the soil of the new plant thoroughly, and to withhold feeding for about 3 months, except for some flowering plants or where there is a burst of new growth.

The slow-release fertiliser granules come in several types lasting from 3–12 months. Plants are seldom tagged to give the purchaser necessary information.

Leaching

Leaching is done mainly to remove unwanted residues from the soil. This is usually to avoid the risk of fertiliser build-up.

It removes slightly toxic substances that may build up in over-wet soil. Leaching can also in a way induce a desirable rest in growth during an acclimatising period.

To leach, stand the plant in water coming nearly to the height of the soil in its container and allow to soak for 10–15 minutes.

Remove it from the water, then when run-off from the drainage holes has almost stopped, slowly pour several litres of water (equivalent to at least twice the volume of the container soil) evenly over the soil.

It is desirable to use water at room temperature or just to remove the chill from tap water. If the water supply is heavily chlorinated (you will then smell it, particularly if hosing with a fine sprinkler on a sunny day) it is better to use either water that has been standing in the sun for a few hours (providing it is not noticeably warm) or hot water that has cooled.

Anthurium crystalinium is a house plant with a long flowering period

Spring-cleaning house plants

In spring some plants may need repotting, but in most cases just a clean-up and gentle feeding will speed recovery.

Start the rejuvenation program by trimming off dead foliage. Dead older leaves may be part of the natural growing process, but with plants such as *dieffenbachia* (dumb cane) it could be due to being too near a cold window during winter nights.

Brown leaf tips are probably due to the over-dry atmosphere of a heated, closed room; remove with sharp scissors angling the cut to match the natural shape of the leaf tip, and no one will guess that you have cheated!

You can also trim the sides of the leaf to get rid of brown blotchy margins also due to dry atmosphere or frequent use of chlorinated or fluoridated water.

Chlorine loses toxicity in heated water so fill your watering device from the hot tap and allow it to cool, or save the unused water from kettles or electric jugs.

Fluoride damage is usually seen as a yellowish or light brown margin extending from the tip to about one-third of the way up the leaf. The spider plant (*chlorophytum*), dracaenas and some palms are particularly prone, so either use distilled or tank water, or water with about half a cup of lime water every 3 or 4 months. Lime water is made by adding 1 teaspoon of hydrated lime to about 2 L of water.

Poor foliage colour and stunted growth suggest that the plant either needs feeding or repotting. Check by tapping the plant from its container. Place the fingers of one hand over the top of the pot to cover most of the soil, invert the pot and gently tap the rim on a table edge or ledge. The soil ball should come out in the hand, especially if soil is rather damp.

Roots wound around the soil ball should be untangled carefully and the plant transferred to a container 2 sizes larger and soil placed below and then gently firmed in between root ball and the pot wall. Finally, give the soil a good soaking by standing the container in a bucket of water which comes almost to soil level.

Do not feed at repotting time. Wait for a few weeks, until new growth begins. There are many good plant foods but, whatever you use, first read directions and be careful not to exceed the dosage. Better to keep a little under than over and water well after feeding.

Before feeding again leach the soil to wash out any unused plant food that could build up to root-damaging strength.

Leach by standing the plant in a bucket of water for 10–15 minutes. Remove and, when most of the water has drained from it, slowly and evenly pour another few litres of water over soil.

Clean the leaves (about once a month) of the larger leathery or glossy foliaged plants, including palms, by holding the pot so that the leaves can be flattened on a table or other solid surface and wiped over, on both sides. Use a piece of towelling liberally moistened with soapy water — not detergent.

This periodical washing allows more light and air to reach the foliage. It removes dust and pests, e.g. red spider mites and scale pests, of various types.

Smaller foliaged plants, except African violets, gloxinias and others with downy leaves, can be inverted with hand over soil and dunked in a sink or bucket of soapy water then rinsed off. Otherwise a syringing with water helps.

If *dieffenbachias,* umbrella trees, Chinese evergreen, cordylines, etc. have become leggy they can be rejuvenated by cutting back.

Planting in baked clay in inner pot

Hydroponics and house plants

House plants can be grown successfully without any soil. There is nothing new about this as the idea has been practised to raise vegetables and flowers at least since the early part of World War II.

The basic principle is to supply the plant roots with water containing an appropriate balance of the nutrients needed for plant growth, using some form of inert substance as a holder for the moisture and support for the roots.

One popular hydroculture system uses small marble-like pieces of baked clay which is solid but has the advantage of absorbing and holding moisture. The plant is supported with this material in an inner container with open mesh sides. This fits snugly into the liquid-holding container. Liquid or nutrient solution is topped up when need is indicated by a small float-type pointer slotted into the container side. This takes the guesswork out of watering and feeding.

There are also larger containers designed for arrangements of numerous plants. Perforated plastic sleeves of appropriate size are spaced between the pebble filling so that plants can easily be interchanged.

A concentrated balanced nutrient is available. This is diluted at the rate of about 1 teaspoon-sized capful to 2 L of water.

Plants being adapted to the hydroculture system must be washed free of soil. They then make a slightly modified type of root system that adapts them to hydroculture.

African violets, spathiphyllums, anthuriums and ruffled Boston fern growing by hydroculture

Controlling pests

The following are pests or diseases that at times could occur on a variety of plants, together with the easiest or least toxic form of effective control.

Ants around plants

Ants around plants should be discouraged as they transport mealy bugs, nurture aphids and also scale pests.

Control: They can be killed with direct contact by Pyrethrum-type sprays which also discourage further invasions for a short period. For more residual effect use Thiodan (Endosulphan). This may also be used to eliminate ants nesting in potting soil. Mix a little weaker than normally recommended spraying strength and either immerse the containers in, or flood the soil with, this mixture.

Aphids

Small soft-bodied insects usually less than match-head size, clustered on new shoots or under leaves. Cause deformation or weaken.
Control: Wash them off with soapy water or using water-based Pyrethrum-type spray.

Caterpillars

Cause damage by eating foliage. Not common indoors but moths can fly in and deposit eggs.
Control: Spray with water-based Pyrethrum-type sprays.

Mealy bugs

Downy white aphid-sized pests clustered where buds or new shoots emerge, under leaf veins or on stems, foliage and at the base of ferns.
Control: Lightly scrubbing off with soapy water or by dabbing each pest with a swab dampened with methylated spirits. Alternatively, move to sheltered outdoor shade and sprinkle Disyston granules around and under plant (toxic fumes rise through foliage).

Red spider or similar mites

Red spider or similar mites cause dull sandblasted foliage appearance, slight webbing may also be present but mites are difficult to see without good light and magnification. Prevalent mainly when atmosphere is warm and dry.
Control: Misting of foliage deters them. If present either sponge foliage with soapy water or immerse head of plant in same. Otherwise move to outdoor shade and spray both sides of foliage with Malathion or use granules as suggested under heading 'Mealy bugs'.

Scale

Scale clustered on stems or flat brown or red scale on foliage.
Control: Gently rub off with soapy cloth or toothbrush on stems. Otherwise move to outdoor shade and spray with Lebaycid plus 2 tablespoons of white oil per 5 L of spray. Do not use white oil on delicate ferns, African violets or other downy foliage plants, including cacti.

White Fly

Small white flies on foliage, cause mottling or yellowing.
Control: Sponge leaves with soapy water to remove scale stage of pest. Mist with

Growing problems and solutions

Problem	Cause	Solution
Yellowing leaves One or two lower leaves yellow and die	Natural process particularly with caney plants as young growth progresses upwards	Cleanly trim off dead foliage
Several lower leaves yellowing, others inclined to sag; stem usually dark, and soil with mossy scum on surface	Too much water	Scratch off surface crust to aerate, then let surface soil dry out between waterings
Leaves yellowing with brown or dead tips and margins	Soil too dry	Water thoroughly whenever surface soil dries out
Leaves with areas gradually paling into yellow or brown, particularly on the side nearest light	Light too intense or sun scorch	Either the plant needs to be gradually conditioned to strong light or is one needing more diffused light
Leaves begin yellowing, then fall suddenly	May be due to relatively dark, warm conditions, such as warm room where blinds are drawn by day	Improve light
Lower leaves yellowing, remainder paler than normal green	May be due to lack of feeding	Leach soil, then saturate with complete water-soluble fertiliser
Yellowing mainly of new growth	Due to alkaline (limey) soil or hard water, especially when plant watered from bottom	Leach soil thoroughly, then dissolve 1 heaped teaspoon of iron sulphate in about 2 L water and slowly pour through soil. If iron sulphate is unavailable, use 2 teaspoons of vinegar to the same amount of water
Leaves with dull yellowish sandblasted appearance, fine webbing may also be present	Red spider mites	Thoroughly sponge all parts of plant with soapy water then an hour or two later gently rinse off, or remove to outdoor shade and spray with either Malathion, Lebaycid or Rogor
Other leaf problems Brown or dead tips or margins of leaves	Atmosphere too dry	Trim off brown areas so that natural leaf shape is retained. Increase humidity as suggested under that heading
Leaves drawn and thin	Temperature too high and soil too moist for the amount of light available	Move to brighter indirect light
Young growth limp	Usually soil too dry but overwetness can cause the same symptom	See heading 'How often should I water?'
Black sootiness on foliage	Usually suggests presence of scale pests but mealy bugs or sometimes aphids may also be responsible	Either sponge foliage thoroughly or spray in outdoor shade with Lebaycid or Rogor
Twisted, blistered or downward crimpled foliage	Usually due to presence of aphids on young growth	Either immerse foliage in soapy water or use Pyrethrum-type spray
Leaves distorted, thickened and brittle	Either broad mite or cyclamen mite	Metasystox is effective but very toxic and unsuitable for indoor use. Alternatively, if plant is too valuable to eliminate from collection, spray thoroughly with Malathion 3 times at intervals of 5–6 days
Areas of foliage eaten	Usually due to caterpillars or in some areas to earwigs	Use Pyrethrum-type insecticide as the pests may be difficult to detect and effectively removed by hand
Small scallops, mainly around leaf margins	Brown vegetable weevil	Use Pyrethrum-type insecticide. Preferably at night
Small downy whitish patches under foliage or in junctions of stems	Mealy bug	Touch each with a camel-hair brush, or small cotton wool swab, moistened with methylated spirits. Alternatively, spray daily with Pyrethrum, for 5 days; with heavy infestations remove outdoors and spray thoroughly with Malathion
Ash-like film over foliage	Powdery mildew	Improve ventilation, spray with Benlate

Problem	Cause	Solution
Tiny, grey to black sandfly-like insects hovering around plant	Mushroom fly, probably from unsterilised spent mushroom compost in potting mixture	Use Pyrethrum-type spray daily for 7–10 days. To destroy larvae which sometimes attack plant roots, flood soil with Malathion or Diazinon mixed at a little less than spray strength
Tiny white flies hover around foliage when disturbed, usually causing some mottling	White fly	Use Pyrethrum-type spray daily while flies are still evident
Black raised scabs, match-head size or larger, mainly on leathery foliaged plants	Black scale	Remove by sponging with soap and water or move to outdoor shade and spray with 1 tablespoon of white oil and 1 teaspoon of Lebaycid or Rogor per 4.5 L of water
Pinhead-size buff to reddish-brown scabs on stems and foliage	Red scale	As above

Growing problems and solutions for individual house plants

Plant	Symptom	Cause	Remedy
Acalypha	Leaf drop	Sudden drop in temperature or natural chill during winter in cooler areas. Poor light may also have similar effect	Keep in warm bright position, not too close to glass during winter. If winter deciduous reduce watering and prune back to about half in early spring
	Loss of foliage colour	Insufficient light	Very bright light needed, even direct sun through glass, if plant accustomed to same
Achimenes	Failure to flower	May be due to excessive heat (over 85 F), 32 C, especially if light is restricted	Move to bright shade, with good ventilation
African violet	Failure to flower	Due to insufficient light or plant food lacking in phosphorus	Move to bright indirect light. If feeding with soluble plant foods, supply the extra phosphorus needed by sprinkling about one-quarter teaspoon of superphosphate evenly below foliage and water in well — about once very 3 months. Allow soil surface to dry out between waterings
	Cream to pale brown markings on leaves	Watering with water too cold, or water on foliage exposed to bright light	Use room-temperature water, apply carefully below leaves
	Thin drawn foliage	Too little light	Move to bright indirect light
	Foliage short and clumpy and pale	Too much light	Move a little further from direct light
	Clumpy foliage, distorted, thickened and brittle	Broad mite or cyclamen mite	See 'Controlling pests'
	Small downy whitish patches	Mealy bugs	See 'Controlling pests'
	Ash-like film on foliage	Mildew	See 'Controlling pests'
Aglaonema	See Chinese Evergreen	see Chinese Evergreen	See Chinese Evergreen
Anthurium	No flowers	Poor light	Move into moderate to bright light
	Foliage yellowing	Light may be too severe. Also check red spider in general section	Moderate to bright light is preferable
Alphelandra	Leaf fall	Either sudden drops in temperature or build-up of soluble salts in soil	Leach soil. Move away from glass window at night
Asparagus Fern	Leaf drop	Light too low in relation to temperature	Move to brigher situation
Azalea	No flowers	Poor light	Plant needs to be moved outdoors when flowering finishes
	Dull mottled or silvery-bronze leaves	Lace bug or red spider mite when plant grown under cover	Remove outdoors and spray both sides of foliage with Malathion or Rogor

Pyrethrum-type spray every few days until flies disappear.

Black Fly or Mushroom Fly
Black Fly or Mushroom Fly around soil, maggot can attack plant roots.
Control: Mist frequently with Pyrethrum-type spray as suggested for white fly or for quicker control remove plant to outdoor shade and drench soil with Malathion mixed to normal spray strength.

Mildew
Ash-like patches or film on foliage.
Control: Move outdoors and spray Benlate or improve ventilation.

Plants with generally poor appearance
A plant may look dull, lustreless and generally sick, without showing any of the definite symptoms listed here.

Carefully remove the plant from its pot without disturbing the soil by inverting it, supporting the soil ball with fingers of one hand straddling the base of the plant, then give the rim a sharp tap on the edge of a bench or some other solid object.

Look for the first suspect which is root mealy bug, sometimes referred to as root aphis. This will show quite plainly at the outside of the root ball as patches of whitish powder with clusters of cotton wool-like bodies intermingled.

It is frequently recommended that the soil be removed, the roots carefully washed and the plant repotted in clean soil. However, it is usually possible to kill the pests by saturating the soil with a solution of Malathion or Diazinon, made up to normal spraying strength. Preferably this is done by soaking the container in the solution for 10 minutes or so.

In areas where this pest is troublesome, I also find a few flakes of naphthalene in the base of the pot seems to give immunity for quite a long period.

What to do with over-leggy plants
All caney plants, dracaenas, cordylines, *dieffenbachias,* umbrella trees, etc. eventually become leggy as bottom foliage falls and top growth progresses.

All that can be done to recapture more compact appearance is to cut the tallest canes off, usually close to the base and just above a node or joint where an old leaf has been. Usually they will shoot from the uppermost remaining joint, therefore choose one on the side where growth is preferred.

The best time to cut is spring before new growth normally starts. Keep the plant just a little on the dry side for a few days before and after cutting to minimise sap loss from the cut.

The top section can also be struck as a new plant. Unless you can keep it in a humid atmosphere such as a shaded glass house, first remove most of the foliage to minimise wilting. Bed the section upright, staked if necessary, in a mixture of about 2 parts coarse sand to 1 of peatmoss.

Sections of the stem each cut with 2 or 3 joints can also be partly covered in a similar mixture as cuttings. One shoot will generally appear from one or more of the joints, even though it may take several months.

One tip: it is advisable to make each cut on a slant then trim the bottom straight across before making the next one. This way you know that the slant represents the top of the cutting, otherwise it is very difficult to tell. However, if in doubt, lie them on their side, half covered with soil and they should still eventually shoot.

Potted chrysanthemums are a good substitute for cut flowers. Move outdoors after flowering, but not into direct sun unless first conditioned in light and part shade.

Why cacti do not flower

Few of the spiky Desert-type cacti can be expected to flower if the plant is grown in poor light and kept too warm during the winter period. Many types, particularly the Peanut cactus (*Chamaecereus silvestri*), rarely flower well unless winter temperatures are down to 7–13°C. They will do better if moved out of doors during winter and given protection from frost and overhead shelter from heavy rain. During the cool months, soil should be allowed to almost dry out between waterings. An indoor position may be satisfactory if near to glass that will conduct and transmit the lower outdoor temperatures.

Strap cacti or Jungle cacti, particularly the Crab's Claw type (*Schlumbergera* and *Rhipsalidopsis*), need about a 6-week period where they receive at least 12 hours of darkness per night before flowering is stimulated. During autumn they should be kept away from lighted areas during the evening.

Plant	Symptom	Cause	Remedy
Begonia (all types)	Blackening and shrivelling of leaf	Mildew, especially where ventilation is lacking, can cause leaf shrivel, but foliage shrivelling from base of plant may be caused by leaf eelworm (nematode)	For mildew use Benlate. For eelworm remove and burn affected foliage or spray in sheltered outdoor position with Metasystox, which must be handled with care
Begonia (tuberous)	Buds and leaves falling	Temperatures too high, lack of ventilation	Circulation of fresh air and a temperature that does not fall below 30°C
	Leaves yellowing and falling after flowering	Natural process	Reduce watering; when plant dies, remove tuber, clean and store until spring
Begonia (Rex)	Older leaves shrivelling in autumn	Occurs naturally as temperatures fall	Allow soil to become a little drier between waterings but keep plant in good light
Bromeliad Bilbergia	Plant shrivelling after flowering	Natural process, offshoots should be present at base of old plant	When original plant loses attractiveness carefully remove to encourage shapely growth of offsets, or replant latter
Cacti Chamaecereus Crab's Claw cactus Echinopsis Epiphyllum	Blackening and rotting of plant base	Usually due to too much water during the colder months	Remove healthy top with sharp knife. Keep in dry situation for cut to callus then strike as cutting in fresh soil
	Thin drawn-out growth	Insufficient light, particularly in warm situations	Remove to bright light near a window
	Uneven or one-sided growth	Plant growing toward light	Give container a quarter turn every few weeks
	Corky incrustations particularly on edges of stems or flanges of plant	Usually a nutritional factor rather than a disease, but excessive sunlight may also be a factor	
	Strap cacti with multi-shoots and stunted clumpy appearance	Usually due to fertiliser with excessive high nitrogen content	Leach soil or repot in a coarse potting mixture with just a little rose food or similar complete plant food added
	Small greyish-brown lumps on spines	Scale pests	Rub off with cotton swab moistened with methylated spirits
	Fluffy white incrustations, particularly in crevices of plant	Mealy bug	Carefully touch each with swab moistened with methylated spirits. For large scale infestations spray with Lebaycid or Rogor
	Roots of plant clustered with downy white substance	Root mealy bug	Immerse container or flood root area of plant with either Malathion, Diazinon, Rogor or Lebaycid, made up to normal spraying strength
	Crab's Claw cactus with flaccid purple-tinged foliage	Excessive light and dryness	Water regularly, particularly during spring and summer and move to bright light situation but not direct sunlight
Caladium	Leaves yellowing and dying	May happen with over-watering in poorly lit or cool situations, but is natural after 6–7 months growth or when autumn temperatures drop below about 18°C	In latter case withhold watering. Remove, clean and store tuber in dark airy situation until replanting time in spring
	Shrivelling of leaf	Either draughts or dry atmosphere	Place plant in protected position with bright indirect light and improve humidity
	Colour foliage fading	Insufficient light	Move to bright indirect light
Calathea	Foliage rolling upwards	This can be due to draughts or wind but many species roll foliage at night	Provide shelter if necessary
	Lack of colour	Foliage colour varies with light intensity	For a brighter colour move to moderate to bright indirect light

Plant	Symptom	Cause	Remedy
	Foliage dying or browning in patches	Over-wet soil during winter dormant period	Allow soil surface to dry between waterings, until new growth starts with warmer conditions
	Browning of leaf tips	Over-dry soil or dry atmosphere	Water whenever soil surface becomes dry, improve humidity if necessary
Calceolaria	Plant dying after flowering	Most container growing types are annuals raised from seed sown early the previous summer	Discard plant
Camellia	Plant with thin drawn foliage Lack of flower	Insufficient light	Plants need to be removed to bright outdoor shade after flowering
Chinese Evergreen	Yellowing and leaf fall particularly of variegated types	Too much light	Move to a low to moderate light situation
Chinese Fire Fern	Foliage dropping	Change of environment, particularly light or cold	Move away from window glass during cold conditions, but maintain bright indirect light
Chlorophytum (Spider Plant)	Browning tips	May be excessively dry atmosphere, but is more likely due to chlorine or fluoride in water	See 'Watering house plants'
Clivia	Foliage with brown tips	Direct sunlight	Move to bright indirect light
Coleus	Foliage colour fading	Poor light	Move to bright indirect light
	Foliage falling, plant becoming straggly	Typical behaviour as autumn weather becomes cooler	Perpetuate plant by striking cuttings from healthy shoots
Columnea	Lack of flower	G. gloriosa and other spring-flowering types need long nights and temperatures between 13–18°C to stimulate flowering	Move away from indoor heat and artificial light during winter
Cordyline	Brown patches along leaf margins	Can be due to Perlite in potting mixture or more frequently to water with high fluoride content	If applicable, carefully remove soil and repot in Perlite-free compost, or see treatment under heading 'Watering house plants'
Croton Codiaeum	Leaf drop	Poor light, sudden temperature drop	Give bright light and protection from cold. Reduce water in cold weather
Cryptanthus	Lack of foliage colour	Insufficient light	Move to brighter light
	Parent plant dying	Natural occurrence after flowering	Carefully remove and repot offsets
Cyclamen	Foliage yellowing, buds shrivelling	Night temperatures too high	Move to situation with bright light by day and cool at night
	Foliage yellowing	As above or because increasing temperatures naturally induce dormancy	If latter, reduce watering and when foliage dies, store corm for replanting in mid-summer
	Foliage clumped, distorted, thickened and brittle	Cyclamen mite	Either remove plant and burn, or spray with Meta-systox in outdoor shaded situation
Dieffenbachia (Dumb Cane)	Collapsing foliage with water-soaked appearance	Soil or plant too wet during cold conditions	Move away from cold of window and water only when surface of soil dries out
Dracaena	Lack of foliage colour	Insufficient light	Move to bright indirect light
	Brown patches along leaf edges	See Cordyline	See Cordyline
Eucharis Lily	Lack of flower	Incorrect watering and temperature	Keep a little drier during autumn. Also allow soil to almost dry out for several weeks after new spring growth is well developed
Ficus benjamina	Foliage falling	Room temperature too high for amount of light available	Remove to bright indirect light where blinds are not drawn by day, and improve humidity

Special growing problems

Aucuba japonica
Problem: Scale on stems or foliage.
Solution: Move to outdoor shade and use white oil spray.

Azalea
Problem: Foliage mottling and bronzing lace bug, particularly from the time new growth starts until April.
Solution: Vigorous weekly hosing of foliage usually deters pest, otherwise at first signs of mottling spray Lebaycid or Rogor, repeating in one month.

Begonia
Problem: Powdery Mildew.
Solution: Improve ventilation, reduce water when cold or move to outdoor shade and spray Benlate.

Chrysanthemum
Problem: Black aphids which cluster mainly below buds.
Solution: Rub off or use Pyrethrum-type garden sprays.

Cissus
Problem: In dry atmosphere thrips can cause dry grey mottling of foliage.
Solution: Misting foliage is a deterrent, either sponge foliage with soapy water or use Pyrethrum-type garden sprays as directed at underside of foliage at intervals of 3–4 days until tiny thrips disappear.

Coleus
Problem: Mealy bugs or looper caterpillars which assume appearance of main vein under-leaf.
Solution: Pyrethrum-type garden sprays misted through plant will soon dislodge them.

Cordyline terminalis
Problem: Fluoride in water or perlite in potting mixture can cause brown blotching of leaf margins and tips.

Croton
Problem: Excessive leaf fall.
Solution: Check for scale pests and mealy bug. Excessive leaf fall is due either to poor light or cold, especially if soil is too damp.

Fern
Problem: Drying out is the most common one. Also watch for mealy bugs, soft brown scale on stems and occasionally brown or green aphids may attack young shoots.
Solution: Aphids can usually be eliminated by whipping up a liberal head of soap suds, lifting and gently patting them in to completely cover the fern.

Fuchsia
Problem: Caterpillars in foliage and buds.
Solution: Do not use Bioresmethrin-type sprays — move to outdoor shade and spray Carbaryl or Endosulphan (Thiodan).

Peperomia

Problem: *P. hederaefolia* and similar types rot at base when over-moist.

Solution: Lift remainder of plant and encourage new roots by standing in an almost pure coarse sand in shaded position.

Palm

Problem:

1. Browning and loss of 1 or 2 lower leaves.

Solution: This is natural, trim them off close to the main stem or base. Browning of tips is usually due to under-watering but can occur with very low humidity or in some cases from heavily chlorinated or fluorinated water. To regain appearance, trim these off, cutting to retain natural shape of leaf.

2. Downy white deposits on foliage, usually with yellow spotting on opposite side or small tan-coloured scales on stems and foliage indicate scale.

Solution: It is a good idea to sponge palm foliage once a month, preferably laying the plant so that fronds can be spread on a flat surface. If scale is present use a very soapy cloth then rinse lightly half an hour or so later. If scale persists move to outdoor shade and spray 2 tablespoons of white oil plus 1 teaspoon of either Malathion, Diazinon, Lebaycid or Rogor per 5 L of water.

3. Leaf-stripping caterpillar, a long greenish grey grub that harbours in leaves it webs together.

Solution: Monthly sponging of foliage dislodges them, usually before much damage occurs.

4. Brown patches covering a large area of the leaf are usually due to sunburn, caused when a plant grown in shade or indirect light is suddenly moved to direct light — or frequently when plants moved out to freshen up in the rain are forgotten when the sun comes out.

Solution: Don't move them suddenly to direct light and don't leave them out in the sun after the rain!

Plants preferring an occasional spell outdoors

Give them a well-lighted position, with fresh air, perhaps on a partly-enclosed veranda. Move those marked with an asterisk outdoors after flowering, but not into direct sun unless first conditioned in light and part shade.

Ardisia (Dwarf Berry Tree)
Aucuba (Gold Dust Shrub)
Azalea*
Bamboo
Camellia*
Chlorphytum
Chrysanthemum*
Coprosma (Looking-Glass Plant)
Eucharis (Amazon Lily)
Ligularia (Leopard Begonia)
Nandina (Sacred Bamboo)
Orchid (*Cymbidium* and others)
Portulacaria afra (Jade)
Pseudopanax (New Zealand Aralia)
Primula obconica

Plant	Symptom	Cause	Remedy
Fittonia	Leaves with pale brown patches or flecks	Over-bright or direct light but also check for red spider mite	Remove to moderate light. If necessary see 'Controlling pests'
	Leaves falling	Soil and atmosphere too dry	Water whenever surface of soil begins to feel dry
	Plant and stems rotting at base	Over-wet soil	See above, and strike cuttings from still healthy tip of growth
Fuchsia	Sudden leaf fall	May occur after using Pyrethrum-type or Bio-resmethrin insecticide sprays	Carbaryl or Endosulphan (Thiodan) are safer sprays for caterpillar control
	Gradual leaf fall	Occurs naturally as winter months approach. Indoors may be due to poor light or faulty watering	Fuchsias are better in an outdoor situation with no more than a few days indoors during the flowering period
Geranium	Leggy growth and foliage falling	Poor light and lack of air circulation	Good growth from geraniums is only possible indoors with some direct sunlight and good air circulation
Gloxinia (Florist's gloxinia or sinningia)	Foliage yellowing and falling during autumn	Approaching natural dormancy as temperatures fall	Withhold watering, then when plant dies, store tubers for replanting in spring
	Pale spots on foliage	Bright light on water droplets	Avoid wetting foliage during watering
	Leaf margins shrivelling	Atmosphere too dry	Improve humidity
	Flowering ceases prematurely	Too little light	Give very bright indirect light
Gynura (Velvet Leaf)	New foliage distorted and thickened	Broad mite or cyclamen mite	Either burn plant or remove to outdoor shade and spray with Metasystox
Hippeastrum	Distorted flower buds and foliage, reddish-brown stain at base of latter	Narcissus mite	Remove outdoors and spray with Lebaycid, Rogor or Metasystox
Hoya	Lack of flower	Due to cutting the flower heads the previous season, poor light or lack of maturity	Plants need at least bright direct light, and sometimes several years to establish. Training growth in a lateral manner or on a circular frame can speed flowering
Kalanchoe blossfeldiana	Failure to flower	Too much warmth and artificial light at night during winter	Give about 11 hours darkness per night and preferably temperatures down around 10–13 °C to stimulate flower bud formation. Flowering occurs about 3 months later
Peperomia	Plants rot at base	Over-watering	Strike new plants from leaf cuttings, allow surface of potting mixture to dry out between waterings
Pilea	Foliage falling	Either over-wet soil or fumes from coal gas or oil heaters	Allow surface of potting mix soil to dry out between waterings or, if necessary, remove from atmosphere contaminated by fumes
Poinsettia	Failure to flower the second year	Influence of artificial light at night	Prune back after flowering, then when new growth is established in autumn, remove out of range of artificial light
Pothos	Loss of golden variegation	Insufficient light	Move to bright indirect light
Rhoeo (Moses-in-Cradle)	Poor foliage colour	Insufficient light	Move to very bright indirect light
Roses (miniature)	Foliage falling	Unsuitable for indoor conditions	Move to airy situation with at least half a day's direct sunlight
Sansevieria	Foliage rotting at base	Over-wet during cold conditions	Except in permanently heated rooms allow potting soil to almost completely dry out during winter
Spathiphyllum (Spoon Lily)	Foliage dull yellow	Too much light	Prefer low to moderate light

Raising insect-eating plants

If you haven't yet come across that fascinating range of plants which seems to be part animal you're in for a surprise.

Some have senses so keen they respond to the gentlest touch while others attract and trap insects which they slowly dissolve and absorb.

One well-known 'sensitive' plant is *Mimosa pudica*. This fern-like little plant rapidly folds its leaves whenever they are touched. In Queensland it is often found growing among low grass by the roadside or in rough lawns.

Even more amazing are the numerous carnivorous or insect-eating plants. Many of these are not only capable of movement but trap and devour their insect prey. This might make these unusual plants sound like monsters to be avoided but most are appealing little subjects. Sundews (*drosera*) are beautiful, with every leaf rimmed in tiny tentacles, each carrying a glistening globule of liquid. The stubby Albany pitcher plants (*cephalotus*) are more quaint than beautiful but very fascinating.

Many of these interesting carnivores can be grown in small containers on sunny window-sills or other well-lit indoor situations. They will trap household insects, although the theory that they successfully rid the area of flies is exaggeration.

By far the most spectacular in both formation and action is the Venus fly trap (*Dionaea muscipula*) which hails from North Carolina. It makes a rosette of slender blade-like bright-green leaves, finger length or longer, each suddenly tapering then broadening into a wallet-like trap, both sides edged with teeth-like bristles that interlace when the hinged sides close together.

The trigger mechanism of the trap consists of three scarcely visible but extremely sensitive hairs on either half of the trap. As a safeguard against false alarms caused by small particles of falling debris a hair needs to be touched twice or two adjacent ones touched in turn. The jaws then snap shut and the insect, attracted by coloured glands in the trap base, is ensnared.

Pressure from the insect or chemical reaction from its body then causes the leaf glands to secrete digestive acids which allow the insect's body substances to be absorbed into the leaf. After 6–10 days the trap re-opens and allows the dried residue of the prey to be discharged.

The Sundews (*droseras*) are relatives of the Venus fly trap. Both have the attractively simple flowers with usually five petals that in some droseras are no longer than a match-head, and white or pink. However, one drosera frequently seen in Western Australia has bright orange flowers that often eclipse the surprisingly small rosetted plant.

Droseras do not catch their prey by snap action of the tentacle-like hairs but by the sticky liquid on these hairs and in the centre of their modified leaves or traps. When an insect becomes entangled, the tentacles slowly turn inward to hold it against the digestive fluid.

The Albany pitcher plant (*Cephalotus follicularis*) is extraordinary looking. Each season it makes smooth green spatula-shaped leaves followed by stubby little green or purple-coloured pitchers. The plant's markings attract insects which slip on the smooth rim and fall to the inner cavity where they are digested by the plant fluids.

There are numerous Nepenthes species and hybrids with different colours and markings. Most come from humid tropical areas and in all but similar climates need a glasshouse to grow well.

The Sundews adapt to all but the coldest climates, and even for these areas there are species which die down to a dormant tuber in winter. All prefer moist conditions but adapt to a variety of soils — even wet, muddy ones in sun or part shade.

All others, especially the Venus fly trap, seem to do best in a crumbly soil kept moist with a surface layer of sphagnum moss 2–3 cm deep. The Venus fly trap needs plenty of sun, humidity and fresh air. Leaves die off periodically and are replaced but the plant keeps in better condition if the flower stem is removed before it opens. Albany pitcher plants also need humidity but less sun.

Growing African violets

These charming little plants bring great pleasure, but the number of people who waylay me with African violet problems might suggest that they are one of the hardest plants to grow successfully.

When poor results are reported I query the aspect first. When people claim their failing plants have the good light and freedom from draughts recommended one has to look for the intangibles. As experienced growers will agree, these plants can do well in one spot and poorly in another with seemingly identical conditions.

You could check for the best position by keeping a plant in each of the most likely places for a season.

In any case choose positions just far enough from a window to escape direct sunlight. I get good results by placing plants about 30 cm from a south window that misses direct sunlight entirely.

Sunlight diffused by sheer curtains works well with east or west windows but all-day sun diffused this way can be too strong, and the foliage will be short, thick and clumpy, sometimes with pale, sandy-coloured areas as it is with violets grown on a balcony where direct sunlight reaches them.

On the other hand, in too shaded areas the leaves become thin and drawn.

Watering

Recommendations differ. Professional growers may advise that the soil should be kept moist at all times. This may apply in heated and brightly lit glasshouses but I prefer to water only when the soil feels dry.

The foliage is an indicator of the moisture needed. When too dry it becomes limp and tends to fall slightly at the edges, or if over-watered begins to look excessively waxy.

An African violet is the one plant I do not saturate when watering; I give enough just to dampen the soil, particularly if the container is without drainage.

A large plant in one of those flat violet bowls about 20 cm across would get about one-third cup of water. I spread it, slightly tipping the bowl in both directions as soon as it is poured on the compact surface.

How often you need to water depends on room temperature. It may be every day during summer heat and only once a week during the cooler months — water whenever the soil is dry with *tepid* water. It has been conclusively proved that cold tap water can shock the plant and retard growth. Some people keep the water at room temperature in an indoor container which is refilled after watering.

Alternatively, run in just enough hot water to take the chill off but not enough to feel obviously warm.

You can water from either top or bottom but care must be taken not to wet the leaves or the centre of the plant.

Feeding

Overfeeding can have more serious effects than starvation.

You could use one of the special African violet foods or a complete soluble food at about half the normally recommended strength every 3–4 weeks, except in winter if the plants are then dormant or without flower.

Most of the soluble plant foods contain relatively high percentages of nitrogen which can cause over-leafiness at the expense of flower so sprinkle one-third of a teaspoon of superphosphate around the edge of the container about every 3 months.

Alternatively, the slowly-soluble plant pills or slow-release Osmocote contain enough elements without any need for superphosphate.

Humidity

In hot, dry climates or in any room with a heater or air-conditioning, the atmosphere may become too dry for African violets to grow well.

A popular way to overcome this is to stand the pots on trays with water in the base and a layer of pebbles to keep the pots just above the water (except of course for containers without drainage holes).

Aquariums or fish bowls are excellent for African violets as they protect from draught and keep the atmosphere moist.

Failure to flower

Most strains of African violets will flower for many months when conditions and treatment suit them. Flowering often ceases through the cooler months.

If it is difficult to start them into flower again it could be due to excessive leafiness, so take off every third leaf, and particularly a few of the small ones at the top, remove any runners or new plantlets from the base of the plant and feed with superphosphate.

Plants become less productive when they develop a woody crown or centre stem. Before this occurs it is a good idea to have some new ones coming on.

Strike new plants from the leaves you have thinned out. Stand them with the tip of the leaf stalk in water or in a damp mixture, 2 parts coarse sand with 1 of peatmoss.

Plastic seedling punnets are handy for this as the leaves can be rested along the edges with tips of the stems just buried toward the centre. Four or 5 cm of stem is sufficient, but cut them cleanly with a razor blade or very sharp knife. Cover the glass or jar with aluminium foil, punching holes in it so that the leaf rests on top and the end of the stem just touches the water.

Tiny plantlets will gradually form around the cut stem. When these have made several sets of leaves and are large enough to handle carefully separate from the stem and space 2–3 cm apart in trays of the mixture.

As they develop pot on African violet soil, which is now available in several proprietary brands.

Carnivorous plants Venus fly-trap (left) and Sundew (right) are fascinating house plants

African violets need bright but indirect light and moderate humidity for prolonged flowering

Growing cyclamen

Cyclamen flowers best in fairly cool conditions. As nights become warmer in mid to late spring, flowering ceases, foliage yellows and the plants become dormant for a few months.

This is what happens when a healthy, bud-packed cyclamen is given a position in a warm room, especially one heated during the night. It is the main cause of non-flowering, but there are ways to overcome it: put the cyclamen out each night, or place the plant close to a glass window where the temperature may be low enough because the glass will conduct the lower temperatures from outside.

An hour or two of early morning sun helps to strengthen the plants, so if they are put out at night it may be possible to choose a position where they can benefit from the early sun.

Do not keep cyclamens over-wet. Allow the surface of the soil to dry out between waterings. If they dry to the point of foliage flagging, give a good soak by standing the container in a bucket with water up to the pot rim.

Watering from the top will not hurt cyclamens but it is not advisable to allow water droplets to remain in the crown of the plant during the night.

Cyclamens need feeding during winter because this is their active growing period, but don't rush to feed a newly purchased plant. Give it a good soaking and leave for a few weeks to acclimatise, with plenty of light by day and a cool dark period at night. When the warmth of late spring brings a weak yellowing to cyclamen foliage, just let the soil become drier. After the foliage is lost, store the corms in slightly damp sand or peatmoss until December, then replant when new growth appears.

Cyclamens, waxy and ornately formed, provide colourful winter and early spring flowers

Above: African Violets

Right: Unlike African violets, Cyclamen need cool nights to flower

A reference guide to house plants

Acalpha wilkesiana (Fijian Fire Plant) Popular foliage shrub in warmer temperate coastal to tropical districts. Also known in some areas as Beefsteak Plant and Match-me-if-you-can, because no two leaves have identical markings — some greenish-bronze splashed with black and blotched pink, others basically coppery-salmon with inserts of cream, black or green, etc. Popular overseas as a house plant and could be grown similarly here.

Needs Very bright light, some direct sunlight. Water whenever soil surface dries out while actively growing and conditions are warm, and during that period feed with soluble plant food every 3–4 weeks. Prune back 15–20 cm in late winter–early spring, for bushier growth, pinching out tips of new growth when 12–15 cm long. Syringe during hot weather to improve humidity.

Achimenes Attractive summer-flowering basket or pot plants with arching slightly hairy stems and serrated green foliage carrying smooth, round-petalled, petunia-like pale blue, violet, coral salmon to pink and ruby red flowers. Plants die down in winter, shooting again in early summer from fleshy corms like miniature pine cones which form at the end of roots and base of the stem. Tip cuttings also strike readily and form corms.

Needs Bright to very bright light, not direct sunlight, or outdoors with dappled shade in humid areas. Add about one-quarter rotted leafmould or moistened peatmoss to standard potting soil, keep damp during active growth, feed every 3–4 weeks with half-strength soluble plant food. Needs moderate warmth but extreme heat curtails flowering.

Adiantum (Maiden Hair) see **Ferns**

Aechmea see **Bromeliads**

Aeschynanthus lobbianus (Lipstick Plant) Handsome basket plant with closely set glossy foliage, clusters of long tubular double-lipped red flowers emerging from goblet-like purple bronze silky textured calyx cups. Under good conditions will trail 1 m. *A. marmoratus* has dark foliage 10 cm long with attractive lighter veining. *A. pulcher* also has bright red flowers but with green calyx.

Needs Warm, fairly humid conditions, down to 15 °C at night, to 30 °C by day, bright light, keep soil damp, only allowing to partly dry out if temperatures drop below suggested minimum. Soil as suggested for *Achimenes*.

African Violet (*Saintpaulias*)

Needs African Violets make healthy growth in moderate light but most varieties need bright but indirect light to encourage or prolong flowering. They are happy with only moderate humidity, therefore there should be no need to worry about this factor except in hot dry climates or where heaters are used in closed rooms. See **Humidity**. Preference is for average to warm temperatures (16°– 30°C). Allow surface of soil to become dry

between waterings but avoid complete drying out. Use room temperature, not cold tap water. There is frequent controversy about watering soil from the top but this does no harm providing water does not remain on foliage for long periods as this may cause spotting.

Feed every 3–4 weeks while temperatures remain above the suggested minimum, using soluble plant foods diluted to half normal strength. Note that many of the soluble preparations sold for general use do not contain sufficient phosphorus to stimulate flower bud formation. If you care to check this, the formula is on the label, usually expressed as N.P.K. — N = nitrogen, P = phosphorus and K = potash (kalium). If the percentage figure for 'P' is less than half of the figure for 'N', then it is advisable to add extra phosphorus to your African Violets.

Do this by sprinkling over the soil toward the rim of the pot a scant quarter-teaspoon of superphosphate about once every three months, watering well afterwards. Beware of heavy plant food concentrations because these can cause root damage. Overleafiness can retard flowering so remove two or three leaves to let more light into the centre of the plant. Remove runners or suckers from plants.

Repotting African Violets that are no longer flowering well and have become very leafy may need repotting. A sure sign is that the plant is beginning to show a section of trunk-like stem between soil level and lower foliage. The best way to rejuvenate it is by gently pressing down with both hands, thumb and forefinger of each held above the base of the lower older and larger leaves to break them from the stem.

Then tap plant from pot, gently shake off some of the soil and with a sharp knife scrape stem clean of old leaf butts. Repot in new African Violet soil (which should be a little coarser and more fibrous than ordinary potting soil), bringing the base of the remaining foliage almost to soil level. This induces new root growth to form from the now bared stem. Keep in just moderate light for a few weeks, then move to bright light and feed occasionally with an African Violet food. Note that in areas where rooms are cold at night it is better to delay general repotting until mid to late spring.

Propagate from leaves with the cut section of the stem just slightly bedded in a mixture of equal parts peatmoss and coarse sand, or with the stem through a hole in a foil cover so that it is just touching water.

Soil for African Violets Coarsen or loosen the standard potting mixtures by adding about one-quarter by volume of moistened peatmoss, milled pine bark or rotted leafmould. African Violet potting soil is commercially available.

Pests Check occasionally for mealy bug or mildew (see **Pest** section).

Aglonema modestum (Chinese Evergreen) Large dark green oval then tapering leathery foliage later developing a caney base. *A. commutatum* Silver King and others have

more slender foliage with attractive feather-like silvery markings over main veins.

Needs *Aglonemas* are among the few plants that prefer only moderate light and adapt well to low light. Water whenever surface soil dries. Feed with half-strength soluble plant food every six weeks only while there are signs of active growth — standard potting soil is suitable.

Aluminium Plant see *Pilea*

Anthurium (Flamingo flower) There are many species and some beautiful hybrids. The one frequently grown for flowers, *A. scherzerianum*, makes clumps of rosetted slender leathery foliage about 25 cm high, and has slightly higher flower stems carrying a plastic textured brilliant scarlet artist's palette-like spathe, topped with a thin finger-like red and often twisted spadex (the fertile part of the flower). *A. andreanum* has larger heart-shaped leaves, and large glossy puckered coral red spathe but in its several varieties colour varies from white to dark red. *A. crystalinum* is grown mainly for its huge ornate dark bronze-green heart-shaped leaves with contrasting silvery veining. There are nearly another hundred species and many hybrids.

Needs *Anthuriums* respond best to moderately bright indirect light — if too bright foliage will pale. They respond well to high humidity and temperatures from between 15 °C and 30 °C but stand occasional colder nights if soil is allowed to dry slightly. Otherwise keep soil damp by watering when surface dries out.

Feed at the first sign of new spring growth with half-strength soluble plant food and repeat every 3–4 weeks during warmer conditions while growth is active. Soil needs to be lightened by the addition of about one-third coarse material like weathered pine bark, pea-size charcoal, rich hulls, granular peatmoss, finely chopped tree fern bark or a mixture of any of these.

Repot when overcrowded or when crowns develop with roots well above soil level. Lightly stake these divisions with the base of the crown (root junctions) about at ground level.

Aphelandra Erect shrubby plant with large elliptical glossy foliage *A. squarrosa* with leaves marked white along cross-veins, sometimes crested with a spiked shell-like orange or yellow bract.

Needs Bright to moderate light, warm, reasonably humid conditions, watering when surface dries out, a little drier if winter temperatures are below 15 °C. Use good peaty potting soil.

Aralia see *Fatsia* and *Dizygotheca*

Ardisia crispa Small shrub with miniature tree form, crest of dark glossy foliage above a shower of cream flowers followed by glossy red berries that last almost throughout the year.

Needs Moderate to bright light, avoiding hot stuffy closed rooms, stands cold down to 5 °C and prefers some fluctuation between night and day temperatures. Ideal for outdoor shade. Water when soil surface dries, feed sparingly with half-strength soluble plant food every 4–6 weeks, leach at least between every third feeding.

Asparagus Numerous varieties, those more frequently grown indoors include *A. plumosus* with tough erect thorny, later twining stems and flat fronds with hair-fine dark green leaflets, *A. sprengeri* with arching stems of tinsel-like bright to light glossy green slender foliage and *A. meyeri Foxi nana* with short, very densely packed tapering sprays of foliage.

Needs Asparagus grows best with fresh air and very bright light but will stand moderate light providing temperatures are not high — resents warm, curtained, stuffy rooms. Needs occasional good soakings but tolerates dryness, especially when light is reduced. Feed every 4–5 weeks when new growth is evident with water-soluble plant foods.

Aspidistra (Cast Iron Plant) As the common name implies, it is probably the toughest and most adaptable house plant. It makes clumps of long-bladed slender dark green leaves to 75 cm in height and 12 to 15 cm wide, sometimes variegated.

Needs Bright to very low light, average home temperatures and humidity, water when soil surface dries out but tolerates near complete dryness for short periods.

Feed occasionally when new growth is evident with half-strength soluble plant food, preferably leaching beforehand. Sponge leaves once a month to keep in top condition.

Aucuba japonica (Gold Dust Shrub) Large leathery elliptical to oval dark green leaves spotted with gold. There are also a larger plain leafed variety and one with leaves heavily blotched with gold. Grows well in outdoor shade where it reaches 1 to 2 m in height. A good plant for shaded porches, etc.

Needs Bright light, stands moderate heat but also has surprising tolerance to cold, accepting temperatures down to 0 °C or lower. Water whenever soil surface dries out, syringe foliage during hot weather — feed 4–6 weekly during spring and summer or when new growth appears.

Azalea In some countries azaleas are rarely grown as house plants but are successful in bright light if night temperatures are moderately cool, and providing plants are returned to outdoors, initially to dappled shade, immediately flowers finish.

Needs Water whenever surface soil dries out, move outdoors and feed only from the time new spring growth commences every 4–5 weeks until mid-summer with half-strength water-soluble plant foods.

BEGONIAS *B. rex* Numerous types grown and their large angular satin texture and beautifully coloured foliage are mainly in combinations of pink, bronze-red, silver and green according to variety. Foliage may die off temporarily during cold conditions.

Needs Bright to moderate light, fresh air (resents stuffy poorly lit rooms), temperatures from 16°–30 °C, water when surface dries, keep a little drier if temperatures are below 16 °C. Feed with half-strength soluble plant food when new spring growth com-

mences every 4–6 weeks while conditions are warm.

Soil Standard potting soil with peatmoss or leafmould or decomposed cow manure added.

B. Elatior Similar to *B. tuberhybrida* but usually smaller and more profuse, does not die down to tuber, propagated from cuttings. Flowers during cooler weather.

Needs Similar to *B. rex* but growth and flowers are better under slightly cooler conditions with moderate humidity.

B. tuberhybrida (Tuberous begonia), large silky petalled flowers like camellias or roses in some single varieties but a percentage of single female flowers may alternate with doubles — also pendulous basket types. Plant dies down to dormant tuber in winter.

Needs Bright light, good ventilation, moderate temperatures from 16 °C to 27 °C, water if soil surface dries, feed every 3–4 weeks with half-strength water-soluble plant food. Soil as *B. rex*. Keep tubers dry during winter, dampen when warmth commences in spring, repot when new shoots appear.

Other Begonias Other types grown mainly for decorative foliage include *B. Cleopatra*, bright light green leaves marked brown. *B. manicata* (*Aureo-maculata*) with hairy red stems and veins, large gold spotted soft green leaves. There are at least another 100 species and hybrids, most suited to *B. rex* conditions and to outdoor shade in all but cool climates.

Billbergia see *Bromeliads*

Brassaia arboracola (Dwarf Umbrella Tree) Caney plant, in outdoor sun bushy and spreading, indoor usually single stemmed, staked to 2 m, with fairly long stemmed (petioles) hand-shaped dark leathery green leaves usually 12–14 cm across, divided into 7–9 leaflets 5–9 cm long. Unlike the Queensland Umbrella Tree (*Schefflera*) it holds foliage well to the base of the stem but for large pots, setting 2 or 3 plants together gives best effect.

Needs Bright to moderately low light, adapts well to most indoor conditions except warm, dark frequently curtained rooms. Water when surface soil dries to about 1 cm down or about 2 cm when night temperatures are low. Feed while making active new growth with half-strength soluble plant foods every 4–6 weeks.

BROMELIADS A large family of remarkable and usually adaptable plants. These include:

Aechmea Embracing popular 40 to 50 cm high vase-shaped silver and darker banded *A. faciata*, producing an erect stemmed cone-shaped head of starry bright pink bracts enclosing the tubular blue flowers. *A. weilbachii* with glossy green foliage, and small deep blue petals forming a peak on the rosy crimson berry-like flowers that carry their striking colours right down into the stem, plus many other distinct species and hybrids.

Annas The pineapple which with the pink variegated form is sometimes grown in very bright indoors.

Billbergias Including well-known garden varieties *B. nutans* or Queen's Tears with clumpy growth, pink-sheathed arching

stems, supporting a pendulous cluster of violet-edged green flowers; bold vase-shaped bright green *B. pyramidalis* with a showy erect spike of crimson-sheathed rose-red and purple-tipped flowers, plus many more species.

Cryptanthus Or Earth Stars, starfish-like, many with dark banded foliage that colours bright coppery pink in very bright light.

Neoregelias Handsomely rosetted foliage.

N. carolinae As the plant matures leaves colour deep red at the base to mark the almost immersed centre flowers, *C. carolinae* Tricolor, a handsome cream variegated form that colours pink in good light.

Nidulariums Resemble *Neoregelias*—some spotted, others with coloured centres or reddish-bronze backed foliage.

Tillandsias Range from thin strappy leafed rosettes, some with ornate fanlike bracts carrying violetlike flowers, to silvery grey Spanish moss that grows on trees and hangs like grey tinsel.

Vriesias Urn-shaped rosettes of foliage. Low growing light green *V. carinata* — the red of its flower stem flares up into the centre of its fan-shaped formation of bright yellow flower bracts. *V. splendens Major* (Flaming Sword) has dark banded showy foliage and a sword-like spike of bright crimson bracts, with occasional golden tubular flowers.

Needs All grow in moderate indoor light but need bright light for good foliage colour and to flower. Most accept temperatures down to 5 °C except a few of the more exotic flowered *Tillandsias* and *V. splendens*. These and most of the others are happiest with a minimum of about 15 °C.

Water needs to be kept in the pitcher-like receptacle formed by the tightly rosetted leaves of the urn-shaped types. Providing this is maintained, humidity is not a factor and soil moisture is of little importance although it can benefit most types. Do not maintain water in the centre of the cold sensitive *Tillandsias* and *Vriesias* in winter in cool areas. Invert during the critical cold period to prevent collection of water that may chill or freeze the plants.

CACTI Are divided into two main groups.

Desert Cacti Spiky and usually covered with spines or hairs, can be small and round or with towering candelabra-like form 5 or 6 m tall.

Strap Cacti are like flattened leafy stems, with hair covered but rarely spiny aeroles in segments of leaves or indentation along the edges.

Strap or Leaf Cacti Include *Epiphyllum, Heliochia* or *Heliocereus, Seleniphyllum* — all known as orchid cactus; *Nopalxochia*, the best known, is German Empress cactus with silvery pink centre petals cupped like a daffodil, now regarded as a hybrid form; *Zygocactus, Rhipsalidopsis* and *Schlumbergera* — often classed as Crab's Claw or under the northern hemisphere name Christmas cactus. Also *Rhipsalis*, usually very branched, some with waxy cylindrical stems and small pearly flowers.

Needs In nature the strap and Crab's Claw

Anthurium scherzerianum

Aglonema modestum (Chinese Evergreen)

Begonia elator

Aphelandra 'Rembrandt'

Aeschyanthus lobbianus (Lipstick Plant)

cacti grow in light jungle country on branches or in forks of trees, usually where leafmould has collected. Therefore they prefer light shade during the heat of the day, or indoors bright indirect light and in the case of orchid cactus very bright light with some direct sunlight.

The Crab's Claw group needs about six weeks of long nights before flower bud formation takes place. Therefore in mid to late autumn move them away from house lights. They prefer a winter night temperature down around 10°C but this is not critical.

Water regularly, allowing the surface of the potting mixture to dry out between waterings. The Orchid and German Empress cacti respond to a rest period for a few weeks during late January or early February when they may be left almost dry.

Soil Although in nature these plants exist on leafmould only, they respond well to standard potting mixtures enriched with about one-quarter part-rotted leafmould or lime-free compost.

Desert Cacti Most need bright to very bright light. Those covered with spines or hairs prefer a large percentage of direct sunlight.

Although of desert origin they appreciate moderate watering when new growth starts and during summer. Allow the surface soil to dry out for the depth of a centimetre or two between waterings. New growth is indicated by lighter or brighter colour of new spines which form in the centre of the plant. During this period they also respond to light feeding — say half-strength liquid plant food every 5 or 6 weeks.

Many types need night temperatures down to about 10°C for several weeks during winter to flower in spring.

Soil Should be crumbly and drain well. A mixture of about two parts coarse river sand and one part garden loam would be suitable. Add about a teaspoon garden lime or dolomite per five litres of soil if the soil is known to be acid as most cacti prefer a slightly acid to neutral soil. A scree of gravel over the surface of the soil is beneficial as it prevents soil splashing and assists drainage.

Caladium Large soft-textured arrow-shaped leaves with beautiful colours and markings. They die down to a dormant crown in winter and reappear during spring.

Needs Bright to very bright indirect light, high humidity and water whenever surface soil dries during the growing season. When foliage yellows in autumn allow soil to become almost dry.

Feed with half-strength soluble plant foods after spring growth commences then at intervals of 4–6 weeks while growth is active.

Calathea (Peacock or Prayer Plant) Beautifully marked oval to oblong foliage clumped in loose rosetted formation on slender stems.

Needs Bright to moderate light and moderate humidity, allow surface of soil to become just dry before watering or a little drier during winter if temperatures are below

Neoregelia carolinea tricolor with Billbergia pyramidalis

Chlorophytum (Spider Plant)

Tree ferns make impressive house plants

15 °C. Feed with half-strength water-soluble plant food every 4–5 weeks during warm conditions while growth is active.

Calceolaria Broad clusters of globular orange or gold flowers, often spotted red. Most of the house plant types sold are annuals and die in summer.

Needs Bright light but fairly cool conditions to prolong flowering. Water if surface soil dries, feed every 3–4 weeks with half-strength soluble plant food.

Camellia Mainly grown outdoors in all but very cold areas but they make imposing house plants.

Needs Treat like *azaleas*, except that feeding may be carried through to flowering time and all but one or two buds per stem may be removed if aiming for flower size and quality rather than quantity.

Ceropegia woodii (**String of Hearts**) Small succulent heart-shaped bronze and silver-grey marbled leaves set in pairs along the trailing thread-like stems, which self-layer and produce a bulblike crown. Suits wall baskets, etc.

Needs Bright light or outdoor shade, water when soil surface dries out but allow to remain drier while growing conditions are cool. Either mulch lightly in spring with leafmould or feed at 6–8-week intervals during spring and summer with half-strength soluble plant foods.

Chinese Evergreen see *Aglonema*

Chinese Fire Fern (*Oxalis hedsarensis*) Attractive bronze red rounded leaflets and stems, small yellow flowers.

Needs Bright light, water when soil surface dries, feed every 4–6 weeks with half-strength soluble plant foods from spring to late summer. Plant tends to become dormant during winter.

Will drop foliage with sudden change of temperature and environment, especially if light is suddenly restricted.

Chlorophytum (**Spider Plant**) Graceful rosettes of slightly succulent tapering ribbon-like foliage, variegated cream and green, tiny white lily-like flowers on tall branching stems that later form plantlets and bend ground-ward to start a colony beyond the parent plant, decorative in hanging baskets.

Needs Moderate to bright light or outdoor shade, water well occasionally — the bulbous storage roots see it through periods of dryness. For extra growth feed with soluble plant foods every four weeks during spring and summer. Brownish tips usually due to excessive chlorine or fluoride in water or atmosphere.

Chrysanthemum Nurseries simulate the shortened days that induce flowering and produce potted plants in bloom at any time of year. Special soil additives are frequently used to keep growth dwarfed. They make colourful and decorative house plants, under reasonable conditions lasting until buds showing colour have opened. In spring and early summer especially, most varieties can be cut back and transferred to the garden when blooms finish, to flower again the following autumn.

Needs Bright to very bright light to bring out unopened buds, otherwise moderate light — water when soil surface dries.

Cissus *C. antarctica* (**Kangaroo Vine**) Glossy green serrated oval leaves, attractive trailer or climber. *C. rhombifolia* has divided dark green holly-like leaves.

Needs Adapts to full sun or moderate light, but requires at least bright light for growth. Any move to direct sunlight should be a gradual one to avoid foliage burn. Water when soil surface becomes dry. To promote growth feed with water-soluble plant food at monthly intervals from spring to autumn — any potting soil. Garden sprays directed at underside of foliage at intervals of 3–4 days until tiny thrips disappear.

Clerodendrum thomsonae Balfouri (**Glory Vine** or **Bleeding Heart Vine**) Twining to shrubby vine with dark oval foliage with small deep crimson flowers 'dripping' from inflated creamy white heart-shaped calyces.

Needs Bright to very bright light or sheltered outdoor shade in mild districts. Keep moist during spring and summer, reduce water and cut back heavily if vine loses foliage in winter. Feed every 3–5 weeks during spring and summer with half-strength soluble plant food.

Clivia Usually grown in outdoor shade, popular as a northern hemisphere house plant and could be used similarly elsewhere. The evergreen dark erect clumps of straplike foliage are attractive. *C. miniata* has heads of upfacing bright orange red flowers in spring. *C. hybrida* larger in every way and usually brighter. *C. nobilis* with pendulous salmon orange, green-tipped funnel-shaped flowers.

Needs Prefers bright airy situations away from direct sunlight, plenty of water and monthly soluble plant food from spring to late summer, drier — late autumn and early winter. Any potting soil will do, container at least 25 cm wide and deep.

Codiaeum see *Croton*

Coleus Branching soft-stemmed plants with coloured velvety foliage, more profuse during warmer months.

Needs Plants exist in moderate light but bright to very bright light is needed for good colour. Water whenever surface soil dries out, feed every 3–5 weeks with water-soluble plant food.

Plants may perish during winter cold. Young plants struck from cuttings during late summer have a better survival rate. Even so, vigour will be better if new plants are raised in spring from tip growths of over-wintered ones.

Columnea gloriosa Trailing basket plants with orange-red *Aeschynanthus*-like flowers but without cylindrical or goblet-like calyx; velvety bronze-green foliage.

Needs Same conditions as *Aeschynanthus*.

Cordyline terminalis Caney stems with a handsome crest of broad straplike foliage — variegated or mostly ruby red, or with cream variegations. Height eventually reaches 2–3 m. *C. terminalis miniata* Baby Ti grows only about 50 cm with short closely set copper-margined green foliage. There is a similar dark bronze form.

Needs Bright light, airy situation, moderate humidity, water whenever soil surface dries — responds to half-strength soluble plant foods every 4–5 weeks while indoor conditions are warm. Standard potting soil but without perlite.

Crab's Claw (*Zygocactus*) see Cacti

Crossandra Small shrubby glossy-foliaged plant with salmon-red partly tubular flowers radiating from a head of greenish bracts.

Needs Prefers brightly lit humid situation, watered when surface soil dries, responds to half-strength water-soluble plant foods every 4–5 weeks while conditions are warm.

Croton Beautiful tropical foliage plants. Long, glossy, leathery leaves with such as coppery-salmon or bronze base, spotted green, gold, etc.

Needs Very bright light, some direct sunlight if possible, water whenever soil surface dries during warm conditions, feed every 3–5 weeks with half-strength soluble plant foods — reduce water and discontinue feeding with cool conditions. Any standard potting soil.

Ctenanthe Resembling *calatheas* or *marantas* but with plantlets or clumps of foliage from reedy stems rather than from a base crown.

Needs Similar to *calathea* but also content with average garden loam and grows in outdoor shade in all but cool districts.

Cussonia spicata Small evergreen *aralia*-like tree with a large rosetted head of attractively cut and lobed leathery green leaflets.

Needs Suits outdoors in all but cold districts or brightly lit indoors. Good plant for large container in shaded porches, etc. Water when soil surface dries, for growth feed with soluble plant foods as often as every 3–4 weeks.

Cycas see **Palms** for general care.

Cyclamen Waxy ornately formed colourful winter and early spring flowers.

Needs Unlike African Violets and many other house plants *cyclamen* need cool nights to continue flowering.

Keep away from heaters and either keep them close to glass where outdoor cold is transmitted or put them out at night with the milk bottles. If they are left out to enjoy an hour or two of early morning sun, so much the better, as they love fresh air and plenty of light.

Let the surface become just dry between thorough waterings but as increasing spring warmth causes foliage to yellow and flower bud formation to cease, allow to almost dry out. Clean and store corm, replanting in new soil during late December. However, not all corms survive dormancy and rarely perform as well the second year.

Use standard potting soil, preferably with a sprinkling of lime or dolomite, and either bone dust or blood and bone added. Feed at fortnightly intervals with complete soluble plant food until flowering commences.

Cymbidium see Orchids
Cyripedium see Orchids
Dendrobium see Orchids

Devil's Ivy see *Scindapsus*

Dieffenbachia (Dumb Cane) Common name refers to irritating sap which causes mouth, tongue, etc to swell and temporarily makes speech impossible.

Decorative caney plants crested with a rosette of oval to oblong bright green foliage, spotted or in some heavily blotched with cream, yellow or silver.

Needs Bright to moderate light, fairly cool indoors but resents extremes during winter. Allow surface soil to become dry between waterings, especially when conditions are cool. To promote growth (which causes them to become taller and eventually leggier especially where light is restricted) feed every 4–6 weeks with half-strength complete soluble plant foods.

Dipladenia Decorative twining plant, carries small clusters of soft rose trumpets 4–5 cm across with a sulphur yellow deep throat flushed green at the base. May be grown in a large pot and trained on arched wire supports, then new growth trimmed back for more compact cover.

Needs Bright to very bright light or outdoor positions in frost-free areas. Water when surface dries out and feed every 4–6 weeks with half-strength soluble plant food while temperatures are above 16°C.

Dizygotheca (Finger Aralia) Erect, elegant plant surrounded by long-stemmed hand-shaped foliage finely divided into slender serrated bronze leaflets.

Needs Brightly to moderately lit airy situation. Water when surface soil dries out, feed at 4–6-weekly intervals with half-strength soluble plant food while conditions are warm. Standard potting soil.

Dracaena Caney plants crested with decorative rosettes of straplike foliage including Happy Plant *D. fragrans* and thin branching dark oval gold spotted leaf *D. godseffiana*. Also slender leafed and usually white variegated *D. deremensis*.

Needs The first two mentioned need very bright to moderate light. *D. deremensis* adapts to low light. Water when surface soil dries. Feed every 4–6 weeks during warm conditions with half-strength soluble plant foods but still less frequently if in low light.

Dumb Cane see *Dieffenbachia*

Epidendrum see Orchids

Epiphyllum see Cacti

Episcia dianthiflora Trailer with rounded velvet-green foliage and trumpet-shaped white flowers fringed around the flared edges. Other hybrids, Flame Violets, have silver variegated deep green or bronze foliage and small bright red tubular flowers.

Needs Bright to moderate light, water when soil surface dries while temperatures are above 16°C, otherwise keep drier. Prefers temperatures 18°C to 27°C. Feed as African Violets.

Eucharis Lily Decorative clump of deep glossy green broad but lance-shaped foliage, head of flowers resembling fragrant waxy white daffodils.

Needs Bright to very bright light, a temperature from 13°C to 21°C. Water when surface soil dries out, except for a near dry rest period when new foliage has just matured and below 13°C. Feed when new growth appears every 4–6 weeks with soluble plant food.

Fatshedera Natural cross between *Fatsia* and *Hedera* (Ivy) with caney but sprawling growth needing support and leaves 3–4 times larger than English ivy and 3–4 times smaller than *Fatsia*.

Needs Bright to low light, outdoors full sun or shade, stands low or high temperatures. Water when surface soil dries. Feed occasionally with soluble plant food to encourage growth.

Fatsia Erect canes with a palm-like crest of long-stemmed large leathery hand-shaped leaves.

Needs Bright to moderate light or outdoor shade, stands high or low temperatures. Feed occasionally to stimulate growth — any loamy potting soil.

FERNS Well-grown and healthy ferns look delightful as individual specimens or as softeners accompanying flowering or foliage plants. Popular house plant types include the Maiden-hair *Adiantums*, various fishbone types such as the Boston fern *Nephrolepis exaltata bostonensis* — lace fern *N. exaltata elegantissima* and finer lacy variety Verona and others, the holly fern *Cyrtomium* with large glossy foliage tolerant of low light, the various hair's foot ferns *Davallias*, different types of strappy-leafed brake ferns *Pteris*, etc.

Needs All are best in bright to moderate light except holly fern which adapts to low light. However, some of the *Nephrolepis* including the giant fishbone *N. ensifolia* and Boston Fern will remain attractive in low light for many months but need a spell in brighter light to rejuvenate.

Most ferns prefer high humidity but moderate comfortable living atmosphere of most homes suits them providing they are kept away from heaters.

Do not wait for the surface to dry out before watering as suggested with many house plants — better to make a habit of watering daily but avoid continuously soggy soil and frequent use of chlorinated water.

Feeding should be done sparingly, as the established growth may appear to respond to some of the standard sprinkle on-type garden fertilisers but the soft fleshy embryo shoots may be burnt at or close to soil level. This may not be noticed until months later. Feed using a complete soluble plant food at about one-third normally recommended strength or a light sprinkling of slow-release granules through the soil when repotting.

Repot at any time providing roots are not disturbed. The safest time to divide is August just before new growth commences. Cut back all remaining fronds, divide by cutting through the clumps, quartering them if necessary; retain new growth from the outer edge of the clump, removing most of the old stubble sections.

Ficus elastica (Rubber Tree) Large leathery-leafed tree adaptable to a variety of indoor situations but like most trees will gradually lose lower foliage and develop a bare trunk. Too often they are then unwisely planted outdoors near buildings or in confined spaces — unwisely because they can grow 30 m high and nearly as wide with penetrating and heavy roots.

Needs Bright to low light — allow surface to dry out between waterings. Feed at 4–5-weekly intervals in spring and summer with soluble plant foods, providing plant is in good light, making new growth.

Ficus benjamina (Weeping Fig) An elegant tree with comparatively small bright green foliage on pendulous outer branches.

Needs Bright to moderate light, fairly average humidity. Except for variety *Exotica*, will drop foliage in closed stuffy rooms with blinds frequently drawn. Water only when surface soil dries, feed as *Ficus elastica* but either leach soil prior to feeding or use only one-third to one-half strength soluble plant food.

Fittonia (Nerve Plant) Low bushing or spreading bronze-green oval-leafed plants with contrasting silver or red leaf veining. Ideal for low table plant or terrariums.

Needs Bright to moderately low light, moderately humid — allow soil to dry to just damp stage before rewatering or surface to dry during winter. Feed 5–6-weekly while conditions are warm with one-third to one-half-strength soluble plant food.

Fuchsias Need very bright airy conditions such as well-ventilated sunroom, or grow in outdoor shade to bring indoors for periods of a few days only.

Needs Water whenever surface is dry. Use bone dust or a complete plant food high in phosphorus in potting mix — apply half-strength soluble plant foods at fortnightly intervals only when flowering starts. If indoors, syringe foliage frequently to deter red spider attack.

Geraniums Beautiful for indoor decoration but need very bright light near a sunny window and fresh air. It is better to grow them in sunny outdoor situations and bring indoors occasionally, or during very frosty winters.

Gloxinias (Florist's gloxinia or *sinningia*) Beautifully marked and showy large open bell flowers arrayed above a rosette of large velvety green foliage. Plants make growth and flower during the warmer months, die down in autumn to a dormant bulb-like corm which usually carries through reliably to the following season.

Needs Very bright to bright light and moderate humidity. Water whenever surface soil dries. Feed every 2–3 weeks with half-strength complete soluble plant food until flowers finish. Diminish water when foliage begins yellowing, then store dry during winter.

Hedera (Ivy) Many decorative types suitable for trailers, low bowls, etc, especially useful for cold to cool situations where warmth-loving plants would not succeed. Among the popular *H. helix* types are Weber's Californian, branching with closely set bright deep green small foliage rounded at the lobes,

Calceolarias

Dieffenbachia (Dumb Cane)

Columnea gloriosa

Impatiens (Busy Lizzy)

Ixora (Prince of Orange)

Odontonema (previously Justicia or Jacobinia)

Pittsburgh, more angular than the latter and slightly darker Parsley Ivy *H. helix crestata* very vigorous, larger than other two, more leathery, crested or crimped edges, leaves not as closely set. Goldheart needs bright light to bring out gold centre, Pinoak and *Pedata* have slender bird's foot-type foliage. Glacier, a number of similar small-leafed types and larger glossy-leafed *Canariensis,* have variegated leaves.

Needs Adapts to bright or fairly low light, bright light best for variegated types, prefers good ventilation, soil surface to dry out between waterings and, for extra growth, feeding with soluble plant foods every 4–6 weeks from spring to autumn, preferably leaching the soil first. Any potting soil.

Hoya **(Wax plant)** Waxy-foliaged twining plants except *H. bella* and *H. sikkimensis* which are branching trailers. Globular clusters of porcelainlike starry flesh-pink to white or buff flowers, many types with another small red or mauve star imposed on the centre of each floret.

Needs Bright to very bright light indoors with good ventilation, moderate temperatures and humidity, allow soil surface to become quite dry between waterings and during late winter to become drier still. Feed sparingly every 4–6 weeks during late spring and summer.

Plants are more likely to flower when growth is brought to lateral position, say with a wire arch supported in the container, also when plant is slightly pot bound, and even then may not flower for several years. The same flower spurs continue to flower for several seasons. Any potting soil that drains well, two parts garden loam, one sand and one rotted leafmould is a good mixture.

Hydrangea Plants brought indoors when flowering commences remain decorative for several weeks.

Needs Grow in outdoor shade or filtered light, some prefer winter temperatures down to at least 10°C. When spring growth commences and throughout summer keep well watered, feeding occasionally with a sprinkling of complete plant food — say a teaspoon per 30 cm square. Prune back each stem to plump double buds in autumn or winter. Lime for pinks, sulphate of aluminium for blue — starting in autumn.

Hypoestes **(Polka-dot Plant)** Soft shrubby plant with white flecked pinkish-bronze oval leaves.

Needs Bright to very bright light, good ventilation, water when soil surface dries, half-strength soluble plant food every 3–5 weeks during warm conditions. To keep compact, prune back in late winter then pinch out tips when shoots are about finger length.

Impatiens **(Busy Lizzy)** Bushy-type balsam with brittle succulent stems, soft foliage and satin-textured purple, red, pink or white flowers, mostly in summer.

Needs Bright to very bright light with good ventilation or outdoor shade, keep soil damp, water with half-strength plant food every 3–4 weeks when flowering com-

Philodendron 'Red Wings'

mences; if leggy, propagate new plants from tip cuttings, pinching out tip growth to encourage branching.

Ixora (Prince of Orange) Tropical shrub, closely set oval leathery foliage, dense rounded showy clusters of orange-red waxy-petalled tubular flowers, mostly in summer.

Needs Very bright light, well-ventilated but humid atmosphere. Water when surface soil dries, feed monthly with soluble plant food from late spring to late summer, keep a little drier during winter.

Jade (*Portulacaria afra*) Shrubby plant, can grow to 3 or 4 m in good conditions, reddish stems, small rounded waxy leaves, inconspicuous pink flowers.

Needs Very bright to bright light, good ventilation, stands dry atmosphere, allow surface soil to become quite dry between waterings, drier still during winter or in only moderately bright light. Feed with half-strength soluble plant food every six weeks after new spring growth starts until early autumn.

Kalanchoe blossfeldiana Compact plants with rosetted broad bright green succulent foliage, showy heads of small bright red flowers, usually in late winter and spring.

Needs Bright to very bright light, long moderately cool nights (12–14 hours) to stimulate flowering, therefore move outdoors during winter except in cold climates. Water when soil surface dries out, feed monthly with soluble plant food in spring and summer.

Kangaroo Vine see *Cissus*
Kentia see Palms
Livistonia see Palms
Maranta Closely related to and resembling *calatheas*. *M. arundinacea* has long wiry-stemmed lance-shaped green or variegated leaves, others like *M. leuconeura* Prayer Plant short-stemmed, broad oval light green leaves with dark blotching between the veins. *M. massangeana* has broad showy blue-green leaves with silver veins running through a dark shadowy reddish-brown centre area.

Needs As *Calatheas*

Monstera deliciosa Huge broad leathery perforated leaves to 1 m in length, thick stem with long cordlike aerial roots. Long leathery-skinned fruits that take about a year to ripen, usually only outdoors.

Needs Adapts to moderately low or very bright light but shade-grown plants may burn if moved to direct sunlight. Water when soil surface dries, drier in winter if less than very bright light. Feed monthly with soluble plant food while conditions are warm.

Neanthe see Palms
Nephrolepis see Ferns
Nidularium see *Bromeliads*
Nopalxochia (German Empress) see Cacti

ORCHIDS Decorative indoors while flowering. Good indoor conditions also suit warmth lovers needing winter protection, such as some Cattleya varieties. The latter may do well indoors in very bright to bright light with fresh air but reasonable humidity

such as sunroom conditions. These, most of the numerous *Dendrobiums* and others with caney growth are kept moderately damp and feed say monthly with half-strength soluble plant food while new growth is developing then, rested without feeding and little water when this growth reaches maturity, usually in autumn.

Epidendrum (Crucifix Orchid) Needs very bright light, some direct sunlight, and requires only moderate watering.

Cymbidium Need about six weeks of cool nights 10–15 °C to set flower spikes. Water frequently and feed only from the time new spring growth starts until mid-autumn then water only when compost is nearly dry. Move to outdoor part sunlight immediately flowers finish. Repot without disturbing roots when the container is filled with growths. Divide only if clumps are congested with back bulbs, preferably when flowering finishes.

Proprietary orchid composts are available for the latter. Caney types prefer compost coarsened with chopped tree fern fibre, or *Oncidiums*, some native *Dendrobiums* also grow on slabs of tree-fern, Ironbark, etc.

Slipper Orchid (*Paphiopedilums* and *Cyripediums*) Need much the same treatment as cymbidiums, preferring humid conditions but flower with less light.

PALMS Elegant and suitable in a variety of situations. The Kentia Palm *Howea* is one of the most adaptable for all but low light situations. Even with the latter, unless light is very dim it usually survives for years but rarely makes growth. The Bangalow Palm, which looks similar but with smooth green trunk, has far less adaptability. The Parlor Palm *Neanthe bella* is more suited to low light situations than most palms.

All palms, including those already mentioned, plus *Livistonia* or Fan Palm, *Cycads*, *Macrozamias*, *Raphis* or Lady Palm, *Cocus plumosa*, *Chamaedorea*, *Chamaerops* and most others will grow in all but low light situations. A few such as Golden-cane or Madagascar Palm *Chrysalidocarpus* need at least bright light, temperatures above 10 °C and moderately high humidity.

Watering is probably the most important factor for success with palms. Many fail because they have been allowed to remain dry for too long, more still because they are over-watered.

As a general rule, allow the potting soil surface to dry out, then give enough water to evenly wet the surface. Dryness can be allowed to extend a little deeper into the soil when light is more restricted (or when blinds are frequently drawn). Never allow excess run-off water to remain in the pot saucer as this can be responsible for root rot.

Feed only when the palm is making new growth. When light is too restricted for growth it is safer not to feed. This applies very definitely to the use of foliage feeders also. Never feed a palm that is ailing. A safe guide to feeding of an actively growing palm is to use either a slow-release plant food applied after new growth is indicated or half-strength water-soluble plant food every 4–6

weeks.

Pedilanthus Flattened green plasticlike zig-zagged stems with small leaves on either side, pinkish in bright light.

Needs Very bright to bright light, allow soil surface to dry out between watering and dryness to extend 2 to 3 cm during winter. Feed with half-strength water-soluble plant food at 4–6-week intervals while conditions are warm.

Pelargonium see Geranium

Pellionia Closely matting pinkish-stemmed trailing plants that attractively drape the side of pot or hanging basket. *P. daveauana* has thin fleshy oval leaves 5–6 cm long, dark bronze with silvery green centre. *P. pulchra* has slightly shorter or rounder grey-green leaves with a network of dark bronze veining.

Needs Bright light, keep soil just damp or allow surface to dry during cold conditions — feed 4–6-weekly with half-strength soluble plant food while indoor temperatures remain warm.

Peperomia Diverse genus, suitable as small table plants. Among the more popular species are the varieties of *P. hederaefolia*, dense rosette of waxy pink stems with shield- to heart-shaped deeply veined glossy foliage in silvery grey-green — variety Pink Lady is variegated and flushed with pink in moderate light. The oval leaves in good light are gold with bronze veining. Blackie is dark olive-green to bronze-black. *P. sandersii* and *P. arifolia* foliage is leathery and smooth with broad rounded base tapering to a point, silvery cream to grey with deep olive veining, *P. caperata* Emerald Ripple is deep green with very sunken veins or tissue between raised, blistered or rippled, *P. obtusifolia* Begonia makes several dark stems with rosetted glossy cream foliage shot through the centre with dark green, *P. scandens* with similar marking but smaller pointed leaves on trailing pinkish bronze stems.

Needs Bright to moderate light, let soil surface dry out between waterings, or drier still during cool periods. Feed sparingly each month when new growth starts with one-third-strength soluble plant food.

Philodendron A variety of quite different forms from the popular trailing or climbing *P. oxycardium* varieties with leathery heart-shaped leaves, others like *P. speciosum* with giant dark satin-textured leaves nearly 2 m long, those that make a woody trunk crested with huge rosettes of deeply divided leaves on stems over a metre long, such as *P. selloum* or *P. undulatum*, and many others.

Needs Most species and hybrids make adaptable house plants growing in very bright to moderate light. Most of the leathery leafed types also survive for a long time in low light.

Water when surface of soil dries, allowing dryness to extend about 2 cm deep during cold conditions. Feed with soluble plant food every 5–6 weeks while conditions are warm, leaching before each feeding, or if not possible, use half-strength plant food.

Pilea cadierie (Aluminium Plant) Oval to pointed glossy silver-grey foliage with dark green veining, *P. involucrata* Friendship Plant, quilted deep green or coppery bronze in very bright light; tiny foliaged Artillery Fern *P. microphylla* and others.

Needs All need very bright to moderate light, moderate humidity and soil kept just damp but not soggy, surface should completely dry during cold conditions. Feed with half-strength soluble plant food at 4–6-week intervals while conditions are warm.

Poinsettia Dwarf strains give long-lasting brilliant colour. Like the chrysanthemums, these are made available at any time of year by artificially shortening daylight hours to stimulate flower buds. Sensitivity to light prevents them from flowering again when growing in artificial light in the home.

Needs Poinsettias keep their colour best in bright to moderate light but even in low light they remain attractive for many weeks. Keep soil damp but not soggy. Feeding is only needed to encourage growth after flowering (occurs naturally with lengthening days). Best to purchase new properly conditioned plants for further display.

Polyscia Tropical caney-stemmed *aralia*-related plants crested with large, long, attractively divided and sometimes variegated leaves.

Needs Very bright to bright light, preferably with moderately high humidity and temperatures above 15°C. Keep away from glass during winter in temperate or cool districts to avoid sudden temperature changes. Keep soil just moist while conditions are warm, drier at other times. Feed monthly with half-strength soluble plant food, only while growth is active during warmth.

Portulacaria see Jade

Pothos The true *Pothos* are trailing or climbing plants with leaves that have a sudden constriction about a third of the way from their base. For variegated heart-shaped types see *Scindapsus*.

Primula obconica Heads of primrose-like flowers in ruby purple, lavender, pale blue, pink or white. Best raised under greenhouse conditions then brought indoors when flowering commences. Their display starts early spring and lasts for 6–10 weeks.

Needs Bright to moderately bright light, keep soil damp but not soggy, feed every 3–4 weeks with half-strength soluble plant food. Note that some people in contact with this plant develop an allergy rash.

Pteris see Ferns

Rhapis see Palms

Rhipsalis see Cacti

Rhoicissus see *Cissus*

Rhoeo discolor (Moses in Cradle) Purple-backed metallic green lance-shaped foliage arranged in a line on either side of a stout fleshy stem, small white flowers in boat or cradle-like bracts.

Needs Bright to very bright light for good colour, allow soil surface to dry between waterings, leave drier still in winter. Feed sparingly when new growth commences in spring then monthly until late summer with about half-strength soluble plant food.

Rubber Plant see *Ficus*

Saintpaulia see African Violet

Sanseviera (Snake Plant or Mother-in-law's tongue). Waxy erect straplike foliage usually margined cream with unusual banding of the grey-green centre.

Needs Stands low to very bright light. Water when surface dries about a centimetre below the surface during warm conditions, leave almost completely dry when growing conditions are cold. Feed with half-strength soluble plant food at no more than monthly intervals during late spring and summer.

Schefflera actinophylla (Queensland Umbrella Tree) Caney tree crested with a rosette of long-stemmed large umbrella-shaped leaves, divided into glossy oval bright green leaflets from 10–20 cm long, depending on development of tree.

Needs Very bright to moderate light, allow soil to become dry a centimetre or two down before watering again, especially during cooler months. Feed with soluble plant food every 6–8 weeks while conditions are warm.

Scindapsus (Devil's Ivy or *Pothos*) Similar to a heart-shaped philodendron with glossier foliage heavily variegated with gold, and thicker yellowish stems. An attractive basket or totem plant. In humid tropical atmosphere it makes large divided adult leaves 10–60 cm long.

Needs Very bright to bright light for good colour, also survives moderate light, allow soil surface to become quite dry between waterings if conditions are cool, otherwise keep moderately damp. Feed at monthly intervals while conditions are warm with half-strength water-soluble plant food.

Selagenella kraussiana (Club Moss) Fine light to yellowish green fern-like spreading carpet, rooting down as growth progresses. Attractive in hanging baskets or around plants in large containers. Some varieties such as *S. martensii* make erect clumps of flat fronds with cord-like segments. *S. unicata* during warm humid conditions is a beautiful metallic blue.

Needs Bright to moderate light and humid atmosphere. Water frequently to keep soil damp. Resents heavily chlorinated water and strong fertiliser. Feeding — give a humus-rich soil or feed with a very diluted organic-type food such as seaweed extract no more than every second month during warm conditions.

Sinningia The popular large bell-flowered florist's *gloxinia* is correctly *sinningia*. Also included are several types with large prominently veined decorative leaves and pendulous tubular flowers.

Needs see *Gloxinia Smithiana* Plants closely related to *Sinningia* but the nodding tubular flowers are on comparatively tall branching stems, usually red or yellow or both.

Needs see *Gloxinia*

Spathiphyllum (Spoonlily or Peacelily) Decorative clumps of large leathery lance-shaped leaves. Inflorescence is an erect spoon shape on tall wiry stems, spathe 8–9 cm long, white, turning green with age and backing a knobby cream spadix. *S. clevelandi* has long-stemmed large leaves to 30 cm high, *S. wallisii* is small, with denser, thinner and

much glossier foliage.

Needs Bright to fairly low light, keep soil damp but not soggy, feed every 4–6 weeks from spring to late summer with half-strength soluble plant food. Leach soil every few months.

Streptocarpus (Cape Primrose) Foliage resembling primrose or polyanthus, flower of smaller types like a large violet on slender erect stems, of larger varieties, bignonia-like, tubular, with outer edges flared to about 5 cm across in violet, pink, purple or white.

Needs They are related to African Violets and need similar bright light to initiate flowers but need a lower temperature range (12 to 24°C), resent excessive heat, need soil to be kept damp but not soggy. Feed with half-strength water-soluble plant foods every 4–6 weeks, add superphosphate as suggested for African Violets every three months unless special African Violet food, bonedust, or other high-phosphorus fertiliser is used.

Syngonium Adaptable and handsome climbing or trailing foliage plants with long heart- to arrow-shaped soft foliage. There are numerous *S. podophyllum* varieties, most with large heart-shaped leaves, mostly a mixture of creamy white and lime green with brighter green margins.

Needs Bright to fairly low light, allow soil surface to dry between waterings, feed while conditions are warm with half-strength soluble plant foods every 4–6 weeks.

Tolmiea (Pig-a-back Plant) Long-stemmed slightly hairy green leaves with plantlets growing on them.

Needs Bright to moderate light but prefers moderately cool rather than warm conditions. Water when soil surface dries out. Feed every 4–6 weeks with half-strength soluble plant foods, preferably leaching beforehand.

Tradescantia Soft-stemmed trailers, popular for baskets, etc, resembling variegated Wandering Jew of the same genus.

Needs Very bright to moderate light, good ventilation and moderate, not excessively hot temperatures. Allow soil surface to dry out between waterings. Feed with half-strength soluble plant foods every 4–6 weeks.

Umbrella Tree (Queensland) see *Schefflera*

Umbrella Tree (Dwarf) see *Brassaia*

Vriesia see Bromeliads

Zanthosma Climbing *philodendron*-like plants with large heart- to arrow-shaped leaves resembling *Syngonium*. *Z. lindenii* is deep green with broad creamy white veining.

Needs see *Syngonium*

Zebrina Closely resembling and related to *Tradescantia* with metallic purple colouring and lighter veining or variegations.

Needs see *Tradescantia*

Zygocactus see Cacti (Crab's Claw)

Xanthosma lindenii

Virginian Creeper with lacy Fishbone Fern

Fishferns must be kept damp

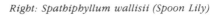

Above: Vriesia splendens (Flaming Sword)

Right: Spathiphyllum wallisii (Spoon Lily)

THE EDIBLE GARDEN

26. Growing fruit, berries, vines and nuts

Growing fruit trees

Planting

Fruit trees now bought in containers can be planted at any time of the year providing the roots are not disturbed. The best times in warm to temperate climates are during spring and autumn and in cool, frosty areas during spring after frosts are over.

Trees, dug from the open ground and sold with bare roots or just with the roots wrapped, should be planted at their dormant stage from late autumn to early spring in warm frost-free areas, or in colder districts during early spring when most frosts are over but before the warmer weather starts.

Soil at planting time must be just damp, not wet or sticky. It is important not to let roots become dry, so do not unwrap bare-rooted trees until ready to plant, then stand them with roots in a bucket of water while the hole is being prepared. In windy areas where atmosphere is dry, pull off at least two-thirds of the leaves, or cut back close to the base leaf to help the tree establish.

Make the planting hole at least twice spade-width so that improved soil or potting soil can be added around the roots to encourage their outward spread. Depth of the hole should only be enough to leave the surface of the container-soil level with the surrounding soil, or for open-ground trees to have only a few cm of soil above the tops of the roots when a mound of topsoil is built up under them to accommodate their spread. In any case the bud union (obvious by a slightly bulbous or elbow-like juction), should be kept about finger length above soil level. Avoid digging into clay sub-soil to achieve the depth needed. It is better to keep the roots at least a few cm above the clay and build up around the tree to get the depth of soil needed.

Fill in over and around the roots with topsoil. If this is clayey or very sandy, mix in up to one-third of moistened peatmoss or well-rotted compost but *not* fertiliser. Firm down by hand (not by treading) as this can cause root damage. Form surplus soil into a water-holding ridge slightly in from the edge of the planting hole and fill the depression with fibrous compost, leafmould or dead grass, then gradually pour a bucketful of water over it.

The fibrous material placed around the tree prior to watering will prevent soil-caking and give better aeration, which in turn will speed the development of healthy new roots.

Staking

In exposed areas where wind may cause movement of open-ground trees, give some support, at least for the first few months, either by driving in a stake before covering the roots or putting one in just beyond the root area. Cross the tree at an angle just below its branches and fasten at that point. In all cases, a tight complete tie should first be made around the stake, then another made loosely around the tree.

Fruit fly control

Contrary to a widely-held opinion, fruit fly does not attack fruit soon after the flowering stage or during its early development. Fruit is not vulnerable until it is at least half grown, or usually 5–6 weeks before ripening or later in the case of tomatoes. Citrus are unlikely to become infested until the fruit begins to ripen.

The adult female fruit fly stings (or deposits) her eggs in or usually below the skin of the fruit. On hatching out the larvae, small (nearly transparent and later white) legless grubs or maggots penetrate toward the centre of the fruit and feed. The area then becomes brown and rotten, even though from the outside the fruit may appear firm.

Some areas are fortunately free from fruit fly, and with co-operation from everyone with fruit trees on their property, it would be possible to eradicate this pest. In fruit fly areas control methods are legally compulsory.

The most widely practised control is to spray apples and pears with either Rogor or Lebaycid 6–8 weeks before fruit is due to ripen, and stone fruits about 5 weeks before. Some fruits, particularly Watt's Early peach, apricots, Meyer lemons, Seville oranges and cumquats are sensitive to Rogor. To be effective, these chemicals must be applied with a sprayer capable of thoroughly and evenly wetting all the fruit. Give a follow-up spraying a week later and a third one a week prior to harvest.

Fruit treated with either spray must not be used within 7 days of harvest and there are difficulties when treating continuously ripening fruits such as tomatoes.

Spray about a week before ripening is anticipated, then 8 days later pick everything that looks like ripening within a week and spray again, repeating this procedure throughout the fruiting period.

There are alternatives to spraying for fruit fly control. The simplest one which suits tomatoes and a number of fruits particularly is to tie waterproof paper bags around the fruit clusters at the time prior to harvest when it is suggested that spraying should be commenced.

A popular bait or lure is the Dak-pot, which is hung in a tree at the beginning of the season. Although this acts as a lure only for the male fruit fly, it does reduce fruit damage.

A lure attractive to both sexes is protein bait, a mixture of 2 teaspoons of protein hydrolysate (non-toxic) with 1 heaped teaspoon of Malathion 25 wettable powder, in about half a cup of water. Using an old paint brush splash this liquid onto an area of the foliage about 25 cm square each week from about 6 weeks before the fruit is due to ripen. Just one patch of liberally-splashed foliage is an effective lure for 10 m or so. Apply the lure to the underside of the foliage (particularly in a section sheltered by overhang of higher branches) so that it is not easily washed off by rain. Should heavy rain fall, apply again immediately foliage dries.

Keep it off fruit, as it might cause burning, but a small amount of damage can be accepted on the foliage.

It is essential and compulsory to rake up and destroy all infected fruit. This should be done as it falls, not at the end of the season as the fruit fly larva leaves fruit before it reaches the pupa stage. Destroy either by boiling or placing the fruit in large, sound plastic bags tied and left in the sun.

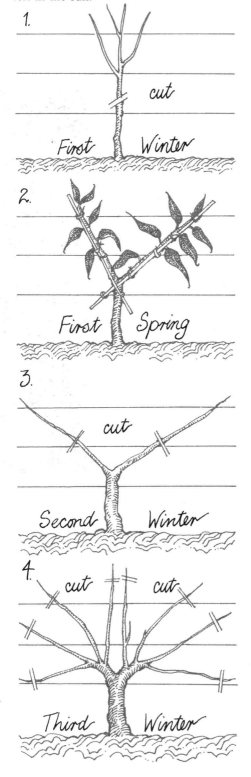

1. cut — First Winter

2. First Spring

3. cut — Second Winter

4. cut — cut — Third Winter

Espaliered fruit trees

Espaliered trees are always admired and are *not* beyond the scope of most home gardeners, though shaping does call for patience.

Fasten wires across the wall, starting 30 cm above the ground and 30 cm apart. Use heavy screws or vertical piping.

The branches can be trained on these wires, horizontally, fan-shaped or like candelabra. Here is a step-by-step guide for a fan-shaped peach tree — the principle is the same for plums, apples and pears.

1. Plant the tree in winter, within 30 cm of the wall, and cut it off a little above the lowest wire.

2. In spring rub off all but one shoot on each side toward the top of the stem. When these are about 30 cm long secure them to light stakes tied to the wires. Even up the growth of the shoots by tying the strongest one in a horizontal position and the weaker one vertically. When they are about even, tie both at about 45° to form a wide V.

3. The following winter cut both canes back to about 40 cm preferably just above a bud on the lower side. During the spring select 4 well-placed shoots on either branch to form the framework of the fan. Aim for three coming from the top of the branch and one from below. All other shoots are rubbed off. The new branches may be evenly spaced by tying them to light stakes as suggested in step 2.

4. The next winter (two years after planting) the eight ribs of the fan are cut back to an average of about 60 cm in length, giving the tree an even fan shape. Make each cut just above a bud pointing in the direction where growth is preferred.

5. During the spring and early summer rub off all unwanted shoots, to leave 3 or 4 well-spaced growths on each of the 8 branches, and you should then have a well-filled espalier covering the wall. Train young sappy growth by tying to light stakes, which are removed once growth matures.

Future care

Peaches fruit on wood made the previous season so keep replacement growth coming on. The fruit grows on laterals along the main branches. Winter pruning is confined to removing excess laterals, and reducing excessively long leaders or ribs by cutting them back to just above a lateral and tying in place to act as 'leader' of the branch.

In spring you will usually find 2 shoots coming from the base of each lateral made the previous season. Rub off one and leave the other to replace the present fruiting lateral which after fruiting should be cut off just above the new shoot at its base.

Plums, apples, pears and, to some extent, apricots continue to fruit for a number of years on the same spurs, so need little pruning. Overcrowded spurs and other congesting growth should be removed. Reduce new growth by pruning back to just above the lowest leaf in late summer; or, if needed for replacement as part of the espalier, tie back to the wires.

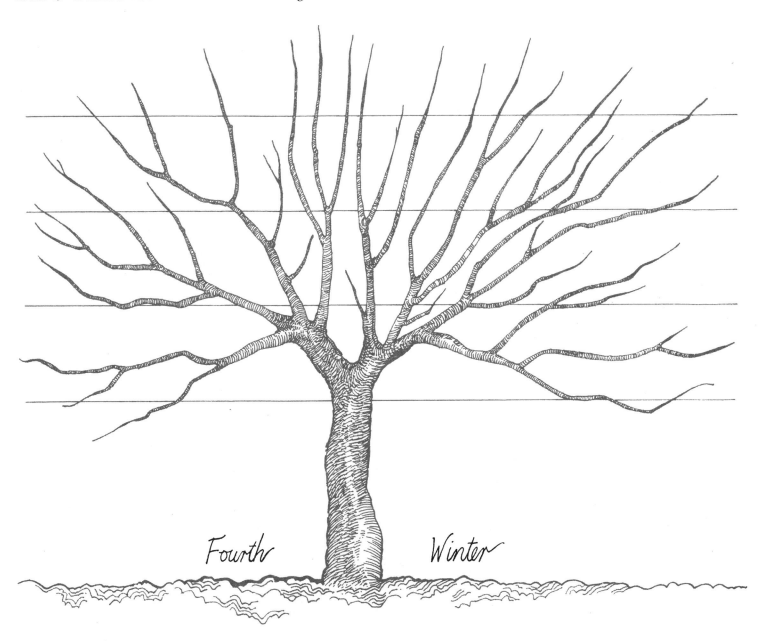

Fourth Winter

A cultivation guide to growing fruit trees

Apple

Although some varieties of apples are successfully grown in tropical to semi-tropical districts, they are more suitable to cool and cooler temperate districts. In very cold areas late frosts may damage flowers and new growth but they are frequently found growing successfully on hillsides above very frosty pockets. Soil moisture is needed during the growing period, but a dry spring is an advantage because black-spot and other fungus diseases are a more serious problem in showery weather.

Requirements

Given an open sunny position with some protection from strong winds they will adapt to a variety of soils, but prefer a well-drained loam that retains moisture. In heavy and slow-drying soil plant them on mounds built up 30 cm or so above the surrounding soil level.

Planting time. Open-ground trees are planted during their winter dormant period, or in very cold districts, in early spring before growth commences. Trees grown in containers can be planted at any time, although the mid-summer period should be avoided because of the difficulty of maintaining constant soil moisture while the trees are developing a wider root spread.

General care

Do not allow to dry out, especially during the spring and summer growing period. In dry weather give the soil a good soaking about once a fortnight, or more frequently in sandy or other quick-drying soils, directing the water mainly at the area below the outer branches. Keep the water away from fruit and foliage as this will dilute or wash off protective sprays used against fungus diseases, codling moth, fruit fly, etc. However, in hot, dry climates occasional misting of the foliage will help to deter red spider mites which are sometimes troublesome during these conditions.

Mulching. Mulch the surface soil with organic material to conserve moisture, improve the condition of the soil and encourage earthworm activity which in turn improves aeration and depth of soil, and induces deeper root growth and greater drought resistance.

Feeding. Apples prefer plant foods relatively high in phosphorus and particularly potassium (potash). Fowl manure is suitable or most of the basic powder or granular-type complete fertilisers. N (nitrogen) 6:P, (phosphorus) 4:K, and (potash) 10 which should be applied at the rate of about 1 handful per sq. m of area below the branch-spread of the tree in early spring and again during early to mid-April. Basic fertilisers usually contain less potash than this so in sandy soils particularly, where this element is more frequently deficient, it would be an advantage to supplement this need by adding a sprinkling of sulphate of potash applied at the rate of 1 handful to about 2 sq. m of area below the branch line.

Soak soil thoroughly before applying manure or fertiliser. Water well after applying and pay extra attention to soil moisture for a couple of weeks afterwards.

These feeding recommendations are for trees growing in open ground. A tree growing in a lawn would benefit from a further feeding in late spring at about half the rate initially suggested. If the lawn was fed in spring and summer with sulphate of ammonia or the usual high nitrogen-type lawn food, feed the tree with a fertiliser made by mixing equal quantities of superphosphate and sulphate of potash, applied at the rate of 1 handful to approximately 1 sq. m. Similar advice applies when other plants are grown below the trees, if these are not fed separately.

Thinning. When a tree carries a heavy crop of fruit, thinning will improve the size and quality of the fruit allowed to remain. Allow one fruit to remain on spurs which can be thinned to about a small span apart. 'Delicious' and some other varieties of apples may only produce a worthwhile crop every second season unless thinned.

Pruning. Pruning for the first few years is aimed at producing a well-shaped tree with a strong framework. A vase or inverted cone shape has been conventionally favoured but there is now a tendency to a pyramid formation which is practical and decorative.

Vase shape. After planting cut back a single-cane tree to about 50 cm, or a little higher if required to double as a shade tree. This encourages formation of shoots from below the cut. The following winter allow 3 or 4 well-spaced side shoots to remain and shorten back to just above a bud about 20 cm from the main trunk or stem. The latter treatment also applies when the new tree already has several branches.

By the next winter the tree will have made a number of branches, hopefully with most of the initial ones branching into two at least. Again, all but those needed to form the main framework of the vase shape should be removed and the remainder shortened back to about 50 cm, with the cut made just above an outward-pointing bud.

During the next season there should be further division of the branches and the following winter the same method of pruning carried out with each of the leaders or main branches shortened back to an outward pointing bud. Excessive branches coming in to the centre of the tree need removing. The exception now is that some of the lesser laterals along the main branches are allowed to remain to produce fruiting spurs.

Shaping a pyramid-type tree. The idea is to encourage tiers of 4 closely-set but well-spaced branches pointing north, south, east and west. Aim to have branches alternating in approximately opposite pairs, in a near lateral position (30–40°) to allow even light penetration into the tree. Remove all branches about 50 cm above the ground. If the young tree does not have a good spread of side branches, shorten back the main stem to about 80 cm above the ground. The following winter, after selection of the 4 evenly-spaced main branches for the first tier, the strongest most upright growth is allowed to take the place of the leader which will ultimately form the erect trunk.

The following season all growth is removed within about 50 cm of the highest branch on the first tier, and the process is repeated until 3 or 4 tiers of well-placed branches have been produced. If necessary, branches in the lower tier may be brought down into a more lateral position by tying them to pegs driven into the ground or, in higher tiers, by tying them down to the lower branches providing these are strong enough.

In this case, all lateral branches already formed are left unpruned in the early stages. Later pruning merely involves thinning out rather than pruning back lateral growths. The more lateral position of the branches is usually sufficient to induce productivity. If necessary, excessive vigour of the central upright lateral or leader may be checked by pruning it back to a weaker side lateral.

General pruning. After the initial shaping is completed give only light pruning. Hard cutting will induce a surge of upward unproductive growth. Should this occur remove it in summer. Better still, anticipate and pinch back over-vigorous growths, or remove unwanted ones during the early stages.

To extend the length of the leader or main branch, cut it back about one-third of its length to just above an outward pointing bud. To restrain growth, prune only lightly, but in all cases shorten back to either an outward pointing bud or side branch. The main aim is to thin out excessive growth, particularly that growing toward the centre of the tree, and to eliminate excessive branching from the tops or ends of the leaders or main branches because this tends to overshade, retard or kill lower growth.

Appreciate that the more vertical a growth the more vegetative and less productive it becomes. Vertical growths draw heavily on the resources of the tree to the detriment of the more productive lateral and lower growth so prune to encourage a lateral general growth of the tree. It is essential to distinguish between fruit and growth buds. The latter are comparatively long and thin, the fruit buds are plump and produced mainly on the spurs (short and stubby growths which branch in several directions with age), or sprigs which are very short twiggy growths, and laterals, which are side shoots from the main branches.

The fruiting habits of different varieties vary. For example, with 'Jonathan', the laterals do not produce fruit until their second year, whereas 'Delicious' and 'Granny Smith' produce fruit on laterals made the previous season, as well as on sprigs and spurs. Therefore the shorter and medium-length laterals on these varieties, if not excessive, are allowed to remain unpruned to produce spurs and fruit.

In other cases the shorter twiggy laterals are left unpruned. All the other medium to strong laterals are pruned back to finger length to encourage the development of fruiting spurs. Where it may be desirable to prune back to one of the stronger outward growing laterals to develop it as a limb of the tree, an exception is made. This lateral then becomes what is known as the leader of a main limb or branch.

Cordon or espalier trees are usually pruned in summer, cutting back any shoots over 20–25 cm long to about the third leaf from the base, and shortening back other side shoots to just above the lowest leaf. Later growth made in autumn is treated similarly.

Varieties

Apples are not completely self-pollinating. Most varieties will produce some fruits without cross-pollination, but for best results have another variety which flowers at the same time growing close by. You can buy a tree budded with two varieties. In this case, it is essential, in the initial shaping, to take care that the wood of one is not removed or excessively reduced. Generally speaking, 'Delicious', 'Granny Smith', 'Jonathan' and 'Red Jonathan' will pollinate well with each other and most other varieties, except very early-flowering types such as 'Willie Sharp' or 'Early Blaze', which fortunately are good pollinators for each other.

Good strains most readily available are:
Delicious — a good eating apple with closely-set reddish streaks over a yellowish skin. Has a distinctive flavour. Inclined to produce good crops only every second year unless fed during early to mid-autumn and fruit is thinned out.
Granny Smith — very popular as a cooking apple in the green-skinned stage once fruit has reached full size, or may be left on the tree until skin develops a yellowish tinge as an excellent eating apple.
Jonathan — a very popular juicy eating apple with attractive clear creamy skin heavily striped with red.
Red Jonathan — a good early eating apple, similar in shape to Jonathan but with very red skin.

Growing problems and solutions

Problem: Small hole, sometimes with slightly webby covering on side of fruit. When the fruit is cut, the point of entry at the calyx end, brown churned up area around seed, and tunnel to side hole are all obvious.
Cause: Codling moth, a small brownish moth which lays its eggs on the blossom end of the embryo fruit. The larva or small grub hatches out and tunnels in through this cavity, feeds around the seed area then, when mature, burrows out through the side of the apple, descends on a fine web then enters its chrysalis stage, usually under loose bark on the trunk of the tree.
Solution: Some compulsory codling moth control regulations say that arsenate of lead should be sprayed to give complete cover of the embryo fruits as soon as the petals have fallen. This is no longer widely practised, and instead Carbaryl is sprayed about a month after the petals have fallen and repeated at intervals of about 3 weeks. In practice, where sprays such as Rogor or Lebaycid are used for fruit fly control, the Carbaryl spray can be discontinued 6 or 7 weeks before fruit ripens, as the former sprays will also give control of codling moth.

An old practice still worthwhile is to put hessian collars around the trunk of the tree to provide an attractive harbour for the chrysalis stage of the larvae. Throughout the season the collars can be periodically removed and cleaned of anything they have caught. These collars are made by tying a 25–30 cm-wide piece of hessian tightly at the lower half, then allowing the top section to lap loosely over. The use of winter oil sprays also helps to kill any of the pupae under loose bark or in crevices of the trunk.

Problem: Brown rotted areas in centre of fruit with small grubs or maggots present.
Cause: Fruit fly.
Solution: See 'Fruit fly control'.

Problem: Small brown pits or sunken areas on fruit.
Cause: This condition, known as 'bitter pit', is a constitutional disease rather than an infection and is usually associated with periods of dryness or excessive nitrogen. The latter could occur when the tree has been given dressings of sulphate of ammonia, urea or is growing in a lawn frequently dressed with lawn food high in nitrogen.
Solution: Mulching and occasionally good soakings, particularly to the area below outer branches of the tree during dry periods. Liberal mulching with compost also helps and occasional light applications of either fowl manure or a complete plant food during early spring and summer.

Problem: Black spots over leaves and fruit. Flower stems are sometimes also affected and fall before fruit is formed.
Cause: Scab or black spot. Spores of the fungus carry over the winter on the remains of infected fallen leaves from the previous season.
Solution: Winter cultivation or mulching to help the breakdown and decomposition of the old infected foliage is a step in the right direction. Good results have been obtained even from spraying the foliage at the time of autumn leaf fall with urea or one of the soluble plant foods, as this speeds its breakdown and usually prevents its carry-over throughout winter. However, the more accepted chemical control is to use copper spray when new spring growth is commencing then later with Captan at intervals of 2 or 3 weeks.

Problem: Powdery film over foliage, leaves tending to curl upwards and brown.
Cause: Powdery mildew.
Solution: Use copper spray when first signs of disease appear.

Problem: Sandblasted appearance on foliage usually worse on lower foliage sheltered by the overhang of the tree.
Cause: Red spider mite.
Solution: Spray with Malathion or fruit fly control sprays such as Rogor or Lebaycid. Repeat spray in a fortnight if necessary. The mottling of the foliage does not disappear quickly so before respraying examine backs of leaves under a magnifying glass in good light to check for presence of minute green or reddish coloured mites.

Problem: Patches of tiny, reddish granules on stems, branches or trunk.
Cause: Byrobia mite.
Solution: If present in winter while tree is still dormant, use winter spraying oil, white oil or lime sulphur, otherwise treat as for red spider mite.

Problem: Downy, white to silvery-grey substance on limbs or in cracks of bark.
Cause: Woolly aphids.
Solution: If present during dormant period, treat as byrobia mite, otherwise spray with Rogor or Lebaycid with the addition of 1 tablespoon of white oil to 4.5 L of spray mixture.

Problem: Branches clustered with tiny grey scabs and possible die-back.
Cause: San José scale.
Solution: Treat as for woolly aphid but increase white oil content to 2 tablespoons per 4.5 L of spray mixture.

Problem: Failure to fruit.
Cause: Apples are self-pollinating but without another variety flowering at the same time to provide cross-pollination, the crop may be very small.

Although apples fruit mainly from spurs on the older wood, very heavy pruning may cause an excess of vegetative top growth which can leave the tree temporarily unproductive.
Solution: Curb any burst of top growth by pruning from early to mid-summer and check any new growth by pinching out the tops, or rubbing the shoots out entirely if unwanted and headed vertically. Once the shape of the tree has been established, little pruning is needed. Failure to fruit could also be due to the presence of black spot or scab — see under that heading.

Apricot

Apricots do best in districts with fairly hot summers and cool winters. They tolerate heavy frosts but, as the trees blossom early, can be damaged by heavy late frosts. They also grow well in the milder temperate coastal areas but may fail to set fruit after an exceptionally mild winter. They are deciduous and make large branching trees spreading to 5 m or so.

Requirements

Apricots need an aspect with at least half sunlight, but preferably more, shelter from strong winds, and should not be enclosed as they need good circulation of air to minimise the risk of fungus diseases.

They grow in a variety of soils providing drainage is good, but prefer a slightly limey soil, so in any but naturally limey areas, work in 1 cupful of garden lime or dolomite per sq. m prior to planting.

Planting time. Open ground or bare-rooted apricots should be planted during the dormant winter period but some nurseries now have container-grown trees which may be planted at any time providing the roots are not disturbed. Avoid mid-summer planting because of the difficulty of keeping up the amount of soil moisture the tree needs to develop a natural root spread.

General care

Apricots require plenty of water especially in spring and throughout the summer and early autumn growing period. Long wet periods during spring and summer are a disadvantage because of the fungus diseases they induce, but during dry periods it is advisable to soak the root area about once a fortnight or more frequently in quick-drying sandy soils, applying the water mainly to the area below the outer branches of the tree.

Mulching. Surface mulching with compost or other organic material helps to conserve moisture and improves the condition of the soil generally.

Feeding. Vigour and fruit quality are improved by a dressing of horse or cow manure during early autumn and again in early spring, or a standard complete plant food applied at the rate of 1 handful per sq. m of area below the branch line of the tree and concentrated mainly on the area below the outer branches rather than close to the trunk. Apply only when the soil is evenly moist and water well afterwards.

Pruning. Initial pruning and shaping of the tree is similar to that suggested for apples. Where possible avoid Y formation of the branches as splitting is liable to occur at the junction.

In areas where bacterial canker is a problem prune in early winter rather than later as infection through the cuts is less likely to occur. Spray with a general fungicide or copper oxychloride immediately after pruning, and seal large cuts with a tree paint.

Some apricots fruit on new wood but it mostly grows on spurs or short laterals from the older wood. Avoid heavy pruning as this would create a flush of new wood. Discourage upright growth by shortening back to comparatively subdued laterals. Leave short laterals along the main branches unpruned, and shorten back moderately vigorous ones to about 20 cm. If there are plenty of short laterals some of the spurs should be nipped out to discourage excessive cropping. Over-vigorous branches can be subdued by pruning them back either to a downward pointing bud or small lateral heading in a downward direction.

Varieties

Apricots are one of the first stone fruits to ripen. The fruiting period of the different varieties spans a period from mid-spring to late summer.

Case's Early — is the first, in warm areas ripening in early to mid-October.

Glengarry — a very popular medium-sized fruit ripens in mid-November.

Newcastle — an attractive red-blushed medium-sized fruit ripens late November.

Trevatt — a strong-growing heavy-bearing type lately used for bottling and drying ripens in late December. These times could be up to a month later in cool districts.

Growing problems and solutions

Problem: Failure to fruit.

Cause: Apricots fruit both from spurs of the old wood and to some extent from the new wood but heavy overall pruning could be responsible for a very small crop the following season.

Solution: Shorten back longer branches to just above an outward pointing lateral or twig. The

longer should be pruned back to about a span in length, and the shorter ones left unpruned.

Problem: Soft brown rot around the fruit stone, with maggots present.

Cause: Fruit fly.

Solution: See heading 'Fruit fly control' but note that apricots are sensitive to some organic phosphate sprays such as Rogor.

Problem: Fruit with soft, rotten patches that spread rapidly.

Cause: Brown rot.

Solution: Use copper spray as flower buds begin to show colour. This disease can be very destructive during a wet spring so spray immediately after weather fines after showery periods or, for more assured control, at fortnightly intervals. Once fruit has formed, Benlate is an effective control and may be alternated with copper spray. Badly affected fruit may become mummified and remain on the tree until the following season. This provides a source of reinfection so any such fruits should be removed and burnt.

Problem: Green to dark freckle-like spots on fruit. Sometimes with cracking of fruit.

Cause: A fungus disease known as freckle.

Solution: Use copper spray when flower buds show colour. The addition of 1 tablespoon of white oil per 4.5 L of spray mixture is helpful. Spray again when petals have fallen, preferably with Mancozeb or Zineb.

Problem: Fruit with raised brown scabs, leaves with reddish-brown spots that fall out leaving shot-hole appearance.

Cause: The fungus condition appropriately known as shot-hole.

Solution: Treat as for freckle on apricots.

Problem: Yellow flecks on leaves with velvety-brown spots on the corresponding underside.

Cause: Rust.

Solution: Control suggested for freckle will also control rust although an application of Zineb or Mancozeb every 2–3 weeks gives more complete control.

Problem: Sunken brown to black lesions in bark with exudation of gum.

Cause: Bacterial canker.

Solution: Spray as suggested for brown rot or freckle as buds begin to show colour then again in autumn as leaves are falling. Reinfection is less likely from early than from late winter pruning and if copper spray is applied thoroughly after pruning and all cuts sealed with a tree paint.

Problem: Clusters of grey scabs on branches.

Cause: San José scale.

Solution: Apply winter spraying oil when tree is dormant, otherwise use 1 teaspoon of Lebaycid plus 2 tablespoons of white oil per 4.5 L of water.

Avocado or Alligator pear

Although the latter name is popularly used this plant bears no relationship to the pear.

The avocado is a handsome evergreen tree which in nature and when grown from seed may reach 8 or 9 m in height, but most of the named varieties, which are available as grafted plants, are more compact and spreading.

Although the avocado is native to tropical

America it can be grown in all but very frosty areas providing adequate water is available during summer. Close to the sea coast it is imperative to give protection from the salt-laden winds.

Avocados grown from seed take at least 7 years to produce fruit. Grafted plants of proven known varieties usually produce their first fruits within 3–4 years, and improve their productivity with age.

Requirements

Avocados need plenty of sunlight and in all but the warm, semi-tropical to tropical districts. Shelter from prevailing cold winter winds.

A well-drained soil is necessary. In slow-draining soils they are subject to phytophthora root rot. This crippling disease can also attack in light soils deficient in organic matter. Therefore add compost at least once a year, or maintain a mulch of slowly-decomposing material below the tree, particularly below the outer branch line, keeping it a span or two out from the trunk.

Planting time. Container-grown avocados can be planted at any time of the year providing roots are not disturbed, but in any but warm areas it is preferable to plant in early spring so that the tree has the longest period of warmth ahead in which to establish itself.

Protect the trunk during the first couple of years of growth by placing several stakes on the sunny side of the tree and arranging them to lean toward the top branches. The stakes can have hessian draped over them so as to give protection, but not to cover the outer foliage.

General care

Plenty of water is needed, particularly during the late spring and summer period. A good gradual soaking at least once a fortnight during dry periods will improve the quality of the fruit.

Feeding. Plenty of nitrogenous fertiliser will help to speed growth during the establishing period. Therefore apply a dressing of animal manure over the mulch in spring or once the young tree is established and showing signs of new growth. Sprinkle a handful of sulphate of ammonia per sq. m or, better still, one of the complete soluble lawn foods, mainly below the outer foliage line, every 6–8 weeks from spring to late summer.

Alternatively, give fortnightly soakings with any of the complete water-soluble plant foods. After about 3 years when a grafted tree should be approaching the fruiting stage, fertiliser containing more phosphorus is needed. During early spring and again in mid-summer apply a dressing of fowl manure or a general complete fertiliser, rose food or a citrus food, using up to one-third cup per sq. m of area below the branch line. In quick-drying sandy soils it is advisable to halve this quantity and apply twice as often. In all cases feed only when the soil is damp and water well afterwards. Do not feed during dry periods when it may be difficult to maintain the soil moisture.

When fruit is picked. Avocados do not ripen on the tree and it is often difficult to determine when the fruits are reaching the ripening stage. After they have obviously reached full growth, pick one or two fruits and store them indoors. If they ripen after 10 days then the remainder of the crop may be picked as required. There is a slightly softer or less 'metallic' feeling once the fruit begins to ripen. Some varieties turn a paler green colour, others turn purple.

Pruning. Very little pruning is needed but some growers remove the top of the tree when it reaches 1–2 m in height to encourage lower branching bushier growth.

The top may be removed from an excessively tall established tree; cut it down to just above a side branch and paint the wound after cutting. Pruning is best done in late winter or just before new growth commences.

Pollination. Avocados produce both male and female flowers but in some cases not always at the one time on the one tree. Therefore, when growing seedling-raised trees, the presence of a second tree may be an advantage. Most grafted varieties available have surer cropping tendencies.

Varieties

Fuerte — a good reliable early-bearing type with fairly large green pear-shaped fruits.

Hass — a late-maturing variety with rounded purple fruits.

Sharwill — a mid-season variety with pear-shaped green fruits.

Growing problems and solutions

Failure to fruit

This is a very common problem because so many of the avocados in home gardens are raised from seed, and seedlings can take from 9–15 years to produce fruit. Also the quality of the fruit that may eventually occur is doubtful because, like most other seedling fruit trees, there is invariably a wide variation of type and they may not retain the same desirable characteristics of the parent tree.

Avocados are self-pollinating but the male and female flowers may occur at different times, so pollination may be better where there are two trees. In any case, grafted trees from known varieties with proven performance are the better proposition as they usually produce quality fruit within about 5 years.

Foliage pale and sparse

This is usually a sign of phytophthora root rot which frequently occurs in poorly drained soils and may also be encountered in avocados where soils are lacking in organic material.

There is no definite cure but where drainage is reasonable it is worth giving the area around the tree a very heavy mulch with compost or well-rotted horse or cow manure. This sometimes encourages the formation of healthy new roots.

Poor growth

In addition to bad drainage and the possibility of root rot described in the preceding paragraphs, this can be due to soil which is over-acid or over-alkaline, or lack of plant food, particularly nitrogen. Soak the soil around the tree during early spring and again about 6 weeks later with one of the water-on-type, complete soluble plant foods.

After about the fourth year when the tree approaches the fruiting stage, use a sprinkle-on-type plant food (rose food is ideal) applied at the rate of about 1 handful per sq. m of area, under foliage and slightly beyond. Give plenty of water during this spring period.

Problem: Leaves wilting and twigs shrivelling.

Cause: Fungus wilt (verticillium wilt).

Solution: Improve growing conditions by supplying plenty of compost to the tree. Using copper spray can sometimes help. Remove the dead branches when new growth commences.

Problem: Small, daisy-like cracks in skin of fruit.

Cause: Physical damage or fruit fly sting.

Solution: See heading 'Fruit fly control'.

Problem: Rotting of fruit during ripening.

Cause: A disease known as anthracnose which is more troublesome during wet seasons. The fruit has actually contracted the infection before harvesting.

Solution: Prune away dead wood from trees on which infection may be carried over and use copper spray immediately after prolonged rain and prior to harvesting.

Banana

Well-cared-for clumps of bananas can look spectacular. They are best suited to tropical and semi-tropical districts but grow with reasonable success in warm temperate districts.

Requirements

A well-drained soil with plenty of water during the summer months.

Planting time. They can be planted at any time of the year but spring is the most suitable in all but tropical areas. They are planted from suckers taken from the old clumps. The strongest suckers are best and are easiest to handle when still folded in cone formation before the leaves develop.

General care

Before planting work in a layer of well-rotted compost and maintain a surface mulch afterwards. Once suckers have established and are producing obvious growth, apply a complete plant food at the rate of 1 handful per sq. m to the area around the plant or clump and repeat every 8–10 weeks in spring and summer. Water thoroughly after feeding.

When the bunches of fruit are fully formed cover with blue, green or yellow plastic sheeting to speed ripening and improve quality if conditions are cool. Once a tree produces fruit it gradually dies, but is replaced by suckers from the base.

Remove trees that have fruited, and all but one or two of the most promising looking suckers. To prevent regrowth of removed suckers, gouge down the centre of the base with something sharp, e.g. an auger, to destroy the embryo growing point, or pierce the base and trickle in a couple of teaspoons of kerosene.

Growing problems and solutions

Problem: Failure to fruit is one of the most common complaints about bananas. As bananas prefer tropical to semi-tropical conditions, there are occasions when the climate can be too cool for them, but in moderately warm, temperate areas fruit will normally set if they are well grown.

Cause: Allowing too many suckers to develop around the parent plant, particularly after the initial bunch is produced, and later throughout the clump generally.

Solution: Cut back all but one or two suckers when they are about 50 cm high, removing them close to ground level. Prevent regrowth by probing down into the centre of the sucker with a broad, sharp screwdriver to destroy the embryo shoots. If growth still persists, pierce the centre again and trickle in about 1 teaspoon of kerosene. Bananas prefer a rich soil with plenty of compost added and an application of fowl manure or about 1 large handful of complete plant food per sq. m scattered around the clump when new growth commences. Plenty of water is also needed during this period.

Problem: Fruit not ripening.

Cause: Cool weather.

Solution: Late summer or autumn bunches should be covered with blue, green or yellow plastic bags.

Problem: Small brown or black spots on leaves which may cause premature browning of the entire leaf.

Solution: Use copper spray or Mancozeb every 4 weeks from mid-summer to early autumn and give an extra spraying after heavy rain.

Cherry

Cherries need a cool to cold winter and a well-drained but deep and friable loamy soil.

They also need more space than most other fruit trees because when mature the average cherry tree is 6–7 m high and as wide.

Requirements

Cherries only crop well in an open sunny position and in a deep, fairly rich crumbly soil. They do not like slow-draining heavy soils, but light soils can be made more suitable by addition of large quantities of well-rotted compost and by maintaining a mulch of organic material over the surface.

Planting time. During their winter dormant period.

General care

Plenty of water is needed during the spring and early summer cropping period but rain or overhead watering of the near mature fruit can cause splitting.

Feeding. Cherries are fairly heavy feeders, so apart from the organic material already suggested they need a liberal dressing of animal manure applied, preferably during autumn, but otherwise in late winter to early spring before growth commences. The alternative is to use a complete plant food or citrus food at the rate of 1 handful per sq. m of area below the branch line of the tree, plus a small handful of sulphate of ammonia to the same area.

Pruning. The initial shaping of cherry trees is similar to that suggested for apples. Later, as cherries continue to flower and produce fruit on old wood, very little pruning is needed except the removal of excessive or old twiggy growth.

Varieties

Cherries are not self-pollinating and some varieties will not pollinate with another. The most widely grown varieties in Australia are:
Burgsdorf — early, large dark-red fruits. Best pollinator is Ron's Seedling.
Ron's Seedling — a good-quality dark-fruited mid-season cherry pollinated best by Burgsdorf.
Early Lyons — a heavy-cropping dark-fruited fairly early variety pollinated satisfactorily by Burgsdorf.
Florence — a large light-red fruited variety which pollinates well with Saint Margaret.
Saint Margaret — a large fruited variety with firm dark flesh, generally later cropping. Pollinator is Florence.

Growing problems and solutions

Cherries suffer from brown rot of fruit, shot-hole, byrobia mite, San José scale and bacterial canker as described under 'Apricot', and in each case the treatment is the same. Other conditions that may occur are:
Problem: Skeletonising of leaves by slug-like grubs.
Cause: Pear and cherry slug.
Solution: Spray with Malathion.

Problem: Dark brown or black insects clustered on new spring growth.
Cause: Black aphids.
Solution: Check to see if ladybirds or their elongated, dragon-like larvae are attacking the aphids. If not, spray with either Pyrethrum, Malathion or Diazinon.

Citrus

Citrus are relatively trouble-free when grown under suitable conditions. They are long-cropping, decorative, can be used as screen or background and can be grown in a container. Most gardeners are happy to find a place for them.

Citrus are most at home in temperate to semi-tropical districts but will withstand moderate frost; they will not tolerate prolonged winter cold or frequent late frosts. In cold districts they can be grown in large containers which can be moved into shelter during the winter or if they are planted close to a sunny wall which gives them protection from cold winds. Some varieties of citrus are more cold-tolerant than others.

Requirements

Citrus require an open sunny position with protection from strong wind. If your garden is exposed, plant wind-resistant shrubbery on their windward side; a temporary screen of brush fencing, twigs threaded through wire netting or bought plastic lattice screenings will give them shelter while the shrubs are becoming established.
Spacing. The ideal situation for a citrus is open ground not overshadowed by other trees or shrubs but, if space is limited, it can take its place in mixed planting and do double duty as a fruit tree and an ornamental.

Citrus planted to screen a wall or fence will give less fruit than those standing free because they become virtually one-sided, but they will be serving a purpose, and some fruit is better than none.

They look best when planted in a group of 3 or 4 but you have to remember that the average orange tree, thorny mandarin or Lisbon and Eureka lemon trees will eventually develop a spread of around 3 m, so don't crowd them. Lemons, particularly Eureka, have an open growth which will allow light penetration so you *could* plant them 3 m apart if you don't mind the trees eventually growing together with subsequent loss of fruit and difficulty of access between them. If you have the space, plant your trees 4–5 m apart.

If space is a problem you could always grow them as espaliers against a wall or as a cordon, a free-standing espalier which can be used as a screen.

Soil

The ideal soil for citrus is a light sandy-type deep loam, which drains freely but holds a reasonable amount of moisture. Heavy clay loams and shallow clay sub-soils that remain wet for long periods after rain cause problems and root rot is likely to occur, particularly with Eureka lemons grafted onto common lemon stock.

Such grafting is necessary because they are not compatible with the rot-resisting trifoliata stock which is used with most other citrus. Even so, no root stock is successful in poorly-drained soils.

Where drainage is suspect, install some type of underground drainage or plant in beds built up about 30 cm to 50 cm above the surrounding soil level. If this is not possible grow your citrus in large containers.

Even though drainage may be reasonable, heavy soil is improved by adding coarse sand and organic material to keep it more open so that aeration and draining properties are improved.

Sandy soils dry too rapidly so add liberal amounts of well-decomposed compost and moistened peatmoss which has excellent water-holding properties.

Surface mulches are invaluable both for heavy and light sandy soils. Used on the latter they help conserve moisture, improve the soil's condition and keep it cool during summer. Sandy soil exposed to long periods of sunlight can become too hot and root growth can be adversely affected. A good supply of organic material on the surface encourages earthworm activity. The tunnelling of these creatures improves aeration and increases the depth of the soil by taking organic material down to the lower levels — a great advantage in heavy soils.

Keep the mulch away from the main stem or trunk, as any moisture-holding materials in this area can induce collar rot.

Citrus in containers

Citrus make decorative container plants and for people without a conventional garden or for gardeners with badly-drained and root-infested soil, growing the fruit in a large container is the perfect answer.

The container should be about 50 cm wide and 50 cm deep — a shallower one would dry out too rapidly. It is safer to have several drain-holes around the base instead of just one in the middle. There is no need to 'crock' and use up good soil space, just put a square of fibreglass insect gauze over each drainage hole and cover with a handful each of charcoal or small pebbles.

Any good proprietary nursery soil will do. Plant tree as suggested for citrus in the soil and raise container on strategically placed bricks to give a few cm clearance above the ground so that the growing roots will not block the drainage holes.

Although the plant needs the sun, position the container so that it has protection against the direct rays, otherwise the soil will become much too hot. Be certain to remember that citrus growing in a container need watering more frequently than those growing in the ground.
Feeding. Use half the amount of fertiliser recommended for plants growing in the soil otherwise you could get root burn; you can give an extra application between the spring and summer feeding time provided growth is active. Flood the soil thoroughly before feeding again to wash out any residue of plant food salts.

General care

Watering. Newly-established trees will need watering well until they are established, but be careful not to over-water. Let the soil dry out to about 1 cm depth before giving a careful, thorough shaking. Water is needed in steady supply from spring to late autumn and any sudden dryness will cause fruit-drop from the embryo state onwards. Washington Navel, particularly, will drop fully-formed fruit.

Most of the active roots are in the ground below the outer perimeter of leaves or even slightly beyond so water should be given there and, since the roots of citrus trees are usually fairly close to the surface, the watered area should be covered with mulch to conserve moisture. During dry periods it is advisable to make periodic checks of the condition of the soil beneath the mulch.

Give the trees water whenever you feed them and for several weeks afterwards — this will prevent a build-up of plant food strong enough to cause root damage.
Feeding. Do not feed newly planted citrus for at least 6 weeks or, in the case of open-ground plantings, until new growth shows that the roots have become established. Young citrus can be killed by over-feeding, so be sparing.

If animal manure is not available give one-third to a half-cup of complete plant food or citrus food to each sq. m from the trunk to the outer perimeter of leaves. Feed in early spring at the first sign of new growth, again in December or January, and again in April, but only when the soil is moist and water well afterwards. It is safer to forgo feeding during dry periods if you cannot give the root area of the trees regular soaking.
Mulching. A permanent surface mulch over the area just out from the trunk of the tree to a little beyond the outer foliage will help to retain moisture and keep the soil in good

condition. Use any organic material but not heavy applications of grass clippings or fresh manure as these may cause root burning. However, both are valuable after they have been heaped for a few weeks to partly decompose. **Pruning.** Citrus need very little pruning especially during the early stages.

Storing lemons

Lemons will hang on the tree for a considerable time but there are advantages in picking them as soon as they are ripe or slightly before, particularly in fruit fly areas where ripe fruit is susceptible to fruit fly attack.

Do not pull the lemons in the usual way: cut them with secateurs and leave 1 or 2 mm of stem. Then line a wooden case or carton with several thicknesses of newspaper, spread about 2 cm of dry sand in the base, pack a layer of lemons over this, spaced so that they are not quite touching, cover with 2 cm of sand and repeat until the case is filled.

Stored this way they will last a couple of months in a reasonably cool situation, and the juice content will improve with storage.

Pruning

Lemons

Carry out progressive pruning by removing fruit-carrying twigs when the lemons are mature. Cut them back to the next good strong-looking shoot on the branchlet. Rejuvenate old lemon trees by cutting back leaving only a framework of branches a metre from the trunk. Seal all cuts with tree paint. New growth that follows hard pruning is often excessive, so thin out by rubbing off all but a well-spaced selection of strong-looking shoots.

Carry out this rejuvenation in late winter or, in frosty areas, during early spring. Some growers cut back in this manner every 10–12 years.

Mandarins

Bushy-growing types fruit much better if the growth is thinned by pruning when the crop finishes. Cut back every fruit-carrying twig to the second or third sturdy shoot from the trunk.

Oranges

Oranges rarely need pruning but if growth becomes dense and fruiting is affected, treat as for mandarins or thin generally. Should the spread of the tree have become too wide, cut the branches well back in late winter–early spring and if necessary treat as suggested for rejuvenating lemons. After such heavy pruning it may be 2 years before the tree comes back into full productivity.

Grapefruit

Treat as for lemons. Pinch out the tip of long sappy growth or bring the cane down in a lateral, arching position to hasten productivity. However, if left to go its own way the tree usually evens itself up.

Varieties

Sweet oranges

Jaffa — large, thin-skinned, oblong fruit in winter. Strong upright growth.
Parramatta — yellow-skinned fruit good for juicing. Strong winter-grower in poor soil.

Late Valencia — large juicy solid fruit with good flavour, ripens late and holds on tree.
Mediterranean — medium-sized, oval juicy fruit with mild flavour and few seeds.
Washington Navel — excellent eating orange, seedless, juicy, flavoursome, but requires regular moisture and nutrition to set a good crop of fruit.

Sour oranges

Chinoti (*Citrus aurantium myrtiolia*) — orange-red fruit over a long period during autumn–winter. Compact growth makes this plant an attractive tub specimen. The fruit may be used for making liqueurs, marmalades, preserves, and can be candied.
Seville — the traditional orange for making marmalade.

Blood oranges

Moro, Sanquinelli, Tarocco — all these oranges have good flavour — a touch of raspberry or strawberry gives an exotic flavour. They grow best in the hot interior regions.

Cumquats

Popular for marmalade or as decorative container-plants frequently grown as standards.
Marumi — compact, comparatively dwarf, with small rounded orange-yellow fruits — excellent container specimens.
Variegated — similar to above with decorative cream and green foliage.
Nagami — strong grower with comparatively sweet, yellow oval fruit.

Grapefruit

Marsh's Seedless — good-quality seedless fruit maturing mainly in late summer and autumn.
Wheeny — strong grower with good cold tolerance, fruiting mainly in late spring and early autumn — sometimes producing a poor crop every second year.

Lemons

Eureka — large juicy fruits throughout the year but most prolific in summer. Practically thornless. Best for temperate areas but subject to root rot in slow-draining soils.
Lisbon — very prolific, particularly in spring, with seedless fruit best picked when ripe. Difficult to peel.
Meyer — Small to medium grower, almost thornless. Good for pot culture. Juicy, thin-skinned fruit during autumn and winter.
Sweet Rind — see Eureka
Villa Franca — similar to Eureka, mainly in summer and autumn. Some thorns. Popular in inland Queensland.

Lime

Mexican — good tropical variety with small, strongly acid fruit and thorny growth; cold sensitive.
Tahitian — large, mild, seedless fruit. Thornless, most suitable for temperate climates but also suits tropics.

Mandarins

Ellendale — large orange-coloured fruit. Easily peeled, juicy with a rich flavour. If left on the tree for too long the fruit tends to granulate.

Emperor — large, very juicy, loose-skinned fruit with a good flavour. Ripens during May and June. The rough skin is almost red.
Hickson — upright growth, large juicy smooth-skinned fruit from May to August.
Kara — spreading growth. Large, juicy bright-orange-skinned fruit with a rich flavour ripening in August.
Thorny — Masses of small, flat, thin-skinned, juicy good-flavoured fruit in autumn.
Unshui — attractive ornamental tree with sweet fruits early in the season, i.e. April to early May.

Tangelo

Cross between tangerine and grapefruit, like large orange-skinned grapefruit, very juicy with slight mandarin aroma, numerous seeds, tart until fully ripe.

Growing problems and solutions

Gall wasps

This Australian native wasp damages citrus trees by depositing its eggs in part of the new spring growth. The larvae which tunnel within the branch cause considerable galling or swelling, weakening the branch involved and restricting its sap flow. In most oranges the galls may be round and about marble size, whereas in grapefruits and lemons (particularly common lemons which seem the most susceptible), they are usually elongated from about 5–18 cm and generally lighter in colour than the remainder of the branch. The adult wasp, which is a little bigger than a small black meat ant, usually emerges from the pupa stage during late winter and burrows its way from the gall, leaving the latter with a pepper-shaker appearance.

There is no effective chemical control for gall wasp, so it is essential to remove the galls by cutting a few cm below them, and then making sure they are burnt thoroughly, otherwise the wasp may still emerge to reinfect the new spring growth. It is vital to go over all citrus trees to make sure that the galls are removed by mid-August or earlier in warm districts.

Fruit problems and solutions

Problem: Lack of fruit. Many home gardeners are concerned about a lack of fruit particularly within the first 2 or 3 years after planting. Concern is still greater when the tree is purchased with fruit on it and it then fails to fruit over the next couple of seasons.
Cause: This behaviour is to be expected as citrus are usually unproductive until the main branches have matured. Fruiting occurs frequently on the young nursery-grown plant in a container because some degree of maturity is encouraged by the restriction of the root growth within the container. When planted out properly and under good conditions, the roots spread rapidly and this encourages a generous flush of new top growth. Fruit production ceases during this vegetative stage and does not commence again until the tree has settled down.
Solution: Expect 2 or 3 years without fruiting, but if longer, refer to the next 'problem'.

Espaliered pear trees take 5–8 years to commence fruiting

Avocados grow in all but cold or very dry areas

Bananas will grow in tropical to temperate areas

Cumquat (left, right), similar to mandarins, but bitter, will grow in tubs or garden

Problem: Well-established trees that continue to produce lush vegetative growth without fruit.

Cause: Over-vegetative, unproductive growth is usually due to an excess of nitrogen in relation to phosphorus in the soil.

Solution: Correct by applying about 1 handful of superphosphate per sq. m of area below the tree and slightly beyond the outer branches, then water in thoroughly.

Problem: Lack of fruit and no growth.

Cause: Oranges in particular may fail to make progress for a year or more after planting. This can be due to being planted in a root-bound state, or in heavily compacted soil, or too deeply. Excessive dryness or root damage due to excessive fertiliser being given at planting time or soon after can also be responsible. Also, some oranges are produced on trifoliata root stock. This is slow growing but has good resistance to root rot.

Solution: When the soil is damp but not sticky, loosen it with a pick to within about a span of the trunk and to a similar depth, even at the risk of injuring already established roots. Then work in a liberal mulch of fibrous compost, leafmould or similarly organic material to keep the soil open and aerated. Give gentle but thorough soakings whenever the surface soil dries out but do not feed until new growth commences and then only sparingly. One-quarter cup of citrus food per sq. m of area surrounding the tree is enough.

If the stem becomes very hardened and bark-bound use a sharp knife or razor blade to make a perpendicular cut, deep enough to penetrate the bark, on either side of the trunk from the graft or bud union upwards. As a precaution against fungus entering the wound paint the cut or the entire trunk with copper spray, mixed with sufficient water to make a paint-like consistency.

Problem: Fruit drop. Some dropping of small fruit is natural, particularly with trees that have set a heavy crop.

Cause: Dropping after reaching about the size of a ten-cent piece can be attributed to dryness or lack of nutrients. Although it may sound contradictory, the latter can occur after over-generous feeding which damages the roots and prevents the intake of nutrients. Unusually hot conditions during mid-summer can cause sudden and heavy dropping of fruit, particularly if soil moisture is lacking.

Washington Navel oranges are especially prone to fruit drop unless an even supply of moisture and nutrients is maintained.

Solution: Give occasional soakings during dry conditions, making sure that moisture penetrates to the sub-soil and is applied evenly to the main root-feeding area below the outer foliage. Mulch the surface in this area to maintain a more even moisture supply. Feed as indicated under 'General care of citrus'. In many areas it will be found that orange varieties such as Valencia, Joppa and Grovely Navel perform much better than Washington Navel although the latter may be nicer to eat.

Problem: Mandarins with dense foliage and very little fruit.

Cause: Foliage becomes so dense, particularly on the thorny variety, that fruiting may cease.

Solution: Prune back to the second or third strong shoot from the fruit cluster or where the fruit has been when fruiting is over.

Problem: Grapefruit failing to fruit.

Cause: Some varieties, particularly Wheeny, only fruit well every second year and may be entirely without fruit during alternate seasons.

Problem: Embryo fruit shrivelling and falling.

Cause: Usually a fungus disease known as lemon scab which attacks the tiny embryo fruit as the petals are shedding during wet periods in mid-summer.

Solution: See distorted lemons.

Problem: Distorted lemons sometimes with several peaky sections or irregular ridges capped with corky scab.

Cause: A fungus that attacks when petals are falling or just after.

Solution: Spray when about half the flower petals have fallen using copper spray adding about 2 tablespoons of white oil per 4.5 L of spray mixture. Mix the white oil separately, gradually adding about 1 L of water, then add this to the already mixed copper spray mixture.

Problem: Excessively thick rind.

Cause: This is common in lemons during the first year of bearing, particularly with the variety Eureka. The fruit becomes more normal with maturity. Thick skin of citrus can also be due to heavy applications of nitrogenous fertiliser such as sulphate of ammonia or urea applied later than mid-summer.

Solution: Use complete fertiliser, citrus food or animal manure, particularly poultry manure. In heavily mulched soils where the nitrogen content may be comparatively high, the application of a small handful of superphosphate per sq. m or about one-third of a cup of bone dust to the same area, applied mainly below outer branches, is recommended.

Problem: Lemons with brown-stained flesh over the seed area when the lemon is cut in cross-section. In more acute cases there are cavities containing a brownish gum between flesh and rind, and heavy woody veins running through the rind.

Cause: Boron deficiency. This can be a temporary deficiency often occurring when dry spells follow prolonged wet periods. (Boron leaches from the soil readily but requires presence of reasonable soil moisture to become available to the plant.) It may also occur after applications of sulphate of ammonia or other highly nitrogenous fertilisers because these tend to depress the deficiency even further by raising the balance in the opposite direction. Other factors such as a very acid soil which reduces the solubility of boron, or heavy liming which makes the boron so soluble that it will leach from the soil quickly, may sometimes be responsbile for the deficiency problems.

Solution: Dissolve 1 tablespoon of borax in about 10 L of water and apply this mainly to the area below the outer foliage of the tree after the soil has been evenly moistened to its full depth. Borax dissolves more readily if first mixed with hot water.

Lemons will normally hang on a tree for a considerable time

Grapefruit maybe treated similarly to lemons

'Tahitian' limes can be grown successfully in temperate areas

Oranges bring a lovely fragrance to the garden

Tangelo seminole trees bear fruit from July–November

> **Note:** It is important not to apply larger quantities of borax than recommended, or to make the application more frequently than once a year, and then only if necessary.

Spots on fruit

Problem: Slightly sunken brown or black spots on fruit.
Cause: Black spot.
Solution: Spray as for citrus scab.
Problem: Brown stain or clusters of tiny brown spots on fruit, leaves and stem, often accompanied by die-back of twigs.
Cause: Melanose.
Solution: Spray as for citrus scab and repeat after 6–8 weeks. Prune off and burn dead wood.
Problem: Clusters of small sunken brown spots, some joined together. Usually more pronounced after winter frosts.
Cause: Brown spot or septoria spot which usually develops during autumn rains.
Solution: Use copper spray during early autumn (usually only frosty inland areas) where this disease becomes troublesome.
Problem: Black sootiness that can be washed off fruit.
Cause: Black sooty mould fungus, which is not a parasite but lives only on 'honeydew', the sugary secretions from scale pests.
Solution: Copper spray will kill the sooty mould fungus but it is preferable to eliminate the cause. See 'Scale' below.
Problem: Flattened, pinhead-sized reddish-brown scabs over fruit.
Cause: Red scale.
Solution: Use white oil spray as directed on container. One teaspoon of Malathion per 4.5 L of spray increases effectiveness of treatment. This scale is less widespread than it was because it is being parasitised by a tiny wasp.
Problem: Tiny puncture in rind usually surrounded by brownish area and sometimes followed by rotting. Maggots may be found in fruit.
Cause: Fruit fly.
Solution: See heading 'Fruit fly control'.
Problem: Brown rotting fruit with unpleasant odour. Sometimes gum may exude from buds.
Cause: Brown rot, which is most likely to be present during warm wet periods when humidity is high, particularly in autumn.
Remedy: Spray with Benlate or Mancozeb to wet all parts of the tree thoroughly. A second spraying in late winter is desirable.

Foliage problems

Problem: Leaves badly distorted or mis-shapen.
Cause: Usually wind damage when the foliage was young and sappy. Infestation by aphids while growth is young can also cause malformation as the foliage matures. See deficiency note.
Solution: This rarely retards the tree seriously. For aphid control use Pyrethrum-type spray or Malathion.
Deficiency note: Deficiencies of molybdenum could cause deformation of young growth but

this is only likely after heavy applications of fertilisers high in nitrogen, or where the soil is very acid. The latter could be corrected by applying half to three-quarters of a cup of garden lime or dolomite per sq. m of area below the spread of the tree and a little further out.
Problem: Pale grey-brown margins or large area of foliage with pale, burnt appearance.
Cause: Wind damage from exposure, particularly prevalent near coast.
Solution: Provide shelter from prevailing winds.

Yellowing leaves

The yellowing of some lower leaves is natural, particularly in early spring when the soil is still cold and sudden warmth triggers off new growth. This applies particularly to lemon trees, which can also yellow and lose foliage with sudden cold changes. Other causes as follows:
Problem: Yellowing of mature leaves. Starts with yellow blotching toward the centre of the leaf on either side of the mid-vein, then enlarges and spreads to leave a definite inverted 'V' of green at the leaf base and extends nearly halfway up the mid-rib. In earlier stages there may be a smaller inverted 'V' at the leaf tip. Branches carrying the most fruit are usually the most affected. Leaves fall prematurely.
Cause: Magnesium deficiency.
Solution: Moisten soil below the area covered by branches of the tree. Dissolve 2 tablespoons of magnesium sulphate (Epsom Salts) in a 10 L can of water and soak into moistened area. For better results retain 1–2 L of the solution and apply as a foliage spray to the tree. Correction of this problem may take several months but will be effective.
Problem: Yellowing, mainly of new foliage, with the fine network of veins standing out in green.
Cause: Iron deficiency, usually indicating that the soil is alkaline or has been limed too heavily. In a home garden some trees may be affected and not others. Rough lemon and Cleopatra mandarin have better tolerance to alkaline soils than other root stocks, e.g. trifoliata.
Solution: Apply iron chelates as a foliage spray and water into the soil at the dilution recommended on the container. Alternatively, about 1 tablespoon per sq. m sulphate of iron may have results depending on the rate of alkalinity. The iron chelates give more positive control.
Problem: Yellowing and distortion with numerous raised, reddish-brown spots, worse toward leaf margins. Dead twigs and distorted young shoots accompany long-standing infestations. Fruit streaked with areas of slightly raised, tiny brown spots.
Cause: Melanose.
Solution: As described for citrus scab, followed by a second application of copper spray about 6 weeks later. Prune off and burn the spore-carrying dead twigs if long-standing infestations have caused die-back. After pruning back to live wood, use copper spray, then seal all cuts with tree paint.
Problem: Leaves small, narrow, on short stems

— giving the appearance of being crowded. Yellow mottling between leaf veins which increases to affect the entire leaf. Some twigs die back, others can have multiple buds with dense shoots giving the tree a bushy and stunted appearance. Fruit is usually pale, elongated and small.
Cause: Zinc deficiency.
Solution: Dissolve 2 tablespoons of zinc sulphate in about 10 L of water, add a wetting agent or 1 tablespoon of white oil and spray to thoroughly wet all parts of the tree and foliage. Results are best if this is done in early spring when new growth is commencing.
Problem: Foliage thinning out, particularly on western side of tree. Remaining leaves eventually pale to dull yellow and die-back of twigs occurs.
Cause: Root rot fungus (phytophthora), a disease mainly of heavy, slow-draining soils or other areas where drainage is poor. As the fungus is only active in wet soil, regrowth may occur during dry periods but then the tree is usually surviving on the surface root system only and so is particularly subject to drying out.

Eureka or sweet rind lemons are the more usually affected, because these are unsuitable on the root stock trifoliata which is resistant to the disease.
Solution: Obtain citrus on trifoliata root stock. Eureka lemons should only be planted in situations where the soil drains readily. Where it is not possible to install a drainage system, use a position where the soil is built up about 1 m above the surrounding level, such as the top of a wide rockery or terraced bed with adequate weep holes at the base of the retaining wall. Alternatively, grow the lemon in a large tub and discourage roots from entering and blocking the drainage holes.
Problem: Young shoots wilting.
Cause: This can occur during dry periods when the tree is existing on the surface root system due to root rot damage as outlined in the preceding paragraphs. Another common cause, particularly from late December to February, is the sap-sucking action of the large oval or later shield-shaped citrus bug.
Solution: See following section.
Problem: Unpleasant-smelling bugs on foliage.
Cause: The mature citrus bug is nearly 3.5 cm long and over 1 cm wide, dark brown or black in colour with an unpleasant 'bean' bug odour. It sucks the sap from young shoots, often causing wilting, and occasionally attacks fruit.
Solution: Use Pyrethrum-type spray to contact the bugs directly or spray liberally with either Malathion or Diazinon. Avoid picking bugs off by hand or attempting to knock them from the tree because they eject acrid fluid that stings the skin and may cause temporary blindness.
Problem: Flat oval buff or orange bugs on citrus.
Cause: This is an earlier stage of the citrus bug described in the preceding paragraph. They go through 8 different stages from egg to adult.
Solution: As for citrus bug.
Problem: Tiny black or brown insects clustered on new twigs and shoots.
Cause: Black aphids.

Solution: Use Pyrethrum-type spray or Malathion.

Coconut

Coconuts are tall, very elegant palms suitable for growing only in humid tropical to semi-tropical regions with plenty of water during summer. There is also a dwarf-growing variety which begins cropping when only 2–3 m high.

Requirements

They are most suitable to situations close to the sea and grow happily in very sandy soils, but their growth is more rapid where plenty of organic material is available.

Planting time. As coconuts are for warm areas only they may be planted at any time. The coconut palm shoots from the end of the coconut and is nurtured initially by the milk or pulp of the nut, but their progress is limited until they are planted into the soil with the nut just covered.

General care

Their main need is plenty of water during the summer months and progress can be speeded at this stage by a light application of animal manure, but young palms in particular can be damaged by heavy feeding.

Custard apple
(Annona and Cherimolia)

The custard apple makes a large shrub or fairly open small tree which sheds a large percentage of its foliage during late winter and early spring. The large fruits weigh up to 1 kg each.

Requirements

Custard apples are best suited to warm tropical to semi-tropical areas with high humidity but are occasionally found growing satisfactorily in sheltered temperate areas near the coast. They need a well-drained and preferably loamy soil rich in organic material.

Planting time. In warm frost-free tropical areas custard apples grown in containers can be planted out any time.

General care

Allow the young tree about 6 weeks to establish itself and then, providing new growth is evident, soak the soil around it every 2–3 weeks with one of the water-soluble complete plant foods, continuing this treatment until late summer. From then on give a liberal dressing of animal manure each spring, or a high-nitrogen-type fertiliser applied at the rate of 1 handful per sq. m of area below the branch line of the tree, first in early spring and then again about mid-summer. In this case a suitable preparation would be complete lawn food, or equal parts of a standard complete fertiliser or citrus food and sulphate of ammonia. Water liberally after feeding and throughout summer.

Varieties

African Pride — one of the most widely-grown varieties. It makes a relatively small compact tree and produces a heavy crop of good-shaped fruits.

Pinks Mammoth — comparatively large with spreading open growth, and produces a moderate crop of unevenly shaped but very good flavoured fruits.

Growing problems and solutions

Problem: Downy white aphid-like insects on young shoots.
Cause: Woolly aphid or mealy bug which can distort the shoots.
Solution: Spray with 1 tablespoon of white oil plus 1 teaspoon of Malathion or Diazinon with 4.5 L of water. Rogor may also be used.
Problem: Brownish or water-soaked spots surrounding small hole in fruit.
Cause: Fruit fly. Larvae (maggots) may be present in the fruit.
Solution: See heading 'Fruit fly control'.

> **Note:** The green shield bug or fruit bug may also cause water-soaked blotching on fruit. If noticed, use Pyrethrum-type sprays or Malathion.

Feijoa
or Pineapple guava

The Feijoa, a very adaptable and decorative shrub or small tree growing to about 4 m in height and nearly as wide, is suitable as a screen or specimen tree. It produces silky-stamened pompon-like flowers mainly in late spring and these are followed by guava-like fruits 8–9 cm in length.

Requirements

The feijoa grows in all but the coldest climates and once established stands heavy frosts.

It is at its best in full sun but also grows reasonably well in half-shade. Any well-drained soil is suitable.

Planting time. Being evergreen, the feijoa is usally purchased as a container-grown plant, so it may be planted any time. Spring planting would be preferable in very frosty areas.

General care

Plenty of water during spring and summer and an occasional scattering of complete plant food will assure more rapid growth.

It needs no pruning but removing the centre of the young plant and later pinching out growing tips will assure more compact growth at an earlier stage.

The feijoa produces fruit from later summer to late autumn. The fruit falls before it is ripe and needs to be stored in a dark airy place until it develops a pineapple-like aroma which signifies that it is ready for eating.
Problem: Fruit fly. Fruits of feijoa are very susceptible to fruit fly attack.
Solution: If grown in fruit fly areas they need to be sprayed when about half-grown with either Lebaycid or Rogor as directed on the container, or baits should be used as suggested under heading 'Fruit fly control'.

Fig

Figs are low-branching large shrubs with fairly open growth and large decorative deciduous foliage. They grow in a variety of climates from sub-tropical to quite cold and dry inland areas.

Requirements

Figs are at their best in an open sunny position. Although they prefer a well-drained soil, they thrive in a situation several metres from drains or seepage areas where their spreading roots can draw on a continuous moisture supply during summer. However, the fruit seems to mature better under dry conditions and most of the commercial-growing areas for figs have a very dry summer period. Heavy rain at fruiting time causes fruit-splitting and sometimes fermentation.

They grow happily in a variety of soils but results will be better if heavy clay soils are broken up with the addition of sand and compost prior to planting, and sandy soils are supplied with a liberal mulch of organic material to conserve moisture and improve the general condition of the soil.

Planting time. Figs are planted during their deciduous winter period but plants in containers can be planted out any time.

General care

Although figs are not demanding, size of fruit and crop will be improved by giving the soil below the branch line occasional good soakings during spring and dry periods in early summer, and a spring application of complete fertiliser using about 1 handful per sq. m of area. This may be repeated again in mid-summer when the embryo fruit first appears.

Pruning. Need very little pruning but if necessary the size of the tree can be reduced by cutting vertical or outward spreading branches back to just above a smaller lateral branch. This is done in mid-winter. Similarly old trees can be rejuvenated by cutting back very hard into the older wood to encourage a flush of new growth from nearer the base. Fruit is formed on the new season's growth.

Figs do not precede their fruit with flowers. The actual flowers are within the fruit and pollination is carried out by a tiny wasp that enters the small aperture at the base of the fruit. Some varieties do not require pollination to fruit.

Varieties

Black Genoa — a very popular large-fruited variety with dark purple to black skin and bright red flesh.

Blue Provence — a very prolific medium-sized blue-green fruit with a purple blush.

Brown Turkey — a very vigorous and heavy-bearing variety with large purplish-brown luscious fruits.

White Genoa — makes a medium-sized tree with good crops of greenish-yellow fruits.

Growing problems and solutions

Problem: Sawdust issuing from trunk at base of tree or sometimes higher in the junction of branches.
Cause: Borer. The larvae of this pest can hollow out a large section of the main trunk or branch.
Solution: At the first sign of sawdust or castings, probe the hole with copper wire and if uncertain that this has killed the borer, use an old eyedropper or venturi tube to inject a few drops of Malathion, other insecticides or even

methylated spirits. Leave for 20 minutes to dry, then paint large areas of damage with copper spray mixed to paint-like consistency and fill the holes with putty or coat areas of exposed wood with tree paint.

Problem: Fruit eaten by birds.
Solution: Drape fine nets or bags over the tree as suggested under 'Fruit fly control'.

Guava

The Strawberry or Cherry Guava (*Psidium cattleianum*) makes a decorative small tree with a smooth greenish-brown trunk and a rounded top of small glossy green evergreen foliage. The fruit is round to pear shape and has deep-red skin and pinkish-white flesh with a pleasant strawberry flavour. The Yellow Guava (*P. guajava*) grows best in tropical to warmer temperate districts where it makes a quick-growing shrubby tree with longer foliage than the Strawberry Guava.

Requirements

Both guavas are at their best in fairly open sunny positions with shelter from strong winds, particularly cold ones. They grow well in any soil but a heavy slow-draining one, but prefer a crumbly to light loam with plenty of organic material added.
Planting time. Being warmth-loving evergreens the guavas are best planted in spring so that they have the maximum period of warm weather ahead in which to establish themselves. In areas with warm winters they may be planted at any time.

Loquat

The loquat is an attractive tree with long, dark glossy green leaves closely set around spreading branchlets. It carries large clusters of luscious golden-orange fruits in late spring. The tree will grow 5–6 m high and if allowed to grow unchecked will reach a similar width. Smaller-growing varieties grafted onto quince stock are becoming available.

Requirements

Loquats grow well in all but cold districts and in a variety of soils, providing drainage is good. Established trees can tolerate quite heavy frosts. They need at least half sun, and plenty of water during spring and early summer.
Planting time. Loquats bought in containers can be replanted safely at any time. Spring planting is best because the trees can become established before hot, dry weather sets in.

General care

If a low-branching tree is required, cut or pinch the growing tip out of single-stem trees soon after planting. Very little feeding is needed in reasonably good soil, but if the trees are slow to establish, apply a good surface mulch of compost under the outer branch line, or in the case of a younger tree about 1 m out from the main stem, then sprinkle over this about 1 handful of complete plant food per sq. m and water in thoroughly. Do this in late winter or early spring. Water well for several weeks after feeding. Do not feed newly-planted trees for at least three months. If fruit is thickly clustered, thin out.

Varieties

Heard's Mammoth — has large rounded yellow fruits almost the size of a hen's egg. A heavy cropper, usually requires thinning.

Growing problems and solutions

Problem: Small brown patches on fruit with maggots inside.
Solution: See heading 'Fruit fly control'.

Lychee (*Nephelium*)

Lychees are attractive glossy-foliaged trees growing 7–8 m high, with plum-sized fruit in a rough thin rind.

Requirements

Lychees grow best in tropical to warmer temperate coastal districts where humidity is high and prefer deep well-drained and well-composted soil. Plenty of moisture is needed during the summer months.
Planting time. Spring is the best planting time, especially in areas where winters are cool.

General care

When planting (in heavy soils particularly) apply a good mulch of fibrous organic material around the tree and knead some into the soil before watering to prevent heavy soil from caking and allow new root growth to establish rapidly. Maintain a surface mulch of compost around the tree but the roots of lychees are sensitive to fertiliser so do not apply other plant foods for at least 6 months, preferably not until the following spring.

If the young trees appear to be lacking in vigour they can then be fed at monthly intervals during spring and early summer with any of the water-soluble plant foods which should be soaked into the area below the outer branch line of the tree. After the first year, if necessary, give light dressings of fowl manure, blood and bone or a preparation (e.g. rose food) containing a high percentage of organic materials applied at the rate of about 1 handful per sq. m of area below the branch line of the tree.

Lychees grown from seed can take 15–20 years to produce fruit which may be of doubtful quality. It is better to buy grafted trees which begin cropping 4–5 years after planting. The outer skin of the fruit turns red on ripening.

Varieties

Brewster — makes a very large tree unsuitable for a small garden. It is a mid-season variety.
Bengal — similar in appearance to Brewster but fruit quality is better.
Haak Ip — a moderate-sized compact grower with a sweet but acid-flavoured fruit.
Kwai Mi — grows into a large spreading tree with sweet-flavoured medium-sized fruit which matures early.
Wai Chi — makes a comparatively small compact tree with late-maturing small fruit.

Growing problems and solutions

Problem: As for loquats and also red felt-like patches under foliage.
Cause: Tiny mites.
Solution: Spray with wettable sulphur or Kelthane during new growth and also when flower buds have formed as flowers also may be damaged by this mite.

Mango

Large spreading evergreens with dark slender foliage and attractive purple-bronze new growth. Their luscious pear-shaped orange fruits vary in size and eating quality according to variety.

Requirements

Mangoes are at home in tropical to semi-tropical districts but grow well in temperate districts if protected from cold winds.

They will grow in most well-drained soils but prefer deep crumbly loam. Very light sandy soils or heavier loams can be made to their liking by the addition of well-rotted organic material. Give young plants shade or fruiting trees full sun.
Planting time. In tropical and semi-tropical districts with mild winters container-grown plants can be planted at any time. Elsewhere spring plantings are preferable. The roots should not be disturbed.

General care

Mangoes need plenty of water during the summer season but may not set their fruit if showery weather is experienced during the late winter or spring-flowering period. Wet at this time induces a fungus which destroys the flowers or embryo fruit. Maintain a surface mulch of organic material but avoid heavy feeding as this encourages excessive growth at the expense of fruit.

Young trees may be fed regularly once new growth commences. Use one of the complete water-soluble plant foods and saturate around the root area every 4 weeks during the warmer months. Once they reach the fruiting stage apply about 1 handful of complete plant food per sq. m of area below the branch line of the tree, first in mid-spring then again in mid to late summer.

Varieties

The largest fruit and best-flavoured mango is known under a variety of names including **Bowen, Strawberry, Peach** and **Kensington.** There are variations because many of these trees produce fairly true-to-type seed, especially the polyembryonic ones which throw several shoots from one seed. (When this happens they are carefully separated and only the stronger ones retained for planting.)

The common mango, or Turpentine mango as it is sometimes called, is a smaller fruit with a stronger flavour usually produced on a larger, more vigorous tree. The flavour can be good but the fruit is usually stringy.

Growing problems and solutions

Problem: Failure to fruit.

Cause: This is the main problem with mangoes. Rarely a problem in northern monsoonal regions where the weather is normally dry at flowering time; wet conditions during the flowering period invariably induce a fungus which either kills the flowers or the embryo fruit. Surviving fruit may rot on ripening.

Solution: Spray the tree with Zineb, Mancozeb or Captan but there is no positive cure — just hope for dry conditions at flowering time.

Problem: Fruit with small, brownish sting marks and maggots inside.

Cause: Fruit fly. See heading 'Fruit fly control'.

Problem: Sooty mould on foliage.

Cause: This is an indication that scale is present, usually pink wax scale.

Solution: Spray with white oil plus Malathion, Rogor or Carbaryl added at the recommended spraying strength. For best results, apply when the scale is in the crawler stage which in warm regions is usually late spring, and in temperate areas early summer.

Monstera

Though grown mainly for its huge ornately perforated leaves the long green-skinned fruits of the plant have pleasant aroma and flavour if eaten when ripe. Ripening occurs from the base up, usually at the rate of only 2–3 cm per day. These fruits may take up to a year to mature. When ripe, the lower skin lifts and a pineapple aroma is given off. Frequently the fruit will then bend or fall.

Requirements

Monsteras are tropical plants which prefer warmth and high humidity but grow well in all but very cold or very hot and dry climates.

Planting time. Container-grown monsteras may be replanted with care at any time. If a plant is being moved from the ground it is desirable to cut off all foliage and make the move in late winter or early spring.

General care

Once established, monsteras survive under the most adverse conditions but grow and fruit better where plenty of moisture is available, particularly in summer. Growth is best in partly shaded but warm areas although they will adapt to full sun. If vigour is lacking or foliage cover is poor, water occasionally with complete soluble plant foods during the warmer months.

Nectarine

The nectarine is really only a smooth-skinned peach although some have a more sugary flavour. For growing conditions and general care see heading 'Peach'.

Pruning. Pruning is different. Some varieties of nectarine carry flower or fruit buds on the outer part of the twigs. Before shortening back these twigs or laterals, distinguish between the fruit and flower buds — the former are plump and oval and the latter comparatively thin. Where clusters of three occur, the centre one is usually a growth bud and the two outer ones flower or fruit buds.

Olive

Olives prefer cool, temperate and semi-tropical areas with wet winters and fairly dry summers and do particularly well in some areas of South Australia, Western Australia and inland districts. They are long-lived and durable trees.

Requirements

To speed establishment of young trees feed in the early stages with nitrogenous fertilisers such as the complete soluble plant foods, slow-release granules or cow manure.

When trees reach maturity confine feeding to either fowl manure or complete fertiliser applying about 1 handful per sq. m of area below the branch line of the tree in winter then again in mid-summer.

Planting time. The container-grown plant may be planted at any time of the year with reasonable safety.

General care

Pruning. At planting time, tall spindly trees are usually headed back to within about 50 cm from the ground, and shoots that follow below the cut are thinned out to 3 or 4 well-spaced ones to provide the main framework of the tree. From then on excessively heavy growth can be thinned, particularly from the centre of the tree to allow penetration of light. After 10–15 years old trees producing a lot of woody growth can be rejuvenated by cutting right back to the main framework or branches of the tree.

Varieties

Only the European olive varieties (*Olea europea*) set edible fruit. These plants can be distinguished by the bluish-grey tinge of the foliage given by the colour of the underside of the leaf. The African olive, which is frequently grown for hedges, occurs often as a self-sown seedling and has become naturalised in some areas but only produces a pea-sized fruit with no edible value. This tree is distinguished by its generally darker foliage and buff to yellowish toning in the new growth, which again comes from the colour of the underside of the leaf.

If growing European olives for cropping purposes it is worth starting with selected grafted strains which include many varieties such as **Verdale, Mission, Sevillano** and many others. It is advisable to check with your nurseryman on the most suitable types available in your district.

Growing problems and solutions

Lack of fruit, a common complaint, is usually due to confusing the African olive which has no value with the European varieties. Only the latter give satisfactory fruit.

Problem: Sooty mould on the branches or foliage.

Cause: Olive scale.

Solution: As suggested for scale on mangoes, but in this case the crawler stage of the scales occurs in late spring rather than in summer. Careful examination of the foliage will disclose the tiny fry or crawler scale, near the mid-rib of the leaf.

Papaw

Papaws are most suited to tropical areas but frequently grow well in temperate areas when given protection from frost and cold winter winds. They are picturesque palm-like trees with long-stemmed attractively divided large leaves. Mature female trees carry large almost stemless flowers attached to the trunk, whereas the non-fruiting male trees have long branching sprays of orange blossom-like flowers. There are also bisexual types, generally with comparatively long thin fruits (Long Toms) which reproduce fairly reliably from seed. These also have branched flower stems similar to the male tree.

With the larger commercial-type papaws, one male is needed to pollinate about 5 or 6 females. Plant a group of seedlings a metre or so apart and when sex is evident remove all but one male.

Requirements

A fairly deep loamy soil, a little on the limey side with good drainage and plenty of organic material added and plenty of water during the summer months.

Planting time. In temperate areas plant out in spring when they have a long period of warmth ahead of them, but in tropical areas with warm winters they may be planted out at any time.

General care

Young seedlings usually make rapid growth during the warmer months when plenty of water is given and the soil contains a reasonable amount of organic material. If growth is slow, feed every 2–3 weeks with one of the soluble plant foods beginning about 6 weeks after planting out and if necessary, continuing while the weather is still warm. Otherwise, the mature trees should be fed about 1 handful per sq. m of complete plant food applied to the area within about 1 m of the trunk in spring, providing soil moisture can be maintained, and given the same again during mid to late summer.

Pruning. Papaw trees are not pruned, except in the case of bunchy top disease or die-back.

Growing problems and solutions

Problem: Foliage pale and bunched, stems shrivelling from the top.

Cause: Die-back, now unfortunately common in papaws.

Solution: Cut the affected stem well below the shrivelled area and just above a side shoot. When no side shoot is present, cut the stem well back into healthy wood, dust the cut with a little copper spray then cover with an inverted clean jam tin large enough to fit the stem. This is to prevent further rotting. The cutting will induce at least one side shoot to develop from lower down on the trunk.

Frost can damage the top of a papaw. Do not cut away the dead top area immediately but leave it as protection for the remainder of the stem until frost danger is over. Recovery cannot be assured. It is better to start new papaw plants in spring as soon as frosts are over so that they have a long period of warmth in which to establish. In colder areas they are unlikely to survive winter unless planted in a warm position, preferably against a northern wall with some protection from a high eave.

Problem: Powdery film on foliage, often accompanied by severe leaf spotting.

Cause: Mildew.

Solution: Use copper spray, wettable sulphur or Benlate.

Problem: Sunken brown pits on fruit, usually in clusters and sometimes joined together causing the ripening fruit to rot.

Solution: Little can be done. Some types of papaws with tough skins are relatively immune to the disease.

Problem: New top leaves wilt, older ones become dry and shrivelled.

Cause: Root rot, common in soils that remain wet for long periods.

Solution: Do not replant in the same position. Choose a well-drained area and add plenty of organic material to the soil, particularly as a surface mulch.

Problem: Failure to fruit.

Cause: Some papaws are bisexual or self-pollinating but the majority are either male or female. The male has comparatively small orange blossom-like flowers on long-branched stems, whereas the female flower is 4–5 cm across and is almost stemless, appearing to sit on the actual trunk of the tree.

Solution: Unless the papaw is known to be a bisexual variety, plant a group of at least 5 plants and when sex is determined remove all males but one.

Peach

One of the most popular deciduous fruit trees which, in small gardens, can also be used as a summer shade tree. Peaches are widely grown in all but tropical and very cold areas, but are at their best in temperate regions where winters are cool enough to mature the wood.

Requirements

Peaches need a well-drained soil and a position with full sun to crop satisfactorily. Plenty of water is needed during the spring and early summer period. In areas with constant rain during this period there are often problems with brown rot or other fungus diseases, therefore the ideal is a dry spring and summer climate with adequate irrigation of the soil.

They can be grown in a variety of soils providing they are well drained. Most suitable is a medium to light loam with plenty of organic material added. In heavy or poor sandy soils the young trees will establish more rapidly if up to one-third organic material or moistened peatmoss is added prior to planting.

Planting time. Most peaches are sold as bare-rooted trees which can only be safely replanted during the winter dormant period.

General care

As peaches fruit on new wood (made the previous season) it is essential to have plenty of growth each year to ensure a worthwhile crop the following season. Feed with fowl manure or complete plant food in late winter to early spring and again about mid-summer.

A plant food or fertiliser containing approximately equal quantities of nitrogen, potassium and phosphorus is ideal and should be applied at the rate of about 1 handful per sq. m of area below the branch line of the tree. Feed only when the soil is moist and water well afterwards to avoid damage to surface roots.

Pruning. Initial pruning for shape is much the same as recommended for apples, then encourage an outward or more lateral type growth by cutting back the more upright leaders or main branches of the tree to a point just above an outward growing lateral or lesser branch each winter. Most of the fruit will grow on laterals or short twigs coming from the main branches.

During the first 5–10 years excessive laterals should be thinned out to give more even spacing, also shorten some of the laterals at winter pruning time, depending on the number of fruit buds the tree is carrying. The flower or fruiting buds can be distinguished from growth buds by their relatively plump and more oval shape. Buds are in groups of three; the two outside larger ones are flower buds and the central thinner one is a growth bud. In shortening back laterals it is advisable to cut to a growth bud.

The more upright growth is vigorous and more vegetative and draws more heavily on the resources of the tree, so to distribute sap to all parts of the tree, encourage lateral growth by pruning back erect leaders to outward-growing laterals or outward-pointing buds.

Varieties

The following are all good home garden varieties of peaches and are all self-pollinating, so one tree alone should perform satisfactorily. They are listed in order of maturity, which for the earlier types commences in early November, the later ones carrying through until February. In both cases later in cool districts.

Bell's November — ripens from the end of the first week in November; white-fleshed semi-cling-stone with good colour.

Fairfax — white-fleshed slip-stone.

Watt's Early Champion — medium to large white-fleshed slip-stone, attractively flushed dark-red; requires heavy pruning and thinning.

Maygold — yellow-fleshed cling-stone; ripening mid-November.

Cardinal — yellow-fleshed cling-stone; ripening early December.

Early Aunt Becky — large white-fleshed slip-stone with attractive red-flushed skin and a good flavour; ripening second week in December.

Coronet — yellow-fleshed semi-cling-stone.

Starking Delicious — yellow cling-stone.

Red Haven — yellow-fleshed semi-cling-stone.

Loring — yellow-fleshed slip-stone.

Hale Haven — large yellow-fleshed slip-stone.

Blackburn — large flushed, yellow-fleshed slip-stone; ripening early new year.

Fragar — large white-fleshed cling-stone with red flush; very heavy bearer with excellent flavour.

Elberta — popular red-skinned slip-stone with yellow flesh; late January.

J.H. Hale — red-flushed, yellow-fleshed slip-stone.

Peach and nectarine
Growing problems and solutions

Nectarines are botanically a smooth-skinned peach and are susceptible to the same disorders.

Problem: Lack of fruit. Both peaches and nectarines carry their fruit on new wood (growth made during the previous spring and summer).

Cause: Badly-drained soil, a poor, dry growing season which prevents the formation of new growth, or heavy pruning of the new wood.

Solution: Learn to recognise the difference between the flower or potential fruit buds (which are oval-shaped or comparatively rounded) and the growth buds (which are thinner and torpedo-shaped). In many cases the buds occur in groups of three — two comparatively plump outer flower buds with a slender growth bud in the centre. If in doubt, leave pruning until the flower appears.

There is one other possible cause of non-fruiting; the most appealing variety — J.H. Hale — needs another variety flowering at the same time for effective pollination.

Problem: Brown patch, usually on the side of the fruit. During moist conditions it spreads rapidly. The soft and rotted fruit may dry out and become mummified on the tree.

Cause: Brown rot.

Solution: When buds begin to show colour, use copper spray with 1 teaspoon of white oil added to every 4.5 L of spray mixture. (**Note:** The white oil must first be mixed separately and added to the bulk of the mixture.) This disease is most troublesome during wet spring conditions so follow the initial spraying with Benlate, Mancozeb or Zineb applied soon after petals fall and immediately after showery or wet periods.

Problem: Patches of black, freckle-like spots on skin of fruit.

Cause: The fungus disease, freckle.

Solution: Spray as for brown rot in preceding paragraph.

Problem: Flesh around stone of fruit rotten and maggoty.

Cause: Fruit fly.

Solution: See heading 'Fruit fly control'.

Problem: Small black weevils in or around the stone.

Cause: Peach weevil.

Solution: This pest is difficult to control as it may enter the fruit in the green stage, before fruit fly control normally occurs. Spraying with Endosulphan when the green peaches are about golf ball-size or a little smaller gives some control but the more important factor is to rake up and dispose of any old fruit or fruit stones from the previous season. Be thorough.

Problem: New foliage badly blistered and distorted, with small green or pink aphids on the underside.

Cause: Peach aphid.

Solution: Spray with Malathion or Lebaycid.

Problem: Patches of foliage with large pink or green blisters, without presence of aphids.

Cause: A fungus disease known as leaf curl or curly leaf. The fungus winters in the scales of the growth buds and infects the young foliage as it emerges.

Solution: Spray with copper spray when flower buds show colour.
Problem: Foliage shows small brown spots that fall out to leave a shot-hole appearance, sometimes gum spots on leaves.
Cause: Shot-hole fungus.
Solution: Use copper spray as flower buds show colour and again when flower petals fall off.
Problem: Yellow flecks on foliage with velvety-brown spots on reverse side.
Cause: Rust.
Solution: Spray with Zineb or Mancozeb and repeat a fortnight later.
Problem: Tips of new spring growth split, brown and exuding gum.
Cause: Peach tip moth borer.
Solution: Spray with Lebaycid.
Problem: Die-back of twigs.
Cause: Brown rot fungus.
Solution: See brown rot control at beginning of peach and nectarine section.

Pear

Pears are long-lived, large attractive trees which prefer similar conditions to apples. They often take 7 years or more to produce their first fruit.

Requirements

Pears are grown satisfactorily in a variety of well-drained soils but prefer fairly heavy clayey loams or soils with clay sub-soil which retain moisture well. They dislike permanently soggy badly-drained soil. The general cultivation, shaping and pruning of pears is similar to that recommended for apples.
Planting time. They are normally sold as bare-rooted trees and are therefore planted during their dormant period in winter.

General care

Feeding requirements are much the same as apples except that they prefer more nitrogen, which can be supplied either by giving dressings of stable manure in addition to the complete fertiliser suggested, or by adding 1 handful of sulphate of ammonia per 2 sq. m of area below the foliage of the tree, or by using one of the slow-release granular fertilisers which has a higher proportion of nitrogen than phosphorus.
Harvesting. Many varieties of pears, particularly **Williams** (Bartlett), deteriorate or break down in the centre of the fruit if allowed to ripen on the tree. Pick them when the fruit is fully formed and showing the first flush of yellow, and wrap them individually and store in the dark indoors until ripe.

Varieties

Pears set a better crop in the vicinity of another variety which flowers at the same time. This will aid pollination. The first two in the following list are suitable pollinators for each other and the same applies to the last two listed.
Beurre Bosc — large brownish-skinned; fine-quality fruits mid-season to late.
Williams (Bartlett) — large, yellow, red-flushed skin, fine musky flavour; mid-season.
Josephine de Malines — greenish-yellow, medium-sized juicy fruit; keeps well, late.

Packham's Triumph — prolific, large yellowish-green, irregular shape, excellent flavour; late.

Growing problems and solutions

Problem: Failure to fruit.
Cause: Lack of fruit from relatively young trees is a common complaint. However, this is to be expected as pears rarely fruit until they have been established for 5–7 years.

Pollination can also be an important factor in fruiting behaviour. Williams, also known as Williams Bon Chretien or Bartlett, is the only variety regarded as self-pollinating, but even so, this produces better crops when accompanied by Beurre Bosc or Winter Cole. Any of these pears can be used as suitable pollinators for each other and also for Packham's Triumph.

Severe black spot infestations may attack flower stems and prevent fruiting. The latter is more likely to occur during a very wet spring.
Problem: Fruit with brown tunnelling from blossom end at base and around the seed. Here a small pinkish caterpillar may be present, or a tunnel will lead to a hole in the side of the fruit which the caterpillar has left to begin its pupa stage.
Cause: Codling moths.
Solution: Spray with Carbaryl approximately 1 month after flower petals have fallen, then every 2–3 weeks, or until spraying for fruit fly control commences. For further details see under apples.
Problem: Brown rot around seed area of fruit with maggots present.
Cause: Fruit fly.
Solution: See heading 'Fruit fly control'.
Problem: Flesh with brownish-grey stain around seed area, but without eaten or grub-damaged area as described under codling moth or fruit fly damage.
Cause: Fruit allowed to ripen on the tree or kept too long in storage. This applies particularly to Williams.
Solution: Pick fruit when skin is fairly green, but starting to show the first flush of yellow, and store individually wrapped until ripe.
Problem: Black spots on leaves and flower stalks.
Cause: Fungus disease known as black spot or pear scab. The problem is worse during a wet or humid spring period and usually disappears in climates with a comparatively dry atmosphere such as Western Australia.
Solution: Spray thoroughly with copper spray as flower buds approach the opening stage, then fortnightly with Captan or Benlate.
Problem: Foliage dull and sandblasted.
Cause: Red spider mite.
Solution: At the first sign of mottling (the more protected foliage is usually the first affected) spray with Lebaycid or Rogor used for control of fruit fly.
Problem: Clusters of dull reddish specks on stems or branches.
Cause: Byrobia mite.
Solution: If apparent before new growth commences during dormant period use winter spraying oil, otherwise treat as red spider mite.
Problem: Tiny grey scabs on twigs, branches

and sometimes on the main limbs and fruit.
Cause: Red José scale.
Solution: Use winter spraying oil during dormant period before growth commences. Otherwise use 2 tablespoons of white oil plus 1 teaspoon of Rogor or Lebaycid per 4.5 L of water when flowering is over and young fruit are well formed.

Persimmon

An attractive umbrella-shaped small tree with large oval foliage that colours beautifully in autumn while the tree is still holding its large showy tomato-like fruits. They grow in all but the coldest and extreme tropical districts and do not mind tough, slow-draining soil.

Requirements

Although persimmons will tolerate heavy clay soils, the young plant will establish more readily if up to about one-third compost or a good soil conditioner is mixed in with the surrounding soil. Once new growth is established in spring they may be fed at monthly intervals with any of the water-soluble plant foods soaked in around the root area.

Mature trees fruit more readily if complete plant food is applied, allowing about one-quarter cup per sq. m of area below the branch line, in late winter or early spring and again in mid-summer. Surface mulching is desirable to conserve moisture during the spring and summer growing period and to eliminate the need for cultivation which would disturb the surface roots of the tree.
Planting time. Persimmons purchased growing in containers can be planted with safety at any time providing the roots are not unduly disturbed, but bare-rooted trees are only planted during their winter deciduous period.

General care

Pruning. This is carried out initially to shape the young tree. If a low-branching effect is preferred, cut back at planting time to about 50 cm above the soil. When new shoots develop below the cut, rub off or thin out all but 3 or 4 evenly-spaced ones headed in different directions. Once trees are established they are usually given a light all-over pruning in winter to encourage new growth which is the fruit-bearing wood.

Varieties

Seedling trees may be either male or female and require another tree close in the vicinity for pollination. It is better to buy grafted trees which are self-pollinating and of known quality such as **Dai Dai Maru, Yemon** and **Tanenashi,** and **Nightingale,** which is a compact grower suitable for small areas.

Growing problems and solutions

Problem: Failure to fruit. Most of the main varieties sold by nurseries these days are self-pollinating. However, it is possible to get a seedling of one of the older varieties which are not.

Persimmons fruit on wood made the current spring; dry weather or heavily-compacted soil can prevent fruiting. Excess nitrogen due to a tree growing in or on the edge of a lawn frequently fed with sulphate of ammonia will cause lush foliage as will compost made largely from lawn clippings, but there will be a shortage of phosphorus which is needed for the production of fruit.

Solution: Offset nitrogen excess by applying 1 handful of superphosphate per sq. m of area below the spread of the tree in early spring to induce fruit for late summer or early autumn.

Problem: Fruit rotting with maggots inside.

Cause: Fruit fly.

Solution: See heading 'Fruit fly control'.

Pineapple

Pineapples are best suited to tropical or semitropical areas but can be grown in the more humid warm temperate areas in sunny positions sheltered from cold winds.

Requirements

Plenty of moisture during the summer-growing period. Progress and fruit size are improved by mulching the soil liberally with organic material and giving a light scattering of complete plant food (approximately 1 handful per sq. m of area surrounding the plant) every 8–10 weeks.

After fruiting the old plant dies out and the offshoots are replanted.

Planting time. In the home garden pineapples can be started from pineapple tops removed from the fruit with a few cm of the top skin or the core present and covered with soil. Commercially they are grown from offshoots of the old plants which may produce fruit 18 months to 2 years after planting.

Plum

Plums, like peaches and other deciduous fruit trees, can be used to provide both summer shade and fruit in small gardens. The European plums require a fairly cool winter to mature their wood and to set a good crop, but the Japanese plums are more adaptable to warmer temperate areas.

Requirements

For soil moisture, feeding and initial pruning and shaping of trees, see apples.

Planting time. Plums are normally sold as bare-rooted trees so should be planted when dormant during winter.

General care

Pruning may vary. Some plums produce flower or fruit on wood made during the previous growing season as well as on spurs from the older wood, so prune mature trees as suggested for apricots.

Varieties

Japanese

Most of these are self-pollinating to a degree and others such as Santa Rosa and Satsuma are completely self-pollinating. Santa Rosa is a suitable pollinator for all other varieties of Japanese plums including:

Donsworth — a large fine-flavoured blood plum ripening in early December.

Mariposa — a very large, dark, heavy-cropping mid-season variety.

Narrabeen — large with red skin and very sweet yellow flesh which is firm and juicy; ripens early February.

Santa Rosa — large oval purplish-crimson with attractive powdery bloom and good light-red flesh; ripens Christmas time. Has an upright growth and so, for more lateral form, needs pruning to side laterals.

Satsuma — generally known as the Japanese blood plum with large fruit and very dark-red flesh. Crops early.

Wickson — very large, heart-shaped slip-stone plum with yellow flesh and skin blushed red. Ripens mid-January and is pollinated by Narrabeen.

Wilson — round, medium-sized yellow-fleshed plum with bright crimson skin; ripening November.

European

Angelina Burdett — dark purple skin with juicy yellow flesh, ripens early. Pollinated by President, Grand Duke or Greengage.

Cherry Plum (Red American) — small to medium with bright-red skin, slip-stone and self-pollinating; very early.

Grand Duke — one of the finest late plums with purplish-black skin and firm yellow flesh. Pollinated by Angelina Burdett.

Greengage — green-skinned, light-yellow flesh, slip-stone, renowned for its distinctive flavour. Needs cool climate to bear well; pollinated by Grand Duke.

Growing problems and solutions

Problem: Failure to fruit.

Cause: Lack of a suitable pollinator — another plum flowering at the same time.

A number of plums, including the Japanese blood plum (Satsuma), Red American Jewel, Monarch and Santa Rosa, are self-pollinating but others such as Narrabeen, Wickson and yellow-fleshed Wilson all need pollinators. Conveniently adaptable and self-pollinating Santa Rosa will also act as a pollinator for the other varieties mentioned.

Problem: Flesh around the stone of the fruit rotted and maggoty.

Cause: Fruit fly.

Solution: See heading 'Fruit fly control'.

Problem: Soft brown rotted patch usually appearing first on side of fruit then rapidly spreading.

Cause: Brown rot.

Solution: When flower buds begin to show colour, use copper spray plus 2 tablespoons of white oil mixed separately, then added to each 4.5 L of spray mixture. If weather is showery, spray with Benlate soon after petals have fallen then fortnightly while moist conditions persist.

Problem: Foliage shows dark spots that fall out to leave a shot-hole appearance.

Cause: Shot-hole fungus.

Solution: Spray as for brown rot at petal fall and repeat copper spray during autumn.

Problem: Yellow spots on foliage, velvety-brown on corresponding underside.

Cause: Rust.

Solution: Use white oil spray as for brown rot initially, then when foliage reaches full size, spray with Zineb or Mancozeb.

Problem: Tiny grey scabs clustered on branches, twigs and sometimes on fruit. Dieback follows long-standing infestation.

Cause: San José scale.

Solution: Spray with winter oil before flowering commences.

Problem: Leaves dull silvery colour and falling prematurely. Where problem persists, branches will show irregular felt-like purplish patches which are the sporing bodies of this destructive disease and will die.

Cause: A branch-invading fungus known as silverleaf.

Solution: If only 1 or 2 branches are affected, prune back into clean unstained wood and carefully burn prunings. Dab all cuts with copper spray mixed with water to paint-like consistency and when dry seal with tree paint.

If the entire tree is affected, chances of recovery are small so it is better to remove and burn all parts rather than leave it as a source of infection.

Quince

Quinces adapt to a wide range of climates from semi-tropical to cool districts. Prolonged rainfall during the spring and early summer-growing period can cause troublesome fungus diseases, particularly 'fleck', which defoliates the trees and spoils the fruit. In very cold districts some protection from late spring frosts is needed.

Requirements

The same as pears or apples. Prune in the same way.

Planting time. Quinces which are normally dug from the open ground (bare-rooted) are planted during the dormant winter period.

Varieties

Although quinces are generally self-pollinating they usually produce a better crop when another variety is grown nearby.

Champion — very large fruit with good-flavoured tender flesh and excellent keeping qualities.

Missouri Mammoth — huge mild-flavoured fruit with smooth skin.

Smyrna — large fruit with good flavour and excellent keeping qualities.

Growing problems and solutions

Problem: Brownish flecks on leaves which yellow and fall prematurely. Fruit may also be spotted.

Cause: Leaf blight or scald — found in humid, coastal districts and more frequently with a wet spring.

Solution: Rake up and burn all fallen leaves then spray to wet all parts of the tree with copper spray. Repeat this treatment particularly after showery periods.

Quinces are also susceptible to codling moth and fruit fly attack. See both problems under apples or pears.

Rosella

Bushy annual shrubs 1 or 2 m high with succulent reddish stems, attractively divided bronze-green foliage, and small cream hibiscus-like flowers which are followed by a fleshy red calyx. This is often used to make jams and jellies. Harvest before it toughens.

Requirements

Rosellas are more suited to tropical and semitropical districts as they need a long summer-growing period. They are best in sunny but sheltered positions with a well-drained, preferably loamy soil.

Add about 1 handful of complete plant food per sq. m to the soil prior to planting out and, after planting, a mulch of compost would be beneficial. Keep well watered during the spring and summer months.

Planting time. Rosellas are raised from seeds sown in spring. Being bushy plants they need to be set out about 150 cm apart or are decorative enough to be used as clumps scattered here and there in the ornamental part of the garden.

Tamarillo — *Tree tomato or Cyphomandra*

Small umbrella-shaped trees up to 4 m in height with pendulous, oval, reddish fruits used mainly as a dessert or for jam. They commence bearing in the second year from seed or seedlings and, under most circumstances, deteriorate after about 5 years, so it is advisable to renew them occasionally. The tree tomato grows in all districts except those with very cold winters.

Requirements

A fairly open sunny position with shelter from strong winds and a well-drained soil. In very sandy or heavy clay soils work in a bucket of well-rotted compost about 50 cm around where the tree will be planted.

Planting time. In frost-prone districts start nursery-grown plants in late spring, elsewhere they may be planted any time of the year. Tree tomatoes may be raised from seed taken from mature fruits and sown when fresh, or left until spring.

General care

After about 6 weeks, if new growth is evident, sprinkle 1 handful of complete plant food in a broad circle starting about 75 cm out from the stem of the plant; rake in lightly and water thoroughly.

Surface mulching is helpful but keep the mulch about a span from the stem. If growth is slow, occasionally soak the root area with one of the complete water-soluble plant foods. After 6–8 months, when the tree is approaching maturity, feed either with dressings of fowl manure or 1 handful per sq. m of complete plant food applied in spring, then again in mid-summer and autumn. Water liberally during the spring and summer-growing periods.

Pruning. Pinch out the tip from the plant when it reaches about 2 m to encourage branching. Lightly prune back the laterals after fruiting to promote new growth but do not cut back heavily into new wood.

Growing problems and solutions

Problem: Ash-like film on foliage.
Cause: Powdery mildew usually troublesome during cool, moist conditions.
Solution: Use copper spray or spray with Benlate.

Problem: Sudden wilting of foliage.
Cause: Root rot, usually only troublesome in badly-drained areas or in heavy soils that remain wet for long periods after rain.
Solution: The disease cannot be cured so the only solution is to replant in a more favourable area.

Problem: Gradual yellowing, loss of foliage and productivity.
Cause: As with passion-fruit this is usually due to a virus disease which shortens the productive life of the tree tomato.
Solution: Theoretically a complete control of aphids would guarantee freedom from the disease but the more practical approach is to plant a replacement tree every 3–4 years.

Grow strawberry guavas in frost-free areas

Yellow-fleshed Elberta peaches ripen in January

The persimmon tree is small, umbrella-shaped

Have fruit in small areas by espaliering the trees

A cultivation guide to growing berries and vines

Currant *(Ribes)*

Currants are only suitable for cool moist climates. The black currant makes a caney plant while the red or white currant grows as single-stemmed bushes.

Requirements

Currants prefer a deep, cool, moist, well-drained soil with plenty of organic material. Once plants are established they may be fed in spring with either fowl manure or about one-third of a cup of citrus or rose food per sq. m of area surrounding the plant.

Planting time. Currants are planted while growth is dormant during winter. When plants are not available they can be propagated from cuttings taken from the current season's wood during late autumn. Use about pencil-length pieces for black currants and at least half as long again for red or white currants. On the latter, all but the top 3 or 4 buds are removed to prevent base suckering. Red and white currants are spaced about 150 cm apart and black currants a little further because of their spreading habit.

General care

Plenty of water during the spring and early summer-growing period is essential.

Pruning:

Black currants. At planting time most of the growth is cut back leaving only one strong bud at the base of the cane. As more canes develop weak and spindly ones should be removed. Fruit comes mainly on canes of the current season's growth. These will produce some fruits the following season also, but the general aim is to remove the canes as they are ageing to make room for plenty of new growth. Older, usually darker canes are cut out just above ground-level.

Red or white currants. When cuttings are planted all buds less than 15 cm from soil-level are removed, leaving only 3 or 4 buds at the top. By the following winter these cutting-grown plants are similar to those normally purchased as planting stock from nurseries. At this stage the canes are cut back to half-size, making the cut just above an outward-pointing bud. The following winter similar procedure is followed, cutting the canes that develop during the current season back to about half or a little harder to leave less buds if the growth is inclined to be weak. During the third winter the canes are reduced to about one-third of their growth. A good well-branched bush should now be established and the current season's canes cut much harder, to just above a bud a few cm from their base.

Summer pruning is also advisable with red and white currants. Rub off or remove any shoots growing toward the centre of the plant. Then when the shoots of the laterals or side growths have lost their sappiness and the wood is starting to turn brown, cut them back to just above the third or fourth leaf from the base.

Growing problems and solutions

Problem: Buds enlarged and distorted, failing to develop further.
Cause: Bud or gall mite.
Solution: Spray with lime sulphur in late winter or early spring, before foliage or flower buds open, or later with wettable sulphur. Galled buds should be removed and burnt.
Problem: Buds failing to develop; dark, shrivelled appearance.
Cause: Eelworm (nematode).
Solution: Remove and burn affected buds or shoots then spray with Rogor or Lebaycid.
Problem: Dark spots on leaves which fall prematurely.
Cause: Leaf spot.
Solution: Use copper spray as flowers begin to open then when most petals have fallen spray with Mancozeb or Benlate.
Problem: Leaves webbed together, inner sections eaten and damaged areas expanding as leaves enlarge.
Cause: A very quick-moving, leaf roller caterpillar.
Solution: Spray with Carbaryl or Endosulphan except when plants are flowering.

Gooseberry

The true gooseberry or bush gooseberry (*Ribes grossularia*) is only suitable for growing in cool climates and the plants can be injured if heavy, late spring frosts occur after new growth has developed.

Requirements

Gooseberries need a well-drained but fairly moist loamy soil which is not too acid (soil that would normally produce pink blooms from untreated hydrangeas). Therefore, in all but naturally limey soils, plants will establish better if three-quarters to one cup of garden lime or dolomite is added to each sq. m of bed prior to planting, and then about every second year afterwards.

Planting time. Gooseberries are planted during their winter dormant period. Plants are normally set in rows with 50–150 cm between each plant in the row.

General care

As gooseberries prefer plant food containing a high rate of potash, most brands of rose food are suitable and should be applied as the first spring growth commences at the rate of about 1 handful per sq. m of area surrounding the plant. Alternatively, one of the standard soluble lawn foods applied at this rate would be suitable.

Commercial growers usually apply a dressing of sulphate of potash in late winter–early spring just before new growth commences. However, these generous applications of potash tend to emphasise magnesium deficiency to which bush gooseberries are particularly sensitive. This deficiency shows by a reddening of the leaf margins which later become pale yellow. If evident, this deficiency can be corrected by liberally watering the plants with a solution of Epsom Salts mixed at the rate of

about 1 tablespoon per 9 L of water. If dolomite is applied instead of lime the magnesium deficiency is less likely to occur.

Pruning. At planting time thin out all but the three strongest stems on the bush, then shorten these back to about a span length. The following winter all the main branches should be shortened back to about half their length and each side shoot taken back to just above the lowest part of the stem. Remove any excess or unwanted growth to allow plenty of sun into the centre of the bush.

When bushes are established shorten back main branches to about one-third or half their length, the stronger side shoots to about finger length and weaker shoots close to the main branches.

Varieties

The three most popular varieties grown in Australia are **Crown Bob** which is a reddish-coloured gooseberry, **Selection** which is yellow, and greenish-yellow **Yorkshire Champion.**

Growing problems and solutions

English gooseberries or Ribes which are grown mainly in cool climates.
Problem: Sudden wilting of foliage. If cut longitudinally lower stems show reddish-purple stain along the conducting tissues of the wood.
Cause: Fungus wilt (*verticillium*).
Solution: Infected plant should be removed and burnt. Do not plant gooseberries in the same patch of soil.
Problem: Leaves gradually turn brown. Serious infestations may kill the bush.
Cause: Botrytis or grey mould, most troublesome during wet or very humid conditions.
Solution: Spray and thoroughly wet the plant with Benlate or Captan.
Problem: Leaves with reddish margins then becoming creamy-yellow on either side of the main vein.
Cause: Magnesium deficiency.
Solution: Dissolve 1 heaped teaspoon of Epsom Salts (magnesium sulphate) in a 10 L can of water and soak in around the root area of the plant. If soil is very acidic, apply about three-quarters of a cup of dolomite per sq. m of area, rake into soil and water well.
Problem: Ash-like film over foliage.
Cause: Powdery mildew.
Solution: Use Benlate or Karathane.
Problem: Brown leaf spotting, usually with angular flecks on underside.
Cause: Leaf spot.
Solution: Use copper spray just prior to bud burst as a preventive or, if already evident, spray with Mancozeb or Zineb.

Cape gooseberry

The Cape gooseberry is a soft-stemmed spreading bush with large, slightly hairy dull-green foliage and orange berries in a lantern-shaped papery husk. The bushes are perennial in warm climates or, sown in spring, and grown as annuals in cooler areas. They are capable of producing fruit the first season from seed.

Requirements

Cape gooseberries are often found growing satisfactorily in partly shaded areas but are at their best in full sun and when given some support similar to that used for tomatoes. They grow well in all but the heaviest soils providing drainage is good.

Planting time. As Cape gooseberries do not transplant well they should be sown in pots, a couple of seeds to each, then thinned out to the strongest seedling and transplanted to the permanent position without root disturbance. Or, 2 or 3 seeds can be sown at intervals of 1 m along a row of trellis and later thinned out to the strongest plant.

General care

Prior to sowing work a dressing of well-rotted compost plus about 1 handful per sq. m of complete plant food into the soil. Keep the surface well mulched and give the soil occasional soakings during dry periods.

Pruning. Little or no pruning is needed until after the first crop of fruits.

Chinese gooseberry

Chinese gooseberries make a large and rather heavy spreading vine which needs substantial trellising at least 2 m in height. Each vine may develop a spread of 3–4 m. Fruit is carried only by the female plants, so a male plant is needed for pollination. One male plant is sufficient to pollinate about 8 females. It is sometimes possible to buy a plant grafted with male and female branches, or to bud a male plant onto a female one, but in either case both sections need clear marking so that one is not removed by pruning. It is also important to obtain male and female varieties which flower at the same time.

Requirements

Chinese gooseberries do best in a sunny position with some shelter from strong winds. They need a well-drained and friable loamy soil with plenty of organic material added.

They normally commence fruiting about 4 years after planting but take 7–8 years to reach full productivity.

Planting time. Plant when the vines are deciduous during their dormant winter period. As the vines are vigorous space them at least 4 m apart.

General care

Soil needs to be kept moist during late spring and summer, and because plants are gross feeders maintain a surface mulch of compost or similar organic material. Feed when new growth commences. Treat them as instructed for avocados, using high nitrogenous fertilisers during the early stages when the plants are establishing, then change to a complete plant food containing more phosphorus as they approach the fruiting stage. Apply the latter at the rate of 1 handful per sq. m when new spring growth commences, then again at intervals of 8–10 weeks during the summer. Always water liberally after feeding.

Pruning. Chinese gooseberries usually make an abundance of growth which needs to be reduced. Select one strong shoot as the main stem and train to the top of the trellis. Allow a shoot to develop in another direction to take the vine along the top of the trellis. Growth that develops along these shoots is then thinned to about 50 cm apart. It is preferable to do this heavy pruning early in winter, otherwise a great deal of sap is lost by 'bleeding' from the pruning cuts.

Further pruning is needed as growth develops. Remove excessive shoots that develop early in the season. Fruit grows only on the lower 4 or 5 buds of new growth which comes from 1-year-old canes. To encourage these to flower and form good-quality fruit it is necessary to shorten back anything in excess of 6 or 7 buds. The following winter these shoots are cut back to about 2 buds from the base.

Water shoots or sappy growths from the main leader cane should be removed except when needed to replace a fruiting cane which is becoming old and woody. The latter is then removed in winter. Fruit usually develops during autumn and early winter. It may be picked when fully developed and stored to ripen in a cool place for 6–8 weeks. This is desirable as in fruit-fly areas fruit softening toward the ripening stage is susceptible to fruit fly attack. However, fruit picked too early will shrivel and have poor flavour.

Varieties

Amongst the best cropping females are **Abbott, Allison, Bruno** and **Montey**. The longest-flowering male variety and therefore the most widely suitable for pollination is **Matua**, but other varieties are being developed, so before purchasing check this point with your nursery.

Growing problems and solutions

Problem: Failure to fruit.
Cause: Only the female vines fruit and a male vine is needed to pollinate every 5–10 females. It is essential to have a male variety that flowers at the same time as the females. Over-leafiness is another cause of poor cropping.
Solution: Thin out excessive growth so that fruit-bearing wood is exposed to the light. Chinese gooseberries are like grapes in that they produce fruit only from the current season's wood, which grows on wood from the previous season. The first 4–5 buds produce the fruit. Remove excess shoots and, after fruiting, any unproductive ones except those that may be needed to replace an old cane during the main pruning time which is mid-winter. Later pruning may result in loss of sap or bleeding of canes.
Problem: Petals and embryo fruit shrivel prematurely.
Cause: Botrytis mould.
Solution: Spray with Captan or Benlate at the first sign of a petal shrivelling and, if necessary, prune back excessive growth to allow air and light to the flowers.
Problem: Small, white, waxy globules on shoots or stems which may later cause disfiguring of fruit.
Cause: Scale.
Solution: Spray with Malathion or Lebaycid.

adding 1 tablespoon of white oil per 4.5 L of spray mixture.
Problem: Fruit furrowed or with large scarred areas.
Cause: Damage by caterpillars.
Solution: Spray with Carbaryl at first signs of attack.

Grape

Grapes make quick-growing, vigorous and decorative vines and are often used for the dual purpose of producing fruits and giving summer shade. In their deciduous stage in winter, sunlight can filter through their branches.

Requirements

Grapes perform best in temperate areas with dry summers. They grow in a variety of soils including very shaley or clayey ones which must be well drained. Although grapes are often found growing in poor soils they will establish more rapidly if, prior to planting, heavy clay soils are broken down with the addition of well-rotted compost, or moistened peatmoss is mixed with very sandy soils, and a surface mulch of organic material applied after planting in both cases.

Planting time. Planted in winter either from cuttings or from established nursery plants in the deciduous stage.

General care

Give plenty of water when new growth commences, and if the soil is poor and compost has not been previously added, scatter a small handful of complete plant food over the sq. m or so of soil surrounding the plant.

Well-established plants will benefit from about twice this quantity of plant food applied in spring and again in autumn.

Pruning. Carried out in mid-winter. The first winter after planting, all but the most vigorous upright cane is cut out and this is cut back to a point just through the third bud from the base. Tie a piece of twine around the swollen section of the base and stretch either to the top wire or top of the trellis. When growth comes from the two lower buds during spring remove the weaker shoot and tie the stronger one carefully to the twine so that it is protected from damage on its way up to the top of the trellis. Pinch out the growing tip about a span above the top of the trellis to induce branching from the sides. When the latter develops, the most convenient side shoots toward the top on either side are trained along the wires to from a T-shaped plant. Any further shoots developing from the main upright cane are rubbed off as they appear.

Pruning during the third year depends on the vigour of the growth produced. If moderately vigorous, cut back the two canes heading along the wire to just beyond the third or fourth bud on each; leave the arms about 30–35 cm in length, then carefully tie them to the wires. When growth commences in spring any surplus buds, particularly those close to the junction of the T or fork, should be rubbed off.

During the third winter untwist and cut back

the lateral canes at the end of each arm of the T-piece to about 3 buds. This procedure is carried out each season to extend the main arms of the vine along the wire until they reach the desired length. Shorten the lateral growth from the remaining buds closer to the T to just above the second bud from the base — if it is a reasonably vigorous lateral — if not, make the cut above the first bud from the base. These buds should produce fruiting wood during the coming season.

The principle of grape pruning. The procedure laid down for pruning grapes may sound involved, but the idea is to establish a strong and permanent framework for the vine. It is easier to appreciate the reason for subsequent pruning once it is realised that grapes produce fruit only on the new season's wood, which grows from the previous season's wood. Any shoots coming from older than 2-year-old canes are classed as water shoots. These are unproductive and are removed unless they are required to replace or renew part of the framework of the vine.

It is also desirable to keep the fruiting arms of the vine on one level, otherwise those on an upper level will draw excessively on the plant's resources and the lower growths will gradually fail.

When planting to cover a pergola, the best idea is to have two plants: one trained to cover the top and the other trained in a fan shape to cover the side.

With bush grapes the general pruning principles already outlined still apply except that the plant should be shortened to produce two main arms by cutting it just above the second bud from the base. During following winters remove excessive growth and cut back all remaining canes or laterals to just above 1 or 2 buds from the base.

Varieties

Except in climates with very dry summers most grapes are subject to several different fungus diseases and can only be grown successfully in humid districts if sprayed regularly.

Isabella is the most disease-resistant grape and the most suitable for humid coastal districts. Is a vigorous grower and prolific producer. The dark rounded fruit has a musky flavour and though not the best eating grape it is good for making jam.

Others reasonably suitable to coastal districts include:

Black Muscat — carries bunches of medium-sized black oval berries with a definite rich muscat flavour; early.

Cardinal — has fleshy red fruits of excellent flavour; early.

Varieties more suited to climates with a dry summer atmosphere include:

Black Lady's Finger (Purple Cornichon) — similar in shape to the well-known Lady's Finger type with dark glossy skin but more resistant to black spot disease. Late-bearing.

Black Sultana — a good black seedless grape; mid-season.

Calmeria — attractive and good-flavoured white fleshy grapes; mid-season.

Gordo Blanco (White Muscat) — a very popular variety with good flavour; late.

Italia — large bunches of large, rounded golden-white berries with excellent eating qualities; late.

Nyora — black fleshy grape most suited to inland climates; mid-season.

Ohanez — large white with good flavour; late.

Sultana — a very popular eating grape with small, oval, very sweet seedless fruits; mid-season.

Waltham Cross — very large bunches of round, thin but very tough-skinned attractive pale-amber fruits with excellent flavour. A late variety particularly suited to warm districts.

Growing problems and solutions

Problem: Lack of fruit.
Cause: Often due to pruning too heavily as grapes bear only from growth from the previous season's wood.
Solution: Prune in winter leaving 2 buds only at the base of the stems made during the previous spring and summer.

Powdery mildew, which shows as an ash-like film on foliage, may also attack flowers and so prevent formation of fruit. This is controlled by using copper spray when new growth first commences then after wet, humid periods.

Problem: Oily or water-soaked patches on grapes which then become soft and brown. Patches of grey mould evident.
Cause: Botrytis or brown mould which is usually only prevalent during wet or humid conditions.
Solution: Watch for signs of rotting during or after wet periods and if evident spray with Captan or Benlate.

Problem: Discoloration of grapes and stalks of the bud. Some grapes shrivel.
Cause: Bunch mite.
Solution: Spray with wettable sulphur or dust with sulphur. In areas where this pest is troublesome, spray with lime sulphur just before spring growth commences to avoid burning off tender leaves.

Problem: Black spotting of foliage and fruit, often with some splitting of the latter.
Cause: Black spot fungus which may occur on some varieties if cool, moist conditions occur in early spring after new growth has started.
Solution: Spray with Zineb or Mancozeb.

Problem: Water-soaked blotches on foliage which turns yellow then shrivels. During moist conditions, white tufts of fungi appear on underside of foliage and sometimes on the grapes.
Cause: Downy mildew.
Solution: Zineb or Mancozeb are the accepted controls for this disease, but copper spray is also helpful against downy, as well as powdery, mildew.

Problem: Blisters on foliage with felt-like creamy-yellow or reddish-brown patches on underside.
Cause: Grape leaf blister mite.
Solution: Spray with wettable sulphur as suggested for bunch mites, or with Kelthane. Malathion applied with a wetting agent also gives some control.

Problem: Foliage skeletonised.
Cause: Caterpillars, usually the blue-grey and yellow-striped grapevine caterpillar.
Solution: When vines are over living areas where poisons are unacceptable, use Pyrethrum-type sprays or substances such as Dipel, a culture of bacillus which affects only true caterpillars, but must be sprayed with a wetting agent to coat all parts of foliage thoroughly. Otherwise Carbaryl, which remains toxic for only 3 days, is most effective.

Grapevines for a cool summer

Grapevines give cool summer shade, plenty of winter sun, stand rugged conditions and bear juicy and delicious fruit. They are happiest in fairly dry districts, although they grow almost anywhere. There are varieties that fruit reliably in all but tropical districts, and grapes are one of the few crops that flourish in poor, tough soil.

Many of the world's fine wine-producing vineyards cling to steep hillsides along the Rhine and in France, Italy and Spain. In most of these areas the soil is rough shale and shingle or tough clay, in which even the native grasses have to struggle miserably.

Districts with low rainfall, particularly those with dry summers, grow the best grapes but types, e.g. Isabella, crop well even in humid areas without any need for frequent spraying. They are musky in flavour, but are relatively free of fungus diseases.

Apart from the fruit, grapevines are worth growing for their beautiful foliage and welcome summer shade, while the vines can be cut right back to their supports during winter, allowing full penetration of sun when it is appreciated.

If growing a grape mainly for summer shade and beauty of foliage, the 'ornamental grape' (*Vitis Alicante Bouchet*) is by far the best choice. It covers rapidly and colours brilliantly in autumn.

Even though grapevines grow well in soils generally considered poor, they still respond to feeding, e.g. a dressing of animal manure applied in autumn or a complete fertiliser containing plenty of potash in spring. Good drainage is essential.

It is simple to grow grapes in large containers, particularly for decoration. Wooden wine casks suit the vines beautifully, but any container over about 35 cm in diameter and at least as deep can support a large vine for a number of years. A vine in a container should not be allowed to become too dry in spring and summer.

Grapes may be grown as relatively low bushes or as high-branching climbers for trellises or pergolas.

In some districts certain varieties may be traditionally grown as bush or trellis types, but the type of growth depends mainly on the training they receive in their first year.

Bush types are cut back to the two lowest buds initially, then pruned back each winter to the lowest of last summer's buds on the canes.

Encourage trellis grapes initially to make one cane, or two if a fan-shaped spread is preferred. The following winter cut back the selected cane or canes to two buds at the top of the trellis where growth is required. Rub off all lower buds or growths that subsequently develop.

Remember when you prune grapes that fruit develops only on the new season's growth, which has come from the previous season's growth.

After a few years of pruning the bush or trellis grape makes a number of cane stubs or spurs, so each of these are usually allowed to carry only 1 or 2 buds each. Eventually some of the older stubs are cut out entirely. Pruning is done during the dormant period.

Ornamental grapes may be cut as lightly or as heavily as needed but it is usually tidier and more convenient for maximum winter sun to keep the main vine framework to the trellis or pergola supports.

Each winter cut all the previous summer's growth back to the lowest bud, much in the same way as suggested for fruiting grapes.

Grapes are normally sold as bare-rooted plants that have been struck from the previous year's cuttings. Therefore these plants can only be transplanted with safety during their dormant winter period.

They are handled in much the same way as roses or bare-rooted summer fruit trees, taking care not to let the roots dry out, and, instead of digging a deep hole, prepare a wide planting hole to encourage a healthy root spread.

Roots are helped by mixing in a little well-rotted compost, or in heavy soils some sand, even though fruit quality is usually best in tough soils.

Do not add fertiliser until the new growth develops in spring — feed only sparingly and water well.

Loganberry

Loganberries could be best described as half-way between blackberries and raspberries, with rather long fleshy fruits on caney growths. They are best suited to cool and temperate areas.

Requirements

An open sunny position with well-drained, preferably loamy or heavy soil lightened by the addition of large amounts of compost. They should be grown on trellises up to 2 m high supported on taller posts about 2 m apart, setting a plant at each post.

Planting time. During the winter dormant period.

General care

The first year allow all growths to grow upright and tie loosely to a post. The next winter arch the canes down and tie along the wires of the trellis which should be one-third to half a metre apart. Canes made during the next growing season are also loosely tied in an upright position ready to replace canes which have finished fruiting. During the next winter cut away the old canes.

Feed in early spring with a dressing of fowl manure or one-third of a cup of complete plant

food per metre of row. Keep well watered during spring and summer.

Growing problems and solutions

Problem: Failure to fruit.
Solution: These berries produce only on canes made the previous season. Loganberries really need to be grown on trellises with the strongest of canes, made the previous season and tied down to the wires during winter. New canes made during spring and summer are usually held together in an upright position. The strongest of these are tied down to the wires the following winter after the old ones that have fruited have been cut away to ground level.

Problem: Fruit becomes dry and split, reddish patches on foliage.
Cause: Downy mildew.
Solution: Spray with lime sulphur after pruning while vines are still dormant, then with Mancozeb or Zineb after flower petals have fallen.

Problem: Fruits misshapen, purplish-grey spots on canes.
Cause: A fungus disease known as cane spot.
Solution: Treat as for downy mildew in previous paragraph then, when new growth commences, use copper spray. As an added precaution spray with Mancozeb after flower petals fall.

Problem: Orange, velvet-like spots that deepen to a chocolate colour on foliage.
Cause: Rust.
Solution: Treat as above.

Mulberry

The English or black mulberry is most suitable to cool or cooler temperate districts, although it is sometimes grown and found cropping well in mild temperate areas. This is a slow-growing tree which produces large black fruits of excellent quality. The Cape mulberry is more suitable to semi-tropical and temperate districts as it resents heavy frost. It is by far the most rapid grower and frequently appears as a volunteer seedling with vigorous and comparatively upright growth. On maturity the small grape-like leaves become much larger and elliptical to heart-shaped. Leaves of both species are fed to silkworms.

Requirements

Both mulberries need a position with at least half sun and plenty of water during spring, and for the English mulberry, in summer also. The latter fruits mainly late summer. The Cape mulberry fruits in spring but with mid-summer rains may produce another crop in autumn.

General care

The Cape mulberry can crop well in moderate or even poor soils with a little feeding. In very poor conditions give a complete plant food early autumn at the rate of 1 handful per sq. m of area below the branch line of the tree. Manures or composts high in nitrogen will encourage excess vegetation. This should be counteracted by giving a small handful of superphosphate per sq. m of area below the branch line.

The English mulberry is slow to establish and should be assisted by soakings around the root area every 3–4 weeks with one of the

Strawberries require sun most of the day

complete water-soluble plant foods, or a dressing of slow-release granular plant food. Once reasonable growth is established, revert to either fowl manure or a complete fertiliser applied in early spring.

Pruning. Mulberries need very little pruning. In the case of the English mulberry prune only when necessary to thin out growth or to remove old growth. If it is necessary to reduce size of Cape mulberry, cut back to immediately above a relatively subdued lower branch in each section of the tree, otherwise an overall general pruning causes a surge of over-vigorous vegetative growth.

Passion-fruit

The purple or black passion-fruit (*Passiflora edulus*) is best suited to tropical and temperate areas where frosts are not severe and humidity is relatively high. They make attractive evergreen vines for covering fences, trellises, etc. but unfortunately rarely remain productive and attractive for more than a few years as they are subject to a virus which gradually debilitates them. Therefore a replacement vine should be planted at least every 2 years.

Requirements

Passion-fruit will grow in half shade but the crop is more prolific in full sunshine. However, the plants can be set out in the shade of a fence to grow up into sun. They are at their best in well-drained light loamy soils where plenty of water is available during spring and summer, but can also be established in heavier soils if rotted composts, preferably some sand or a good soil conditioner, are worked in prior to planting. Over-rich soils heavily supplied with nitrogen produce an abundance of lush vegetative growth at the expense of fruit.

If the soil is poor, speed the growth of young plants by feeding at 3–4-weekly intervals during the warmer months with one of the water-soluble plant foods until they have made a couple of metres of growth or reached the top of their fence or trellising. Then use the standard-type complete plant food which contains more phosphorus. Apply at the rate of 1 handful per sq. m of area for 1–2 m out from the main stem of the plant, every 6–8 weeks from spring to early autumn, providing it is possible to keep the soil reasonably moist during this period.

Planting time. In frost-free warm districts passion-fruit may be planted out at any time, but where winters are cool, spring planting is recommended.

General care

Surface mulching encourages better root growth and helps to maintain moisture needed during the warmer months, but should be kept back 20–25 cm from the main stem. Apply the plant food recommended over the mulch.

Pruning. This is done in early spring in temperate regions or at any time between flushes of fruit in tropical areas. The growth is thinned out by removing laterals which are closer than two-thirds to 1 m apart. Wandering shoots can be curbed by pruning them back to just beyond a side lateral or by arching about

50 cm of the tip growth in a downward position.

Passion-fruits normally crop within 12–18 months of planting but it is possible to obtain some autumn fruits from spring-planted vines.

Varieties

Black Passion-fruit — the black or purple passion-fruit is sold under a variety of names but all are selections from *Passiflora edulus* and are raised from seed and so are bound to vary a little in type.

Grafted passion-fruit are also available but these also are usually produced from seedlings grafted onto a wild passion-fruit stock which is resistant to fusarium fungus disease. This can be a serious pest in areas where the disease has become established, as it causes the stems to collapse and the vines to wilt. These grafted vines are not resistant to virus disease.

Banana Passion-fruit — makes a wider spreading very caney vine with large pendulous pink flowers followed by long torpedo-shaped fruits with a skin like orange-buff felt. The vine is usually wider spreading than the Black passion-fruit, tolerates colder winters and usually takes at least a year longer to bear but, being less susceptible to disease, is more permanent. Cultivation is the same as for Black passion-fruit.

Growing problems and solutions

Problem: Failure to set fruit.
Cause: If the weather is very hot and dry the pollen may dry out and lose its viability. Prolonged wet conditions also create problems with pollination. An excess of sappy vegetative growth due to an over-abundance of nitrogen in the soil and a deficiency in phosphorus essential for productivity. This frequently occurs in soil heavily supplied with compost, largely composed of lawn clippings and other vegetative material. Over-lush growth may also develop due to frequent use of water-soluble fertilisers which contain very large proportions of nitrogen.
Solution: Apply a large handful of superphosphate per sq. m of area surrounding the vine at a radius of at least 2 m from the trunk. Prune back some of the main and more vigorous laterals to a lesser side branch or curve the ends of the vigorous laterals or canes downwards.
Problem: Brown spots on leaves, fruit and stems. Fruit shrivels and falls prematurely.
Cause: Fungus disease due to warm, humid conditions.
Solution: Control by using copper spray at the first signs of leaf spotting.
Problem: Foliage wilt.
Cause: Fusarium wilt which attacks the stem of the plant.
Solution: Paint the affected base of the stem near ground-level with copper spray made up to a paste-like consistency at the first signs of wilting, but there is no positive cure for the disease. It can be prevented by planting vines which have been grafted onto fusarium-resistant, wild passion-fruit stocks. These plants are more expensive but worthwhile in areas where this particular disease is prevalent. Only fusarium-resistant passion-fruit should be

replanted in areas previously affected by the disease.
Problem: Vines becoming woody, unproductive; fruit small, very woody and malformed.
Cause: Woody virus or bullet, caused by a virus transmitted from affected to healthy vine by aphids or leaf hoppers.
Solution: Unfortunately there is no cure. This disease shortens the productive life of passion-fruit to 2 or 3 years so the only solution is to plant a replacement vine approximately every second year.
Problem: Corky brown scabs on the skins of passion-fruit.
Cause: Fruit flies stinging the fruits in their greener stage; their larvae does not normally penetrate the skin of the purple passion-fruit. Green shield bugs sucking the fruit may also cause scabbiness, or a small water-soaked area that gradually subsides and becomes thin.
Solution: If bugs are present, use a Pyrethrum-type spray or Malathion.

Raspberry

Raspberries are best suited to areas with cold winters and fairly cool springs and summers. They are caney plants growing 1–2 m high and bear fruit on 2-year-old canes.

Requirements

A well-drained slightly acid soil with protection from strong winds.
Planting time. Plant while dormant during winter and spaced 50 cm apart in rows 2–3 m apart.

General care

Feed in late winter to early spring with fowl manure or one-third of a cup of complete plant food per metre of row. Water well from the time new spring growth appears.

To save rows becoming congested hoe out the old canes after fruiting or cut back to ground-level in winter and thin out new suckers.

Growing problems and solutions

Problem: Failure to fruit. This may occur when the winter has been very mild (raspberries are best in cool climates) or when the planting becomes too congested.
Solution: Canes that have fruited should be cut out at ground level and others thinned out to about a span apart. Suckers from the side of the rows should also be chipped out as these tend to congest.

For other conditions that may affect raspberries, see loganberries.

Strawberry

Apart from their luscious fruit, strawberries are decorative so, where space is limited, they can be used in borders, casks or large hanging baskets. Strawberries grow well in all but extreme tropical districts.

Requirements

They will produce some fruit in half shade, but position in full sun gives best results. They like a reasonably rich soil. Heavy clay or poor sand can be made more to their liking by adding well-decomposed organic material. Mulch the surface soil after planting to prolong fruiting and keep plants and fruit clean.

Very acid soils benefit from the addition of three-quarters of a cup of garden lime or dolomite and one-quarter cup per sq. m of complete plant food prior to planting.

Avoid frequent use of the highly nitrogenous water-soluble fertilisers as these induce excessive leafiness. Correct the condition by clipping off the higher leaves to allow better penetration of light to the crown and scatter about 1 handful of superphosphate per sq. m between the plants and water in thoroughly. **Planting time.** Although strawberries are often regarded as a winter-planting crop, they do better from autumn planting as they then have a longer time in which to establish before spring cropping. When grown in large quantities, they are best set out in rows 30 cm apart with a span between each plant.

General care
Strawberries resent over-wet conditions but should never be allowed to dry out completely. Give a good soaking to about 1 cm down whenever the surface soil dries.

Remove runners showing before late summer. Although these can produce the replacement plants for future seasons, they curtail cropping if allowed to form.

Because of the prevalence of strawberry virus discard old plants and purchase new virus-free stock every second year. If replanting from the increase of your own stock, choose the younger plants formed from runners with a crown about finger thickness. When planting out trim off most of the foliage and cut long roots to finger length.

Varieties
Improved varieties of strawberries seem to be evolved every few years. **Torrey, Red Gauntlet** and **Redlands Crimson** are among the most adaptable and stronger-growing large-rooted varieties. **Kendall** also does well in some coastal districts, has excellent flavour but poor keeping qualities.

Growing problems and solutions
Problem: The berry or part of it becomes soft and watery, then pale and dry.
Cause: Fungus disease known as Botrytis, encouraged by moist, sheltered conditions and when frequent applications of liquid manures have encouraged lush leaf growth.
Solution: Pruning off some of the higher leaves, then spray either with copper spray or, after picking all fruit liable to ripen within a few days, spray with Benlate.
Problem: Brown spots on leaves.
Cause: Fungus disease known as leaf spot.
Solution: Spray with Zineb or Mancozeb.
Problem: Brownish-grey spots with a purple border, often accompanied by hard dry patches on fruit. Shrivelling of flower stems may also accompany severe attacks of this disease. A similar infection known as leaf spot (*Mycospharella*) gives spots surrounded with a reddish-purple zone but usually the centre of the spot is white or pale grey.
Cause: Leaf spot or hard rot.
Solution: Use copper spray for both conditions.
Problem: Ash-like film on foliage. In some cases accompanied by a cracking of the fruit.
Cause: Powdery mildew.
Solution: Use Benlate or dust with sulphur.
Problem: Leaves crinkled and distorted with yellowing patches and a general lack of vigour.
Cause: Strawberry virus spread by aphids.
Solution: Spray regularly with Malathion to eliminate aphids but once the disease is in the neighbourhood it is better to lift and burn all plants as soon as cropping has finished and to start with new virus-free plants the next season.
Problem: Dull mottling of leaves which may later develop a dull sandblasted appearance.
Cause: Red spider mites which can only be detected with the aid of a magnifying glass in good strong light. It usually occurs during very dry conditions or when plants are grown under protection from the weather.
Solution: Dust with sulphur or spray with wettable sulphur (both non-toxic), or spray the undersides of foliage with Malathion providing fruit is not harvested for at least 4 days afterwards, or with Rogor or Lebaycid at least 7 days before harvest.

Harvest your own strawberries
Strawberries are conventionally bedded down in part of the vegetable garden but they are attractive enough for borders edging flower gardens, ground cover below roses or on balconies and patios in troughs, barrels or ornamental strawberry pots. I have also had them growing attractively in hanging baskets which is an effective way to trick the slugs and snails.

Strawberries are a satisfying crop to grow. With feeding and regular watering they will begin producing a few months after planting. It is possible to buy packs of pre-chilled plants that fruit within weeks of planting. Because strawberries normally commence flowering with the first warmth of spring, the chilling acts as an artificial winter and the plants begin flowering soon after planting out, even during winter except in the coldest districts. These plants will fruit again in spring.

Strawberries used to be planted in winter but autumn plantings are now preferred because the plants establish better before spring cropping. However, winter is the next best time, especially if the pre-chilled, winter-fruiting plants are available. In tropical areas they are planted in late summer to crop through the cool months.

Strawberries can grow and make reasonable fruit in the part shade of other plants but are stronger and more prolific in full sunlight. They adapt to a variety of soils providing drainage is good but establish more rapidly if heavy clayey soils are broken down by adding a liberal dressing of either well-rotted compost, weathered horse manure or spent mushroom compost. Poor sandy soils can be made more productive by adding compost or especially moistened peatmoss which improves their water-holding ability.

They prefer slightly acid conditions, which means that in most of our more acid soils, such as where azaleas thrive and hydrangeas are normally blue without treatment, a light liming is beneficial.

Half to two-thirds of a cup of garden lime or dolomite would be enough to use unless you know that the soil is extremely acid. Also mix in about half a cup of bone dust or one-third of a cup of complete plant food per sq. m.

If growing strawberries in containers, most of the proprietary potting soils will be suitable. However, grown in tall, narrow, unglazed strawberry jars it is advisable to add up to one-quarter part of peatmoss to increase the soil's water-holding ability because these pots dry out quickly.

For hanging baskets, use a peaty soil or better still, line the basket with a 2–4 cm thick layer of sphagnum moss which holds far more water than bark or fibre. Another advantage of this is that the plants are easily poked through the moss at the sides of the basket which allows better spacing and they look so attractive growing this way.

If growing strawberries in a single row as a border or in clumps of only 3 or 4 plants, they can be spaced as close as a good span apart but allow a little more space if they are to be in blocks of several rows and stagger the plants.

The good virus-free plants sold by most nurseries should be ready for planting as they are. If separating clumps in your own or a friend's garden, discard the old original plant at the centre of the clump. Select younger outside ones formed from runners that have thickened up at the base crown to at least pencil width. Trim the roots back cleanly to 7 or 8 cm and trim back most of the foliage. Otherwise it will draw too heavily on the plant.

Water thoroughly but gently so that the soil does not become puddled and set hard. Break the crust occasionally to keep the soil open and eliminate weeds.

As the plants become established, mulch liberally between them with a fibrous compost, leafmould, straw or even partly decomposed grass clippings to keep the soil cool (which prolongs cropping), improves root growth and plant quality.

Water thoroughly whenever the soil surface below the mulch becomes dry but minimise overhead watering while fruit is forming as this may encourage fruit mould. Should soft watery rot, shrivelling berries or leaf spots occur, pick heavily then spray with copper oxychloride or Bordeaux.

Strawberry virus gradually weakens the plants and reduces productivity. It is transmitted from infected to healthy plants. Runners from infected plants carry the disease so discard and destroy all plants after a few years.

A cultivation guide to growing nuts

Almond

The almond is a deciduous tree resembling the peach in habit and foliage but generally more upright and larger, growing 5–6 m high and as wide. It grows best in temperate areas where most of the rainfall is in the winter and summers are fairly dry. It flowers early, usually in late winter to early spring, and so is not recommended for very cold districts because heavy frosts may damage buds and flowers.

Requirements

Almonds are grown successfully in a variety of soils but are at their best in fairly light well-drained sandy loams or volcanic soils.

Harvesting is during late summer and early autumn when the leathery downy skins or hulls enclosing the shells split open. These hulls are then removed and the shells dried in the sun.

Unlike peaches, almonds are not self-pollinating, therefore two varieties flowering at the same time are essential for crop.

Planting time. Plant while dormant during winter. For good results, almonds need occasional soaking around the root area while in active growth during late winter and early spring. Constant rain during the warmer months of summer may induce diseases and prevent maturing.

General care

Feeding. Almonds respond to light applications of fertiliser in late autumn and early spring. Use 1–2 handfuls of complete plant food per sq. m of area below outer branches and water in thoroughly.

Pruning. Shape the trees initially as suggested for peaches and other stoned fruits. From then on little pruning is needed except the removal of excessive old wood, and over-vigorous upright growths which should be shortened back to just above a lateral growth.

Excessive growth developing during summer, especially in the centre of the tree, can either be pinched back or rubbed off in the early stages.

Varieties

Two popular varieties are **Brand's Jordan,** a popular strong-growing thin-shelled variety, and **Chellaston** which has upright growth and medium-sized thin shells.

Cashew

The cashew or cashew apple makes a handsome, glossy-foliaged umbrella-shaped small to medium-sized tree. The cashew nut forms on the end of an unusual oval apple-like fruit which is very sour and sometimes regarded as poisonous.

Requirements

Cashews need well-drained loamy soil with plenty of organic matter added and a generous supply of water during the summer months.

General care

Feed as suggested for avocados.

Macadamia
Queensland or Bauble Nut

Attractive pyramid-shaped trees growing to about 6 m in height with dark glossy evergreen foliage and decked in spring with sprays of small cream or mauve flowers which are followed by bunches of rounded green-husked nuts. In most varieties the nuts are very hard shelled but of excellent flavour.

Requirements

Macadamias grow in tropical, semi-tropical and temperate districts. In the latter they need shelter from cold winter winds. Soil-tolerant providing drainage is good. Results are better when heavy loamy soils or light sandy soils are liberally mulched with organic material.

Planting time. Macadamias are grown in containers, so may be planted at any time of the year providing the roots are not disturbed, but in climates with cool winters, spring planting is preferable.

General care

Give plenty of water from the time flower bunches appear in spring until cropping is finished in late summer. Except for the addition of compost, do not feed newly-planted trees the first season. Once established they will respond well to the feeding suggested for apples.

Varieties

There are two definite species of macadamia: **M. tetrafolia** which has serrated, slightly prickly leaves in sets of four and nuts with smooth hard shells and **M. integrifolia** which has smooth-edged very glossy leaves and the more restrained growth of the two species. Nuts are usually slightly warted and generally thinner shelled. Both species come true from seed with possible minor variations in type and producing some relatively thin-shelled varieties with desirably large kernels. Grafted stocks of the better types should be available. *M. ternifolia* is an unofficial name that was once loosely applied to both species.

Growing problems and solutions

Problem: Sawdust-like castings toward base of new shoots, latter may die.
Cause: A small borer which enters the stem or a small grub which may girdle the stems and attack foliage.
Solution: Spray with Carbaryl or Endosulphan

Macadamia

at weekly intervals for 3 weeks after the first sign of damage or, as a precaution, spray when new growth commences.

Peanut

Peanuts are produced from a small bushy plant less than 1 m high, belonging to the Pea family. The nuts are formed on the end of long string-like peduncles originating from the lower branches and pushing down into the soil. They are grown like potatoes in both tropical and temperate districts.

Requirements

Deep well-drained light soils are best for peanuts. Results are best when a liberal dressing, say about one-third of a cup per sq. m of complete plant food, is raked into the soil prior to planting. When plants are about 30 cm high, the soil between the rows is raked in and hilled up around them in much the same manner as potatoes. Mulching between the rows and another light sprinkling of complete plant food and occasional good soakings help at this stage. Plants are dug like potatoes when the foliage begins to deteriorate in late autumn or early winter. Nuts are removed, dried on trays for several weeks, then roasted in the shell.

Varieties

Valencia Bunch is a popular variety sometimes available from seed merchants. However, when seed peanuts are difficult to obtain, unroasted ones will usually germinate. If planting a large area sow 10 seeds in a small area to check the percentage of germination; allow 2 per spacing.

Walnut

Walnuts make large, spreading trees suitable to cool or temperate climates with cool winters. Seedlings of walnuts take at least 10 years, perhaps longer, to produce nuts that may or may not be of good quality. Grafted plants normally produce quality nuts in about 8 years, or under good conditions in 5, if other trees are available to supply pollen because the female flowers are often produced at an earlier age than the male flowers.

Requirements

Deep loamy well-drained soil. Otherwise make a planting hole about 1 m wide and mix up to one-third peatmoss or well-rotted compost with the soil around the root area.

The main requirement for a good crop is plenty of water during the spring period. Heavy surface mulching will conserve moisture and improve soil conditions generally.

Planting time. Walnuts are frequently sold as bare-rooted trees which need to be planted during their winter dormant period. Container-grown trees can be planted at any time but establish more rapidly if started during winter.

General care

Do not fertilise during the first year but from then on give several good soakings of the root area during spring with one of the complete water-soluble plant foods. During the years following, feed as suggested for pears.

Grow your own coffee

Coffee beans come from a glossy-foliaged shrub or small tree which looks attractive in the garden or as an indoor plant.

You'd have an interesting talking-point and could drink the crop too, although there mightn't be so many berries on the house plant.

The 'beans' are the seeds in the berries, usually two to each.

The commercially popular Arabian coffee, or *Coffea arabica*, grows 3–5 m in height but indoors it remains pot size.

Raising your own coffee can be fun if you have the right conditions.

Any reasonable aspect with light shade would suit it in many parts of Queensland, but farther south it needs a warm corner protected from cold winds and with at least half-a-day's sunlight.

Coffee bushes need plenty of water, particularly from spring to autumn, and prefer a moist atmosphere. This rules out many parts of Western and South Australia and most inland districts unless plants are grown in an enclosed courtyard where evaporation creates humidity. A slightly acid soil with plenty of compost is desirable. Bushes can be planted 1.5–2 m apart.

Don't imagine that one tree will keep you and your friends supplied wih coffee. A small nursery pot-size tree will produce a few beans after 2 or 3 years, then after 6 or 7 years it would average about 0.7 kg of cured coffee under reasonable growing conditions, although twice this amount is possible when a tree is really happy.

Plants are usually tip pruned or cut back to about half when 1 m or so high, to encourage low bushy growth.

Coffee beans take 7 or 8 months to mature. The fragrant white flowers come mainly in spring and form berries which turn red toward harvest time. The seeds are fermented in tanks or wooden boxes for 12–18 hours to remove sugary substances, then washed and dried in the sun for about 3 weeks. The drying has to be gradual.

Finally remove the parchment or hull, and the beans are ready for their roasting and grinding.

If you don't have a coffee climate, then try chicory which used to be a popular coffee additive or substitute. The parsnip-like root is dried and ground. Young leaves can be blanched and used as a salad. Chicory grows easily as a weed and has an attractive little blue flower. It grows easily from seed sown in spring or summer in fairly rich, deep soil.

Grow your own tea

Tea growing is usually associated with tropical areas because most of the world's plantations are in Sri Lanka or India. Australia's only large and commercially successful tea plantation is in tropical north Queensland, but tea adapts well to any of the not-too-dry temperate districts.

The plant, with rich green glossy foliage, is worthy of a place amongst the ornamentals in any garden. If left alone it makes a small tree 5–6 m high, but occasional clipping (or harvesting) keeps it down to a compact, densely-foliaged 1–1.5 m shrub.

It surprises many people to learn that tea is a camellia (*Camellia sinensis*). By camellia standards its flowers are small. They are creamy-white with yellow stamen-clustered centres, no way as eye-catching as most *Camellia japonica* or *C. sasanqua cultivars* but quite acceptable in the general shrub range.

At Nerada, Australia's first large-scale and financially successful tea plantation, hundreds of trimly clipped rows of tea cover the gently undulating valley floor and disappear into the cloud-wreathed blue hills.

The soil is deep volcanic loam that gives the good drainage needed for successful tea growing.

You can even grow tea as far south as Sydney. Apart from good drainage, tea needs an acid soil (pH 5.5 to 6.5) such as occurs along most of the eastern Australian coast, also Melbourne and the Adelaide hills. Avoid unnecessarily acidifying the soil with sulphates of iron or aluminium, as excessive acidity retards growth.

Keep the soil well mulched with compost and water plants occasionally during spring and summer with one of the complete soluble plant foods, a complete organic plant food, or a camellia and azalea food. If using the latter, 1 tablespoon per sq. m of area around the tree is plenty, applied 3 or 4 times a year and watered thoroughly afterwards.

Plenty of water during spring and summer ensures an abundance of new top growth. To gain bushy growth with plenty of shoots, begin pinching tips from main growth when plants are about 35 cm high.

A tea plant should grow happily in a 25 cm nursery bucket-sized container for a few years, then would be best transferred to a tub 35–40 cm across. Any good proprietary potting soil would be suitable or mix about 5 parts of good crumbly garden loam with 2 parts moistened peatmoss and 3 parts coarse sand.

To treat the leaves after picking, wither them on hessian for a few hours then mince and leave in a cool place for another few hours. Dry in the oven at 120°C for about 40 minutes until crisp, dry and dark.

Right: Tea growing at Nerada, Qld. Even in the quick growing climate of Nerada it takes about 3 years for tea to reach harvesting stage.

27. Growing herbs for flavour and fragrance

A traditional herb garden has charm and interest. Many herbs give strength to others, which is a good argument for gathering them together in a herb garden, but they help other vegetables and flowers too, so can be scattered about where they do the most good.

All these delightful plants can be grown successfully on balconies or terraces, in pots, rockeries, troughs, window boxes and strawberry pots or can be used to border rose gardens or vegetable plots.

Aspect

Irrespective of the neighbouring plants, the first consideration is the soil, moisture and preference of these plants for sunlight. They need good soil and a light airy place, preferably with direct sunlight for at least half a day.

Don't try to grow herbs indoors, except perhaps on the sill of a very sunny window; even then success would be doubtful with chives, thyme, sage and other greyish-foliaged herbs unless the window was open most of the time.

Almost any type of plant container is suitable as long as it has drainage holes, as most herbs resent an over-wet soil — mint is an exception.

The strawberry pot or jar is an excellent container for growing a variety of herbs in a small space, e.g. a corner of a sunny balcony. Thyme, chives and other herbs that prefer drier conditions can be planted in the higher compartments of the pot while mint, parsley and basil are happier in the lower and damper places.

One of the most unusual herb-growing ideas I have seen is a hanging garden that acts as a screen between the front and back areas of a garden. Two posts about 2 m apart support a dozen baskets of herbs hung alternately at high and low levels from cross-bars which extend about 1 m beyond each post.

A hedge of clipped rosemary is below the baskets, with a well-shaped bay tree in a tub at either end.

Plastic hanging baskets are the easiest to use, and trailing herbs such as the prostrate thyme, oregano and peppermint look most attractive when growth spills over sufficiently to hide the container. The baskets with water-holding drip trays are good for mint, but the trays should be removed for sage, thyme and other herbs that need to dry out between waterings.

Wall baskets enable you to grow a collection of herbs on a sunny wall.

Deep wire baskets can be used, e.g. strawberry pots, with herbs planted through the sides as well as in the top. Line the baskets with bark or moss, then with black plastic sheeting. Make drainage holes through the plastic.

Plant as you fill the soil up from the bottom, much the same as with a strawberry pot; but with plastic-lined baskets the slits for planting are cut when and where they are wanted. For pot-grown herbs it is easiest to roll the tops of plants in paper and thread them out through the slits from the inside.

Foam plastic troughs make convenient containers for a collection of herbs for balconies or terraces and can often be fitted onto a sunny window-ledge.

Out in the garden, rockeries make excellent herb gardens as plants can be placed in the higher or lower levels according to their soil-moisture preference.

Sage and thyme do better with a layer of gravel spread over the soil. Wet earth splashed onto the plants in warm and humid weather can induce fungus rot.

There are some lovely designs for formal herb gardens; but after all only a few of each different plant, or perhaps even one, will satisfy most needs so the same result can be achieved in a very small corner.

To bring one classic design down to a small scale, divide a rectangle about 2 m square with diagonals from opposite corners, then by cross-lines from the centre of each side, 'Union Jack' style. This gives 8 triangular beds which can be separated by bricks or timber. A small square or circular bed may be isolated in the centre.

A circle may be segmented similarly — perhaps you could use an old cartwheel set in the soil, with every second spoke removed. An old wheelbarrow or handcart filled with soil can also make a novel herb garden.

Herbs that prefer a fairly dry soil

The following herbs prefer soil with a good drainage and a quick-drying or gritty surface. Let the surface dry out to the depth of 1–2 cm between watering. They do well in half to three-quarters sun in warm to temperate climates, but prefer full sun in cool districts.

Marjoram *(Origanum marjorana)* 30 cm high, perennial, is a popular flavouring for seasoning many meat dishes; reputed to flavour growth of all plants it surrounds. Propagate from seed sown in spring or autumn, from layers of low outer bracts, or from tip cuttings taken when new growth loses sappiness.

Oregano *(Oreganum vulgare)* 50 cm high, considered a wild form of marjoram, but with larger foliage, usually sharper aroma, though this varies according to growing conditions. Similar use to marjoram, favoured for meat and sauces. Other properties similar to marjoram; repels insects, particularly beetles, at close quarters.

Rosemary Shrubby perennial 1–1.5 m, or may be clipped as hedge to 50 cm height. Prefers limey soil; used for flavouring lamb and other dishes. Propagate from seed or tip cuttings.

Sage *(Salvia officinalis)* Bush perennial, 50–75 cm high. Used in poultry, pork or beef seasoning and as a gargle for sore throats. As a companion plant is reputed to improve eating quality of cabbages and to repel cabbage butterfly.

Winter Savory *(Satureia montana)* Prostrate carpeting perennial that adapts to reasonably moist soil but prefers a gritty scree or pebble surface. Attractive rockery trailer. Used as flavour for bean salad, fish or veal dishes. Propagate from seed sown in spring or autumn from tip cuttings or stems in contact with soil. Some repellent properties; deters germination of weeds and other seeds.

Summer Savory *(Satureia hortense)* Summer-growing annual, 60 cm high, used as above. Propagate from spring-sown seed.

Thyme *(Thymus vulgaris)* Height 25 cm. The popular culinary thyme is used for flavouring chicken. Lemon thyme is greener and is available in cream variegated form, decorative in the garden and used for flavouring duck. There is also a variety of low-carpeting thyme delightful for rockeries or between flagging. Propagate as marjoram.

For average, moderately moist soil

Basil *(Ocimum basilieum)* 60–70 cm high; annual, growing only during the warmer months. Delicious aroma and used for flavouring tomato, egg, beef, fish and salads. Bright-green foliage. Assists growth of tomatoes, beans and all plants except rue (possibly also antagonistic to diosma and some boronias). Repels flies and mosquitoes. I have also used it successfully to repel white fly with some effect up to about 1 m in distance. Sow seed from spring to early summer; harvest and dry before nights become cold.

Bay *(Laurus nobilis)* The classical laurel used for wreaths crowning victorious Greeks. Dense-foliaged bushy evergreen to 5 m, but may be clipped to about 1 m or as a standard — grows in all but tropical districts. Pleasant flavouring for meat dishes, gravies and marinades. Leaves repel weevils in stored grain. Propagate from finger-length tip-cuttings taken when new growth loses softness, or from base suckers carefully removed during cool months.

Bergamot *(Monarda didyma)* Herbaceous perennial 60 cm–1 m. Leaves and scented flower heads used for tea, flavouring salads, jellies and fruit dishes. Propagated by dividing clumps in late winter, or by seed.

Borage Vigorous annual with flower stems to 1 m. The large hairy leaves have a cucumber flavour and can be added to drinks or boiled with spinach. Blue flowers are candied for cake or sweet decoration. Sow seed any time, self-sows readily — beneficial in compost.

Burnet *(Sanquisorbia minor)* Clumpy perennial to 25 cm with interesting fern-like foliage, mild cucumber flavour for salads or drinks. Propagate from clump division or seed.

Chervil *(Anthriscus cerefolium)* Like a flat-leafed soft-foliaged parsley, 30–40 cm. Annual, used like parsley, but it has a more delicate aniseed aroma. Prefers fairly moist soil and semi-shade in summer. Sow in spring and in frost-free areas; also during autumn.

Coriander (Chinese Parsley) 40 cm tall, annual, resembling parsley but with sharper taste — the seeds are used for curry and confections or for flavouring bread.

Chives Grow in pots or clumps in convenient parts of the garden — best with about half sun and well-drained, slightly limey soil. The taller, flatter-leafed garlic chive is also worth growing. Both seem to repel green rose but not black aphids. Both are good neighbours for cabbages, tomatoes, beets and lettuce but not beans or peas. Increase by dividing clumps in winter allowing about 10 bulbs per pot or clump, or from seed sown in spring or in warm areas; autumn also.

Dill Quick-growing annual, reaches 1 m in height. Fern-like foliage, can be chopped for potato salad and fish sauces, seeds are used to flavour gherkins and pickles. Good neighbour for most plants but can retard growth of carrots. Sow seed direct where plants are to remain, preferably in spring, but any time in warm districts.

Garlic Clumps of broad foliage up to 1 m high; perennial, dies down after flowering. Bulbs are dried for culinary use. Some divisions (or cloves) are planted back to provide next season's clumps. Sunny, well-drained soil.

Lemon Balm *(Melissa officinalis)* Bushy perennial, 50–60 cm. A mint with sweet lemon fragrance and flavour. Propagate by division of clumps in late winter, spring or summer-sown seed. Best cut back in winter.

Lemon Grass Clumpy perennial bladed grass with a strong lemon aroma — a substitute for lemon in tea or cooking; also refreshing to crush and smell. Grows to 1 m and dies back by late winter. Propagate by division.

Parsley Indispensable biennial, grows to 40 cm. Appetising flavour and very high in Vitamin A, C and iron. Prefers a slightly acid (unlimed) soil and at least half sun but makes moderate growth in shade or even in a pot or trough on a window-sill. Can last 2 years before going to seed, but it is better to start some new plants each year from spring to late summer.

Parsley usually takes 3–4 weeks to germinate but fresh seed often comes through in about 10 days if pressed or scratched into the surface of a fairly sandy soil, covered with a piece of towelling and about 1 L of near-boiling water. Leave it covered until the first signs of germination, checking in about a week. Feed established seedlings each month with soluble plant food. Pick only outer leaves after plants reach 12–15 cm, allowing 3 or 4 mature leaves to remain on each plant.

Tarragon 60–90 cm high, perennial, used in salads, sauces, cheese dishes and to make tarragon vinegar for salad dressings. Needs plenty of sun and good, moderately-moist soil. Sow seed direct in clumps or rows from spring to early summer.

Herbs that will grow in wet soil

Mint *(Mentha)* Freely-suckering perennial to 50 cm high. Grows in average garden soil but is more luxuriant if grown in damp areas. Mint is sometimes available from seed sown in spring but is usually started from rhizomes or divisions of clumps in late winter or early spring. Tip cuttings can also be grown successfully.

Apple Mint *(M. rotundifolia)* Rounded light-green foliage, sometimes variegated cream, used in mint sauce, fruit salad and finely chopped to coat bananas for frying. It grows well in moderately dry situations.

Eau-de-Cologne *(M. piperata citrata)* Heavy but refreshing eau-de-cologne aroma when brushed or crushed. Used to scent baths and in very small quantities in jellies or ice cubes for drinks. Suckers freely and vigorously in even moderately dry soils and could be grown in containers bedded into the garden.

Peppermint *(M. piperita)* Slightly bronze, narrow foliage supplies the oil of peppermint for confections and makes a refreshing drink.

Pennyroyal *(M. pulegium)* Has a strong aroma, repels ants and mosquitoes if rubbed on skin, and is used as a flea-repellent under kennel mats.

Spearmint *(M. spicata* of *M. crispa)* slender or rounded deeply crinkled foliage; are in greatest demand for flavouring peas, lamb, mint sauce, pineapple and cool drinks.

Sorrel Perennial growing to 60 cm. The flattish, light-green spinach-like leaves give a sharp, acid bite when added to salads — and can also be used in soups, stews and meat dishes. Needs at least half sun, grows best in moist soil. Propagate from seed sown direct into permanent positions from spring to early summer, placing 3 or 4 seeds at spacings about 20 cm apart.

Propagation

Most common herbs are easily propagated by one or more of the usual methods of plant propagation — seeds, cuttings, division or layering. Listed here are the herbs best suited to each method.

Seed

Sow these annuals indoors or outdoors after soil has warmed in spring: anise, basil, borage, caraway, coriander, dill, fennel, pot marigold and summer savory. Biennials to grow from seed include burnet, feverfew and clary sage. Perennials include catnip, sweet cicely, horehound, hyssop, lovage, marjoram, winter savory and common thyme.

Angelica seeds are short-lived, so sow them in late summer as soon as they are mature. The seeds of parsley are slow to germinate — soaking in water before planting helps. Seeds of sweet cicely require exposure to cold for good germination, so plant them in autumn to come up the following spring.

Cuttings

Herbs that can be propagated by cuttings include scented geraniums, germander, horehound, bay laurel, lavender, lemon balm, lemon verbena, oregano, rosemary, sage, pineapple sage, santolina, sweet marjoram, winter savory, common thyme, southernwood and wormwood.

Division or layering

Herbs easily propagated by division include burnet, chives, sweet flag, germander, horehound, lady's bedstraw, lemon balm, pot marjoram, wild marjoram, mints, iris, sorrel, tansy, tarragon, creeping thyme, lemon thyme, sweet violets, sweet woodruff and yarrow.

Layering is a common method for propagating thyme, santolina, lemon balm, winter savory, sage and mint.

Propagation by seed
Outdoors

Sowing seeds in rows makes it easy to distinguish the seedlings from weeds, but broadcasting is easier, especially with tiny seeds. Herbs that do not transplant well, such as dill, fennel, borage and pot marigold, should be sown where you want them to grow. In spring, as the soil begins to warm, they will germinate and begin to grow.

In mild climates, many biennials such as coriander and parsley do best planted in autumn; planted in spring they may bypass their 2-year cycle and flower too soon.

Indoors

Sow seeds in 5 or 10 cm pots or flats. Use light, well-drained soil mix or a sterilised commercial mix that prevents seedling disease. Allow 6–8 weeks for seedlings to develop to transplant size.

Propagation by cuttings

A cutting is a piece of stem that is planted like a seed. It forms roots and eventually becomes a plant identical to its parent. Cut a piece of stem 7.5–12.5 cm long with 2 or more nodes from the tip or side shoot of a healthy, well-established plant any time during spring or summer. Autumn cuttings take longer to root and the stem may rot before roots form. Plant the cutting in a light, fast-draining soil mix and cover with plastic to retain humidity. Keep it out of direct sun until roots form. Check the soil occasionally to be sure it is damp but not wet. Roots will form in 3–6 weeks.

Root cutting

Angelica, comfrey and horseradish are propagated by root cuttings. The principle is the same, except the cutting comes from below ground and makes new shoots.

Propagation by division or layering

These methods are generally more successful than propagation by cuttings, because the parent plant provides sustenance and moisture until new roots form.

Division

Simply dig down the middle of a clump with a shovel or trowel until you can pull away a section. Do this in spring just before the cycle of vigorous growth begins.

Layering

Any time in spring or summer, take a vigorous flexible branch and bend it into the soil and out again. Pile soil over it and secure it with stakes or a rock. Be sure the mounded soil remains moist. Check after a month for roots. If they are present, cut the layered stem from the parent and plant.

Transplanting

Whether purchased at a nursery or grown at home, all propagated herbs will need transplanting. Be sure they are not rootbound, old or sickly in appearance. Look for compact, stocky and vigorous plants.

Seedlings started from seeds should be transplanted when they develop their first 'true' leaves — those with the characteristic shape and colour of the mature herb. Handle them carefully; they have a critical area at the *neck*, the part of the stem just above the soil. A pencil, knife or similar tool will make it easier to reach under and lift the seedling's roots.

Wait until frost danger has passed in spring before transplanting, and most seedlings will benefit if you provide some shade and wind protection for a few days.

Borage

Chives

Parsley, silverbeet and celery combine with flowers

Put a little ginger in your garden

Green ginger has gained popularity for Chinese dishes, making condiments for flavouring and even as a medicinal herb. You can buy it from a greengrocer and raise your own plants. The woody rhizomes may not look very promising but usually need little more than warmth and moisture to make them sprout. If they are large, with more than two branches, then they may be cut into several sections before planting.

They grow best in a warm but lightly-shaded position, with good soil, rich in organic material.

Divisions are usually set 30–40 cm apart in furrows about 1 m apart, but if you are trying a small amount, set 3 or 4 divisions in a circle about 30 cm across or two in a large flower pot.

Make a furrow about finger depth and lightly cover each division after firming it into good contact with the soil. After shoots develop, gradually fill the furrow. Water sparingly until growth starts, then use water generously.

Note that the normal replanting time for ginger is in spring. Roots that have been well stored should still produce some growth months later. The normal procedure is to plant in spring and harvest from late summer to winter, although parts of well-established clumps can be dug at any time.

They can be left in the ground through winter in all but very cold districts.

Ginger of commerce (*Zingiber officinale*) is more restrained in growth than yellow or white ginger (*Hedychium*) or shell ginger (*Alpinia*). The young rhizomes may be washed and scraped soon after digging and preserved in syrup.

Ginger

Bay tree

Chrysanthemum parthenium

Lemon grass

28. How to grow vegetables

Many gardens have space which could be easily converted into a vegetable garden. There can be more lawn than is needed and an area of the turf could be removed to make an attractive and productive garden. If appearance bothers you why not enclose the vegetable area with a small neat hedge of herbs? Rosemary, thyme, sage and marjoram would be particularly appealing and appropriate. Some gardens surround the vegetable plot with low-growing annuals; the petite marigold is not only decorative but useful, for it will repel nematodes (the root-damaging eel worms.)

Many vegetables have attractive leaves and clumps of carrots, parsley, beetroot, lettuce, artichokes, capsicum, eggplant and dwarf tomatoes can look quite at home among your flowers.

Planning for continuous vegetable growing

A family of four can maintain a continual supply of fresh vegetables from a small 'conventional' garden plot measuring only 8 m by 3.5 m. The area can be sub-divided into 6 beds each measuring 3 m x 1 m, plus one larger bed for 'special' growings. Retain the overall borders of the plot by brick or timber to prevent the intrusion of grass and provide for access paths between the beds (wood chip or pebbles are ideal all-weather materials for pathways). A vegetable plot of this size could occupy the corner of a large suburban garden, or a small city garden, provided it has essential sunshine.

If you plant or sow too much you can be faced with a glut at harvest time; the secret of success is always to have enough and to have one crop of a vegetable following the crop of a different one in smooth succession. Family preferences are important. If lettuce and beans are in constant demand give them a whole bed to themselves, but systematically replace each harvested space with a sowing of carrots or onions, etc. so that the soil is not completely robbed of the same sort of nutrient. This change also minimises build up of organisms that may attack one type of vegetable.

Crop rotation was once an important factor in successful vegetable growing, as some plants demand far more of a particular mineral or food than others, so deficiencies were likely to occur where the same crops were replanted in the soil.

This is no longer a problem now that there are well-balanced plant foods available, many of them containing a complete trace element balance.

However, disease is still a consideration, so it is better to vary the plantings, and where possible to follow each crop with vegetables from a different family, whether they happen to be root or leaf vegetables.

For example, cabbages, cauliflowers, broccoli, brussels sprouts and turnips are all members of the same family (brassicas), and subject to similar diseases.

Potatoes, tomatoes, capsicums and egg-plant belong to another. The first two in this group may seem to have little in common, but root diseases can be a problem when one follows the other, or either are planted for several seasons in the same bed.

Preparing for planting
Choosing the site

Most people would put good soil at the top of the list of essentials for making a good vegetable garden: you can improve poor soil but you cannot change the position of the sun! Sunlight is the most important factor in successful vegetable growing. Full sunlight is ideal — sun for half to two-thirds of the day is essential. A few crops such as rhubarb, parsley, mint and, to some extent, chives will grow quite well in indirect light but they do even better in the sun. Cress and mushrooms are the only vegetables which prefer shade.

Choose an open part of the garden which, preferably, should face north or north-east to get the best of the sun, and arrange to have the vegetable beds and the rows within the beds running from north to south. If you have a sloping site, terrace the bed across the slope in step fashion, retaining the soil with wood, brick or concrete but making sure that seepage holes are left at the base of the retaining material so that water can seep away down the slope.

Drainage is important. If your soil is heavy clay it might be as well to take the initial trouble of laying drains. Otherwise lighten the soil by adding plenty of well-rotted compost or other organic material. The water-holding properties of light, sandy soil will be improved in the same way.

Make certain you have easy access to water; vegetables have to be grown quickly without setbacks to be able to enjoy them at their best. A fixed hose and sprinkler or a perforated hose which can be laid along the ground will give the best opportunities for the slow, gentle, thorough and regular watering which gives the best results.

One of the most important things to remember is that even good soil will be unproductive if handled badly. Only work   soil when it is damp, never when it is wet, otherwise when it dries you are likely to find you have a crusted, caked surface, impervious to air, which will inhibit the healthy root growth of your plants.

The soil

It is more important for the soil to be in a good crumbly physical condition than rich in plant foods which can easily be added. If the soil packs tightly it not only prevents the easy access of water but also of oxygen from the air both of which are essential for healthy root growth. Heavy clay soils are not the only ones that pack tightly; some alluvial loams that appear gritty when dry and actually crumble up, will pack down very tightly when watered and become comparatively airless. The finer the soil particles, the closer they pack together and so the spaces between them become correspondingly smaller. It is only through these spaces between the soil particles that the movement of water and air is possible.

Even very fine sand which will never set hard can pack down so densely that it is very difficult to get water to penetrate once it becomes quite dry. The most important point when handling any soil with a clay content is to dig, weed or generally cultivate only when it is in the just damp stage. Only then is it possible to get it to crumble.

If clay soils are disturbed when they are wet and sticky they will set harder when dry. When agitated, the wet fine clay particles are forced into solution with the soil water. The result is mud, which when dry is airless and too dense to allow development of healthy plant roots.

Test. Before disturbing clay soils after rain or watering, give them a simple test by taking a small handful of the soil and moulding it together to form a ball. If in a reasonable condition to cultivate, the ball of soil should be dry enough to crumble on impact. If it clings together or shows signs of stickiness, then delay cultivation or planting for another day, then test again.

The only type of soil that may not react as described in the test is pure clay, which when damp will mould into a ball but is too tenacious to shatter on impact.

What type of soil is yours?

The soil so often recommended for vegetable growing is a 'good loam'. Loam is a very variable term that refers to a mixture of different soil ingredients, usually clay, sand and humus together with other organic material. Clay loams, those that remain sticky for a long period after watering and are inclined to pack very hard when dry, contain more clay than sand. Inversely sandy soils contain more sand than clay.

The ideal soil is a medium to light loam, containing sufficient clay to hold reasonable amounts of moisture but enough organic material and sand to allow easy crumbling and help it keep that way.

> **Refer:** The Fertile Soil p. 62 for details on how to prepare soil, soil types, acidity and alkalinity, composting, etc.

Preparing the beds

Raising the beds about 10–15 cm above the surrounding soil will make certain that heavy rain will drain away more easily and that puddling will be prevented. Beds should be about 1 m wide so that access from 25–30 cm paths on either side is easy and comfortable.

Mark out the position of the beds and paths then shovel an 8 cm depth of soil from the paths and pile it on the beds and rake smooth. On a sloping site with paths and beds running across the slope, the soil shovelled from a path will be used to build up the low side of the bed above it.

Preparing to plant

Dig in well-rotted compost and rake the soil over. Any fibrous material large enough to be picked up by the rake can be piled on one side for use as mulch later.

If preparing the ground for root vegetables mix the decomposed material with the top layer of soil as evenly as possible and then turn it in to about fork-depth, half turning the soil several times to ensure the mixing is thorough. Do not add complete fertiliser close to planting time unless you make certain to mix it in exceptionally well.

Most vegetables like a fairly alkaline soil. An addition of half to two-thirds of a cup of garden lime or dolomite per sq. m once a year would benefit all soils that are not naturally alkaline. It is quite safe to add fertiliser at the same time. Beans, peas, onions, lettuce, cabbage and beetroot all appreciate lime; rhubarb, parsley, tomatoes and radishes do not. Take care with potatoes — don't use lime unless you are certain the soil is very acid.

Fertilising

Feeding with complete fertiliser prior to sowing or planting out is good practice even in fairly well-composted soil and in addition to nitrogen and potash, it supplies the phosphorus so frequently lacking locally and so essential for good germination, root growth and maturity. About one-third cup per sq. m is enough for most crops but peas and beans can take a little more — up to half a cup.

Alternatives to complete fertiliser are complete organic plant foods (usually well balanced with phosphorus) and animal manures which are also excellent (except for carrots and parsnips, where they should not be used directly, but only 'second-hand' from a previous crop). Fresh horse manure, and to some extent cow manure, have only a low percentage of phosphorus compared to nitrogen, so except for leaf crops they need balancing with superphosphate or fowl manure.

Heap fresh animal manures for a few weeks before using. The amount needed to give appreciable benefit would be 7–10 L per sq. m of soil and about half this amount if using fowl manure. However, reasonably well-weathered or partly decomposed horse or cow manure can be piled 3–4 cm thick as a surface mulch.

Spent mushroom compost is also an excellent soil improver and contains a good balance of plant foods — use it as a surface mulch or lightly knead it into the surface.

The benefit of having a good, coarse, open-structured soil has been well stressed, but if it is too 'fluffed up' there will not be sufficient contact between the new roots of seed or seedling and the moisture surrounding the soil particles. After mixing in compost and fertiliser, water the ground very gently and leave it for a week to 'settle'. If you are in a desperate hurry to plant, tread the soil down very lightly when it is just damp *not* when it is wet or even sticky, and gently rake even. That way soil and young

root will be able to make contact when planting or sowing is made.

But the best way is to prepare the beds well ahead of planting time and, after watering, to leave them for a couple of weeks so that any weed seeds will germinate and show themselves. Any but the bulbous weeds can then be destroyed by scuffling the soil to cut their roots just below the surface. You can sow or plant in beds that will be weed-free for a considerable time thus avoiding much fiddly and tedious later weeding between the new little plants.

Earthworms

The physical tunnelling of earthworms helps to aerate the soil. They do also help to combine organic material with clay and soil particles by mixing them all thoroughly together as it passes through their bodies. Their activity also tends to deepen the top soil because as they tunnel deeper during the drier periods they take organic material down to these levels.

They also increase soil fertility. They ingest soil, pass it through their bodies, expelling it as castings that are richer in nutrients than the original soil. It has been discovered that worm castings contain 5 times more nitrogen, 7 times more available phosphorus, 11 times more potash and 40% more humus than the surrounding top soil.

However, because of the relative fineness of their castings they can interfere with drainage so are to be discouraged for container gardening. The best way to encourage earthworms in the garden is by maintaining a surface mulch. Also be discriminate with the use of artificial fertilisers.

Sowing and planting

Root vegetables, e.g. carrots and parsnips, do not transplant well and should be sown where they are to grow. Beetroot and onions transplant well. Peas and beans do not enjoy transplanting — sow direct. Lettuce, cabbage and cauliflower are amenable, but lettuce are less likely to run to seed during summer if spared the shock of transplanting.

Growing from seed

If seed is to germinate it needs moisture, oxygen and the correct temperature. You will find, in early spring in temperate to cool climates, that beans, cucumbers and vine crops will not germinate because although the air temperature is reasonably warm the soil is still too cool. Inversely, during summer the soil temperature may be too hot for lettuce and other seeds to germinate.

Seeds cannot germinate if they are covered too deeply. Twice their own depth is sensible. Large seeds like those of beans, pumpkin, etc. should just be pressed into the soil; peas and beans can be sown in 'drills'. Root crops such as carrots, parsnips, beetroot, radish, etc. should be sown in shallow depressions 1 cm deep. Some people

tap them from the seed packet; I tip some seed into my left hand and then scatter it, a pinch at a time, along the furrow and press down with the back of the rake. Careful spacing at this stage will save thinning later. The ways seeds are covered is important.

Crumbly garden soil will do, but fibrous compost or spent mushroom compost is a better topping as it makes a good buffer against disturbance by heavy rain and holds needed moisture. Vermiculite, which I like to use, is even better. It is very light, holds a surprising amount of water, allows maximum air penetration to growing roots and is highly visible so that not only is it easy to tell where the seed has been sown but it helps to make identification of weeds easier. We have all known the frustration of decapitating seedlings under the mistaken impression they were weeds!

Spaced sowing

Lettuce, cabbage, cauliflower, silver beet, etc. can be transplanted but, if sown with an eye to spacing, can grow *in situ* and thereby avoid the shock of being lifted and having to re-establish themselves.

Mark out the rows and also the space within the row. You can cross each row in grid formation or stagger the plantings. At each marked spot sow 3 or 4 seeds, cover, and firm down the soil. If all the seeds germinate you can make a judicious thinning leaving the strongest plant to grow at the correct distance from the next.

Fluid sowing

Apart from 'sowing aids' such as vermiculite and compressed peat pots, fluid sowing is probably the most notable departure from seed-sowing tradition since man started cultivating the soil.

Seeds are pre-sprouted by sprinkling them on wet filter paper (or some other absorbent, but not too open, material), enclosing them to maintain moisture and keeping in a warm place until germination begins.

The sprouting seed is then carefully washed in a fine sieve, tapped into a prepared fluid gel, poured into a plastic squeeze bottle with a suitably large nozzle, or into a plastic bag with one corner nicked off. And then, with slight pressure, is extruded along the rows of soil prepared for sowing like icing being piped onto a cake and it is finally lightly covered and watered.

The advantages of fluid sowing are that at indoor temperatures, germination time is halved, you know how much seed is viable and have a good idea of the germination rate before sowing — and it is much easier to control the spacing and so avoid unnecessary thinning of carrots, parsnips and onions later.

You can practise this fascinating process by purchasing a 'fluid sowing kit' with its supply of gel. Some overseas experts recommend wallpaper paste for making gel but I find that most types available here contain fungicides that retard germination and growth. Try making a thin mixture with arrowroot or even cornflour but keep the gel thin or it will take too long to dissipate in the soil.

Transplanting seedlings

All plants receive some shock or setback when transplanting so it is a great advantage to transplant carefully to minimise this shock. Seedlings that have been kept in containers indoors, or even kept shaded for a few days, are likely to wilt and shrivel if planted straight out into hot sunlight. It is therefore an advantage to condition them to sunlight before planting out by giving them, say, a few hours direct sun the first day, then half a day's full sun, etc. at the same time being conscious of the fact that in this situation they will suddenly use a lot more water and dry out a lot more rapidly.

If it is essential to plant out immediately and if there is doubt about the seedlings being conditioned, the ideal time is on a dull day or late in the evening. The latter is good practice in all cases. It also helps the seedlings overcome transplanting shock if they are shaded for a few days until the disturbed or injured roots are again able to function properly. A few twigs, especially dry twigs, provide a good type of shading.

During very hot conditions terracotta pots large enough to comfortably cover the foliage of the seedlings are excellent, because after watering the evaporation from their porous surface cools the inside air around the seedlings. To prevent the seedlings from becoming too drawn they should only be applied during the heat of the day. Quite good sun shelters can be made by cutting plastic ice-cream containers into equal halves or quarters for larger ones, inverting the sections and pressing them into the soil on the sunny side of each seedling.

Also, it is possible to buy plastic shade cloth that can be supported on wire hoops above the seedlings or even to make a few tunnel-shaped covers of wire netting and drape the shade cloth on the sunny side of the seedlings. These same wire netting shapes can double as protection from cat or bird damage.

The actual process of transplanting or introducing the seedling into its permanent position may seem rather basic but numerous trials have shown that the way this is handled can make quite a difference to the progress of the seedling. This applies particularly to lettuce and other seedlings with a fibrous root system.

The conventional practice has been to dibble a comparatively deep cone-shaped hole, suspend the seedling with the lowest leaves or crown at about ground-level, then press the soil evenly inwards from all sides to firm the seedling into position.

The objection to this rather conventional method is that it pushes all roots into a central column or close around the tap root and then the seedling makes little progress until it regains a spreading root system. Development has proved much quicker, especially with fibrous rooted plants, when a comparatively wide shallow depression is made, almost with the same action drawing up a small hump of soil in the centre and spreading the roots nearly laterally over this before raking in the disturbed soil to cover them, then firming downward gently.

It is also important to have the soil just damp at transplanting time. If surface mulching is available, place it around the seedlings immediately after transplanting and before watering. This prevents the inevitable surface caking in heavy soils and in very light sandy soils keeps the shallow roots of the seedlings much cooler during summer as well as preventing the loss by washing of organic particles in the sand.

Planting Guide

When to sow

Vegetable	Temperate areas	Sub-tropical	Cool
Broad Bean	April to August	April & May	July to September
Bean (other than above)	Late September to late February	All seasons	October to late January
Beetroot	August to April	All seasons	September to March
Broccoli	January to March	January to March	January to March
Brussels Sprout	December to March	Not suitable	December to February
Cabbage	August to May	March to July	August to April
Capsicum	October to November	September to February	October
Carrot	August to April	March to August	August to March
Cauliflower	December to March	February to March (quick maturing types)	November to March
Celery	August to January	November to March	August to January
Chive	March to July	March to May	Autumn & Spring
Cucumber	September to December	September to February	October & November
Dill	All seasons	All seasons	All seasons
Egg Plant	October to November	September to January	Not suitable
Endive	August to April	March to August	August to March
Herb Thyme, Marjoram, Sage, etc.	August to March	All seasons	August to March
Kohlrabi	April to August	April to June	March & August
Leek	August to March	February to April	August to March
Lettuce	All seasons	All seasons	All seasons
Marrow & Squash	October to January	September to February	October & November
Melon	October to December	September to February	October & November
Mustard & Cress	All seasons	All seasons	August to April
Okra	September to February	September to May	October to January
Onion	March to July	March to May	Autumn & Spring
Parsley	August to March	January to April	September to March
Parsnip	August to March	February to April	September to February
Pea	February to November	March to July	August to February
Potato	Feb. & July to August	February to April	September to November
Pumpkin	September to January	September to February	October to November
Raddish	All seasons	All seasons	September to March
Rhubarb (seed)	June to November	November to February	September to January
Rosella	October & November	September to December	Not suitable
Salsify	March to October	Not suitable	All seasons
Silverbeet	All seasons	March to August	August to March
Spinach	April to July	May & June	April to August
Sweet Corn	September to February	September to February	October to January
Sweet Potato (cuttings)	September to December	September to December	October to November
Tomato	August to December	All seasons	September to October
Turnip	February to September	March to July	February to March & August to September
Turnip Swede	January to April	March to May	January to April

How to plant

Vegetable	Sow = S Transplant = T	Spacing cm Between Rows	In Rows	Seed To Sow 15 m Row Grams	Seeds Per Gram	Depth To Sow mm	Time To Harvest From Sowing or Planting Days	Period over which Crop can be picked Weeks	Yield Per 15 m Row Kilograms	Quantity Needed Per Person Per Year Plants	Row in m.
Artichoke Globe	S.T.	120	75	8	7	12	1 yr Plus	2	5	5	3
Jerusalem	T	75	35	(tubers) 2 kg	—	100	140	20	45	10	4
Asparagus	S.T.	75	45	16	20	12	S = 3 yrs P = 2 yrs	12	12	15	8
Aubergine (Egg Plant)	S.T.	90	45	1	200	7	100	12	12	8	4
Beans Broad	S	90	10	200	1	25	100	4	35	—	15
Runner	S	180	15	200	1	30	80	6	35	—	8
Beetroot	S	35	8	50	7	12	70	4	22	—	4
Broccoli (Calabrese)	S.T.	60	40	1	300	7	100	4	22	20	8
Brussels Sprout	S.T.	75	50	1	300	7	140	12	22	20	8
Cabbage	S.T.	75	50	1	300	7	80	4	22	20	8
Carrot	S	35	5	1	700	7	80	4	22	—	8
Cauliflower	S.T.	65	45	1	300	7	100	4	22	20	8
Celery	S.T.	25	25	0.1	2500	3	100	4	12	25	8
Chinese Cabbage	S.T.	60	35	1	350	7	65	2	12	12	4
Cress Salad	S	—	—	—	250	Do not cover	10	1	—	—	—
Cucumber	S.T.	90	45	1	30	12	80	8	45	4	3
Endive	S.T.	45	30	1	500	3	60	3	20	25	8
Kohlrabi	S.T.	40	25	1	350	7	50	4	20	20	3
Leek	S.T.	40	15	1	300	7	120	12	20	50	8
Lettuce	S.T.	30	30	1	700	7	60	2	18	25	8
Cos	S.T.	30	25	1	700	7	70	2	20	25	8
Marrow Bush	S.T.	120	60	15	7	12	100	8	100	2	2
Trailing	S.T.	180	60	15	7	12	100	8	100	2	2
Melon Rock	S.T.	150	100	15	10	12	120	4	40	2	2
Water	S.T.	200	100	15	7	12	120	4	50	2	3
Okra (Gumbo)	S.T.	100	75	1	100	12	110	4	7	4	2
Onion Bulbs	S.T.	30	10	1	300	12	120	24	20	100	15
Spring	S	30	2	1	300	12	80	4	5	300	4
Parsnip	S	30	10	1	250	12	100	16	20	20	3
Pea	S	90	4	500	4	25	70	2	25	—	15
Pepper (Capsicum)	S.T.	60	50	1	200	7	100	12	10	8	4
Potato Early	T	75	30	Tubers 2.5 kg	—	100	100	4	70	25	8
Maincrop	T	100	40	Tubers 2 kg	—	100	120	20	90	40	15
Pumpkin (and squash)	S.T.	400	200	25	5	25	100	20	100	2	2
Radish	S	10	3	8	100	12	30	1	5	—	2
Rhubarb	S.T.	90	60	1	50	7	—	12	15	2	2
Shallot	T	25	10	Bulbs 1 kg	—	12	150	24	20	20	3
Silverbeet	S.T.	45	25	8	100	12	50	4	20	10	3
Spinach	S	40	15	8	100	12	45	2	10	20	3
Swede	S	30	15	1	350	7	60	12	20	20	3
Sweet Corn	S.T.	40	15	25	4	25	100	3	12	16	4
Sweet potato (Kumera)	T	100	400	Rooted cuttings	—	—	100	24	45	20	8
Tomato Bush	S.T.	200	100	0.5	200	7	100	12	60	6	4
Staked	S.T.	150	40	0.5	200	7	100	12	75	9	4
Turnip	S	30	15	1	350	7	60	12	20	20	3

Growing the vegetables

Thinning out the seedlings

When sowing direct, it pays to thin out at the earliest possible stage, preferably as soon as the seedlings begin to make their second or true leaves. Spaces needed between the seedlings are given in the accompanying vegetable growing guide which shows minimum spacing where a restricted area makes crowding desirable. (Conventional spacing is given on the seed packets.)

I find the easiest way to thin crowded seedlings is to use a thin stick or pencil to hold aside the plants you want to keep so that you can more easily remove the unwanted ones.

thinning out seedlings

Damping off

This common disease of seedlings is encouraged by close planting as the fungus survives best in dark, moist, enclosed conditions and needs a microscopic film of moisture on the surface through which to travel from plant to plant. The snake-like mycelium invades a stem near ground-level and the seedling collapses.

Prevent the disease from taking hold by thinning seedlings, or by planting them in rows so that there is plenty of light and air penetration between them. Avoid watering late in the day. The soil surface should not remain wet at night. Wet the seedlings and surrounding soil by watering with Captan or a similar fungicide. Use vermiculite as a topping for the seed of susceptible seedlings.

Although vermiculite granules hold large quantities of water, it is held within the particle, while the outside remains fairly dry and the loose nature of the vermiculite prevents the fungus from travelling through it.

Watering

As a general rule let the soil surface dry out then give the soil a good soaking, if possible by using a fine spray that does not agitate or puddle the soil. Leave it on for about an hour but use a trowel in several parts of the garden to check whether the moisture has penetrated well down into the soil.

Growing problems and solutions

Do not be discouraged by the numerous trouble symptoms listed here; these are not necessarily regular occurrences but mostly things that can happen during some seasons or sets of circumstances.

Plant	Symptom	Cause	Remedy
Beans (Broad)	Shiny black insects clustered toward tip of stem	Black aphids	Spray Pyrethrum-type preparation or Malathion
	Brown spots on leaves	Chocolate leaf spot	Spray with Zineb
	Velvety brown pustules on leaves	Rust	As above
	Brownish-grey spots on foliage, sunken on stem	Leaf spot	Complete fungicide or copper spray
Beans (French) Dwarf and Climbing types	Poor germination of seed	Sowing when ground is too cold, or too deeply in wet soil	In wet or heavy soil sow no deeper than 2–3 cm and water only when surface dries out. During wet humid conditions dust seed with fungicide prior to sowing
	Plants collapse, rotting with red discoloration, near soil-level	Fusarium or damping-off fungus	Drench soil around surviving plants with Fongarid, do not replant beans in same soil for 2 years
	Brown tunnelling in stems, some plants collapsing	Bean-fly prevalent in warmer temperate to tropical districts	Spray with Rogor or Lebaycid
	Leaves with dull sand-blasted appearance, some faint webbing	Red spider mites	Spray with Rogor or Lebaycid. Frequent misting with water also deters this pest
	Yellow spotting with brownish pustules on underside	Rust	Spray with Zineb
	Brown spots surrounded by yellow halo	Blight	Remove infested plants and use copper spray at intervals of 10 days
Beetroot	Whitish tracery through leaves	Leaf miner	Spray Rogor or Lebaycid at least 7 days before harvest
	Pale to dark brown spots on leaves	Leaf spot fungus	Use copper spray
	Whitish mould on inner foliage	Mildew	Use sulphur dust or Benlate
	Brown sunken canker on root	Boron deficiency	Dissolve 1 teaspoon Borax per 10 L of water and soak into 2 or 3 m of row when replanting
Broccoli	Loose flavourless heads	Cutting delayed too long	Cut before buds or heads begin separating, best when matured during cooler months
For other broccoli problems see cabbage and cauliflower			
Carrot	Small green insects on foliage	Aphids	Pyrethrum-type spray or Malathion
	Pale stunted foliage	If drainage is satisfactory, usually due to carrot virus	Aphids transmit this disease, but most modern quicker-growing types are resistant
	Brown or black spots on leaves	Fungus leaf spot	Spray Zineb or Mancozeb
	Shallow holes eaten in roots	Carrot weevil	Water rows with Carbaryl or Malathion at first signs of damage
	Deformed lumpy roots with bead-like swellings on root heads	Root eelworm (nematode)	Avoid by treating soil prior to planting. See heading 'Eelworm control'
Note: Twining or forking can be due to stony soil, delayed thinning or fertiliser unevenly mixed through soil			
Cabbage and Cauliflower	Small dull grey insects clustered mainly on back of foliage	Cabbage aphid	Spray with garlic spray, Pyrethrum-type sprays or use cabbage dust
	Areas of leaf eaten	Caterpillars of cabbage moth or white butterfly (apart from slugs and snails)	Use Pyrethrum-type sprays, Carbaryl or cabbage dust
	Greyish film on foliage (mainly on seedlings)	Mildew	Use copper spray
	Black streaking from base of leaf down stem	Bacterial rot (fortunately an infrequent seed-borne disease)	Hot water treatment of seed is needed to prevent this (50°C for 20 minutes)

Plant	Symptom	Cause	Remedy
Cabbage and Cauliflower cont.	Badly stunted growth, bead-like knots on plant roots	Eelworm (nematode). Unfavourable close neighbours (particularly strawberries) cause stunting	For eelworm treat soil prior to planting. See heading 'Eelworm control'
	Large swelling on roots	Club root	Lime soil liberally prior to planting
	Cauliflowers with long thin twisted foliage	Whiptail (molybdenum deficiency)	See heading 'Molybdenum' in 'Get to know your garden' chapter
Chinese cabbage	Running to seed without hearting properly	Maturing when weather is warming	Plant early in winter to mature in cold or, in cool districts, during mid to late spring
Capsicum	Brown spots on fruit or foliage	Fungus spot or blight	Copper spray or Zineb
	Small green insects under leaves	Aphid	Use Pyrethrum-type spray or Malathion
	Creamy-white maggots causing rotting of fruit	Fruit fly	See 'Tomato'
Celery	Brown or black spots followed by rotting of leaves	Leaf spot	Use copper spray or Benlate
Cucumber	Grey film over foliage	Powdery mildew	Benlate
	Foliage shrivelling, whitish tufts of fungus on underside	Downy mildew	Spray with Zineb or Mancozeb
	Leaf skeletonised	28-spot ladybird or its larvae (like a spiny grub)	Pyrethrum-type spray or Carbaryl
	Leaf skeletonised	Pumpkin beetle (4 large spots and a longer body than above)	As above
	Dull mottling of foliage, numerous small white flies	White fly	Pyrethrum-type spray or Malathion. See 'Tomato'
	Dull sandblasted appearance of foliage	Red spider mites	Spray either Malathion, Rogor or Lebaycid. Frequent misting of foliage also helps
Egg-plant	Powdery film on foliage	Mildew	Benlate
Kohlrabi — *for leaf damage see Cabbage*			
Leek	Shrivelling of leaf tips	Downy mildew	Spray Zineb
	Silvery grey streaking of foliage	Thrip	Spray Malathion or Rogor
	Roots rotted with white fungus growth	White rot	Dig root with surrounding soil and burn to prevent spore bodies remaining in soil
Lettuce	Leaves deformed with small green insects clustered	Aphid	Pyrethrum-type spray or Malathion
	Angular pale then brown spots on leaves. Downy tufts on underside	Downy mildew	Spray Zineb or Mancozeb
	Foliage eaten	Slugs, snails or birds	Place snail baits, arch lengths of wire netting over rows to keep birds off
	Bolting to seed without hearting	Usually due to check in growth through temporary dryness or transplanting shock	Sow direct or transplant carefully during hot weather. Keep liberally watered and well fed, and use sure-hearting varieties such as 'Lakes' types during hot months
Marrow and Squash — *For leaf pests and diseases see Cucumber*	Failure to set fruit	Usually faulty pollination	Pick male flowers, strip petals and rub anthers into female flowers, preferably during early morning when they are open. Female flowers are distinguished by a bulbous swelling (embryo fruit between petals and stem)
Melon (rock) *For other foliage problems see Cucumber and Marrow*	Grey film over foliage	Powdery mildew	Benlate. Some varieties such as Hales' Best are resistant

Feeding the growing crop

Carrots and parsnips normally carry through to maturity without extra feeding. The 'side dressings' recommended for other vegetables can cause 'forking' or root distortion. Frequent use of soluble plant foods can result in thick tops and very little root.

Beets, potatoes and turnips will respond to a light dressing — sprinkled on either side of the row — of mixed plant food after about 6 weeks of growth. So will onions as bulbing commences and peas and beans when flowering starts.

Liquid feeding

Complete soluble plant foods have largely replaced the 'dry mix' side dressings but, depending on the plant food balance of the soil, can cause excessive leafiness because of their high content of nitrogen. Predominance of leaf at the expense of fruit is likely to be a factor with tomato, capsicum, egg-plant, okra, pea, bean, marrow, zucchini, melon and potato, but if detected early enough in the season can be counteracted by raking and watering in superphosphate at the rate of 1 tablespoon per sq. m of area surrounding the plant. The complete dry mix fertilisers do not cause this problem because of their relatively high content of phosphorus (superphosphate).

Some of these preparations contain too much phosphorus in relation to nitrogen for leaf crops such as lettuce, cabbage, Chinese cabbage, celery, silver beet and spinach. Give these soluble plant food applied every week from the time seedlings become established.

Liquid manure

'Liquid manure' is made by suspending or floating a sugar bag of fresh animal manure in a drum of water for 3 or 4 weeks — a practice still favoured by some gardeners, though in a closely settled area the aroma generated is unlikely to make you a popular neighbour! Before applying the brew dilute it to weak tea consistency and colour.

Seaweed extract is a good substitute for the old liquid manure brew and is generally more acceptable. Both forms of liquid feeding receive criticism from people who assess plant foods on their content of nitrogen, phosphorus and potash because these liquid preparations contain low percentages of those elements in relation to standard commercial fertilisers.

However, it is obvious from the results obtained by gardeners for several centuries that these organically-charged solutions contain substances that act as catalysts, and help intake and conversion of available nutrients, and encourage growth of algae-type soil organisms which utilise atmospheric nitrogen and carbon dioxide, and make these elements available to the plants. So try the mystery brews and if you get good results, stay with them.

Liquefied meat extracts and fish emulsion have also proved worthwhile but are also in the 'low analysis' category. Some suppliers are 'fortifying' these with urea and potassium salts to improve the analysis so it is as well to keep to the dilution recommended on the label.

Eelworm control

Nematodes — Some nematodes in the soil perform a useful task of decomposing organic material, while less desirable ones are plant parasites. Some invade the leaves of chrysanthemums, bulbs and other perennials but the more common parasitic types invade plant roots.

Eelworm infestation of roots causes knots or galls, sometimes tiny and bead-like, sometimes a chain of longer bulb swellings which seriously affect root functioning and plants are small and stunted or wilt readily because they cannot take in enough water to keep pace with their needs and the amount lost through their foliage.

Natural controls — Where this is a high population of the beneficial or non-parasitic eelworms, development of the parasitic types seems to be inhibited. These parasites are probably also inhibited by the presence of other useful micro-organisms, e.g. protozoa and some kinds of bacteria and fungi. Therefore soils containing large quantities of organic matter which fosters the development of useful organisms are less likely to be troubled by parasitic eelworms. Just keeping a surface mulch of compost or of grass cuttings that have been heaped for a few weeks prior to spreading will help.

Some plants exude substances from their roots which deter the activity of parasitic eelworms, others lure them from a crop that may otherwise be attacked.

In some overseas bulb farms marigolds used as a green crop the season prior to bulb planting have proved successful deterrents. They have also given good results when planted in alternate rows with cauliflowers, cabbages, tomatoes and other vegetables in soils where eelworms were a serious problem. See 'Companion planting'. Retarding of nematodes is not the total answer to the problem but it does help.

Chemical control — Methyl bromide is sometimes used to rid the soil of nematodes. This is a lethal gas, expensive and for qualified operators only. Nemacur granules can be mixed in soil before planting.

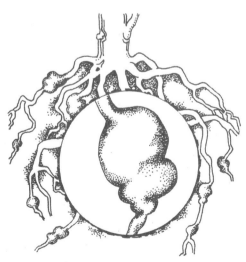

Nematode damage

Plant	Symptom	Cause	Remedy
	Yellow splotching and shrivelling of foliage, with tufts of white fungus on underside	Downy mildew	Spray with Zineb or Mancozeb
Melon (water)	Wilting of foliage and rotting of stem at ground-level	Fusarium wilt	Do not plant crop in same ground for at least 5 years. Sow resistant varieties.
	Wilting with rotting of stems and fruit	Anthracnose	As above. Varieties such as Candy Red and Charleston Grey are resistant to both diseases
Mushroom	Cropping ceases prematurely	Either too dry, or temperatures above 20°C	Sprinkle with water to moisten peat covering or, if warm weather approaches, grow summer varieties only
	Tiny fly present over compost, mushrooms or stems tunnelled by small maggots	Mushroom fly	Lightly mist each day with Pyrethrum-type spray, remove old stems and infected mushrooms
Onion	Running to seed before making bulbs	Wrong planting time for the variety. If early types are about half grown when heavy frosts occur a mass seeding may follow rapidly	Plant earlier or later
	Tops of foliage shrivelling	Downy mildew	Spray with Zineb or Mancozeb
	White flecks or streaks on foliage	Thrip	Spray either Malathion, Diazinon or Endosulphan
	Rotting bulbs enveloped in white fungus	White rot	See Leek
Parsley	Foliage eaten	Looper caterpillar, slugs or snails	Place snail baits, spray with Pyrethrum-type sprays for caterpillars
Parsnip	Grey film on foliage	Powdery mildew	Use Benlate
	Black spots on leaves, rotting at base of stem	Leaf spot	Spray with Benlate
	Roots cracking and splitting	Irregular watering. Dryness	During dry periods give good soaking at least weekly
Peanut	Dead areas on foliage	Leaf spot	Spray with Benlate
	Foliage with dull sand-blasted appearance	Red spider mite	Spray with Malathion or dust with sulphur
	Plant wilting with rot and white fungus at base of stems	Stem rot	Water plants and surrounding soil with Zineb at normal spray strength
	Plants inclined to wilt easily, underground areas damaged by grey or white grubs	Scarab or black beetle larvae	Flood soil either with Diazinon, Malathion or Carbaryl at normal spraying strength
Pea	Poor germination or emerged seedlings rotting	Deep planting or over-wet soil which produces seed-rotting fungus	Dust seed prior to sowing with either Zineb, copper spray or complete fungicide powder and do not plant deeper than 2 cm except when dry conditions are expected
	Yellow to buff dull patches	Red spider mite	Spray either Malathion, Rogor, or dust with sulphur
	Foliage shrivelling with tiny mites at base of plant	Red-legged earth mite	Spray Malathion, Lebaycid or Rogor. Tomato Dust
	Dark spotting on leaves and pods	Leaf spot	Use copper spray or Benlate
	Flowers or pods blackened, and possibly empty	Early frost damage	Sow no earlier than 8 weeks before the end of frosts is expected
Potato	Caterpillars in rolled edges of leaves, tubers may also be tunnelled	Potato moth	At first signs of damage spray with Carbaryl or Endosulphan. Hill soil to protect expanding tubers
	Foliage skeletonised	28-spot ladybird	Spray with Carbaryl
	Dark spotting on leaves also apparently 'water-soaked areas', mainly during cool, wet conditions	Blight	Spray with Zineb or Mancozeb

Plant	Symptom	Cause	Remedy
Potato cont.	Numerous corky scabs over skin of tuber	Bacterial scab	Avoid liming soil prior to planting, add plenty of well-rotted compost
	End of tuber glassy when cut	Due to second growth such as when rain follows dry period close to maturity of tubers	Maintain more even supply of moisture
	Objectionable kerosene-like odour and taste when tubers are cooked	Use of B.H.C. insecticides. Residues may remain in soil and taint for up to 12 months	Use either Carbaryl or Endosulphan to control potato moth, not B.H.C.
Pumpkin *See Marrow and Squash for pest, disease or pollination problems*			
Radish	Small grey or green insects clustered on backs of leaves and new growth	Aphid	Spray Pyrethrum-type sprays or Malathion
	Caterpillars eating large holes in foliage	Cabbage moth or white butterfly larvae	Spray with Carbaryl or Pyrethrum-type preparations
	Yellow blotches on foliage with downy patches on underside	Downy mildew	Spray with Zineb
Rhubarb	Yellow then later brown spotting on foliage	Fungus spot	Spray with Zineb
	Crown of plant rotting, young growth shrivelling	Bacterial crown rot	Dig and burn affected plants, protect others by watering centre and surrounding soil with copper spray. Water less.
Silver Beet (commonly called spinach)	Numerous small brown spots surrounded by yellow zone	Fungus leaf spot	Use copper spray or Benlate and feed liberally with water-soluble plant foods
	Grey scribble-like markings on leaf	Leaf miner	Spray with Rogor or Lebaycid at least 7 days before harvest
Spinach (true or English)	Plants run to seed rapidly	Weather too warm at maturity	In all but cool districts sow in autumn to mature during cooler months
Squash *see Marrow and Squash*			
Sweet Corn	Small greenish-grey insects clustered in uppermost leaves	Aphid	Spray with Malathion or Diazinon
	Caterpillar burrowing into cobs and eating kernels	Corn earworm	Liberally spray Carbaryl directed at cobs as silks begin withering
	Young seedlings severed, others with poor restricted growth	Cutworms which sever older plants at soil-level, or larvae of black beetle which devour roots	Either scatter Carbaryl dust along furrows when sowing or water plants and surrounding soil with Carbaryl made to spraying strength
	Poor germination or young seedlings rotting at soil level	Damping-off fungi	Dust seed with fungicide prior to planting
Sweet Potato	Large areas of foliage eaten	Either looper or night-feeding cutworm	Spray plants liberally with Carbaryl
Tomato	Vigorous healthy plants but few blossoms and no fruit	Excess nitrogen, low phosphorus — usually happens when only water-soluble plant foods or nitrogen-rich compost is used	Scatter 1 handful of super-phosphate per sq. m around plants and water in well
	Blossoms falling	Due either to low spring temperatures or excess heat in summer	Crinkly skinned 'rogue' or Chinese types set fruit more readily during cool conditions
	Base or end of fruit sunken and blackened	Blossom-end rot, a calcium deficiency usually because there is insufficient water to transport this element to extremities of plant	Mulch soil to maintain more even water supply or in very acid soils add a dusting of lime
	Large caterpillar tunnels into stalk end of fruit	Tomato caterpillar	Spray with Carbaryl
	Numerous small white flies over foliage some-times with sooty mould or sticky substance present	White fly	Spray each day for several days with Pyrethrum-type sprays. Basil planted between plants usually repels for about 1 m

Globe Artichokes (cynaria)

Dwarf beans ready to pick

Scarlet runner beans are best suited to cool climates

Nemagon and Nemacur are simpler and quite effective controls for root-infesting eelworms. The latter is available in a shaker-can containing impregnated vermiculite granules which are sprinkled onto the soil and lightly forked in prior to planting. This treatment gives immunity from most types of eelworms for the growing season.

Tomato wilt

There are two main types of wilt in tomatoes. Fungus wilts attack the stem and cut off or retard the plant's water supply, and virus wilt which causes a general debility of the entire plant. Verticillium wilt, or sleepy disease, is a fungus invasion of the plant stem. If the latter is cut longitudinally a brown discoloration of the sap-conducting tissues is seen; this discoloration runs right down to the roots. Affected plants wilt more readily on warm days before more serious deterioration sets in.

Fusarium wilt usually attacks the stem at ground-level and also causes rotting and sudden wilting. In either case infected plants should be burnt and stems of those remaining liberally watered with fungicide such as Zineb or Captan. This treatment is only a mild deterrent, not a cure or definite preventive. Tomatoes should not be grown in this same area again until the soil has either been sterilised or used for other crops for several years with plenty of compost added at regular intervals.

Virus wilt, also known as spotted wilt or bronze wilt, appears first as bronze pin-point-size spots over the foliage which increase until all the leaves have a bronze flush and gradually wilt and die. The fruit may remain on the plant but will have yellow bird's-eye-like concentric markings.

There is no cure; the disease is carried by thrips that have fed on infected plants during their infancy. The insects cannot pass the virus on until it has undergone a 5-day cycle in their intestines so it is obvious that with regular insect control the incidence of virus wilt can be kept down. See 'Thrips'.

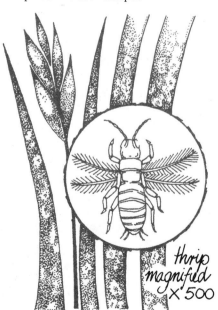

thrip
magnified
x 500

Plant	Symptom	Cause	Remedy
	Interior of fruit infested with maggots, usually followed by rotting	Fruit fly	Apply fruit fly baits to foliage as directed at weekly intervals, or adopt a program of picking all fruit that will ripen within 1 week. Spray remainder with Rogor or Lebaycid and do not pick again for at least a week. Also see 'Fruit fly control' in 'Fruit and nuts' chapter
	Brown spotting of foliage usually surrounded by yellow zones	Can be several types of blight or target spot	Spray with Zineb or Mancozeb or use Tomato Dust regularly
	Silvering of foliage which droops and curls	Tomato mite	Dust with sulphur or spray wettable sulphur or Rogor or Lebaycid
	Plant wilting, rotted at base of stem	Probably fusarium wilt	See heading 'Tomato wilt'
	Tiny metallic bronze spots on foliage gradually spreading and causing wilting	Bronze or spotted wilt, a virus disease	See heading 'Tomato wilt'

Zucchini *see Marrow and Squash*

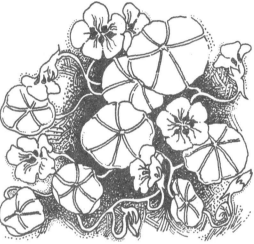

Nasturtiums are rampant growers but, before you succumb to the impulse to rip them out, consider the good they do.

Orange-coloured nasturtiums repel aphids. If you leave them to grow under, and even to twine up, apple trees, they will control the spread of the woolly aphid.

Nasturtiums grown in the greenhouse will protect more precious plants against white-fly.

Nasturtiums secrete a mustard oil which insects find attractive and they will seek them out in preference to any cabbage, cauliflower, broccoli, brussels sprouts, kohlrabi and turnips growing nearby. It therefore makes good sense to let them wander between these crops to act not only as a ground cover to keep the soil moist but as a decoy for insects and as a flavour-improving agent for your crops. They are particularly good for giving radish a good hot taste, and for keeping away cucumber beetles.

Companion planting

One of the as yet not understood principles which govern successful gardening is that of biodynamics. Some plants grow well in the proximity of others but will fail and die if given companions of a different sort. Plants have the ability to repel or attract different insects, fungi and soil organisms.

Vegetable	Plants that help their growth	Antagonistic plants
Asparagus	Tomatoes, parsley	
Basil	Most plants	Rue
Bean	Carrots, beet, cauliflower	Onions, garlic
Beet	Dwarf beans, onions	Climbing beans, mustard
Broad bean	Potatoes	Fennel
Broccoli		
Cabbage	Beet, dill, celery	Strawberries
Carrot	Radish, leeks	Dill
Cauliflower		
Celery	Leeks, tomatoes, beans	
Egg-plant	Dwarf beans	
Kohlrabi	Beets, onions	Tomatoes
Leek	Onions, celery, carrots	
Lettuce	Carrots, strawberries	
Onion	Beets	
Pea	Carrots, cucumber, turnips	Onions, garlic
Potato	Cabbage, peas, broad beans	Dill
Pumpkin	Sweet corn	Potatoes
Radish	Lettuce, peas	Hyssop
Tomato	Parsley, asparagus, chives, carrots	Kohlrabi, potatoes, fennel

A cultivation guide to vegetables

Artichoke
Globe

The globe-shaped flower buds are picked at the bluish-green stage just before the flowers open. The plant is very decorative with large silvery-grey scotch thistle-type leaves. They are perennials, normally cropping for about 5 years, mostly from early winter to mid-summer.

Requirements

Globe artichokes need a rich well-drained soil and an open sunny position.
Planting time. Most growers propagate by taking suckers early in spring from plants proved to yield consistently and provide good quality heads. Otherwise raise from seed sown early in spring and retain plants that give the best performance for propagation.

Cultivation

Allow about 75 cm between plants. Four to 5 plants usually sufficient for the average family and continuity of productive plants is assured by replanting 1 or 2 suckers from the best stock plant every 2–3 years. Apply a dressing of poultry manure or complete plant food each spring.

Jerusalem

This perennial form of sunflower produces edible tubers like rough irregular potatoes.

Requirements

Any well-prepared and well-drained soil with half to full sunlight.
Planting time. Plant in mid to late winter. Each year save some of the best types for replanting in July.

Cultivation

Enrich the soil with a dressing of poultry manure or complete plant food. Set tubers 30–40 cm apart about 10 cm deep. Keep reasonably moist once growth commences. Mulch with compost. Removing flower buds improves tuber quality. Tubers are dug from 4–5 months after planting until mid-winter.

Asparagus

A good asparagus crop needs lengthy preparation and patience but if given extra initial care it will crop well for many years.

Requirements

An open sunny position and well-drained soil.
Planting time. Two-year-old asparagus crowns in winter. Otherwise raise crowns from seed sown in spring.

Cultivation

Before planting, trench or deeply dig soil to the depth of about 35 cm at the same time turning a liberal layer of well-rotted compost or animal manure, plus a dressing of lime. Allow to settle down for about a week then make trenches 60–70 cm apart, about 25 cm wide and 20 cm deep. Scatter a handful of complete plant food per sq. m along the trench base and lightly hoe into the soil. Make a slight ridge of top soil over this to take the spread of the crown roots, which should be spaced about 35 cm apart and covered with a few cm of soil. Gradually fill in as growth progresses and mulch the surface with fibrous compost or similar organic material.

The first spring the growth is usually left to mature and later to yellow naturally but it is permissible to cut spears for the first weeks. If white spears are preferred, soil is hilled up about 15 cm around them. To avoid damage to later growth, cut by feeling down toward the spear base with a long-bladed knife and hold the tip in the other hand.

The next and following years cutting ceases about mid-December. Water fortnightly with soluble plant foods while harvesting. When mature canes yellow they are cut and left as a weed-retarding mulch over the rows. Dress during early spring before new growth develops with a little lime and complete plant food, if possible, also with compost.
Planting time. Sow in spring, first soaking the seed in water overnight to speed germination which normally takes about 3 weeks. Sow seeds about 2 cm deep in rows 20–25 cm apart, thinning seedlings in the early stages to 8–10 cm apart. Female plants which usually produce inferior spears are culled out. These are distinguished by their lower branching growth and their berries. The remaining plants are then set out as indicated for crowns during the following winter.

Bean

Beans are a most satisfying crop to grow because they are quick growing and relatively trouble-free.

Requirements

A well-drained preferably limey soil and at least half sunlight.
Planting time. In tropical districts sow all seasons, in temperate areas from late September to late February and in cool climates from October to January.

Cultivation

Prior to sowing lightly dig in a dressing of fowl manure that has been heaped for several weeks or about half a cup of complete plant food per sq. m. Some growers prefer to confine the fertiliser to a strip scattered along the base of furrows made 4–5 cm either side of the seed.

If sowing in built-up beds allow 2 rows per metre-wide bed, setting each row about 20 cm from the edge. Two to 3 m of single row would normally supply enough beans for a family of four for 2–3 weeks; for long beds it would be preferable to plant each row 2–3 weeks apart.

For continuity of supply it is a good idea to sow at these intervals or in temperate areas until about late February. To minimise gaps in the rows, sow 2 seeds about 2 cm apart every 10 cm along the row. No need for thinning if both seeds germinate in each planting.

General care

Hill the soil up around the base of dwarf beans when they reach the half-grown stage or about 25 cm high. Give a thorough but gentle soaking when the soil dries out for 1–2 cm below the surface. Quantity and quality of the beans will be improved if given a soaking with water-soluble plant food when the first beans have formed. Lightly misting the foliage at the end of a hot, dry day helps setting of flowers and deters red spider. These mites are difficult to pick with the naked eye but their presence is indicated by a dull yellowing or a dry sand-blasted appearance to the foliage. If the infestation is heavy, there may be some webbing and a reddish zone where the mites are clustered near the leaf margins. If chemical control is needed, use Malathion, spraying the underside of the leaf or use penetrating insecticides, e.g Lebaycid or Rogor. Before spraying, read label and observe the directions.

Varieties

There are numerous varieties of dwarf beans. All available in packet seed are worthwhile and have a reasonably good disease resistance. Those such as **Pioneer** and **Tendergreen** are popular because they are stringless but string types are thought to have better flavour.
Climbing beans. Are the answer where space is limited and can often be conveniently planted in areas where the ground is shaded but where plants can climb up to the sun. Conventional spacing is 1.5–2 m between rows and about 12 cm between the plants but it is possible to have a dozen or so plants in a circle only 25–30 cm across providing there is plenty of sun surrounding this column of plants. Two or three plants can be grown reasonably well in a bucket-sized pot of soil. Probably the most popular climbing stringless bean is still **Blue Lake,** which for many years has held the record for heavy cropping. **Purple King** is also popular for its good flavour and although the fresh beans are purple, they cook a good green colour. **Westralia** is popular because of its rust resistance.
Broad beans. Have a distinctive nutty flavour and can be served either boiled, in sauces, sautéed, cold in salads, or as green beans, slicing pod and all before seeds fill out. Some people also cook the tips of the plants.

Requirements

Broad beans are one of the few vegetables that show a preference for clay soils but still do reasonably well in loamy soils, even in nearly pure sand. However, they need good drainage and preferably full sunlight.
Planting time. Because of their need to set pods during moderately mild conditions, broad beans are sown in warm to semi-tropical districts during autumn to mature during the mild months and in cold districts late autumn–early winter to mature when spring nights are losing their chill. Late autumn is a good planting time in most temperate districts. They take 4–5 months to mature. It is common practice to pinch out the tips once flowering commences to induce the setting of pods. This may have some slight effect but has little bearing on the overall crop that forms when temperatures are suitable.

Cultivation

Prepare the soil with complete plant food and lime as suggested for French beans. Broad beans do well when planted in sets of double rows with about 25 cm between them, and if growing large quantities allow about 1 m between each set of rows. Space the seeds about 15 cm apart approximately 3 cm deep in heavy moist soil and about 5 cm in light soils. Allow the soil to dry out to about 2 cm below the surface between soakings.

A light scattering of complete plant food on either side of the rows when the plants are about half-grown, or as flowering commences, is beneficial in light sandy soils, but in heavy soils the initial preparation suggested should be sufficient to set them to maturity, except perhaps when prolonged rain has been experienced.

Beetroot

Fresh home-grown beetroot is delicious and is a pleasant change when used raw for salads in the young stage, either sliced or grated.

Requirements

Beetroot needs at least half sun and adapts readily to practically any soil except very tough sticky clays which need to be broken down well. It also grows well in salty soils and in fact seems to have preference for them.

Planting time. In tropical districts beetroot may be sown or planted out during all seasons, in temperate districts from late winter to mid-autumn and in cool districts from spring to early autumn.

Cultivation

Where possible give beetroot a position that has been manured for a previous crop such as lettuce, cabbage, etc. Add about a quarter-cup of complete plant food per sq. m but, in soil not cultivated for some time, use twice this amount. If not limed for the previous crop mix half a cup of lime per sq. m with the fertiliser. Rake the mixture backward and forward into the fairly dry soil then fork the bed over a couple of times.

Level the bed ready for sowing and leave until the soil has had a good soaking and been allowed to stand for a week to settle it down and allow quick-germinating weeds to be destroyed, and give distribution of the plant foods through the soil.

Soak the seed in water overnight, allow it to drain but not to dry out completely then sow in shallow furrows about 2 cm deep and 15 cm apart if only two furrows are being sown. Otherwise leave a space of about 25 cm between each pair of furrows. As the seed is fairly large it can be individually spaced at intervals of 5 cm along each furrow. This allows for approximately every second plant to be transplanted. Beetroot transplants quite well.

Cover the seeds with about 1 cm of crumbly soil then gently firm down to ensure good soil contact and to make a slight furrow which will direct water down around the seeds. If the soil is kept reasonably moist the seedlings should come through in about 10–12 days and take 10–12 weeks to mature.

A root crop like beetroot appreciates fairly large amounts of nitrogen so may be fed at fortnightly intervals from the time the plants are about 10 cm high with one of the complete water-soluble plant foods. As suggested earlier it is also improved by the presence of salt. Therefore, during the week between the water-soluble plant food applications, water with a weak salt solution by dissolving 1 teaspoon of common salt in 4–5 L of water.

Varieties

Both **Derwent Globe** and **Turnip Rooted** have excellent quality, deeply-coloured roots. **Early Wonder** is the most popular market variety in states where the beetroot is sold in the bunch, mainly because it retains freshness of its foliage longer than other types.

Special problems

Beetroot is relatively free from pests. Canker or scabbiness of the roots may occur in acid soils or others heavily limed prior to prolonged rainfall which results in a boron deficiency which can be corrected by dissolving a heaped teaspoon of borax in about 10 L of water and soaking this into a double 3-m long row. Avoid repeating this treatment in the same soil within a year or boron toxicity may occur.

Broccoli

A distinctively flavoured green vegetable with a high nutritional value, and appetisingly tender if used before the stems become fibrous. After harvesting the main centre head, most garden varieties continue to produce edible side shoots for several weeks.

Requirements

Broccoli needs at least two-thirds sun and limey well-drained soil as suggested for cabbages.
Planting time. As broccoli needs to mature during cool conditions it is unsuitable for tropical districts. In temperate areas it needs to be planted out by mid-autumn. Therefore, if planting from seed, it should be sown by February. In cool districts planting times are much the same but slightly later plantings are also satisfactory where there is a long cool spring. For cultivation and special problems see 'Cabbage'.

Brussels sprout

Have a definite and pleasant flavour especially when grown to mature during frosty conditions.

Requirements

Basic preparation of the soil for growing brussels sprouts is much the same as recommended for cabbages but they prefer a much firmer or heavier soil.
Planting time. Early-maturing varieties of brussels sprouts, e.g. Long Island, need to be sown in cold districts from November to early January or in milder districts in early December to late January. Later varieties, e.g. Fillbasket, are more suited to cool districts with a late spring and are best sown during late February.

Cultivation

Unless the soil is heavy tread it down prior to planting only when it is just damp. Instead of digging fibrous compost through the soil, apply as a surface mulch after planting. Give

lime and a good dressing of fowl manure or complete plant food prior to planting, and a very light sprinkling of either every 4–6 weeks during the growing period and water moderately. Do not apply water-soluble or other high-nitrogenous fertilisers such as sulphate of ammonia until the first picking of sprouts, otherwise they tend to lose their firmness and quality.

During mild conditions while reasonable growth is continuing the sprouts are picked every 8–10 days but during cold conditions there may be lapses of 2–3 weeks before the next batch is ready. Pick in batches of 5–6 from the base upwards.

Cabbage

Some hybrid types, e.g. Superette, are quick maturing and offer continuous cropping. They produce small cabbages within about 8 weeks from transplanting while those that were not transplanted gain size over the next month or so. Other popular quick-maturing types, e.g. Sugarloaf, may be planted in small batches 3 or 4 weeks apart to give continuity.

Requirements

Cabbages need a well-drained and preferably limey soil and if possible a full day's sunlight.
Planting time. Many of the hybrid cabbages such as Ballhead and Superette can be sown throughout the year in mild districts. However, the main sowing times for most varieties are in temperate districts from August through to May, in cold districts from August to April and in tropical regions from March to July. If the older Drumhead or Ballhead types are exposed to frosty winters, particularly when the plants are in the half-grown stage, they will run to seed as soon as the warm weather occurs. This applies less to conical or Sugarloaf types such as Enfield Market, Eastham, Irish, etc. which in cooler districts are known as 'springheading' or 'spring-maturing' types.

Long-maturing types such as Savoy and Drumhead which are mainly grown for winter maturity are sown during November or December for planting out in late January and February. This applies particularly in the cooler districts where they need to make the most of their growth before winter.

Cultivation

Soils that are known to be acid and have not been limed during the past season will benefit from the addition of about a quarter-cup of garden lime or dolomite per sq. m. Also add about one-third cup of complete plant food or a shovel of dried poultry manure to the same area. A bucketful per sq. m of well-rotted compost is also beneficial especially in very sandy or clay soils. Dig this in with the lime and fertiliser if most of it is well decomposed, or otherwise use as a surface mulch after planting.

In sandy soils particularly it is an advantage to give very light sprinklings (say 1 level dessertspoon per sq. m) of complete plant food every 4–6 weeks and in all cases water when the surface soil dries out. When plants are starting to form hearts, give fortnightly watering with either liquid animal manure or any of the complete soluble plant foods.

Special problems

Slugs, snails and the caterpillars of white cabbage moths can devastate the foliage of cabbages. Make regular use of snail baits or spray and applications of cabbage dust which will also control grey aphids. Club root — a fungus disease causing distorted knobbly roots — may occur in some areas. This disease is unusual in limey prepared soils as suggested but where it has previously been a problem it is advisable to apply burnt limestone (quicklime) or hydrated lime 5–6 weeks prior to planting out.

Browning and shrivelling of the leaf margin indicates a deficiency in potash. This is more likely to occur in sandy soils where complete plant foods have not been used, in unlimed acid soils or occasionally where prolonged rainfall followed heavy liming which had increased the solubility of potash, and made it more readily leached from the soil. Correct by scattering about 1 level tablespoon per sq. m of sulphate of potash or muriate of potash around the plants and water in well.

Long 'burpless' cucumbers

Grow carrots year round in mild climates

Capsicum

Capsicums have a higher source of Vitamin C than any other vegetable, add a tremendous flavour to salads and variety in cooked dishes, and are attractive in growth. The most popular and widely grown are the sweet or bell peppers including Californian Wonder and Yolo. These are also referred to as Bullnose types. Sweet Banana is a long yellow or banana-shaped variety. The hot peppers, e.g. Long Red Cayenne and Tabasco, are popular for pickles, chutneys, curries, etc.

Requirements

Capsicums are warmth-lovers needing much the same conditions as tomatoes. Although not to be confused with ornamental chillies which are not edible, capsicums are very decorative as pot plants or in any sunny, not too root-infested, area of the ornamental garden.

Planting time. As capsicums need 4–5 months of warm conditions, they should be planted in both cool and cooler temperate districts as soon as nights have lost their chill. Sow seed indoors or in warm sheltered corners during early spring, because seeds do not germinate readily until temperatures are above 20°C. In warmer temperate areas they may be planted out as late as November or early December, in warm semi-tropical areas until February and in the extreme north during mid-autumn or as soon as the wet conditions are over.

Cultivation

As plenty of air circulation is desirable leave about 50 cm between plants. Prepare the soil with a compost and complete plant food as suggested for tomatoes and water whenever the soil surface dries out. Sweet peppers can be picked at any time but are best when the fruits have reached full size and are firm and crisp. All except the yellow types are green initially then turn red when ripe but may be used at either stage.

Special problems

Sometimes fruit fly protection is needed (see

Savoy hybrid cabbages

Green gold cabbages

tomatoes). The setting of the fruits may be affected by sudden cold changes, heat-wave conditions or extreme dryness. If spotting of fruit or foliage occurs use copper spray or Zineb. Tomato dust will also control these and pest problems.

Chinese cabbage

The green in the foliage has the texture of lettuce and the broad white centre ribs of the leaf a tender crispness when sliced in salads.

Requirements

Chinese cabbage needs to be grown quickly without setback. Therefore maintain an even supply of plant foods and water as suggested for lettuce. A similar aspect is also required.

Planting time. In warmer temperate climates sow during August and September and then again from early March to late April. In cool districts during late February to March and again during October and November; in tropical districts from March to June.

Cultivation

As lettuce.

Special problems

Except for slugs and snails, few pests or diseases attack Chinese cabbage. Some plants almost reach the hearting stage and then run to seed. In temperate areas this usually occurs during early spring. In cooler districts it can be at the same period or later following a sudden cold change. Therefore in these districts delay sowings until conditions are settled, or sow to mature during the cooler months.

Carrot

Carrots are an excellent proposition for home gardeners because so many can be grown in a small space. Two to 3 m of row will keep the average family supplied for 8–10 weeks. When only two rows are sown they can be as close as 10–15 cm apart. They are decorative in the foreground of the ornamental garden if small clumps are sown in circles 20–30 cm in diameter. They can also be grown in bucket-sized nursery pots. See 'Container gardening'.

Requirements

Carrots need a well-drained position where they have at least half sun — preferably more. Long-shaped varieties particularly require a deeply dug stone-free soil, ideally well manured from a previous crop. However, poor or previously unprepared soil can be improved by digging in plenty of well-rotted compost and a complete plant food within a week or two of sowing, providing it is mixed evenly through the soil. To do this it should be raked in and mixed with the surface soil first, and then forked over 2 or 3 times.

To overcome the problem of a stony soil, I make a thorough mixture of soil, fertiliser and compost. The soil comes from a spade-depth wedge-shaped trench which runs the length of the row. After thorough mixing it is then sifted back into the trench through bird wire to remove stones, fibrous compost and other coarse material. It needs to be heaped a few cm above the surrounding soil-level to allow for settlement.

After firming the soil it is then gently watered and allowed to settle for a couple of days before the seed is sown. Use the same principle for planting in bucket-size nursery pots.

Planting time. In areas with cold winters sow from August to March because carrots which mature when spring weather is approaching tend to bolt to seed. In temperate areas varieties such as All-The-Year-Round can be sown throughout the year but August to March are the main sowing times. In tropical districts, sow from March (or whenever the wet season finishes) until about August.

Cultivation

Prepare the soil adding about half a cup of garden lime or dolomite per sq. m unless the soil is naturally limey or has been limed in the previous year. Distribute deeply and evenly through the soil.

Carrots in their early stages are difficult to weed by hand so prepare the soil, water it and allow to stand for a week or two so the weeds that emerge can be destroyed by surface scuffling on a hot day before planting takes place. For easy weed control sow the carrots in a perfectly straight row made by pressing the straight edge of a piece of timber into the soil to a depth of 1 cm.

Germination is retarded when soil crusts over the seed row so cover the lightly-sown furrow with either vermiculite, shredded compost or, in moist clay loams that do not dry out rapidly, with coarse sand. Vermiculite or sand remain visible and make weeding easier by clearly defining the sown row.

Vermiculite is very light and will blow about or wash away so after nearly filling the furrow run forefinger and thumb along either side of the row to pull in slight shoulder of the soil on either side of the vermiculite strip. The latter will remain just visible when the soil is patted down. Then water gently so as not to dislodge the seed. Heavy watering causes clay soils to cake.

Some gardeners overcome the problem of soil caking and crusting by sowing a radish seed with the carrots. Radishes come up very rapidly and break the crusty surface soil and allow the comparatively frail carrots through. Carrots and radishes are good companion plants and one seems to help the other to grow.

Special problems

Most modern varieties are virus resistant, so this once common disease is no longer a problem. Aphids can cause a downward crimping, distortion and slight yellowing of the foliage but can be eliminated by spraying with Pyrethrum or Malathion.

Root rot may affect Western Red during humid autumn conditions but Topweight, All-The-Year-Round, Progress and most other varieties have resistance to this problem. Carrot maggot, the larvae of the carrot fly which may attack the roots of the carrots, can be deterred by hilling to cover the tops of the roots or, if the problem is evident, by watering with Carbaryl or Malathion.

Forking is often attributed to stony ground

but fertilisers which have not been mixed in evenly can also be the cause. Splitting may occur when prolonged wet follows a fairly dry period.

Cauliflower

Cauliflowers were once considered a very exacting crop but modern varieties are far more adaptable, and there are miniature types that may be planted at any time, require a minimum of space and crop quickly.

Requirements

The same as recommended for cabbages.

Planting time. The old 'phenomenal' types have to be sown to mature before mid to late winter. They require about 6 months from planting out time *not* sowing time. Therefore, the Phenomenal Six Months need to be sown by late November or early December; Phenomenal Four Months by late January, etc. Paleface and other modern medium-sized cauliflowers are less sensitive to lengthening days and can be planted at any time, from late summer to late autumn. Miniature types can be sown at any time but avoid a mid-summer maturity.

As new types are continuously being developed, it is as well to check information on the seed packet. Seedlings sold by reputable suppliers will naturally be suitable for planting at the time of sale.

Cultivation

As for cabbages, leaving at least 50 cm spacing between medium to large types and 15–18 cm between the miniatures.

Special problems

Cauliflowers are subject to the same problems as cabbages. An additional one is a condition known as Whiptail which causes elongated and deformed foliage, and in serious cases a breakdown of the curd of the cauliflower. This is due to molybdenum deficiency which is more likely to occur when large amounts of fertiliser containing only major elements are used, and particularly heavy applications of sulphate of ammonia. Avoid the problem by using a complete fertiliser containing trace elements, and for liquid feeding one of the complete water-soluble plant foods rather than sulphate of ammonia alone. If detected early the molybdenum deficiency can be corrected by spraying the plants with 1 level teaspoon of sodium or ammonium molybdate dissolved in about 5 L of water. Molybdenum is an essential trace element but is only required in minute quantities; 1 or 2 teaspoonfuls per year would be sufficient for the needs of the average home garden.

Celery

Celery is sometimes regarded as a crop for the professional grower but good-quality celery can be grown in the average home garden.

Requirements

A sunny position, well-drained soil with plenty of well-rotted compost or animal manure added, and given a dressing of lime or dolomite and complete plant food.

Planting time. In cool to temperate areas from August to February, in warmer temperate and semi-tropical areas with mild winters it can be planted almost throughout the year. March–April is the main planting time in northern monsoonal areas.

Cultivation
Plants can be set out 15 cm apart with only 22 cm between the rows. After the seedlings have had a week or so to establish, feed at fortnightly intervals with one of the complete water-soluble plant foods.

When plants are nearly fully grown the stems can be whitened by covering them to the foliage with lengths of board held by stakes on either side of the row or by wrapping individual plants in brown paper.

Special problems
At the first sign of brown leaf spotting spray with Bordeaux mixture or copper oxychloride and repeat every 10 days. Sprayed plants are safe to use within 4 days of harvest.

Chives
Chives are always useful for sandwiches, savouries, sauces, etc.

Requirements
Chives can be grown indoors in a sunny window-sill but do better in an open sunny part of the garden or in pots 15–20 cm in diameter.
Planting time. Can be grown from seeds sown in spring or autumn or by division of whole clumps at that time. Trim back the foliage to at least half before replanting.

Cultivation
Chives prefer a slightly limey soil with a sprinkling of complete plant food or a light dressing of poultry manure prior to planting out. Keep well watered and feed occasionally with a complete water-soluble plant food.

Cress
Cress is nutritious and gives freshness to salads, sandwiches, etc.

Requirements
Garden cress, sometimes known as mustard cress, can be sown in the shaded part of the garden or shallow seed trays on a shaded balcony. It needs plenty of moisture.
Planting time. Sow at any time.

Cultivation
Sow the seed thickly using 1 teaspoonful to a seed tray 30 cm square. Cover with paper or moist sacking which should be removed just before the plants appear (10–12 days). Then water with a complete soluble plant food. Harvest with scissors at ground-level in 2–4 weeks.

Land cress can be grown from seed or by finger-length cuttings struck in moist sand. Leafy tip sections are harvested similarly to water cress.

Water cress
Water cress usually grows in a running stream but can be raised near a dripping tap or in other constantly moist positions.

Sometimes plants are hard to obtain but are easily propagated by striking about finger length, preferably tip sections of the stem in moist sand or in a jar of water.

Cucumber
Cucumbers give freshness to salads, sandwiches and drinks.

Requirements
Cucumbers crop best in a well-drained sunny position in a slightly limey soil enriched by dried fowl manure or about one-third cup per sq. m of complete plant food. Well-rotted compost mixed in or applied later as a surface mulch is an added advantage.
Planting time. In temperate districts you can sow cucumbers from September–December and to the end of January in warmer spots. In cool districts they can be sown from October–December. In semi-tropical areas from September–February and in more northern monsoonal areas during autumn.

Cultivation
Cucumbers are normally sown on 1 m mounds raised 12–15 cm above the surrounding soil and dished slightly in the centre. Groups of 2 or 3 seeds are sown 2 cm deep at 50 cm intervals around the mound toward the edge, then after germination the strongest plant in each planting is removed. Many people prefer to train the long green cucumbers on trellises 1.5 m high with the plants spaced about 30 cm apart along the trellising. Don't keep the soil continuously moist but give a good soaking whenever it becomes dry to 1–2 cm below the surface.

Special problems
Germination, often a problem early in the season, is usually due to cold soil conditions, over-wet soil and deep planting. Powdery mildew (an ash-like film) can be controlled by spraying with Bordeaux mixture or copper oxychloride. Downy mildew (small white tufts below shrivelled foliage) is checked by spraying with Zineb or Mancozeb. Some cucumber strains are resistant to mildew and this will be indicated on the seed packet.

Egg-plant
Aubergine
The plants and large glossy purple fruits are decorative, and the fruit appetising sliced and fried or used in casseroles, etc.

Requirements
As for tomatoes.
Planting time. Egg-plants need a long, warm growing season so in temperate regions are sown or planted during October or November; in cool areas during October, and in semi-tropical regions from September–February.

Cultivation
Because of their need for a long growing period and because they do not transplant well, egg-plants are usually sown 3 or 4 seeds per pot and the strongest seedling is planted out when nights have lost their chill. Peat pots are an excellent starting medium. Plants should be set out about 50 cm apart and, if more than 2 rows are being planted, allow 1 m between the rows. Stake plants in windy areas or pinch the tips from the plant when 15–20 cm tall to force lower branching and make the plants a little more self-supporting.

Harvest fruit when deep purple. Regular picking encourages longer cropping.

Special problems
Tomato dusts control any pests liable to attack the plants.

Endive
Very similar to lettuce but with thinly divided or cut leaves and often grown in hot climates where lettuce can be difficult.

Requirements
As for lettuce.
Planting time. In temperate climates sow from August–April; in cool areas from August–March, and in tropical or semi-tropical districts throughout the year.

Cultivation
As for lettuce. Plants are blanched by lifting the foliage and tying it together, or covering with a cardboard box for about 10 days. Only blanch as needed because plants quickly run to seed afterwards.

Kohlrabi
Looks like a purple-top turnip but tastes like sweet fresh cabbage, especially if grown quickly through the cool weather.
Planting time. In temperate districts sow from March–August; in cool districts from February–April and again in late winter–early spring, and tropical areas in autumn. It matures in three-and-a-half months from sowing.

Cultivation
Sow direct, spacing a pinch of 2–3 seeds about every 10 cm along the row, then thin to the strongest one in each spacing. If growing only 2 rows space only 15 cm apart. Once the seedlings have established, water fortnightly with complete water-soluble fertiliser.

Special problems
As for cabbage.

Leek
Boiled leeks have a flavour somewhere between onions and asparagus. They suit cool and tropical areas where onions are difficult to grow.

Requirements
Sow in a sunny position, preferably in a deeply dug soil with plenty of well-rotted compost. If the soil is acid add lime or dolomite and a dressing of fowl manure, or one-third cup per sq. m of complete plant food.
Planting time. In both cool and temperate areas leeks are best grown through the warm weather, from August–March. In tropical districts they are sown from late summer to autumn.

Cultivation
Sow seeds thinly in seed boxes or seed beds. Prepare garden soil and allow to settle. Make furrows about 50 cm apart and 12 cm deep and plant seedlings along the furrows about 10 cm apart, and as growth progresses, fill soil around the plants almost to the base of the leaves. Water occasionally with complete water-soluble plant food. Leeks mature 24–28 weeks from the time seed is sown. They crop over a period of about 12 weeks.

Butterhead, a small loose-headed lettuce, has excellent flavour

Two rows of lettuce (3 weeks old) divided by carrots with potatoes and strawberries behind

Onion tops bending just before harvest

Lettuce

Freshly harvested home-grown lettuce makes salads and sandwiches much more appetising.

Requirements

It is generally considered that lettuce needs an open sunny position, but during the summer they can be grown in as little as half a day's sunshine. They need a limey soil, preferably with a little dressing of well-rotted compost or animal manure dug in prior to planting.

Planting time. Can be sown throughout the year providing the right varieties are chosen. Imperial 615 and Triumph only grow well through the cooler months; Great Lakes types, Valverdie and Yadesdale, through the warmer ones. Small loose-hearting types such as Mignonette and Butterhead are reliable at any time of the year and though they may not heart well all but the outer foliage is pleasantly flavoured and textured. Imperial 847, a fine-textured lettuce for sowing most of the year, does not heart as reliably during hot weather as Great Lakes types. Different varieties vary in performance from district to district. For example, all but Original Strain Great Lakes may be prone to a condition known as 'sliming' in summer. Check with your local supplier or consult the seed packet.

Cultivation

To get a good heart lettuce it should be sown quickly without setback. Thin out the unwanted seedlings as early and as carefully as possible. Keep lettuce growing rapidly by not allowing more than the surface soil to dry out and by feeding moderately, but constantly, with complete water-soluble plant foods at the recommended strength as frequently as once per week. Avoid any more than light surface scuffling as deep cultivation usually destroys surface roots and results in growth check. Mulch the surface with fibrous compost not only for soil improvement and moisture conservation but because it keeps soil cool which is the way lettuce likes it.

Special problems

Guard against slugs and snails, the main enemies of lettuce. In some areas birds can be a problem. Some gardeners combat this problem by stretching black cotton about 20 cm above the plants but the easiest and best protection against birds and beasts is to make half-cylinder or tunnel shapes of wire netting to cover the rows. These are easily transferred as needed.

Marrow, zucchini and squash

The bush varieties have gained popularity now it is appreciated how much nicer they are when used young, cooked whole or sliced for sauté or salads.

Requirements

Warm conditions; a sunny well-drained aspect with the soil prepared as suggested for cucumbers.

Planting time. In temperate climates sow or plant out from October–January; in cooler areas from October–December; in semi-tropical regions from September–February, and in the extreme north from autumn to spring.

Cultivation

In slow-draining soils and particularly when sowing seed early in the season, sow or plant as suggested for cucumbers or plant in clumps of 3 or 4 plants or in rows, leaving 75 cm between the plants. When the fruits are to be used young, pick every second day to maintain an even size and prolong cropping.

Special problems

Check for powdery mildew as suggested for cucumbers. Failure of fruit to set can be due to lack of bees so hand-pollinate by picking the male flowers, breaking them away from the petals then dusting the centre stamens over the stigma or centre of the female flower which can be distinguished by the bulbous embryo fruit at the base of the flower. Pollination is best carried out early in the cool of the day. Some plants produce a succession of up to 10 male or female flowers and pollination is less of a problem when you have a number of plants. Shrivelling of embryo fruit due to mildew can be controlled by adding 1 tablespoon of sulphate of potash per sq. m of soil around the plants when flowering commences and watering in.

Melon
Rockmelon or cantaloup

Dwarf or bush varieties now available do not take up too much space.

Requirements

Rockmelons are at their best in dry inland climates but some of the new dwarf types and particularly Hale's Best which is resistant to downy mildew grow well in coastal areas. Some varieties, e.g. Honeydew, have much better flavour when grown in hot, dry districts, and may lose some of their flavour should wet or humid conditions occur when the fruit is ripening.

Planting time. Similar to marrows, except that most varieties take about 1 month longer to mature, therefore sowing should cease 1 month earlier in both temperate and cool climates.

Okra

Bushy plants about 1 m high. Related to hibiscus, are grown for their fleshy green pods which are used in soups, sauces and as a thickening agent. It is essential that these pods be picked before they become stringy.

Requirements, planting time and cultivation

Similar to beans.

Onion

Although onions take at least 6 months to mature, they can be planted out thickly and used as shallots from the half-grown stage onwards. Thin them out progressively until the remaining plants are 7–10 cm apart and leave these to mature.

Requirements

A well-drained limey soil in an open sunny position because partly shaded plants tend to run to seed. Prepare soil as suggested for cab-

Radishes are quick and easy to grow

Tomatoes crop in hottest part of summer

Rainbow chard (coloured stemmed silverbeet)

Zucchinis (Golden Corgettes), best picked young

bages. Compost or animal manure should be dug in a couple of weeks before sowing or planting, otherwise they tend to attract onion flies.

Planting time. In temperate and semi-tropical climates, most varieties of onions are sown from mid-autumn to mid-winter. The early salad or bunching types such as Early Barletta, White Rocket, etc. are usually sown a little earlier, from February–March, but the danger is that heavy frosts when the plants are about half-grown (20–30 cm) may cause most of them to run to seed. This can also apply to some of the early globe types such as Early Lockyer, Crystal Grano, etc. Plants sown in April are not affected this way. Keeping onions, e.g. brown or white Spanish, are sown from May–July. The large late onions, e.g. Prizetaker and Ailsa Craig, are sown from July–September. Cool climate sowing times are much the same as those already mentioned excepting that brown Spanish and other keeping types are safer planted during July rather than May and large types such as Ailsa Craig and Prizetaker should not be sown before August.

Cultivation

Sow or transplant into double rows 15 cm apart. If more than 2 rows are sown, allow 20–25 cm between each set of rows. Scatter the seeds thinly along the rows and when the young seedlings emerge from the hooked-over stage, thin out to about 2 cm apart.

Seedlings may be planted at the same spacing then, from the time they reach lead pencil thickness, thin and use as shallots until about 10 cm apart, then leave remainder to mature.

Salad onions can be improved by watering every 3–4 weeks with a complete water-soluble plant food. This treatment is not recommended for keeping types as the extra nitrogen reduces both keeping qualities and strength of flavour.

When transplanting seedlings they will be easier to handle and will establish better if the tips are trimmed to half-length and the roots to about 4 cm.

Special problems

Shrivelling of the leaf tips can be due to downy mildew which is controlled by spraying with Zineb or Mancozeb. Leaf tip shrivelling accompanied by a white streakiness of the remaining foliage is usually due to attack by onion thrips. These pests develop resistance to chemicals so it is better to alternate sprays, using Thiodan or Carbaryl one week and Malathion or Lebaycid the next.

Parsnip

Parsnips take 5–6 months to mature but can be harvested over a period of about 3 months.

Requirements

A deeply-dug well-prepared soil as suggested for carrots.

Planting time. In temperate districts parsnips are sown from August through to March. In cold districts from September through to February and in tropical regions from late summer to early winter.

Cultivation

Parsnip seeds need good contact with soil moisture to germinate. The best procedure is to allow the soil to settle for a week or two after preparing. Have the surface only just lightly crumbly, then after lightly sowing the seed along the rows and covering with a few mm of soil, use a flat board to press it down into good contact with the soil. After germination thin out and cultivate as suggested for carrots.

If you are interested in growing giant show-bench parsnips, use a crowbar to widen a cone-shaped hole 75 cm deep, fill with a mixture of equal parts of light soil and well-rotted compost, firm down, sow 2–3 seeds close to the centre then as growth becomes evident remove all but the strongest shoot.

Parsley

Parsley has many uses and is very nutritious. Its growth is decorative, so can be combined with ornamentals. This is very convenient because parsley prefers a slightly more acid soil than do most vegetables.

Requirements

Parsley will grow in a partly shaded area but is stronger and better flavoured when it has at least half a day's sun. It is very adaptable but growth is better when heavy or very sandy soil is improved by the addition of well-rotted compost.

Planting time. Sow or plant out almost any time. The best times are August–March for temperate areas; September–March for cold districts and January–April for tropical areas.

Cultivation

Most households need only a few plants so it is often more convenient to purchase seedlings. Seed often takes 3–4 weeks to germinate but it can be speeded up by sowing in a 12–15 cm diameter pot, firming the seed into the surface, then covering with a piece of towelling. Over this pour near-boiling water then leave to stand with the towelling intact, if necessary, watering through the towelling should it dry out. Lift the towelling to check for germination from about the eighth day onward, then remove it at the first sign of sprouting. This method will encourage germination in about 10 days.

Do not weaken parsley by picking plants too early and too hard. Pick only the outer leaves as they reach full size, leaving 4 mature ones in the centre of the plant.

Pea

Peas are usually grown in the home garden during the months too cold for beans. Compared to the latter they are often regarded a poor proposition. There are now a number of prolific and long-cropping climbing types, including the sugar or snow peas which have edible and palatable pods.

Requirements

Same as for beans.

Planting time. Sow in all but very frosty areas from early autumn until spring. The pods rather than the vines are damaged by heavy frosts, therefore in cold winter areas sowing

can be timed to give maturity when frosts are likely to be over. The average time from sowing to maturity is 12–15 weeks.

Cultivation

Climbing peas can be sown like beans, spacing 2 seeds about 2 m apart every 8–10 cm along a row or base of a trellis. Dwarf peas are set quite closely in a broad row about a span wide with the seeds only 3–4 cm apart.

Sow peas by making a spade-width furrow 5–6 cm deep, sprinkle the base with complete fertiliser using about half a cup for every 2 m of furrow and cover with 3 cm of soil. Sprinkle the seed over it 3–4 cm apart, cover with 2 cm of soil, gently firm down and, provided the soil is already damp, give only a light watering.

Germination is often poor during wet conditions, especially if the seed is planted deeper than 2 cm. This problem can be minimised by dusting the seed with copper oxychloride, Zineb, Captan or similar fungicide immediately prior to sowing. Do this by adding half a teaspoon of the fungicide powder to the seed in the packet, close and slightly balloon the pack and shake until the seed is evenly coated. This gives some protection against fungi which could destroy the seed during cold, wet and airless soil conditions.

A few twigs placed along the row will keep the peas upright and make them easier to manage. Peas picked and used when the pods have just filled out have the best flavour. When left on the vine or stored, flavour deteriorates as the natural sugars turn into starch.

Special problems

Powdery mildew (an ash-like film over the foliage) can be controlled by spraying with Bordeaux mixture or copper oxychloride. Red-legged earth mites, tiny black insects with red legs which cause the shrivelling and collapse of vines, can be controlled by spraying with Lebaycid or Rogor.

Potato

Potatoes are often regarded as only being suitable for large gardens but a space 4 m square can accommodate about 3 kg seed potatoes, and produce at least 50 kg new potatoes, or more, under good growth conditions. One plant grown in a 20–25 L drum can produce surprising results. People wishing to plant only a small area need not buy seed potatoes. Healthy-looking eating potatoes that have begun to sprout can be used; the eyes (sprouts) removed with a thick section of peel will soon make plants if covered lightly with moist soil.

Requirements

Potatoes need a well-drained position and at least half a day's sun, preferably more. They adapt to a wide range of soils and are frequently used to break up heavy soil. A slightly acid soil is best because fungus diseases are more prevalent in limey soils. Only add lime if the soil is known to be very acid then only use about half a cup of dolomite or garden lime per sq. m.

Planting time. In comparatively warm frost-free areas, plant from June–August; elsewhere planting should be delayed until 3–4 weeks before frosts are expected to end. (Will normally stand up to 4–5 frostings after initial growth shows.) They can also be planted in February. If seed potatoes are not available, sprouting of mature ones can be induced by storing them in a plastic bag in a dark place.

Cultivation
Vigour of the tubers is improved if they are spread out a week prior to planting, in a brightly lit position, but not in direct sunlight. Turn them after a few days to green them evenly. Tubers less than 8 cm in diameter are planted whole. Larger ones are cut with an even distribution of eyes on each section by halving them cross-wise between the root and the tip end where the largest number of eyes are. Cut through again. Compost the soil and, if necessary, lime.

Dig the soil deeply about 1 month prior to planting, partly turning the clods and leaving them in a loosely packed state so that air can circulate freely through them. About 1 week prior to planting, dig the soil over again to break down the clods and add one-third cup of plant food per sq. m. Make furrows 50–70 cm apart and 15 cm deep. Space the seed potatoes or cuts 30 cm apart along the furrows and cover with 2–5 cm of soil. As shoots progress, fill in soil around them. About 6 weeks after planting give another light sprinkling of complete plant food (quarter-cup per sq. m) and chip this lightly into the soil. As growth progresses use soil from between the furrows to hill up around the base of the plants to encourage more roots and so more potatoes.

Be careful not to expose already formed potatoes as they then turn green and become toxic. If the rows must be spaced more closely apply a mulch of straw around the plants and during dry periods give the ground a good gentle soaking about once a week. Allow the surface soil to dry out before watering again.

Harvest
Dig potatoes from the time the lower leaves begin to yellow. Plants are allowed to die down prior to digging if potatoes are to be stored. Do not leave dug potatoes exposed to light as this causes toxic greening.

Special problems
Leaf-eating ladybirds which skeletonise foliage, and all caterpillars, can be controlled by spraying or dusting with Carbaryl. Do not use B.H.C. on potatoes as this causes tainting of the tubers. Brown spotting or water-soaked areas of the foliage indicate need to spray with copper oxychloride or Zineb.

Pumpkin
Plant breeders have introduced several good bush types each one covering an area of only about 1 m square. Intermediate varieties, e.g. butternut, spread only about 2 m so are suitable for relatively small gardens. Larger varieties such as Queensland Blue, Crown Prince and Triamble are likely to spread 4–5 m in each direction so do need more space. However, over-venturesome runners can be restrained by pinching the tips or heading them back toward the centre of the plant by carefully bending them around and holding in position with a small stake.

Requirements
The same as for marrows and zucchinis.
Planting time. Plant in spring when soil is warming up and, in temperate climates, continue sowing until January or early February with quick-maturing Butternut and bush types. In cool climates the latter can be sown until December while the larger late-maturing types should not be planted after late November. In the extreme north the main sowing season for pumpkins is from late March until May.

Cultivation and special problems
See marrows.

Radish
Radishes are amongst the easiest vegetables to grow, germinating and growing to maturity 6 weeks after sowing.

Requirements
Any well-drained soil with about half a day's sunlight will suit them.
Planting time. Sow at any time. They are nicest used fresh so sow 50 cm of row each fortnight.

Cultivation
At the earliest opportunity thin the young plants 4–5 cm apart. Keep well watered and after the first set of true leaves has formed apply liquid manure or a complete water-soluble plant food once a fortnight.

Special problems
The same as for cabbages.

Rhubarb
Rhubarb clumps can remain productive for many years so it is better to keep them in separate beds.

Requirements
A lime-free soil and full sunlight but will grow in half shade.
Planting time. Most rhubarb is grown from crowns planted during the winter months. It can also be raised from seed sown in spring.

Cultivation
Mulch the soil liberally with well-rotted compost or manure prior to planting out, and maintain a good surface mulch of these materials around the plant. Keep well watered and do not over-pick. Remove outer leaves only with an outward and downward twist, leave at least 4 new mature leaves in the centre of each crown. Remove any seed heads. If vigour is lacking, water about once a fortnight with a complete water-soluble plant food.

Space seedlings 15–20 cm apart as soon as they are large enough. As they develop keep only those that show good red sturdy stems and discard the rest. Transplant into their permanent position during winter. Propagate from good clumps by dividing the crowns during winter. Good colour and size depend on selection rather than special feeding.

Special problems
If leaf spotting occurs spray with Zineb or copper oxychloride.

Silverbeet
Silverbeet is a useful long-lasting and nutri-tious stand-by vegetable. Sometimes sold as spinach but the latter is a much softer textured, narrow-stemmed plant that grows well in cool conditions.

Requirements
Choose a position with at least half sunlight and well-drained limey soil containing plenty of organic material.
Planting time. Can be sown or planted out at any time. Where cold winters are experienced, autumn and winter sowings are inclined to run to seed in spring. In tropical areas sowing is from early autumn through to spring.

Cultivation
Six to 8 plants are sufficient for the average family. Seed germinates readily if soaked overnight prior to sowing. Better to sow in a container or seed bed then transplant about 20 cm apart in rows as individual seeds may produce several seedlings that need thinning to a single plant.

Allow the seedlings a few weeks to establish then encourage lush leafy growth by feeding each fortnight with a water-soluble plant food. When harvesting, remove the entire leaf by twisting downwards and outwards. Always leave 4 well-formed leaves in the centre of the plant as over-picking weakens.

Special problems
Small yellow spots that turn brown may occur during wet conditions due to a fungus infection. Remove the worst infected leaves and spray the remainder with copper oxychloride. Grey scribble-like tracery through the foliage is caused by the tunnelling of leaf miner fly larvae. Control by spraying with Lebaycid or Rogor and do not harvest for at least a week afterwards.

Spinach
In some cases this is confused with silverbeet — see above.

Requirements
Similar to lettuce.
Planting time. In temperate districts sow from March–May; in semi-tropical areas from May–June only, and in cool districts from late February–September.

Cultivation
Spinach is best sown direct in rows about 25 cm apart, placing 2–3 seeds every 20 cm, thin out later to 1 or 2 plants per spacing. Keep well watered and feed at weekly intervals with water-soluble plant food.

Sweet corn
Growing sweet corn in the home garden allows you to enjoy the freshness of cobs harvested at the correct time. These are much nicer than market sweet corn because the latter loses its creamy succulence in transit and storage. Many of the modern hybrids mature in 8–9 weeks instead of 12, and the semi-dwarf varieties demand little space.

Requirements
A sunny position and a well-drained soil with plenty of organic material added plus either fowl manure or a dressing of complete plant food. The addition of lime or dolomite is also an advantage in all but naturally limey soils or

those limed within the previous 12 months. Plant in a block of several short rows to assure better pollination. Pollen from the tassels at the tops of the plants must reach the silks at the tip of the cobs to achieve pollination of each kernel.

Planting time. In tropical districts with warm winters sweet corn can be sown at any time. In semi-tropical and warm temperate areas it is sown from early spring until February or with the quick-maturing types until March. In cool districts it is best to wait until October and continue through to January or until February for the quick-maturing 60-day types.

Cultivation

Sow seeds 2–3 cm deep and 8–10 cm apart in short rows about 50 cm apart. Keep well watered and apply a light dressing of fowl manure or complete plant food when plants are about half-grown.

Crops are ready to harvest when the silks shrivel. A more definite test is to peel back the sheath and puncture a kernel toward the base of the cob. It should exude a creamy juice. If thin and milky the cobs are still immature, or if not present the corn is over-mature and will be tough.

Special problems

The corn earworm or caterpillar sometimes enters the cobs and eats out sections. Once it gains entry it is difficult to control but at first sign of its presence spray liberally with Carbaryl to protect the later maturing cobs.

Sweet potato

Sweet potatoes are only worthwhile in a garden where space is plentiful and they can occupy the ground the entire summer season. They need 5 months of warm weather between planting and maturity.

Requirements

Sweet potatoes grow well in almost any well-drained sunny position but for best results prepare the soil as suggested for potatoes.

Planting time. In both cool and temperate districts set the plants out as soon as the soil has warmed up in spring, and certainly by November. In warmer semi-tropical districts they can be planted satisfactorily until December.

Cultivation

Plants are raised by striking shoots from the tubers as cuttings. If buying the tubers during winter to produce cuttings, they should be first thoroughly washed in case they have been treated with shoot-retarding compound, then kept moist preferably in a warm indoor position. When shoots have developed, match-length sections with a leaf or two attached are struck in moist sand. Plants are set out in rows about 1 m apart with at least 50 cm between them. Give occasional good soakings during dry periods. Tubers will form from the original roots of the cuttings, and the formation is assisted if the vines are lifted occasionally with a fork to prevent the stems from forming roots in the soil.

Tomato

Garden-fresh tomatoes have a special flavour.

Although the tallest staking varieties are most often grown, there are self-supporting dwarf types ideal for container growing.

Requirements

Tomatoes are a warm-weather crop. They suit well-drained soil with plenty of organic material added, and at least half sun, preferably more.

Planting time. In warm tropical and semi-tropical districts, tomatoes may be grown all the year round. Elsewhere they can be planted out in spring as soon as frosts are over; until about late December in temperate districts, but only until early November in cold areas.

If raising your own seedlings start them in a warm sunny indoor area, transfer them to peat pots or other small individual containers as soon as large enough, then keep them in an outdoor sheltered sunny position until they are ready to go out into the garden or into large growing containers.

Cultivation

Prepare the bed with well-rotted compost or animal manure as early as possible prior to planting out. If fowl manure has not been used in initial preparations mix in about one-third cup of complete plant food per sq. m. Lime is not recommended unless the soil is known to be very acidy.

If grown in single rows, set plants 50 cm apart. For larger areas allow a little more space and about 1.5 m between the rows.

Tall types such as Grosse Lisse need stakes at least 2 m tall, preferably driven in prior to planting. Make a wide hole extending out about a small span from the base of the stake, and set the roots of the seedling at the farthest point 4–5 cm deep and with the stem angled toward the stake. Cover the stem with well-rotted compost or soil as growth progresses. Unlike other seedlings, tomatoes will make extra roots from the stem and the plant will gain extra vigour.

As growth progresses carefully tie the stem to the stake at intervals of about 25–30 cm. Make a separate firm tie around the stake and another loose one around the stem of the plant. The tall-growing varieties should be pruned as growth progresses to prevent over-bushiness and to improve fruit quality.

Pruning consists of removing the small shoot or lateral that develops in the junction of leaf and stem. Sometimes the lowest one is left to provide an extra main stem which is trained diagonally across the trellis or stake or to a separate stake.

Give good soakings whenever the surface dries out. When the first fruits are formed plants gain extra vigour if one of the complete water-soluble plant foods is applied about once a fortnight.

Special problems

Over-leafy plants with very little flower or fruit sometimes occur. This is due to feeding either with complete water-soluble plant food or other highly nitrogenous material which is lacking in phosphorus. This can be counteracted by sprinkling a handful of superphosphate per sq. m around the plants and watering well.

Blossom End rot, a collapsed sunken and usually black area at the base of the fruit, is caused by there being insufficient water to carry calcium to all parts of the plant. It can be overcome by regular watering and a surface mulch of compost to conserve soil moisture. Deep cultivation around the plants can have a similar effect by destroying feeder roots and retarding the plant's moisture intake.

Tomatoes are subject to several leaf and fruit spotting fungus diseases and attack by leaf- or fruit-burrowing caterpillars. These can be controlled by regular use of tomato dust.

Fruit fly is a serious pest of tomatoes in some areas. Spray with Lebaycid or Rogor every 8–10 days from the time the first fruits begin changing from deep to limey green. Do not harvest any fruits for at least 7 days after spraying. Repeat the spray program every 10 days after picking everything that looks like ripening within that time.

Fruit fly baits are effective if freshly mixed and splashed on a 25 cm square area of the foliage once a week, choosing a sheltered lower area of the plant. They lure fruit flies from a distance of about 15 m.

Another fruit fly control is to cover the fruit clusters with paper bags fairly securely tied when the first fruits show their lighter colour change.

Swede turnip

Unlike table turnips these are used for their stronger flavour or for storing. However, they are comparatively mild and sweet if used in the younger stages.

Requirements

As for table turnips.

Planting time. In tropical districts sow March–May, elsewhere from January–April.

Cultivation

Treat like table turnips but allow about 20 cm between rows and 12 cm between plants. They take 14–18 weeks to mature.

Table turnip

These are often confused with the much stronger-flavoured swedes. They are sweet and succulent, especially if grown quickly and used while young. Try harvesting them 8–10 weeks from sowing and using as an hors d'oeuvre as popular in Europe, or slicing thinly for salads.

Requirements

A sunny position with well-drained limey soil as prepared for cabbages.

Planting time. Table turnips grow best through the cooler months. In temperate districts sow in February and March and again in August and September. In tropical districts sow during autumn and early winter.

Special problems

As with cabbages they are subject to grey aphids, cabbage moth or white butterfly caterpillar and slugs or snails. These problems can be controlled by using cabbage dust and, if necessary, snail bait.

Zucchini

See marrow and squash.

GARDEN CARE
AND MAINTENANCE

29. The art of watering

The way you water your soil is more important than generally realised; it can make a lot of difference to your plants, your soil — and your pocket!

Some people use far more water than is needed; others water more frequently than is necessary but still leave their plants thirsty.

Then there are the 'get-it-on-quickly' types who pound the soil with a hefty jet of water and turn clayey soil into mud which sets so hard it stifles plant roots and reduces the absorption rate of the soil so that much of the water they are supplying is lost in run-off.

Even if you are among the minority who water lightly and thoroughly, you could still be overdoing the water. Plant roots need air as well as water if they are to function properly.

The air on which they depend enters the soil through the spaces between the soil particles. Water is held in a thin film around these particles. As extra water is added the film becomes thicker; when too much water is added it becomes so thick that there is no room for the much-needed air.

Plants are like people; if water cuts off their air supply, they drown. It will take 4 or 5 days for the drowning to be accomplished and then the roots will rot.

Sandy soil absorbs water more rapidly than a clay soil can, but there are only small air spaces between fine sand particles and this hinders both water and air passage. Sand coated with decomposed organic substance can become greasy if allowed to dry out. Always water sand with a fine, mist-like spray over a long period of time. A surface mulch of coarse organic material is mandatory no matter whether your soil is light or heavy.

If you give plants a daily watering they will become dependent on this regular freshener and their roots will grow upward toward the moist surface of the soil. If there is a sudden heat-wave or you have to be away from home for a time they will suffer from the lack of moisture on which they have come to rely and will be damaged by the heat of the surface soil.

To be fair to your plants you should help them to become more self-reliant; they need a strong root system which runs deep and can tap water beneath the soil. Allow the surface of the soil to dry out to a depth of 2–3 cm. Do not induce the roots to grow upward. Test the dryness of the soil by trowelling down, then soak the soil, gently and very thoroughly, so that the water will go down . . . and down . . . and down. If you have agricultural pipes laid for drainage, watch the outlets and if water is beginning to run you know the soil is thoroughly wet. You may need to use a sprinkler for half a day to get moisture down to where it is needed.

Newly planted seedlings and germinating seeds should be treated differently; they need a steady, reliable watering to enable them to establish their roots. Once they are established and the plant is growing well, water as prescribed.

Plants should not be left without water until their foliage hangs limp, but plants allowed to show a little stress before being given water will flower well. Until experience gives you the 'feel' of the mild stress signs which say 'Water!' take your guide from examination of the soil a few cm below the surface. Trowel up a small sample; if it is damp, leave watering for a few days. By very, very gradually extending the time between waterings, you can make your plants less and less dependent on a supplementary water supply and thereby free yourself from the chore of watering so often.

There is nothing like rain for watering soil; it falls gently, as a rule, and does not compact the soil so that plant roots are starved of oxygen. If you must water, sprinkle, and let the sprinkling be long and slow. It can take as long as 2 hours for a light spray of water to penetrate the soil to any significant depth.

If shrubs or trees need water take the nozzle off your hosepipe, lay the pipe down near the trunk and let the water run out gently and leave until the ground is soaked but not swamped. Whenever you water, do it thoroughly; give your plants enough to sustain them for a week at least. Before watering again check that the soil has dried out to at least 2–3 cm.

WATER CORRECTLY
The illustration far left shows what happens when a plant is given frequent, shallow waterings. Roots grow in the upper soil surface where there is water. During periods of warm windy weather the plant is unable to absorb the water it needs. The plant at left is given deep, regular waterings. The roots penetrate deeply into the soil so they have a greater reservoir of water and nutrients to draw upon.

When to water

It has often been said that watering should never be done in the heat of the day. If you have been unwise enough to let your plants get into trouble, soak them as soon as you see their distress. If you were racked with thirst would you want to wait any longer than necessary? But make certain you give a thoroughly good soaking so that roots are not enticed to grow upward to the heat of the surface, because this would do them harm rather than good.

In summer it is wisest to water annuals and perennials with an overhead sprinkler before the sun gets hot in the morning and late in the afternoon after the heat has died down. Don't wet the plants and then leave them in the hot sun. Drops of water on leaf and blossom will be 'boiled' by the fierce rays and the plant will be damaged. A hot sun will evaporate water falling in a fine spray so your plants will not get all the water for which you are paying to provide for them. Any watering done during the hot parts of the day should be confined to soaking the ground.

In winter, watering should be kept to late morning and early afternoon. Water left on plants overnight could turn to ice or at least become cold enough to shock young growth. Lunch-time sprinkling should provide all the moisture needed as none will be lost by evaporation.

Dormant perennials and shrubs do not need much water during winter; if you give them too much they could become chilled or rotted; on the other hand the evergreens which flower in winter or spring need quite a lot — a good watering once or even twice a week could be necessary.

Equipment

The experienced gardener rarely waters the garden soil by hand — seed and seedlings growing in boxes are another matter.

Every garden needs a convenient source of water — taps should be provided at strategic points so that watering is made simple and not a job to be shirked. Hosepipe and watering cans are useful but better still are the sprays and sprinklers which rotate or swing and can be easily moved from one spot to another as the ground becomes moistened to the requisite depth. When using fixed sprinklers, always place them to overlap the outer limit of their range so that all sections receive equal water. A long piece of rubber tubing with holes at regular spacing can be used too.

You can easily build up a good watering system from the many devices on offer these days. You can be as elaborate or as basic as you wish. The expense involved is one you are not likely to regret for few garden 'helps' offer such a saving of labour for the gardener or better assistance to the healthy growth of the plants.

Mulching

The importance of mulching has been stressed again and again throughout this book and once more emphasis is laid on the benefits it gives.

Weed and water your soil well before putting down a mulch.

Make certain the mulch you put down is permeable — it should not be so deep or so dense that rain or water cannot get through it to the soil beneath or that air cannot penetrate. Choice of mulch is wide — peatmoss, sawdust, pine needles, well-rotted grass cuttings, well-composted leaves, straw, seaweed, fibrous compost will all eventually rot down and become part of the soil; gravel or small white stones will not, of course, although they can look very nice and be useful in places where they will not take up heat from the sun and make the soil even hotter. They should be used for purely cosmetic effect and the earth beneath them should be given a liberal layer of organic material before they are put down. Black plastic laid beneath pebbles or gravel — and perforated so that water can reach the soil — can help to retain water and keep the soil from becoming impacted.

Causes of water loss

1. Evaporation — high temperatures combined with low humidity cause surface water to be absorbed into the atmosphere.

2. Transpiration — water taken in by the roots of plants is given off as vapour primarily through the leaves, affecting heavily vegetated areas in particular.

3. Drainage — coarse, free-draining soils retain less moisture than close-grained, heavy loams.

4. Surface run-off — dry, compact soils which do not allow surface water to percolate.

5. Porous brick walls — these attract water out of the soil which may then evaporate.

30. Propagation

How to raise your own plants

Most gardeners take great joy in raising plants by their own efforts and enthusiastically sow seed, take cuttings, layer and graft. A little basic knowledge takes all the guesswork out of these enterprises. For instance, knowing that seeds need not only warmth and moisture to germinate and grow, but oxygen too, could make all the difference between failure and success.

Plants raised from seed

The soil chosen for seed-raising is all important. The finely-sieved mixtures so many people mistakenly use have soil particles so tightly packed that there is no space between them for water to escape, and, once the soil becomes permanently saturated, there is no room for the oxygen so essential to the survival of the germinating seed.

If you use bought seed-raising mixture choose one which contains vermiculite. The soil will be open enough for roots to penetrate it easily and for air to circulate and it will hold water without becoming soggy. You could make your own mixture by adding 1 part of well-moistened and squeezed-out crumbly peatmoss to 4 parts of vermiculite and adding that to an equal part of coarse river sand. Since there is nothing to feed a plant in the mixture you would have to water it with soluble liquid food used at half strength. The dosage would be about 500 mL to every 5 L container of the mixture.

A soil that does not contain nutrient could be prepared by mixing 2 parts coarse river sand with 1 part moistened peatmoss. If the peatmoss is dry and difficult to wet, pour hot water over it, leave for a while then squeeze out the surplus moisture when it is cool enough to handle. If you add 1 part of good garden loam that has been baked at 65°C for 20 minutes to sterilise it and kill any weed seeds present, you will have a mixture not only suitable for raising seeds but for growing-on seedlings in their early stages.

Sowing seed

If you use a vermiculite-based mixture there is no need to provide drainage in the container used. For other soils use shallow wooden or plastic trays between 5–10 cm deep with drainage holes at each corner and at 8 cm intervals along the base. If you use a wooden seed-tray with wide spaces between the base slats, place a sheet of newspaper over the slats to retain the soil. Don't use crocks; you will find them more trouble than they are worth.

Firm the damp soil mixture to within 1 cm of the top of the tray ensuring it is pressed well down into the corners before evening the surface. Fine seed will only need pressing into the surface of the soil, larger seed should be sown in rows about 1–2 cm apart.

Define the rows by pressing the edge of a ruler into the soil surface, making the depression just a little deeper than the size of the seeds, then sprinkle the seeds evenly along the rows and gently draw the soil over them. Large seeds need a soil covering of twice their own thickness, so use your judgement when making the depth of the rows.

The fine seeds of poppies, primula, petunias and begonias present problems in handling and the best way to get an even distribution is to mix the seeds with 1 teaspoon of fine sand per row you have to fill, and either sprinkle the mixture along the rows or angle a ruler against the edge of the furrow and, with a steady hand, trickle the seed along it. Firm the soil down gently with a flat board. Stand the trays in water to half their depth until water has crept evenly over the surface of the soil; lift them carefully and allow to drain. The seed should not be disturbed.

Keeping growing seed moist

Enclose the tray in a plastic bag. Place it in good indirect light *but not direct sunlight* as hot sun through the plastic would shrivel the germinating seed.

As soon as the seedlings begin to show, ease away the plastic and gradually accustom the young growth to stronger and stronger light; if left in dim light it will become spindly. However, cineraria, primula and seedlings of plants that grow best in light shade will be quite happy with indirect light.

I make a tent-shaped envelope of fibreglass or insect-proof gauze, held together with pins or staples and closed at one end with a clothes-peg, and fit it over the seed-tray, as this not only reduces the intensity of the sunlight and gives protection against heavy rain and injudicious watering but also keeps out slugs, snails and other night marauders likely to attack the tender young seedlings.

Transplanting seedlings

It is important to thin or space seedlings correctly. If they are left in a crowded condition they cannot make progress. When they have made their second leaves, either thin or transplant. Thin by removing all but the most promising ones which should be left at 1.2 cm spacing, or transplant — at the same spacing — into seed beds in the garden or into other trays of soil. Do not replant at more than the previous depth; if the seedlings fall over they will soon right themselves. Tomatoes and, to some extent, marigolds are exceptions to this rule.

When transplanting fibrous-rooted seedlings do not bunch the roots together and bury in a narrow 'dibbled' hole; spread them out in a shallow depression and gently firm the soil over them. They will then be able to grow outward and establish themselves quickly and easily.

Never water seedlings heavily; you could create an airtight, root-growth-inhibiting crust of soil. Watering, though thorough, should always be gentle and a covering of fibrous compost or other organic material between the little plants will give them protection against both heavy rain and injudicious watering.

1. Plant large seeds about .75 cm deep with 2.5–5 cm between seeds. Firm soil. Scatter tiny seeds over firmed soil, then press into soil with flat of your hand.

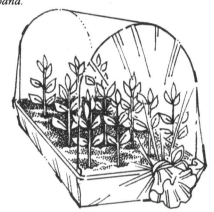

2. A plastic cover or sheet of glass retains humidity and keeps seeds from drying out. Some seeds germinate best in darkness. Cover with newspaper or board.

3. Transfer seedlings to pots or, weather permitting, move larger seedlings into garden.

Plants from cuttings

Increasing your stock from cuttings is easy but it entails more than just shoving a cutting into the ground at any time and expecting it to grow. The knowledge required is simple, but basic. Timing is all important.

Deciduous plants. Use large pieces of stem while the plant is dormant in winter.

Summer-flowering evergreens — hibiscus, oleander, hydrangea. Use stem cuttings (pencil-thick growth made during the previous summer), late winter to early spring.

Other evergreens. Use cuttings or new growth with a heel of older wood taken in late spring when the sappiness has gone out of the new growth.

Spring-flowering evergreens — azalea, camellia and many native shrubs. Take cuttings in early summer.

Late spring or summer flowerers — grevillea, veronica, prostanthera, etc. In late summer.

The young wood of evergreens roots rapidly but wilts more quickly than cuttings taken from older wood. The quick root growth uses up moisture just as quickly. Nurserymen raise cuttings in glass houses with a misting system which keeps the air damp, a heating system which keeps the soil warm and they use a coarse river sand in which to strike the cuttings; the enthusiastic amateur will do surprisingly well with soil previously suggested, the plastic bag and judicious watering.

How to do it step by step

1. Take the cuttings, and unless ready to plant immediately, sprinkle with water, seal in a plastic bag and keep cool and shaded.
2. Wash several 10–15 cm pots. Six to 18 cuttings will fit into one pot, depending on size.
3. Fill pot with coarse sand and moistened peatmoss mixture firming it down thoroughly, but keeping it slightly mounded above the rim.
4. Using a razor blade take 5–8 cm long tip cuttings through or fractionally below the junction of a leaf.
5. Trim or rub foliage from the lower half to one-third of the stem.
6. Set the cuttings to about one-third of their depth, 2–4 cm apart, close to the side of the pot, first dibbling a hole for them with a toothpick or skewer.
7. Press soil down and sideways to firm it around the cuttings toward the wall of the pot; good contact between cutting and soil is essential.
8. Stand the pot to about half its depth in water until moisture rises to the soil surface.
9. Place pot in a plastic bag, tie at the top, and hang it so that the pot stands upright with plenty of space above the cuttings. Or arch several wire hoops above the cutting tops, with ends wedged in soil between them, and cover with a plastic bag, closed tightly around the side of the pot with a rubber band.
10. Keep shaded for a week, then move to indirect light. Sun on the plastic could 'cook' the cuttings.
11. Check soft-wooded or young growth cuttings for signs of roots after 4–5 weeks

(camellias may take as many months) by inverting the pot and tapping the moistened soil ball loose. Woody perennials such as marguerites, Kingfisher daisies, carnations, etc. are quick to root. I prefer to bunch the foliage of these cuttings forward and trim it back by half. This reduces moisture loss and the new growth that commences at the same time as root growth will be obvious above the cut foliage. Cuttings from these plants and from geraniums can be set straight into small individual pots.

Geraniums usually need renewing at least every second year. New plants are easily started from chunky tip cuttings from 7–10 cm long. Remove lower leaves and firm cuttings to about half their depth in sandy soil with some initial protection from strong winds or full sun.

Train the newly struck geranium cuttings into attractively compact branching plants by pinching out the tips as soon as they reach about finger length in height. Repeat the process when new side shoots develop until good bush plants form.

Marguerites, Kingfisher daisies and lavenders are also better if the plants are kept young by replacing them as suggested for geraniums.

A few tips

Geraldton wax, tea-tree and other wiry-stemmed cuttings can be taken with a heel of the old wood. Short side growth is removed by bending them back to crack them at their junction with the main stem. Wispy bark trailing from the 'toe' of the cutting is trimmed back to just above where the wood starts below.

Cuttings taken from hibiscus and other deciduous shrubs in winter (pencil-thick pieces of the young growth made during the previous summer) should be struck in the same way as tip cuttings, but bed the pot into warm soil rather than enclose the cutting in plastic. Warm soil and cool air will encourage root formation before new leaves appear; this, of course, is preferable.

Root growth only occurs from the cambium, the smooth, silky tissue between bark and wood. Although the roots emerge through the bark, they originate in this tissue and you could speed matters by lightly shaving a little of the bark down, or bevelling the base of the cutting to expose a little more of the cambium.

Before planting, cuttings could be dipped in hormone powders or solutions to stimulate root growth. Most garden stores sell these preparations.

2. Hormone rooting powders speed root formation on some cuttings. Make a fresh cut on stem, moisten the base of cutting and lightly coat tip with hormone powder.

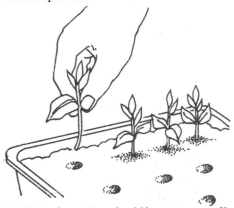

3. Soil mix for cuttings should be very porous. Use perlite alone or perlite plus small amounts of vermiculite or peatmoss.

4. High humidity provided by the plastic tent ensures successful rooting.

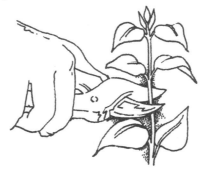

1. Make 7.5–12.5 cm long cuttings ending just below a leaf node. Cut off oldest leaves.

5. After 4 or 5 weeks, gently tug on the cuttings. If there is resistance, they are ready to transfer to a larger pot.

Division

The easiest way to increase spring- and summer-flowering perennials is to divide the clumps by taking young and healthy shoots from the main plant and replanting each one to make a separate plant. Divide polyanthus and crowded clumps of bearded iris in autumn; Japanese iris after foliage has died down in early autumn, and herbaceous summer flowerers, e.g. asters and phlox, in early spring when the new young shoots appear.

Bearded irises usually separate easily when the clump is lifted and soil shaken off. Trim off any section of old spongy rhizome. Trim roots and shorten foliage to compensate, making an inverted 'V'-cut starting 12–14 cm on outer foliage of fan-like formation and angled up to 17 or 18 cm in the centre.

Japanese irises need to be carefully cut between crowns and through their fibrous root mass, trimming off any dead foliage. Replant before they dry out, especially if new white roots are already beginning to form.

Shasta daisies re-establish better if leaves and roots of the new divisions are trimmed to about one-third of their length and excessively long rhizomes are trimmed back leaving a few roots near the foliage.

Day lilies and pokers (*Kniphofia*) require the lifting of the entire clump and the cutting through of woody tissue at the base of the foliage to separate the clump into 1–3 crowns. Trim back foliage to 20–25 cm from the base and shorten roots to about finger length.

The lovely polyanthus primrose, especially modern strains, e.g. the large-flowered Pacific giants, are generally regarded as not worth keeping after the first season. However, they can be coaxed to give a creditable performance the following year if divided so that only new outer growths are retained and the old woody centre crown divided.

To keep clumps that have flowered in a good condition, move them to a shaded part of the garden by late spring. If foliage becomes brown and dry from red spider attack or distorted by aphids or mealy bugs, control by watering to wet foliage with Lebaycid or Rogor.

Then lift about late April when new side shoots should then be showing the start of their independent root systems. Cut these shoots from the old woody crown, leaving as little of the latter tissue as possible. Then plant them up in sheltered seed bed conditions until sufficiently established to take their place in the garden.

The majority of the other perennials are much easier to divide successfully. Campanulas and especially the semi-evergreen trailing types can be cut through the clumps or just pulled apart and replanted. Cut off excess foliage to prevent wilting. Ajuga is just as easy to divide.

Layering

Some plants self-layer; instances range from trailing perennials such as verbena, arabis and alpine phlox, through shrubby perennials such as Kingfisher daisy and marguerite, to shrubs

LAYERING

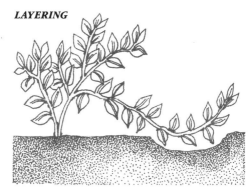

Normal layering consists of scooping out a hollow under a suitable 1–2-year-old shoot. This is either done during autumn for deciduous woody plants or in spring for many evergreens.

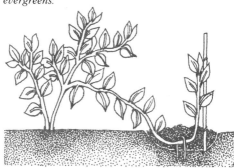

Bend the branch into the hollow. Bend the shoot at the point it is pegged down. Cover with a thin layer of fine soil. Tie the tip of the layer to a short piece of bamboo cane.

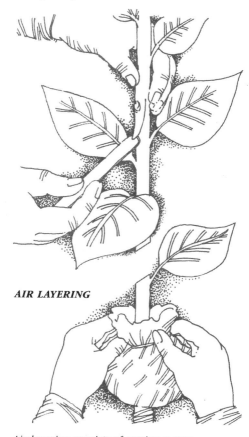

AIR LAYERING

Air layering consists of cutting a stem obliquely, applying rooting hormone and wrapping in moist moss, kept in place with polythene. When roots are visible, cut off the tops complete with roots.

such as azalea and rhododendron. Nature can be assisted and layering encouraged in shrubs with tough branches by selecting a low branch, making an upward cut halfway into the bark, plugging the cut to keep it open by a pebble, a piece of charcoal or a piece of sphagnum moss, and then bending the branch over so that the cut can be covered by a few cm of soil which has been improved by the addition of coarse sand and moistened peatmoss, so that roots formed at the site of the cut will find penetration into the soil easy.

Keep the branch in position for several months; if necessary you can arc a piece of pliable wood over it and keep in place by a brick at either side or plug it with a V-shaped piece of wire pushed well down into the soil at either end. Carefully check root progression by easing the plant from the ground very, very gently when you think roots should have become established. If they are not doing well, tuck back into the soil and be prepared to wait a little longer; if they are, just wait a week or two and then sever the newly rooted stem from the parent plant. Keep watered and, after a month or so, lift and plant in a permanent position. Time this process for winter for most plants and late winter to early spring for warmth-lovers such as citrus, gardenias and hibiscus.

Air layering

Plants without branches close to the ground can be air layered.

Make a cut in the stem as described for soil layering, plug the cut open and surround it with sphagnum moss kept in place with plastic sheeting tied above and below the cut in a bonbon-like shape. Alternatively, you could use plastic sheeting, cut to surround the serration like a cone, secured at the base and then filled with the peatmoss and sand mixture recommended for growing cuttings and then tightly wrapped and secured at the top so that the soil mixture is firmed against the cut in the branch.

Marcottage grafting

This is a different way of air layering.

Ring the stem with 2 cuts 5 cm apart and peel away the bark between to disclose the silky cambium layer. Then ring again, 1 cm above the bottom of the ringed area, and scrape away all the cambium layer between the ringing and the bottom of the previously ringed area. Wrap the whole of the treated area with moistened sphagnum moss or treat as just described, and seal with plastic tied at both ends.

Staking or some support will be needed to prevent the branch from breaking at the weakened point of the layer. Staking is usually done from the soil below but there are times when it might be easier to lash the top of a stake to the branch above and tie the layered section to this. Where possible, make this support before starting the layer. When roots are well formed the layer is severed and potted up or replanted. This is a good way to produce mature-looking stock for bonsai.

Budding and grafting

Budding

Budding is a method of producing plants on stronger and quicker-growing rootstock than would develop from cuttings of their own wood. Roses, for instance, are budded on briar rootstock and citrus on common lemon or trifoliate seedling stock.

Both budding and grafting require skill and patient attention to detail but the results are well worthwhile — you can even have two sorts of flowers or fruit growing on the one plant!

The plant to be propagated is called the 'scion'; the growing plant to which it will be attached is called the 'stock'. The object of the exercise is to unite the cambium layer of the two plants. It is done when plump but still dormant buds are evident on the plant you wish to propagate; roses are usually budded in late spring. You can also bud them in February, using a bud from a plump stem which has already produced flowers. Camellias are budded in June. As a rough guide, choose either spring or early autumn for budding citrus, deciduous fruits or roses.

Method

Only bud when conditions are moist and there is no likelihood of the bud drying out.

First make a perpendicular cut (about 2–4 cm long) well down on the stock you are budding on to, then make a cut at the top of this to form a 'T'. With a sharp knife, slice the scion bud with a shield-shaped piece of bark and outer wood behind it, starting the cut just above the bud when slicing down cleanly to finish about 1 cm below it.

If you have taken more than a shaving of wood behind the bark and if you can do it cleanly and safely without damaging the bud (or slicing your finger), thin it down a little. If there is a leaf stalk below the bud leave it there as a 'handle'.

Slip the shield-like piece of stem with the bud centred well down into the flap made

BUDDING

Remove a thin sliver of bark, together with healthy bud and leaf, of the scion variety which is being budded onto a rootstock.

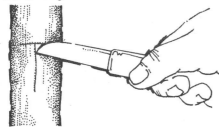

Make a T-shaped cut close to soil-level in pencil-thick stems of rootstocks, to the depth of the bark.

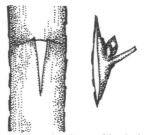

Cut off the leaf on the sliver of bark, leaving a piece of stalk, and open up the back of the rootstock.

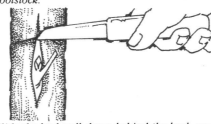

Slide the bud well down behind the bark and trim off the tail of the sliver level with the top of the T cut.

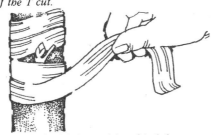

When the bud is in position, bind the stem with budding tape to prevent it drying out and avoid movement of the bud.

GRAFTING

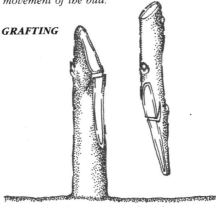

Make a slanting cut about 4 cm long, a vertical nick in pencil-thick rootstocks. Prepare a short scion of similar thickness with a matching cut at the bottom end.

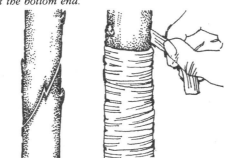

The matching cuts on scion and stock should be cleanly made to ensure good contact and the wood should intermesh at the nicks when the scion is pressed down. Bind the scion and stock firmly at the join, using grafting tape. Make sure the scion does not slip and the cuts are covered.

when the bark either side of the cut in the stock is carefully lifted. Make the cut a little longer if the top of the shield does not come just below the T, or if this top is long, trim it a little so that all of the cut area is in contact with exposed wood of the stock.

Then carefully bind with grafting tape or raffia, starting at the base of the cut and finishing above the bud, with the latter protruding between the ties. A little grafting mastic can be used to complete the seal but take care that it does not penetrate behind the bud or it will spoil any chance of uniting. Grafting tape expands and allows for developing growth but less flexible ties should be cut away when the bud begins to swell or shows other signs of growth.

Grafting

There are several ways to graft but the object is always the same — to unite the cambium layers of the plants.

Whip-tongue

This is done toward the end of the dormant season when stock and scion are approximately the same thickness — about 2.5 cm.

Make a long tapering cut on the scion, starting at below a bud and tapering it upward to a point about 5–8 cm above the bud on the opposite side of the stem.

Cut the stock in the same slant so that the two cuts will fit when placed together. Trim each stem back a little to give maximum exposure of the cambium layer then place together and bind with raffia or preferably grafting tape, making the seal strong and airtight. If you use grafting mastic it is imperative to prevent it entering the cut.

Cleft

This is used when the stock is much larger than the scion, such as young camellia wood onto an older plant or when 'reworking' a summer fruit tree (grafting young laterals onto heavily cut-back branches or framework). Saw the stock first with a cut angled at about 45° then cut the top horizontally to form a small platform a little longer than the thickness of the scion — then make a downward cut to halve the platform on top of the stock and continue through the angled cut.

Hold this cut open with a screwdriver and insert the scion which has first been tapered to a wedge. The latter should be placed so that its bark (on one side) lines up with that of the scion. The stock is then bound near the top to keep the scion firmly wedged. Cover with a large glass jar or plastic bag held clear of the scion by hooped wire, but shade it with a firmly secured brown paper bag or similar covering.

Crown

This graft is used to graft more than one scion onto stock more than 2.5 cm in diameter.

Prepare scions of 10–15 cm with a wedge-shaped tapered cut at the base of each one.

Saw off the stock branch at right angles, make a cut deep enough for each scion to be inserted with the cambium exposed by the slanting cut in contact with the cambium of the stock plant. Bind, as previously described, again taking care with the mastic.

31. Pruning

Why prune?

1. To remove diseased, dead or broken branches.
2. To shape the plant.
3. To eliminate suckers and wild growth.
4. To renew old plants.
5. To produce new autumn growth for colour.
6. To ensure you obtain better fruit, blossoms or flowers.

Pruning takes place when doing other tasks

Trimming. This is essentially for shaping plants like hedges. No thinning out is practised.

Training. When training grapes or roses on to trellises and walls, the plants must first be pruned and then trained on to supports. Creepers can be trained in a pattern and superfluous growth removed.

Transplanting. When transplanting deciduous woody plants, the roots will be cut and the top should be reduced accordingly. Evergreens may only require slight trimming or stripping of leaves.

Repairing. This is known as tree surgery. It involves reshaping old, mature or decrepit trees and repairing broken, badly pruned or decayed trees.

Cutting flowers. When cutting roses for the vase, we cut above an outward-facing bud and follow the principles of pruning. When cutting flowering shrubs for the vase, we do not destroy the shape of the bush.

Basic pruning tools

Hand pruning shears or secateurs — for pruning shrubs, etc. which have a pair of crossed, short, curved blades, and a spring for returning them to the open position.

Lopping shears — which have long handles giving good leverage to cut branches as thick as 32 mm. This is the tool to use for branches over 13 mm in diameter.

Hedge shears — can be used on hedges with wood up to 13 mm thick. The blades range in length, longer blades cut more accurately on a level plane.

Pruning saws — are small curved saws and can cut branches up to 51 mm thick. The teeth are angled back and are able to cut green wood without clogging. These saws cut on the backward instead of the forward stroke.

Bow saws — have thinner blades and cut more quickly than pruning saws. However, they can be too wide to fit in some tight places.

Disinfecting pruning tools

Bacterial diseases can be transmitted from sick to healthy plants by the tools used for pruning.

Pruning techniques

Cutting back — some plants, either all the way to the ground or only partway, stimulates new growth.

Heading back — removes the growing tips of branches. Repeated heading back gives the plant a full dense, sculpted look.

Pinching — is a type of heading back. It removes the terminal bud, forcing growth back into the lateral buds. Pinched plants become more dense. Pinching off some of the flower buds on a plant diverts energy to the remaining buds to make larger flowers.

Shearing — removes many growing points at once. Plants for which shearing is appropriate then release many dormant buds at the same time, resulting in dense growth with a sculpted look.

Thinning — takes out entire branches, giving a lighter, more open look. The growing energy is then distributed among the remaining branches causing them to grow longer. When wind is a problem, thinning branches can help reduce the wind load of the plant.

Suckers — should be removed especially when they come from roots below a bud union or a graft, since the sucker will be of a different form than the scion.

Dead heading — is the removal of the spent flowers on plants such as roses, rhododendrons and dahlias. It increases flower production. If the effort to produce seed is removed, the plant puts extra energy into producing more flowers.

Pruning trees

After a tree reaches the shape you like, prune only to remove broken or diseased branches and occasionally to thin. Also remove suckers and watersprouts.

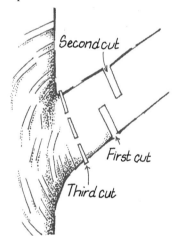

Remove heavy branches in 3 cuts to keep from tearing the bark.

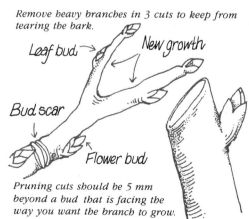

Pruning cuts should be 5 mm beyond a bud that is facing the way you want the branch to grow.

How to prune

Make thinning cuts close to the trunk or larger branch. When using secateurs lay the blade against the trunk with the blade cutting upwards. When cutting with a saw make a similar close cut just outside the bulge at the base of the branch. Proper cuts will start outward. If a cut is too flush, it is larger than necessary.

Prune large branches with three cuts. Make the first 8–30 cm from the trunk. Cut from the bottom of the branch, about a quarter of the way through the branch. The second cut is from the top of the branch, about 2 cm beyond the first. The third cut removes the stub. Finally paint or spray the wound with tree paint to keep out fungus and encourage bark to grow over the wound.

Pruning fruit trees

Pruning aims to regulate growth of the branches, allow light to enter the framework and encourage flowers and fruit. Generally, trees are pruned in winter and usually hard for the first few years to build up a sturdy framework and to shape the tree. Later, the main concern of pruning is to remove dead and diseased wood, ingrowing branches, thin overcrowded growth and to cut back leaders or main limbs.

Different fruit trees have their own growth habits. Some fruit may set on current spring growth, on wood from the previous year's growth or on fruiting spurs which may bear for several years.

As a general rule fruit with poor colour is an indication that pruning is needed. Remove branches that are heavily shaded as these will bear very few spurs.

Training fruit trees

Central leader system

Sometimes referred to as the pyramid form, the central leader system means a single central trunk is allowed to predominate while lateral or scaffold branches develop at regular intervals. Trees tend to withstand heavy weather and heavy fruit. Thin annually, so the centre of the tree gets good light.

Open centre system

A central leader does not dominate. Three or 4 main limbs of similar size are encouraged to grow at wide angles. In turn, these branch outward with 6 or so secondary limbs. Peach, nectarine, apricot and plum are adaptable to this system.

Modified central leader system

The central leader and lateral branches are equally important in the modified central leader method. If branched one- or two-year-old trees are planted, then pruning involves selecting 3 or 4 widely spaced, wide-angled branches and removing the rest. The leader or any scaffold branch should not be allowed to dominate for the first 2 years.

Easy rules for pruning fruit trees or roses

1. Remove dead wood
   This is now useless and will only deprive the plant of sunlight and room for growth as well as harbour pests. It often causes the healthy wood below it to die back.
2. Remove old wood
   Nature starves and discards old wood. We hasten its removal so that growth can be directed into the production of new, vigorous flowering wood.
3. Remove weak twigs
   These only clutter the plant and use some of the nutrition which should be conserved for the strong stems that produce good flowers or fruit.
4. Remove superfluous wood
   This includes branches that cross over or rub up against one another or branches that fill up the centre of the tree and exclude light. Thin out some good growths in order to space remaining branches into a strong framework.

5. Shorten the remaining stems
   Shortening the main stems keeps the fruit tree low for harvesting. Shortening leaders and side branches by half strengthens the remaining portion and stimulates new growth from the top bud below the cut.

> **Do not**
> 1. **Overprune.**
> 2. **Cut into old wood unless absolutely essential.**
> 3. **Remove old wood if there is no new wood to take its place.**

Pruning roses

Roses are categorised according to whether they bloom on wood produced in the current or previous year.

Roses that bloom on the previous year's wood should be pruned after flowering, before new shoots emerge. Most of these roses produce flowers in spring and are not repeat bloomers.

Most roses in modern gardens are continuous-blooming varieties that produce flowers on the current season's growth. This group includes most of the modern hybrid tea, floribunda and grandiflora roses. They should be pruned when the plant is dormant but when the buds have begun to swell.

Pruning in frost-free districts can be started in June or early July. In other temperate areas with only occasional moderate frosts, mid-to late July is preferable.

In colder districts it is better to leave pruning until as late as possible in August or until early September. This is because pruning tends to stimulate new growth which can be burnt by heavy, late frosts. However, our climate is anything but consistent. If unusually mild weather makes the eyes (on the rose canes) swell and they look like bursting into growth, then prune without delay, even at the risk of late frost damage.

Hybrid tea & Grandiflora types

• **Newly planted.** Cut dead shoots cleanly back to a main stem. When in doubt, scrape the bark with your thumbnail or knife and, if the stem is green beneath, there is still life. Shorten weak canes back to 1 bud. Prune strong canes back leaving 2 or 3 good buds (eyes).

• **Established.** Prune according to vigour, cutting weaker plants harder than vigorous ones. Remove dead or old canes carrying only weak growth. Prune plump newer canes back to leave 2 to 4 good buds (eyes), preferably with the top one pointing in the direction where growth is preferred.

Floribunda (small flowered cluster types)

• **Newly Planted.** Treat in a similar manner to hybrid tea varieties. However to promote more base shoots these are often cut back to about 15 cm from ground.

• **Established.** Some growers treat these similarly to Hybrid tea & Grandiflora types. Others prefer to cut them back each winter

to a dormant bud within 10 to 15 cm of ground level. This is more likely to promote canes carrying larger flower clusters but generally with less continuity of colour. After flowering these canes are cut back to a lower bud.

Shrub roses

• **Newly planted.** Prune when buds are starting to grow but before the first leaves open, the date will depend on the site and season.

• **Established.** Shorten one-third of the stems by half. Remove weak shoots and soft tips on any others after flowering for average growth.

Climbing roses

Most climbing roses flower on year-old wood. Don't prune them for 2 or 3 years, except to remove dead wood. They need this amount of time to establish mature canes for flowering.

Long canes grow from the bud union. Don't tip these canes. The long canes don't flower, but flowers appear the next year on the laterals of these canes. Prune back to 3 to 5 young canes. Prune the laterals on these canes back to 2 or 3 buds.

Standard roses

Standard roses should be pruned to maintain their tree shape. Remove suckers from the trunk and base of the plant. Thin out the head, and shorten canes to strong buds that are pointed in the direction you want the cane to grow.

32. Pests and Diseases

Don't let a few bugs spoil your gardening pleasures — remember that you are bigger than they are! You might argue that there are more of them than us. This may be true, but although at times the numbers of some pests may seem formidable, don't think that they are going to overrun the earth, or even your garden.

Take heart in the fact that there are at least as many friends in the insect world as there are enemies. 'Friends' is not an exaggeration, because they are the natural predators of other and usually less desirable insects.

Most gardeners appreciate the presence of ladybirds because their main diet is aphids. An adult ladybird beetle eats 50–60 aphids a day and the slightly ominous-looking and surprisingly long-bodied wingless larvae consume at least 25. They also feed on cottony cushion scale and, because they are usually found where the less definable scale is causing problems, are unfortunately regarded as culprit rather than friend.

The praying mantis is also a friend because if feeds on a great variety of insects — as are the green or brown lace-wing flies that often come indoors at night, and their ugly but useful little 'ant lion' larvae, the May flies, tachinid flies and small ichneumon flies or wasps that eat caterpillars, beetles and 'eggs' or scales of tiny pests such as the white fly. Last, but by no means least, there are the insect-eating birds and the less attractive, but important, spiders, centipedes and lizards.

Nature has its own way of keeping everything in control and when they get out of hand, it is often due to man's interference. This does not mean that you should sit back and let your plants be devoured — take action by all means but don't kill every creature in the garden just to get rid of a few aphis or caterpillars. After these indiscriminate massacres the troublesome insects get a hold and reach plague proportions before the predators beneficial to the garden return.

There are parallels to the red spider problem that occurred during the 20 years or so following World War II, when DDT and similar hydrocarbons were so widely used. These preparations affected the true insects only. The minute red spider mites and other spiders are technically arachnids, not insects, so when sprays were used which wiped out their natural predators they increased out of all proportion.

Many of the high-powered chemicals available to the gardener are as toxic to man as they are to plant pests. Some are absorbed through the skin without sign of any adverse symptom or reaction until the intake builds up to danger level. The naive who believe they have an immunity to these poisons are in great danger.

These chemicals, though toxic, have their uses but the precautions on their labels should be closely noted. Always take the less drastic approach first: quite often an innocuous-sounding non-toxic treatment turns out to be the most effective one.

Before you spray, study the problem to see whether it is actually due to pests and diseases or to some other factor. There is no point in using pesticides for a fungus disease problem or fungicides against insect pests.

In the following 'Advice' section suggestions for natural or relatively non-toxic treatment are given first, followed by standard remedies.

Pests
Aphis
Rub or hose the insects off stems below flower bud. If too widespread or amongst foliage spray with soapy water or garlic. More effective still are the relatively non-toxic Pyrethrum-type sprays; if using these in pressure packs, hold them at forearm length from plant.

Malathion, Rogor and Lebaycid are effective, the latter two remain toxic for about 1 week, Malathion for 4 days. None of them should be used on hibiscus. Malathion should not be used on petunias, sweet peas, pileas, ferns, snapdragons and zinnias and Rogor should not be used on asters, chrysanthemums, Myer lemons or early peaches.

Caterpillar
Cutworms, loopers and others can tear away large areas of foliage in a short time. Loopers assume leaf colouring and often the form of a leaf-vein or stem and can be difficult to detect. Cutworms shelter below soil by day and eat at night. Remove them by hand if possible.

Pyrethrum or Bioresmethrin aerosols are effective and do not leave toxic residues, so are safe for vegetables close to harvest. If held at forearm length from foliage they are safe to plants (except some softer varieties of fuchsias and hydrangeas) but are toxic to fish, so aquariums should be covered before the sprays are used.

Bacterial derivatives, e.g. Dipel, if sprayed on with a spreader to cover all parts of foliage, will prevent caterpillars from feeding within a few hours and usually kill them within 2 days without affecting other insects or animals.

Carbaryl is effective against caterpillars and other chewing insects and safe to use within 7 days of harvest, except on some tender-foliaged ornamentals.

Endosulphan (Thiodan), effective against caterpillars, remains toxic for 7 days.

Beetle
Pyrethrum and Bioresmethrin sprays are effective on contact. Carbaryl, Endosulphan and, to some extent, Malathion also give control — see their residual effects under 'Aphis' and 'Caterpillar'. Lawn beetle granules are frequently used against beetles in lawns or Christmas beetle larvae under gum trees. Flooding soil with Endosulphan or Malathion mixed to spray strength is also effective.

Borer
There are several types.

Ringbarking borer covers the stem section under attack with fabric and eats out bark and soft tissue beneath, eventually girdling the stem or branch. It makes a hole between 4–8 cm deep into which it retreats when fabric is disturbed. If you inject a few drops of Malathion or methylated spirits into the hole the grub may emerge. Putty the hole and paint the damaged bark with tree paint — this often induces bark to regrow and repair the damage.

Pine weevil can cause death of conifer branches. Hose vigorously each spring to remove build-up of old foliage in crotches of branches and trunk, and if there is evidence of infestation, spray with Endosulphan or similar insecticide while bark is still damp.

Longicorn borer. Adult is a beetle up to 7 cm long with even longer antennae. The cream to grey grubs channel below bark of trees, eating softer outer wood. Patches of flaking or lifting bark and gum indicate presence.

Treat by removing loose bark, hosing to clear away loose matter, etc. When dry, putty any holes then paint or spray wounded area with tree paint. Longicorns sometimes burrow straight through branches of pittosporum, causing them to snap. Cut cleanly, as close as possible to trunk or where another branch emerges, and coat the wound with tree paint.

Other borers may tunnel deeply into a tree. When holes are noticed, the grub has passed through the pupae stage and the adult beetle has emerged, but as a precaution inject Malathion and putty the holes to prevent entry of water and consequent fungus problems.

Precautions
Constantly spraying trees with insecticide to prevent borer attack through the late spring and summer period is tedious and undesirable for the ecology.

Borers mainly attack trees weakened either by removal of leafmould (which then prevents the recycling of their natural foods) or by a build-up of soil over the root area, or by excavation, sullage (particularly with detergents) and redirection of drainage by excavation.

Forestry researchers say that healthy trees can form sufficient resins and kinos to engulf borer larvae in its very early stages. Feeding in spring with complete fertiliser containing a full trace element mix is recommended to restore vigour, using about 1 handful per sq. m of area below the entire foliage spread of the tree. Native trees will benefit too.

Bug
Citrus, Shield, Bean, Harlequin and Rutherglen
Pyrethrum or Bioresmethrin sprays (detailed under 'Aphis' and 'Caterpillar') are more effective than most toxic preparations. Malathion has some effect; can be added to white oil sprays in December–January if these are

needed for scale control and citrus bug. Do not remove large brown or black citrus bugs by hand as they eject a stinging fluid that can cause temporary blindness.

Codling moth

Codling moth attacks apples, pears and quinces but not stone fruit. In winter remove any loose bark from base of the trees (where pupae usually harbour) and spray with dormant or winter spraying oil. A collar of corrugated cardboard around the trunk from midsummer onwards will collect the larvae. The collars can be removed and burnt in late autumn.

Spray with Malathion each week after petalfall, then after a month spray monthly with Carbaryl (except on quinces), in all cases directing spray at base of fruit clusters. Eggs are laid at blossom-end of fruit; larvae penetrate the core and, when fully fed, burrow out through the flesh.

Cutworm

Spray or water plants and surrounding soil with Carbaryl or Endosulphan at strength recommended on container.

Earwig

Trap in jam tins or jars loosely filled with damp paper, or containing bait made by mixing 1 teaspoon of Carbaryl or BHC powder per cup of powdered (not pelleted) snail bait. Chopped potato peelings or moistened bran may be substituted for the snail bait. Remove and burn infested flowers.

Eelworm

See Nematode.

Fruit fly

Use baits made by mixing 4 teaspoons of protein hydrolysate (non-toxic liquid lure) with 2 teaspoons of Malathion 25 wettable powder and 1 cup of water; splash it liberally on a patch of foliage about 25 cm square each week (repeat after rain) from the time fruit reaches the half-grown stage. Treat only every second or third tree as the solution lures for 10 m or more. Dak pots hung in trees trap the male flies.

A more standard treatment is to spray with Rogor or Lebaycid starting 5 or 6 weeks before fruit is due to ripen, then a week later and again a week before harvest. Good coverage of fruit is essential. Observe warnings on the label regarding effect on sensitive trees — Rogor on Myer lemons and Watt's Early peaches, apricots, etc.

Gall wasp

These cause marble-like woody galls on orange branches, finger-length or larger ones on lemon and grapefruit. Cut off and burn before August because adult wasps emerge as weather warms and lay eggs in the new spring growth.

Grasshopper

Spray Carbaryl or Endosulphan.

Jassid

Eats foliage on marigolds, dahlias, etc. leaving it mottled. Use Pyrethrum, Bioresmethrin or Malathion as suggested for aphis.

Lace Bug (Azaleas)

This tiny bug with comparatively large flat wings sucks foliage, causes mottling and turns the leaves grey bronze. It is active at about 20°C temperatures in all but semi-tropical areas from late September–April only. Watch for the first signs of mottling on the new spring growth and if evident spray Pyrethrum-based preparations, directly under foliage, repeating twice at weekly intervals; or spray with Rogor or Lebaycid. A weekly vigorous hosing of the foliage often helps. This pest usually does the most damage where foliage is protected from rain.

Leaf hopper

See Jassid.

Leaf roller

These roll new tips of camellias, citrus, etc. often destroying shoots or leaving holes in enclosed leaves. Watch for and destroy when new spring growth commences, if necessary spray with Endosulphan (Thiodan) to stop the reinfestation of other shoots. Rogor and Lebaycid are also effective.
Note: Cup your hand below base of shoot before unfolding leaves, as the small quickmoving grey or green grub often sneaks out of the 'back door' at any signs of disturbance, sometimes suspending itself on a 50 cm fine web.

Mealy bug

Found on ferns or potted plants under shelter but may infest daphne, polyanthus and other perennials. For small-scale attacks sponge them off with a soapy cloth or touch with a cotton wool swab or camel-hair brush moistened with methylated spirits. Invert pot plants, hold back the soil ball with your hand and immerse the foliage and stems in soapy water. Folimat is also effective.

For large-scale treatment of shrubs use 1 tablespoon of white oil mixed with 4 L of water and 1 teaspoon of Malathion. Ants transmit and nurture mealy bugs so baiting and spraying for these with insecticides can minimise the problem.

Nematode (eelworm)

Some types attack roots, causing galling and distortion which weakens or kills the plant. Others feed on decomposing or organic material and appear to attack or inhibit the growth of the types infesting live plants. Therefore the addition of compost or organic matter can help to deter harmful nematode activity. Plants such as marigolds exude a root subtance that inhibits nematodes or, in other cases, attracts them away from a crop they might otherwise infest. Preparations which are watered into the soil (or granules that are mixed in) prior to planting to protect plants from nematodes are available.

For nematodes in bulbs see chapter on 'Bulbs'.

Leaf miner

Small fly or moth larvae that tunnels between the leaf tissue leaving a scribble-like tracery. Pull off and burn the infected leaves or leaf sections, spraying every second or third day for 2–3 weeks with Pyrethrum or Bioresmethrin, or spray every 10 days with Carbaryl or Endosulphan. Lebaycid or Rogor are also effective

but the latter should not be used on asters, chrysanthemums, etc. Check tolerance on label.

Leaf nematode

These cause blackening of foliage, starting from the base of chrysanthemums; dark wedged-shaped areas or banding on ferns. Watering to wet foliage with Metasystox is a positive cure. This substance is very toxic so it is essential to avoid skin contact or inhalation. Lebaycid may also be used.

Pumpkin beetle

Spray with Pyrethrum, Bioresmethrin or Carbaryl.

Peach tip moth

Spray Carbaryl, Lebaycid or Rogor.

Red spider

Hundreds of these tiny mites may be on the back of a small leaf but can only be seen clearly with a magnifying glass in good daylight. They do the worst damage when atmosphere is warm and dry.

Frequent misting of foliage with water helps to deter them — soapy water also helps. The least toxic chemical treatment is dusting with sulphur or spraying wettable sulphur. Kelthane is a specific red spider spray, or miticide, effective only against these pests. Malathion, Rogor and Lebaycid also control red spider and other mites.

Scale

White wax scale of citrus can be brushed off with soapy water. For complete treatment use white oil, as directed on container, during December and again in late January, at the latter stage using about 2 tablespoons of washing soda per 5 L of spray mix. At this period the minute young brood of scale (fry) is mobile and unprotected on foliage. For red scale, olive scale, etc. use Malathion or Rogor at normal spraying strength with white oil.

Rose scale is covered in the 'Roses' section. Brown or soft scale on ferns and house plants (and palm scale) is best removed with a soapy cloth.

Slater

Treat as earwigs or spray their haunts or waterinfested compost with Malathion at normal spraying strength.

Slugs and snails

These familiar and destructive marauders do considerable damage at night then disappear during the day to havens below stones, pots, or foliage of plants. Slugs may even hide below loose clods of moist soil. Both leave a telltale slime trail which can be difficult to detect on some plants, and they are most active during warm, dewy nights.

You can catch them by torchlight but most gardeners use snail baits. These baits are either metaldehyde mixed with bran (or a similar meal, either in powder or pelleted form) or pellets of Methiocarb.

Pellets are the more tempting to these creatures, and are most effective if scattered among dense growth frequented by snails — used this way they involve little risk to birds or pets. Powdered baits can be placed in small heaps covered by inverted flower pots, or pieces of propped-up board. To be effective amongst seedlings they need be no more than 50 cm apart.

The cannibal or 'killer' snail has a flatter and glossier shell than the more common vegetarian species and actually attacks other snails so it is worth protecting. Lizards and some of the larger birds also help to keep snails in check.

Thrip
These spoil foliage and flowers of carnations, roses, gladioli and foliage of onions, the evergreen viburnums, rhododendrons, fuchsias, cissus, holly, etc. causing symptoms similar to azalea lace bugs and red spider, but usually leave silvery marks rather than bronze. Spray with Endosulphan (Thiodan) to thoroughly wet foliage. Alternate with Rogor or Lebaycid.

Gladioli need spraying every 10–14 days from the four-leaf stage onwards; spray both sides of foliage thoroughly.

Web worm
These attack tea-trees, bottle-brush, melaleucas and some other shrubs, congregating within a protective tent of webbing. Break the webbing with a stake or strong hose-jet, then spray with Carbaryl or Endosulphan. Rogor and Lebaycid are effective against some of the leaf-infesting saw flies.

White fly
Treat as for aphis with Bioresmethrin or Pyrethrum. I find that this has a better end result than most toxic substances and is less damaging to the scales or egg-like larvae that have been parasitised by a tiny wasp. These eggs, usually green or white and just visible under the leaf, will be black if parasitised. Basil seems to repel white fly within 1 m and is worth planting between tomatoes.

Woolly aphis
Spray with Malathion, Folimat, Rogor or Lebaycid, with a heaped teaspoon of white oil added to each 4 L of spray.

Diseases

Brown rot
This affects stone fruit in wet periods, spreading rapidly and leaving most of the fruit soft and brown. Some fruits eventually dry and mummify on tree. Freckles in apricot, shot-hole of foliage and other fruit rots are caused by similar fungi.

Remove and destroy infected fruit. Spray with Bordeaux in June, again at bud swell as flower buds show first colour, then spray with Macrozeb from stage fruit is half formed.

Black patches on leaves
See heading 'Black spot' in 'Roses' chapter.

For apples, spray with a systemic fungicide when flower petals fall. See also 'Bacterial diseases'.

Collar rot
On citrus attacks bark then the trunk near ground-level causing bark to flake and wood to rot. The rot is soft when wet.

Treat by scraping down to clean wood and painting surface with Bordeaux powder mixed with just enough water to make a paint-like consistency. When it is dry coat with tree paint to encourage regrowth of bark.

Flaking of bark, or 'scaly bark', is only a constitutional condition, not a fungus disease. In this case you will find sound, green bark below the scales — if doubtful, paint with Bordeaux.

Crown rot
This can be caused by sclerotina or similar fungi but in trailing or carpeting perennials often by a damping-off-type fungus. Control by removing dead foliage, then watering the entire plant with either Bordeaux, Captan, Benlate or a complete fungicide. To play it safe, strike cuttings from healthier outer growths of plant.

Curly leaf
Attacks stone fruits, causing blister-like distortion of foliage. Spray with Bordeaux when flower buds show colour (as for brown rot). If found on azaleas, see 'Leaf gall'.

Damping off
Fungus common amongst seedlings, especially when closely-planted as the fungus travels over the soil in the thin layer of surface moisture, usually during darkness.

Avoid by thinning seedlings early; using a topping of vermiculite over the soil also helps, as the moisture is held only within the particle instead of in the film outside it. Avoid watering late in the day so that soil is dry at night. At the first signs remove infected plants and those closely surrounding them, then water remainder with Fongarid, Mancozeb or Zineb.

Leaf gall
Rubbery, sometimes powdery, thickening and distortion of azalea and camellia sasanqua leaves. Remove and burn infected parts and spray with Bordeaux.

Leaf spot
Leaf spots on tomatoes, celery, lemons, house plants and a number of ornamentals are caused by fungi and sometimes bacteria. The latter, particularly, may be difficult to control but spraying with Bordeaux gives a fairly general though mild control of most likely diseases.

Mildew
Grey to white patches on foliage.

Powdery mildew shows as an ash-like film or spots on foliage and sometimes on buds of roses and crepe myrtles. Spray with Benlate, Bayleton or with Karathane — use a spreader with the latter to avoid burning. Wettable sulphur or dusting sulphur is also effective.

Downy mildew makes small, less obvious tufts of mycelium, usually under the leaf. Grape leaves and other plants infected will usually brown and shrivel from the leaf edge; onion tips shrivel. Bordeaux gives some control here, but Zineb or Mancozeb are more potent against this type of mildew.

Petal blight
Causes brown or transparent flecks on azaleas and some other flower petals; flowers shrivel prematurely and remain fused to the plant. Seed-like black sclerots (or resting bodies) of the fungus form in the petals, eventually falling to the ground. These then develop a mush-room-like mycelium growth in the soil which eventually produces small toadstool-type fruiting bodies that release dust-like spores into the air. The ugly cycle will start again unless there is a deposit of fungicide on the petals to halt the progress.

Systemic fungicides, such as Bayleton (triadimefon), give the more positive control because they translocate throughout the petals. Spray every 10 days from the time the buds show colour until the flowers finish. Spray the ground around the plants also, as this can eliminate the spore-carrying toadstools.

Some growers find soil fungicides effective, but success depends on the environment as spores can blow in from neighbouring gardens. Avoid overhead watering as much as possible.

Rust
On geraniums
Rust causes yellow spots on the top side of foliage, circular, tan rust-like spots on the underside. When general yellowing occurs, earlier yellow spots often revert to green. Pull off and burn obviously infected foliage; spray remainder with Zineb, repeating at least monthly as a preventive spray.
On calendulas and bellis (English daisy)
Rust shows as bright orange pustule-like spore clusters. Treat as for geraniums.
On snapdragons (*antirrhinum*)
Rust is more devastating here. Spraying each 5–7 days with Zineb is a good preventive but infected plants usually die so they might as well be pulled up and burnt. Some strains of flowers show a little more resistance, but overseas rust-resistant strains are not immune to the Australian-type rusts.
On gerberas
Raised, creamy spots on foliage. Control by spraying with lime-sulphur spray.
On other plants
Treat as for geraniums.

Bacterial diseases
Fortunately these are not common. Occasionally they attack some types of ivy, other house plants and ivy geraniums. One type is responsible for black rot in cauliflowers, cabbages and stock, and another for canker in tomatoes and apricots. In tomatoes, stock, cauliflowers, etc. the disease is often seed-borne. Reliable seed merchants treat their seed with hot water and acetic acid.

Cut away and burn the infected parts of perennial plants (these show as blackish-brown marginal blotches in the leaf or as light brown sunken areas in ivy geraniums), then spray with Bordeaux.

Virus diseases
There are various types causing streaking or variegation in stock and tulips; greening of gerberas and perennial phlox; big bud in Iceland poppies; browning and drying of sweet pea plants; unproductive passion-fruit vines; bronze or spotted wilt of tomatoes, and mosaic-like markings in leaves of orchids, liliums and other bulbs.

There is no cure for virus diseases. Most are

A quick guide to garden pests

The chart identifies most of the common garden pests and gives ways of controlling them. You can choose between non-toxic remedies or more potent, poisonous pesticides. (The period these remain toxic is given in brackets. Don't use them closer to harvest than this.) In nature, birds and useful predatory insects help keep pests under control, so it is more prudent to pick off a caterpillar or rub aphis from a rosebud than to use a spray that kills both pest and predator.

Symptoms to watch for: Distorted or downward-cupped foliage — suspect aphis, or mildew. If foliage is silvery-mottled or dull — thrips, lace bug, red spider. If there are holes in leaves — suspect slugs, snails. If you see silvery trails, use snail baits; if not suspect caterpillars, loopers, cutworms, beetles. If daphne buds are falling, ferns shrivelling, check for mealy bug. For yellowing foliage — see 'Fungus diseases', but it could be a virus disease. There's no cure, but aphis and thrips carry it. Yellowing in house plants may mean over-watering in cold weather or bad drainage. Or element deficiency — give liquid plant food. ALWAYS read directions on pesticides. (Note: sketches of insects not to scale.)

Insect	How it looks	What it does	How to combat
Aphis	Small green, grey or black usually wingless insects clustered on young shoots, buds or under foliage	Sucks sap, deforms buds and petals of gerberas and other daisies, causes foliage of stocks, ageratum, pansies, etc. to contort and cup downward. Carries virus diseases	Non-toxic: Soapy water, Pyrethrum, Derris dust. Short-term toxic: Malathion (3 days), Rogor (7 days) or Lebaycid (14 days). On hibiscus use Thiodan
Caterpillars: Cabbage Moth / Looper	Small or large, fleshy or hairy 'grubs' in a variety of colours / Fleshy caterpillars with centre set of legs missing, giving them a looping action. Camouflaged in leaf-green colour or as brown or grey twig	Loopers and caterpillars devour foliage. Tomato grub bores into fruit. Small loopers often skeletonise leaf by eating away fleshy sections between veins. They usually stay under the leaf and may be hard to find	Non-toxic: Dipel, Pyrethrum, Derris. Short-term toxic: Carbaryl (3 days)
Pumpkin beetle	1 cm long, oval, red and black beetle	Skeletonises leaves of pumpkins, marrows and other vine crops	Non-toxic: Pyrethrum, Derris. Short-term toxic: Carbaryl (3 days)
Dendrobium beetle	Dull orange and black beetle, 1 cm long, shield-shaped	Chews petals of orchids, eats away green tissue from young dendrobium leaves. Larva tunnels in and kills bulbous stems	Non-toxic: Pyrethrum, Derris. Short-term toxic: Carbaryl (3 days)
Earwig	Greenish-brown, 1–2.5 cm long	Eats flowers and foliage at night	Non-toxic: Trap in old cans loosely filled with damp paper. Short-term toxic: Spray Carbaryl double strength (3 days)
Grasshopper	Long green or brown insects	Devour all types of growth	Short-term toxic: Carbaryl (3 days)
Hibiscus beetle	Small purplish-black beetle	Eats small holes in leaves of hibiscus and other shrubs	Short-term toxic: Carbaryl (3 days). Long-term toxic: Thiodan

transmitted by aphis and leafhoppers (in the case of bronze wilt of tomatoes and dahlias, by thrips) so remove and burn infected plants as they remain a source of reinfection.

Virus is rarely transmitted by seed. In annual plants it usually only occurs when insects transmit it from a perennial 'host' plant. The broad bean virus which also attacks sweet peas is carried by aphids from plantain, a perennial weed. Getting rid of plantain should give freedom from this disease.

Mosaic virus in lettuce is harboured by one of the large prickly thistles. Spotted wilt of tomatoes also infects dahlias, where it shows only as yellowish concentric 'bird's-eye' markings but does not seem to affect the flower as seriously as it does tomatoes. It is transmitted only by thrips which have fed on infected plants during their early development, and has undergone a 5-day cycle in the thrips' intestines before it becomes active.

Solving the problem

When something goes wrong in the plant world, searching for the answer through long lists of various pests and diseases leaves most people utterly confused.

Therefore the symptoms that may be encountered are listed here together with the most likely cause of the problem so you can find the safest and least toxic as well as the standard remedy — the choice is yours.

Symptoms

Holes in leaves or large sections eaten
First suspect: slugs and snails. If you see silvery tracks here and there, see heading 'Snails and slugs'. Caterpillars are the next likely cause: examine below leaves but looper caterpillars are difficult to detect, see headings 'Caterpillar' and 'Cutworm'.

Large curved gaps in leaf edges could be caused by grasshoppers. Birds occasionally help themselves to succulent garden greenery but in this case they usually concentrate on the more upright tips.

Leaves rolled. On citrus and some varieties of tomatoes leaf roll can be due to cold. Tight rolling, especially of young tips, could be caused by leaf roller.

Downward-cupped and distorted leaves on stocks, ageratum or violas, see 'Aphis'. Long-drawn deformed leaves on cauliflowers is due to molybdenum deficiency.

Unevenly scalloped or deformed leaves. Citrus foliage is likely to be deformed like this if exposed to wind when young and soft. Aphis attack in the young, sappy stages can result in a similar but usually more blistered appearance when the leaves mature.

Camellias can be similarly affected. In either case it does not seriously affect the tree.

Curled leaves on peaches — see 'Curly leaf'.

Blistered rubbery leaves on azaleas — see 'Leaf gall'.

Yellow leaves. This can be due to lack of nitrogen or to lack of iron if only new growth is yellow or pale and lack of magnesium if pale or yellow between veins, mainly on lower growth.

Yellowing can also be due to dryness, over-wet soil that retards root action, or even from overfeeding.

Note that on many shrubs and trees it is natural for the lower leaves to yellow before they fall. On gardenias it is common if the soil is still cold when sudden rises in air temperature start new growth.

Mottled leaves. Pinhead-size pale spots on marigolds, dahlias, tomatoes — see 'Jassid'.

Gladioli with whitish mottling at base of leaves — see 'Thrip'.

Geranium leaves with scattered pale spots — see 'Rust'.

Azalea leaves with light irregular mottling, later followed by overall grey to pale bronze appearance, brownish spots beneath — see 'Lace bug'.

Fuchsias, rhododendrons, viburnums and cissus with patchy pale mottling then overall or large patches of silvery grey — see 'Thrip'.

Dull, sandblasted appearance of roses, fuchsias, polyanthus, beans, squash, etc. Close inspection in bright light or magnifying glass shows sand grain-size green or reddish-brown mites — see 'Red spider'.

Mottling of orchids, lilium, passion-fruit and other foliage, usually angular and between veins — see 'Virus'.

Black patches on rose leaves — see 'Black spot' in 'Roses' chapter.

Brown patches on foliage. Large browned areas may be due to sunburn when shelter has been removed from above a plant or a potted plant is moved from shade to sun.

Brown patches on edges of leaves and leaf tips on house plants or palms can be due to dry atmosphere or fluoride damage, on edges of dracena to perlite in potting mix — see also 'Bacterial diseases'.

Brown patches. Definite oval-to-circular brown patches, especially on house plants or daphne, can be scale: see if it can be scraped off with a finger-nail; if so, see 'Scale' — if not, see 'Leaf spot'.

Fern leaves with dark angular patches or banding — see 'Nematode'.

Black sooty mould on citrus, gardenias, holly and other evergreens — see 'Scale' as this is responsible for fungus living on sugary scale secretions. (Note: Mealy bug may also secrete similarly.)

Grey or white patches on plants. A powdery film on leaves — see 'Mildew'.

Clusters of down in junctions of leaf and stem, under or between foliage. See 'Mealy bug'.

Downy patches in cracks of bark, stem junction, etc. or base of trunk, particularly on apple trees — see 'Woolly aphis'.

Brown shrivelling of margins, curled under on grapes, rock-melons, etc. — see 'Downy mildew' under 'Mildew'. If curled inwards on cabbages and many other plants is likely to be potash deficiency. Water in about 1 level tablespoon of sulphate of potash per sq. m of garden. On deciduous magnolias, poplars, maples and birch it can be due to excessive water loss during hot, dry days but this condition can also be linked with potash deficiency.

Woody lumps on stems — see 'Gall wasp'.

Insect	How it looks	What it does	How to combat
Black beetle	Black beetle of lawns; shiny, black, 1–2 cm long	See Chafer grub	Short-term toxic: Carbaryl (3 days). Or lawn beetle granules.
Shield beetle or bean bug	Adults are green shield-shaped about 1 cm long, pungent smell. Also light or dark brown in earlier stages of development	Sucks beans, tomatoes, etc. causing distortion, wilting or blotching	Non-toxic: Pyrethrum (most effective). Short-term toxic: Malathion (3 days). Needs generous dousing
Citrus bug (Similar shape to shield beetle)	Twice the size of above, brown or black; when disturbed may emit fluid which irritates skin or causes temporary blindness	Causes young shoots of citrus to wilt	As above
Harlequin bug	Similar to shield beetle, usually with red and black markings	Sap sucking; mostly found on dahlias and other ornamentals	As for shield beetle
Cutworm	Fleshy grey-brown caterpillar; hides in soil by day, curls wheel-shaped if disturbed	Severs seedlings at ground-level or devours foliage near ground	Pyrethrum. Short-term toxic: Carbaryl (3 days) or dust soil around plants with cabbage dust (residual effect shown on container, according to ingredients)
Chafer grub	Dirty white, 2.5–4 cm long; plump grub with brown or orange head and legs. Larva of black beetle has similar appearance, but is more slender	Ringbarks plants below soil-level, damages roots	Short-term toxic: Water soil generously with Carbaryl mixed to spraying strength
Mealy bug	Downy, whitish aphis-like insect on ferns, daphne, and some perennials	Causes slow die-back of fronds, loss of buds, weakening of foliage	On house plants, sponge with soapy water or dab with methylated spirits. Otherwise spray Folimat
Leaf miner	Tiny larva embedded in leaf tissue. Adult miner fly is not often seen	Tunnels a winding course through leaf, leaving a light-coloured trail	Non-toxic: Pyrethrum, sprayed twice weekly. Toxic: Lebaycid
Staghorn beetle	Tiny round black beetle	Makes shot-holes or indentations in staghorn or elkhorn fronds	Malathion or Pyrethrum are least likely to burn foliage. Also saturate back of plant with spray

Insect	How it looks	What it does	How to combat
Thrip	Slender, black or brown cigar-shaped insect about 1 mm long. More often seen during hot, dry conditions	Rasps away green tissue from gladioli, onions and other foliage, leaving silver streaking. Flowers damage similarly — marking more noticeable on dark carnations, roses, etc.	Non-toxic: Pyrethrum — gives some control. Short-term toxic: Malathion alternated weekly with Carbaryl (both 3 days)
Lace bug	Resembles large sandfly with delicate lacy wings. Found on underside of foliage	Attacks underside of foliage, especially azaleas, causing pale flecks then an all-over light bronze or silver appearance. Small, treacle-like spots usually present. Similar to thrip damage.	Non-toxic: Pyrethrum sprayed below foliage. Short-term toxic: Rogor (1 week), Lebaycid (2 weeks)
Red spider and mites	Hard to see without a magnifying glass; reddish-brown to transparent. In colonies, usually on underside of foliage	Foliage loses lustre, becomes closely mottled, then turns dull yellow or light brown	Non-toxic: Sulphur dust. Frequent misting with water or soapy-water sprays deters the pest. Short-term toxic: Kelthane (7 days), Malathion (3 days), Rogor (7 days),
Scale pests	White wax scale is common on holly, box thorn, gardenias and citrus, in some areas	Weakens plant. Heavy infestation causes die-back. Black sooty mould is fungus living on honeydew, a sugary substance secreted by scale pests	Non-toxic: Spray with white oil in late December, and again a month later. Malathion (3 days) may be added to spray. If white wax is already evident also add 100 gm washing soda to each 4.5 L of spray
White wax scale	Red scale on citrus and ornamentals shows as pin-head-sized brownish scales; oleander scale as brownish or black swellings on stems	As white scale	Spray with white oil and Malathion when noticed
	Cottony cushion scale leaves soft, cushion-like sacs surrounded by fluffy substance along twigs or under foliage	Attacks wattles, hydrangeas, fruit trees and ornamentals, causing die-back	Spray with white oil

The cup moth caterpillar also makes hard, smooth grey-brown woody cocoons like small acorns.

Woody or fleshy lumps on leaves. Leaf gall — no definite cure and not of serious consequence.

Soft, grey-brown match-head-size eggs clustered on stems of gum trees are gum tree scale. Treat as 'Scale' (they usually only affect young trees).

Safety

Before using any pesticide, read the directions carefully. Never use more than the quantity recommended. Observe all safety precautions, especially the use of protective clothing where recommended. Always wash gloves and shower off waterproof clothing before removing.

How safe are garden chemicals?
Fertilisers

None of the widely-used fertilisers or plant foods could be regarded as toxic. Some, like sulphate of ammonia, muriate, or sulphate of potash, will burn or leave the skin very dry, especially if in contact with wet hands. They would be unpleasant to the taste and could make a person ill but would not poison.

Commercial insecticides (listed in approximate order of safety)

Pyrethrum is a natural insecticide extracted from the pyrethrum flower and is toxic to insects but not to humans or warm-blooded animals. Inhaling appreciable quantities may cause mild irritation and depress respiration, but it is considered safe for application right up to harvest time. It is, however, toxic to fish, so ponds or aquariums should be covered before spraying. Some varieties of fuchsia and hydrangea may also be sensitive to it.

Bioresmethrin is similar in action and safety to Pyrethrum and is particularly effective against caterpillars, shield bugs, aphis and white fly.

Dipel is another 'natural' product of bacterial origin, effective only against caterpillars that have ingested it, so it needs applying with a spreading or wetting agent so that it covers the foliage evenly. (Caterpillars stop eating within a few hours of consuming Dipel then die a few days later.) It is non-toxic so can be applied at any time.

Chemical pesticides

Malathion is effective against aphis, red spider, lace bug, mealy bug, most scale pests and, to some extent, thrip and white fly. It is the least toxic of the organic phosphate group and can be used up to 4 days of harvest.

Carbaryl is particularly effective against chewing insects which include caterpillars, cutworms, beetles and earwigs; although toxic it is generally considered safe to use on vegetables to within 4 days of harvest.

Rogor and **Lebaycid** are both organic phosphates, semi-systemic in action. They usually penetrate a leaf or through skin of fruit, so are popular for fruit fly control, lace bug on azaleas, red spider, scale and mealy bug. They are toxic but considered safe to use up to 7 days prior to harvest. Check labels as some plants are sensitive to them.

Endosulphan (Thiodan) is used mostly against caterpillars and other chewing insects and ants. Toxic, but considered safe up to 7 days prior to harvest.

Diazinon, an organic phosphate, is effective against aphis, scale, caterpillar, red spider, and also has some effect on caterpillar and white fly. Toxic, should not be used within 14 days of harvest.

B.H.C. and **Lindane** (chlorinated hydrocarbons) are effective against aphis and chewing insects, especially cutworms and other soil grubs. However, they are not recommended for the vegetable garden. B.H.C., particularly, causes tainting of cucumbers and other vine crops and can taint root crops growing in the soil a year after its use.

Chlordane — Highly toxic, still used in some areas for control of ants and spiders but generally eliminated from the home garden range.

Dieldrin — now eliminated from the home garden range — was widely used for control of borers, termites, ants, lawn beetles and spiders. It is highly toxic, readily absorbed through the skin and can remain toxic in the soil for many years.

Folimat (omethoate) controls sucking insects including aphids, mealy bugs, mites, white fly, also thrips, codlin moth, lace bugs etc. Toxic for 7 days.

Fungicides

Bordeaux. The original formula, developed last century in France, is a mixture of powdered copper sulphate and hydrated lime. This rapidly solidifies so copper oxychloride is generally sold as a substitute under various names sounding like 'Bordeaux'. It is a general fungicide effective against powdery mildew, numerous soft rots but is not particularly potent against black spot on roses or apples, or rust. Bordeaux or its substitutes also have some bactericidal effect. Only mildly toxic at normal spray strength. Vegetables may be used a few days after treatment if they are washed first.

T.M.T.D. (Thiram), **Zineb** and **Mancozeb** are dithiocarbymates. Zineb is widely used for rust, especially of geraniums, various leaf spots and downy mildew; Mancozeb for petal blight and diseases of turf. Although only mildly toxic they can cause irritation of skin, eyes and nasal passages.

Benomyl, a systemic fungicide effective against black spot, mildew, various moulds and damping off diseases, although the chemical can deteriorate and lose effectiveness with age. Avoid inhalation and skin contact. Do not use on vegetables.

Other fungicides include **Karathane,** specifically for powdery mildew and **Captan,** used for damping-off and other fungus diseases but not powdery mildew.

Sulphur is effective against powdery mildew, red spider and tomato mite but can burn tender foliage.

Lime-sulphur (a general fungicide) is a useful miticide for roses and fruit trees during the winter dormant period and is also effective against rose scale. It may burn tender foliage. Triadimelon (Bayleton) may be used for the control of azalea petal blight and is effective against powdery mildew.

Fungus diseases

Disease	How it looks	What it does	How to combat
Powdery mildew	Ash-like growth over foliage	Deforms young shoots of cucumbers, melons, marrows, crepe myrtles, roses, etc. May also cause foliage to fall	Spray with Bordeaux or copper oxychloride (each 1 day)
Downy mildew (not illustrated)	Tufts of whitish mycelium under foliage	Leaves of grapes, melons, etc. go brown and crimp downward, usually first at edges. Onion foliage withers from tips	Zineb, Maneb (7 days), Bordeaux (1 day) or combination sprays (see packet for toxicity time)
Black spot (Roses)	Black spots, rather feathered at the edge, later surrounded by yellow areas	Leaves fall prematurely	Spray Zineb, Captan or combination rose spray to prevent spread of disease
Rust	Rust-coloured pustules under leaves. On geraniums the tiny pustules are in circular formation; on calendulas in large orange tufts	Foliage yellows and plant weakens. Snap-dragons collapse when infection becomes severe	No positive cure for snapdragon and calendula rust, but spray with Zineb to prevent it. For geraniums, roses, beans, etc. remove infected leaves, spray with Zineb (7 days) to check spread

SPECIALISED GARDENING

33. Growing orchids

Growing orchids is easy . . . if you can find the aspect that suits them. It is much easier to find an orchid that suits the area you have available than to find an area for a particular orchid. There are hundreds of different orchids from different parts of the world. Some are at home in cool foothills, others on the steamy jungle floor of the tropics, some in cool sheltered valleys while others are native to relatively dry open plains and hillsides.

Orchids are usually regarded as delicate and demanding, but most are surprisingly tough.

Orchid types

Orchids are divided into terrestrial and epiphytic orchids, which are cultivated differently.

Terrestrial orchids

May be grown in loamy soil in the garden provided the temperature is not too cold in winter or they may be grown in pots containing leaf-mould and soil.

Epiphyte orchids

In nature grow on trees, not as parasites but taking food from rotted wood or leaves and from the air. Rock orchids are also epiphytes.

Most epiphyte orchids also do well in pots of spongy but not-too-soft decomposed wood, with marble-sized pieces of charcoal, sandstone, or similar material to provide a permanent grip for roots.

Many epiphytes will grow on a piece of porous wood, on an old stump, or on the bark of a tree. They need a fairly moist atmosphere for the summer growth, but most will grow under similar conditions to cymbidiums, preferring lightly broken sunlight.

Some flower in almost full shade (the same environment as ferns) — the beech orchid, pink rocklily, pencil and spider orchids among them.

Growing on wood

A piece of branch 35 cm to 70 cm long, 12 cm to 17 cm in diameter, will house one or two epiphyte orchids. Suspend it by wire in a fernery on a tree branch; move indoors for brief periods when flowering.

Use wood with long-lasting but spongy bark. Nail sleeve of bark to wood so it doesn't fall off later, and then bind with thin copper wire so it won't split.

Secure the plant firmly with nylon fishing line or thin copper wire. Or rest the plant on two thin nails projecting from the bark, then bind short pieces of bark or tree fern fibre over the roots on either side of the crown.

Let loose roots spread in natural growth, but bring them into close contact with the bark by covering with a soft pad of sphagnum moss or teased-out tree fern fibre, binding firmly but carefully so the binding doesn't cut.

Once roots find their way into the bark, the plant becomes self-supporting. Plants already growing on small pieces of wood are merely fixed to a post.

If establishing plants on growing trees, choose ones that don't shed bark — such as 'old-man' banksia (*B. serrulata*), whose corky bark is ideal; casuarina (or she-oak), ironbark, jacaranda, podocarpus; or smooth-barked trees such as coachwood, Christmas bush, Illawarra flame, coral tree, ash, or even peach, apricot, or plum.

Orchids for warm, frost-free areas

E — Epiphyte   T — Terrestrial

Most of these orchids require an even but not necessarily high temperature. In cool climates they will grow in a house which is centrally heated during the winter or in a glass house and outdoors in tropical and semi-tropical areas.

They need a winter temperature between 10–15° C.

The problem of low humidity in a heated home can be overcome by grouping tropical orchids with other plants well away from warm air inlets or standing them on trays of moist pebbles. Someone I know of has several orchids flourishing in a well-lit bathroom.

What I do with plants needing warmth and humidity indoors is stand them in an old fish tank; the acquarium pebbles in the base are kept wet by the run-off from the pot plants. This is also an excellent propagating box.

However, to flower well, exotic orchids also need bright but well-diffused light. Specialist growers usually use white painted glass, but you could place them near a bright window screened by a white sheer curtain.

Give these types of orchids plenty of water and an occasional feed of a complete plant food after flowering is over but while growth is still active. In the dormant period during the coolest months reduce watering and do not feed.

Aracnanthe (Spider Orchid) **E.** They prefer a higher winter temperature than many other types. Flowers are yellow with browny-red blotches hanging from the spikes opening one at a time as the stem elongates to about 30 cm. The strange flower-shape gives the orchid its common name.

Cattleya **T.** Many varieties, many different types, but all of them showy. The flowers can be spectacular. Tall plants to 75 cm.

Cattleyas need plenty of light and high humidity. The ideal temperature should vary between 10–32° C. Always water the plants from the top, soaking the pot and spraying the leaves. They must have good drainage so that the pots can dry rapidly in spite of being watered frequently.

Cattleyas need to be repotted about once in three years when they have grown too large for the pot. Divide the rhizome into 4 segments per piece.

Epidendrum (Crucifix Orchid) **T.** Do well in the open garden given full sun and plenty of water. They have dome-shaped heads of numerous small flowers shaped like a crucifix in many colours. 90 cm.

Laelia and ***Laeliocattleya*** **E.** There are hundreds of varieties — all beautiful.

Miltonia (Pansy Orchid) **T.** Crimson, white, brown, deep gold, pink or purple single flowers which look like pansies. 45 cm. Need winter temperatures above 5° C.

Odontoglossum **T.** Most have spiky flowers, many with pale mauve, buff and brown tonings and markings.

Oncidium (Dancing Lady Orchid) **E.** Large branching cascades dainty flowers, usually gold. Brown, red, pink and white hybrids. 120 cm.

Paphiopedilum (Slipper Orchid) **T.** Grow in the same outdoor conditions as cymbidium but will take more shade. They look beautiful in a low container. They are very adaptable.

I once came across a number of clumps of large showy slipper orchids growing profusely in a garden on the edge of high cliffs above the sea. Most were in wide shallow containers, some with as many as 30 flowers fluttering in the breeze.

They were in aspects ranging from full shade to open sunlight, but all protected from severe sea winds by trees and shrubs.

The slipper orchids are in some ways even more adaptable than the graceful long-spiked cymbidiums as most seem to flower well in positions too shaded for cymbidiums.

Another point about slippers is that different species flower at different times, and so it is possible to have flowers throughout the year. For example, predominantly yellow *Paphiopedilum aueram*, purplish-brown and green *P. hirsutissimum*, large brown and white *P. leeanum* and others flower mainly in spring; reddish *P. guardianum*, pale green and white *P. lawrenceanum* with its contrasting striped dorsal petal, and *P. mandiae* flower from spring to autumn, while the various *P. insigne* types flower in winter.

The majority of the slipper orchids are naturally terrestrial or semi-terrestrial, found in leafmould on the soil surface or in rocky pockets. They do well in most cymbidium composts or average potting soils with about one-third of granulated charcoal or weathered pine bark added. If you prefer to make up your own mixture add equal parts of leafmould and weathered pine bark with about half a part of coarse gritty sand or granulated charcoal.

They need very little extra feeding when plenty of organic material is present, but the addition of a little blood-and-bone or bone dust is beneficial. Otherwise they can have a light sprinkling of slow-release fertiliser such as Osmocote applied when new growth appears, which is generally in spring, or occasional waterings with water-soluble foods such as Zest, Aquasol or Liquifert applied at about half the normally recommended strength.

Phaleaenopsis (Butterfly Orchid). Some people call them Moth Orchids. The round-petalled, delicate flowers move in the wind and since the plant has few leaves they look like delicate insects in flight.

Vanda **E.** Tall, erect spikes, flowers rose, burgundy, blue. Need staking. All these plants need high humidity.

Orchids for temperate areas

E — Epiphyte   T — Terrestrial

These plants will tolerate quite high summer temperature if the humidity is high, and winter temperatures are down to around 5° C. and they are protected against frost, especially when budding.

Coelogyne (Angel Orchid) **T.** Pure white large flowers, wavy-petalled with golden throats. Cascading sprays. Only flower well in pots if crowded. They are exceptionally cold tolerant.

Cymbidium **T.** With their handsome, strap-like foliage and gracefully arching flower sprays, are undoubtedly the most popular and widely grown orchids. They flourish in temperate and sub-tropical climates, provided they are not exposed to heavy frosts or hot, dry winds.

The plants will survive for years almost anywhere, but they do need shelter from mid-summer sun, and sunlight that is only lightly broken at other times.

They generally grow well under the shelter of light-foliaged, deciduous trees such as peach or cherry. Tall gums or other evergreens are usually satisfactory. Here they can be placed so that they have more shade during mid-summer, when the sun is at a high angle, but have the winter sun, which comes in at a lower angle.

The light requirements of cymbidiums vary, but, if in doubt, err toward too much sun rather than too much shade. While some plants do not flower regularly every season, abnormal lack of flower is often due to too much shade.

Flower colour is influenced by the amount of light on the unopened buds. Yellows and reds are intensified by plenty of sun at this stage. Pale greens and whites are improved by shade, and enthusiastic growers move these into a more shaded area when the buds emerge from the sheath.

Atmosphere: Orchids revel in a humid atmosphere. Keeping the soil below the pots moist will help. If possible, during the summer, water foliage, pots and surrounds at least daily.

This treatment, combined with the partial shade, will also create favourable conditions for ferns such as maidenhair, hare's foot and feathery green lycopodium, which makes a delightful, moisture-holding ground cover. Protection from wind is necessary, ideally.

Containers: Large pots with tapering sides are best, as the plants can be removed easily for re-potting.

Use plenty of loose drainage material in the base, as the plants need easy movement of air as well as moisture through the soil. Where shelving isn't used, stand the pots on bricks, asbestos-cement sheeting, crushed tile or gravel, or roots and soil may eventually combine to block drainage holes.

Wooden tubs or half-casks also make attractive containers for large clumps.

Pots need not be regimented or herded together. For best effect they could stand at the base of a tree, or complement a shrub or other plantings where the environment is suitable.

Bushland settings: Cymbidiums lend themselves to natural bushland settings. If you have such an area, naturalise the orchids in old tree stumps, hollow logs, or in pockets between boulders.

By moving a few stones here and there, these pockets can be built up to appear like natural formations. A depth of 26–30 cm is sufficient, as the roots will spread and fossick between the rocks. Under these conditions, I have found roots in pockets of leafmould 2.5 m from the plant.

Compost filling the pockets or containers should be similar to that used for potting, with only a small percentage of soil, otherwise the plants cannot make healthy root growth.

Hollow logs or old, partly hollowed stumps can make ideal containers. Pack them with plenty of coarse compost, otherwise the plant may sink too deeply before its roots take hold.

When growing orchids under trees, watch that leaves and twigs don't build up too heavily around the base of the foliage. They may deter bud formation.

Flower quantity: Blooms out of doors are subject to a certain amount of petal-curling and weather-spotting, and naturally won't be the quality of those moved under cover. However, this is of little consequence unless the blooms are being grown for sale or exhibition. They will still look delightful in the garden, and give a lot of pleasure.

Miniatures: Cymbidiums are available in miniature forms. They grow under the same conditions as the conventional cymbidiums, flower just as freely in a similar colour range, and with as many blooms to the spray, but in miniature.

They should be popular for indoor decoration, as they are less cumbersome than the normal large type. A fully grown plant with several flower spikes need only occupy a 13 cm flower pot.

Dendrobium **E.** May grow and flower well in dappled sunlight without special attention.

D. densiflorum — From Burma. Gold-centred cream flowers hanging in dense bunches.

D. fimbriatum — Golden-orange flowers.

D. nobile — From Assam, purple and white flowers.

Sarcobilus ciliatus (Fairy Orchid) **E.** Small, dainty lilac-coloured flowers, mid-summer.

Growing Australian native orchids

Most of the great range of Australian tree and rock orchids are surprisingly easy to grow, in partly sheltered outdoor situations and especially in the comparatively humid coastal and mountain areas.

In hot dry parts they would need bush-house or fernhouse conditions.

Among the most endearing of these little charmers is the pink rock lily, with its short spikes of small waxy-petalled flowers. The orange blossom orchid is more retiring but even more beautiful; in the pendulous sprays of dainty blooms the smoothly rounded petals are like elongated pearls around a small opal centrepiece.

blooms the smoothly rounded petals are like elongated pearls around a small opal centrepiece.

There are many other little natives with big appeal, if not all for their beauty then for their personality.

One of the great things about the tree- and rock-dwellers is that a mature plant will continue to exist happily for many years on a piece of tree-fern fibre no larger than your hand. This means that a collection of 20 or so plants can be hung like a picture on a wall.

They also grow well in pots of orchid compost coarsened with cubes of tree-fern fibre, charcoal, weathered pine bark or similar material.

I have many of mine, which are mostly forms of *D. kingianum*, scrambling over rocks in a fairly moist south-sloping bushland setting. They were started by anchoring roots of small clumps to the rock with pieces of flattish stone up to matchbox size, plus a light scattering of leafmould.

Other clumps were started on steeper rocks from quite small pieces that looked as though they might make a shoot. These were wedged into a crack with a little moss.

Over more recent years I have been fortunate enough to have seedlings establish on rocks from seed scattered in the natural moss. However, don't pin too much hope on this method as you need the right conditions, and orchid seedlings in nature are very slow.

Enthusiasts raise them in sterile flasks of agar with regulated temperatures, then gradually accustom them to a natural environment. Even then, this is done mainly with seed from hybrids, not just for plant increase. Except for the ground orchids, increase is by plant division, or for the more sophisticated by tissue culture which needs laboratory techniques.

On the subject of plant division, it is helpful for hobby growers to understand a simple process known as back cutting.

To appreciate the process, look first at the way these tree and rock orchids grow. The new shoot grows away from the old plant, then thickens and forms a bulbous storage stem, or pseudobulb. From its base in the next growing season a new shoot emerges, in some species progressing only a centimetre or two before making another pseudobulb.

Notice that after the second season a pseudobulb usually loses its foliage, then a year or two later it gradually dies away. By this time the vigorously growing part of the plant has crept some distance, perhaps close to the top of your little tree-fern fibre block or right to the edge of the container. You can't stop the outward movement but by back cutting you can induce new productive growth from the old part of the plant.

All you do is cut the stem connecting the last still leafy pseudobulb and the older dormant one behind it. Then, instead of shrivelling away, the pseudobulb just behind the cut usually sends out another shoot.

With this treatment the clump increases in size instead of merely changing its position; moreover any of these severed sections that are growing can be taken off as new plants.

Lycaste Orchid

Dendrobium nobeli hybrid

Exotic Cattleya hybrid

Australian Rock lily (Dendrobium speciosum) needs at least one third sunlight to flower well

Some easily grown native orchids

Cymbidium sauve. Dark green foliage 27–32 cm long, flower spikes to 35 cm clustered with small green/golden-buff blooms about 2.5 cm across; soft fragrance. Do best in pots or hollow logs filled with composts of about 75 per cent brown rotted wood from the centre of old logs. Need constant moisture until established; don't over-water in winter.

C. albuciflorum. Similar to *C. sauve*, with foliage up to 1 m long; mainly from coastal area of Queensland, northern N.S.W.

C. canaliculatum. Similar to *C. albuciflorum* but more rigid growth, and open flowers have white rather than greenish-brown labellum.

Dendrobium (Rock Lily). Best known is *D. speciosum*, the king orchid or rock lily, with feathery sprays of creamy flowers 3–6 cm across, in spring. Established clumps may have 20 or more spikes. Best when roots are wedged between rocks or loose rubble, with a little leafmould over the rocks, but not touching the roots. Failure often results from using too much soil.

Lack of flowers usually means too much shade, especially with varieties other than *hillii* (from N.S.W. rain forests). They need at least half sunlight and enjoy a dry winter.

D. kingianum (Pink Rock Lily). Found on rocks and rotted tree stumps, with small, oval, glossy foliage, and usually pinkish spikes of 4 to 8 small, rose-pink flowers. These flower in fairly shaded places, but are best in broken sunlight. Establish on rocks as for rock lily, on moist tree stumps, or pots of the wood-and-stone mixture; in standard cymbidium compost.

D. falcorostrum (Beech Orchid). Like small rock lily, with 17 cm spikes of white, slightly fragrant. Grows in rain forests, N.S.W. to southern Queensland, chiefly on Australian beech; hence its name. Also known as Dorrigo orchid, because of prevalence in that district. It will grow in the wood/stone compost, but is best on tree fern fibre, tea-tree, or live banksias, with a covering of sphagnum moss until new roots establish. Flowers in full shade, best in broken sunlight.

D. gracilicaule. Similar to beech orchid, with smaller, creamy flowers with metallic sheen, usually spotted on outside.

D. aemulum (Ironbark Orchid). Again similar to beech orchid, but with long, thin white petals.

D. linguiforme. Rock-dweller from eastern Australia with woody leaves like green almond kernels pressed close against the rock, and feathery white spikes of spidery flowers; spring. Can be bound to tea-tree or established on semi-shaded rocks with small pieces of stone over roots to anchor. Dislikes soil.

D. tetragonum (Spider Orchid). Usually found on tea-trees of east coast, with pendulous, four-sided stems 3 cm long, small foliage at tips. Spidery, buff, fragrant flowers hang from the fleshy stems. Establish as beech orchid.

D. teretifolium (Pencil Orchid or Bridal Veil). Slender, pendulous leaves to 35 cm long, cascade of feathery white flowers in spring. Best bound to tea-tree or tree fern fibre, without soil; part shade.

D. bigibbum (Cooktown Orchid). Long, spectacular sprays of broad-petalled, rosy-pink flowers, 6 cm across; in autumn. In coastal tropical areas will grow on trees, bound with tree fern fibre; or in woody compost. Hard to establish and flower in temperate areas without heat.

Sarcochilus. Includes some beautiful species. Usually on spongy-barked timber such as banksia, tea-tree, or tree fern fibre; also grows in woody compost or coarse cymbidium compost.

S. falcatus (Orange-blossom Orchid). Waxy, strap-like fans of 12 cm leaves, pendulous sprays of dainty white flowers.

S. hartmannii has more upright sprays, yellow-centred, creamy white flowers.

S. fitzgeraldii has dainty, open flowers, mauve-pink at base of petals.

Growing hints

Use proprietary cymbidium compost or make a mixture containing at least one-third coarse material that does not decompose readily, such as one part partly rotted leafmould, one part weathered pine bark varying from pea- to small walnut-size, one part rotted cow manure and one part coarse sand or lightly crushed sandstone (both of which are fairly stable).

Divide or repot?

Cymbidiums do not need to be divided frequently; the less they are disturbed the better they flower. If the plant is filling its container then carefully tap it out and transfer it to one about two sizes larger — first adding enough new orchid compost to the base to bring the original root ball to about 1 cm below the container rim. With the aid of a dowel or wooden spoon, gently but firmly pack more new compost to fill around the sides.

Repotting ('potting on' as often referred to in orchid circles) can be done at any time of the year providing roots are not disturbed but obviously more care is needed when flower spikes have been formed.

Dividing is only necessary when a plant is cluttered with back bulbs and then should be done before new mid- to late spring growth commences. Better to do it during the flowering season, removing and enjoying any flower spikes present as cut flowers rather than leaving them to linger on the plant until late in the season.

Divide with the idea of removing most back bulbs but keeping the plant segments as large as possible. This will mean leaving the back bulb closest to two or more still leafy adjoining growths because removing it will usually part these.

Separate between divisions and wanted and unwanted back bulbs by removing the plant from its container holding a number of leaves then vigorously shake out the roots and compost adhering to them.

When a point for division is decided, pull the two sections far enough apart to feel down between them with a sharp knife or secateurs and cut the woody connecting tissue at the base.

Old roots are trimmed off but most of these automatically come away with the old back bulbs. The remaining one or two could be trimmed — old roots are brownish grey and spongy, new ones whitish and firm, particularly at the tips.

As orchids should not be overpotted it is likely that the divisions of the old plant would be more suited to smaller pots. When repotting these, hold them in position and feed the compost in around them with the other hand in such a way that roots remain spread, not pushed together. Pause several times during the filling, slightly lifting and tamping the pot on its base to firm the compost. Quite often a thin stake and tie will be needed to support the plant until new roots have established. Water initially and then only sparingly for a few weeks, at the same time keeping the plant lightly shaded.

Crocking in the base of the pot is not needed unless you are using the older type pot with only one comparatively large centre hole in the base rather than slits at the base of the wall. Compost should contain enough coarse material to keep it reasonably aerated and allow excess water to drain through rapidly.

Feeding orchids

Established orchid plants usually benefit from feeding several times during the growing period. With most species this is from flowering time until autumn. Complete soluble plant or orchid foods are usually used, applied when the compost is already damp.

Back cutting

Dendrobiums and other epiphytes (tree-dwellers) tend to grow away from the old canes (pseudobulbs) in one direction, usually upwards, and the older part of the plant lingers as a storage system, then gradually shrivels and dies. This can be prevented and the original centre of the plant kept more attractive and productive by 'back cutting'.

This means severing the woody rhizome connecting older and new growth just behind the last, well-matured and still leafy pseudobulb to induce at least one new growth from the base of the severed pseudobulb. It is usually done at flowering time (or just afterwards), before new growth begins.

Extending growing area

Epiphytes that grow beyond their tree-fern or back blocks can be given an extended area to grow by nailing them onto a larger board, then butting another piece of fibre against the old one.

Start most epiphytes toward the base of the fibre. New plants can be easily attached to fibre by binding them with a few strands of fishing line, cushioned where it crosses the roots with a little sphagnum moss or shredded fibre.

It would take several volumes to record all the finer points advocated by orchid enthusiasts, but you can enjoy success by starting with the basic steps outlined here, and join an orchid society.

Slipper orchid (Paphiopedilum).

Tongue Orchid (Dendrobium lingulform)

Pansy orchid (Miltonia)

These Cymbidiums have been flowering for many years in this garden without dividing. They were started in pockets of leaf mould and sandstone.

Growing problems and solutions

Problem	Cause	Solution
Leaves yellowing and falling.	Normal if confined only to one or two older pseudobulbs or canes.	Avoid feeding or over-watering during resting period.
Yellowish/green foliage on cymbidiums.	Excessive sunlight.	Allow only 60–70% sunlight.
Foliage with dull sandblasted appearance.	Red spider mites.	Spray with Malathion or Folimat
Pale yellow mottling between veins, translucent against light.	Probably virus.	It is wisest to remove and destroy infected plants. No cure but a warmer, sunnier position may allay disease.
Circular black markings, some in 'target' formation	Ringspot virus.	As above.
Yellow spotting of foliage	Check opposite side of leaf for small flattened buff or dark glossy brown scales.	Rub off with a soapy cloth or for large infestations use Metasystox.
Irregular dark sunken patches in leaves.	Check virus but may also be due to fungus infection.	Spray Benlate or copper spray.
Dendrobiums, areas of new growth with only veins remaining.	Dendrobium beetle.	See heading *Dendrobium beetle*.
Canes of dendrobium with brown or eaten out patches.	Dendrobium beetle.	See heading *Dendrobium beetle*.
Mature flowers of cymbidiums eaten.	May be slugs, snails or caterpillars, but frequently dendrobium beetle.	See heading *Dendrobium beetle*.
Flower buds, particularly of cymbidiums, eaten or with large holes.	Cutworm-type caterpillar or grasshoppers.	Look for grasshoppers or night-feeding cutworm-type caterpillars by torchlight or spray with Carbaryl.
Sugary substance or black sooty mould on foliage or canes.	Usually scale but downy white mealy bugs can also cause these secretions.	For mealy bug spray with Malathion plus a wetting agent or with Folimat
Ants infesting flowers.	May be aphids present but sugary exudates from the flowers could be the attraction.	To avoid spray marking the flowers, use a collar of insecticide-soaked cotton wool on the stem well below buds.

Dendrobium beetle

This pest is about 8 mm long, almost oval in shape, orange-tan in colour with dark blotches usually at either end of the wings. It emerges from the chrysalis stage about the time the dendrobiums make new growth. If this growth has not yet developed, it may be found feeding on the old flowers of cymbidiums or, resting, well camouflaged at the base of the flower lip. It may also attack young growth of coelogyne and other orchids. When feeding on the young foliage it completely strips the green tissue from the top of the leaf leaving only the veins. Worse still, the females lay their eggs either on or in the pseudobulb and the tunnelling of the larvae (a creamy white grub) sometimes causes complete collapse.

When the adult dendrobium beetle is disturbed feeding on the leaf, it drops to the ground and is hard to find, or takes flight. You can remove them by hand if you approach cautiously. Carefully cup one hand below the feeding beetles in case they drop, then make your grab with the other. If they do take flight they usually take a circular course and soon return to their point of departure.

The alternative control is to spray old cymbidium flower spikes, then young growth of dendrobiums etc. using either Carbaryl which gives protection for about 7 days, or with Endosulphan which has a life of about 14 days. Heavy rain or watering following application will naturally dilute the chemical.

Why orchids do not flower
Cymbidiums

Non-flowering can be due to several causes. Some cymbidiums only flower every 2 years. Congestion in the containers can also be a factor. If the orchid clump completely fills the pot, and is not carrying an excessive number of back-bulbs, then it needs 'potting on' into a container one or two sizes larger. If the clump is heavily cluttered with back-bulbs or pseudo-bulbs (the old bulbs without foliage), then the clump needs dividing immediately after flowering to remove all the old back-bulbs except the one closest to the leafy growths. Dividing should not be a yearly ritual but only undertaken under the circumstances described. Excessive dividing will result in lack of flower until the plant again becomes well established.

The most common cause of non-flowering in cymbidiums is insufficient sunlight. Quite often the containers are kept indoors too long after the flower spikes have passed their prime, or have been kept in too much shade. Some growers expose their plants to full sunlight after removing the ageing flower spikes, but this may result in foliage burn or yellowing if the plants have been kept excessively shaded. A happy medium is a position with half to two-thirds sunlight. An ideal situation is one with a few hours direct sunlight in the morning.

Cymbidiums need temperatures down around the 10° C mark to produce flowers; that is why they do not flower in semi-tropical to tropical districts.

Dendrobiums

Many of the Australian native dendrobiums will flower in quite shaded areas. These include such as the pink rock lily (*D. kingianum, D. falcorostrum, D. gracillimum*), and the numerous hybrids of these species. Others like the King Orchid or Rock Lily (*D. speciosum*) need at least half sun to flower well although there do seem to be other factors like hot dry summers which can stimulate flowering, both in these and cymbidiums.

Tropical dendrobiums such as *D. biggibum* and *D. undulalum* will only grow in heated houses because their flowering is mainly during late autumn when outdoor conditions are usually too cool. Other semi-tropical orchids like cattleyas and some of the vandas need a definite resting period to flower well. To stimulate this, water must be withheld for a 5–6-week period after the new growth is well established.

34. Bonsai and Saikei

Records show that bonsai was practised at least 700 years ago — originally by the Chinese then adapted and probably perfected by the Japanese.

The word bonsai means 'tree in a shallow container'. However, nature has been creating bonsai for millions of years. It is a delicate and precise method of controlling nature. In bonsai all growth is small, but perfectly represents the specimen chosen in miniature form.

Natural bonsai occur where a seed falls and grows in a small rock pocket of soil. The limited size of the growing area restricts root growth which in turn causes dwarfing of top growth. Quite often the plant on a rocky crag is contorted by the wind, or by the way it must find its way around rocks or ledges to gain light or achieve its natural tendency toward upright growth.

Some of Australia's earlier bonsai were Moreton Bay and Port Jackson figs that grew for years where soil or composted material was trapped at the base of phoenix or date palm fronds.

After the fronds fell the little trees clung to the near-bare trunk, nurtured by a few string-like roots that had found a little compost.

The bonsai subject is usually one element of the natural landscape — a grand feature tree mellowed and matured by time.

Then there are group plantings of maple, birch or elm that run the gamut of change of seasons as the beautiful filigree of bare winter branches is adorned with silky puffs of young spring growth, which turns into a verdant summer canopy that gradually takes on the rich glowing colours of autumn.

Volumes have been written on the fascinating art of bonsai, but that does not mean that you must be steeped in its tradition before trying your hand at it. Nor do you have to wait years to see satisfying results.

There are several ways to achieve 'aged' bonsai specimens without waiting patiently for years. One is to buy advanced specimens that could be reduced to small proportions. One well-known bonsai enthusiast has the most beautiful Japanese maple that was at least 25 years old when saved from the bulldozer at a demolition site.

The trunk was cut down to nearly 35 cm and roots pruned back so that they would fit a large bonsai pot (with the upper parts or those roots nearest the surface left exposed to give an immediate impression of great age). The required balance of branches was easily selected from the burst of shoots that followed the heavy cutting.

The same could be done with camellias, conifers and many other shrubs. The right time to do this is in late winter or early spring — several weeks before new growth is due to start.

You can steal time by air-layering a branch that looks as though it might make an interesting dwarf tree.

The general principle of bonsai is to restrict growth to a minimum by pruning both top and root growth. Cruel? It is really little different to cutting the grass or clipping a hedge. The small container keeps the plants small by restricting root growth. Natural bonsais of normally large trees are sometimes found where a seed has grown in a tiny rock pocket of soil.

Root pruning allows the plant to remain healthy and active without actually becoming root-bound. Root pruning is done every 2 or 3 years for maples and many other deciduous trees or for ficus and some other tough evergreens only every 4 or 5 years. The plant is removed from container, the soil loosened, about one-third of the roots pruned off, mostly from the base (but surface roots may also be thinned out or cut back).

Bonsai methods

You can 'dwarf' a tree just by leaving it to grow in a small container but the result is seldom pleasing, for when growth is halted by a root-bound condition the lower branches usually die.

Far better and kinder is to keep the plant healthy but dwarfed by top and root pruning. With root pruning and good care, the bonsai tree may outlive another of its kind growing in good soil with an unrestricted root run. Some very beautiful bonsai specimens are several hundreds of years old and still flourishing.

Root pruning induces the growth of new fibrous roots and keeps the system open and active. Shaping of small nursery-grown seedlings can start when they are about finger length by wiring the branches and then bending them — but you can bend the stem of a young plant just by laying the pot on its side, for the new growth will automatically turn upward and when the bend is sufficient the pot can be set upright again. This is often done to create a one-sided or windswept appearance.

There are a number of accepted types of bonsai:

Formal upright

An erect tapering trunk with fairly evenly-spaced branches in an overall triangular or pyramid shape. The tree is positioned in the centre of a squat container.

Informal upright

Very similar to the formal upright but with gentle twists to the trunk and branches, triangular in overall form.

Slanting

The trunk slants well over one end of an oblong or oval container with a low branch heading in the opposite direction.

Semi-cascade

The trunk arches over one side of container and branches bend slightly below rim of container which needs to be relatively high.

Cascade

The trunk bends outwards over the rim of the container and growth descends below container base. This needs a deep container on a stand.

Initial shaping

Follow any design that pleases you, even though it may not conform with traditional bonsai. Except for semi-cascade or cascade shapes, aim to have the first or lowest branch starting nearly a third of the way up the trunk to the right or left. Choose the largest and most dominant branch. The second branch should be a little higher on the opposite side and kept a little shorter than the first.

To give depth, a branch heading to the back of the tree is desirable, preferably from somewhere between the lowest and second lowest side branch. The higher branches would then alternate in opposite directions, spaced fairly evenly or diminishing toward the top, and their length reducing similarly.

Instant bonsai

It is possible to transform a bushy little nursery plant into an interesting-looking small tree immediately. Start with a conifer, buxus or other bushy, small-foliaged plant with fairly well-formed branches.

First remove branches not needed for the general framework of the tree. Then clip off all unwanted foliage and twiggy growth using side cutters which are like pincers with the cutting blades bowed to one side so that they cut closely without leaving a stub.

Next, trim the foliage of each branch back to isolate each one and give it individuality. Aim for the broad undulating clusters of foliage as carried by a mature tree. A dense compact foliage line can be built up gradually by clipping, or pinching out the tips of each young shoot.

Wiring or spacing to improve the general line of the tree can be decided after positioning it in its container.

Root pruning

Root pruning is done toward the end of the plant's dormant period, which in most cases is late winter or early spring. It is done initially when the new bonsai is transferred to its container and then usually every second year or even less often when the tree matures. Rapidly-growing plants in small containers may need yearly root pruning. With a new bonsai particularly, it is safest to top prune at the same time, as this reduces demand on the depleted root system.

To root prune, remove the plant from the container and use a pointed stick to separate roots and remove soil from between them, then cut back the roots by about one-third; they may be pruned more drastically if it is possible to compensate by reducing top growth accordingly. When you are ready to plant, determine the angle of the trunk and general position of the tree in relation to container. Cover each drainage hole with a square of fibreglass insect screen which eliminates need for crocking.

The pleasant effect of maturity is gained by setting the tree on a slight mound exposing heavy roots close to the trunk. Use a small stick to pack soil between the roots. It needs to be a little on the dry side so that it filters easily into all areas. Water gently but thoroughly, if necessary supporting the plant with wire stays fixed to the base of the pot.

Wiring

Use copper wire or soft, flexible, but not springy, steel wire. Secure it at the trunk then carefully wind spirally along the branches or the flexible part of the trunk or main stem. The wire must not be rigid enough to bruise or cut into the limbs or trunk.

When wiring is completed, gradually and gently bend with both thumb and first two fingers, firmly holding either side of the stem or branchlet. Confine bending to flexible growth only. If the wire is not firm enough to hold the branch in the desired position, it may be tied down with fishing line to a wire encircling the container, or attached to two small weights, but be careful not to overburden the branch. Upward twists or bends can be achieved by binding the branch to fine bamboo stakes or similar supports set in the container or bound to the trunk.

Excessive bends or twists should be avoided as these do not improve the overall effect. Just aim to reproduce a tree shape that looks graceful and natural.

Close branches may be spaced by twisting two pieces of fairly rigid wire together so that a fork is formed at either end. This is then wedged between the two branches or between trunk and branch. Widely-spaced branches may be brought closer by a figure-of-eight-type tie tightened until the desired distance is finally reached.

Wired branches generally set shape in 3–6 months, depending on maturity of wood — the wiring should not be left on for more than 9–12 months. Remove by carefully unwinding after cutting in several places.

General care

Bonsais need sunshine or at least good bright light outdoors to keep them healthy and compact. However, they may be enjoyed indoors for periods of a few days in well-lit rooms. Avoid bringing them into a much warmer environment than outdoors because this can induce a burst of new growth which will be thin and weak if made in poor light.

Give protection from hot midday and afternoon sun, especially for Japanese maples and azaleas. Protect from strong wind to avoid rapid drying of the soil and leaf burn, especially of deciduous trees.

Water whenever the surface of the soil dries out using a sprinkler to wet all the soil evenly, or immerse plant and container in water deeper than the soil-level and wait till air bubbles cease.

Further pruning should be done progressively as new growth occurs, rubbing off unwanted shoots and encouraging compact growth by pinching out the growing tip of others.

Bonsai can be raised from seed and it is possible to propagate well-advanced and mature material by layering branchlets of trees and shrubs.

Saikei

Saikei is another living art form that complements bonsai using ordinary nursery stock.

It depicts all the elements of the natural landscape with small gnarled rocks to depict craggy mountainsides or deep ravines, gravel for river beds, and moss as grass or low scrub. Trees are positioned and shaped as they would be found in nature.

These trees can be tied and fixed with mud and compost or peat-type mixtures to grow as they would in a small pocket of clifftop soil. Alternatively they may be formed into leafy arcades over moss-lined streams, or bow to the wind on an exposed shoreline.

Saikei is especially for the creative who do not have the patience to wait for bonsai trees to materialise into full glory.

With saikei it is possible to create natural landscape immediately, using small inexpensive nursery stock and whatever feature rock material you can find. The other great thing about it is that each planting in a saikei or group arrangement is a potential bonsai specimen.

Don't be too adventurous at first. Start with a small grove of maples or upright conifers in a wide bowl with soil mounded to form a gentle hill. Prune each individual plant in the saikei planting with the idea of using them as single bonsai specimens in the future.

35. Shadehouse and glasshouse gardening

Making a bushhouse

Where the atmosphere is naturally moist, in sheltered coastal areas, bushhouse conditions can be created below the light shade of over-hanging trees and shrubbery. Drier inland districts usually call for a little more planning.

Choose a site already protected from wind. It is as well to avoid dense shade, as this reduces the scope of plantings, but if there is already some surrounding shade from trees or tall shrubbery, so much the better. The protection of a building on the western or southern side of the bushhouse would be an advantage.

A minimum size of 4 m by 7 m is sometimes laid down, but this applies only in rather open areas, where size is needed to create a cool, moist micro-climate.

In the average garden, with plenty of shelter from trees and shrubbery, even a corner about 1 m across can be converted to a small 'bushhouse'.

However, in dry, inland districts it helps to have the bushhouse as large as possible. Make it a cool oasis, with space for relaxation on hot summer days, a haven for shade-loving plants.

The structure

The floor needs to hold moisture, as the evaporation from this provides the desired moist atmosphere. Ordinary moist earth is satisfactory, but muddiness is avoided and appearance improved by covering with a layer of blue-metal screenings, fine gravel, clinker ash, shavings, or even leafmould. Brick is also very absorbent, and an attractive, practical flooring.

For walls, a pleasantly rustic structure can be made with saplings as uprights and roof supports, covered with wire-netting and tea-tree brush.

The tea-tree is cut in 70 cm lengths and loosely woven between the netting. Work from the outside, starting along the bottom and working upward as you would thatching a roof.

The top pieces then overlap the bottom, so that drips are carried off and don't erode the soil in the pots or disturb the floor. The house may be a little dark after the brush is put on but will lighten as leaves fall.

Another attractive bushhouse has a sawn-hardwood timber frame covered with 2.5 cm-wide laths tacked about 2.5 cm apart.

The materials in both these bushhouses are ideal, as they absorb or hold appreciable amounts of water. Hosed over on a hot, dry day, they evaporate large quantities of water to the passing breeze, cooling and moistening the inside air.

Prefabricated steel-mesh bushhouses which are available can be covered with material such as tea-tree brush or plastic shade cloth.

The roof

The roof needs some pitch to take off drips, but keep it between 15 and 30 degrees in slope. The lower the roof the more moist the atmosphere of the house, so start at about head height, increasing height gradually toward the centre.

Although there is little weight in the roof, it is worth having supports strong enough to take a man's weight so repairs can be carried out by placing a ladder or plank across the supports or rafters. The rafters also need to take the weight of fern baskets.

Plastic shade cloth has advantages for the roof, as it breaks up and diffuses heavy rain, sheds water well, gives an even degree of shade, is long lasting.

There are varying grades, designed to give different degrees of shade from 28 to 80 per cent. The 80 per cent is satisfactory for most ferns and many exotic plants but is too dense for cymbidiums to flower well. They would prefer the 28 per cent one, but a 50 per cent shade cloth is a happy medium — enough for ferns, and lets orchids flower quite well.

Or perhaps you might have lighter shade at one end for cymbidiums and a denser one for ferns at the other. This denser shade would also be good to make a cool outdoor living area.

Shelving

Shelves are best within 1 m of the ground, as most plants appreciate moist air rising round them. In this case, have the shelves of fairly open material such as 5 cm wooden slats spaced about 4 cm apart. These also would be less enticing to slugs and slaters than unbroken, moist timber.

Some growers do prefer to line the shelves with metal or plastic, surrounding them with a 2 cm lip, then filling this tray-like section with crushed sandstone or gravel. Water is held in the base, the pebbles keeping the pots just above it — a system recommended in areas with low humidity.

It also overcomes earthworm problems that normally occur when pots are directly on the soil. Worms are beneficial in soil, but they can damage pot plants by silting up the drainage holes.

Small pools help increase the humidity of bushhouses and give them pleasant atmosphere. These are made easily by lining saucer-shaped depressions with heavy plastic sheeting. Bush stones will camouflage and anchor the sides.

Let some of the stones touch the water. This will cause some loss of water by seepage and mean more frequent filling, but it does increase evaporation and help keep the atmosphere moist.

Lacey Fishbone and Boston fern both accept light or dense shade.

Glasshouse gardening

A glasshouse or even a glass frame broadens a gardener's world into the lush field of tropical exotics.

It also provides a recovery area where tired house plants can regain their vigour and beauty, and is the ideal place to propagate cuttings of many shrubs or trees and to raise seedlings rapidly, with protection from heavy rain, drying winds, frost, birds and possums.

With this protection, vegetables such as tomatoes, cucumbers, capsicums and other warmth lovers can be grown right through winter and other high-price periods.

These summer vegetables, and flowers too, can be enjoyed earlier in the season by growing the potted seedlings to a good size under glass, then moving them into the open garden when the weather is warm enough. At the other end of the season, vegetables grown in large containers out of doors during late summer and early autumn can be moved under glass as nights become cooler.

Tomatoes can be grown under glass during winter without need for heaters in all but very cold districts. The extra warmth behind glass by day is enough to mature varieties such as Rouge de Marmande, Small Fry, Australian Large Red, Potentate and other hybrids developed for the purpose.

These and other vegetables can be grown directly into the soil on the glasshouse floor, or in plastic bucket-size containers of soil, or by hydroponics. (Hydroponic culture is gaining favour particularly in glasshouses, partly as a way to eliminate soil-borne diseases but also because plants constantly fed this way need less root area and so can be grown closer.)

One of the many advantages of a glasshouse is that you can work or potter in comfort with your plants during rain or biting winds. It can be a haven during bleak winter days but still quite bearable in summer because of ventilation normally provided and, if necessary, extra shading.

There is a lean-to model available which some people in exposed windy areas are erecting over an outside door, particularly where living or dining-room opens on to the garden.

The effect is a little like the conservatory or plant room popular in the Victorian era. It extends the room, giving a pleasant outdoor feeling without discomfort from the wind. The amount of air entering is regulated by the louvred ventilators or sliding door of the glasshouse.

Glasshouse construction has been simplified since timber framing has been replaced by strong but light cast aluminium which does not warp or rust and is unaffected by moisture. Prefabricated kits are available.

The size you choose depends on the need you have for a glasshouse, space available and your pocket. A small glass frame with a lift top would be suitable for balcony gardens or for raising seedlings or cuttings in the garden.

Operation of a glasshouse can sound complicated but it mainly comes down to increasing ventilation as temperatures rise. In most cases ventilators remain open during summer, especially through the heat of the day, and during the warmer days of autumn and spring. Automatic controls are available to open or close vents according to temperature.

In temperate areas there is no problem about growing most tropical plants without heating in the glasshouse, and even in mildly cool areas tuberous begonias, rex begonias, cinerarias, schizanthus, coleus, pelargoniums or geraniums, most ferns, gloxinias, *Primula obconica*, fuchsias, cacti, cymbidiums and most dendrobium orchids, gardenias, fuchsias, tomatoes and cucumbers, crotons, columnea, African violets and most of the warmth-loving house plants will all grow without heat.

Some tropical plants need plenty of water during summer but fairly dry soil in winter and in a weather-protected glasshouse they can be certain of ideal conditions.

If you want to use the glasshouse for mist propagation and need relatively dry areas as well, you can separate the sections with screens of clear plastic sheeting without appreciably reducing light.

Brake fern (Pteris) adapts to most aspects.

The fronds of Boston ferns are always longer in heavy shaded situations.

36. Hydroponic gardening

Hydroponic gardening means plants are regularly fed with nutrient solutions that supply much the same foods as good soil. They are set out in deep trays or shallow tanks filled with sand, gravel, vermiculite, charcoal, perlite, or similar material which acts as a support and a conveyor for the nutrient solution.

'Hydroponic' suggests growing in water, which actually was the original practice. I remember when the idea gained some popularity just after World War II. Enthusiasts had plants supported on frames of wire with a loose packing of coconut fibre, the roots permanently dangling in nutrient-charged water. However it is easier to plant in one of the solid media such as sand or gravel. They can be saturated just often enough to keep roots moist. Results are better because partial drying between irrigation allows vital oxygen to reach the roots more freely than it could in water.

Easily assembled hydroponic garden kits are now readily available. Most are complete with tank, liner, frame, sand, vermiculite, gravel, nutrient powder and instructions. All you supply are the plants and water.

Alternatively you can make your own hydroponic garden, any size from a small dish to a bed of many square metres. Even a fruit case lined with a plastic sheet offers possibilities, or you could build something more permanent and substantial.

To demonstrate the variety of scope of hydroponic systems it is worth mentioning that there are successful large-scale growing areas where lettuce and other vegetables are produced by what is sometimes referred to as trickle irrigation or nutrient film technique. One of these has very large areas of gently sloping corrugated asbestos sheeting with a controlled flow of nutrient solution trickling into each corrugation at the higher end. Over this is flat sheeting which leaves plants supported at normal spacing in holes above each groove. Enough solution is continuously circulating to keep the roots moist without actually being immersed in liquid.

Unless you are prepared to install automatic pumps that are to reticulate at predetermined times, it is far easier to plant in one of the semi-absorbent growing media already suggested. However there are many variations. For example, other than applying this by water-can as you would conventionally in the garden, there is no reason why a suitable water trough could not be fitted with a hose in the base attached to a 15-L container of nutrient solution. This could be suspended for an hour or two above the tank to irrigate and then lowered below the growing trough to drain off excess solution. In an extensive hydroponic garden I have visited, the growing tank is like a brick-sided garden bed 8–9 m long, about 1.5 m wide, lined with cement waterproofed by bitumen paint, and nearly filled to its 30 cm depth with vermiculite. The bottom slopes gradually to a drain plug at one end, emptying into a sunken 110 L drum fitted with a pump

to return excess nutrient-charged water to the nutrient storage tank at the high end.

This storage tank is a painted 110 L drum on a metre-high stand, with a base fitting for two hoses which run down either side of the bed and are punctured by fan-shaped nozzles every 30 cm or so. Initially this storage tank is filled with water four times. About 110 L runs off into the drainage tank and is pumped back, which means that the large bed holds about 340 L of solution.

The solution must be kept topped up with water. The nutrient is recharged each week during summer, monthly during winter or after flooding rains.

How often you irrigate the bed depends on temperature, closeness of crops and speed of growth; once a week is plenty during winter, but daily irrigation is usual during summer.

Early books on hydroponics listed separate chemical formulae for each different crop, but now the one mixture can suit all crops. The extra nitrogen needed by lettuce, cabbage, silverbeet and other leafy crops can be supplied by watering with proprietary soluble foods.

Some hydroponic gardeners use only these proprietary mixtures for their nutrient solutions. Phastrogen and Zest suit general crops such as beans, tomatoes, onions, carrots, flowers etc. Thrive suits lettuce, cabbages and similar leafy crops.

The mixture used for the large tank is a good cup-and-a-half of superphosphate, three-quarters of a cup of sulphate of ammonia, and three-quarters of a cup of sulphate of potash, plus a trace-element mix. The latter mixes vary in strength. Use the proportions recommended for mixing with standard fertiliser.

As superphosphate is only partly soluble, the mixture is enclosed in a glass fibre gauze insect bag and suspended in a tank, rather like a giant tea bag.

This quantity of fertiliser makes about 340 L of nutrient solution so needs to be reduced proportionally for smaller tanks.

Sowings are made direct into the bed where the plants are to remain, thinning out if necessary when the seedlings are large enough. Some growers buy seedlings and transplant, as in a conventional garden. Plants such as lettuce and cabbages need room to spread without crowding, but beans, root vegetables and tomatoes seem to need only about half the spacing normally recommended.

To grow plants successfully by hydroponics you need the same amount of sunlight and wind protection as you would for crops in the soil, and much the same methods of pest control.

A less ambitious but very prolific enterprise I have seen was a simply constructed but very productive ground-level hydroponic bed with a wire fence to keep out animals and an overhead awning of shade cloth, to catch leaves and heavy rain, but high enough to allow sunlight below it.

The sides were built up 40–50 cm with brick (the same could be done with timber) and the base was the natural earth. Waterproofing was achieved by lining first with the heavy blue plastic used for above-ground swimming pools, then placing over this a protective sheet of black plastic.

This made a growing tank 2 m long, 1.3 m wide and 15 cm deep. Over the base of the tank was a 4–5 cm deep layer of gravel, then about 4 cm of sand, topped with approximately 6 cm of vermiculite.

Vermiculite was the most expensive ingredient used, but relatively large quantities are much cheaper than small bag lots and are available from some of the larger garden suppliers or from plaster companies or builders' hardware stores. Vermiculite has no nutrient value but absorbs large quantities of liquid which are held within the flaky particles, allowing maximum penetration of air between the particles.

The bed was drained through a hose fitted into the base. The 55 L drum catching the nutrient solution was in a lined pit at the lowest end of the bed. When irrigation was needed again, this was raised to gravity feed back to the tank. However results are better when at least some of the nutrient is watered over the surface.

To compensate for water evaporated and used by the plants, the solution is topped up before each application, then discarded and replenished after 10–12 days. At that stage it still has some nutrient value, so is used on the plants in other parts of the garden.

Another, smaller tank garden in a discarded bathtub was brimming with silverbeet and zucchini.

One of the simplest beds or trays for home gardens is a trough, such as a long, wooden case, lined with plastic. One end of a flexible pipe is glued with liquid plastic into the base of the trough, the other end in the base of a 10–15 L can or light drum. The container of nutrient solution is raised on a hook above the trough to irrigate it, then is lowered to drain off the solution.

When growing soil-raised seedlings in a hydroponic tank, first carefully wash the soil from roots. Seed may be sown direct by bedding it on coarse sand, and covering to about twice its depth with vermiculite, which holds water in contact with the seed but also allows good aeration.

Some people feel there is something synthetic about hydroponic growing and condemn the use of chemical nutrients. Although a strong supporter of organic gardening, I must concede that the soluble nutrients essential for plant growth are in much the same form, whether they come from well-made compost or from a packet.

Soil organisms must convert organic material to inorganic water-soluble salts before it can be absorbed by plant roots. When feeding artificially, success depends mainly in applying a good balance of all essential plant foods.

One advantage of hydroponic growing is that if the dreaded die-back, fausarium disease, is detected, the tray in which the affected plants are growing can be totally discarded. Hydroponic gardening is simple gardening.

An easy way to sow lettuce or cabbages without transplanting, either in hydroponic beds or the garden, is to mark out the normal spacing required, place a pinch of 3 or 4 seeds at each spacing, cover each with either vermiculite, perlite or sand, then pat down gently and keep moist. When seedlings emerge, pull out all but the strongest one at each spacing.

When transplanting seedlings grown in soil or conventional seedling punnet mixtures into hydroponic beds, it is necessary to wash all soil from their roots then transplant in the usual way, spreading roots as much as possible.

The roots in hydroponic trays or beds are usually much shorter than in soil because there is no need for them to spread in search of moisture or nutrients. For this reason much shallower containers can be used than with soil. Plants with comparatively upright rather than spreading top growth, such as onions, beetroots and carrots, can be set closer than in soil. Naturally only short or baby carrots can be grown in trays.

Get the greatest number per tray of cabbages, lettuce and other vegetables with spreading tops by placing them close to the edges of the tray. Start with one in each corner, so that nearly half of the top overlaps the tray.

Growing pot plants by hydroculture

You can do away with soil entirely and still enjoy healthy house plants by using a modern but well-tried method which eliminates the usual hassles about under- or over-watering.

Just one top-up with water can keep a large house plant happy for weeks. When the water supply gets low, a little indicator tells you how much more to add.

The Luwasa system of hydroculture has been tried in Australia for several years. It was initially developed in Switzerland and rapidly gained popularity in Europe.

Hydroculture is one of the many methods of hydroponics — the growing of plants in nutrient-charged water rather than soil.

In the Luwasa method, the plants are supported in a perforated container filled with expanded clay pieces about the size of small marbles.

Being very absorbent, the expanded baked clay transmits a continuous supply of water and dissolved nutrients to the roots, and at the same time allows air to enter freely. The latter is important because it assures a continuous supply of oxygen, which is essential for healthy root functioning.

The perforated container (cultivation pot) holding the expanded clay and plant fits snugly into a decorative, imported ceramic or plastic pot which holds the nutrient solution.

For group planting in large containers or planter boxes, there is a special slotted sleeve to fit each cultivation pot. The arrangement can be changed and plants moved about easily

without disturbing the gravel or expanded clay filling between the pots.

Since water and plant food are readily available, the plant roots are not stimulated to expand at the same rate as they do in soil mixtures, and large plants will remain healthy and attractive for years in comparatively small containers.

With the guesswork removed from watering, feeding and soil type, the only other need to keep your house plants beautiful is sufficient light.

Soil-grown house plants can be converted to the hydroculture method:
1. Select a healthy plant, then carefully wash all soil from its roots.
2. One-third fill the cultivation pot with expanded clay that has been washed thoroughly in warm water. Any roots reaching beyond the clay should be trimmed back.
3. After positioning the plant carefully, cover roots and fill the pot with the washed expanded clay.
4. Place the cultivation pot in its outer container and pour lukewarm water over the clay until the indicator needle reaches the bottom of the frosted section.

For the first week or two keep the plant in a fairly well-lit, moderately warm position (20–25º C) and mist foliage occasionally. This careful nursing is desirable until the plant has made 'water roots'.

When the indicator shows that all the water has been used, the nutrient solution is watered over the clay.

Plants need transferring to larger containers only when they either become top-heavy or need refilling with water every few days.

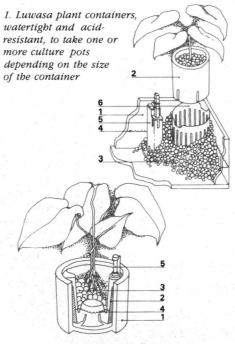

1. Luwasa plant containers, watertight and acid-resistant, to take one or more culture pots depending on the size of the container

2. Cultivation pot for growing Luwasa Hydroculture plants — interchangeable in seconds
3. Expanded clay instead of earth
4. Luwasa nutrient solution, the complete nutrient specially developed for Luwasa Hydroculture
5. Water-level indicator for supervision of the nutrient solution reserve

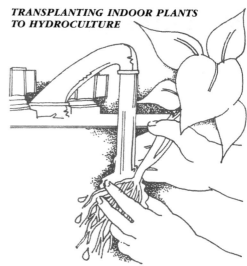

Select healthy young, robust plants and wash all earth from the roots with lukewarm water. Trim back any long roots.

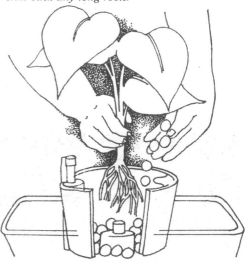

Wash the expanded clay well before putting it into the pot. Cover the floor of the cultivation pot with the clay balls then place the plant carefully in the pot and fill to the brim with expanded clay. Then place the cultivation pot into the outer container and pour in lukewarm water until the water-level indicator reaches the halfway mark.

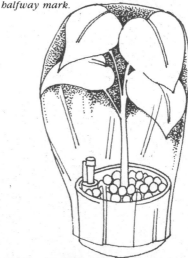

Freshly transplanted plants will be grateful for being sprayed with lukewarm water during the first weeks and covered with a transparent plastic bag.

37. Organic gardening

A great deal has been written in recent years in support of organic gardening, and there is now wide and successful use of hydroponics — the growing of crops without soil, fed only by chemical or inorganic plant nutrients.

Although organic material is essential for healthy soil, there is far less difference between organic and inorganic feeding than most people realise.

Plant roots cannot absorb nutrients from compost or other organic material until it has undergone complete decomposition, first by various fungi, then by bacteria that convert it from organic to soluble inorganic salts — nitrates, phosphates and potassium salts which are in much the same form as packeted chemicals.

The main advantage of organic feeding is that the decomposition process is a gradual one, making a slow release of the chemical or inorganic plant foods which then minimises danger of root damage from overdosage. There are substances present in organic material that act as beneficial enzymes or catalysts aiding the assimilation of other nutrients. However, if plant matter is grown on soil with mineral deficiencies, then the compost made from it will be similarly deficient unless compensating fertilisers are added to it.

Chemical feeding, if applied in moderation and with a proper balance of nutrients, is equally as good as organic feeding but does nothing for the physical condition of the soil. If soil is poor, then root growth is often poor and plants cannot receive full benefit from the nutrients applied. Also, the heavy and repeated applications of chemical fertilisers (particularly in agriculture in recent years) are strong enough to kill or discourage earthworm activity. This is a debit, as these small creatures keep the soil aerated and improve its depth by transferring organic materials to different levels.

Realisation of the long-term effect over-use of some chemicals, coinciding with concern for the dangers to the environment, has led many 'organic' gardeners to reject the use of any insecticide or fertiliser artificially produced.

Compost or organic material supports the teeming population of micro-organisms necessary to keep the soil healthy. The main role of these microscopic creatures is to recycle spent plant material, converting the organic to inorganic so that it can be used again by plant life. These useful organisms are able to attack, or repress, the development of the comparatively small population of organisms that cause damping-off, or root rots, and also the parasitic eelworms or nematodes (most species of the latter are useful recyclers).

To sum up, compost is essential to keep soil healthy and in a good physical condition, especially when the supply is maintained as a surface mulch. Chemical fertilisers are useful too and can be used to advantage providing they are applied as a complete or well-balanced mixture, and always in moderation. The best approach is to use only about half the quantity recommended on the package but twice as often (instead of a handful per sq. m every 8–10 weeks, apply this to 2 sq. m every 4–5 weeks).

If you prefer not to use any chemical fertilisers, maintain a surface mulch of compost between your plants, then supplement phosphorus and potash deficient in many Australian soils with light sprinklings of fowl manure, applied every 4–6 weeks during the growing season, over the compost mulch, then watered in. Let earthworms do the digging for you.

Flowers flourish as well as vegetables in an organic garden.

Straw gardening

You need never use a spade again! Forget about impossible weed growth and poor soil: You can now grow a garden on top of it. In fact, you can even grow a bumper crop of vegetables on a concrete slab without using chemicals.

The answer is not soilless gardening but a straw garden, a 'no-dig' method using only organic materials. I have seen lush beds of vegetables and flowers apparently surrounded by trim kikuyu lawns. Actually the gardens are placed on top of the kikuyu.

The garden was once a wilderness littered with tyres and other old car parts and overgrown with kikuyu but the rubbish was cleared, the grass mowed and a garden established on the kikuyu without turning a sod of the tough, compacted soil beneath it.

Some of the large beds are designed on a commercial scale. Bales of reject-quality meadow hay have been placed end to end to make large enclosures for vegetable growing. Others on a home garden scale are from 2 sq. m.

These are made of easily assembled hardwood frames which give the gardens a height of about 25 cm.

'No dig' beds are prepared by lining the base of the enclosure with a layer of newspaper 1.5 cm thick and covering with a 5 cm thick layer of lucerne hay, as it is 'flaked' from the compressed bale. This is covered with a thin layer of poultry manure, followed by about 20 cm of straw and a layer of compost sufficiently deep to start seedlings and the garden is watered well to commence growth.

For a bed of 2 sq. m you need 1 bale each of straw and lucerne hay (a cheaper grade of hay and straw will do), plus a small bag of poultry manure and 2 barrows of compost.

With lawn clippings, leaves, vegetable peelings and other garden refuse you can make compost in 8–10 weeks, or, for an immediate start, you can buy large bags of spent mushroom compost from most garden suppliers.

Although the initial outlay for materials to make a straw garden may sound considerable, these gardens will last for many years. Just add a little compost each season as the material subsides.

Maintaining a surface mulch of straw is a worthwhile alternative, as it acts as a buffer against heavy rain or watering, gives extra support to the plants, conserves moisture and revitalises the bed as it gradually decomposes.

Light scattering of complete plant food may be added, particularly for beans, zucchinis and similar podding or fruiting plants that need more phosphorus than supplied by the poultry manure.

This method of gardening also offers a way to regain productive soil in subdivisions where the topsoil has been removed in the initial grading process.

One of two beds could be moved about each season to systematically produce a layer of top-soil over otherwise inert and stubborn clay.

But a sunny aspect is needed.

Above; Below: Straw gardening is a form of organic gardening with the straw and lucerne hay decomposing into compost. Results can be spectacular and otherwise none productive areas made productive.

A month-by-month flower guide

January flowers

Trees and shrubs
Abelia
Abutilon
Acalypha
Beloperone
Calodendrum capense
Cassia fistula
Ceratostigma willmottianum
Clerodendrum ugandense
Cuphea
Delonix regia
Duranta
Fuchsia
Gardenia
Hebe
Hibiscus
Hydrangea
Lagerstroemia
Lavender
Malvaviscus
Murraya
Mussaenda
Nerium (Oleander)
Pentas
Plumbago
Plumeria
Punica
Rose
Russelia
Tecomaria
Tibouchina
Vitex

Flowers
Alyssum
Aster
Begonia
Daisy (Marguerite, Shasta, Pyrethrum)
Felicia
Geranium
Impatiens
Perennial Phlox
Petunia
Marigold
Stokesia
Verbena
Zinnia

Bulbs
Agapanthus
Canna
Crinum
Dahlia
Gladiolus
Gloriosa Lily
Hemerocallis
Ismene
Lilium species

Climbers and creepers
Allamanda
Antigonon
Beaumontia
Bougainvillaea
Campsis
Clerodendrum
Doxantha

Lonicera
Mandevilla
Murraya
Solandra (Cup of Gold)

Natives
Acacia elata
  A. implexa
  A. longissima
  A. maidenii
Brachychiton populneus
Ceratopetalum gummiferum
Crotalaria
Grevillea spp.
Hibbertia scandens
Hibiscus splendens
  H. tileaceus (Cotton Tree)
Sturt's Desert Rose

February flowers
Trees and shrubs
Abelia
Begonia coccinea
Buddleia
Ceratostigma
Clerodendrum
Cuphea
Fuchsia
Gardenia
Heliotrope
Hibiscus
Lagerstroemia
Lantana — hybrids
Malvaviscus
Nerium
Penta
Plumbago
Pomegranate
Rose
Thevetia
Tibouchina (Lassiandra)

Flowers
Alyssum
Amaranthus
Aster
Balsam
Begonia
Brachycome
Calliopsis
Celosia
Cosmos
Eschscholtzia
Geranium
Gomphrena
Impatiens
Marigold
Petunia
Phlox
Portulaca
Salvia
Torenia
Verbena
Zinnia

Bulbs
Amaryllis

Canna
Crinum
Dahlia
Dietes
Hemerocallis
Tigridia
Zephyranthes

Climbers and creepers
Allamanda
Antigonon
Aristolochia
Bougainvillaea
Cobaea scandens
Mandevilla
Maurandya
Mina lobata
Morning Glory
Quisqualis
Solandra

Natives
Crotalaria
Epacris
Grevillea — hybrids
Hakea
Helichrysum
Hibbertia
Indigofera
Melastoma
Rhododendron
Scaevola
Senecio
Tristania

March flowers
Trees and shrubs
Abelia
Azalea (early varieties)
Begonia coccinea
Camellia sasanqua
Cassia
Ceratostigma
Clerodendrum ugandense
Cuphea
Frangipani
Fuchsia
Gordonia
Hibiscus
Holmskoldia
Lagerstroemia
Melaleuca quinquenervia
Plumbago
Rose
Tecomaria
Tibouchina granulosa

Flowers
Aster
Chrysanthemum
Dahlia
Hedychium
Helianthus
Impatiens
Marigold
Petunia
Phlox (perennial)
Physostegia

Plectranthus
Rose
Rudbeckia

Bulbs

Belladonna Lily
Canna
Colchicum
Day Lily
Liriope
Nerine
Sternbergia
Zephyranthes

Climbers and creepers

Antigonon
Podranea
Quisqualis
Solandra
Thunbergia

Natives

Acacia terminalis
Banksia
Epacris
Stenocarpus

April flowers

Trees and shrubs

Alyssum
Azalea
Camellia sasanqua
Ceratostigma (Skybush)
Gordonia
Hibiscus
Plectranthus

Flowers

Anemone hupehensis (Japanese Windflower)
Chrysanthemum
Dahlia
Day Lily
Easter Daisy
Goldenrod (*Solidago*)
Michaelmas Daisy (Perennial Aster)
Nerine
Pansy
Torenia
Viola

Climbers and creepers

Allamanda
Ampelopsis (Chinese Ornamental Grape
    — in berry)
Antigonon
Holmskoldia
Manettia
Maurandya
Polygonum
Tecomaria
Vitis coignetiae (Crimson Glory Vine
    — in autumn foliage)

Natives

Acacia terminalis (Wattle)
Banksia ericifolia
Crowea
Epacris
Lagunaria (Norfolk Island Hibiscus)
Stenocarpus (Queensland Firewheel Tree)

May flowers

Trees and shrubs

Arbutus
Azalea
Camellia sasanqua
    C. sasanqua japonica — varieties
Cassia
Ceratostigma (Skybush)
Daphne
Euphorbia
Gordonia
Holmskoldia
Luculia
Reinwardtia

Flowers

Chrysanthemum
Marigold
Michaelmas Daisy
Strelitzia
Violet

Bulbs

Iris stylosa
Jonquil
Narcissus
Nerine

Creepers and climbers

Minalobata

Natives

Callistemon citrinus
Correa
Crowea (Waxflower)
Epacris (Native Fuchsia)
Grevillea triloba
Thryptomene

June flowers

Trees and shrubs

Azalea
Buddleia salvifolia
Camellia sasanqua
    C. japonica
Chimonanthus praecox (Winter Sweet)
Daphne
Erica
Erythrina (Coral Tree)
Euphorbia (Poinsettia)
Garrya
Gordonia
Hamamelis mollis (Witch-hazel)
Hebe
Jasminum mesnyi
Lavendula dentata (French Lavender)
Luculia
Osmanthus fragrans
Prunus mume
Reinwardtia
Salvia leucantha
Senecio
Thryptomene

Berries and fruit on

Arbutus
Ardisia
Aronia
Aucuba
Berberis

Callicarpa
Cotoneaster
Crataegus
Elaeagnus
Elaeocarpus
Eugenia (Lilly-pilly)
Euonymus
Ilex (Holly)
Nandina
Pyracantha (Fire-thorn)
Ruscus (Butcher's Broom)
Symphoricarpos (Snow Berry)

Flowers

Bergenia
Euryops
French Marigold (*Tagete*)
Helleborus
Iceland Poppy
Kalanchoe
Primula
Schlumbergera (Christmas Cactus)
Strelitzia
Zygocactus

July flowers

Trees and shrubs

Azalea
Buddleia salvifolia
Camellia
Daphne
Diosma
Erythrina (Coral Tree)
Euphorbia (Poinsettia)
Gordonia
Hebe
Japonica
Lavendula dentata (French Lavender)
Luculia
Magnolia
Podalyria sericea
Polygala
Prunus
Reinwardtia
Viburnum tinus

Berries on:

Ardisia
Cotoneaster
Euonymus
Hawthorn
Holly
Melia
Nandina
Pyracantha

Flowers

Bergenia
Calendula
Helleborus
Iceland Poppy
Kalanchoe
Mignonette
Pansy
Primula
Rochea
Stock
Violet
Wallflower
Zygocactus

English daisies (Bellis) and polyanthus attractively border azaleas and rhododendrons.

Bulbs
Daffodil
Hyacinth
Iris stylosa
Jonquil
Narcissus
Snowflake

Climbers and creepers

Clerodendrum splendens
C. speciosissimum
Pyrostegia

Natives
Acacia baileyana (Cootamundra Wattle)
Boronialedifolia
Epacris

Trees and shrubs
Azalea
Buddleia salvifolia
Camellia (*japonica* and *reticulata* varieties)
Crassula
Diosma
Garrya
Japonica
Lantana montevidensis
Magnolia
Michelia
Polygala
Prunus
Psoralea

Flowers
Helleborus
Iceland Poppy
Marguerite
Pansy
Polyanthus
Primula
Ruellia
Viola
Violet

Bulbs
Daffodil
Freesia
Hyacinth
Lachenalia
Narcissus
Triteteia

Climbers and creepers

Akebia
Clerodendrum splendens
Jasminum polyanthum
Pyrostegia venusta
Thunbergia grandiflora

Natives
Acacia
Boronia
Chamaelaucium (Geraldton Wax)
Clematis aristata
Correa
Crotalaria (Bird Flower)
Epacris
Eriostemon
Grevillea
Hardenbergia
Prostanthera (Mint Bush)
Thryptomene

A spring riot of white Arabis, Alipine phlox and Wisteria.

Cymbidium orchids growing happily in a lightly shaded temperate garden

September flowers

Trees and shrubs

Agonis
Azalea
Bauhinia
Beloperone
Camellia
Cersis
Cornus (Dogwood)
Datura
Diosma
Eupatorium
Fuchsia
Jasminum mesnyi
Lavender (French)
Magnolia
Malus
Philadelphus (Mock Orange)
Pieris
Prunus
Rhododendron
Robinia
Rondeletia
Rose
Spiraea
Syringa
Viburnum
Virgilia

Flowers

Alyssum
Antirrhinum (Snapdragon)
Aubrieta
Bellis
Campanula
Centaurea (Cornflower)
Cheiranthus
Cineraria
Daisy (Marguerite — *Bellis perennis*)
Eschscholtzia
Forget-me-Not
Gazania
Gerbera
Gypsophila
Linaria
Lobelia
Mignonette
Nemesia
Nigella
Polyanthus (Primrose)
Poppy
Primula
Schizanthus
Statice
Stock
Sweet Pea

Bulbs

Anemone
Babiana
Clivia
Crocus
Daffodil
Freesia
Hyacinth
Iris (Bearded and Dutch)
Ixia
Lachenalia
Narcissus

Ranunculus
Scilla (Bluebells)
Sparaxis
Tulip
Watsonia

Climbers and creepers

Bougainvillaea
Clematis
Doxanthus
Gelsemium (Carolina Jasmine)
Jasminum polyanthum
Wistaria

Natives

Acacia
Actinotis (Flannel Flower)
Anigozanthus (Kangaroo Paw)
Banksia
Bauera
Boronia
Callistemon (Bottlebrush)
Dendrobium (Rock Lily)
Epacris
Eriostemon
Grevillea
Hakea
Hardenbergia
Hovea
Isopogon
Leptospermum
Leschenaultia
Pittosporum
Prostanthera (Mint Bush)
Pultenaea (Bacon and Eggs)
Tetratheca
Thryptomene
Westringia (Coast Rosemary)

October flowers

Trees and shrubs

Azalea
Bauhinia
Beloperone
Brunfelsia
Camellia
Catalpa
Deutzia
Diosma
Eupatorium
Fuchsia
Jasminum
Laburnum
Lavender
Malus (Crab Apple)
Philadelphus (Mock Orange)
Pieris
Prunus (Flowering Cherry)
Rhododendron
Robinia
Rondeletia
Rose
Spartium (Spanish Broom)
Spiraea
Syringa (Lilac)
Viburnum
Virgilia
Weigela

Flowers

Alyssum

Antirrhinum
Aquilegia
Armeria (Thrift)
Aubrieta
Campanula
Centaurea (Cornflower)
Cheiranthus (Wallflower)
Cineraria
Daisy (*Bellis perennis*)
Delphinium
Echium
Eschscholtzia
Forget-me-not
Foxglove
Gazania
Geranium
Gerbera
Gypsophila
Linaria
Lobelia
Nemesia
Nigella
Penstemon
Peony
Poppy
Statice
Stock
Vinca

Bulbs

Babiana
Iris (*Dutch*)
Iris
Ixia
Scilla
Sparaxis
Tulip

Climbers and creepers

Bougainvillea
Clematis
Doxantha
Gelsemium (Carolina Jasmine)
Jasminum polyanthum
Trachelospermum
Wisteria

Natives

Banksia
Bauera
Boronia
Brachychiton acerifolium
Callistemon
Chamaelaucium
Chorizema
Epacris
Eriostemon
Grevillea
Hakea
Hardenbergia
Hovea
Hymenosporum (Native Frangipani)
Isopogon
Lambertia
Leptospermum
Melia (white cedar)
Prostanthera (Mint Bush)
Sollya (Bluebell Creeper)
Telopea (Waratah)
Thryptomene
Viola (Native Violet)
Westringia (Coast Rosemary)

November flowers

Trees and shrubs
Abutilon
Berberis
Brunfelsia
Calliandra
Calodendron (Cape Chestnut)
Catalpa
Ceanothus
Choisya
Dais
Deutzia
Duranta
Erythrina crista-galli (Cockspur Coral Tree)
Escallonia
Felicia
Fuchsia
Gardenia
Heliotrope
Hibiscus
Hypericum
Jacaranda
Kalmia
Lantana hybrids
Lavender
Leonotis (Lion's Ear)
Magnolia grandiflora
Metrosideros (New Zealand Christmas bush)
Murraya
Philadelphus (Mock Orange)
Plumbago
Raphiolepis (Indian Hawthorn)
Rhododendron
Russelia
Spartium (Spanish Broom)
Spiraea bumalda (pink May)
Stenotobium
Tamarix
Virgilia

Flowers
Ageratum
Antirrhinum (Snapdragon)
Campanula
Cerastium
Delphinium
Dianthus
Gazania
Gerbera
Kentranthus
Lobelia
Nepeta
Petunia
Phlox sublata
Phlox (annual)
Portulaca
Salvia
Tagetes (Marigold)
Tropaeolum (Nasturtium)

Bulbs
Allium
Agapanthus
Calla (Arum)
Canna
Gladiolus
Hippeastrum
Iris
Lilium (Madonna and November Lily)
Watsonia

Climbers and creepers
Beaumontia
Bougainvillaea
Campsis
Clytostoma
Cobaea
Dolichos
Doxantha (Cat's Claw)
Jasminum
Lonicera (Honeysuckle)
Manettia
Phaedranthus (Disticis)
Stephanotis
Thunbergia
Trachelospermum (Star Jasmine)

Natives
Acacia mollissima
Agonis (Willow Myrtle)
Angophora cordifolia
Boronia mollis
Brachychiton (Flame Tree)
Calicoma (Black Wattle)
Callistemon (Bottlebrush)
Castenospermum
Ceratopetalum
Chamaelaucium
Grevillea robusta (Silky Oak)
Hymenosporum flavum
Kunzia
Lagunaria
Melaleuca
Sollya

December flowers

Trees and shrubs
Abelia
Abutilon
Beloperone
Bauhinia galpini
Buddleia davidii (Summer Lilac)
Calodendrum capense (Cape Chestnut)
Cistus
Cuphea
Delonix (Poinciana)
Duranta
Escallonia
Frangipani
Fuchsia
Gardenia
Heliotrope
Hibiscus
Hydrangea
Hypericum
Jacaranda
Lantana hybrids
Lavender
Nerium (Oleander)
Osmanthus
Pentas
Plumbago
Protea
Rose
Russelia
Salvia
Spirea bumalda (Anthony Waterer)
Stenolobium

Flowers
Acanthus
Ageratum
Alyssum

Antirrhinum
Aster
Candytuft
Canterbury Bells
Carnation
Centaurea
Cerastium (Snow-in-Summer)
Clarkia
Cleome
Dahlia
Daisy *(Marguerite, Pyrethrum and Shasta)*
Echium
Erigeron
Gazania
Geranium
Gerbera
Globe Amaranth
Hollyhocks
Hosta
Isoloma
Linaria
Lobelia
Marigold
Nasturtium
Nepeta
Petunia
Phlox
Pinks
Salvia
Stokesia (Stoke's Aster)
Sweet William
Torenia
Verbena
Zinnia

Bulbs
Agapanthus
Canna
Crinum
Day Lily
Dierama
Dietes
Gladiolus
Gloxinia
Hippeastrum
Jacobean Lily
Lilium
Liriope
Tiger Lily
Tigridia
Tulbaghia
Zephyranthus

Climbers and creepers
Antigonon
Aristolochia (Dutchman's Pipe)
Bougainvillaea
Campsis
Convolvulus
Lonicera (Honeysuckle)
Mandevilla
Maurandia
Pandorea
Phaseolus (Snail Creeper)
Podranea ricasolina
Quisqualis (Rangoon Creeper)

Glossary

Acid soil — The opposite to alkaline. Soil with a pH less than 7 but over 6 would be regarded as slightly acid, pH6 to 5 moderately acid and below pH5 very acid. Most plants prefer slightly acid soils.

Aeration — Penetration of air. Desirable in soil because oxygen is needed for healthy root growth and germination.

Aerosol — Substance (insecticide, foliage food, leaf gloss or fungicide) combined with a compressed gas or propellent. The latter may cause damage if released closer than 45–50 cm from the foliage.

Alkaline soil — Opposite to acid soil (above pH7) — see 'Acid soil'. Elements including iron and manganese become unavailable in alkaline soils. Reduce alkalinity by adding iron or aluminium sulphates or sulphur.

Alpine — Strictly speaking, plants from above the treeline of alpine regions, usually growing from rock crevices or in a gravelly scree. The term is loosely applied to most cool-climate rock plants.

Amitrole (amino-trizole) — Herbicide that acts by preventing the formation of chlorophyll. Initial effect is a whitening or variegation of the leaf.

Ammonium sulphate (sulphate of ammonia) — One of the most widely-used sources of nitrogen. Contains approximately 21% N (nitrogen) in its pure form. Popularly used for lawn feeding and to 'burn out' weeds.

Ammonia — A water-soluble gaseous combination of nitrogen and hydrogen (NH_4), either synthetic or occurring with the decomposition of organic matter. A major source of nitrogen.

Anemone-centre — Flowers like daisies with central florets elongated to form a pincushion-like centre.

Annual — A plant that lives only one year.

Ant — Nature's scavengers. In the garden they usually do more harm than good by nurturing aphids, scale pests and mealy bugs. They may also transport mealy bugs to suitable host plants. Ants can also be responsible for non-germination of seeds which they carry off to underground storage areas. Even moderately large seeds such as those of lettuce, asters and carrots can be systematically removed by them.

All insecticides such as Pyrethrum, Carbaryl, Malathion or Endosulphan, etc., will kill ants. Longer lasting effect comes from the latter. One idea for protecting seed from ants is to rub them prior to sowing in a rag dampened with Kerosene. Alternatively dust the sown seed box or bed with cabbage dust or Endosulphan. Endosulphan sprayed over sown seed beds or boxes should give ant protection until seeds germinate.

Aphid — Sap-sucking insects, usually less than match-head-size, generally clustered on new shoots or under foliage which they sometimes deform. Apart from direct damage, they are often responsible for transmitting virus diseases from infected to healthy plants. Their main predators are ladybirds and their larvae, lace wing fly and larvae, mantis and birds including silver-eyes and wrens. Otherwise all but black aphis (found mainly on citrus, chrysanthemums and onions) can be controlled by spraying with soapy water or garlic spray. More widely effective sprays, listed in order of low toxicity and residual effect, are Pyrethrum or Bioresmethrin, Malathion, all-purpose sprays such as Rogor or Lebaycid and Metasystox.

Ash — Wood ash, incinerator ash, etc. Alkaline in action, should be used only sparingly on azaleas and other acid-loving plants. Content of potassium (potash) depends on material burned. Foliage and twigs may provide appreciable potash; heartwood very little. Ash can be added to compost, helps to replace lime. Coal ash is not generally recommended for gardens.

Bacteria — Microscopic and relatively primitive form of plant life that lives mainly on organic rather than inorganic substances. A few types of bacteria such as black rot of cabbages, stocks and other brassicas are plant parasites but most live on decomposing tissues, helping their corrosion to inorganic chemicals to support the growth of higher plants. Root nodule-forming bacteria of peas, beans, clovers and other legumes are capable of converting free atmospheric nitrogen for the use of their host plants.

Bamboo — This decorative plant can become a garden pest unless confined to containers or beds surrounded with a concrete mower strip 25 cm deep or similar solid retainer. Removal, especially when spread first commences, is usually easy as most of the tough caney runners are just below soil surface and can be lifted with a mattock. Remove chemically by using Zero or Roundup as directed or by cutting down the plants and flooding the soil with T.C.A. (500 gm to 10 sq. m of area) after the ground has been evenly moistened. Both chemical treatments may take 4–6 weeks to become effective.

Bark bound — During a long period of inactive growth the bark of some ornamentals (particularly camellias) and fruit trees becomes so toughened it restricts sap flow to the branches.

Bean fly — Sometimes troublesome in tropical districts. The small fly lays its egg on or below stem surface of the bean seedling then the larva tunnels through the stem often causing collapse of the plant. Combat with Endosulphan, Diazinon, Rogor or Lebaycid spray at first sign of damage.

Bean weevil — Often destroys bean seed. Prevent by dusting seeds with Carbaryl or similar insecticide prior to storing.

Beard — Tuft of hairs down the centre of the lower petals such as found on bearded iris.

Bedding plant — Any compact annual used for massed display.

Beetle — Many forms attack plants. Larvae of lawn black beetle (a greyish grub) eats grass roots and underground stems. Larvae of scarab beetle and Christmas beetle also attack roots and adults may devour foliage.

Benlate — see 'Benomel'.

Benomel — Benlate, a fungicide with some systemic properties, useful for control of various mildews and black spot, especially in ornamentals. Has a residual effect for 7–8 days.

BHC — Benzine hexachloride. Insecticide effective against chewing and sucking insects. Residual effect for about 30 days but can taint root crops grown within 12 months.

Biennial — A plant that usually lives for two years.

Bioresmethrin — A relatively safe chemical similar to Pyrethrum, with a residual effect of only one day. Gives good control of caterpillars, other leaf-eating insects, aphids and citrus or shield bugs. Do not use on fuchsias.

Bitter pit — A constitutional disease of apples, usually related to faulty nutrition.

Black fly — Sometimes refers to black aphis, which mainly attack citrus or chrysanthemums or to compost or mushroom fly — a tiny insect often found hovering around pot plants, especially those where spent mushroom compost is contained in the potting mixture. Control by spraying daily, while troublesome, with Pyrethrum or Bioresmethrin and flooding potting soil with Malathion to destroy larvae.

Black rot — A bacterial disease of cabbages, cauliflowers, stocks and other brassicas. There is no positive control except to burn infected plants and to avoid growing (for at least 4 years) these crops in soil where infection has been.

Black spot of apples — Also known as scab.

Black spot of citrus — see under 'Citrus'.

Black spot of roses — A leaf-invading fungus, troublesome mainly in districts with humid summers. For details and control see 'Roses'.

Blight — Several different bacterial and fungal infections are referred to as blight. Especially serious in potatoes and common in tomatoes. See charts under these respective headings in 'Vegetable' section.

Blind — A stem or plant that fails to develop a flower bud or growing tip.

Blister leaf sawfly — Larvae of small moth-like fly that tunnels between leaf tissue (particularly eucalyptus) causing blistered and scorched appearance.

Blossom-end rot — A disease of tomatoes where the base or blossom end of the fruit collapses, becoming sunken or flattened and blackened, usually with secondary fungal infection. Initial breakdown is due to a calcium deficiency, often caused by erratic watering, which prevents sufficient calcium reaching the more distant cells. Mulch to maintain an even moisture supply. Apply lime sparingly (one-third of a cup per sq. m) only if soil is known to be very acid.

Bonsai — The art of dwarfing trees, giving them the character of specimens in miniature.

Bordeaux — An old remedy adopted initially to control mildew in grapes, but has some control of other fungus and bacterial diseases.

The original mixture is equivalent to 6 level teaspoons of powdered bluestone (copper sulphate) and 3 level tablespoons of hydrated lime to 4.5 L of water, but may be difficult to dissolve unless freshly mixed. Therefore, copper oxychloride is often used as a more convenient and equally effective substitute. Sold under names sounding like Bordeaux, i.e. Bordo and Bordone — also as copper spray.

Bordo, Bordone — see Bordeaux.

Boron — A trace element required by plants only in small quantities (3–4 kg per .405 ha) and sometimes used in comparatively heavy concentrations as a herbicide. See details under 'Boron'.

Botanical name — The official name registered according to the Vienna Institute's Code of Nomenclature. Plants with similar characteristics, particularly those with the same pattern in flower make-up, are broadly classified in divisions and orders, and then family, genus and species.

Genus — is equivalent to the surname, Species — the christian name, but expressed botanically back to front. For example, native wax is Eriostemon (genus) myoporoides (species) which belongs to the family Rutaceae.

Rutaceae have common 'field characteristics', e.g. oil-glands in foliage, and some, such as boronia and diosma, share a musky or spicy aroma. Botanically they have flower characteristics in common, such as the ovary above the petals (hypogenus) and an even pattern in petal and stamen numbers — either 4 petals and 8 stamens (boronia), 4 petals and 4 stamens (zieria), 5 petals and 10 stamens (eriostemon).

The **Species** of a genus may be determined by a variation in foliage, petal size or general appearance. Species names are either descriptive or honour a person such as the discoverer or a patron of botany.

As an example, one of the many acacia species, following botanical tradition, is expressed as *A. baileyana*.

Botany — The scientific study of plants.

Brassica — Members of the *cruciferae* family, including cabbage, cauliflower, sprouts, broccoli, mustard kale and stocks.

Broad mite — A microscopic mite that causes thickening and deformation of leaves and limbs, particularly of African violets, chrysanthemums, cyclamens and gynura. Highly toxic, organic phosphate sprays, give the most positive control, or remove and destroy infected plants in your collection.

Bromophos — An organic phosphate dust not always available for control of soil insects, particularly cutworms and root maggot of carrots, cabbages and onions.

Brown rot — A fungal disease of stone fruits causing soft rot of fruit and die-back of twigs.

Bud swell — When the growth buds are swelling just prior to bursting. On stone fruits, apples, etc. this usually coincides with the time flower buds are showing colour, which is a more obvious sign. This is the time to spray for fungus diseases like leaf curl, black spot, etc.

Bugs — Shield bug of citrus, bean or green shield bug, harlequin bug, Rutherglen bug, etc. These are distinct from beetles as they hatch from their eggs as bugs but undergo several changes before reaching maturity, e.g. citrus bug in earlier stages is round to oval, buff or orange-coloured, then shield-shaped, brown or black. Most suck foliage or fruit, causing distortion or wilting. The assassin bug, dull red with trunk-like probiscus, is a useful predator. Parasitic types are effectively controlled with Pyrethrum or Bioresmethrin sprays.

Bulb — A term also loosely applied to corms and tubers. A true bulb is a mass of closely-folded swollen storage leaves attached to a button-like base of stem tissue — from which new growth and roots develop, e.g. daffodils, tulips, hyacinths, liliums, etc.

Bulbil — A tiny bulb, forming from the base tissue, or with some liliums from the stems below soil-level or in leaf axils (tiger lily).

Bulb fibre— A mixture of inert 'non-souring' materials such as coconut fibre, peatmoss, charcoal, grit, etc. (but *not* soil) used for growing bulbs in bowls without drainage.

Byrobia mite — Resembling red spider, can be identified by masses of reddish eggs on stems of deciduous fruit trees. Spray winter oil or see 'Red spider mite'.

Cabbage aphid — A grey aphid prevalent on cabbages, cauliflowers, turnips, radishes and other brassicas. Controlled by chemicals listed under cabbage moth or with Malathion or Diazinon.

Cabbage moth — A brownish moth, the larvae (caterpillar) skeletonises leaves of cabbages, cauliflowers and related plants. Controlled by derris, Pyrethrum sprays, Carbaryl and cabbage dust.

Cabbage white butterfly — The larvae causes similar damage to that of cabbage moth and is controlled by the same chemicals.

Calcium — An essential ingredient of plants. Lime is the main source.

Cambium — A layer of silky tissue in stems or trunks found just below the soft conducting tissue directly under the bark. It is the growth substance from which shoots or roots arise and the cambium layer of each plant must be united when grafting.

Capsid bug — Fast-moving green or brown bug that causes distortion of flower petals and shoots of ornamentals and apples. Controlled by Lebaycid, Rogor and Carbaryl.

Captan — A fungicide effective for control of damping off diseases and soft rot of flowers and vegetable botrytis, also with some effect against other fungus diseases, except powdery mildew.

Carbamate — A group of insecticides, Carbaryl being the one with the widest application.

Carbaryl — An insecticide effective against all chewing insects including caterpillars, beetles, weevils, earwigs, codling moths, etc. For use on all but tender foliage plants. Toxic to bees so avoid spraying on flowers. Residual up to 3 weeks but may be used within 3 days of harvest. A wettable powder or dust. Also sold as Sevin.

Carrot fly — The larvae or maggot of this fly burrows into the roots of carrots, causing wilting and inducing fungus. Rarely a problem.

Can be controlled by soaking plants with Carbaryl or Malathion.

Caterpillar — Larvae, or first stage from the egg, of moths or butterflies. They are destructive to plant foliage. Controlled by Pyrethrum, Bioresmethrin, Dipel, Carbaryl, Endosulphan, Lindane or BHC.

Chafer — The larva of beetles. Often large grub, creamy-white to grey with wiry legs and tan head. The cockchafer may ringbark large roots or stems of shrubs below soil-level — black beetle larvae eat grass roots and sometimes underground stems. Drench soil with Carbaryl or Endosulphan or use black beetle lawn granules.

Chelate — Element surrounded by organic molecule which prevents it combining and becoming insoluble with other elements. Iron and manganese are more readily available to plants in this form.

Chlordane — A powerful insecticide for control of ants, Argentine ants, earwigs, lawn grubs and black beetles, spiders and centipedes. Not for use on edible crops.

Chlorine — Element used mainly to purify water. Essential to plants in minute quantities, toxic to most plants in swimming pool concentration. Effective for killing moss on paths.

Chlorophyll — The green pigment of leaves which is able to use the sun's rays as energy for combining carbon dioxide and water to make sugar.

Chocolate spot — A disease of broad beans. May be controlled with Zineb spray.

Citrus — Oranges, lemons, grapefruit, cumquats, mandarins and limes.

Club root — A root-enlarging and distorting fungus disease of brassicas (cabbages, stocks, etc.). Less troublesome in limey soil.

Codling moth — A small brown to buff moth, lays its eggs at blossom-end of apples, pears or quinces. The small grub then hatches in core and emerges through side of fruit.

Compost — Decomposing leaves, grass, vegetable matter and other organic material which later reaches an inorganic state so that it can be absorbed by plant roots. Excellent when used to improve the physical quality of soil.

Contact herbicide — A herbicide that kills on contact with stems or foliage rather than by root absorption.

Contact insecticide — Kills insects when absorbed through body, without need for ingestion.

Copper oxychloride — A greenish-blue powder dispersible in water to make a fungicide particularly effective against some fungal diseases. A convenient substitute for the copper sulphate and lime Bordeaux.

Corm — Swollen stem tissue with storage and dormant buds (cyclamens, freesias, sparaxis, gladioli, anemones, etc.).

Cotyledon — First leaf or leaves, present in the seed and which emerge on germination.

Crown gall — Bacterial infection causing swelling at the base of some fruit trees, rhododendrons, pelargoniums and others. No cure, but rarely has serious effect on plant.

Cut worm — Caterpillars, usually hairless, that shelter in soil or plant debris by day and sever stems or foliage at night. Control by watering or dusting base of plant liberally with Carbaryl.

Cyclamen mite — Microscopic mite that causes thickening and distortion of cyclamen, African violet, and some other foliage. Remove infected plant from others and destroy or water to wet foliage with Metasystox.

Dalapon — A grass killer absorbed mainly through foliage. May take 5 or 6 weeks to kill.

Damping off — Sudden collapse, particularly of seedling, caused by stem penetration of a fungus that travels on soil in a film of surface moisture. Control by better spacing to improve air circulation and light penetration, by topping seed bed or box with vermiculite — avoid watering late in day. Drench with Captan or Benlate at first sign of attack.

Dak pot — Artificial lures for male fruit flies.

Deciduous — A plant which loses all foliage during its dormant season.

Dendrobium beetle — see 'Orchids'. Pumpkin beetle and 28-spot ladybird attack foliage and stems — also see 'Borer'. Spray with Carbaryl (gives control for about 7 days which should be effective enough to break cycle of foliage-feeding types). Flooding Fenamiphos lawn granules will control those feeding below ground.

Derris — A mild organic insecticide produced from the ground roots of an American weed (*Tephrosia*). Active ingredient is rotenone. May be used within 1 day of harvest.

Diazinon — An organophosphorous insecticide that controls aphids, scale, red spider, mealy bug and white fly. Has a residual effect of about 2 weeks. Do not use on maidenhair fern.

Dibble — Poke a hole for seedlings or bulbs with a dibbler — usually like a broad trowel handle tapered to a cone.

Dicamba — Herbicide effective against many broad-leafed weeds, used with M.C.P.A., etc. in lawn weed killers to broaden range of weeds controlled.

Dimethoate — Controls aphids, mealy bugs, white fly, scale, red spider mites and fruit fly. Sold as Rogor. Do not use on Meyer lemons, Seville oranges, apricots, Watt's early peach, chrysanthemums, asters, sage, salvia pilea or ornamental prunus.

Dincocap — A fungicide for control of powdery mildew on roses and other ornamentals (Karathane). May be used up to 21 days from harvest.

Disbudding — Removing surplus buds, usually to improve the size or quality of those left to mature.

Dithocarbamate — A group of fungicides including Zineb, Maneb and Mancozeb. Effective against most common fungal diseases except powdery mildew.

Division — Sections of a clump of rhizomes, of a woody crown, of evergreen bulbs (cliveas, agapanthus, orchids) or of tubers.

Dollar spot — Lawn fungus causing circular brown spots from 5 cm across.

Dormant — Inactive period during plant's life.

Dowpon — see Dalapon (similar composition).

Drainage — Good drainage is essential for most plants except willows, poplars, swamp cypress (*taxodium*), paper barks (some types of *melaleuca*), water irises, nile grass, astilbe, flavidus varieties of kangaroo paw, etc. As a test, if water remains in a 40–50 cm deep hole for more than 36 hours after soaking rains or watering, some drainage system is needed.

Dry mix fertiliser — Those that are applied direct to the soil.

D.S.M.A. — Disodium methyl arsenate. Used for selective killing of paspalum, summer grass and Mullumbimby couch in couch or brown top bent lawns.

Earthworm — Useful in the garden to aerate and deepen soil but not to be encouraged in containers because they often upset drainage. Rapidly killed by most insecticides and strong fertilisers.

Earwig — Crawling and sometimes flying insects 2–3 cm long with 2 prominent pincer-like appendages at the rear. Night feeding on foliage and flowers, often causing considerable damage to dahlias, etc. Control by spraying with Carbaryl or Endosulphan, or trap with slightly moistened crumpled newspaper in flower pots or jam tins (lay them on their sides, which will attract earwigs as hiding places during the day).

Ecology — Relationship of plants to their environment, now often used to imply general surroundings.

Eelworm — Microscopic (nematode) worms, some species are plant parasites causing knots or galls on roots or collapse of leaf tissue. See 'Flowers', 'Bulbs' and 'Gardenias'.

Endosulphan — An insecticide effective for control of most insects including aphids, thrips, caterpillars and beetles, particularly on ornamentals. It should not be used within 21 days of harvest. Sold also as Thiodan and hibiscus spray.

Epiphyte — Plant that in nature grows on a tree but not a parasite — some orchids, bromeliads and ferns.

Espalier — Tree or shrub trained in one plane — usually with branches fastened against fence or wall.

Evergreen — A plant that retains a good covering of foliage throughout the year.

Eye — A dormant or semi-dormant bud, in a left axil, above where a leaf has been or on a corm or tuber.

Ferthion — Insecticide and miticide that controls fruit fly, codling moth, lace bugs, mealy bugs, red spider, aphids, thrips, etc. May be used within 7 days of harvest. Sold as Lebaycid.

Ferbam — or one of the Ditho-carbamate fungicides (more popular in North America than Australia) for control of black spot on roses and rust on apples.

Fire blight — A fungus disease of tulips.

Fly (fruit flies) — A serious summer fruit and tomato pest in some districts.

Formalin — Volatile liquid used mainly for sterilising implements and containers to kill fungi and bacteria.

Fungicide — Chemicals used in a concentration that kills only lower plants (fungi). In greater than recommended concentration they can also damage plants that they are designed to protect.

Fungus — A lower or less-specialised plant, either parasitic on other plants or capable of decomposing and obtaining its own nutrients from other organic material.

Fusarium — A fungus causing one type of tomato wilt, carnation die-back and similar diseases, also snow patch or fusarium patch in lawns. Some types live in soil for many years, are difficult to completely control chemically, so replanting of crops is not recommended for at least 4 years.

Gall mite — Microscopic mite causing swelling and distortion of flower buds, particularly chrysanthemums and arabis, also blistering of leaves and dense clusters of minute foliage on some trees. Control with Lebaycid or Metasystox spray.

Garlic spray — A non-toxic spray effective against rose and cabbage aphis and a deterrent against some other sucking and chewing pests. Also appears to retard downy mildew plus several other fungal and bacterial diseases. Made by mincing a clove of garlic with about 4 L of water. The addition of soap and a teaspoon of well-emulsified paraffin will also extend control to black aphids of citrus, chrysanthemums and the onion family.

Germination — The actual sprouting of roots or shoots from seed after contact with moisture, suitable temperature and sometimes darkness.

Green fly — A common U.S.A. and U.K. term for aphids.

Grey mould (botrytis) — Affects double or clumpy flowers, causing rotting when conditions are moist, also of some vegetables and causes type of leaf spot. Controlled by Captan or Benlate.

Gumnosis — Gum exuding from bark of fruit trees. May be due to borer damage, over-wet soil or planting too deeply, peach tip moth or, in citrus, to copper deficiency. If applicable, treat as for 'Borer', otherwise improve drainage and apply copper spray liberally.

Halo blight — Seed-borne disease, initially showing brown spots surrounded by yellowish halo on leaves and water-soaked patches on pods, then death of plants. Remove and burn plants as symptoms show, then apply copper spray.

Hardy — In most cool climates means frost-resistant plant but also used to imply tough or tolerant to adverse conditions.

Herbaceous — Generally a plant (non-woody) with top growth dying back annually.

Honeydew — Normally refers to the sugary secretions from scale pests, aphids, or mealy bugs.

Hormone — Substances that stimulate growth and other behaviour, also refers to cutting powders or selective herbicides of 2.4-D-type that kill by overstimulating and altering metabolisms of some plants.

Hormone weed killer — 2.4-D, 2.45-T, M.G.P.A., Dicamba, etc.

Horticulture — The art of cultivating plants.

Humidity — Atmospheric moisture.

Hybrid — The result of a cross between two different species.

Hydroponics — Growing plants with nutrient solutions, not in soil.

Inorganic — The chemical section of the

carbon cycle where organic substances have been broken down to carbon and soluble salts of elements. Also refers to mined or factory-processed chemicals rather than those processed by soil organisms.

Insect — True insects (in their adult stage) have 3 pairs of legs attached to the thorax of their 3-segmented bodies, whereas mites and spiders have 8 legs. This is of significance as many insecticides will not kill mites.

Insecticide — Substances that kill insects.

Iron — One of the trace elements essential to plants. Its absence shows as a yellowing of new growth.

Kelthane (Dicofol) — A miticide that is relatively harmless to true insects, for use at least 7 days before harvest.

Lace bug — A bug, in the adult stage resembling a sand fly, with large lacy wings. Causes mottling and later a complete bronzing or silvering of azalea leaves. Damage more pronounced on weather-sheltered parts of azaleas because the delicate bug is dislodged by heavy rain. Vigorous hosing of plants therefore gives some control. Otherwise water or spray to thoroughly wet foliage with Lebaycid or Rogor when signs of mottling appear on new growth between mid- to late spring and late autumn. Do not spray unnecessarily as natural predators are lace wing fly larvae, ladybirds, small spiders, etc.

Lace wing fly — Both brown and particularly the green lace wings are elegant flies with slender bodies to 1 cm long and much longer transparent wings with a beautiful filigree of fine veining. Their clusters of whitish eggs are individually suspended on long, silvery hairs and the clumsy-looking larvae adorns its body with the dead remains of aphids, small beetles, moths and other prey. The adult is also a useful predator, unfortunately attracted by light so is often unintentionally destroyed by household insecticides.

Lateral — Side branches from the main branch or stem of a tree or shrub — generally the productive, or fruit-carrying, branches of summer fruit trees.

Lawn sand — A mixture of sulphate of ammonia, sulphate of iron and sand, used at the rate of one-third cup per sq. m to kill out soft weeds and moss with only temporary burning to grass.

Leach — To wash out various mineral salts from the soil.

Lebaycid — see 'Ferthion'.

Legume — Plants that produce pods with pea-type flowers: beans, peas, clover, lucerne. Previously a family name (*Leguminoseae*) which included wattles (acacias), cassias, bauhinias, etc. as well as pea-flowers.

Lime — Garden or agricultural lime or ground limestone is calcium carbonate. When burnt sufficiently to expel the carbon dioxide it becomes quicklime (calcium oxide) when soaked or with water added in calcium hydroxide which again readily absorbs carbon dioxide to revert to its original form (calcium carbonate).

Lime-sulphur — A powerful fungicide, miticide and cure for louse scale, made by boiling hydrated lime and sulphur. Pungent but can be regarded as non-toxic, it will burn tender growth, especially if a warm sunny day follows application. Available under names such as Harola.

Limey soil — Naturally limey or made limey by the addition of lime. The opposite to acid soil.

Lindane — A purified form of B.H.C. (Benzine hexachloride).

Loam — A mixture of clay, sand, sometimes silt and organic matter. If clay exceeds sand content it is classed as clayey loam, or sandy loam when sand is in excess.

Magnesium — Classed as a minor element but vital to plant functioning because it is the key atom of the chlorophyll molecule.

Malathion (Maldison) — An organophosphate pesticide with relatively low toxicity to man or animals. Effective against sucking insects such as aphids, leaf hoppers, scale pests (when unprotected by heavy wax coating), mealy bugs and red spider mites. May be used within 4 days of harvest.

Maldison — see 'Malathion'.

Mancozeb — A fungicide of the dithiocarbamate group. Effective for control of lawn fungus diseases, damping off in seedlings, downy mildew (particularly of onions and lettuce), rust, blight of potatoes and tomatoes and various leaf spots. Although only mildly toxic it should not be used on leaf vegetables or apples within 14 days of harvest.

Manganese — A trace element likely to become deficient in alkaline soils or present in toxic excesses under acid soil conditions.

M.C.P.A. — Selective hormone-type herbicide for control of many broad-leafed weeds in lawns.

Mealy bug — Grey to pink insects covered in whitish down, oval, flattish, rarely longer than the width of a match in the adult stage. Related to scale, damage plants by sap sucking. Natural predators are ladybirds and tiny predatory wasps, hence they are usually more troublesome indoors. Control by touching each pest with a cotton-wool swab or camel-hair brush moistened with methylated spirits, or use Pyrethrum or Bioresmethrin spray every second day while they still persist. Malathion, Carbaryl, Lebaycid, Rogor and Metasystox are more potent controls.

Mercury fungicides — Once standard treatments for lawn fungus and as bulb dips but now largely replaced by less toxic and biodegradable preparations such as Folimat and T.M.T.D.

Metaldehyde — A poison and attractant for slugs and snails, combined with bran or similar material to produce a standard-type snail bait, e.g. 1 pulverised 'meta' fuel tablet mixed with 1 cup of bran. Toxic to birds and animals so place baits with care.

Methiocarb — Used similarly to metaldehyde as a slug and snail bait, usually with longer-lasting toxicity. Also available as a foliage spray.

Mildew — A fungus parasite in plants. Powdery mildew seen as an ash-like film over roses, crepe myrtle, cucumber, pumpkin and foliage. Downy mildew, causing shrivelling of onion foliage and grape, brown flecking of lettuce (in this case the spore-carrying mycelium if visible in tufts below foliage).

Mosaic — Translucent or yellow patches usually between veins of foliage caused by different types of viruses, e.g. cucumber mosaic, which also causes streaking of petunia flowers, orchid mosaic common in cymbidiums.

Moth — The adult stage of caterpillars where mating, egg laying and wider transmission of the species occurs.

Mould — Colonies of fungi responsible for decomposition of organic waste or sometimes parasitic on plants such as grey mould (botrytis) of flowers and leaf vegetables during moist conditions. Controlled by Captan or similar fungicides.

Mulch — Any protective covering for the soil, plastic sheeting, gravel or more usually organic material (compost, etc.).

Mycelium — Web or thread-like branches of a fungus plant.

Natural insecticide — Plant substances which repel or destroy certain plant pests such as garlic spray (made from crushed cloves of garlic and soapy water) which is repellent to all but some black aphids; powdered derris root which yields roterone, toxic to aphids, flies and mildly so to caterpillars and weevils; Pyrethrins which are contained in appreciable quantities in dried pyrethrum flowers, grown in some areas, toxic to most sucking and chewing insects; boiled rhubarb leaves which produce a stomach poison; boiled tobacco which yields nicotine toxic to all sucking insects including mealy bugs.

Nitrate — Salt produced by the action of nitric acid on metal or at the final stage of decomposition by bacteria. Nitrogen in its fully soluble form and immediately available to plants.

Nitrogen — An essential growth substance, component of chlorophyll and protein. Free nitrogen is an atmospheric gas but the greater part used by plants is absorbed through roots as nitrates — see 'Nitrates' — or as urea.

Node — The point of a stem where a leaf or leaves arise, usually with a dormant or potential bud in the axil.

Nutrient — All major, minor and trace elements.

Organic — Plant or animal tissue (i.e. non-artificial) either petrified (as peat) or before complete decomposition.

Organophosphate insecticide — Malathion, Diazinon, Lebaycid, Rogor and Metasystox all control mites as well as true insects and should be used with care as either extensive or gradual absorption through skin or by inhalation inhibits or reduces presence of an enzyme (chlorinesterase) essential for nerve functioning.

Osmosis — A natural force causing passage of molecules or dissolved substances from a weaker to stronger solution through a semipermeable membrane such as the walls of plant cells. By this process, dissolved nutrients move from root cells throughout the plant.

Paraquat — A powerful contact insecticide that kills all green foliage it wets. Highly toxic to man and animals but breaks down within a day or so in contact with soil.

Peatmoss — Sphagnum moss or sedge grasses that have undergone a long period in an airless state which prevented decomposition (in sedges often buried below their own regrowth) leaving them in a petrified state. Valuable for their water-holding capacity.

Perennial — A plant with a normal life of more than 2 years.

pH — Stands for percentage Hydrogen ion, measured on a scale from 1–14. 1 is extremely acid, 14 extremely alkaline and both figures are beyond the range where plants would grow; pH7 is neutral, important because around this point (pH6–7.5) most soil nutrients are in their most soluble state and so are more readily available to plants.

Phosphate — A salt created by the action of phosphoric acid on a metal. The major naturally occurring phosphate is rock phosphate (moncalcic phosphate), rendered more soluble when treated with sulphuric acid to form superphosphate (dicalcicphosphate).

Phosphorus — One of the three major elements essential for healthy root growth, development of flowers, fruit and maturity generally. Main processed sources are superphosphate and for soluble foods mono or di-ammonium phosphate and natural sources, bone meal, rock phosphate, fish meal, poultry manure, raw sugar waste, cotton seed meal, banana, apple and citrus skin.

Photosynthesis — Combining of simple organic substances to form an inorganic substance. Example: 6 parts of CO_2 (carbon dioxide) + 6 parts of H_2O (water) = $C_6H_{12}O_6$ (glucose) + 6 parts of O_2 (oxygen). This combination occurs in the protoplasm of a plant cell containing the green pigment chlorophyll which uses the sun's rays as energy for the process.

Pinching-out or pinching-back — Pinching out the growing tip of a stem with a blade or your fingers to encourage side-shoots.

Plant food — either inorganic, immediately available plant nutrients, or organic material which will release plant nutrients after it decomposes to inorganic soluble form.

Planting out — Planting seed bed — or container-raised seedlings into their permanent positions in the garden.

Pollination — Fertilisation of the flower ovary by pollen grains from the male stamens.

Polyquat — like Paraquat with broader herbicidal properties.

Potting mixture — Mixture of soil and organic material, usually loamy soil, peat and sand — suitable for potting.

Potting on — Moving a plant into a pot 1 or 2 sizes larger.

Pricking out — Replanting recently-germinated, closely-sown seedlings into spaced growing position.

Privet — Vigorous quick-growing shrub once popular for hedging. Spreads rapidly from seeds carried by birds, now serious threat to bushland and other areas.

Propon — see 'Dalapon' (a similar composition).

Pyrethrins — A natural insecticide from dried and ground pyrethrum flowers. Toxic to most insects and fish but relatively non-toxic to animals and man.

Red-legged earth mite — A winter pest, adult about 1 mm long with bright red legs, causing a general foliage silvering starting from close to base of peas, sweet peas, lettuce, silverbeet, beetroot and turnips. For control see 'Red spider mite'.

Red spider mite — Foliage-sucking mites, can only be seen clearly under a magnifying glass in strong light. Causes a dull buff mottling or overall sandblasted appearance, more likely to be troublesome in weather-protected areas or dry conditions. Also where DDT-type sprays are used (as these kill their natural predators but not the mites). Controlled by frequent misting with water, sulphur dust or spray with Kelthane, Lebaycid, Rogor or Folimat.

Rhizome — Underground stems by which some plants spread, and which act as a storage organ during dormancy (bearded irises, couch grass, etc.).

Rogor — see 'Dimethoate'.

Root aphis — A mealy bug-like aphid which attacks roots, particularly of woody perennials, dandelions, rhubarb, potted plants and other plants in rarely disturbed soil. Control by saturating soil with Malathion, Diazinon, Lebaycid or Rogor. A few flakes of naphthalene in the bottom of the pot usually deters them.

Root nematode — Root knot nematodes or eelworms.

Rotenone — Active ingredient of ground derris root.

Rust — A fungus disease attacking, particularly, calendulas, bellis, snapdragons, geraniums, oxalis, some varieties of beans and sometimes roses. Identified by orange spots or clusters of spores on foliage and stems, usually accompanied by yellowing, or collapse (in snapdragons). Controlled but rarely cured by spraying with Zineb or Mancozeb.

Salt — Usually refers to sodium chloride or sea salt, also various salts found in soil from fertiliser use or decomposition of organic material in organic substances. Harmful if percentage of soluble salts exceeds that of root cell sap (which may be as little as 4 per cent for azaleas and other related plants).

Sawfly — Resembles an elongated blowfly, so-called because of the saw-like appendage used for opening leaves to insert eggs. Larvae of eucalyptus sawfly (spitfires — because they emit a yellowish liquid) is blue-black, up to 2 cm long, and often found in clusters when not feeding on leaves. Other types vary in colour and size. Control by removing and destroying clusters or spraying Carbaryl.

Scab — Usually refers to a fungus disease causing ridged scabs or distortions of lemons, or sometimes destroying embryo fruit. Also alternative name for black spot of apples or pears.

Scale — Tiny insects, coccids that attack plants and weaken them by sap sucking. Most types have a protective covering of white wax, shell-like crust or scab. Some types are controlled naturally, e.g. tiny parasite wasps, or even by fungus. Otherwise they may be scrubbed off with a brush and soapy water. For more extensive infestation, spray with white oil as directed on container with the addition of Malathion, Lebaycid or Rogor at normal spraying strength. The most effective time to spray is in late spring to early summer when the fry, or young, is in the unprotected crawler stage, then give a repeat spraying 4–6 weeks later. The adult females die after the fry develops. For San José scale see 'Pears' and for rose scale see 'Roses'.

Scree — Gravel-like material formed when the surface of rock is crumbled as the water it contains is expanded by freezing — hence the natural mulch for most alpine plants.

Seedling — Young plant soon after germination.

Selective herbicide — One that kills only certain weeds, as D.S.M.A. kills paspalum and summer grass but not common couch and bent, or 2.4-D which kills most broad-leafed lawns but not all lawn grasses.

Selective insecticide — One that kills only certain insects. Unfortunately there is little that kills pests and not predators, except Dipel which is lethal when ingested by caterpillars — those from moths or butterflies.

Sequestrene — A brand of chelate.

Sevin — A trade name for Carbaryl.

Silver leaf — A destructive fungal disease, particularly of prunus.

Simazine — Pre-emergence weedacide, or used on tolerant plants after emergence to prevent germination of weeds or other seeds in the soil.

Slater — see 'Wood lice'.

Slug — Can be described as shell-less snails controlled mainly by selective baits.

Snail — Control as slugs.

Sodium borate — A commercial source of boron.

Sooty mould — Soot-like covering caused by non-parasitic fungus living on sugary secretions from scale, mealy bugs or other plant-sucking insects.

Sowing direct — Sowing seed direct into its permanent position in the garden.

Sphagnum moss — A sedge moss capable of holding very large quantities of water in its large cell structure. Could be described as one of nature's reservoirs, as it often grows on plateaux and regulates the water supply to lower areas for a long period after rain — valuable for propagation, air layers, etc.

Stone fruit — Fruits with a single large kernel — peach, apricot, plum, cherry, etc.

Sub-soil — The inert soil below the surface layer of topsoil (which is usually mixed with organic material). In the case of clay loams it is usually solid clay or sometimes shale.

Sulphur — An essential minor element and control for mites and some fungal diseases. Foliage-burn may result if hot conditions follow application. Some apples, pears and rockmelons are sensitive to sulphur.

Systemic fungicide — Absorbed into the plant and translocated through sap stream.

Systemic insecticide — As systemic fungicide, e.g. Metasystox. Some insecticides (Lebaycid and Rogor) are semi-systemic, being absorbed but not appreciably translocated.

T.C.A. — A herbicide, chiefly grass killer, which is absorbed through roots rather than foliage, therefore is more concentrated in plant when high growth is cut down before treatment. Takes about 6 weeks to kill and leaves soil toxic for approximately 3 months.

Tendril — Modified leaf stems used by climbing plants to entwine support within reach (sweet peas, passion-fruit, choko, etc.).

Terrarium — An enclosed glass vessel where plants can grow in a moist-protected microclimate. Evaporating moisture condenses on the glass and returns to the soil.

Thrip — Tiny insects, winged in adult stages, that rasp outer tissue from petals or foliage causing silvering or browning. Also carry tomato bronze wilt virus.

Tip-pruning — Pinching out the growing tip of young shoots to stimulate further shoots from their leaf axils — encourages bushier, more compact growth.

Topsoil — The upper, more fertile soil layer which is usually as far down as humus and other organic matter and silt penetrates.

Tortrix moth — Small, green, quick-moving caterpillars that web or roll young leaves together, drop on a web when disturbed, eat out tip growth and penetrate rose buds. Control with Thiodan, Lebaycid or Rogor.

Total herbicide — A non-selective preparation that kills all growth.

Transpiration — Surplus water from leaf cells evaporated through stomata (pores) into the atmosphere.

Tree paint — Tar-like paint for damaged areas of trees; bark will continue to grow over it.

Tuber — Swollen storage roots (in the case of dahlias and ranunculi) or storage stems (potatoes, sweet potatoes).

Tulip fire (Fire blight or *Botrytis tulipae*) — Destructive fungus causing irregular grey or scorched foliage or distortion of plant in early growth. Affected plants should be carefully removed and burnt, survivors sprayed with Captan or Benlate.

Variety — Variation of a species, often obtained by selection.

Vegetable weevil — Brown to grey tiny weevil 4–5 mm long, feeds at night, scalloping edges of leaves. Difficult to detect as it matches dead margin of damaged foliage. The legless larvae or maggot also causes damage, usually below soil surface. Control by spraying at least every third night with Pyrethrum or Bioresmethrin while damage persists or weekly with Carbaryl or Thiodan. Also drench soil with these or Malathion for larvae control.

Vermiculite — Particles of mica exploded in a furnace enabling them to retain up to 14 times their own weight in water; inert physical medium with no food value but useful covering for seeds.

Verticillium — Stem-invading fungus causing wilt of tomatoes and other plants.

Virus — Minute organism, too small for normal microscopic detection but can be transmitted to healthy plants by infected sap, manually, or by insects.

Causes foliage mottling, distortion, general debility, lack of productivity and sometimes gradual wilting of plants. No direct chemical cure. In most cases it is prudent to destroy infected plants to deter insect or manual transmission. Some host plants may carry certain viruses without showing conspicuous symptoms, e.g. plantain weed carrying broadbean virus, dahlia spotted wilt virus of tomato, wild thistle, the mosaic virus of lettuce, etc.

Wasp — Most are useful predators from large spider or cicada hunter to minute creatures that parasitise caterpillars, scale and even the eggs of various moths and flies. Others cause galling of citrus or eucalyptus foliage.

Water — The major component of living plants, accounting for 80–90% of their weight.

Watering — Correct watering is a science, not just a matter of pointing the jet of a hose at the soil. For best results, water should be applied long enough to penetrate the sub-soil, but gently enough not to agitate or puddle the soil surface. Note that mulches make it easier to water without damaging soil structure.

Waterlogging — Soil saturated with water which excludes entry of oxygen, if prolonged, preventing root functioning and causing rotting in all but bog or sedge plants.

Weed killer — Substances which kill plants by contact or root absorption. See 'Chemical control', also 'Hormone weed killers'.

Weevil — Beetle-like insects, usually comparatively small, larvae is usually legless. Most are plant pests. Others attack large seeds in storage, particularly beans and grain. Eggs are usually present prior to storage but damage can be controlled by dusting seeds for planting (not edible) with Carbaryl prior to storage.

Wettable powder — Dry powder which mixes readily with water to form an emulsion. Unless directed otherwise, most need creaming with a small quantity of water before the bulk is added, then agitating occasionally to keep in suspension throughout the water.

Wetting agent — Substance that reduces surface tension of a liquid, allowing it to spread or wet evenly over a surface rather than remain in droplets on a leaf or other surface.

White fly — The adult of a scale-like leaf-sucking insect. The more juvenile scale stage (which appear to be eggs) are often parasitised by a tiny wasp. They then turn black. Control by misting flying adults with Pyrethrum or Bioresmethrin each day while trouble persists, rather than by more penetrating chemicals that also kill larvae of parasitic wasps. Basil repels white fly within a range of about 1 m.

Wilt — Excessive loss of water from plant or particularly leaf cells which cause leaves to become limp or, in extreme cases, to collapse. Due to plant being unable to take up sufficient moisture to compensate for transpiration of leaves, by reason of dry soil or damage to roots (root rot, eelworm or insect damage or fungus such as fusarium or verticillium invading conducting tissues of stem).

Wood lice (slaters) — Oval, grey creatures that frequent compost and other decomposing material but also likely to attack tender shoots or seedlings. Control by watering haunts with Carbaryl or Malathion, or placing baits prepared by adding 1 teaspoon of Carbaryl or Malathion wettable powder to 1 cup of non-pelleted snail bait. Place small heaps in damp, sheltered positions protected from pets or birds.

Zineb — A fungicide sold as a wettable powder, gives control of rust, blight, botrytis, leaf spots and downy (but not powdery) mildew.

Climatic zones of Australia

Spathodea — tropical climate

Dogwood — cold climate

Heliconia— tropical climate

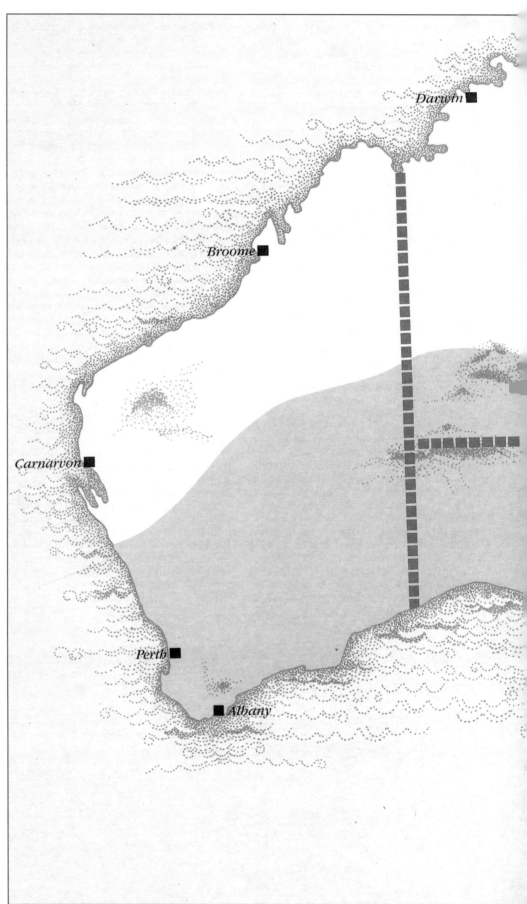

Key | Tropical/Subtropical | *Temperate* | *Cold*

Cairns

Townsville

Mackay

Rockhampton

Bundaberg

Springs

Dalby

Brisbane

Armidale

Coffs Harbour

Mudgee

Bathurst

Sydney

Canberra

Adelaide

Bendigo

Melbourne

Hobart

Bougainvillea — tropical/subtropical climate

Syringa vulgaris (Lilac) — cold/temperate climate

Frangipanni — tropical to warmer temperate climate

Index